Using Paradox for Windows

Special Edition

JAMES J. TOWNSEND

JENIFER LINDSAY

Using Paradox for Windows, Special Edition

Copyright© 1993 by Que® Corporation

All rights reserved. Printed in the United States of America. No part of this book may be used or reproduced in any form or by any means, or stored in a database or retrieval system, without prior written permission of the publisher except in the case of brief quotations embodied in critical articles and reviews. Making copies of any part of this book for any purpose other than your own personal use is a violation of United States copyright laws. For information, address Que Corporation, 11711 N. College Ave., Carmel, IN 46032.

Library of Congress Catalog No.: 91-68381

ISBN: 0-88022-823-7

This book is sold *as is*, without warranty of any kind, either express or implied, respecting the contents of this book, including but not limited to implied warranties for the book's quality, performance, merchantability, or fitness for any particular purpose. Neither Que Corporation nor its dealers or distributors shall be liable to the purchaser or any other person or entity with respect to any liability, loss, or damage caused or alleged to be caused directly or indirectly by this book.

95 94 93   5 4 3 2

Interpretation of the printing code: the rightmost double-digit number is the year of the book's printing; the rightmost single-digit number, the number of the book's printing. For example, a printing code of 93-1 shows that the first printing of the book occurred in 1993.

Screen reproductions in this book were created using Collage Plus from Inner Media, Inc., Hollis, NH.

Using Paradox for Windows, Special Edition, is based on Paradox for Windows, Version 1.0.

Publisher: Lloyd J. Short

Associate Publisher: Rick Ranucci

Publishing Plan Manager: Thomas H. Bennett

Operations Manager: Sheila Cunningham

Book Designer: Scott Cook

Production Team: Jeff Baker, Claudia Bell, Julie Brown, Jodie Cantwell, Paula Carroll, Michelle Cleary, Brook Farling, Bob LaRoche, Jay Lesandrini, Cindy Phipps, Caroline Roop, Linda Seifert, Michelle Self, Susan Shepard, Tina Trettin, Phil Worthington

DEDICATION

To Mom and Dad—JT
To Dana—JL

CREDITS

Title Manager
Walter R. Bruce III

Acquisitions Editor
Chris Katsaropoulos

Production Editor
Lori A. Lyons

Editors
Sara Kurtz Allaei
Louise Lambert
Diana R. Moore
Susan Pink
Kathy Simpson

Technical Editor
Ken Merson

Composed in *Cheltenham* and *MCPdigital*
by Que Corporation

ABOUT THE AUTHORS

James J. Townsend is author of Que's *Introduction to Databases*. He is president of Information Strategies, a database consulting firm in Washington, DC. He designs custom database applications and teaches database design. James may be contacted at (202) 462-1290 or via CompuServe address 70304,2750.

Jenifer Lindsay has been programming with Paradox and writing about Paradox and Paradox for Windows for four years. She worked as a technical writer at Borland International, writing about Paradox and Borland C++. She went on to become a PAL programmer and systems analyst at a major publishing company. She has designed and installed networks and network PAL applications, including a forecasting and sales tracking system and an inventory control system. Over the last year, Jenifer has been consulting for Borland and writing example ObjectPAL programs for Paradox for Windows. Jenifer holds degrees in English and Computer Science.

ACKNOWLEDGMENTS

Thanks to Que Corporation for support during the ups and downs of the software beta process. Special thanks to:

Walt Bruce, for the example offered by his Paradox books and for encouragement throughout the project.

Chris Katsaropoulos, for asking me to take on this project.

The editors, for tireless editing of a constantly changing and ongoing subject.

I am grateful to Joe Carpentiere, Jeff Chapski, Jon Phillips, and especially Marcella Townsend for keeping the business afloat during my absences. — Jim

Thanks to Marie Scanlon, Robert Hall, Margaret Dumas, and the entire Borland Paradox for Windows team. — Jenifer

Trademarks

All terms mentioned in this book that are known to be trademarks or service marks have been appropriately capitalized. Que Corporation cannot attest to the accuracy of this information. Use of a term in this book should not be regarded as affecting the validity of any trademark or service mark.

CONVENTIONS

The conventions used in this book have been established to help you learn to use Paradox for Windows quickly and easily.

Material you are to type appears in **bold** type. Terms that are introduced for the first time are set in *italic* type. Messages that appear on-screen are in a `special typeface`.

Hot-key letters you can press in combination with the Alt key to access commands and menu options are underlined. For example, to access the File menu, you press Alt+F.

Key combinations you enter to perform Windows operations are indicated by combining the keys with a plus sign, as in Alt+F4. This indicates that you press and hold the Alt key while pressing the F4 function key. In the rare cases in which you must press and release a control key, then enter another key, they are separated by a comma, as in Alt,F4.

Tips, Notes, and Cautions provide important information about a subject and appear in boxes. Marginal icons indicate where SpeedBar buttons are first introduced in the text.

CONTENTS AT A GLANCE

Introduction 1

Part I: Paradox for Windows Fundamentals

    Quick Start 1: Starting Your First
        Paradox for Windows Session 13
1 Navigating Paradox 39
2 Designing Paradox Tables and Databases 67
3 Entering, Editing, and Viewing Data 121
4 Getting Started with Query By Example 169
5 Getting Started with Forms 205
6 Getting Started with Reports 265

Part II: Paradox for Windows Power Techniques

    Quick Start 2: Exploring Advanced
        Paradox Features 311
7 Using Advanced Form Techniques 335
8 Using Advanced Query By Example 365
9 Using Power Entry and Editing Features 397
10 Creating Crosstabs and Graphs 421
11 Exchanging Data with Other Applications 455
12 Working with Your Files 473

Part III: Programming Paradox for Windows

13 Getting Started with ObjectPAL 513
14 Understanding ObjectPAL Basics 551
15 Sample Application: Using ObjectPAL 605
16 Sample Application: Working with Multiple Forms ... 629
17 Sample Application: Working with Dialog Boxes
    and Tables 651
18 Sample Application: Adding Menus 667

A Installing Paradox for Windows 701
B Using the Graphical User Interface 709

    Index 731

TABLE OF CONTENTS

Introduction 1
    What Is Paradox for Windows? 2
    The Heart of Paradox: Query By Example 2
    Features for the Power User and Application
        Developer 3
    What's New in Paradox for Windows? 4
    What Should Your System Have? 4
    Who Should Read This Book? 5
    What Is Covered in This Book? 6
        Part I: Paradox for Windows Fundamentals 7
        Part II: Paradox for Windows Power Techniques ... 7
        Part III: Programming Paradox for Windows 8
        Using the Appendixes 9

I Paradox for Windows Fundamentals

Quick Start 1: Starting Your First Paradox for Windows Session 13
    Launching the Paradox Desktop from Windows 14
    Creating a Table 17
    Entering Data in the Table 22
        Resizing Table Columns 26
        Moving Table Columns 27
    Entering Data in Form View 27
    Using Query By Example 30
    Printing a Quick Report 35
    Closing Paradox for Windows 37
    Quick Start Summary 37

1 Navigating Paradox 39
    Using the Desktop 40
        The Title Bar 41
        The Control Menu 41

        The Maximize and Minimize Icons 42
        The Menu Bar 42
        The SpeedBar 44
        The Message Area 46
Using the Mouse and the Keyboard 46
Understanding Objects 49
        Tables 50
        Forms 51
        Reports 51
        Queries 52
        Scripts 53
        Design Objects 54
Working with Objects 56
        Finding Objects with the File Browser 59
Communicating with Paradox 59
        Using Dialog Boxes 60
        Using Selection Lists 61
        Using Buttons 61
        Responding to Prompts 61
Working in Multiple Windows 62
Getting Help 63
Chapter Summary 64

2 Designing Paradox Tables and Databases 67

Understanding Database Terminology 67
        What Is a Relational Database? 68
        What Is a Table? 69
        What Is a Primary Key? 70
        What Is a Relationship? 71
        What Is Referential Integrity? 72
Planning a Table 72
        Using the Album Tracking
            Database Example 73
        Using Multiple Tables 73
        Eliminating Repeated Fields 74
        Consolidating Duplicate Tables 76
Creating a Paradox Table 76
        Choosing the Table Type 77
        Specifying Field Names 79
        Specifying Field Type 82
        Specifying Field Sizes 89
        Defining a Primary Key 90
        Saving a Table 93

Understanding Indexes, Validity Checks,
    and Referential Integrity 95
        Using Indexes 95
        Specifying Validity Checks 99
        Borrowing a Table Structure 104
Restructuring a Table 111
    Changing a Field Type 114
    Inserting a Field 118
    Deleting a Field 118
    Moving a Field 118
Chapter Summary 119

3 Entering, Editing, and Viewing Data 121

Opening a Table 122
Paradox Data-Entry Modes 123
    Choosing Table View or Form View 124
    Choosing View Mode or Edit Mode 125
    Using Field View 128
Using the SpeedBar 130
Entering Data with Special Field Types 132
    Entering Data in Date Fields 132
    Entering Data in Memo Fields 133
    Entering Data in Formatted Memo Fields 136
    Entering Data in Graphic Fields 137
    Entering Data in OLE Fields 142
    Using Ditto To Repeat Entries 142
Editing Data in Edit Mode 143
    Cutting, Copying, and Pasting Values 143
    Using Undo 144
    Deleting Records 145
Using Search To Find Fields, Records, and Values 145
    Searching for a Field 146
    Searching for a Value 147
    Searching for a Record Number 149
    Searching and Replacing Values 150
Inserting Records in Edit Mode 152
Entering and Editing Data with Multiuser Settings 153
    Locking Options 154
    Data-Entry Locks 155
Changing a Table's On-Screen Appearance 156
    Resizing a Column 157
    Changing the Row Height 159
    Viewing Table Properties 159
Chapter Summary 168

4 Getting Started with Query By Example 169

- The Benefits of Query By Example 170
- Getting Started with Queries 171
  - The Query Editor Dialog Box 172
  - Adding a Table to a Query 174
  - Removing a Table from a Query 175
  - The Query Menu 175
  - Handling Query Errors 176
  - The Query SpeedBar 177
- Selecting Fields 178
  - The Check Mark 178
  - Displaying Duplicate Values 179
  - Sorting 181
- Restricting the Search 184
  - Exact Match 185
  - Approximate Match 186
  - Range of Values 189
  - Intersection 191
  - Union 193
  - The AS Operator: Changing a Field Name 195
  - The NOT Operator: Finding Unmatching
    Values 196
  - The BLANK Operator: Finding Blank Values 196
  - Searching in Exotic Field Types 197
  - The TODAY Operator and Date Arithmetic 198
- Understanding the Answer Table 200
  - Sorting the Answer Table 201
  - Editing the Answer Table 201
  - Printing the Answer Table 203
- Saving the Query 203
- Chapter Summary 204

5 Getting Started with Forms 205

- What Is a Paradox Form? 206
- What Is Form Design? 207
- Creating a New Form 207
  - Choosing Design Layout for Fields 210
  - Selecting a Style 211
- Working in the Form Design Window 215
  - Selecting Objects 217
  - Displaying Object Properties 218
  - Displaying Tool Properties 218
  - Drawing Boxes, Ellipses, and Lines 219

  Adding Text 222
  Adding a Graphic 229
 Adding OLE Objects 237
 Adding Buttons 237
 Adding Fields 237
  Placing Regular Fields 237
  Placing Read Only Fields 238
  Placing Calculated Fields 238
  Placing the Record-Number and
   Other System Fields 240
  Placing Special Fields 240
  Erasing Fields from the Form 241
  Reformatting a Field 242
  Adding a Table Object 242
  Adding a Multi-Record Region 242
  Adding a Graph 243
  Adding a Crosstab 243
  The Data Model Tool 243
  The Object Tree 243
 General Design Considerations 244
 Working with Multiple Objects 247
  Using Shared Property Menus 247
  Understanding Embedding 247
  Grouping Objects 248
  Adjusting Alignment, Size, and Spacing 249
  Designer Properties 252
 Using Rulers and Grids 253
  The Rulers 254
  The Expanded Ruler 255
  The Grid 257
 Using Zoom 258
 Saving the Form Design 259
 Testing the Form 260
 Guidelines for Text and Field Labels 262
 Screen Layout 263
 Chapter Summary 264

6 Getting Started with Reports 265

 Examining Types of Reports 266
 Understanding Paradox Reports 266
 Printing a Quick Report 266
 Creating a Report 267
  Selecting a Report Layout 267
  Setting the Page Layout 270
  Choosing the Layout Style 271

- Working in the Report Design Window 272
  - Selecting Objects 274
  - Displaying Object Properties 275
  - Displaying Tool Properties 275
  - Drawing Boxes, Ellipses, and Lines 276
  - Adding Text 278
  - Adding a Graphic 278
- Adding OLE Objects 279
- Adding Fields 280
  - Placing Regular Fields 280
  - Placing Calculated Fields 280
  - Placing the Record-Number and Other Special Fields 281
  - Reformatting a Field 282
  - Adding a Table Object 282
  - Adding a Multi-Record Region 283
  - Adding a Graph 283
  - Using the Data Model Tool 283
  - Using the Object Tree 283
- Understanding Bands 284
  - Resizing Bands 285
  - Deleting a Band 285
  - Specifying Report Headers and Footers 286
  - Specifying Page Headers and Footers 286
- Working with Fields 287
  - Placing a Regular Field 287
  - Deleting a Field 288
- Manipulating the Table Object 288
  - Resizing the Table Object 289
  - Resizing a Column 289
  - Moving, Adding, and Deleting a Column 289
  - Changing the Row Height 290
  - Viewing Report Table Properties 290
- Previewing and Saving a Report 291
- Printing a Report 292
  - Controlling the Printer 293
  - Printer Orientation 294
- Examining Some Typical Paradox Reports 295
  - Mailing Labels 295
  - Items in Groups 299
- Creating Multi-Table Reports 302
- Planning a Report 302
  - Easy on the Eyes 303
  - Clear and Concise 303
  - Meaningful 305

Examining Report Style 305
Chapter Summary 306

II Paradox for Windows Power Techniques

Quick Start 2: Exploring Advanced Paradox Features 311

Creating Sample Tables 311
Linking Tables as a Database 313
    What Is a Secondary Index? 314
    What Is Referential Integrity? 316
    What Is Table Lookup? 318
    What Is a Validity Check? 322
        Required Fields 323
        Minimum and Maximum Values 323
        Default Values 324
Creating a Multi-Table Form 324
Creating a Multi-Table Query 326
    Using Example Elements To Link Tables 327
Creating a Crosstab 330
Creating a Graph 332
Chapter Summary 334

7 Using Advanced Form Techniques 335

Creating Multi-Table Forms 336
    Understanding Relationships 339
    Defining and Modifying a Secondary Index 346
    Creating Nested Multi-Table Forms 348
Defining Special Form Fields 351
    Using the Button Tool To Define Forms 360
Working with Table Objects 361
    Setting Filters 362
    Placing Graphs in Forms 364
Chapter Summary 364

8 Using Advanced Query By Example 365

Creating Multi-Table Queries 366
    Understanding Relationships 368
    Using Example Elements 369
Specifying Multiple Conditions
    in Multi-Table Queries 373
    Creating AND Conditions 374
    Creating OR Conditions 374

xv

- Creating Inner and Outer Joins 376
- Performing Calculations in Queries 379
    - Performing Calculations within a Record 380
    - Using Summary Operators and Grouping Records 382
- Comparing Sets of Records 385
    - Constructing Set Queries 386
- Changing Tables with Queries 388
    - Inserting Records 389
    - Deleting Records 392
    - Changing Records 393
- Chapter Summary 394

9 Using Power Entry and Editing Features 397

- Using Validity Checks 398
    - Entering Values in Required Fields 399
    - Setting Minimum and Maximum Values 400
    - Accepting or Changing a Default Value 400
- Assisting Data Entry with Pictures 401
- Using Table Lookup 403
- Understanding Referential Integrity 410
    - Updating across Linked Tables 413
    - Deleting Referential Integrity 413
    - Modifying Referential Integrity 414
- Defining Password Protection 414
    - Table Rights 415
    - Field Rights 417
- Handling Key Violations 417
- Chapter Summary 418

10 Creating Crosstabs and Graphs 421

- Creating Crosstabs 422
    - Defining a Crosstab 422
    - Understanding Types of Crosstabs 422
        - One-Dimensional Crosstabs 422
        - Two-Dimensional Crosstabs 428
    - Defining Aggregators 432
    - Customizing Crosstab Settings 433
    - Using the Data Model 435
- Creating Graphs 436
    - Understanding the Parts of a Graph 437
    - Understanding Types of Graphs 438
    - Placing and Defining a Graph Object 442

Customizing Graph Settings 443
    Customizing Series Settings 450
    Customizing Pie and Bar Settings 450
Printing a Graph 451
Chapter Summary 453

11 Exchanging Data with Other Applications 455

What Is DDE? 456
    Using DDE To Get Values 457
    Using DDE To Send Values 460
What Is OLE? 461
    Placing OLE Objects in Design Documents 462
    Placing OLE Fields in Tables 467
    Changing an OLE Object's Properties 469
Chapter Summary 471

12 Working with Your Files 473

Using the File Browser 474
Table Utilities 477
    Transferring Records from One Table
      to Another 478
    Subtracting Records in One Table
      from Another 480
Renaming Paradox Objects 481
    Restructuring and Sorting Tables 481
Importing and Exporting Data 485
    Importing from a Spreadsheet 486
    Importing Text Files 488
    Exporting Paradox Tables to Spreadsheets 492
    Renaming Tables 495
    Renaming Forms, Reports, Scripts,
      and Queries 496
Copying Paradox Tables 496
Deleting Objects and Emptying a Table 497
Defining Aliases 498
    Changing the Working Directory 500
    Creating Private Directories 501
Using Multiuser (Network) Features 502
    Viewing File Locks 502
    Setting Locks on Tables 503
    Displaying Your User Name 504
    Viewing User Names 505

| Setting Retry Intervals 506
   Getting System Information 506
      Using Auto Refresh 507
      Blank as Zero 508
      Viewing Database Drivers 508
      Viewing ODAPI Information 509
   Chapter Summary 510

III Programming Paradox for Windows

13 Getting Started with ObjectPAL 513

   What Is ObjectPAL? 515
      ObjectPAL Is Object-Based 516
      ObjectPAL Is Event-Driven 517
      ObjectPAL Is Easy: An Example 519
      ObjectPAL Is Modular 524
      ObjectPAL Is Visual 525
   The ObjectPAL Environment 527
      The ObjectPAL Editor 527
      ObjectPAL Debugger 537
   Adding a Program with ObjectPAL 538
   A Quick Overview for Programmers 547
      Language Features 547
      Control Features 548
      Objects in ObjectPAL 549
   Chapter Summary 550

14 Understanding ObjectPAL Basics 551

   Understanding Program Style Basics 552
      Spaces 552
      Maximum Characters 552
   Using Uppercase and Lowercase 553
      Comments 554
      Indentation 554
   Declaring Variables 555
      Variable Types 556
      Variable Declarations 557
      Types 560
   Declaring Constants 564
   Creating Data Types and Records 566
   Understanding Scope 567
      Scope and the Containership Hierarchy 567

      Var Section Declarations 568
      Var Window Declarations 570
      Scoping Variables and Constants 574
Using Operators 575
Creating Control Structures 578
      If Statements 578
      Immediate If Statements 580
      Switch Statements 581
      Try Statements 581
      For Loops 582
      Scan Loops 583
      While Loops 585
Calling Methods and Procedures 587
      Understanding Parameters and Arguments 588
      Understanding Return Values 589
      Calling Methods 589
      Calling Procedures 591
Calling DLL Functions 591
Creating Custom Procedures 594
Creating Custom Methods 596
Working with Arrays 599
      Declaring Fixed Arrays 599
      Declaring Resizable Arrays 600
      Declaring Dynamic Arrays 602
Chapter Summary 603

15 Sample Application: Using ObjectPAL 605

Designing a Graphical Interface 606
Interacting with the User 608
      Creating and Naming Objects
         for the Mortgage Calculator 609
      Using Messages To Describe Objects 613
      Defining the Calculate Button 620
Checking Data Entry 624
Chapter Summary 628

16 Sample Application: Working with Multiple Forms 629

Creating the Payment Calculator Form 630
      Defining the Calculations 633
      recalcButton Methods 634
      calcButton Methods 636
      OKButton Method 641
      cancButton Method 641

      A Starting Value for maxDI 642
    Calling the Payment Calculator from the
      Mortgage Calculator 643
          getPayment Methods 643
          calcLoanButton Methods 646
    Chapter Summary 649

17 Sample Application: Working with Dialog Boxes and Tables 651

    Opening the Payment Calculator as a Dialog Box 652
          Modal versus Non-Modal Forms 652
          Layer 653
          Form Window Characteristics 653
          Calling the Dialog Box 655
    Using Tables with the Mortgage Calculator 658
    Controlling Data Entry in the Mortgage Calculator ... 664
    Chapter Summary 666

18 Sample Application: Adding Menus 667

    Understanding Menus 667
    Creating Menus 668
    Handling Menu Actions 671
          Closing the Form with fileExitM 673
          Restoring a Record with undoEditM 675
          Searching for a Record with searchM 676
          Printing the Current Form with printCurrM 681
          Printing a Client Report with printAllCM 686
          Getting Help with getHelpM 687
          Showing an Animated About Box
            with showAboutM 692
    Improving the Mortgage Calculator Application 698
    Chapter Summary 700

A Installing Paradox for Windows 701

    Installation Requirements 701
    Making a Backup Copy of the Program Disks 703
    Running the Install Program 703
          Installing Sample Files 704
          Installing SHARE 706

Modifying CONFIG.SYS and AUTOEXEC.BAT
Files 707
Viewing the README File 708
Deinstalling Paradox for Windows 708

B Using the Graphical User Interface 709

Customizing Database Objects 710
Using the Mouse 711
Using the Control Menus 713
Changing the Size and Position of a Window 715
Maximizing and Restoring a Window 716
Minimizing a Window 716
Sizing a Window 717
Moving a Window 718
Closing a Window 718
Accessing the Task List 718
Manipulating Windows 719
Cascading Windows 721
Tiling Windows 721
Choosing a Window Display Mode 721
Making Another Window Active 722
Using the Paradox for Windows
Main Menu 723
Using Pull-Down Menus and Cascade Menus 723
Using Object Inspectors 724
Using Dialog Boxes 725
Navigating within a Dialog Box.............................. 725
Entering Information in a Dialog Box 727
Moving a Dialog Box 729
Using SpeedBars 729

Index 731

Introduction

Welcome to *Using Paradox for Windows*, Special Edition. This book contains nearly everything you need to develop professional applications with Paradox for Windows. The rest will come from you: the desire to use a relational database to meet your information needs.

Paradox for Windows is a dramatic departure from its DOS predecessor. While many of the commands will remain familiar to DOS users, the entire program has been overhauled, with no module left untouched. The power of Paradox for DOS has been supplemented with new capabilities, and the Paradox programming language (now called ObjectPAL) has been completely replaced in Paradox for Windows. Paradox for Windows moves closer to the relational model with a number of new features.

Although much has changed, the fundamental look and feel of Paradox remain. If you are experienced with Paradox for DOS, the concepts, commands, and menus of Paradox for Windows will be easy to learn.

Learning any software package, especially a full-featured database management system such as Paradox for Windows, can be a long, lonely path. This book maps out Paradox for Windows, with detailed instructions for difficult concepts and operations. This book will serve as your companion on the road to mastery of Paradox for Windows. Equally important, this book will spur you to come up with creative ways to apply Paradox for Windows to solve your business problems.

What Is Paradox for Windows?

Paradox for Windows is a relational database management system developed by Borland International, the world's largest PC database software company. Paradox for Windows is used to store, sort, and produce reports on data for a wide range of applications. In addition to standard database reporting capabilities, Paradox for Windows also includes integrated business graphics so that you may generate bar graphs, pie charts, and other graphics from your data.

Paradox for Windows allows you great control over how information is entered, stored, and manipulated. This program uses an interface similar to Lotus 1-2-3 and other spreadsheets for interactive manipulation of data, complemented by a programming language for more complex procedures. Because it is written for Windows, Paradox for Windows takes advantage of the ease of learning offered by Windows applications and the inherent support for graphics and communication among Windows software packages.

By the time you finish building your first application, you will not only be adept at Paradox for Windows, but you will have a deeper understanding of your data and the ways that your organization operates. Because it is such a productive way to create applications, Paradox for Windows will enable you to spend more time analyzing your business rules and the problems you intend to solve rather than struggling with tedious command syntax and program debugging.

The Heart of Paradox: Query By Example

Paradox for Windows further enhances one of Paradox's strongest features—query by example (QBE). QBE enables users to retrieve information from data tables without writing a single line of programming code, even from incomplete or mispelled searches.

Query by example is visual and does not require you to memorize commands or query syntax. You can easily refine a query if it does not yield the group of records you were looking for. QBE is the heart of interactive Paradox for Windows.

Just because QBE is easy to learn doesn't mean that it cannot handle difficult tasks. QBE may be used for complex searches using multiple criteria or for retrieval from more than one table at a time. For instance, you can write a query to retrieve all customers who have purchased at least $1,000 worth of products, along with a listing of their most recent orders. Using QBE, you can retrieve in seconds information from your database that would have required hours to write and debug a program with other database software.

Features for the Power User and Application Developer

Paradox for Windows contains eye-popping new features that will move even the most jaded database programmer. Forms design has been enhanced to use all the capabilities of the Windows environment, with such enhancements as radio buttons, integrated graphics, and full control of fonts and colors of objects. Using a Paradox for Windows database can be a multimedia experience, including graphic images or even sound.

Tables now include range limits, default derivation formulas, and referential integrity checks without writing a program. These features safeguard the accuracy of your data, preventing invalid entries. For instance, you can set up the state field to reject invalid state abbreviations, and check the ZIP codes against a range of valid ZIP codes for each state. Referential integrity ensures that a change in one table will be reflected in related tables. You may set up rules, for example, to prevent a user from deleting a customer record as long as any outstanding orders exist for that customer. Indexes may be specified for secondary indexes (such as foreign keys) as well as key fields and composite keys, boosting performance for searching and sorting data.

The most far-reaching change for the advanced programmer in Paradox for Windows is the adoption of object-oriented programming technology. Object-oriented programming can condense hundreds of lines of program code into dozens and includes functions impossible to perform in low-level programming languages. Borland has long been a pioneer in delivering object-oriented programming languages, and the advent of ObjectPAL brings their benefits to the PC database world.

What's New in Paradox for Windows?

A large number of enhancements have been added to Paradox for Windows from Paradox for DOS. Many of these are inherent in any Windows application. Some features of Paradox for DOS have been dropped altogether, such as the Image concept and the Personal Programmer. Table I.1 summarizes key changes in the program.

Table I.1. New Features in Paradox for Windows

Category	Enhancement
Navigation	Mouse support
	Compliance with Windows standards
New data types	Graphic
	OLE
	Access to dBASE tables
Data integrity	Field level rules, table lookup, referential integrity
Object-orientation	ObjectPAL (not compatible with PAL)
Extendability	Ability to write dynamic link libraries (DLLs) in C, C++ or Pascal
GUI features	Object linking and embedding (OLE)
	Dynamic data exchange (DDE)
	Graphics in forms and reports
	Access to all Windows fonts in form and report design

What Should Your System Have?

To run Paradox for Windows on a single-user PC, your IBM-compatible system must run Windows 3.0 or higher. This means that you need the extended memory support available on Intel 80286, 386, and 486 processors. Paradox for Windows, like all relational databases for Windows, requires quite a bit of memory and processing power to perform well. If you will be doing a significant amount of database work, you will be rewarded for investing in the fastest machine you can afford.

In addition, you need high-resolution graphics (such as EGA or VGA) to adequately display this and other Windows applications. A color monitor is optional, but highly desirable. Paradox for Windows takes advantage of color in many parts of the program and even enables you to customize the screen colors for tables, forms, and other display items.

A mouse is required to design screen elements, but is optional for data-entry. As with all Windows programs, a mouse greatly simplifies working with the program. Another pointing device such as a trackball may be used in place of the mouse, as long as it is compatible with mouse drivers supported by Windows. Most pointing devices include drivers that emulate popular mice such as those produced by Microsoft and Logitech.

For use on a local area network, Paradox for Windows supports the following networks:

- Novell Advanced NetWare
- Banyan Vines
- 3COM 3Plus/3Plus Open
- Microsoft LAN Manager
- Other 100% Windows compatible networks

Additional memory and a math coprocessor will improve performance of the system.

A graphics printer is required to print Paradox for Windows graphs. Consult your Windows documentation for additional information on printer support.

Who Should Read This Book?

Using Paradox for Windows, Special Edition, is divided into three main parts. Part I is designed to meet the needs of first-time Paradox users and those who desire a step-by-step introduction to Paradox for Windows. Part II is tailored toward advanced Paradox for Windows techniques. Part III explores the programming language for Paradox for Windows—ObjectPAL.

Unlike some other database software, you do not have to be a programmer to build databases with Paradox for Windows. This book assumes no prior training or experience with computer databases. This book includes background on relational database concepts, design practices, and even the new discipline of object-oriented programming.

The keys to success in building your own Paradox for Windows application are a solid understanding of your business needs and the desire to learn the tools to tailor your database to those needs. Through its examples, *Using Paradox for Windows*, Special Edition, will help you develop the analytical skills to create your first Paradox for Windows database.

First-time users should read through Part I and follow along with its examples as they explore the program. After you finish Part I, you may want to work on your database for some time before deciding how much further you would like to advance.

Experienced Paradox users may boldly skip to Part II. Part II contains advanced techniques for form design, report writing, and other Paradox elements. Even for advanced users, Chapter 1 is strongly recommended. This chapter defines key concepts and shows how to move around in the program.

Part III is devoted to ObjectPAL, the programming language of Paradox for Windows. Part III also contains an introduction to object-oriented programming. This is the most difficult section to master, especially if you have little or no programming experience. Luckily, you may build quite sophisticated applications without ever resorting to ObjectPAL.

What Is Covered in This Book?

This book is divided into three major parts: Part I, "Paradox for Windows Fundamentals"; Part II, "Paradox for Windows Power Techniques"; and Part III, "Programming Paradox for Windows." Additional reference information is contained in the appendixes. Parts I and II begin with Quick Start sections that highlight the topics to be discussed, with samples from actual Paradox for Windows sessions.

INTRODUCTION

Part I: Paradox for Windows Fundamentals

The first part of the book lays the groundwork for all the sections that follow. Part I discusses key terminology, Paradox for Windows objects, relational database concepts, and illustrates all the operations of interactive Paradox. This part of the book contains sufficient instruction to create your first complete database application.

Main database functions covered in this part include creating tables, defining fields, entering and editing data, querying the database, and printing simple reports.

Quick Start 1, "Starting Your First Paradox for Windows Session," shows how to start Paradox for Windows and guides you through the creation of a database table. You enter some data in the table and retrieve it using instant reports.

Chapter 1, "Navigating Paradox," explains how to use the keyboard, mouse, and menus to wind your way through the corridors of Paradox for Windows.

Chapter 2, "Designing Paradox Tables and Databases," shows how to define and modify the structure of the Paradox tables that make up a database.

Chapter 3, "Entering, Editing, and Viewing Data," examines the basics of entering, editing, and sorting data.

Chapter 4, "Getting Started with Query By Example," describes the most identifiable feature of Paradox—allowing powerful database queries to be created without programming.

Chapter 5, "Getting Started with Forms," introduces the use of forms to improve the ease and accuracy of data entry into tables.

Chapter 6, "Getting Started with Reports," shows how to create tabular reports from database tables.

Part II: Paradox for Windows Power Techniques

This part of the book takes each of the sections in Paradox Fundamentals a step further, teaching advanced techniques for greater control over your application.

Quick Start 2, "Exploring Advanced Paradox Features," introduces you to advanced Paradox for Windows features, including multi-table forms and queries, crosstabs, and graphs.

Chapter 7, "Using Advanced Form Techniques," explains multi-record and multi-table forms, as well as field validation techniques.

Chapter 8, "Using Advanced Query By Example," expands on queries with multiple record selection criteria and set operations.

Chapter 9, "Using Power Entry and Editing Features," describes how to enter and modify data in Paradox tables. This chapter includes hints for manipulating the screen for more productive data entry, and provides keyboard shortcuts for quick entry without reaching for the mouse.

Chapter 10, "Creating Crosstabs and Graphs," deals with creating cross tabulations and graphs to show your numerical data.

Chapter 11, "Exchanging Data with Other Applications," explores OLE (Object Linking and Embedding) to move data among Paradox for Windows and other software packages, such as spreadsheets, graphics, and word processors.

Chapter 12, "Working with Your Files," discusses the types of files Paradox for Windows creates, along with file compatibility for imports and exports.

Part III: Programming Paradox for Windows

The final part of the book is devoted to the object-oriented programming language used in Paradox for Windows—ObjectPAL. First, object-oriented programming is defined and compared to traditional programming languages. ObjectPAL is compared to its predecessor, PAL. Finally, ObjectPAL commands and functions are described along with sample programs you can use in your database application.

Chapter 13, "Getting Started with ObjectPAL," helps you decide when it is appropriate to write a program rather than use interactive Paradox for Windows. This chapter discusses the basic concepts of object-oriented programming.

Chapter 14, "Understanding ObjectPAL Basics," lists all commands and functions and shows how they work in the context of actual programs.

Chapter 15, "Sample Application: Using ObjectPAL," along with the next three chapters, takes you through the steps of building a Paradox for Windows application with ObjectPAL. In these chapters, you learn how to interact with the user with fields, messages, and dialog boxes.

Chapter 16, "Sample Application: Working with Multiple Forms," describes how to work with multiple forms under ObjectPAL control.

Chapter 17, "Sample Application: Working with Dialog Boxes and Tables," illustrates how to open a form as a dialog box, how tables and forms interact under ObjectPAL control, and how to control data entry to a form.

Chapter 18, "Sample Application: Adding Menus," shows you how to replace the default menu with custom menus.

Using the Appendixes

The appendixes provide additional reference and background information. Appendix A, "Installing Paradox for Windows," describes how to install and configure Paradox for Windows on your computer. Appendix B, "Using the Graphical User Interface," explains how to navigate through Windows programs and use the mouse, icons, and menus.

Now it is time to roll up your sleeves and enter the exciting world of Paradox for Windows. After you take the time to learn the Paradox mindset, your work with Paradox for Windows will be much more rewarding.

Paradox for Windows Fundamentals

PART 1

OUTLINE

Quick Start 1: Starting Your First Paradox for Windows Session

Navigating Paradox

Designing Paradox Tables and Databases

Entering, Editing, and Viewing Data

Getting Started with Query By Example

Getting Started with Forms

Getting Started with Reports

1
QUICK START

Starting Your First Paradox for Windows Session

This chapter is the first of two quick start chapters in this book. The quick starts are designed to provide instant immersion into Paradox for Windows through simple hands-on exercises. The text contains step-by-step instructions and images of the computer screen at each stage of the lesson.

Not all commands or options are covered in the quick starts, but chapter references are provided so that you can quickly find the help you need.

This quick start gives you a taste of the features discussed in Part 1 of this book and encourages you to learn Paradox for Windows in the most direct way: by using the program. As you complete the exercises, you create simple database tables for a business application, enter a few records, perform a query, and produce a report.

Before you perform the exercises in this chapter, you must install Paradox for Windows on your computer. Appendix A contains installation instructions.

I — PARADOX FOR WINDOWS FUNDAMENTALS

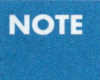 If Paradox for Windows is your first Windows application, remember that you must install Windows before you install Paradox for Windows.

If you are a first-time Windows user, you may want to read Appendix B, "Using the Graphical User Interface," before continuing this chapter. The appendix describes key Windows features; offers timesaving hints for finding your way through screens and menus; and defines Windows terms such as dialog boxes, windows, and icons.

This Paradox session introduces basic commands and explains how to enter and store data in the program. Each topic in this chapter is discussed in detail in Part 1.

 If you are an experienced Paradox for Windows user, you may want to skip to the second quick start, which introduces the intermediate Paradox techniques described in Part II. If you read no other chapter in Part I, however, you should read Chapter 2, which provides essential information on designing a relational database. You must understand relational-database principles before tackling the advanced relational techniques in Part II.

Launching the Paradox Desktop from Windows

To access Paradox for Windows, you first must invoke Windows by typing **win** at the DOS prompt and pressing Enter. You start Paradox for Windows the same way you start all Windows applications—by double-clicking the program icon in the Windows Program Manager. To display the Paradox desktop, follow these steps:

1. If the Program Manager window is not on your screen, double-click the Program Manager icon or press Ctrl+Esc and switch to the Program Manager. The Program Manager window appears, displaying the Windows programs you have installed on your computer (see fig. QS1.1).

   Programs are organized into program groups, such as Word Processing or Accessories, which are represented on-screen by squares filled with tiny figures.

QUICK START 1 — STARTING YOUR FIRST PARADOX FOR WINDOWS SESSION

2. If the Paradox for Windows program group is minimized, double-click the icon of the program group that contains the Paradox icon. The Paradox for Windows program group appears, containing three icons for Paradox programs (see fig. QS1.1). The first icon is for Paradox for Windows. The second icon is the Configuration Utility used to set up the program. The third icon is Table Repair Utility, used for data recovery.

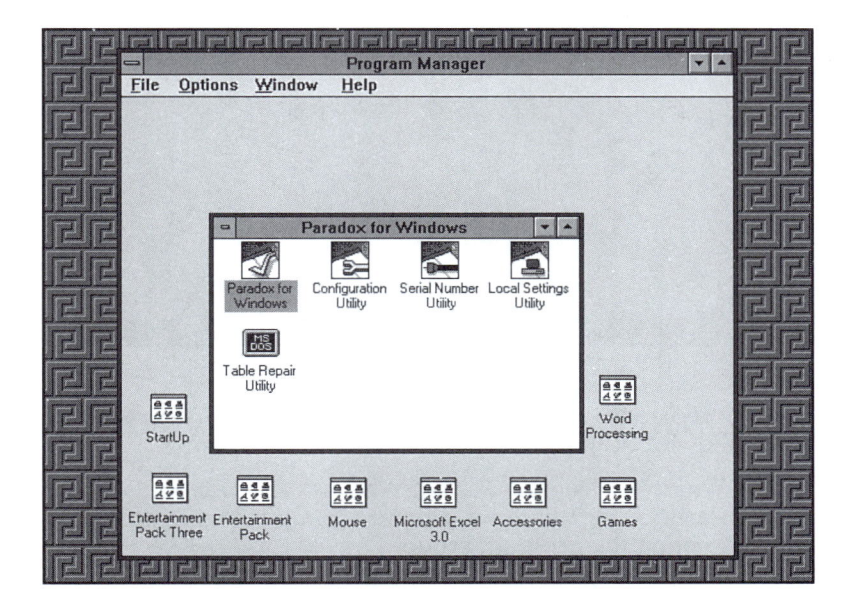

FIG. QS1.1

The Windows Program Manager with the Paradox for Windows program group.

NOTE The installation program creates a program group called Paradox for Windows and places the Paradox for Windows icon there by default. You can move the program to another group or rename the icon if you want.

3. After Windows displays the program group, double-click the Paradox for Windows icon. The Paradox Desktop appears (see fig. QS1.2).

NOTE Be patient. Depending on your hardware configuration, your computer may take a minute or more to start Paradox for Windows.

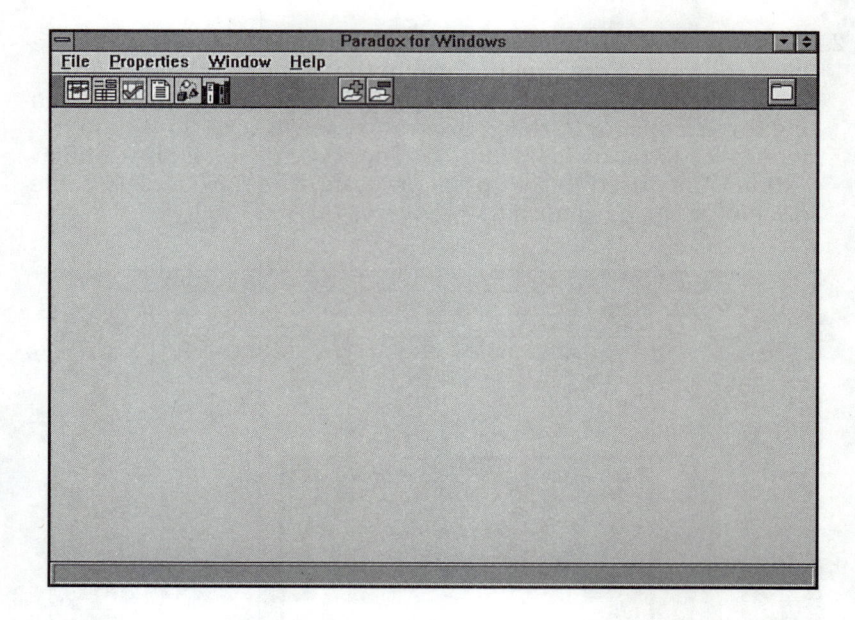

I — PARADOX FOR WINDOWS FUNDAMENTALS

FIG. QS1.2
The Paradox for Windows desktop.

If you prefer to use the keyboard to start Paradox for Windows, complete the following steps:

1. In the Windows Program Manager, press Ctrl+Tab until the name of the Paradox for Windows program group is highlighted. Press Enter to open the program group.

2. Use the arrow keys to move to the Paradox for Windows icon. Windows highlights the first icon in the group by default, so you may not have to move to choose Paradox for Windows.

3. Press Enter or choose File from the Program Manager menu by pressing Alt+F, then Open.

You see a small title screen indicating that Paradox for Windows is being loaded. After the program is loaded, the Paradox for Windows desktop appears (see fig. QS1.2).

NOTE Nearly every Windows command has a keyboard equivalent. You press and hold the Alt key while you press the underlined letter (the "hot key") of a menu choice. Throughout this book, hot keys are indicated with the underline character, such as File. To choose the File menu, press Alt+F.

The desktop is where you begin every Paradox for Windows session. The third bar from the top of the desktop contains buttons that represent tools. In most Windows applications, this area is called the toolbar; Paradox calls this the *SpeedBar*. The tool buttons on the SpeedBar may be different in different windows. For example, some tools available for reports are not available for queries and vice versa. Chapter 1, "Navigating Paradox," discusses Paradox menus and the SpeedBar in depth.

Creating a Table

The purpose of a database is to store information; the place where data is stored is called a *table*. Tables may track information about concrete items such as products and people or abstract things such as transactions and assignments. Items that you track are called *entities*.

Each entity you track in a database has a corresponding table. A fund-raising database, for example, might contain separate tables for donors, contributions, campaigns, and fund-raising events. A project management table might contact project name, project leader, start date, completion date, and budget.

A table consists of rows and columns. Each row constitutes an entry, or *record*, in the table. A table that tracks customers, for example, would include a record for each customer.

Each column in a table constitutes a piece of data, or *field*, in the table. Fields contain the attributes of the entities that you track in the table. In a donor table, donors' last names would be stored in a last-name field.

Because they are laid out in rows and columns, tables superficially resemble spreadsheets. Like spreadsheet cells, table fields may be set up to accept only certain types of entries, such as numbers or dates. Unlike spreadsheets, however, a column in a table must have the same data type and meaning for the entire table. Another difference is that database tables may be virtually unlimited in the number of rows they contain, storing millions or even billions of records.

When you create a table, you specify field names, field types, and field lengths. To create a table called CUSTOMER, start from the Paradox for Windows desktop and follow these steps:

1. Choose the File menu by clicking it or by pressing Alt+F. The menu choices drop down when you choose the menu.

I — PARADOX FOR WINDOWS FUNDAMENTALS

2. Choose New from the File menu. The arrow to the right of the menu choice indicates that a submenu is available. The File New submenu opens (see fig. QS1.3).

3. Choose Table from the File New submenu. The Table Type dialog box appears (see fig. QS1.4).

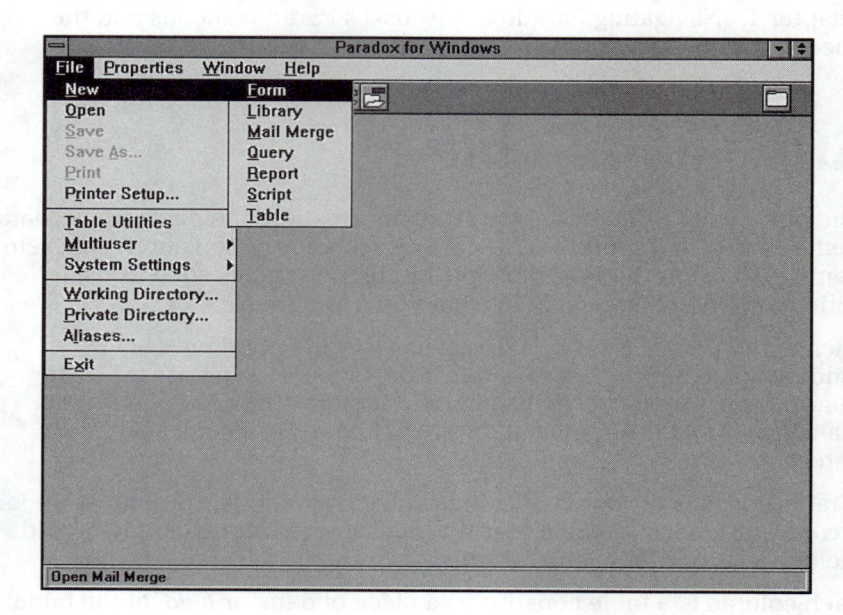

FIG. QS1.3

The File New submenu.

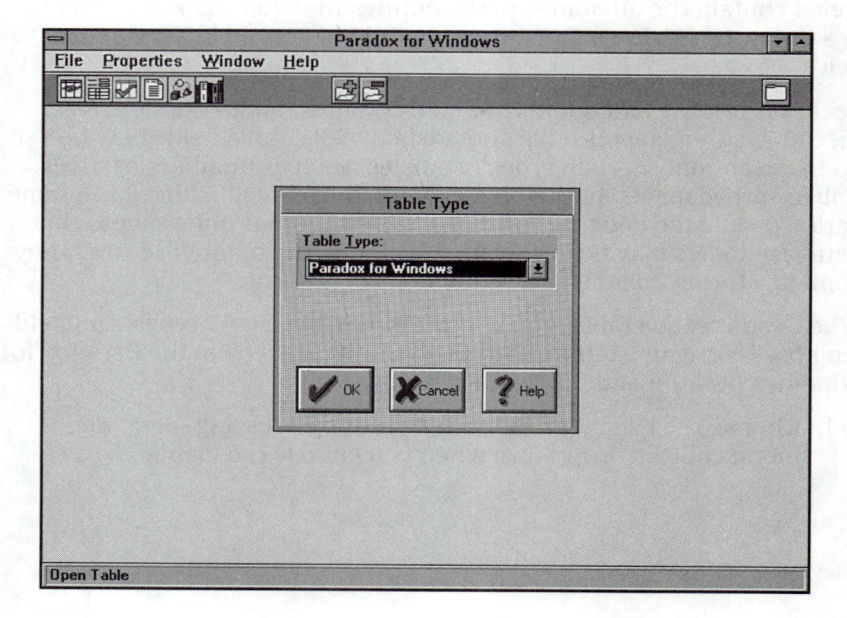

FIG. QS1.4

The Table Type dialog box.

QUICK START 1 — STARTING YOUR FIRST PARADOX FOR WINDOWS SESSION

4. Paradox for Windows enables you to create several types of database tables, including dBASE and Paradox 3.5 tables. To choose a table type other than Paradox for Windows, click the arrow next to Table Type to activate the pull-down menu (see fig. QS1.5). Click the desired table type to make your choice. For this exercise, however, choose Paradox for Windows as the table type.

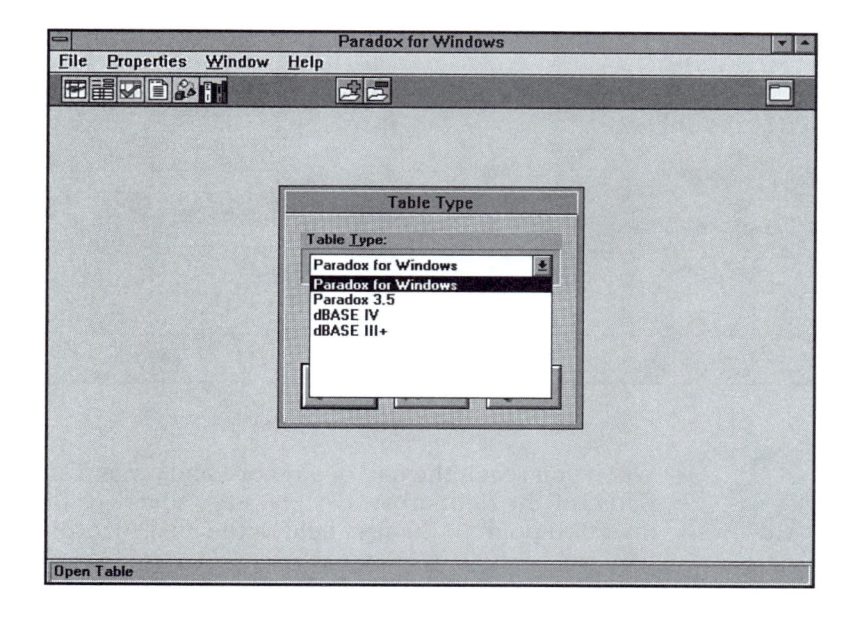

FIG. QS1.5

The Paradox Table Type pull-down menu.

5. Click the OK button to continue. The Create Paradox for Windows Table dialog box appears (see fig. QS1.6).

6. Type **lname** in the Field Name column. If you make a mistake, use the Backspace key to correct your entry.

7. Advance to the Type column by pressing Tab, Enter, or the right-arrow key. Enter the field type in this column. Press the space bar or right-click to see a list of valid field types, as shown in figure QS1.7. Press **A** (for Alphanumeric) as the field type.

8. Advance to the Size column and enter **20** as the field length.

9. Advance to the Key column. In this column, you designate *key fields*, which determine the rules for duplicate entries and the standard sort order of the table. The Key column uses an asterisk to indicate a key field. Press any character or double-click in the Key column to make LNAME the key field. The key column acts like a toggle switch. To remove a key, press any character or double-click in the Key column.

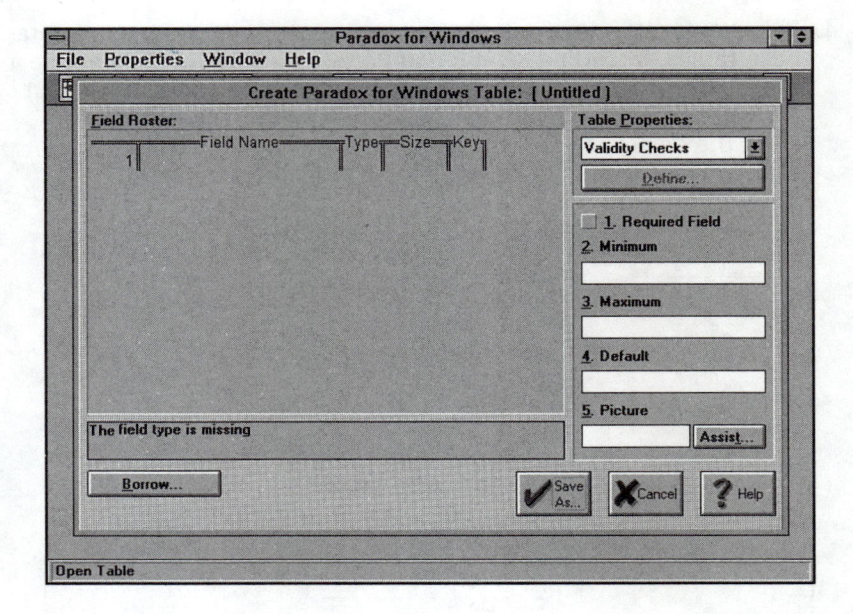

20   I — PARADOX FOR WINDOWS FUNDAMENTALS

FIG. QS1.6

The Create Paradox for Windows Table dialog box.

NOTE When you reach the end of a record and press Tab, Enter, or the right-arrow key, Paradox advances the insertion point to the first field of the next record.

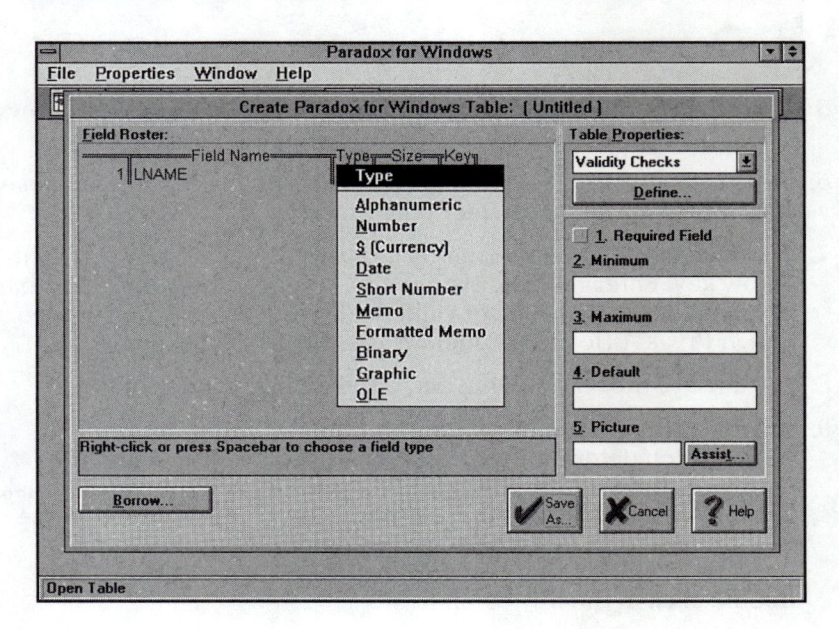

FIG. QS1.7

Field types in the Create Paradox for Windows Table dialog box.

QUICK START 1 — STARTING YOUR FIRST PARADOX FOR WINDOWS SESSION

10. Repeat steps 6-9 to enter additional fields, using the field names, lengths, and types shown in figure QS1.8. Note that the Date field type does not require a field length. Leave the Key column blank for these fields.

11. When you finish entering field data, click the Save As button to save and name the table. The Save Table As dialog box appears (see fig. QS1.9).

12. Type **customer** as the table name in the New Table Name text box and click the OK button. After you save the table, the Paradox for Windows desktop reappears.

> **T I P**
>
> Paradox table names are limited by DOS to eight characters and cannot include spaces. Try to use meaningful table names so that you can remember them.

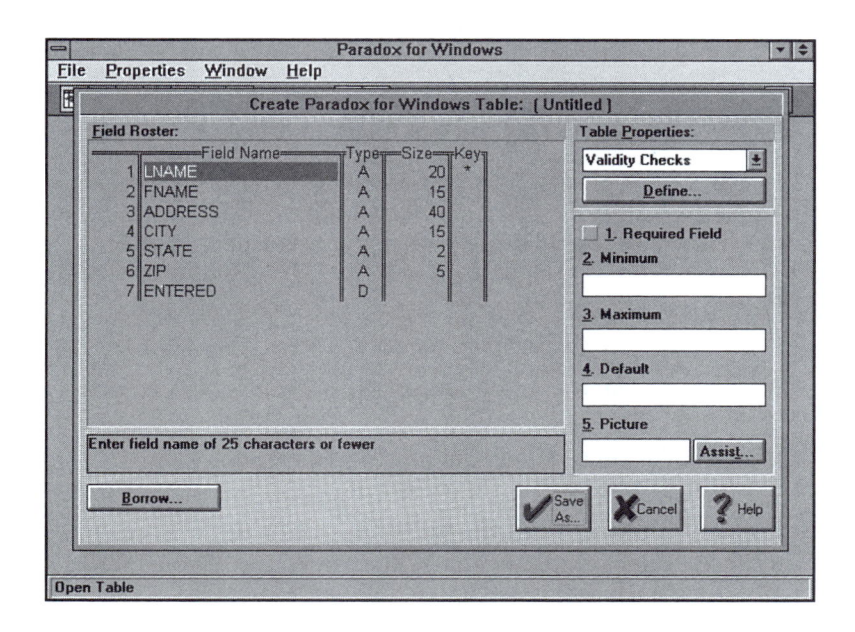

FIG. QS1.8

Table definition fields.

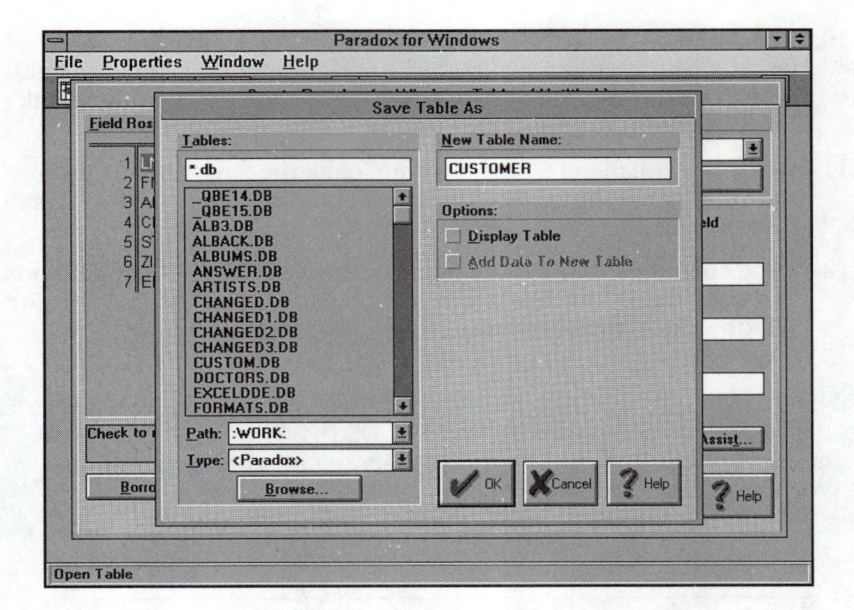

I — PARADOX FOR WINDOWS FUNDAMENTALS

FIG. QS1.9

The Save Table As dialog box.

Entering Data in the Table

Now that you have created the CUSTOMER table, you can enter data into the table. You can enter data in Paradox tables in two ways: in *Table view* (the default), which shows many records at a time; or in *Form view*, which shows one record at a time. This section describes Table view.

To open the CUSTOMER table, follow these steps:

1. Choose File from the menu bar on the Paradox for Windows desktop.

2. Choose Open from the File menu. The File Open submenu appears (see fig. QS1.10).

3. Choose Table from the submenu. You can click the Table button on the SpeedBar rather than use the File, Open, Table menus. The Open a Table dialog box appears (see fig. QS1.11).

TIP If you're not sure of a button name, the message area at the bottom of the screen gives you the name when you place the mouse pointer on the button.

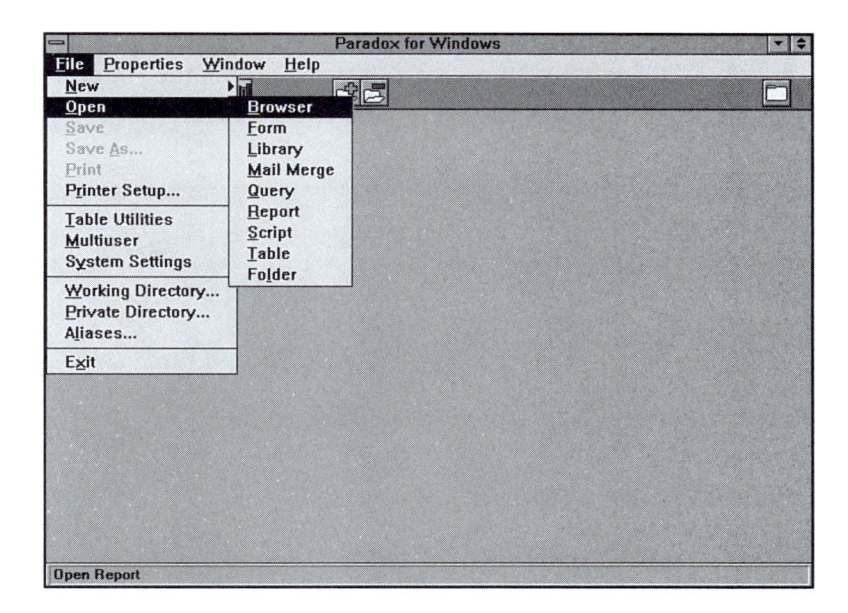

QUICK START 1 — STARTING YOUR FIRST PARADOX FOR WINDOWS SESSION

FIG. QS1.10

The File Open submenu.

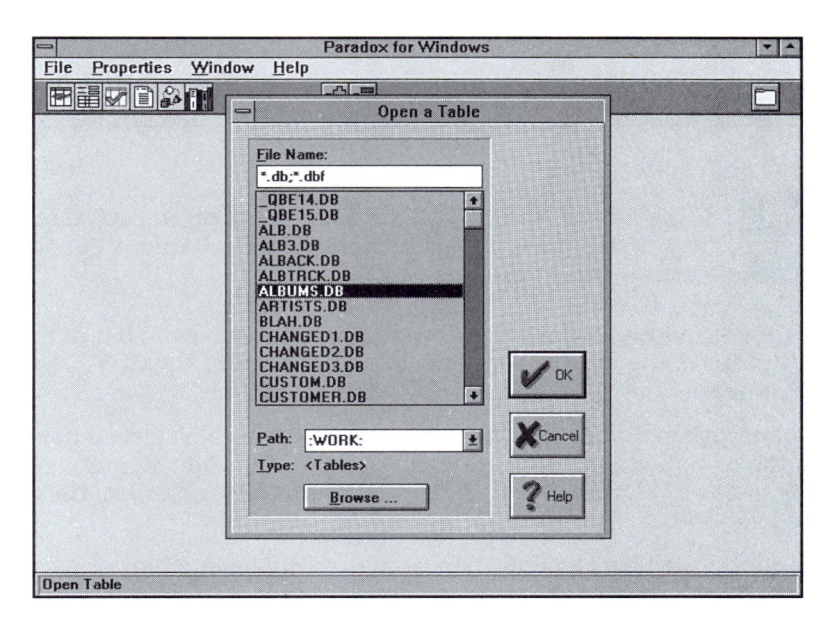

FIG. QS.11

The Open a Table dialog box.

I — PARADOX FOR WINDOWS FUNDAMENTALS

4. Select CUSTOMER.DB from the File Name list by double-clicking it, or by clicking the table name and then clicking the OK button. The Table window appears, with the file name in the title bar (see fig. QS1.12).

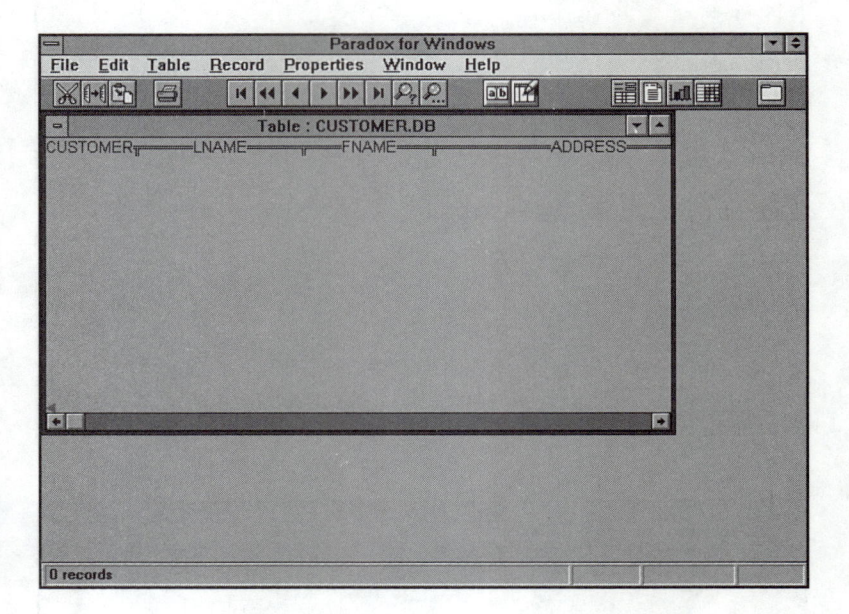

FIG. QS1.12
The Table window.

NOTE Table names, like all DOS file names, appear in capital letters. If you enter file names as lowercase, Paradox converts them to uppercase.

The Table window displays new menu options in the menu bar and new tool buttons in the SpeedBar. The column headers for the CUSTOMER table appear in the window.

You can work with tables in View mode or Edit mode. You read data in View mode and add, modify, or delete data in Edit mode. Paradox only opens tables in View mode. To switch to Edit mode, use one of the following methods:

Choose Table, then Edit Data from the Table menu bar.

or

Press F9 to switch between View and Edit modes.

or

Click the Edit Data button in the SpeedBar (it looks like a pencil writing on a ledger).

QUICK START 1 — STARTING YOUR FIRST PARADOX FOR WINDOWS SESSION

The current mode is shown in the second box from the left of the message line at the bottom of the window. The Edit Data button is now depressed, as shown in figure QS1.13.

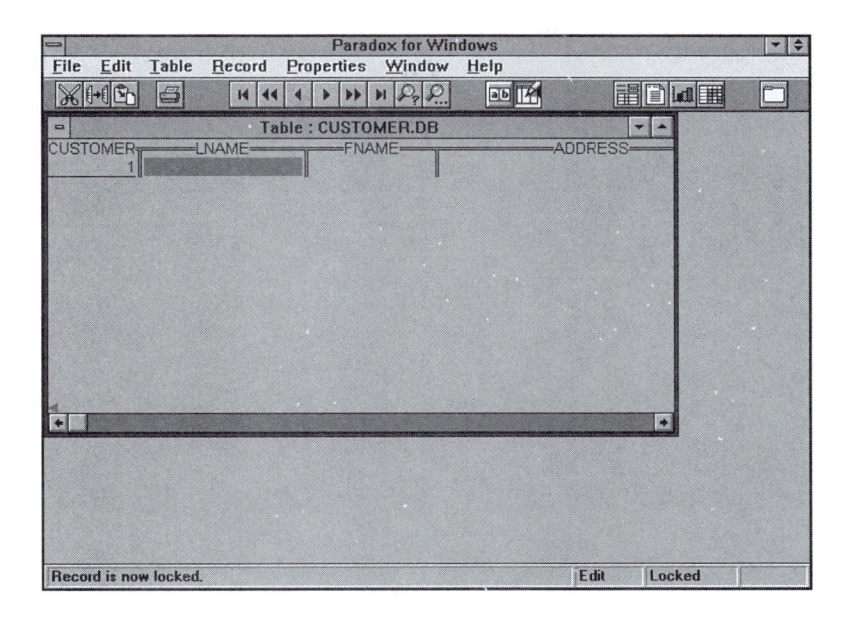

FIG. QS1.13
The Table window in Edit Mode.

The insertion point appears in the first field of the table, LNAME. The first column of the table displays the record number—1. Paradox increments this number as you add records to the table.

To enter data in the CUSTOMER table, follow these steps:

1. Type **Jenkins** in the LNAME field and then press Tab, Enter, or the right-arrow key to advance to the FNAME field.

2. Type **William** in the FNAME field and then advance to the ADDRESS field.

3. Type **3431 N. 35th St.** in the ADDRESS field and then advance to the CITY field.

4. Type **Glenville** in the CITY field and then advance to the STATE field.

5. Type **NY** in the STATE field and then advance to the ZIP field.

6. Type **10200** in the ZIP field and then advance to the ENTERED field.

7. Type **Jan-01-92** in the ENTERED field and then press Tab, Enter, or the right-arrow key to advance to the start of the next record.

NOTE Paradox saves all your work as you go along. You do not have to press any special key to save a record.

8. Repeat steps 1 through 7 to enter the other three records shown in figure QS1.14.

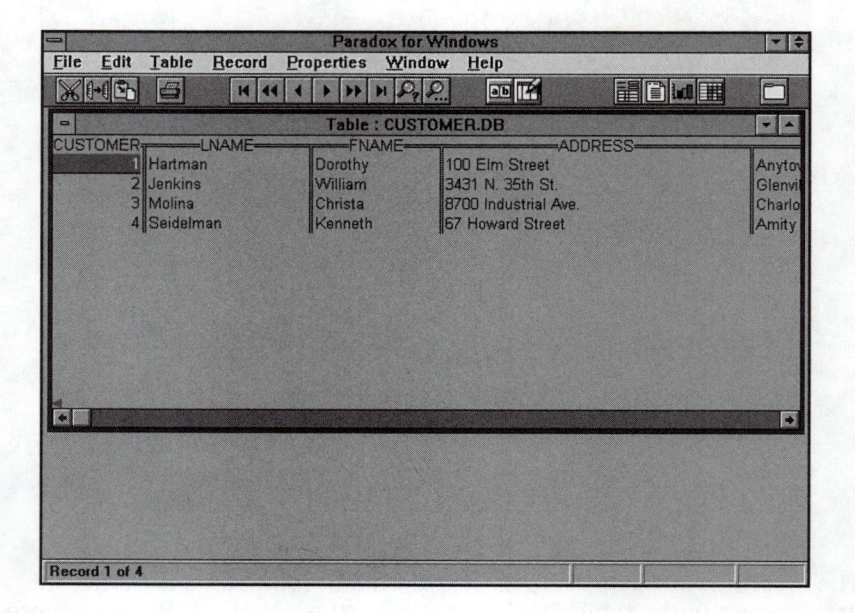

FIG. QS1.14

The CUSTOMER table with sample data.

Paradox for Windows accepts dates entered in several different formats but converts all date entries to a standard display format. You can enter January 1, 1992 as Jan-01-92, 1/1/92, or 01/01/1992, for example, but Paradox displays all of them as 1/1/92.

Paradox sorts the records alphabetically, using the LNAME field you specified as the key field. Although you entered Jenkins first, that name now appears after Hartman.

Resizing Table Columns

Paradox for Windows gives you extensive control of the appearance of the table. In this example, you reduce the size of the first column of the CUSTOMER table, which shows the last name, to make more of the table visible.

QUICK START 1 — STARTING YOUR FIRST PARADOX FOR WINDOWS SESSION

To resize the first column, follow these steps:

1. Move the pointer to the top of the vertical border between the first column (LNAME) and the second column (FNAME).

2. When the pointer becomes a two-headed arrow, click the mouse and hold down the left mouse button. After you click, `Resizing column width` appears in the message line at the bottom of the screen.

3. Drag the column margin to the left.

4. When the column is the desired width, release the mouse button. All columns to the right shift accordingly.

Moving Table Columns

Sometimes you may want to view the columns in a different order. For instance, you may want to move the STATE field so that you can see where a customer is located without scrolling to the right to view the STATE field. You can accomplish this by moving the STATE column between the FNAME and ADDRESS columns.

To move the STATE column, follow these steps:

1. Move the cursor to the top of the STATE column.

   The pointer becomes a tiny rectangle with a vertical line in the upper left side of its top.

2. When you click, the pointer becomes a double arrow. Drag the column to its new position.

3. Release the mouse button. Your screen should look like figure QS1.15.

When you finish entering data, you can close the Table window by double-clicking the Control menu, clicking the Control menu and choosing Close, or choosing E*x*it from the *F*ile menu. If you want to continue with the next exercise, however, do not close the Table window.

Entering Data in Form View

Paradox for Windows enables you to enter and view records one at a time rather than in a table. This is called Form view. You can change from Table view to Form view by pressing F7. A new window appears, showing all the fields of your table, with each field on a separate line (see fig. QS1.16).

I — PARADOX FOR WINDOWS FUNDAMENTALS

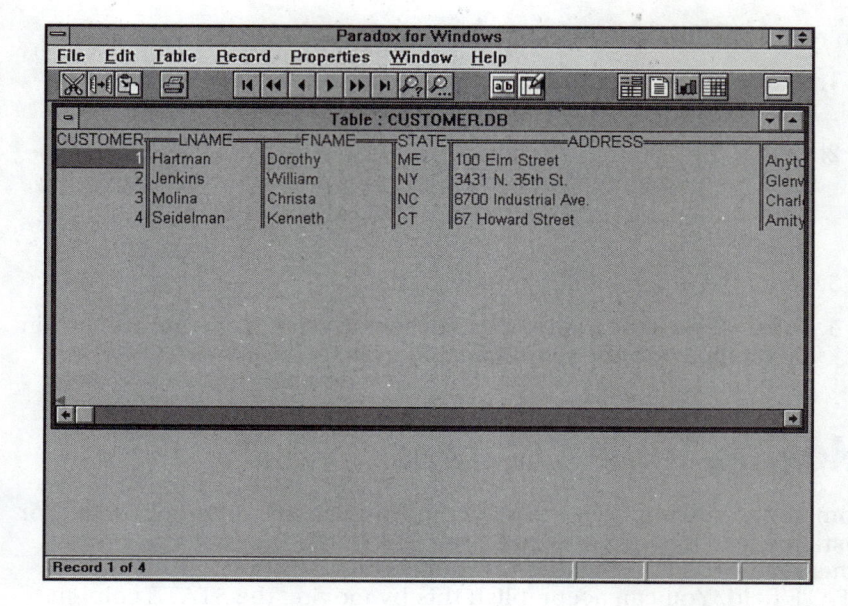

FIG. QS1.15

Moved and resized columns.

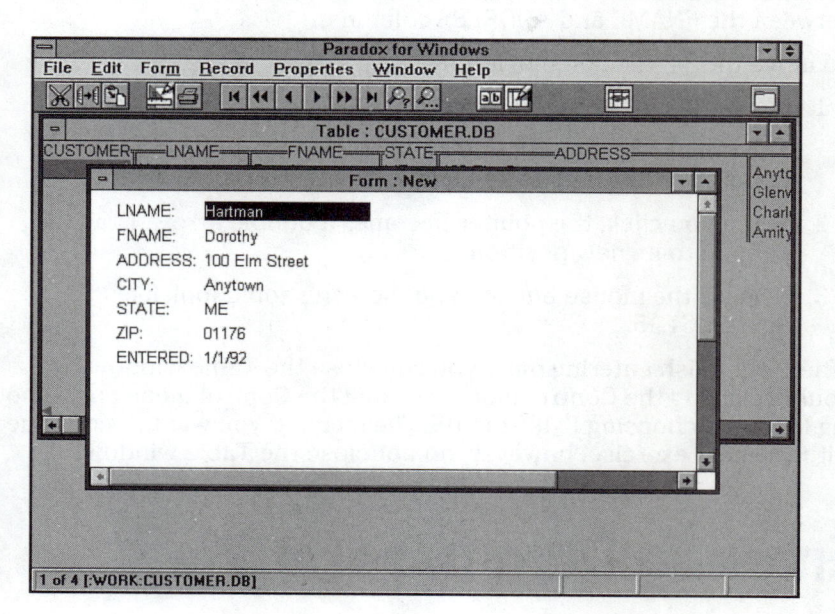

FIG. QS1.16

A Quick form for the CUSTOMER table.

QUICK START 1 — STARTING YOUR FIRST PARADOX FOR WINDOWS SESSION

NOTE The F7 key is a toggle switch that moves you back and forth from the Table view window to the Form view window. You also can switch between Form and Table view by clicking on the window you want or by clicking the Quick Form (a sheet of paper with lines and fields) and Table View (a ledger with a lightning bolt) buttons in the SpeedBar. When you switch from Table view to Form view, both windows remain on-screen.

Use the quick form to enter three more records, using the names and addresses of family members or friends. Entering data in a form is much the same as entering data in a table.

To enter records in Form view, follow these steps:

1. Type data in each field, pressing Tab, Enter, or the down-arrow key to move to the next field. You also can use the mouse to move from one field to another by clicking in the desired field.

   Press PgDn or F12 to move to the next record and PgUp or F11 to move to the preceding record. You also can use the arrow buttons on the SpeedBar to move through one record at a time, to move through a group of records, or to move directly to the first or last record. When you reach the end of a record, press the Ins key to clear the form so that you can enter the next record.

2. When you finish entering data, close the Form window. Click the Control menu in the upper left corner of the Form window, and then choose Close or double-click the Control menu.

3. Double-click the Control menu of the Table window to close the window.

   The dialog box shown in figure QS1.17 appears, asking whether you want to save the form you have created. If you have changed table properties, you also are asked whether you want to save your changes.

4. For this exercise, choose No.

   Because you changed the display properties of the table, a second dialog box appears, asking whether you want to save these changes. For this exercise, choose No. You are returned to the Paradox desktop.

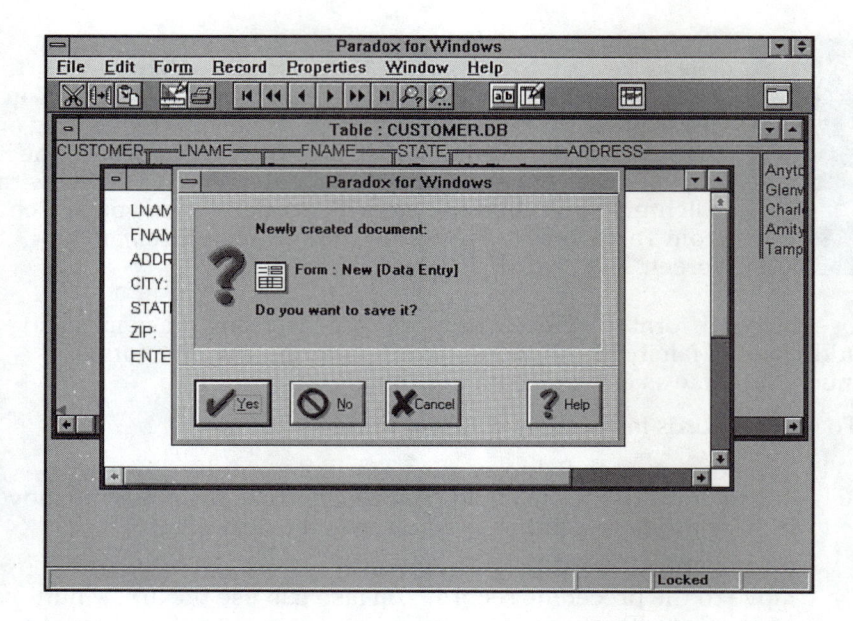

FIG. QS1.17

The save newly created document dialog box.

Using Query By Example

In a small table, you can search for records by scanning through all the entries to see whether they meet your criteria. As a table grows, however, this method becomes impractical. Imagine reading through a hundred, a thousand, or ten thousand customer records to find the records you want. Paradox for Windows provides a simple, but powerful, search feature called query by example (QBE). The QBE feature enables you to search a table based on the data in one or more fields.

QBE is one of the features that made Paradox for DOS so successful because information is retrieved easily without programming.

To write a query to retrieve all customers from New York from the CUSTOMER table, follow these steps:

1. Choose File from the desktop menu bar. The File menu opens.

2. Choose New from the File menu. The New submenu appears.

3. Choose Query from the New submenu.

    The Query window opens, showing a small, empty window below the SpeedBar. This window is where you enter your search. Paradox immediately displays the Select File dialog box so that you can choose the table to use for the query (see fig. QS1.18).

QUICK START 1 — STARTING YOUR FIRST PARADOX FOR WINDOWS SESSION

4. Choose CUSTOMER.DB from the list by clicking the file name, and then clicking the OK button. If you do not see CUSTOMER.DB in the file list, use the scroll bars to display additional tables.

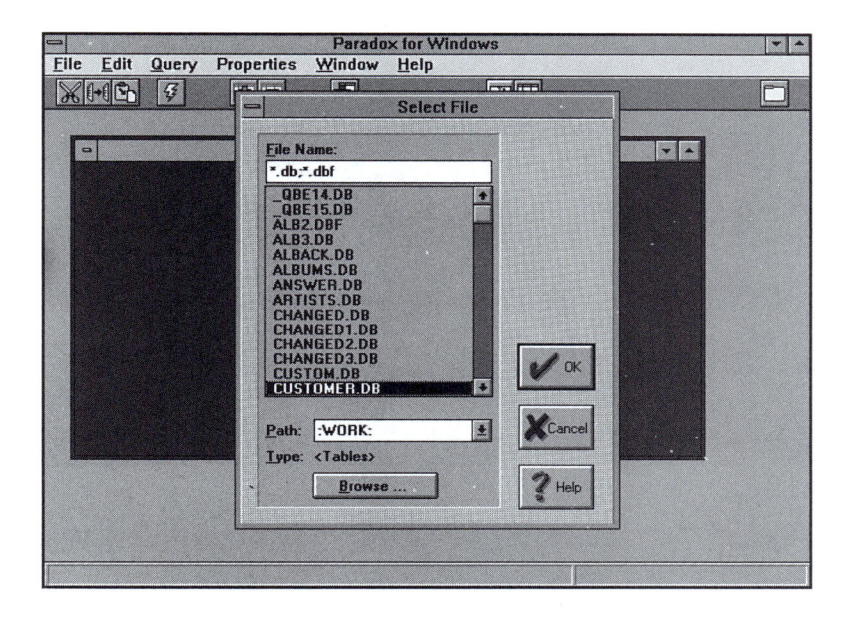

FIG. QS1.18

The Query window.

A blank version of the CUSTOMER table appears in the query window (see fig. QS1.19). The columns are in the same order as in the data table, but no records are displayed. An empty check box appears under each column heading.

5. Click the check boxes for the LNAME, FNAME, and CITY fields. These are the fields that will be retrieved in the query.

Paradox provides several kinds of check marks that produce different query results. This exercise uses the standard check mark. Other check marks are covered in depth in Chapter 4, "Getting Started with Query By Example."

TIP

If you check a field by mistake, simply click the check box again to clear the check mark.

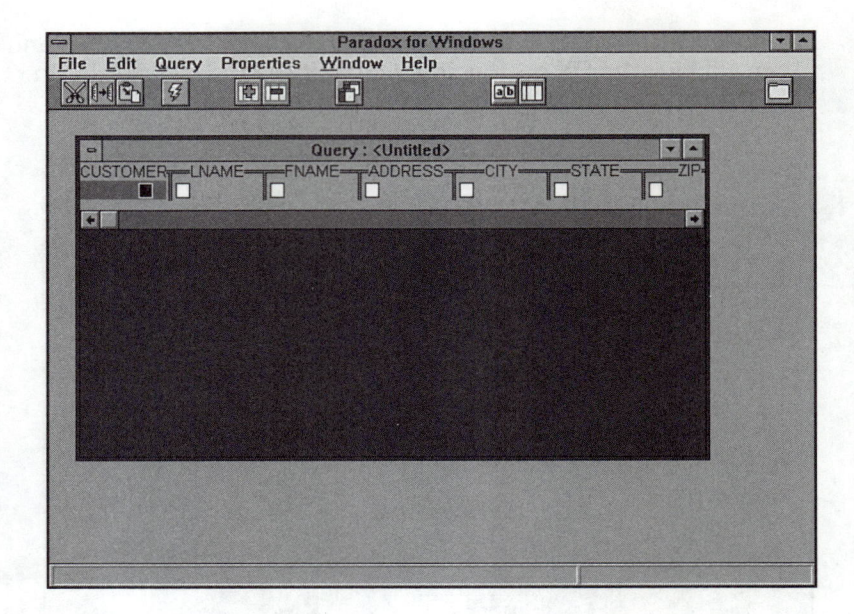

I — PARADOX FOR WINDOWS FUNDAMENTALS

FIG. QS1.19

The CUSTOMER table in the Query window.

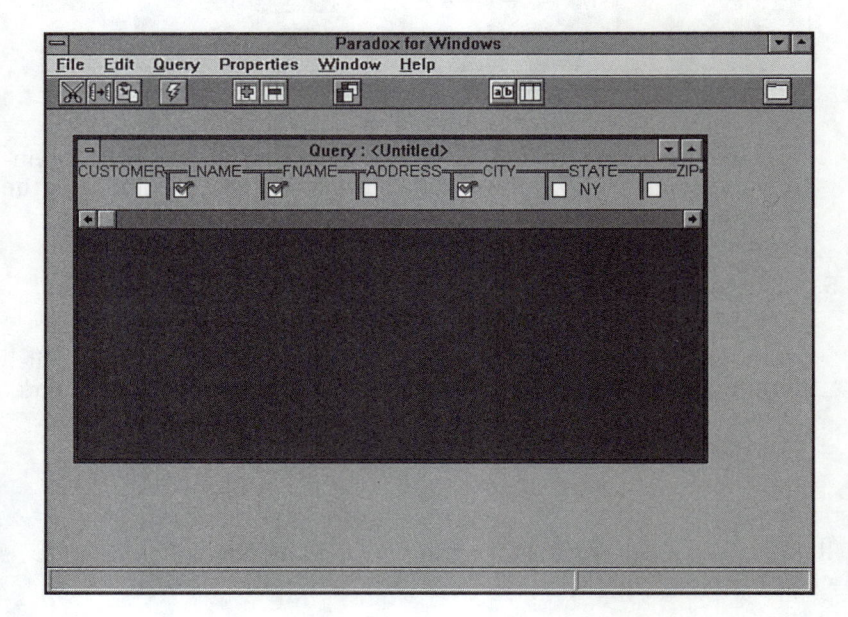

FIG. QS1.20

The completed query for New York customers.

QUICK START 1 — STARTING YOUR FIRST PARADOX FOR WINDOWS SESSION

6. Enter **NY** in the state field to select only those customers from New York, as shown in figure QS1.20. To do this, click the state field. The cursor becomes a text insertion marker. Type **NY**. Be sure to properly capitalize search criteria, because Paradox for Windows is case-sensitive.

7. Run the query by clicking the Run Query button in the SpeedBar (looks like a lightning bolt). The Answer table lists data from all records with NY entered as the state (see fig. QS1.21).

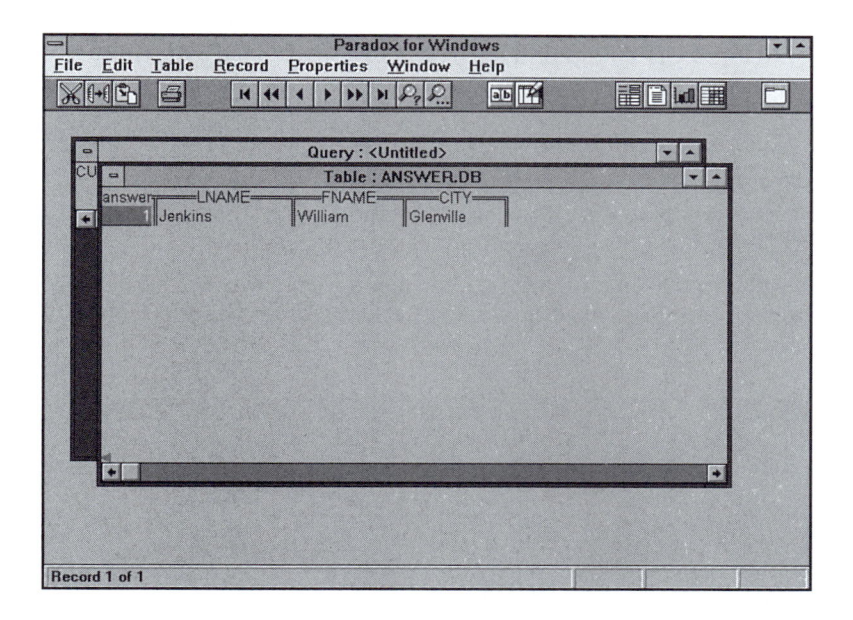

FIG. QS1.21

The Answer table.

For now, leave the Query window open so that you can proceed to the next exercises.

You can search more than one field at a time by entering multiple search criteria in the query. (Multiple search criteria and query operators are discussed in detail in Chapter 4.)

Paradox also enables you to run queries based on incomplete or misspelled information by using special query operators. The two handiest query operators are LIKE and .. (two periods).

You use the LIKE operator to find entries that are similar to the entry for which you are searching. If you use LIKE SMITH in a query, Paradox could retrieve Smythe, Smithe, or Smith.

I — PARADOX FOR WINDOWS FUNDAMENTALS

You use the .. operator, which is a wild-card operator, in place of an unknown letter or letters. To search for all cities whose names begin with the word New, for example, you would type **New..** as the value to match. Paradox might retrieve New York, New Orleans, and Newtown Square.

To search the CUSTOMER table for the records of all customers from cities whose names start with the letter A, follow these steps:

1. Clear the preceding search criterion by clicking in the STATE field and pressing the Backspace key to delete NY.

2. Click the CITY field and enter **A..** as your search criterion.

3. Click the Run Query button to run the query.

4. The Answer table shows the records retrieved (see fig. QS1.22).

5. To close the Answer table, double-click the Control menu. To close the Query window, double-click its Control menu. The Save This Object? dialog box appears (see fig. QS1.23).

You can use this dialog box to save a query for reuse later. For now, click No. Paradox closes the dialog box and returns you to the desktop.

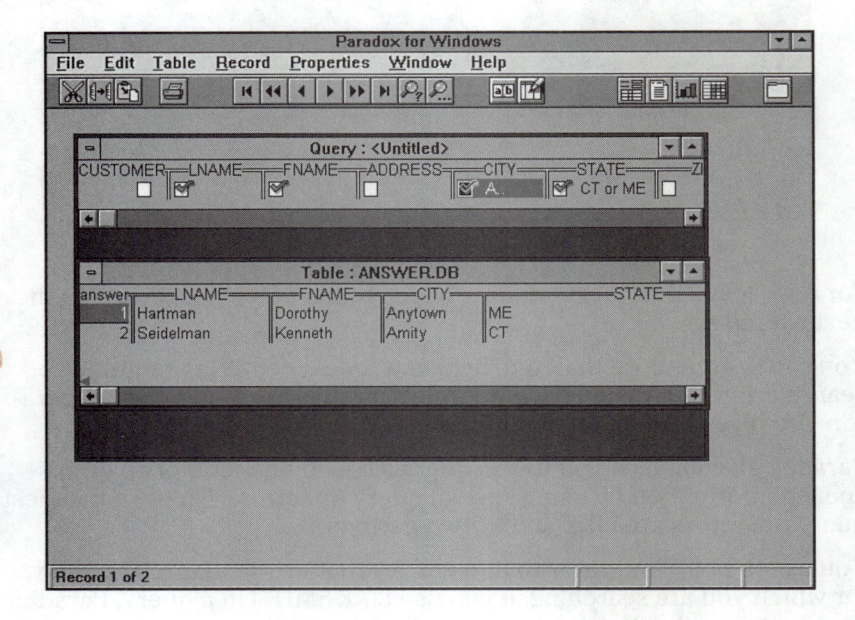

FIG. QS1.22

The Answer table for the A.. city search.

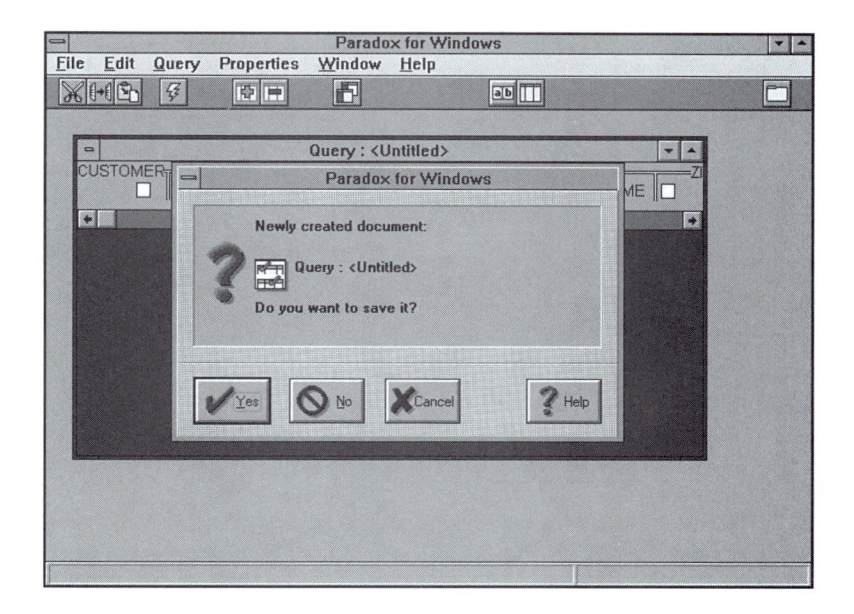

QUICK START 1 — STARTING YOUR FIRST PARADOX FOR WINDOWS SESSION

FIG. QS1.23
The Save This Object? dialog box.

Printing a Quick Report

Now you know how to create a table, enter some records using Form or Table view, and search for information with a query. But what if someone else needs information from your database? What if you need to send a fax of your customer list to Cincinnati? Paradox for Windows enables you to produce printed output from the database.

The simplest way to print a report is to create a quick report. To create a quick report, follow these steps:

1. From the desktop, open the CUSTOMER table by choosing File, Open, Table.

2. Select CUSTOMER and click OK. The Table window appears (refer to earlier fig. QS1.12).

3. Click the Quick Report button in the SpeedBar (this icon is on the right side of the SpeedBar and looks like a few lines on a white piece of paper), press Shift+F7, or choose Table, Quick Report from the menu. The Print the File dialog box appears, as shown in figure QS1.24.

I — PARADOX FOR WINDOWS FUNDAMENTALS

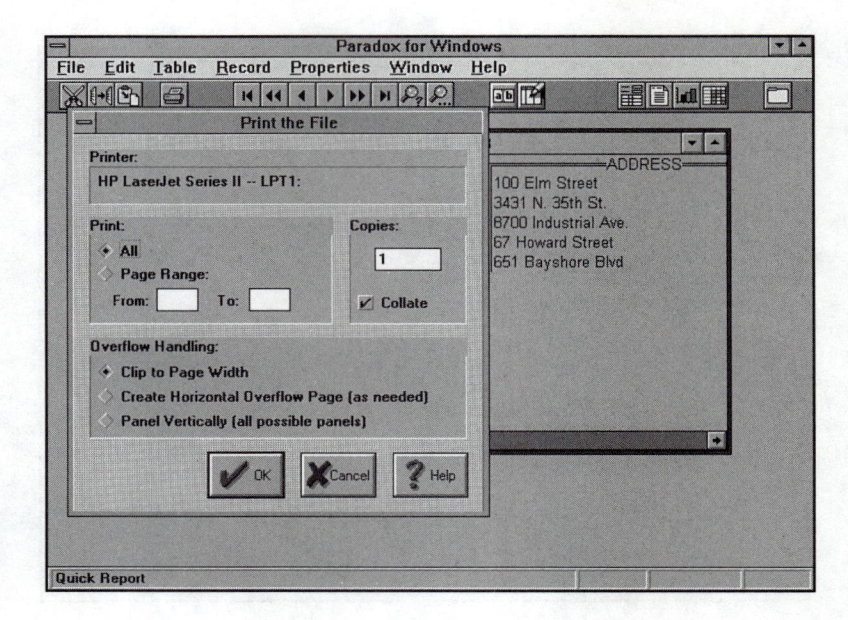

FIG. QS1.24

The Print the File dialog box.

This dialog box enables you to choose printer options and to specify the number of pages to be printed.

4. Make sure that your printer is on-line. Click the OK box to accept the default setting—one copy of all pages. The quick report prints all the fields for all the records in the table, as shown in figure QS1.25.

FIG. QS1.25

The printed Quick Report for CUSTOMER.DB.

A quick report may not be the most elegant format available but is difficult to beat for speedy results. To learn how to create custom reports, see Chapter 6, "Getting Started with Reports."

Closing Paradox for Windows

No matter how much you enjoy working with Paradox for Windows, you eventually must leave the program so that you can participate in other activities. When you finish a Paradox for Windows session, you can close the program in any of the following ways:

- Choose File, Exit.
- Click the Control menu of the open window and then choose Close, or just double-click the Control menu.
- Press Alt+F4 (the keyboard equivalent for Close).

When you exit the program, Paradox for Windows saves all the files you worked on during the session and returns you to the Windows Program Manager.

If you plan to resume your Paradox for Windows session, you may want to *minimize* the window rather than close it. To minimize a window, click the window's Control menu and then choose Minimize, or click the Minimize button (a downward pointing arrow) in the upper right corner of the window. The window closes and the Paradox for Windows icon is shown on your Windows desktop.

To resume your Paradox for Windows session, either double-click the icon or press Ctrl+Esc to move from one window to another.

Quick Start Summary

In this quick start, you defined a table, entered records, retrieved data, and created a printed report.

Part I expands on the functions discussed in this chapter. The following chapters cover topics ranging from navigating through the program to designing sophisticated tables, forms, and queries.

CHAPTER 1

Navigating Paradox

Paradox for Windows offers a complex but productive environment for programmers and end users. Like other Windows applications, Paradox for Windows is complex because it offers many different ways to perform the same tasks. Paradox for Windows is productive due to its visual nature, enabling you to point and click your way quickly through a job. This chapter introduces the fundamental terms and concepts you need to use Paradox for Windows and illustrates how you will interact with the program through its menus, windows, and dialog boxes.

If Paradox for Windows is your first database program, many of the concepts introduced in this chapter will be new to you. If you are experienced with databases but Paradox for Windows is your first graphical user interface (GUI) program, you will need to spend time learning how to use Windows. Although some of the techniques of Paradox for Windows may seem foreign at first, after some experimentation you may wonder how you ever used a non-GUI database. For a primer on Windows, read Appendix B, "Using the Graphical User Interface," which covers Windows basics.

Even if you are an experienced Paradox for DOS user, you may need some time to unlearn the DOS commands and become accustomed to new menus, dialog boxes, and other Windows features. Paradox for Windows is fundamentally different from its DOS predecessor and operates from a distinctly Windows perspective.

I — PARADOX FOR WINDOWS FUNDAMENTALS

NOTE If you plan to read the other chapters in Part I in order, you can skip this chapter. The step-by-step instructions that accompany the examples later in the book restate the necessary keystrokes and mouse movements. If you want to explore Paradox for Windows with a minimum of reading, take the time to work through this chapter so that you can familiarize yourself with the program.

TIP The most painless way to learn how to use Windows is to play the games included with Windows. Start with Solitaire. Practice moving and resizing the window, using the mouse to move the cards from one stack to another, pulling down menus for help and options, and minimizing the window when your boss enters the room. Pull down each of the menus of the game and try changing all the options you can find.

This chapter is divided into three parts. The first part of this chapter offers a map showing of Paradox windows. The second part defines key object types in Paradox. The last part of this chapter describes the *user interface* (the way that the application communicates with you).

You may want to refer to Paradox for Windows on-screen while you read this chapter. If you have not yet installed Paradox for Windows, refer to Appendix A for detailed installation instructions.

Using the Desktop

The Desktop is the first screen that appears when you open Paradox for Windows (see fig. 1.1). From the Desktop you can create new database objects, open existing objects, or access menus containing network or database utility functions. When you close a Paradox window, you return to the Paradox for Windows Desktop.

The Paradox interface consists of a number of windows devoted to particular database functions, such as editing tables, writing queries, and creating graphs. Because several windows can be displayed on-screen at one time, you can switch easily from one database task to another. With Paradox, as with all Windows applications, you can switch back and forth to other programs, such as your favorite word processor or spreadsheet, and even cut and paste objects into Paradox that you create in another program.

1 — NAVIGATING PARADOX

FIG. 1.1
The Paradox for Windows Desktop.

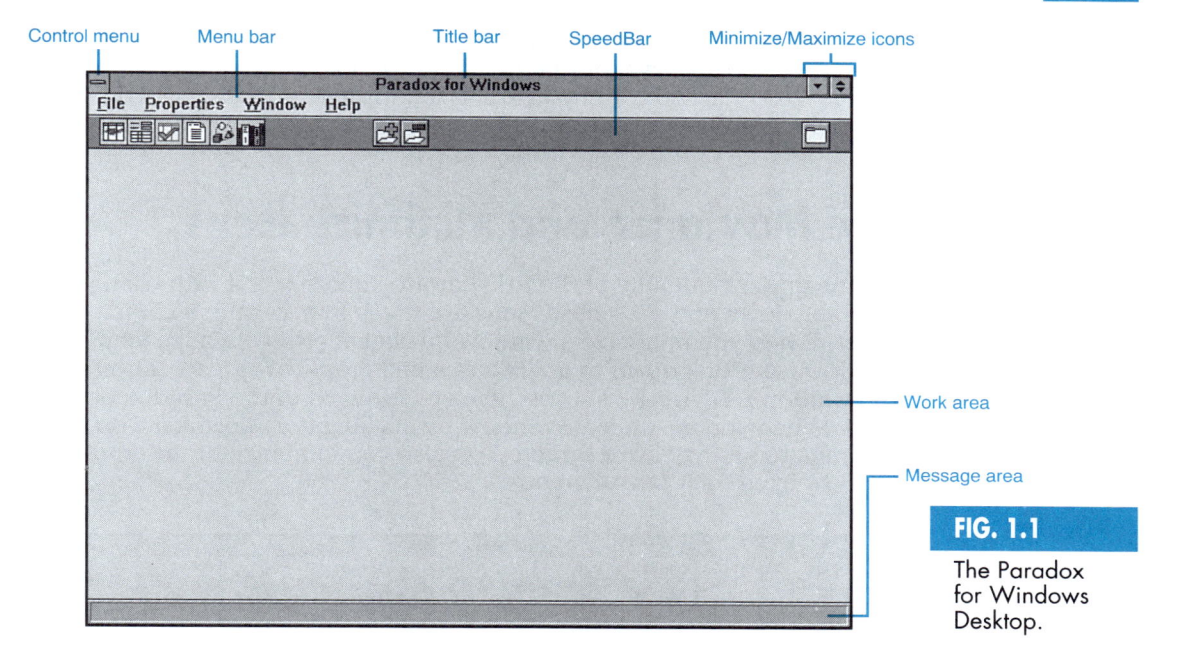

The Desktop is divided into six areas: the title bar, the Control menu, the menu bar, the SpeedBar, the work area, and the message area. The following sections describe each of these areas.

The Title Bar

The uppermost line of the screen is the Desktop *title bar*, which contains the name of the program you are running (in this case, Paradox for Windows). When you perform different actions in Paradox for Windows, new windows are opened. The title bars of these windows show the name of the current window. If you are editing a table, for example, the title bar displays [Edit - TABLE.DB], where TABLE.DB is the name of the table. If you minimize the Paradox for Windows window while you are in the middle of an operation, the title remains with the Paradox for Windows icon to identify the window.

The Control Menu

In the upper left corner of the Desktop is the square icon for the Control menu. You use the Control menu to exit from Paradox or to switch to another Windows application. Click the Control menu icon to reveal the Control menu. You can choose options from the Control menu with the mouse, arrow keys, or function keys. Double-clicking the Control menu closes Paradox, and you are asked to save any changes you made since the last time you saved.

The Maximize and Minimize Icons

On the upper right side of the title bar are square icons with triangles pointing down and up. These icons are the *Minimize* and *Maximize* icons. When you minimize a window by clicking the Minimize icon, the window is shrunk down to an icon (a small graphic representation of the window). Figure 1.2 shows the icons for each of the Paradox objects. When you maximize a window by clicking the Maximize icon, it expands to fill the entire screen. You also can minimize or maximize a window from the Control menu.

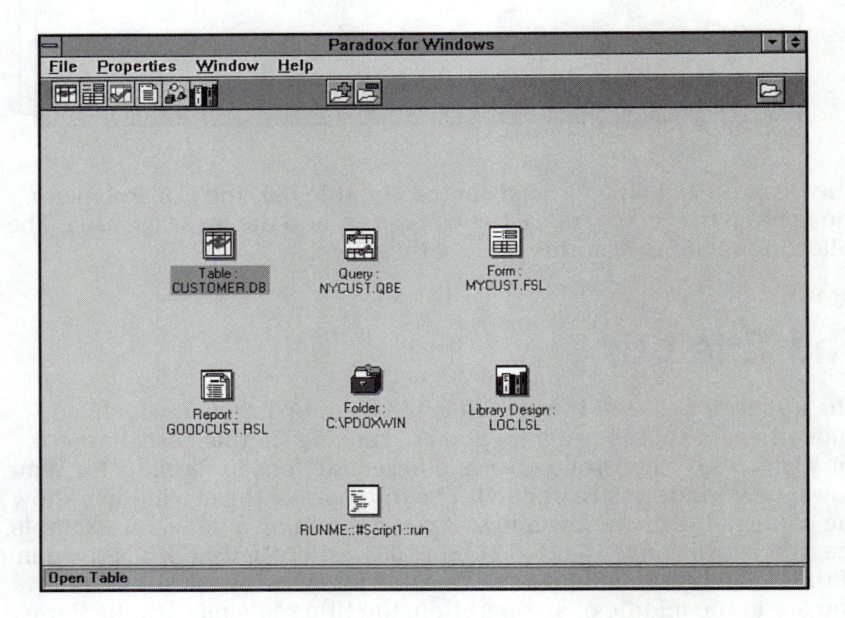

FIG. 1.2

Paradox for Windows object icons.

The Menu Bar

From the Desktop you can open a number of different menus, submenus, and windows. You control the size, position, and relationship (layering or tiling) of windows. In layering, windows are placed in a stack, one on top of the other. In tiling, windows are set side by side so that they do not overlap.

1 — NAVIGATING PARADOX

The second line of the screen is the *menu bar*. The menu bar lists each of the menus, with one letter in each menu name underlined. You can select an option from the menu bar by clicking on the option, or by pressing the Alt key and the underscored letter (called the *hot key*) of the menu. For example, Alt+F pulls down the File menu, and Alt+W pulls down the Window menu. You also can move the cursor to the menu bar by pressing F10 and then use the arrow keys to select a menu. Pressing the Alt key also takes you to the menu bar.

The Paradox for Windows Desktop offers four menus: File, Properties, Window, and Help. The available menus differ from one Paradox window to the next. Windows contain menus with options unique to their function. The Table window, for example, contains menus to move forward or backward through database records, or to search for a specific record. Some menus (such as File, Window, and Help) are available in all windows.

When you pull down a menu, a list of its options appears. Figure 1.3 shows the File menu pulled down. Paradox has three kinds of options that can be listed on a menu: options that call other menus, options that invoke dialog boxes, and options that directly perform the action you select. Menu options can be active or inactive. The options displayed in bold letters are currently active. The dimmer (usually gray) menu options are inactive and therefore cannot be used—usually because the menu option does not apply at this time. The Paste option, for example, is inactive until you have cut or copied an object.

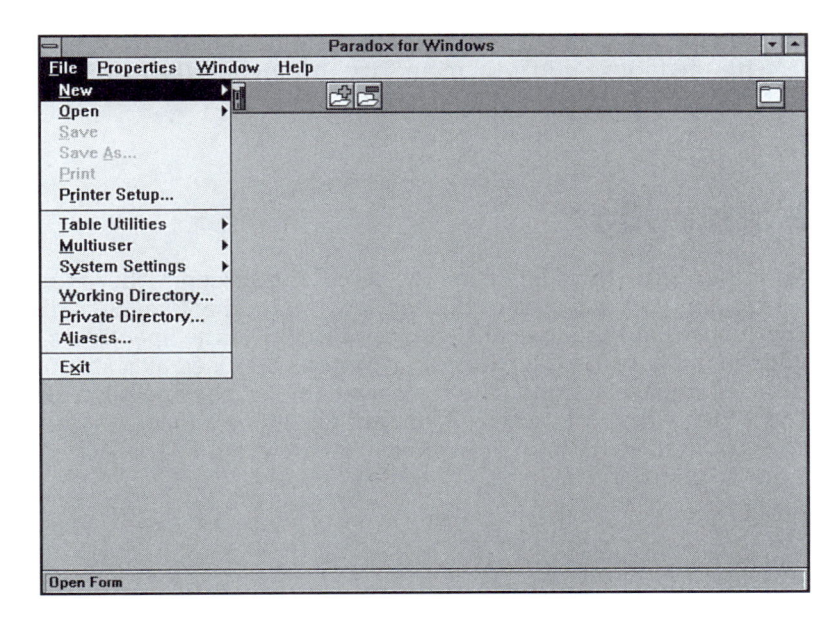

FIG. 1.3

The File menu.

You can choose menu options by using a hot key, clicking the menu option, or moving to the menu option with the arrow keys and pressing Enter.

Some menu options call up submenus. Menu choices with submenus are marked with a small triangle after the menu option. You can make submenu choices by clicking the choice with the mouse or using a hot key (if available). All options on the menu bar have hot keys (Alt plus the underlined letter), but not all choices on menus or submenus have hot keys.

Menu options that invoke dialog boxes are marked with an ellipsis (...) after the menu option. After you choose the menu option, a dialog box prompts you for additional information. The Open Document dialog box, for example, enables you to enter or choose the file name, and the Print File dialog box enables you to enter the page range and number of copies to be printed.

If a menu option is not marked with an ellipsis, choosing that option performs the action without additional menus, dialog boxes, or other prompts. Choosing the Exit choice on the File menu, for example, closes the Paradox Desktop.

T I P The hot keys used for menu names and menu choices are not always intuitive. This is especially true for menus whose options start with the same letters. Be sure to look at the menu before pressing what seems to be the obvious hot key. You may want to choose from menus with the mouse until you memorize the keyboard shortcuts.

The SpeedBar

The *SpeedBar* is the third line from the top of the screen. Other Windows programs call this area of the window the toolbar. The SpeedBar displays icons that Paradox calls *buttons* or *tools*. All the SpeedBars are reproduced in figure 1.4. The SpeedBar buttons are used as a shortcut to perform database actions. The tools available on the SpeedBar depend on which window is active. If you are designing a form, for example, you can have tools to draw boxes, create graphs, or switch from one mode to another.

1 — NAVIGATING PARADOX

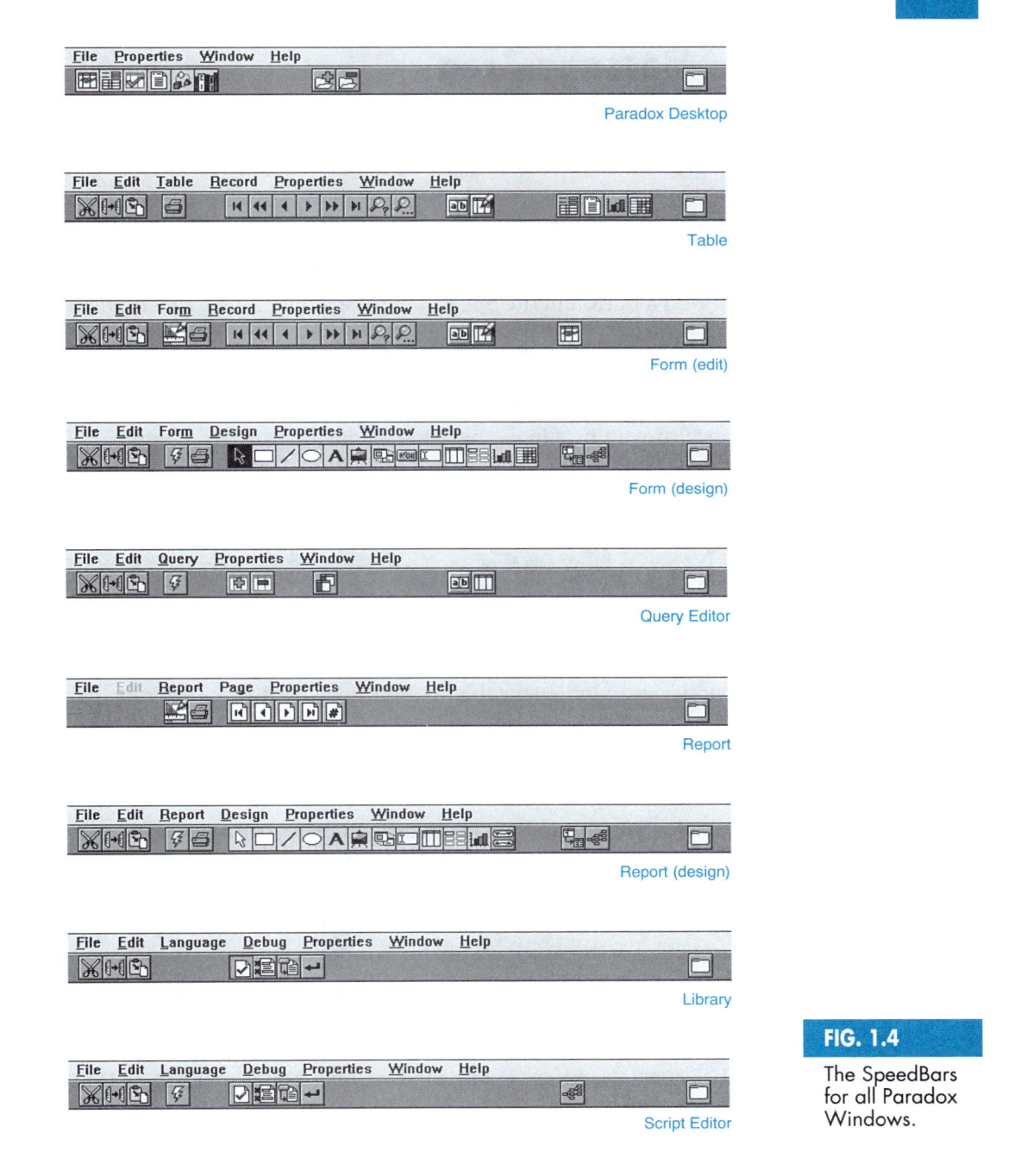

Paradox Desktop

Table

Form (edit)

Form (design)

Query Editor

Report

Report (design)

Library

Script Editor

FIG. 1.4

The SpeedBars for all Paradox Windows.

The Message Area

The *message area* is the bottom line of the window. This area displays messages from Paradox for Windows, such as status reports and error messages. When you use the mouse to perform a function, the message area often displays a description of the current action, such as `Resizing column width`.

The message area is divided into three sections. The left section shows SpeedBar help and status information. When you place the mouse pointer on a button in the SpeedBar, for example, the name of the button is displayed in the message area. The middle section of the message area shows the record number of the record you are viewing or editing. This section of the message area usually is blank. The right side of the message area shows the mode (such as Edit or View mode).

All Paradox windows have the same elements: title bar, menu bar, SpeedBar, work area, and message area. After you learn to work with one window, you can easily learn to work with them all.

Using the Mouse and the Keyboard

The mouse is an indispensable tool for developing applications in Paradox for Windows. Using the mouse often is the fastest way—and in some cases the only way—to accomplish many common database tasks. For most Paradox applications, the mouse alone is insufficient; you must use the keyboard to type data into fields.

Paradox for Windows offers keyboard equivalents for many mouse actions and menu options. Table 1.1 shows the keyboard equivalents for some Paradox for Windows commands. Keyboard shortcuts (especially the function keys) enable the experienced user to save some mouse movements. Throughout this book, both methods of navigation are explained with each Paradox for Windows function.

You use the keyboard most frequently when you define tables, enter data, and perform queries, and most mouse commands have keyboard equivalents.

Another special keyboard command is *Super Tab*. Super Tab (F4) is the equivalent of a number of individual tab keystrokes. With Super Tab, you can jump from one multi-region area (such as a multi-record table) to another without placing the cursor in each intervening field individually. Using Shift and Super Tab returns you to the previous multi-region area.

Table 1.1. Paradox Keyboard Shortcuts

Key	Action
Menu commands	
Alt	Highlights first menu item
Alt-underlined letter	Selects menu item
Alt-space bar	Opens Paradox Control menu
Alt-hyphen	Opens Control menu of current window
Alt-Esc	Moves to next Windows application on Desktop
Alt-Tab	Restores minimized application
Alt-F4	Closes the application window
Alt-H	Opens the Help window
F1	Accesses context-sensitive help
Ctrl-Esc	Switches to another application without closing the previous application
Esc	Closes a menu
Edit menu equivalents	
Alt-Backspace	Edit/Undo
Shift-Del	Edit/Cut
Ctrl-Ins	Edit/Copy
Shift-Ins	Edit/Paste
Del	Edit/Clear or Edit/Delete
Table operations	
Ctrl-A	Search Next
Ctrl-D	Repeat last entry (ditto)
Ctrl-F	Field view
Ctrl-G	Grid menu
Ctrl-H	Heading properties for current column
Shift-Ctrl-H	Heading properties for all columns
Ctrl-L	Lock record
Shift-Ctrl-L	Commit record

continues

Table 1.1. Continued

Key	Action
Ctrl-M	Field properties for current column
Shift-Ctrl-M	Field properties for all columns
Ctrl-R	Rotate columns
Ctrl-T	Memo view
Ctrl-Z	Locate value
Shift-Ctrl-Z	Locate and replace

Design Window (Form, Report) operations

Key	Action
Ctrl-C	Copy selected object
Ctrl-D	Repeat last entry (ditto)
Ctrl-L	Lock record
Shift-Ctrl-L	Commit record
Ctrl-M	Field properties for current object
Ctrl-R	Rotate columns on table object
Ctrl-T	Memo view
Ctrl-Z	Locate value
Shift-Ctrl-Z	Locate and replace

Super tab operations

Key	Action
Ctrl-Enter	Super tab
Shift-Ctrl-Enter	Super backtab

Function key operations

	Table	Form	Query
F1	Help	Help	Help
F2	Field view	Field view	Field view
Shift-F2	Memo view	Memo view	
Ctrl-F2	Persistent Field view	Persistent Field view	
F3	Super back tab	Super back tab	Up image
Shift-F3	Page back	Page back	
F4	Super tab	Super tab	Down image
Shift-F4	Page forward	Page forward	

Key	Action		
	Table	*Form*	*Query*
F5	Lock record	Lock record	New example
Shift-F5	Commit record	Commit record	
Ctrl-F5	Post/Keep locked	Post/Keep locked	
F6	Inspect properties	Inspect properties	Check mark
Shift-F6	Multi-object inspect	Multi-object inspect	Cycle checks
F7	Quick form	Table View toggle	
Shift-F7	Quick report		
Ctrl-F7	Quick graph		
F8		View data/form	Run query design toggle
Shift-F8		Object properties	
F9	Enter/exit edit mode	Enter/exit edit mode	
F10	Menu	Menu	Menu
F11	Previous record	Previous record	Copy example
Shift-F11	Previous set	Previous set	
Ctrl-F11	First record	First record	
F12	Next record	Next record	Paste example
Shift-F12	Next set	Next set	
Ctrl-F12	Last record	Last record	

Understanding Objects

Paradox considers nearly everything in a database as an object. Although each object has different attributes, it belongs to a class of objects that share the same attributes. The *major object* types are tables, forms, queries, reports, and scripts. Paradox calls these major objects because they are the larger database elements. Major objects can consist of smaller objects, such as fields, boxes, buttons, or graphs, which Paradox calls *design objects*. You will spend most of your development time defining or using both major and design objects.

You probably have used objects in other programs, although you may not have called them by that name. The main object created by a word processor, for example, is a text document. Spreadsheet programs create spreadsheets and graphs as objects.

Each object shares fundamental characteristics with all other objects of the same type (or class). Text objects, for example, have certain characteristics, such as typeface, size, and color. Paradox calls these characteristics *properties*.

Paradox for Windows offers a rich set of properties to control the appearance of objects. To make your work easier, Paradox uses the same techniques to modify all kinds of objects. The steps you follow to enlarge a box, for example, are the same steps you follow to enlarge an ellipse. Changing the font for a text box is the same as changing the font of an alphanumeric field.

Tables

Tables are the fundamental building blocks of a relational database. A table stores information entered by users. Figure 1.5 shows a table that tracks invoices. The columns from left to right are record number, invoice number, customer number, invoice date, ship date, subtotal, tax, shipping cost, and invoice total.

A table consists of rows and columns. A row, also called a *record*, contains information about each item you are tracking in a table. A Supplier table, for example, would contain a record for each company from which you buy. A column, also known as a *field*, stores each characteristic you are tracking in the table. The Supplier table, for example, would contain a field for Company Name.

Although tables superficially resemble spreadsheets, tables have some special properties that spreadsheets lack. The meaning of each column in a database table must remain the same from the beginning of the table to the end, whereas the data type or meaning of cells in a spreadsheet column can change. The number of columns in a database table is constant for all the rows in the table. If no data is available for a particular column, that column is left blank. With a spreadsheet, however, you can change the structure of columns for different rows. Another special property of tables is the *primary key*, a field that determines whether a record is unique so that Paradox prevents you from entering duplicate records in a table. Key fields are discussed at length in Chapter 2, "Designing Paradox Tables and Databases."

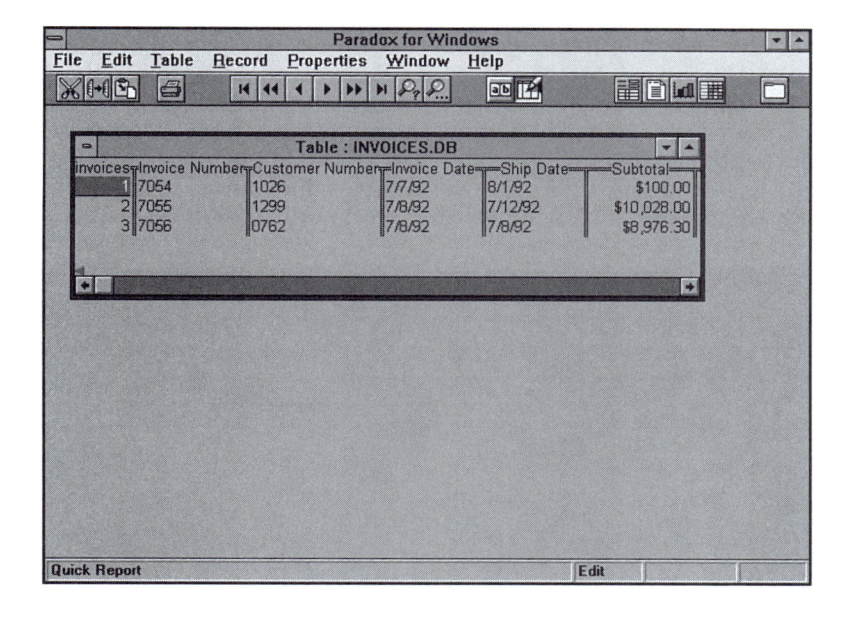

1 — NAVIGATING PARADOX

FIG. 1.5
The Invoices table.

Most tables are created by the database designer. Paradox also creates its own temporary tables for some database operations. The results of a Paradox query, for example, are stored in the Answer table.

Forms

Forms offer another way to access information in database tables. Forms often display the same fields as tables, but they display only one record at a time. Paradox for Windows enables you to create custom forms that show more than one record, or even more than one table, on one screen.

Figure 1.6 shows a form based on the invoices table in figure 1.5. Forms can include several types of Paradox objects, including text, fields, tables, graphs, and graphics. Chapter 5, "Getting Started with Forms," and Chapter 7, "Using Advanced Form Techniques," explain how to create forms.

Reports

To retrieve information from the database, you use a *report*. A report is a procedure that extracts information in the database, formats the information along with background text, and sends it to an output device (usually the printer). You can ask Paradox to retrieve some or all of the fields in the table and search for records based on the values in one or more fields. Figure 1.7 shows a simple report drawn from the invoices table, listing invoice dates and amounts. Reports can draw on information from one table or several tables and can be sent to the screen, the printer, a disk file, or any Windows print device.

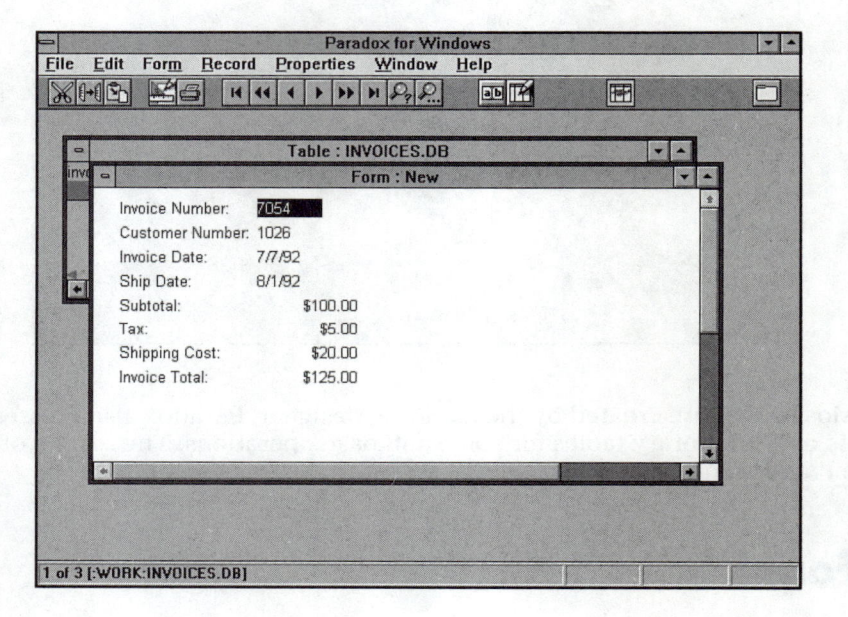

FIG. 1.6

The Invoices form.

Nearly every database application needs reports. Reports are commonly used in order processing, such as invoices and packing lists. Summary reports calculate totals and averages; examples include monthly or quarterly financial reports and the expense summary you receive from your credit card company. Chapter 6, "Getting Started with Reports," discusses reports in detail.

Queries

Queries are quick, interactive ways to retrieve information from the database. For example, you can track your sales and employees in a Paradox database. You can write queries to look up the least popular inventory items or to find all employees who did not receive a ten percent salary increase in the past year. Figure 1.8 shows a query listing all customers from New York or Florida.

FIG. 1.7

The invoice list report.

You also can use queries to insert, delete, or modify information in your tables. For example, a query can give a twenty percent raise to everyone in the technical support department who has worked with your company for more than five years. Chapter 4, "Getting Started with Query By Example," and Chapter 8, "Using Advanced Query By Example," provide more information on using queries.

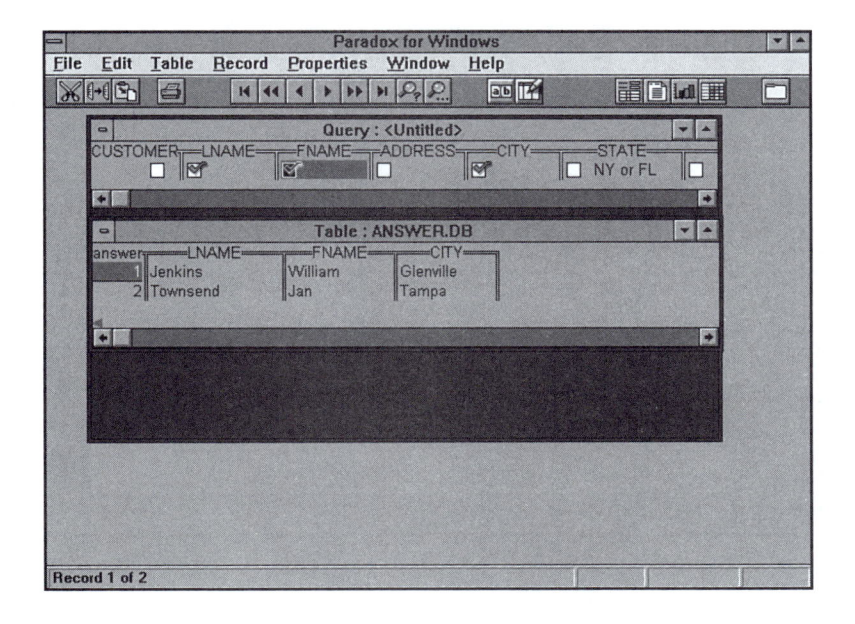

FIG. 1.8

A query: customers from NY or FL.

Scripts

You can use *scripts* to automate repetitive or complicated tasks. A script is like a program that combines a number of actions. Paradox for Windows uses a language called ObjectPAL to write scripts. Part III covers the ObjectPAL language.

For example, you might write a script to control the behavior of a button on a form so that pressing the button runs a report or prompts the user for information to perform a search.

Design Objects

Several design objects are used in screen displays, such as Paradox forms and reports (see fig. 1.9). Design objects generate output from the database or present data to the user. They can be moved about the screen and manipulated by changing their size or shape. Because Paradox for Windows is a graphical database, a wide range of design objects, including graphic images, are available.

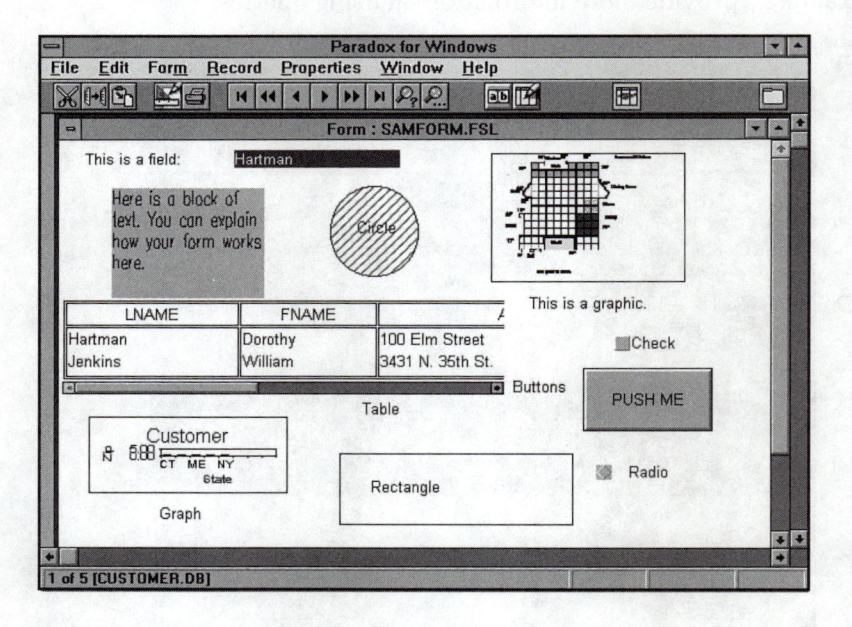

FIG. 1.9

A sample of design objects.

The following list describes all the types of design objects:

- *Text*. Text is used to label fields and other areas on a display document. You can control the size, color, and font (typeface) of text to enhance the appearance of a form.

- *Boxes, lines, and ellipses*. To highlight areas on-screen (or a printed report), you can draw boxes, lines, and ellipses (circles and ovals) of various sizes and colors. The drawing capabilities of Paradox for Windows are similar to the drawing capabilities in paint programs.

- *Fields.* Fields are used to enter data into columns in database tables. Like text properties, you can change field properties to enhance the look of a form. Some data types, such as numbers and dates, offer several display formats.

- *Tables.* Table display objects show several records at a time. Each field is shown as a column and each record as a row. Table display objects (sometimes called table frames) are used in reports to show detailed records, such as line items for an invoice.

- *Graphs.* You can build business graphs (such as pie charts, plots, or bar graphs) based on data in Paradox for Windows tables as part of a form or report. Figure 1.9 shows a bar graph chart created with Paradox for Windows.

- *Crosstabs.* Another database object, the crosstab (short for cross tabulation), offers a special way to look at your data. A crosstab is similar to a spreadsheet; it presents a matrix of cells for each combination of factors. For example, you might count the membership of your association based on state and academic degree. A crosstab creates a display using these factors listed at the top and the left side of the screen, as shown in figure 1.9.

  Crosstabs are powerful tools for computing numerical data because they can tabulate two or more factors. You can use a crosstab, for example, to show a breakdown of automobile accidents by time of day and weather, and the total number of accidents for each time period and weather condition.

- *Multi-record objects.* A multi-record object is similar to a table in that you can use it to display several records from a table on a data-entry form. A multi-record object, however, can list the fields in any format you desire—not just in rows and columns like a table. For example, you can use a multi-record object to print mailing labels three across by repeating the format for a label three times.

- *Graphics.* Graphics are scanned or drawn images, such as a corporate logo. Most graphics are bit-mapped images (the location of every dot on-screen is recorded) and can require significant disk space for storage.

- *Buttons.* Buttons provide one of the fastest, most direct ways to communicate with the user. To activate a button, click your selection with the mouse. You can define several kinds of buttons, including radio buttons, pushbuttons, and check boxes. You can show a button's function by adding text or graphics to it. Figure 1.9 shows several button types used in Paradox for Windows. To define buttons, you must use ObjectPAL, the programming language of Paradox for Windows. Because buttons are used interactively, they are available only in forms, not in reports. Buttons are discussed in Chapter 7, "Using Advanced Form Techniques."

- *OLE objects*. Object linking and embedding, or OLE, enables two Windows applications to communicate. OLE objects look like ordinary Paradox objects, but their content is controlled by another program. An OLE object is connected to the application that created it; changes made to the object in the original program are reflected automatically in Paradox for Windows.

Working with Objects

Paradox offers tools and techniques for handling each type of object. The mouse is used primarily to choose from menus, select objects, and move objects. The mouse is probably your best choice for fine movement of objects.

To select an object, click the mouse on the object. The object is highlighted after you select it. The exact way the object is highlighted—by changing its color, adding handles, or other ways—depends on the object type and the current mode.

Selected objects show small squares called *handles* around their perimeter (see fig. 1.10). You use these handles to drag or stretch the object to the desired size or shape.

You can select several objects at once by clicking the objects you want to select, one after the other, while holding down the Shift key. To select all the objects in an area, hold down the Shift key, click on one corner of the area to be selected, and then move to the opposite (diagonal) corner of the selected area. A box appears around the area while you are selecting it. When you release the mouse button, all objects within the rectangle will be selected.

One of the characteristics of object-oriented programs is that objects have certain inherent attributes. These attributes are called *properties*. The specific properties are different for each type of object. Boxes, for example, have the properties of color, frame (or border), and pattern (see fig. 1.11). You can view these object properties by right-clicking (pressing the right mouse button) the object. To change a property, click the appropriate option on the pop-up properties menu and change it.

You can modify an object's size, shape, and other properties. Position the mouse pointer on the object, click it, and then pull or drag to manipulate the object.

1 — NAVIGATING PARADOX

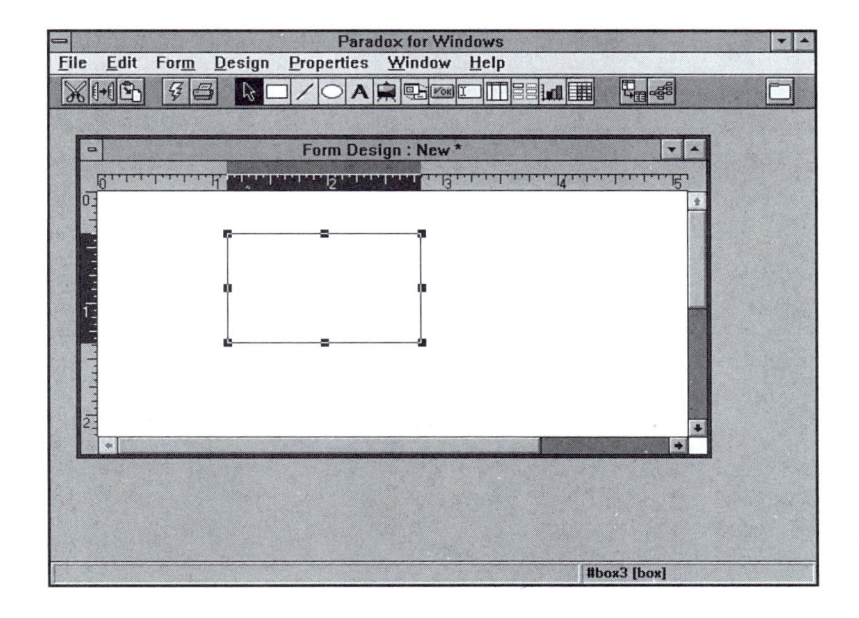

FIG. 1.10

Handles on a box object.

Viewing the properties of an object is called *inspecting* in Paradox for Windows. To inspect an object, right-click the object, or select the object and press Shift+F8.

The following example shows how to create an object, move it, change its shape, examine its properties, and change its color. This example uses a square in the form window, but the same techniques apply to other objects in other Paradox windows.

To create the box, follow these steps:

1. From the Paradox desktop, choose File, New, Form. The Data Model dialog box appears.

2. For this example, no data table is required. Click OK to continue. If a data table were required, you would choose it from the list that appears in the Data Model dialog box.

3. The Page Layout dialog box appears. Click OK to accept the default settings.

4. The Create Form window appears. The SpeedBar shows all the tools available to create forms (refer to earlier fig. 1.4).

5. Click the Box tool, the seventh button from the left on the SpeedBar. The mouse pointer changes to a box symbol to indicate which tool you are using.

I — PARADOX FOR WINDOWS FUNDAMENTALS

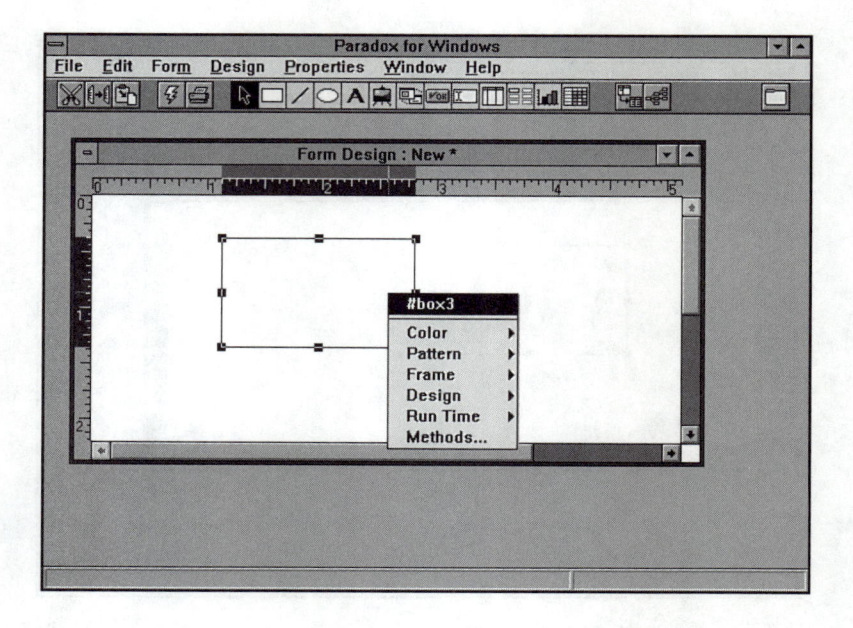

FIG. 1.11

The properties of a box.

6. Move the mouse pointer to the center of the window. Click and drag the mouse down and to the right, until the box is a rectangle about two inches wide and one inch tall.

7. Release the mouse button and the box is displayed, with square handles on all sides. Your box should look something like the one shown earlier in figure 1.10.

To move the box you have created, do the following:

1. Click in the center of the box and drag the box to a new location.

   When you move the box, only its outline is displayed.

2. Release the mouse button when you have positioned the box.

To resize the box, complete these steps:

1. Click on the handle in the middle of the left side of the box and drag the handle to the left or right.

   When you place the mouse pointer on the handle, it changes from an arrow to a two-sided arrow, indicating the directions in which you can move the handle. When you move the handle, the side of the box moves, enlarging or shrinking the box.

2. Release the mouse button when the box is the desired size.

   You can use the handles on the corners of the box to change the height and width of the box at the same time. If you use a corner handle, the mouse pointer changes to a diagonal two-sided arrow to indicate how you can move the handle.

To change the color of the box, follow these steps:

1. Place the mouse pointer on the box and right-click to inspect its properties.
2. From the pop-up properties menu, select Color. The Color property controls the background color of the object.
3. Choose light blue by clicking the light blue color swatch in the color palette. The properties of a box are shown in figure 1.11.

   The color of the box immediately changes to the new color you selected. If you don't like this color, repeat step 3 to change it.

To close the Form window, do the following:

1. When you are finished with this example, double-click the Control menu of the Form window, or click the Control menu and choose E*x*it.
2. A dialog box appears, asking `File is new. Save it?` If you click Yes, you are asked for the name of the form. If you don't want to save the form, click No.

Finding Objects with the File Browser

With all these objects stored throughout your database, you can easily lose track of where you place them. Luckily, Paradox for Windows provides quick access to all files on your computer with the File Browser. Dialog boxes that prompt you for a file name include a button to open the File Browser. Figure 1.12 shows the File Browser window.

The File Browser window shows a directory tree on the left side of the window, the individual files on the right side of the window, and graphical symbols for each file.

You can access the File Browser from inside dialog boxes that have a Browse button. The Select File dialog box, for example, contains a button to take you to the File Browser.

Communicating with Paradox

Like all computer programs, Paradox constantly is asking the user for direction. The main ways that Paradox communicates with you are dialog boxes, selection boxes, prompts, and buttons. The method used depends on how much information Paradox needs at a time to perform an action. Sometimes Paradox uses several of these techniques at once. The Create Table dialog box, for example, contains fields, buttons, and selection boxes.

Using Dialog Boxes

The most detailed means of interaction is through dialog boxes. Dialog boxes can be simple—for example, asking for confirmation to continue an action—or complex. The Create Paradox for Windows Table dialog box, for example, contains quite a few fields that you fill in to create a new data table (see fig. 1.13).

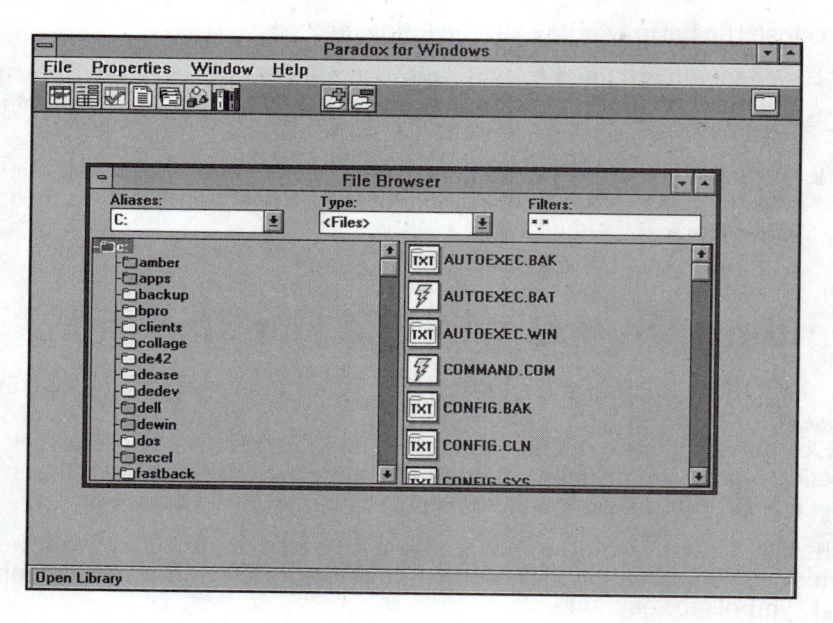

FIG. 1.12

The File Browser window.

T I P

Dialog boxes are quite similar to windows, but you can easily distinguish them from each other if you are familiar with some of the fundamental differences between them. Windows usually contain a workspace in which you place text, fields, or other objects, but dialog boxes never contain a workspace. Windows contain a menu bar; dialog boxes do not. You cannot resize or minimize a dialog box. To leave the dialog box, you must close it by completing it and selecting OK, cancelling, or closing the dialog box from its Control menu.

Using Selection Lists

Another form of communication is through check boxes. These boxes use check marks to record your preferences for a number of options at a time. You choose options by clicking the box to check or uncheck the option. The Designer Properties dialog box shown in figure 1.14, for example, contains a list of check boxes.

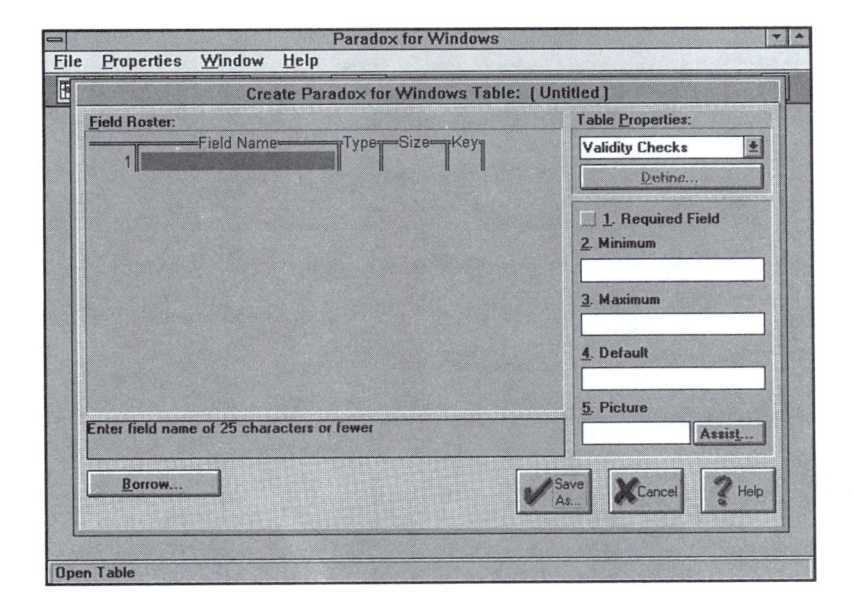

FIG. 1.13

The Create Paradox Table dialog box.

Using Buttons

You also can communicate with the user by using buttons. You can use buttons for a number of different functions, including calling other menus, choosing tools, and entering choices in tables.

Some forms use special button types. Radio buttons, for example, resemble the buttons on a car radio. Radio buttons are good for questions that can have only one answer because you can choose only one button at a time.

Responding to Prompts

When Paradox needs only a yes or no answer, it uses a prompt. For example, Paradox may ask whether you want to save your changes

I — PARADOX FOR WINDOWS FUNDAMENTALS

when you leave a window. When you respond to a prompt, you click the mouse button on Yes or No, or you press Enter.

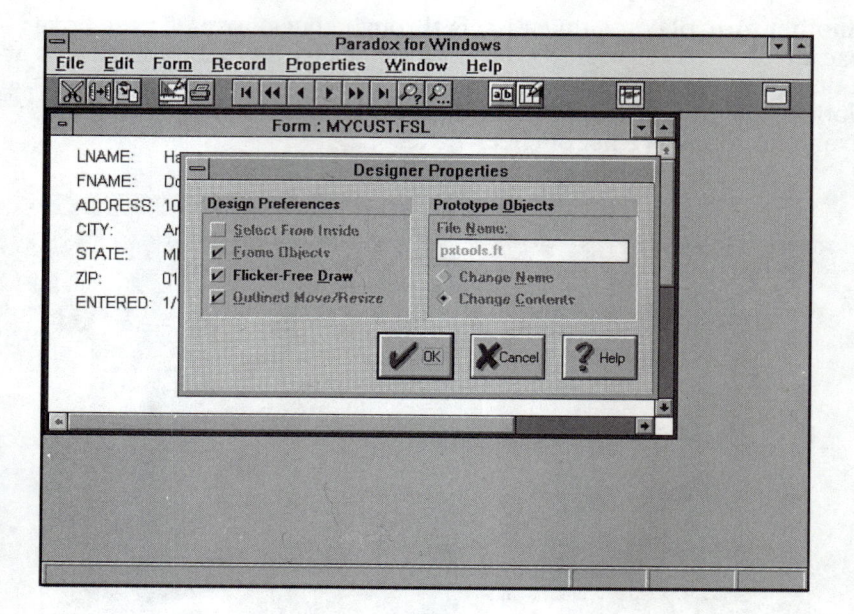

FIG. 1.14

The Designer Properties dialog box.

Working in Multiple Windows

Paradox for Windows takes full advantage of Windows' capabilities, including the capability to have multiple windows open at the same time. You can open a form, for example, and then open a query or run a report in another window without closing the form window. You can switch from one task to another and move the windows in the workspace to get the best possible view of your work.

You can switch among windows in several ways:

- Choose the Window menu and select the window you want to activate.
- If you can see the window you want to use, click the mouse on it to activate the window.
- If you have shrunk a window to an icon, double-click the icon to open the window.

To switch to another application, such as your word processor, use the Control menu in the upper left corner of the Paradox for Windows window or press Alt+Tab to activate the next application window.

1 — NAVIGATING PARADOX

If you find yourself lost in all these windows or unable to recall how to access a particular Paradox function, you can turn to on-line help, as described in the next section.

Getting Help

You can get help from Paradox in several ways without hunting down the user manuals. The on-line help is context-sensitive (the help information displayed depends on the action you are performing when you ask for help).

Press F1 to display a help screen that pertains to your current action. The help screen shown in figure 1.15 appears when you press the Help button on the Designer Properties dialog box.

Paradox for Windows contains standard Windows help, with many pages of detailed background material and assistance. If you have used help for other Windows applications, or for Windows itself, you will recognize the layout of Paradox for Windows help.

From the main Paradox for Windows window, choose Help, and then choose Map. The map for the help screen is displayed, as shown in figure 1.16.

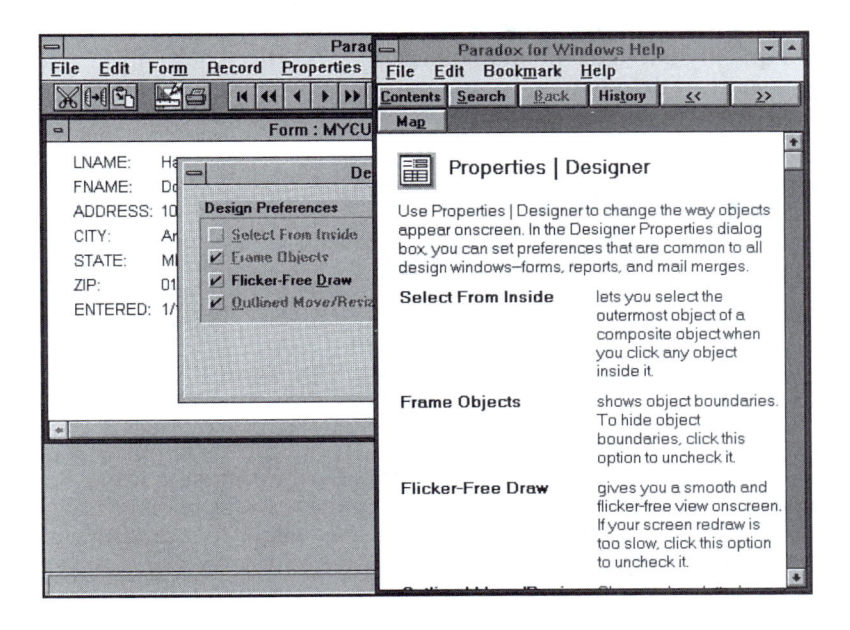

FIG. 1.15
Help screen from Desktop window.

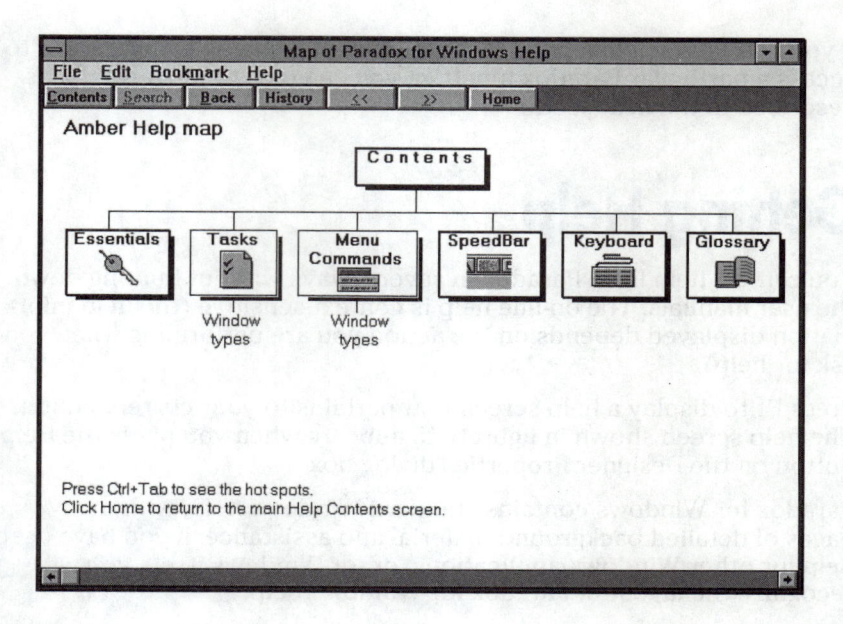

FIG. 1.16

Help screen map.

Use the buttons at the top of the screen to page through topics. You can even define a bookmark in Help so that you can find your place later. To move from one help screen to other related topics, click the topic list at the bottom of the screen. This branching feature enables you to quickly find just the help you need. To print a help topic, choose Print from the File menu.

Chapter Summary

Paradox for Windows interacts with you through windows, dialog boxes, and prompts. A Paradox session begins at the Desktop, from which you can access various windows and menus. Paradox windows accessed from the Desktop are Table (edit data), Form, Define Form, Query, Report, Script, and Folder. Paradox submenus accessed from the Desktop are Utilities, Net, and Info.

Paradox often provides more than one method for accomplishing the same task. You can use the mouse or keyboard for most actions. Some commands have function key equivalents; these function keys are particularly useful in record entry. The mouse is easier to learn but the keyboard can sometimes produce results more quickly.

Paradox calls database elements *objects*. Major objects include tables, forms, reports, scripts, crosstabs, and graphs. Minor objects include text, graphics, fields, lines, boxes, and ellipses. Each type of object has a set of characteristics, or *properties*. You can select one or more objects to work with at a time. Generally, you can select objects by clicking the mouse. A right-click reveals the object's properties. You can move objects on the workspace by clicking and dragging.

Now that you have learned how to navigate Paradox, you are ready to put these skills to work designing your own database. The first step is to build data tables, as discussed in Chapter 2.

CHAPTER 2

Designing Paradox Tables and Databases

Planning and creating tables are the first steps in building a Paradox database. Without tables, you have no place to store the data you need for forms, reports, queries, graphs, and other database output. After a brief discussion of database terminology, this chapter explains each step in the process of defining a table in Paradox. You learn how to create a new table, modify an existing table, borrow the structure of a table, and use features such as validity checks and referential integrity.

For information on some advanced table techniques, see Chapter 7, "Using Advanced Form Techniques," and Chapter 12, "Working with Your Files."

Understanding Database Terminology

Before you can build a table, you need to understand some relational basics. The better you understand relational database concepts, the better you can structure your Paradox databases. Each principle discussed in this section has important practical implications.

What Is a Relational Database?

A *database* is a collection of information that you can search systematically. Several types of database management systems (DBMS) are available. The most popular DBMS for personal computers are flat-file databases (such as Borland's Reflex or Symantec's Q&A) and relational databases. Flat-file databases are designed to work with only one table at a time and are more limited in handling sophisticated data structures than relational databases. Paradox is a relational database management structure.

Relational databases are based on the relational model developed by Dr. Edgar F. Codd and other researchers at IBM in the late 1960s and early 1970s. Rooted in mathematics and logic, the relational model provides a set of guidelines for the way users interact with data. For example, the relational model accesses data by its contents rather than its physical location in the file. In a relational database, you would not have to know the record number or disk drive track and sector in order to look up the address of a particular customer. Instead, you would enter the customer's name to perform the search.

A relational database is powerful and flexible, offering a simple structure for data storage, features that protect the accuracy of data, and a predictable method for retrieving and manipulating data. Paradox for Windows, which contains many key features of the relational model, easily handles multitable operations such as forms, queries, and reports.

A relational database prevents duplicate records from being entered in data tables using a key field; you cannot accidentally enter a customer or invoice twice. Paradox also enforces some forms of referential integrity to ensure that data is changed in all affected tables (see "What Is Referential Integrity?" later in the chapter). Referential integrity is an important feature in a relational database. Paradox also supports the relational feature of set operations, providing a means of searching for groups of records. For example, you may want to retrieve all prospects you met at the COMDEX trade show who need a consultant and currently are not clients.

What Is a Table?

A *table* is the building block of a database, describing the items, or *entities*, that you are tracking. (Another term for table is *relation*—hence, relational databases.) A table consists of rows and columns, as shown in figure 2.1.

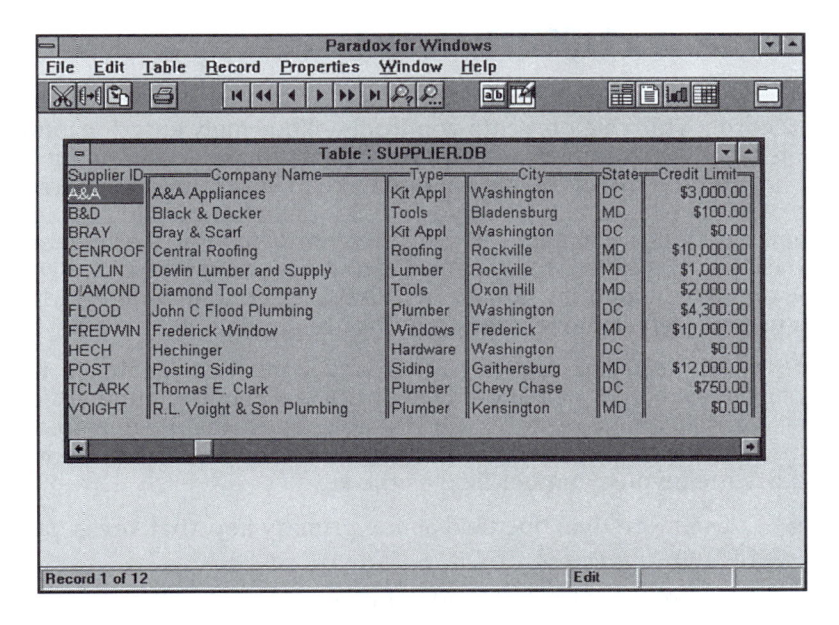

FIG. 2.1

The Supplier table.

A row, also called a *record*, contains information about an entity that you enter in a table. The Supplier table shown in figure 2.1, for example, contains a record for each supplier, such as the record for Diamond Tool Company. If you read across the row, you see all the fields for this particular record.

A column, also known as a *field*, lists certain characteristics of the entities you are entering. The Supplier table, for example, contains a Company Name field. If you read down this column, you see the company name for each of the records.

A database can consist of one or more related tables. If you want to track retail sales, for example, you can create a table for customers (customer names and addresses) and a table for purchases (information on each purchase). A relational database ties these tables together, enabling you to retrieve information from either table at any time. Storing data in many small tables can be much more efficient and accurate than using a single large table, because searches on small files are faster than searches on large files.

> **NOTE** If you have used dBASE or dBASE-compatible programs, you may have referred to tables as "databases." In relational databases such as Paradox, a database consists of one or more tables.

What Is a Primary Key?

A fundamental rule of relational databases is that you may not duplicate records. This rule prevents you from unknowingly entering information several times, thereby cluttering the database and harming the accuracy or integrity of the data. If you were to enter the same person more than once in a mailing list, you would waste letters and postage by sending duplicate mailings. Duplicate records in a sales or inventory database could lead to double counting of sales or expenses and wreak havoc on your accounting. Relational databases contain *primary keys*—fields used to determine whether records are duplicates.

To prevent the entry of duplicate records, you must designate a primary key in each table. You could use the Social Security number field as the key in an employee table, for example, because no two employees should have the same Social Security number. In a sales file, you could use the invoice number field as the key.

When you use more than one field as the primary key, that key is called a *composite key*.

Primary keys are essential to Paradox tables and to all SQL server-based tables used with Paradox. SQL stands for Structured Query Language and refers to powerful database software that can be used in conjunction with Paradox for Windows. You cannot, however, designate keys in dBASE-type tables.

The steps for designating key fields and rules for determining primary keys are discussed later in this chapter in the section "Defining a Primary Key."

In addition to a primary key, a table may contain a *foreign key*—a field that is the primary key in a related table. For example, you might have a Customer table that contains customer number (the primary key), customer name, customer address, and the initials of the sales representative assigned to the customers. In a second table, Staff, you might have a record for each sales representative, including initials (the primary key), full name, commission rate, and other information. In this scenario, the Sales Rep field in the Customer table would be a foreign key.

Paradox uses foreign keys to create relationships between tables, often assigning secondary indexes to foreign keys as a means of boosting performance. Secondary indexes are discussed later in this chapter.

What Is a Relationship?

Relationships (sometimes called *links*) describe how two tables are related. In a Sales table, for example, customers may be related to purchases by a customer number; invoices may be related to line items by an invoice number. Paradox uses its Data Model feature to draw the links between tables.

You can use the following kinds of relationships in Paradox:

- *One-to-one.* Each record in Table A is related to one record in Table B, and each record in Table B is related to one record in Table A. You could, for example, create a one-to-one relationship between Customers and Accounts.

- *One-to-many.* Each record in Table A is related to multiple records in Table B, and each record in Table B is related to one record in Table A. You could create a one-to-many relationship between Customers and Invoices.

    Sometimes, a one-to-many relationship is called a *many-to-one* relationship. The two relationships are identical.

- *Many-to-many.* Each record in Table A is related to multiple records in Table B, and each record in Table B is related to multiple records in Table A. You could create a many-to-many relationship between Sales Staff and Customers, if each customer is assigned multiple sales representatives and each sales representative has multiple customers.

    One challenge for the database designer is to identify many-to-many relationships. These relationships can make data entry and information retrieval problematic, because the separate relationships are based on different sets of fields. Techniques for handling many-to-many relationships are discussed later in this chapter and in Chapter 7, "Using Advanced Form Techniques."

For Related Information
▶▶ "Understanding Relationships," p. 339.

FROM HERE...

To define relationships on paper, you specify the related entities and (if possible at this point) the field or fields that relate to those entities. For now, your goal is to identify and categorize the relationships that link the tables. Be sure to write down the relationships. You use relationships later to create multitable forms, queries, and reports.

A relationship statement might read, "Invoices are related to customers when the customer number in the invoice equals the customer number in the Customers table." For step-by-step instructions on defining relationships, see Quick Start 2.

What Is Referential Integrity?

Referential integrity refers to features that protect the database from inconsistencies which arise when data is modified in one table but not modified in related tables by a user or a program.

Suppose that you have a personnel database and use employee numbers to relate the Employee, Payroll, Insurance, and Dependents tables. What happens if an employee number changes? If the employee number changes in the Employee table but not in the other tables, that employee's payroll records are no longer related to his employee records. As a result, the Payroll table contains "orphan" records.

When you define a table in Paradox for Windows, you can specify both relationships and referential integrity (where it applies). After you define referential integrity, Paradox tracks all changes that may affect referential integrity and automatically changes the data in related tables accordingly. When you change the invoice number of a record in the Invoices table, for example, Paradox for Windows automatically changes the invoice number of related records in the Invoice Line Item table.

The steps for setting up referential integrity are discussed in Chapter 7, "Using Advanced Form Techniques." Nonetheless, keep referential integrity in mind as you design your tables.

Planning a Table

Planning your database tables before you create them pays dividends. You can correct badly written reports or queries, but you may have to perform extensive revisions to repair a badly organized table after you enter data into that table.

Writing your table plan before you build Paradox tables can be helpful because you can use that written plan as a checklist when you create the tables on-screen. You may want to consider the following items when planning tables:

- Names of tables
- Field names, types, and lengths
- The common fields in table relationships

Using the Album Tracking Database Example

This book provides many examples to illustrate the features of Paradox for Windows. One example, however, appears throughout the book: a database that tracks a collection of records, tapes, and compact discs.

If you are a music lover, you want to be able to quickly find a certain sonata, aria, or heavy-metal recording; perhaps you also want to produce inventory reports or cassette labels. Paradox can help you accomplish these tasks. With a little imagination, you can apply the principles of the example database to databases that track everything from videotapes and baseball cards to artworks. (The example database also illustrates many relational features of Paradox for Windows, including multitable forms, queries, and reports.)

In planning a database for tracking recordings, you must identify the entities you want to track and the attributes that describe the entity. The entities become tables in the database, and the attributes become fields.

Using Multiple Tables

Although the saying "divide and conquer" was coined in another context, it applies to relational-database design. You achieve better results by dividing your data into several small tables instead of lumping many items together in a single behemoth table.

After you split your data into many tables, Paradox enables you to combine the data from these tables for use in queries, reports, and other output. Multitable forms enable you to enter or view information from more than one table on a single screen, but first you must build the tables.

A database application consists of all the tables, forms, queries, reports, and ObjectPAL scripts needed for a database. Although some small applications track only one entity and therefore require only one table, those applications are the exception. Most business databases deal with several related entities, so the user can benefit by using multiple-database tables.

When you use multiple tables, you can create a more realistic model of business activity than you can in a single table. Multiple tables ensure data integrity (accuracy and completeness) and simplify data entry and reporting by minimizing redundant data.

Using tables also can make your database more flexible. Suppose that you use a database that tracks employee time sheets and calculates payroll. A table called Timesheets contains daily time-sheet records for each employee.

You can set up the database to perform pay calculations in either of two ways. One method is to create an hourly pay-rate field in each time-sheet record. This method, however, involves redundant data (the pay rate), which must be entered properly in every record.

The other method is to create a second table, Employee, that contains employee names, hourly wages, and other pertinent information. You could link the Timesheets table to the Employee table through employees' Social Security numbers and use a query to multiply the hours in Timesheets by the pay rate in Employee. This method involves entering the pay rate only once for each employee.

Even if you use several tables to present your data, you can view that data in a single data-entry form. Defining forms is discussed in Chapter 5, "Getting Started with Forms," and Chapter 7, "Using Advanced Form Techniques."

Eliminating Repeated Fields

Database experts have developed several methods of organizing data. One of these methods is called *normalization*, which streamlines relational databases.

To understand the benefits of normalization, consider the drawbacks of not using this method. Suppose that you want your database to store information about each recording you own and also about each song on each recording. You probably want to include the name of each song, its length in minutes and seconds, and its order in the recording (for example, Track 5).

One way to add this level of detail is to create new fields in the Albums table—for example, Track Number, Song Title, Minutes, and Seconds. You would need several sets of these fields to accommodate all the songs, however—for example, Song Title2, Song Title3, and so on.

Figure 2.2 shows part of a table that contains these fields. The table is not normalized, because it contains repeating groups of fields.

One problem with using this table, however, is that you cannot anticipate how many song-title fields you need in each record. If you create 10 sets of song-title fields, you would have no space in the table to enter an 11th song title.

You could create many song-title fields in every record, but if you are overly generous with those fields, you would waste a great deal of space. On the other hand, if you are stingy with song-title fields, you would have to exclude some song titles from the table.

2 — DESIGNING PARADOX TABLES AND DATABASES

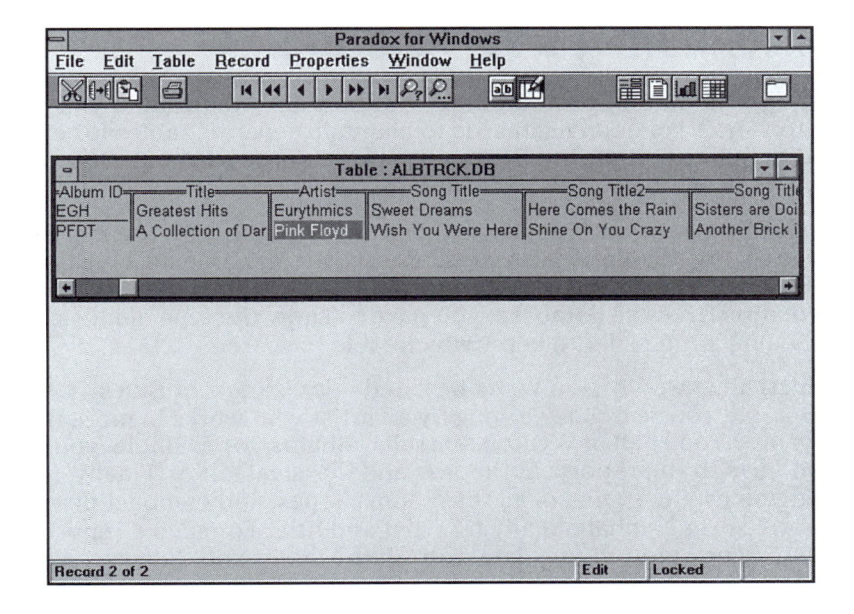

FIG. 2.2

Albums and tracks in one table.

Duplicate fields not only waste space, but also make data extraction more difficult. To find out how many versions of "Moon River" you have in your collection, for example, you would have to check each song-title field in each record of each table. Checking a table with 10 song-title fields takes longer than checking a table with 1 song-title field.

Furthermore, if you want to print a list of those versions in alphabetical order, you would have to compare each song title in that list with every other song title in that list. A 10-field query or report is more complex than a single-field query or report.

In order to store information on the songs in your recordings, therefore, you should create two tables: Albums and Tracks. You could use a common field—Album ID—to relate the tables.

This streamlining, or normalization, makes reporting data much easier. Although the Albums and Tracks tables contain more records than the old Albums table, each table contains only one song-title field. To print a list of titles in alphabetical order, then, you would have to sort only one field of all those records.

For additional information on normalization, see Que's book *Introduction to Databases*.

Consolidating Duplicate Tables

Splitting your database into multiple tables is a good idea that you can take too far. A common mistake is to maintain separate tables for entities that fundamentally are the same. One database can contain apparently identical tables with subtle differences.

Suppose that you create separate tables for each music genre in your collection: one for classical recordings, one for jazz, one for blues, and one for rock. The problem with this system is the difficulty of retrieving information from the database; you have to know the type of music you are looking for in order to know which table to search.

In which table would Tom Waits be listed—Jazz, Rock, or Blues? Which table would you search for a song by an artist who works in more than one genre? To list all of Wynton Marsalis' albums, for example, you would have to run reports in the Jazz and Classical tables. Finally, how would you produce a list of all the albums, tapes, and compact discs you own, sorted alphabetically by artist and title? For such a report, you would have to retrieve data from all the tables and then sort all that data.

The solution to this dilemma is to combine Classical, Jazz, Blues, and Rock into a single table—Albums—and to add a field that lists the type of music contained in each recording. The next section describes how to create such a table in Paradox.

Creating a Paradox Table

This section shows you how to create the Albums Tracking table. To create any Paradox table, you follow these basic steps:

1. Choose the table type.
2. Specify field names.
3. Specify field types.
4. Specify field length.
5. Designate a primary key.
6. Save and name the table.

The following sections explain these steps in detail.

Choosing the Table Type

The first step in creating a table is choosing the table type. To choose a table type, begin at the Paradox desktop and complete the following steps:

1. If you have not already done so, start Paradox by clicking the Paradox for Windows icon in the Paradox for Windows program group in the Windows File Manager.

   The Paradox desktop appears.

2. Choose File, New, and Table. The Table Type dialog box appears, as shown in figure 2.3.

   NOTE If you right-click the Table button, you get the choice of New or Open.

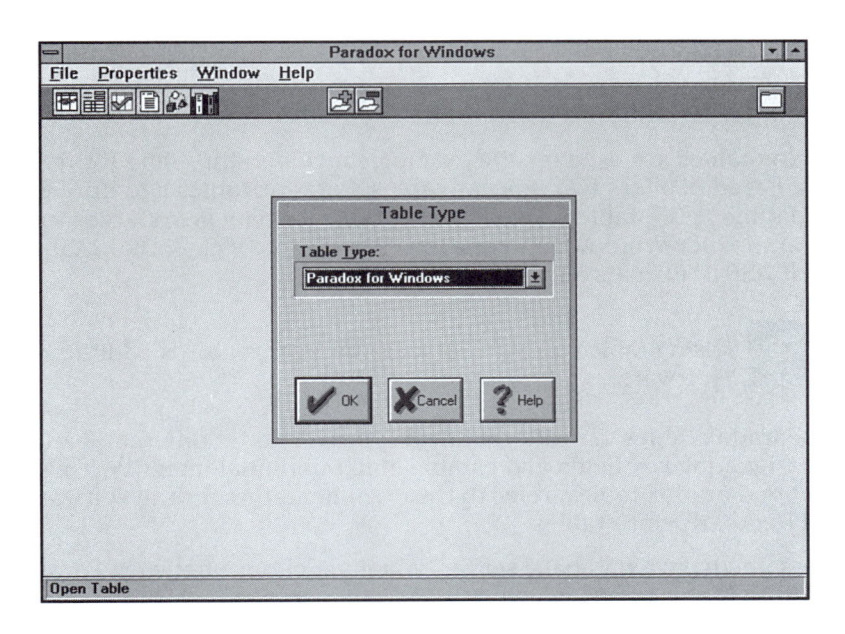

   FIG. 2.3
   The Table Type dialog box.

   This dialog box enables you to choose Paradox (the default) or dBASE.

3. To choose the Paradox table type, simply click OK. To choose table types other than Paradox, click the Table Type pull-down menu box and then select a type in the menu that appears (fig. 2.4).

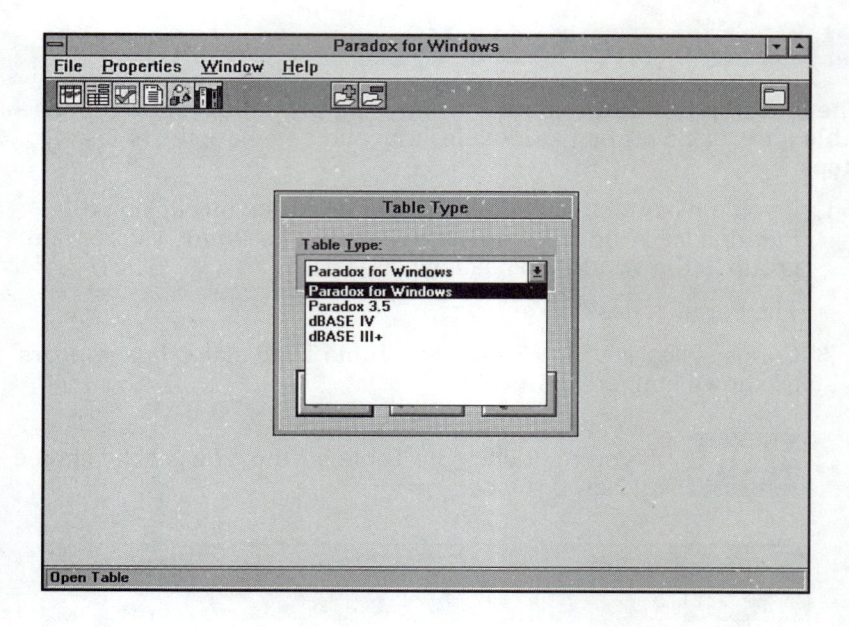

FIG. 2.4

The Table Type pull-down menu.

Paradox tables are used for the examples included throughout this book. Paradox offers two types of tables: Paradox tables and dBASE-compatible (DBF) tables. Two Paradox table formats are offered—one for Paradox for Windows and one for Paradox for DOS. Both dBASE III and dBASE IV formats also are supported.

> **NOTE** Using tables on SQL database servers requires additional software.

Non-Paradox tables use different field types and offer different features for designating key fields and establishing referential integrity. To work with non-Paradox tables, refer to the documentation for the software used to create those tables.

Unless you have a database server, you must choose between Paradox and dBASE table types, which table 2.1 compares.

Table 2.1. Paradox and dBASE Table Types

Feature	Paradox	dBASE
Logical fields	No	Yes
View deleted records	No	Yes
Graphics fields	Yes	No

Feature	Paradox	dBASE
Binary fields	Yes	No
Formatted memo fields	Yes	No
25-character field names	Yes	No
OLE fields	Yes	No
Primary keys	Yes	No
Table sorted by key	Yes	No
Validity checks	Yes	No
Table lookup	Yes	No
Referential integrity	Yes	No

Each table type has its strengths and weaknesses. One of the dBASE table type's strengths is its compatibility with many software programs. You can use dBASE files with Clipper, FoxPro, and other dBASE-compatible programs, as well as with dBASE itself. dBASE tables also offer logical fields, a field type not available in Paradox. Field types are explained in detail in the later section, "Specifying Field Types."

The dBASE table type, however, does not offer Paradox's advanced features, such as table lookups and referential integrity, and also lacks many field types available in Paradox, such as graphics and binary. Most important, dBASE files do not support primary keys. Therefore, unless dBASE compatibility is a consideration, Paradox tables are superior to dBASE tables in a Paradox database.

For the Albums table, you have chosen Paradox in the Table Type dialog box. Now proceed to the next section.

Specifying Field Names

After you choose a table type and click OK, the Create Paradox for Windows Table dialog box appears (see fig. 2.5).

NOTE You can use the mouse and keyboard commands to move around the Create Table dialog box.

This dialog box enables you to specify field names, types, lengths, and special field characteristics such as data validation. In this section, you learn how to specify field names.

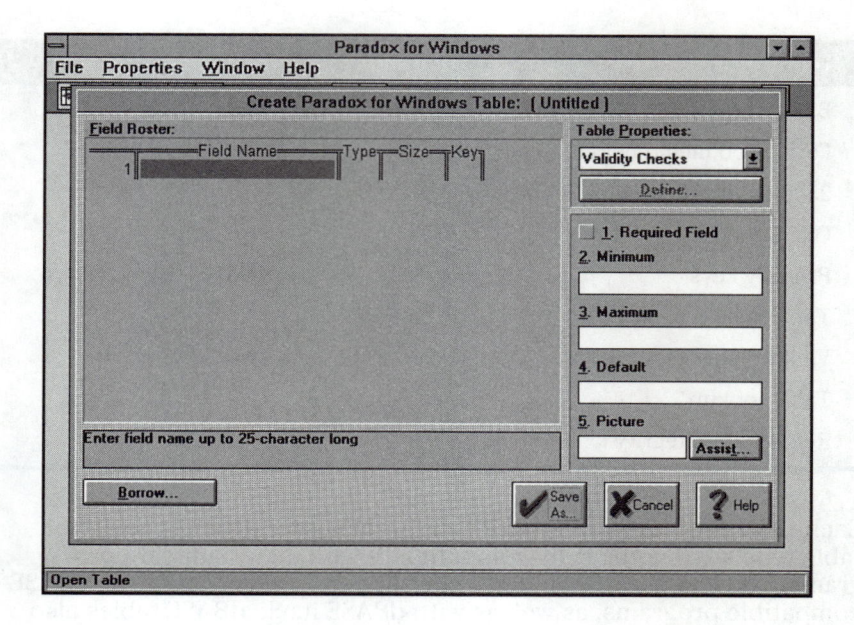

FIG. 2.5

The Create Paradox for Windows Table dialog box.

Paradox for Windows field names can be up to 25 characters long and can contain any printable character except the following symbols:

" "	Quotation marks
[ ]	Square brackets
{ }	Curly braces
( )	Parentheses
->	Hyphen followed by a greater-than symbol
#	Pound sign

Although you can use spaces in a Paradox field name, you cannot start a field name with a space.

Make field names as descriptive as possible. Avoid acronyms and jargon. (CUSTOMERNAME reads better than CSTNM, for example.) Using descriptive words also reduces the possibility of misspellings in field names.

Avoid using punctuation marks in field names. Although you may use spaces in field names, some programmers prefer to use the underscore character (_) to make field names more readable but keep the field name as one "word." You may want to use letters rather than numbers in designating fields, especially where mathematical functions will be performed, to avoid confusing fields with numeric constants. For example, having fields named 25 or 100, which themselves contain numbers, might be confusing.

TIP

Force yourself to use consistent field names throughout your database. For example, decide whether you want to use FNAME, FirstName, or FIRST for a first-name field and use your choice in every table.

For Related Information

▶▶ "Renaming Tables," p. 495.

CAUTION: Field names must be unique within a table. You cannot create two fields and name both of them Address. If you need a second address field, give the second field a name based on the first field's name—for example, Address2.

For the Albums table, enter the following field names under Field Name in the Create Table dialog box:

- *Album ID.* A unique identifier assigned to each album, tape, or compact disc—perhaps a letter that identifies the record label, followed by the number of the recording.
- *Title.* The title of the recording.
- *Artist.* The name of the recording artist or group.
- *Year.* Date when the recording was made or released.
- *Genre.* The category—for example, rock, opera, or country—into which the recording falls. You might use this field frequently in searches.
- *Price.* The price you paid for the recording.
- *Format.* The recording medium (cassette tape, compact disc, or album).
- *Value.* The current market value of the recording.
- *Cover.* A graphics image of the recording's cover.
- *In Print.* The recording's status: in print or out of print.

I — PARADOX FOR WINDOWS FUNDAMENTALS

- *Review.* A brief review of the recording. This field could contain a memo field (discussed in the "Specifying Paradox for Windows Field Types" section) so that you could enter longer reviews in each record of the table.

- *Date Purchased.* The date you bought the recording.

To create these fields, complete the following steps:

1. In the Create Paradox for Windows Table dialog box, enter the field name under Field Name of the field roster.

2. Press Tab to advance to the field type. To display a list of field types, press the space bar. Choose the field type by entering the first character, clicking the field type with the mouse, or highlighting the field type with the arrow keys and pressing Enter. Field types include Alphanumeric, Number, $ (Currency), Date, and so on.

3. Specify the field size, if prompted to do so. If you choose a field type for which the field length is not applicable, you will skip over the field length to the key field.

4. For the Album ID, press the space bar in the Key column to turn on the key indicator so that you can designate key fields. For non-key fields, press Enter to advance to the next row.

5. Repeat these steps to create each of the fields for the Albums table.

Figure 2.6 shows the field names, types, and lengths for the Albums table. The following sections offer general guidelines for specifying field types and field size.

Specifying Field Type

Databases support several types of fields for storing different kinds of information. Choosing the correct field type makes validating and calculating data easier. This section describes how each field type is used.

When you choose field types, remember that sorting has different effects on different types of fields, even if those fields contain the same value. For example, Paradox would list 1,642 before 2 in sorted alphanumeric fields; the program alphabetizes from left to right, and 1 comes before 2. In sorted number fields, however, Paradox would list 2 before 1,642; the program sorts numbers in ascending order from negative to positive. Paradox sorts date fields in chronological order.

2 — DESIGNING PARADOX TABLES AND DATABASES

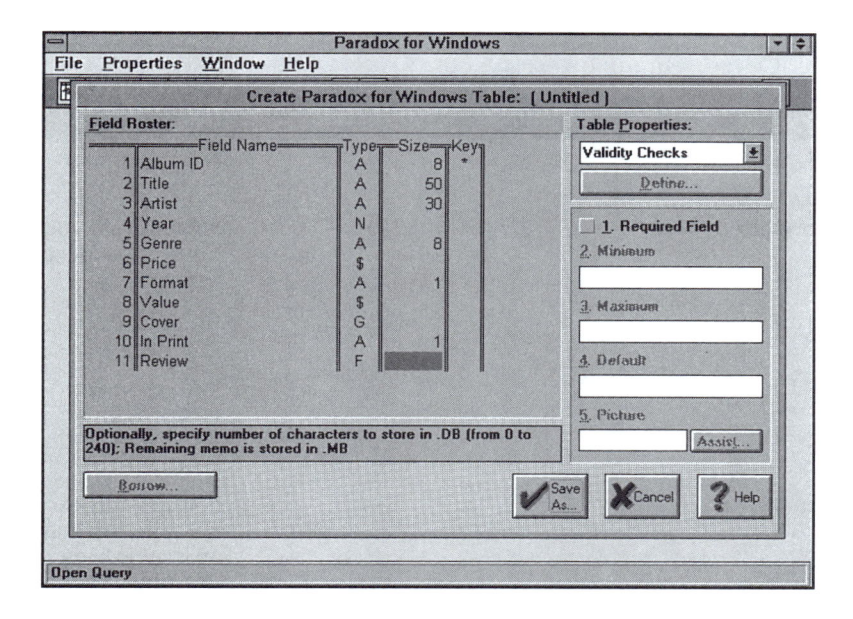

FIG. 2.6

The Albums table structure.

Specifying Paradox for Windows Field Types

You can choose any of 10 field types for tables you create in Paradox for Windows, as shown in table 2.2. The most commonly used field types are alphanumeric, number, and date.

Table 2.2. Paradox for Windows Field Types

Type	Symbol	Size limit	Use
Alphanumeric	A	255	Text, spaces, and other characters
Number	N	N/A	Integers, fixed and floating-point numbers
Short Number	S	N/A	Special number fields containing whole numbers ranging from –32,767 to 32,767
Currency	$	N/A	Monetary amounts
Date	D	N/A	Calendar dates

continues

Table 2.2. Continued

Type	Symbol	Size limit	Use
Memo	M	240	Long text information
Formatted Memo	F	240	Similar to Memo, but with a special format
Graphic	G	N/A	Bit-mapped graphic image
OLE	O	N/A	Linked object from another Windows program
Binary	B	N/A	Foreign nontext data file, such as an engineering drawing or sound

You enter the field symbol, which is shorthand for the field type, in the Type field of the Create Table dialog box. Each field type is suited for a particular kind of data, as the following sections explain.

Alphanumeric Fields

Alphanumeric is the most general field type. Alphanumeric fields accept letters, numbers, punctuation marks, spaces, and all ASCII (American Standard Code for Information Interchange) characters except null or control characters such as Tab. You may store up to 255 characters in a text field.

Number Fields

Use *number fields* for data that represents quantities or values to be used in calculations.

Paradox enables you to display numbers in several different formats. You can, for example, display a number as an *integer* (a positive or negative whole number) or with fixed or floating decimal points. If you specify a *fixed decimal point*, you can define the number of digits to the left and right of the decimal point. If you specify a *floating decimal point*, the number of digits on either side of the decimal point can vary (within the maximum field length). Floating-point number fields often are used for storing precise measurements or the results of complex calculations.

Short Number Fields

Paradox *short number fields*, which occupy less space in a table than ordinary number fields, store numbers ranging from –32,767 to 32,767. This range is not the result of a programmer's whim. Computers store data as a combination of *1*s and *0*s (each *1* or *0* constituting a *bit*) and need several bits to store large numbers. As it happens, 32,768 is 2^{15} power, or 2 multiplied by itself 15 times. A computer needs 15 bits to store such a number and a 16th bit to indicate the sign (positive or negative).

> **T I P**
>
> Not all numbers represent quantities or values for use in calculations. When you need to enter Social Security numbers, phone numbers, or serial numbers, for example, you should define the field as an alphanumeric field and use a template that restricts entry to numerals only. (Templates are explained later in this chapter.)

Currency Fields

Currency fields contain monetary values and are formatted to store currency amounts. A currency field is equivalent to a fixed-point number field.

Date Fields

Date fields are formatted with slashes to accommodate dates. Paradox for Windows enables you to use several different date formats, including MM/DD/YY (month, day, year), DD/MM/YY (standard international format), DD-MON-YYYY (with the month written as three alphabetic characters), and YY-MM-DD (metric format). The format is a property of each field and may be changed by inspecting the field properties and changing the display format, as discussed in Chapter 3, "Entering, Editing, and Viewing Data."

You also can define your own custom date formats, converting dates to text (for example, 9/01/67 to September 1, 1967) or to days of the week (for example, Saturday).

Paradox dates can range from January 1, 100, to December 31, 9999. If you omit the century in a date, the twentieth century is assumed.

You can use date fields to perform calendar calculations. For example, you can calculate the turnaround time for an order by subtracting the shipment date from the order date.

Memo Fields

Memo fields enable you to add long text entries to a record without adding a series of text fields to the table.

You can store virtually an infinite amount of data in a memo field (up to your available disk space). Up to 255 characters of a formatted memo or 240 characters of a memo field may be stored in the table itself. Paradox stores the rest of the text in a separate file with the extension MB. When you access the memo field, Paradox automatically opens the MB file and places you in the appropriate place.

Formatted Memo Fields

Formatted memo fields are similar to memo fields but give you greater control of text format. In the Albums table, for example, you could use a memo field to store reviews, which follow no standard format.

Graphic Fields

Graphic fields, which contain graphic images, are new features in Paradox for Windows. You create the images by using a drawing program or by scanning a photo or a piece of artwork.

You can view graphic fields during record entry and use them for applications ranging from parts inventory to personnel. The serious drawback to using images, however, is that image files tend to be large—as much as a megabyte or more for a detailed drawing. Consequently, image files quickly use up disk space and can create a need for high-capacity storage systems such as optical disks (similar to audio compact discs).

Database programs do not yet enable you to search directly for the contents of graphic fields, so you must cross-index these fields with text entries.

OLE Object Fields

Another new field type in Paradox for Windows is *object linking and embedding* (OLE). OLE fields contain objects from other Windows applications, enabling you to use data from more than one program in a table.

For example, a Paradox for Windows table can contain a field you created in a spreadsheet program. When you access the table, Paradox for Windows goes to the spreadsheet to check the current value for the field.

Binary Fields

Binary fields also are new in Paradox for Windows. These fields store binary information (stored as zeros and ones and unintelligible to most humans), such as digitized speech for use in a voice-mail system. In the Albums table, you could use binary fields to store a sample of each song (assuming that you have a sound card, synthesizer, or other means to digitally record and play back sound).

You must access a binary field through ObjectPAL, the programming language of Paradox for Windows; you cannot display or manipulate such a field through interactive Paradox.

Binary fields are most often used in advanced applications, in conjunction with ObjectPAL programming. For example, you could create a database to show locations of all your offices, and allow users to click a button and hear travel directions for each office.

Specifying dBASE Field Types

dBASE-type tables support six field types, five of which are identical or similar to Paradox field types. dBASE includes the logical yes/no field not offered by Paradox.

Table 2.3 shows dBASE field types.

Table 2.3. dBASE Field Types

Type	Symbol	Use
Character	C	Same as a Paradox alphanumeric field
Number	N	Similar to a Paradox number field
Float Number	F	Less precise than a number field
Date	D	Calendar date
Logic	L	Yes or No, True or False
Memo	M	Similar to a Paradox memo field

The following list explains the six field types:

- *Character.* dBASE *character* fields are the same as Paradox alphanumeric fields. Character fields can contain letters, numbers, spaces, and most other ASCII characters.
- *Number.* dBASE number fields are similar to Paradox number fields. In dBASE, however, you may specify the length of the number to be stored.
- *Float Number. Float-number* fields for dBASE tables are similar to Paradox number fields. Float-number fields, however, store numbers to the full precision allowed by the system rather than rounding to the length of the field as in a Number field. For instance, 1/3 would be stored as 0.333333333333. Not all the digits of the float number are necessarily displayed on-screen. Float numbers are used for scientific and technical applications where high precision is needed. They can cause problems for calculations with money, where the result should be rounded to the nearest penny. For storing dollar amounts, use Number fields.
- *Date. Date* fields are the same in Paradox and in dBASE. You can change the display format of a dBASE date field the same way you change the display format of a Paradox date field.
- *Logic. Logic* fields contain yes/no or true/false values and are suitable for storing survey results or checklists. You can use logic fields in Paradox tables only if you choose the dBASE table type.
- *Memo.* Like their Paradox counterparts, dBASE *memo* fields contain long text entries.

Specifying Unsupported Field Types

Although Paradox for Windows supports several field types, including a few that are unavailable in the DOS version of Paradox, the program does not support these field types: time fields, logical fields, and choice fields. If you need to use unsupported field types in Paradox tables, you must create alternatives, using the available field types.

Some databases need to store information about clock times. A lawyer, for example, could use time fields to log the hours for which he or she bills clients. You also may want to indicate when a record was entered or modified, using the time from the system clock. Unfortunately, Paradox does not provide a field type that stores times.

Although Paradox for Windows does not support time fields directly, you can enter a time in a number field by converting the hours and minutes to the number of seconds. For instance, 10:30:55 am would be stored as 37,855 (10 hours * 3600 seconds/hour + 30 minutes * 60 + 55 seconds). Remember that this number must be converted back into a time to be more meaningful to a user.

Variable-length text fields, which expand or contract to fit the data you enter, also are not available in Paradox. These fields are useful for storing entire documents or extensive excerpts from documents. In Paradox, you can substitute memo fields for variable-length text fields.

Specifying Field Sizes

For three field types—alphanumeric, formatted memo, and memo—you must specify field length, or *size*.

Alphanumeric, formatted memo, graphic, OLE, and binary fields (the portion stored in Paradox tables) cannot exceed 255 characters. Memo fields have a limit of 250 characters. The contents of both types of memo fields can be larger (limited only by disk space), but the data these fields contain that exceeds the field length is stored outside the table and cannot be searched in a query. For instance, if you define a memo field length of 50 characters and you enter 2,000 characters, the first 50 characters are stored with the table and all 2,000 appear in the memo file.

A Paradox number field accommodates all entries up to its limits; you cannot specify a field length. Number and short number fields have different capacities. Number fields can contain -10^{307} to 10^{307} (15 significant digits). Short number fields range from –32,767 to 32,767. Therefore, as you might expect from their names, number fields can store much larger entries than short number fields.

The lengths of Paradox date, graphic, OLE object, and binary fields also are fixed. Paradox stores date fields, for example, in a standard format, so you cannot specify the length of a date field. Likewise, you do not have to specify the lengths of graphic, binary, and OLE object fields; Paradox stores the contents of these fields outside the table itself.

Although you cannot specify the length of certain field types, you can specify the formatting of data in those fields. For example, you can use any of several date formats in tables, forms, and reports. The display type does not affect the length of the date as Paradox stores the date in the table.

Defining a Primary Key

After you define field names, types, and lengths, your next task is to designate a primary key.

The choice of a key field is not always obvious. Using a person's name as a key field, for example, is risky for several reasons. First, Paradox cannot detect duplicate variations on the name; the program would consider *Bob*, for example, to be different from *Robert*. Second, if a person's name changes for any reason, such as marriage, Paradox considers the changed name to belong to a different person. Finally, a large list may include two different people who happen to have the same name. In such a case, one field is not enough to establish uniqueness. In a personnel file, employee names, Social Security numbers, and home addresses could serve as key fields.

Each possible key field is called a *candidate key*. To choose a primary key from several candidate keys, apply the following criteria:

- The primary key must be unique. No two records may have the same value in the key field.

- The key field must never be blank (null). If you use a Social Security number field as a key field, you must enter a number in this field for each record. Otherwise, you risk duplication of data in your table because Paradox cannot differentiate between two records with blank keys.

- The key field should be as short as possible. Shorter fields boost database performance because their index files are smaller, resulting in quicker searching and sorting.

- The key field should be meaningful, describing the entity tracked in the table. Using arbitrarily assigned customer numbers as key fields does not help you determine uniqueness, because you could unintentionally assign two different numbers to one customer.

When you designate a primary key, Paradox not only detects duplications of records but also displays the records in primary-key order. If you use the company-name field as the primary key in a Customers table, for example, Paradox displays the records in alphabetical order by company name. If you use the Social Security number field as the primary key in an Employee table, Paradox displays the records in numerical order by Social Security number.

2 — DESIGNING PARADOX TABLES AND DATABASES

> **CAUTION:** You can use only alphanumeric, date, and number fields (including currency and short number fields) as key fields. You cannot designate a memo, binary, or graphic field as a key field because the contents of these fields are stored outside the table and Paradox cannot evaluate those contents to determine uniqueness.

Creating a Single-Field Key

The *key indicator* in the Key column of the Create Table dialog box shows whether a field is the key (or part of a composite key) for the table. To activate the key indicator, press the space bar or double-click the Key column. Paradox displays an asterisk in the Key column of the record containing the key field.

Figure 2.7 shows a table named Salesrep. Rep ID (initials of the sales representative) is the primary key for this table. The primary key establishes the sort order for the table and prevents duplicate entries with the same key value.

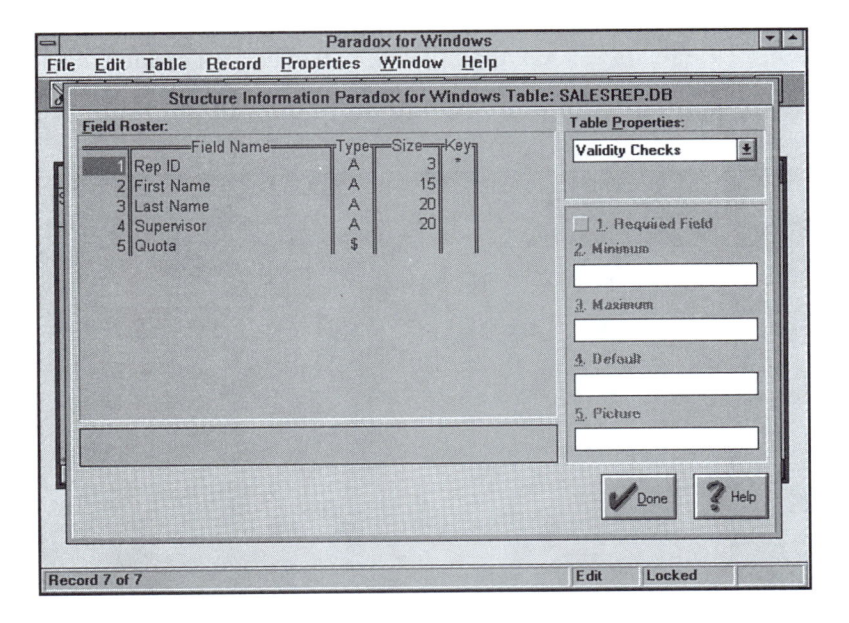

FIG. 2.7

Using the key indicator.

Creating a Composite Key

Two or more fields may constitute the key field. If you use the invoice-number field as the key field in an Invoices table, for example, you could enter only one item per invoice; and if you used the stock-number field as the key field, you could enter only one record per stock number. Using both fields as a composite key, however, would enable you to enter many records for each invoice, because no two line items from the same invoice would have the same stock number.

To designate a composite key, make the key fields the first fields in the table, and check the key column with a mouse click or a press of the space bar.

Composite keys work essentially the way single-field keys do, detecting duplications and sorting records in key order. If you add a field to track the individual songs on each album (calling the new table Tracks), you would need a composite key to prevent the same song from being entered twice. Figure 2.8 shows that the Album ID and Song Title fields are the composite key for the Tracks table.

You almost always need composite keys for tables related to a master table. The Tracks table, for example, contains data related to the Albums table. If you used Album ID as the key field in the Tracks table, you could enter only one track per recording. If you use the Album ID and Song Title fields as a composite key, however, you can make as many track entries as you want, as long as no two records contain the same Album ID and Song Title entries.

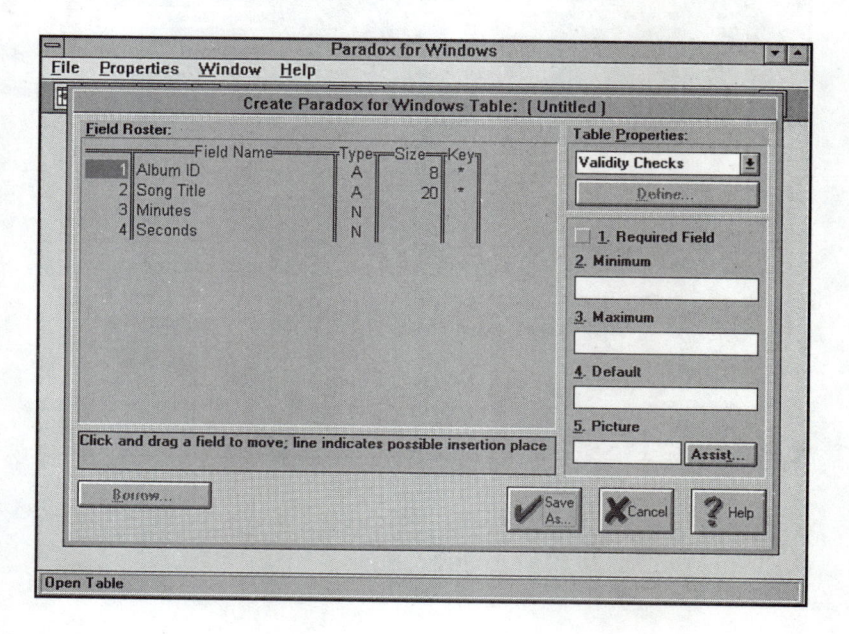

FIG. 2.8

A table with a composite key.

NOTE Key fields must appear before nonkey fields in the table specification. If you make the third field in a table the key field, Paradox also makes the first and second fields key fields, assuming that you want to use a composite key for the table. If you do not want to use a composite key, move your intended key field to the top of the table by clicking and dragging it with the mouse.

To designate a composite key, place the key fields at the top of the table specification and check the Key column for the key indicators. The key fields must appear at the top of the list.

Saving a Table

When you complete the fields in the Create Table dialog box, save the table by clicking the Save button. At this point, you also must name the table. The following sections explain Paradox table names.

Choosing a Table Name

Paradox for Windows table names can be up to eight characters long, with no spaces. This constraint is based on the eight-character limit for DOS file names. You can, however, use longer names for tables created in Paradox-compatible programs such as Oracle and Sybase.

Whenever possible, use descriptive table names—for example, CUSTOMER, INVOICES, and LINEITEM in a sales database. If you use abbreviations, choose abbreviations that other users can understand; avoid using cryptic or arbitrary names such as ST1028 and FR1HY.

Many users give plural names (such as Invoices, Clients, and Trips) to tables and singular names (such as Invoice Number, First Name, and Destination) to fields. Unfortunately, the eight-character limit on table names prevents you from using plurals for table names such as Customer and Employee.

Some database servers enable you to use *aliases*—alternative names that refer to database tables. You may find aliases useful because you may be able to make those names longer (and thus more descriptive) than the eight-character DOS file names. If your server supports aliases, you are asked to provide the alias when you create the table.

Avoiding Reserved Words

Although you enjoy creative license in most aspects of database design, some restrictions apply to naming database elements. All programs reserve certain words for commands; you should not use these *reserved words* in the names of tables, fields, views, indexes, and memory variables. If you use reserved words, the program may not be capable of differentiating commands from database objects.

For example, you could create a table for storing ski-race results, including fields called Average and Sum for average and total scores, respectively. Because AVERAGE and SUM are reserved for Paradox for Windows queries, however, your queries may go astray if you use these reserved words as field names.

The following list contains the reserved words in Paradox for Windows. If you use other table types, such as dBASE or Oracle, consult the software documentation for a list of reserved words in those programs.

Words Reserved for Queries		
ALL	EVERY	NOT
AS	EXACTLY	ONLY
AVERAGE	FIND	OR
BLANK	INSERT	SET
CALC	LIKE	SUM
CHANGETO	MAX	TODAY
COUNT	MIN	UNIQUE
DELETE	NO	

In some cases, you can get away with using reserved words as table or field names, but why take chances? The prudent approach is to steer clear of names that Paradox can misinterpret.

You can display a list of words reserved for ObjectPAL by choosing the Keywords option on the Language menu in the ObjectPAL Editor (see Part III, "Programming Paradox for Windows."

For Related Information

▶▶ "Creating Data Types and Records," p. 566.

Understanding Indexes, Validity Checks, and Referential Integrity

So far, this chapter has discussed the mandatory steps involved in defining a table: choosing a table type; defining field names, types, and lengths; designating a primary key; and saving and naming the table. Paradox also offers options that enhance the performance and reliability of tables. These options include indexes, validity checks, and referential integrity.

Using Indexes

Paradox for Windows uses indexes to speed access to tables. You can define indexes when you create or restructure tables. For example, you may want to add an Artists table to the Albums database for storing additional information on recording artists. To add that table, you restructure the Albums table and create a secondary index in the Artist field.

A database index is similar to a book index. Rather than read an entire book from the first page to the last, you can refer to the index to find a topic. The index provides *pointers* (page numbers) that show you where to find information on certain topics.

Using Indexes in Paradox Tables

Paradox automatically creates and maintains indexes for fields used as primary keys. You can define *secondary indexes* that link the table with other tables and establish alternative sort orders. Secondary indexes are useful for establishing relationships among tables and for defining multitable forms.

NOTE Before you can assign a secondary index, you must define a primary key.

To define a secondary index, follow these steps:

1. If you are creating a new table, go to the Create Paradox for Windows Table dialog box by selecting File, New, Table from the

I — PARADOX FOR WINDOWS FUNDAMENTALS

Paradox Desktop and choosing the Paradox for Windows table type or right-clicking the Table button in the SpeedBar and choosing New. The Create Paradox for Windows Table dialog box appears.

To define a secondary index on an existing table, use File, Open, Table from the Paradox Desktop, select the table, and then choose Restructure from the Table menu. The Restructure a Paradox for Windows Table dialog box appears.

2. Pull down the menu for Table Properties from the Create (or Restructure) Table dialog box and choose Secondary Indexes (see fig. 2.9).

3. Click the Define button directly below the Table Properties menu. The Define Secondary Index dialog box appears (see fig. 2.10).

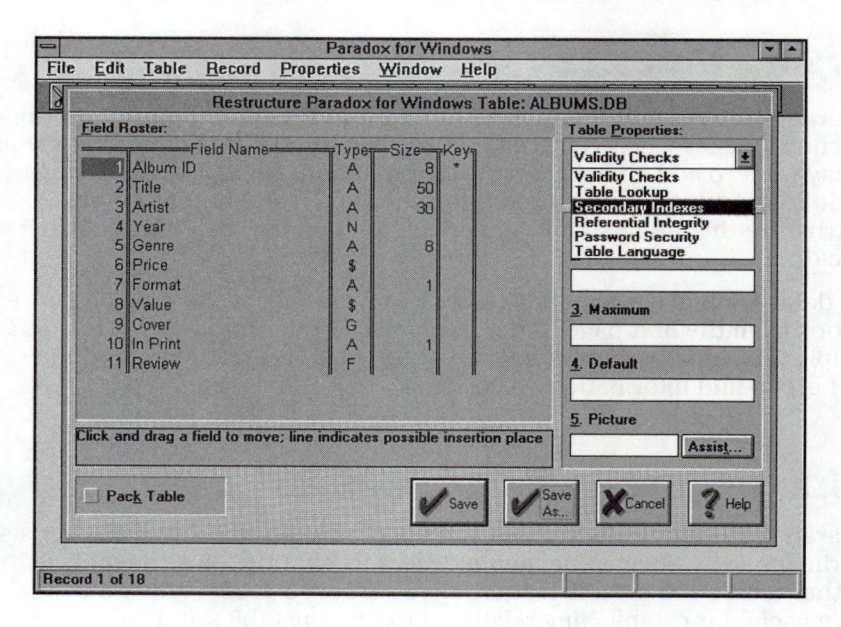

FIG. 2.9

The Table Properties menu (Paradox table).

4. Choose the field you want to index by highlighting the field name in the Fields list box and clicking the right-arrow box after each selection. You also may choose whether the index is automatically Maintained or Case Sensitive by checking the Index Options boxes in lower left side of the dialog box.

5. When you have completed your selections, click OK to save the secondary index.

2 — DESIGNING PARADOX TABLES AND DATABASES

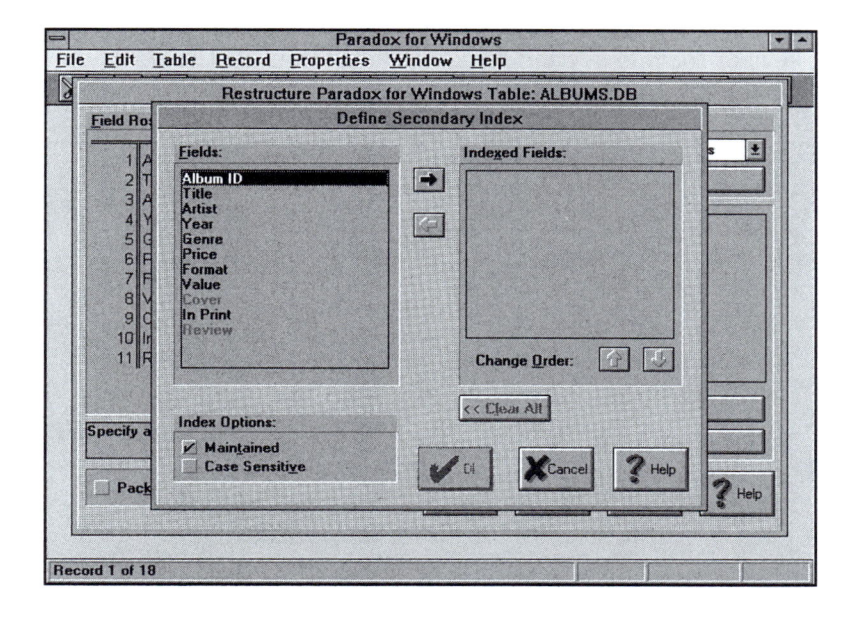

FIG. 2.10
The Define Secondary Index dialog box (Paradox table).

Notice that the names of fields you cannot use for an index (memo fields, in this example) are dimmed.

Rules for defining secondary indexes are discussed in detail in Chapter 7, "Using Advanced Form Techniques."

Using Indexes in dBASE Tables

Index options for dBASE-type tables differ from the options for native Paradox tables. For example, you can define a unique index for a dBASE table. A *unique index* contains one entry for each unique value in a field, whether or not other fields in the table contain duplicates of that value; if you use a unique index to search for a value, you find only the first occurrence of a value.

To define a dBASE IV index, follow these steps:

1. If you are creating a new table, go to the Create dBASE IV Table dialog box by selecting File, New, Table from the Paradox Desktop and choosing the dBASE IV table type. The Create dBASE IV Table dialog box appears.

   To define a secondary index on an existing table, use File, Open, Table from the Paradox Desktop, select the table, then choose Restructure from the Table menu. The Restructure dBASE IV Table dialog box appears.

I — PARADOX FOR WINDOWS FUNDAMENTALS

2. Highlight the name of the field you want to index (with the arrow keys or the mouse) and click the Define button. The Define Index dialog box appears (see fig. 2.11).

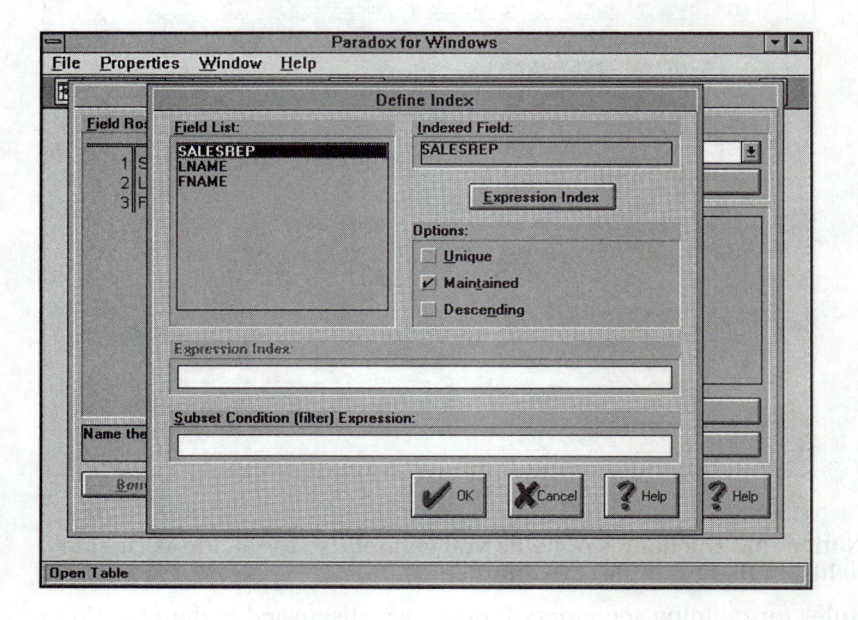

FIG. 2.11

The Define Index dialog box (dBASE table).

3. Click the field to be indexed so that it appears in the Indexed Field field. You also have options to make the index Unique, Maintained, or Descending, as well as Expression Index and Subset Condition (Filter) Expressions. Complete the dialog box and click OK to save the index. The Save Index As dialog box appears (see fig. 2.12).

4. You must provide a name (up to eight characters) for each dBASE index you create. Paradox uses a default index name of the table name. If you want to use another index name, enter the name of the index in the Index File Name field of the Save Index As dialog box. Click OK to save the new index.

5. Use the Save or Save As buttons from the Create (Restructure) dBASE IV Table dialog box to save your changes.

See Chapter 7, "Using Advanced Form Techniques," for more information on using dBASE index options.

FIG. 2.12

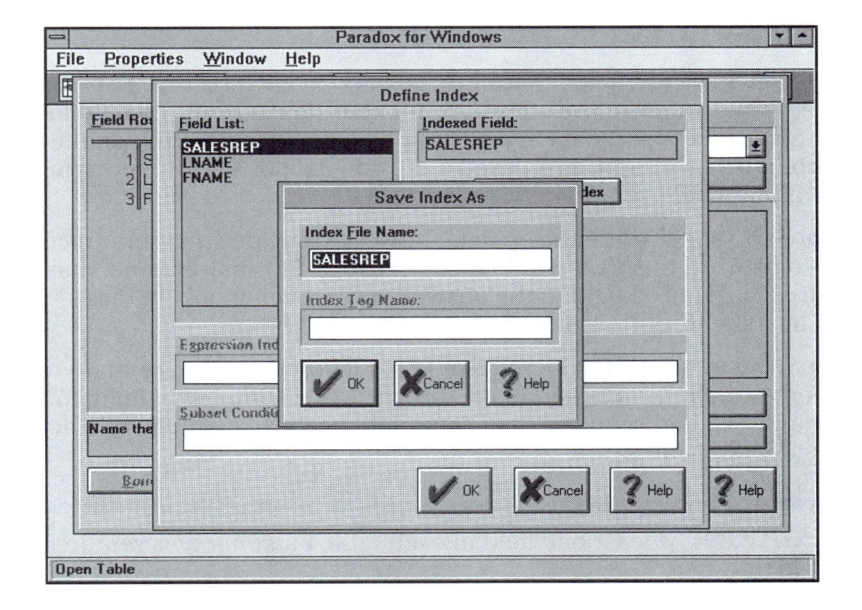

The Save Index As dialog box (dBASE table).

Specifying Validity Checks

The best way to guarantee the quality of your data is to prevent the entry of invalid data. *Validity checks* enable you to define tests for each field. Table 2.4 lists the validity checks available in Paradox for Windows.

Table 2.4. Validity Checks	
Check	**Meaning**
Required Field	Every record in the table must have a value in this field
Minimum	The smallest acceptable value in the field
Maximum	The largest acceptable value in the field
Default	The value Paradox is to enter if you do not enter a value in the field
Picture	A character string that is a template for the values entered in the field

The following sections explain these validity checks.

Specifying Required Fields

Required fields are fields that must be filled in each record. For example, you can make the telephone-number field a required field in a Customer table so that each customer record includes a telephone number. If you specify a required field, you cannot save a record in which that field is empty.

Before you specify a required field, however, decide whether a record with a blank in this field would make sense. If the answer is no, make the field a required field. If the answer is yes, even if only in rare circumstances, don't make the field a required field.

Also avoid making a field a required field if you are not sure that you can enter data in each field of each record. A middle-initial field, for example, is a bad required-field candidate because many people do not have middle names.

> **CAUTION:** At least one field in each table must *not* be a required field.

In the Albums table, make the Album ID, Artist, and Title fields required fields by following these steps:

1. Choose File, Open, Table from the Paradox Desktop, select the table, and then choose Restructure from the Table menu. The Restructure Paradox for Windows Table dialog box appears (see fig. 2.13).

2. Highlight the Album ID field in the Restructure Table dialog box.

3. Click the check box next to Required Field or press Alt-1. A check mark appears in the check box, indicating that the highlighted field now is a required field.

4. Repeat these steps for the Title and Artist fields.

5. When you finish, you can click the Save button to save the modified table. To continue with entering other validity checks discussed below, don't save the table yet.

Specifying Minimum and Maximum Values

Paradox for Windows enables you to establish upper and lower limits for the values in a field with the Minimum and Maximum options. You can specify limits to prevent invoices from being dated with future dates, for example, or to restrict the amount of credit extended to a customer.

2 — DESIGNING PARADOX TABLES AND DATABASES

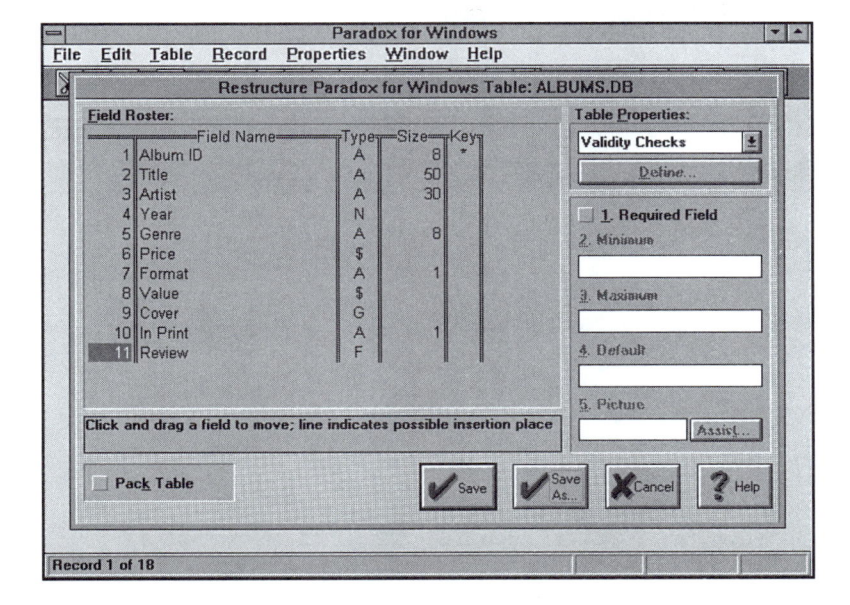

FIG. 2.13

The Restructure Paradox for Windows table dialog box.

To set minimum and maximum values for fields in the Albums table, follow these steps:

1. In the Restructure (or Define) Paradox for Windows Table dialog box, highlight the field for which you want to set minimum and maximum values. For this example, choose the Value field in the Albums table.

2. Click the Minimum box or press Alt+2, and enter **0** to establish $0 as the minimum limit.

3. Click the Maximum box or press Alt+3, and type **1000** to establish $1,000 as the maximum limit.

    The dialog box should look like figure 2.14.

4. Normally, you would close the Restructure Paradox for Windows Table dialog box by clicking the Save (or Save As) button. Again, leave this dialog box open if you want to continue with the next type of validity check.

Specifying Default Values

A field default is the value Paradox enters when you leave a field blank. If you are running a business in Seattle and most of your customers are local, you can specify WA as the state field default. To override the default for an out-of-state customer, simply type the correct value in that field.

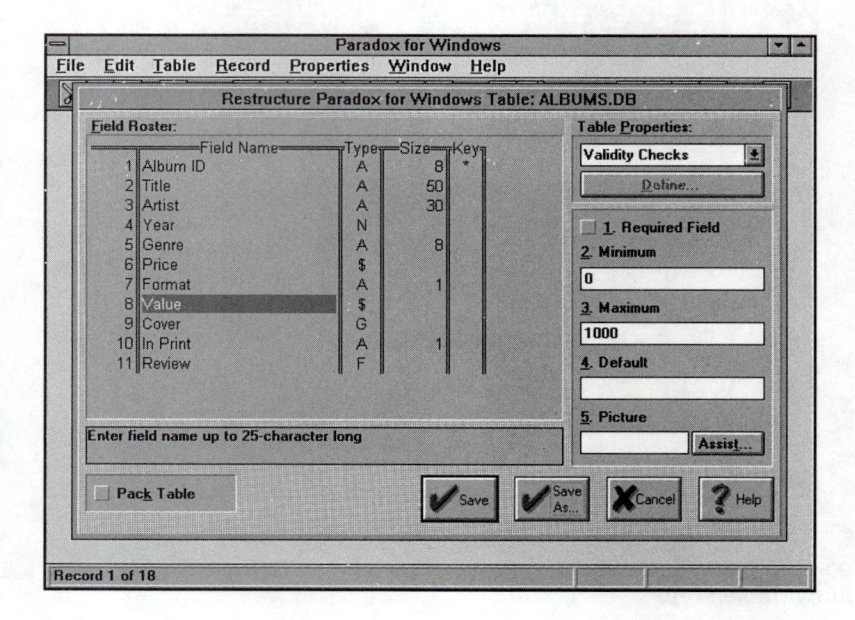

FIG. 2.14

The Albums table with minimum and maximum amounts for the Value field.

To specify a default in the Albums table, follow these steps:

1. In the Restructure (or Define) Paradox for Windows Table dialog box, highlight the field for which you want to establish the default value. For this example, choose the Format field in the Albums table. This is the field that specifies whether a recording is an album, compact disc, or tape.

2. Click the Default or press Alt+4, and enter C to establish Compact disc as the field default (see fig. 2.15).

3. Normally, you would close the Restructure Paradox for Windows Table dialog box by clicking the Save (or Save As) button. Leave this dialog box open if you want to continue with the next type of validity check.

Specifying Picture Characters

The Picture option defines the type of character that should appear in each position of a field. Many fields, such as ZIP codes and telephone numbers, have special formats you should follow when you enter data.

2 — DESIGNING PARADOX TABLES AND DATABASES

The Picture option makes formatting simpler; Paradox supplies formatting characters as needed and displays error messages if you attempt to make invalid entries.

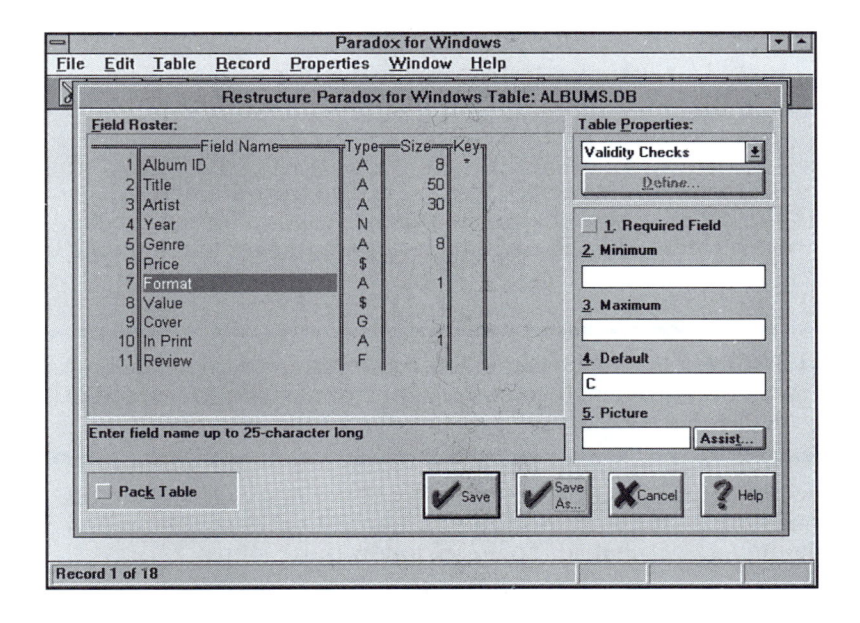

FIG. 2.15
The Albums table with C as the default for Format.

Table 2.5 lists the Picture characters in Paradox for Windows.

Table 2.5. Picture Characters

Character	Use
#	Digit
?	Any letter (uppercase or lowercase)
&	Any character (convert to uppercase)
@	Any character (convert to lowercase)
;	A literal character, not a picture-string character
*	Following character can be repeated any number of times
[]	Optional items enclosed
{}	Grouping operators
,	Alternative values

Following are examples of some common uses of picture characters:

#####[-####]	Zip code with optional four-digit code
######	Invoice number
(###)-###-####[x####]	Phone number with optional extension
&&	State

Paradox interprets characters that are not picture characters as constants—in other words, characters that are used to format the field but are not entered by the user, such as parentheses in telephone numbers.

> **CAUTION:** You must enter data precisely in picture fields. If you type a lowercase **l** instead of the digit 1 or a capital **O** instead of the digit 0, Paradox displays an error message.

Suppose that you want to restrict entry of the Album ID field in the Albums table to numbers only, with a hyphen between the second and third numbers of the field. To do so, follow these steps:

1. In the Restructure (or Define) Paradox for Windows Table dialog box, highlight the field for which you want to establish a picture. For this example, choose the Album ID field in the Albums table. This is a character field that uniquely identifies each album.

2. Enter ##-###### in the Picture field (Alt+5 is the hot key for this option). The result is shown in figure 2.16.

    You also can ask Paradox for help in defining a picture by pressing the Assist button next to the Picture field. The Picture Assistance dialog box appears (see fig. 2.17). To check the syntax of the picture, click the Verify Syntax button. You also can choose from Sample Pictures provided by Paradox or add your own sample pictures. Click OK to return to the Restructure Table dialog box.

3. Close the Restructure Paradox for Windows Table dialog box by clicking the Save (or Save As) button.

Borrowing a Table Structure

You do not have to start from scratch when you design a table; you can use an existing table as the basis for a new table. Paradox for Windows enables you to copy the structure of a table into a new table and then add or delete fields as necessary.

2 — DESIGNING PARADOX TABLES AND DATABASES

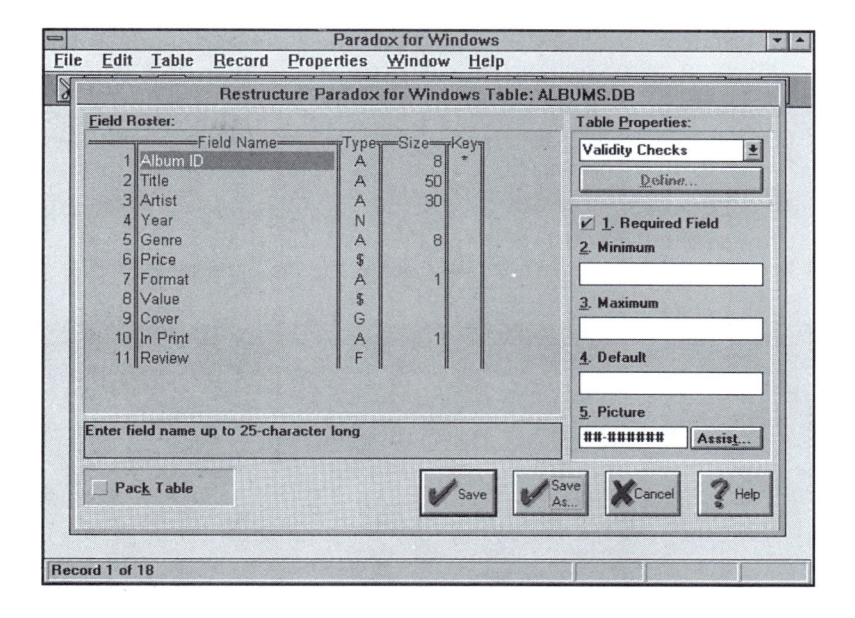

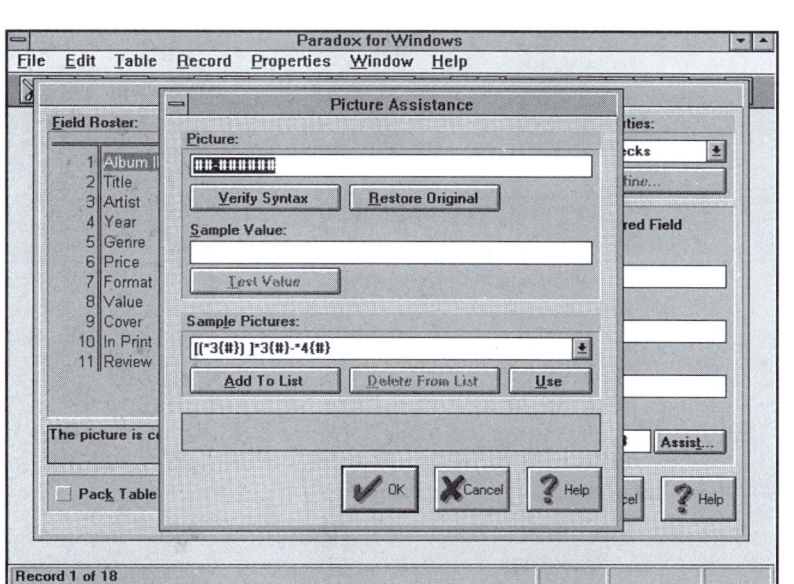

FIG. 2.16

The Albums table with a picture in the Album ID field.

FIG. 2.17

The Picture Assistance dialog box.

I — PARADOX FOR WINDOWS FUNDAMENTALS

You can create a Tracks table, based on the Albums table, to store information on each song or track. To create this table, follow these steps:

1. Choose File, New, Table from the Paradox Desktop, select the Paradox for Windows table type. The Create a Paradox for Windows Table dialog box appears.

2. Choose the Borrow box in the Create Table dialog box. The Borrow Table Structure dialog box appears (see fig. 2.18).

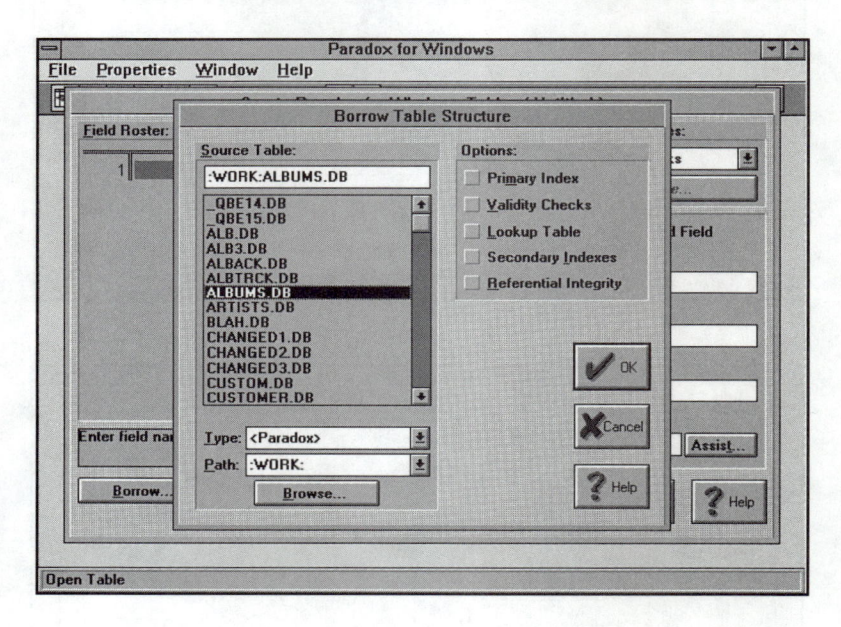

FIG. 2.18

The Borrow Table Structure dialog box.

3. Choose the name of the table to borrow—ALBUMS.DB for this example—by clicking the table name under Source Table.

4. You can check the Options boxes to copy the Primary Index, Validity Checks, Lookup Table, Secondary Indexes, and Referential Integrity of the source table. By default, Paradox does not copy these characteristics of the table.

5. Click OK to confirm your choice and copy the table. The Create Paradox for Windows Table dialog box reappears, containing all the fields from the table you have borrowed (see fig. 2.19). Now you may add, delete, or modify the fields as needed. Unlike Paradox for DOS, Paradox for Windows does not allow you to borrow more than one table at a time.

2 — DESIGNING PARADOX TABLES AND DATABASES

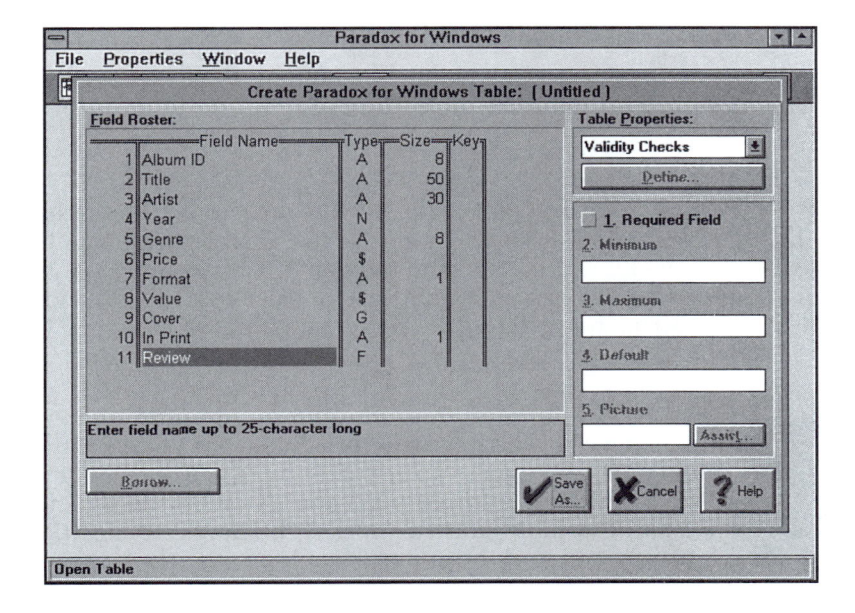

FIG. 2.19

The Create Paradox for Windows Table dialog box with borrowed table.

6. Delete the fields you do not need for the Tracks table (all the fields except for Album ID) by highlighting the field and pressing Ctrl-Del.

7. Make the Album ID a key field by pressing the space bar in the Key column of the field roster.

8. Add the new fields for the table. Press the down-arrow key to open a new row in the field roster and enter the following fields (see fig. 2.20 for the finished field roster):

   ■ *Track Number.* Indicates the order in which the track appears in the recording. If the recording is a record album or a cassette, the numeric sequence starts from side 1 and continues through side 2; if the recording is a compact disc, tracks are numbered in a single sequence.

   Album ID and Track Number are the composite key for the Tracks table; both are key fields.

   ■ *Song Title.* Title of the track.

   ■ *Minutes.* The track's playing time. Because Paradox for Windows does not support time fields, you enter playing-time values in two separate fields: Minutes and Seconds.

I — PARADOX FOR WINDOWS FUNDAMENTALS

■ *Seconds.* The companion field for minutes.

9. When you finish creating the table definition, click Save As to save the new table, naming the table TRACKS.

> **TIP**
>
> When you create related tables, borrow the structure of the first table you create so that you do not have to re-create fields in other tables. To save time, create a large table that contains fields you commonly use (such as mailing-address or sales-total fields) and then borrow from this table when you create new tables.

> **NOTE**
>
> You can borrow a table structure only from a table of the same type as the one you are creating. If you are building a dBASE table, for example, you cannot borrow the structure of a Paradox table, and vice versa. The Borrow dialog box lists only tables of the appropriate type.

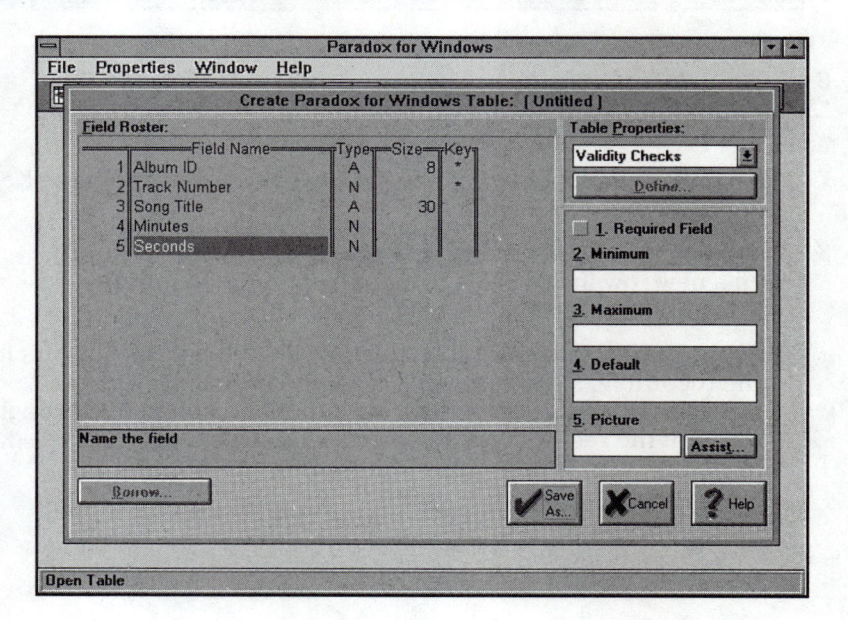

FIG. 2.20

The finished field roster for the TRACKS table.

Displaying the Table Structure

To display the structure of a table, open the table by choosing File, Open, Table from the Paradox Desktop. Select the table from the Open a Table dialog box, then choose Info Structure from the Table menu.

The Structure Information Paradox for Windows Table dialog box appears (see fig. 2.21). This dialog box is similar to the Create (Restructure) Paradox for Windows Table dialog box, but it does not allow you to change the structure of the table but only to view it. To see the validity checks for a field, highlight the field by clicking it.

When you finish viewing the table structure, click Done to return to the Table Edit window.

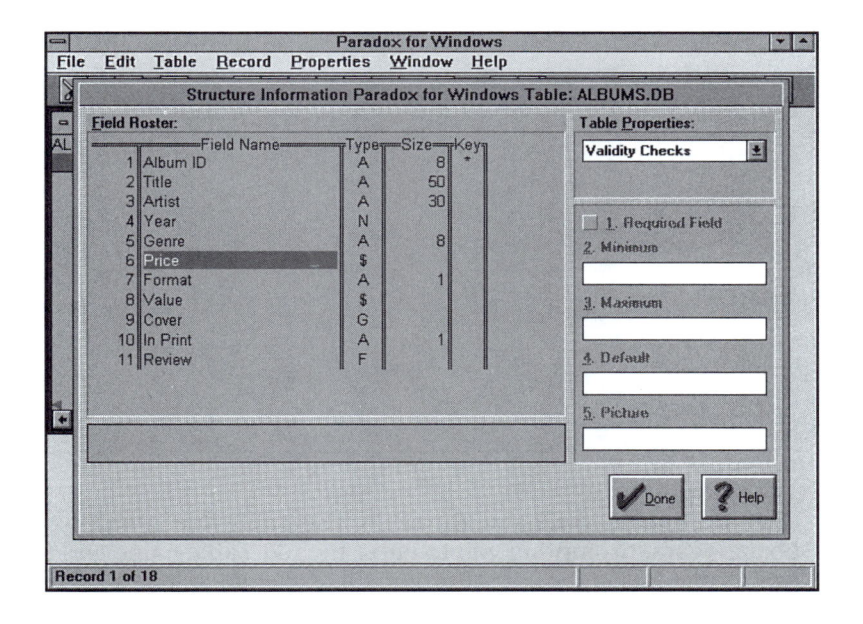

FIG. 2.21

The Structure Information Paradox for Windows Table dialog box for the Albums table.

Using Save As with a Table

Paradox for Windows enables you to use either of two commands when you save an existing table. As you have already seen, the Save command replaces the old structure and overwrites the old file. The Save As command creates a new table with a modified structure, along with data from the old table converted to the new structure; the old table remains unchanged. You use Save As after changing an existing table rather than clicking the Save button.

I — PARADOX FOR WINDOWS FUNDAMENTALS

Use Save As if you are worried about the effect of your changes on existing data. If you run into problems in the new file, the old structure remains intact. After you resolve any problems, simply rename the new table by following these steps:

1. From the Paradox Desktop, choose File.
2. Choose Utilities. The Table Utilities submenu appears (see fig. 2.22).

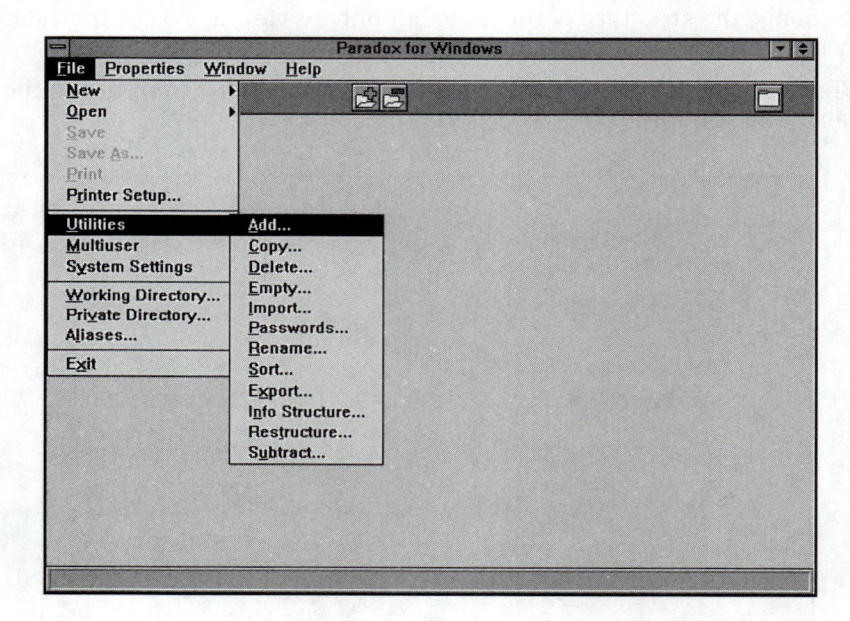

FIG. 2.22

The Table Utilities submenu.

3. Choose Rename to rename the table. The Table Rename dialog box appears, prompting you to enter the old Table name and the New Name (see fig. 2.23). After you fill in the old and new table names, click the Rename button and the table is renamed.

For Related Information

▶▶ "Defining and Modifying a Secondary Index," p. 346.

▶▶ "Using Validity Checks," p. 398.

▶▶ "Assisting Data Entry with Pictures," p. 401.

2 — DESIGNING PARADOX TABLES AND DATABASES

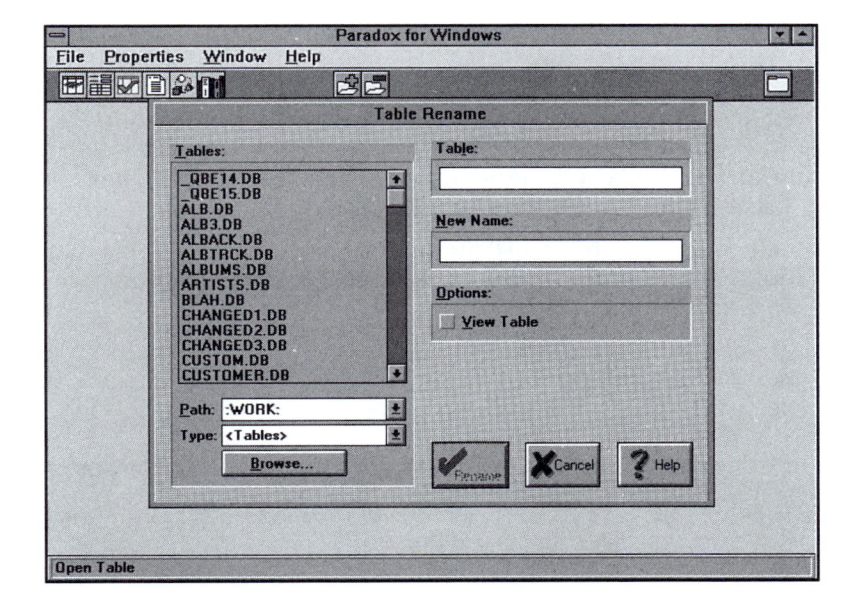

FIG. 2.23

The Table Rename dialog box.

Restructuring a Table

Over time, you often need to change the structure of a table. You may have to add or delete fields, lengthen or shorten fields, or change fields from one type to another. Paradox enables you to make such changes after you begin entering data.

The process of changing a table is called *restructuring*. Paradox automatically handles many aspects of restructuring (such as converting your data to the new structure) and warns you about potential data loss or inconsistency that may arise from your changes.

> **CAUTION:** Restructuring is one of the most dangerous things you can do to a table. You could permanently lose data in fields that you change, so think carefully about how the restructuring will affect your database. Restructuring can also affect reports, forms, and other objects related to the table. To prevent data loss, make a backup of your database before you begin a significant restructuring effort.

I — PARADOX FOR WINDOWS FUNDAMENTALS

Restructuring a table is similar to creating a new table. You do most of the work in the Restructure Table dialog box, which is identical to the Create Table dialog box.

To restructure the Albums table, follow these steps:

1. From the Paradox desktop, choose File, Open, Table. The Open a Table dialog box appears (see fig. 2.24).

2. Select the table to be restructured from the Open a Table dialog box. For this example, select ALBUMS. The Table: Albums window appears (see fig. 2.25).

3. Choose Table from the menu and then choose Restructure. The Restructure Paradox for Windows Table dialog box appears (see fig. 2.26).

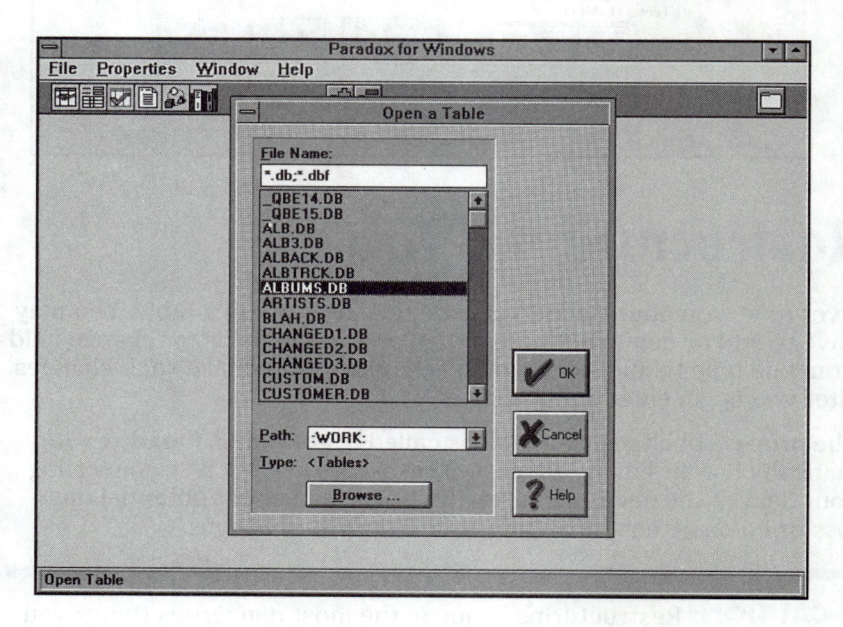

FIG. 2.24

The Open a Table dialog box.

4. Add a new field, Recording Method, to the table between field 5 (Genre) and field 6 (Price). Recording Method indicates whether the album used digital or analog recording.

   To add this field, place the pointer on field 6 and then press Ins to insert a blank line. Paradox inserts a blank line above field 6. Paradox automatically renumbers the fields if you add or delete a field.

5. In the blank line, type the name of the new field, **Recording Method**.

2 — DESIGNING PARADOX TABLES AND DATABASES

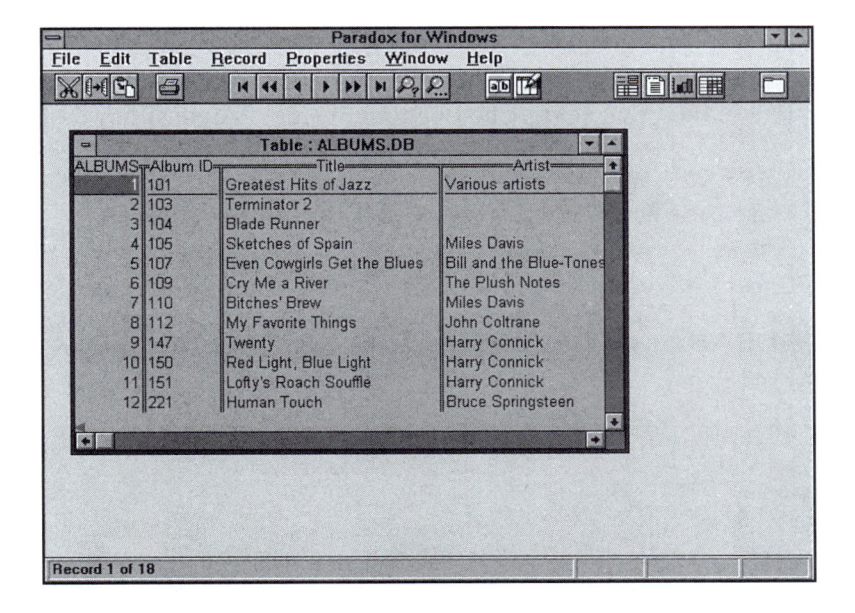

FIG. 2.25

The Table Edit window.

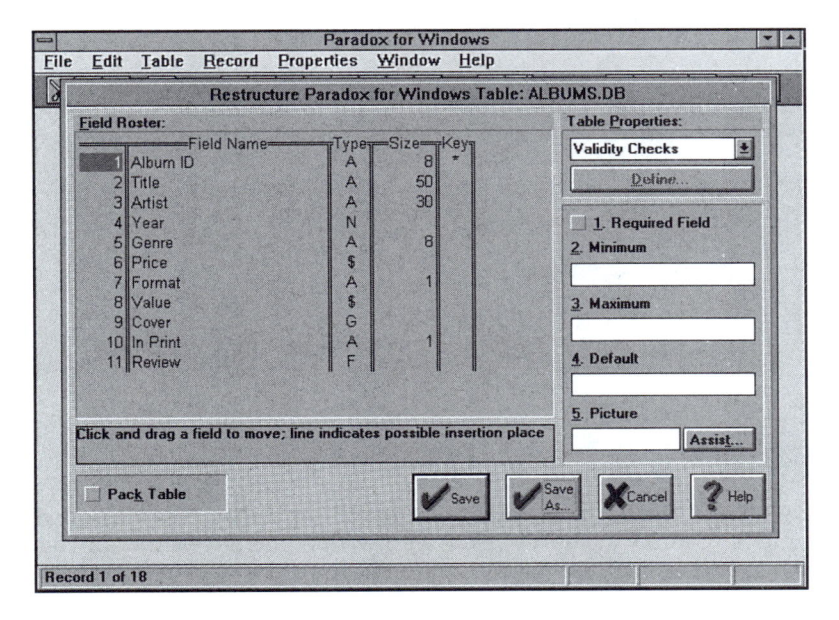

FIG. 2.26

The Restructure Paradox for Windows Table dialog box.

I — PARADOX FOR WINDOWS FUNDAMENTALS

6. Specify Alphanumeric as the field type by entering **A** in the field Type column and specify **3** as the field Size.

7. Delete the Price field by highlighting the field name and pressing Ctrl+Del. The Recording Method field is now located between the Genre and Format fields.

8. Make the Year field a number field by typing **N** in the Type column.

9. Click the Save As button. The Save Table As dialog box appears (see fig. 2.27). Name the new table ALBUMS2 by entering **ALBUMS2** in the New Table Name field, and then click the OK button.

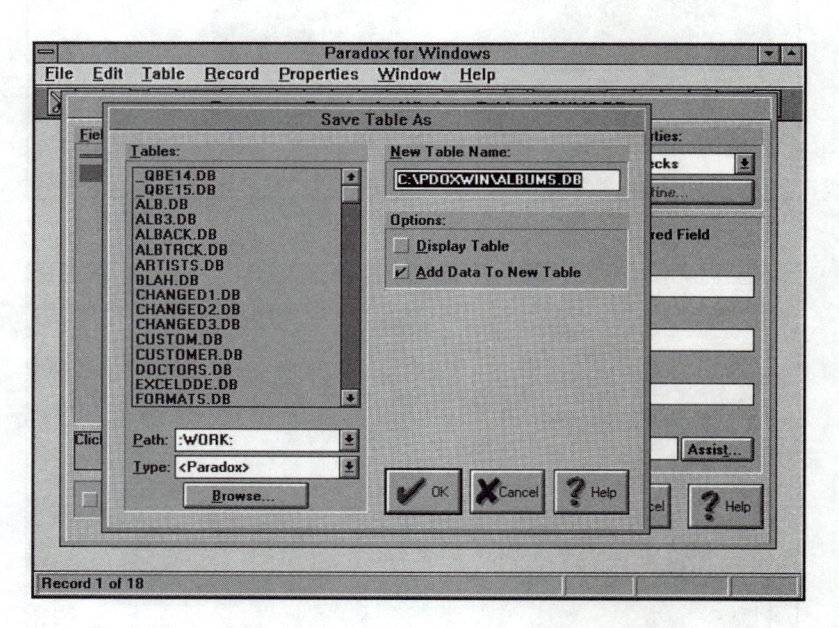

FIG. 2.27
The Save Table As dialog box.

Changing a Field Type

Changing a field type is as easy as highlighting the field name and changing the entry in the Type column. When you save the table again, Paradox modifies all the data in that field to fit the new field type.

Changing the field type can create problems if existing entries are incompatible with the new field type. Paradox warns you if your change of field type may result in data loss. If you change a text field to a number field, for example, entries that contain letters become invalid.

2 — DESIGNING PARADOX TABLES AND DATABASES

Rather than discard these entries, however, Paradox for Windows creates a temporary table called Problems for records that must be modified to fit the new field type. You can edit these records and then transfer them into the main table.

Because changing a field type can create data inconsistency, examine your entries before making the change. For an extra measure of security, copy the table and change the copy; replace the original table only when you are certain that your changes are successful.

Table 2.6 shows the results of field type conversions. (For an explanation of Paradox field types, see table 2.2).

Table 2.6. Paradox Field Type Conversions

Old field Type	New field Type								
	A	N	C	S	D	M/F	G	O	B
Alphanumeric	—	P	P	P	P	Yes	No	No	No
Number	Yes	—	Yes	Yes	Yes	Yes	No	No	No
Currency	Yes	Yes	—	Yes	Yes	Yes	No	No	No
Short	Yes	Yes	Yes	—	No	Yes	No	No	No
Date	Yes	No	No	No	—	Yes	No	No	No
Memo/ Formatted Memo	P	No	No	No	No	—	No	No	Yes
Graphic	No	No	No	No	No	No	—	No	Yes
OLE Object	No	No	No	No	No	No	No	—	Yes

A	Alphanumeric		G	Graphic
B	Binary		M	Memo
C	Currency		N	Number
D	Date		O	OLE Object
F	Formatted memo		S	Short number
Yes	Conversion is allowed but may result in some trimming			
No	Conversion is not allowed			
P	Conversion is allowed but almost always generates the Problems table			
—	Not applicable			

Similar considerations apply to restructuring dBASE tables. Table 2.7 shows the effects of changing from one dBASE field type to another.

Table 2.7. dBASE Field Type Conversions

Old field Type	New field Type					
	C	**F**	**N**	**D**	**L**	**M**
Character	—	P	P	P	Yes	Yes
Floating-point number	Yes	—	Yes	No	Yes	No
Number	Yes	Yes	—	No	Yes	No
Date	Yes	No	No	—	No	No
Logic	Yes	Yes	Yes	No	—	No
Memo	Yes	No	No	No	No	—

C	Character	D	Date
F	Floating-point number	L	Logic
N	Number	M	Memo
Yes	Conversion is allowed, but may result in some trimming		
No	Conversion is not allowed		
P	Conversion is allowed, but almost always generates the Problems table		
—	Not applicable		

One of the conclusions you may draw from tables 2.6 and 2.7 is that converting from more specialized to less specialized field types is easier than converting from less specialized to more specialized field types. You can convert most field types to text fields easily because text fields can accommodate nearly any character, including numbers used in dates. On the other hand, converting dates stored as text to date fields can create problems because you can format dates many ways in text fields. Even when formatted properly, however, you could make entries in text fields that date fields would reject.

When you convert a field to a date field, you must enter the alphanumeric strings to be converted in one of the accepted Paradox for Windows date formats. The following list shows the six formats you can use to enter Bastille Day:

> 07/14/1789
> 07/14/89
> 14-Jul-1789
> Jul-14-1789
> 14.07.1789
> 14.07.89

The formats that include only two digits for the year assume that the century is the twentieth.

2 — DESIGNING PARADOX TABLES AND DATABASES

117

Paradox for Windows does not convert dates expressed in other formats, such as July 14, 1789.

Restructuring is particularly dangerous when you shorten fields, because you can lose data if the existing fields are longer than the restructured ones. In such a case, Paradox displays a dialog box to warn you of potential data loss. If you delete the Price field and save the Albums table, for example, a warning dialog box appears (see fig. 2.28).

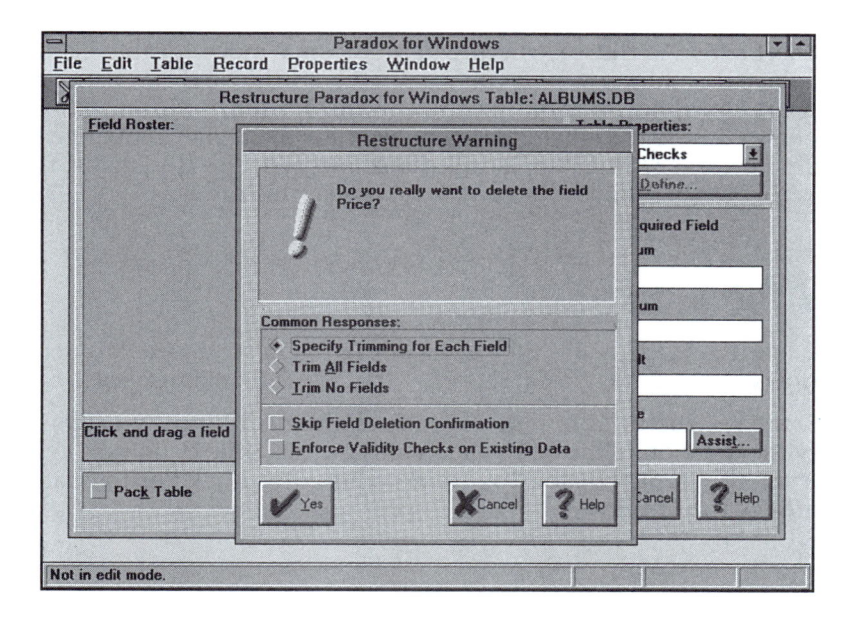

FIG. 2.28

The Restructure Warning dialog box.

The Restructure Warning dialog box gives you several options for handling potential data loss from table restructuring. By default, you must confirm changes or deletions of each field. By choosing Trim All Fields or Trim No Fields, you will not be prompted for each individual field. Similarly, if you check the Skip Field Deletion Confirmation option, you will not be prompted to confirm the deletion of fields. When you add a new validity check to a table, old data is not affected unless you choose the Enforce Validity Checks On Existing Data option.

> **NOTE** If you add a field when you restructure a table, Paradox does not add the new field to existing forms or reports associated with the table. You must add the new field to each document in which you want to include the field.

Inserting a Field

To insert a field in the Restructure Paradox for Windows Table dialog box, place the pointer where you want to insert the field and press Ins. To insert a field between the second and third fields, for example, place the cursor on the third field. Paradox inserts a blank line above the line where the cursor is located. In this blank line, type the field name, type, and size. To insert more than one field, repeat this process.

Deleting a Field

To delete a field, highlight the field name in the Restructure Paradox for Windows Table dialog box and press Ctrl+Del. The field disappears.

If you are restructuring an existing table, Paradox prompts you to verify the deletion of the field when you save the table definition in the Restructure Warning dialog box (refer to fig. 2.28). Click Yes to confirm deletion of the field.

Moving a Field

To move a field in the Restructure Paradox for Windows Table dialog box, click the row number of the field and then drag the field to its new location. (When you place the pointer on the row number, the pointer becomes an arrow.)

Remember that key fields must be the first fields listed in a table, so you should not move them farther down in the field list.

Chapter Summary

In this chapter, you learned the concepts and techniques used to create and modify tables in Paradox for Windows. You learned the importance of key fields to database design and how to determine which tables and fields you need. You learned how to define Paradox for Windows field types and learned the appropriate applications for each type. Next you learned that you can easily change Paradox tables as your business needs change by restructuring. You can add new fields, delete fields, change field types, and change the order of fields within a table.

Now that you have created some tables, the next step is to enter data. Chapter 3 shows how to take advantage of all the data entry facilities of Paradox for Windows.

CHAPTER 3

Entering, Editing, and Viewing Data

This chapter shows you how to add, edit, delete, and view data in Paradox for Windows tables. You learn the essentials of Paradox modes, SpeedBar tools, menus, and keyboard shortcuts (including function keys) that relate to data entry. Some advanced techniques are presented in Chapter 9, "Using Power Entry and Editing Features." You also may use queries to manipulate records (see Chapter 4, "Getting Started with Query by Example").

Compared to other database packages, Paradox for Windows offers a large set of data-entry features. The good news is that you have many commands and options at your disposal. You may use the keyboard, the mouse, menus, SpeedBar icons, or function keys to accomplish the same tasks. The bad news is that learning all these options and deciding which method is best for you takes longer.

The descriptions in this chapter build on concepts introduced in Chapters 1 and 2. If you are not familiar with basic Paradox for Windows terminology or do not know how to create a Paradox table, review Chapters 1 and 2 before you read this chapter.

I — PARADOX FOR WINDOWS FUNDAMENTALS

Opening a Table

As discussed in Chapter 2, "Designing Paradox Tables and Databases," all Paradox data is stored in tables. Therefore, the starting point for record entry is either the table itself or a form based on the table. This chapter explores data entry in both tables and forms, starting with tables. First, open a table by following these steps:

1. From the Paradox Desktop, choose File, Open, Table or click the Open Table button in the SpeedBar. The Open Table button is on the far left of the SpeedBar and resembles a sheet of paper marked into columns with a lightning bolt.

2. The Open a Table dialog box appears (see fig. 3.1). This dialog box contains a list of database tables in your current directory. If you do not see the table you want, use the scroll bars to reveal the rest of the list. To change to another directory, click the Browse button.

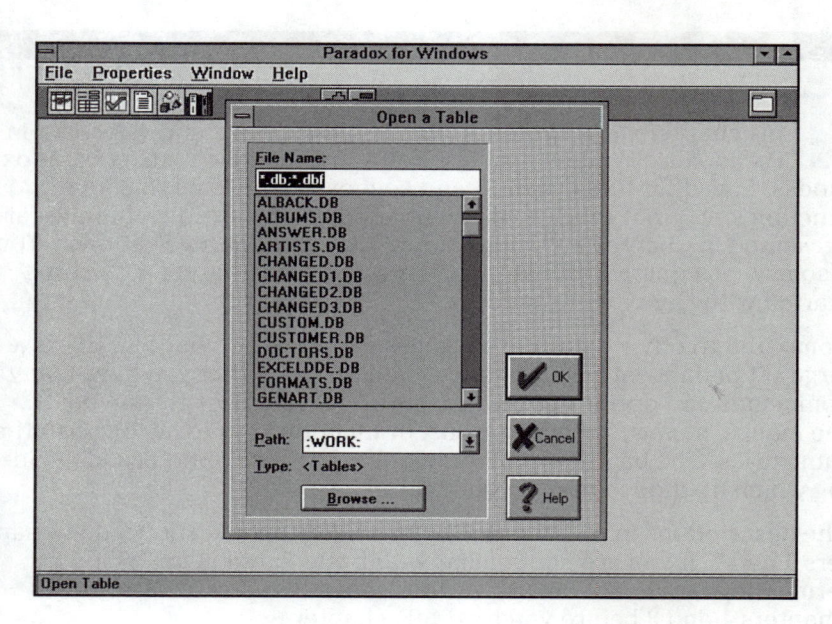

FIG. 3.1

The Open a Table dialog box.

3. Choose the name of the table you want to view or edit, then click OK. To open the Albums table introduced in Chapter 2, for example, choose ALBUMS.DB from the list and click OK.

4. The table appears in a window. If you choose ALBUMS.DB, for example, the Albums table shown in figure 3.2 appears.

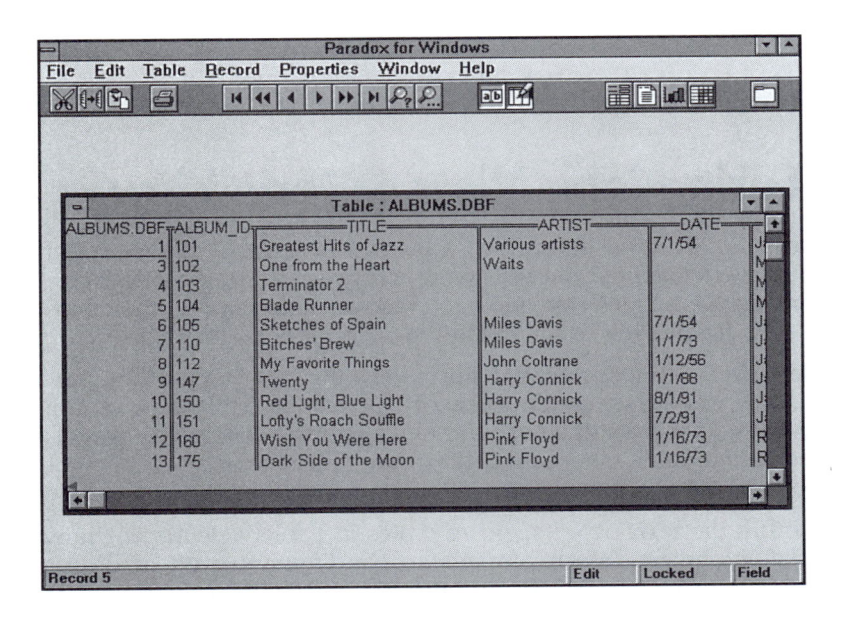

FIG. 3.2

The Albums table in Table view.

The window shows the first records in the table. From this table window, you may view records, search for records, and add, edit, and delete records.

Paradox Data-Entry Modes

Paradox operates in several modes so that you can perform different data-entry operations. Paradox has three levels of data-entry modes, with six possible combinations between them. These modes may be confusing at first, especially Edit mode, which itself contains two modes.

Figure 3.3 shows a diagram of all record-entry modes. The first level is the type of view. You may be in either Table view or Form view. Within table or Form view, you may be in View mode or Edit mode. Finally, in Edit mode you may be in Field view or Non-field view. Each of these modes is explained in this chapter, along with the commands to change from one mode to another.

FIG. 3.3

The Paradox data-entry modes.

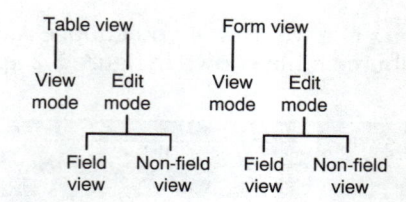

```
              Table view              Form view
              ┌────┴────┐             ┌────┴────┐
            View      Edit          View      Edit
            mode      mode          mode      mode
                      ┌──┴──┐                 ┌──┴──┐
                    Field  Non-field        Field  Non-field
                    view   view             view   view
```

Choosing Table View or Form View

Paradox for Windows offers two ways to view data: Table view and Form view. *Table view* shows several records at a time, with each record displayed as a row and each field as a column, as shown in figure 3.2. Table view is the default view in Paradox for Windows.

Table view is often better than Form view for entering multiple records, especially when they are short records, because Table view groups the fields more closely and gives your eye a shorter distance to travel between fields. Table view can display many records at a time, so you can take in the data at a glance.

Like other Paradox objects, entire tables in Table view may be moved, resized, minimized (shrunk to an icon), and manipulated. In addition, their columns can be resized and moved, and the row height can be modified. This helps you see more of the table and arrange the fields in a more useful order without restructuring the table.

Form view is an alternative to Table view, as shown in figure 3.4. Form view shows all the fields of one record on a single screen (or on multiple screens if the fields cannot fit on one screen), rather than several records in a window.

To switch from Table view to Form view, press F7. Paradox automatically creates a standard (default) form for you. Press F7 again to return to Table view.

You have greater control over the order and appearance of the fields in Form view, which usually shows more fields at one time. Form view is especially useful for tables with long fields, such as an address list. In Table view, you might see only the name and first line or two of the address, but Form view can use the entire window to show all the fields.

Paradox Form view resembles a paper form more closely than Table view. Data entry can be facilitated by designing Paradox forms that copy the flow of paper forms. With Form view, you also can include tools such as buttons and pull-down menus to speed data entry and minimize mistakes. As a result, many users find Form view easier to work with.

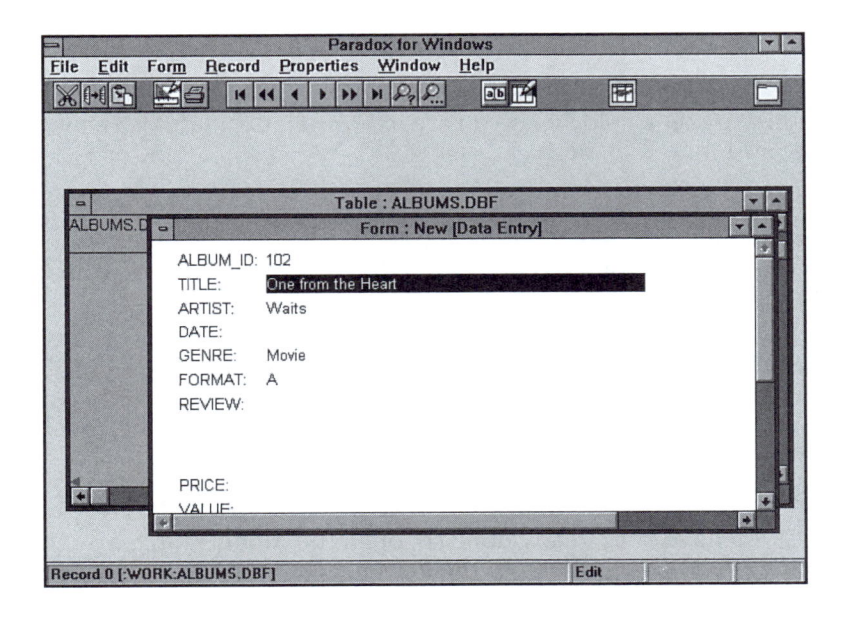

FIG. 3.4

The Albums table in Form view.

If you want to design your own form, you can include graphics or even fields from multiple tables in the same form, as shown in Chapter 5, "Getting Started with Forms" and Chapter 7, "Using Advanced Form Techniques."

Choosing View Mode or Edit Mode

For both Form view and Table view, Paradox has two data-entry modes: View mode and Edit mode. In *View mode*, you can scan through a table but you cannot add new records or change records. View mode is the default. In *Edit mode*, you can browse through a table, and you can also add, edit, or delete records. The current mode is displayed in the title bar of the window, immediately before the table name, and on the right side of the message line at the bottom of the window.

You can use any of these three methods to change between View mode and Edit mode:

■ Toggle with the F9 key.

I — PARADOX FOR WINDOWS FUNDAMENTALS

- Click the Edit Data button (which looks like a pencil on a ledger) in the SpeedBar.
- Choose Table from the menu. Then select Edit Data to switch to Edit mode or Table and End Data Entry to switch to View mode.

T I P If you try to edit a field when you are in View mode, Paradox reminds you to switch to Edit mode.

When you open a table, Paradox automatically displays the table in View mode. If you want to enter or modify records, you must switch to Edit mode.

In Edit mode, you may add new records by filling in the fields in a blank record. A newly created table contains no records, and you can begin entering data on the first line of the table. In a table that already contains records, you must begin by moving the cursor to the bottom of the table or by pressing Ins to insert a blank line.

Follow these steps to enter some records into the Albums table:

1. If you have not already done so, open the Albums table by choosing File, Open, Table from the Paradox Desktop.
2. Choose ALBUMS.DB from the Open a Table dialog box.
3. Switch from View mode to Edit mode by pressing F9.
4. Press Ins to open an empty row in the table.
5. Fill in each field in the table, pressing Tab to move to the next field. Don't worry about making errors; you can edit them later.
6. Repeat steps 4 and 5 to enter three or four records.

To move from field to field, press Tab, Enter, or the arrow keys, or use the mouse to click the cursor on the desired location. (Shift+Tab moves the cursor to the previous field.) In most cases, you will use the mouse or standard cursor-movement keys (the arrow keys, Tab, and Enter) to move around the table. Paradox for Windows offers additional keyboard shortcuts that can simplify cursor movement, as listed in table 3.1.

Table 3.1. Data-Entry Cursor Movement

Key combination	Form view	Table view
Enter Tab Right arrow	Next field	Next field
Shift+Tab Left arrow	Previous field	Previous field
Up arrow	Previous field	Previous record
Down arrow	Next field	Next record
Home	First field of current record	First field of current record
End	Last field of current record	Last field of current record
Ctrl+Home	First field of first record	First field of first record
Ctrl+End	Last field of last record	Last field of last record

TIP

When you enter data, make your job easier by showing as much of the table as possible. You can do this by *maximizing* the data entry window. To maximize a window, click the Maximize button in the upper right corner of the window (or double-click the title bar of the window or click the Control menu button in the upper left corner of the window and choose Maximize). If you are working in a child window (a window within a window), you may need to maximize the parent window as well. Maximizing is especially handy for Table view, when you want to see many records at a time.

To clear a field, press Del or choose Edit, Delete from the menu. Either of these methods will delete the contents of the field you are editing. Note that clearing a field is different from deleting an entire record (Ctrl+Del). If you press Esc while editing a field, your changes will be discarded.

Using Field View

Within Edit mode, Paradox for Windows has two modes for editing the contents of a field in a form or table: Field view and Non-field view. By default, when you place your cursor in a field and begin typing, the existing field entry disappears and your new entry replaces it. This default mode is *Non-field view*. If you want to edit the value in a field rather than replace it, you should use *Field view*. You can use four ways to switch from Non-field view to Field view:

- Choose Field View from the Table or Form menu.
- Press F2
- Click the Field View button
- Double-click the field you want to edit

Your mouse pointer changes to resemble a vertical bar, and may be moved with the Backspace key, Delete key, or arrow keys. To exit Field view, repeat one of the commands you used to enter Field view or, more simply, move to another field. As soon as you leave the field you are working on, the data is saved in the table, and Paradox resumes Non-field view in the next field.

If you want to stay in Field view for each field, press Ctrl+F2 for persistent Field view. The message `Persist` is displayed on the right side of the message bar. You will remain in persistent Field view until you press Ctrl+F2 again to deactivate the feature. Persistent Field view can be handy for an intensive editing session, so you don't have to keep clicking back into Edit mode.

When Field view has been activated, you can position the cursor with the arrow keys or the mouse. The Backspace key deletes characters as it moves backwards within the field. In addition, you can use special Field view keyboard shortcuts to move within a field, as shown in table 3.2.

Table 3.2. Keyboard Shortcuts in Field View

Key	Result
Home	Beginning of field
End	End of field
Ctrl+Home	Beginning of field
Ctrl+End	End of field
Ctrl+right arrow	First letter in next word

3 — ENTERING, EDITING, AND VIEWING DATA

Key	Result
Ctrl+left arrow	First letter in previous word
Ctrl+Backspace	Delete word to left of cursor
Del	Delete selected block of text or character to right of the insertion point

As mentioned, you exit Field view using one of the following options you used to get into Field view:

- Click the Field View button
- Press F2
- Choose Table (or Form if you are in Form view), then select Field View
- Move the cursor to another field and click once to select it
- Double-click the field

Try out Field view by editing the Title field in the Albums table. Use the Tab key or the mouse to move to the field, then double-click to enter Field view. The mouse pointer changes to a text insertion point. Field view is shown in figure 3.5. You may move around inside the field, adding or deleting characters as needed to edit the entry. To delete several characters in a field, click and drag the mouse to mark the block and press Del.

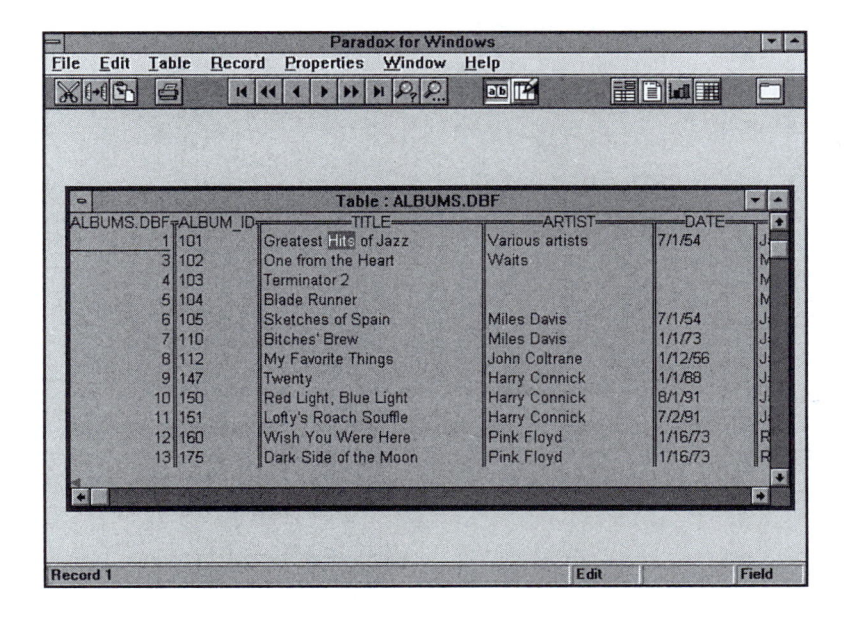

FIG. 3.5

Field view in the Title field of the Albums table.

NOTE You cannot edit the contents of exotic field types such as graphic, binary, and OLE (object linking and embedding) in Field view. You can, however, edit the contents of memo fields in Field view.

Using the SpeedBar

The SpeedBar contains special tools for viewing and editing data. Different SpeedBar tools are available in Table view and Form view, as shown in figures 3.6 and 3.7, and tables 3.3 and 3.4. Both modes, however, share the record navigation buttons on the left side of the SpeedBar. When you change to Form view, the icons for quick report, graph, and crosstab disappear.

FIG. 3.6

The SpeedBar in Table view.

Table 3.3. Buttons on the Table SpeedBar

Button	Name
	Cut to Clipboard
	Copy to Clipboard
	Paste from Clipboard
	Print
	First Record
	Previous Set of Records
	Previous Record
	Next Record
	Next Set of Records
	Last Record
	Locate Field Value
	Locate Next
	Field View

3 — ENTERING, EDITING, AND VIEWING DATA

Button	Name
	Edit Data
	Quick Form
	Quick Report
	Quick Graph
	Quick Crosstab
	Open Folder

FIG. 3.7
The SpeedBar in Form view.

Table 3.4. Buttons on the Form SpeedBar

Button	Name
	Cut to Clipboard
	Copy to Clipboard
	Paste from Clipboard
	Design
	Print
	First record
	Previous set of records
	Previous record
	Next record
	Next set of records
	Last record
	Locate field value
	Locate next
	Field view
	Edit data
	Table view
	Open folder

I — PARADOX FOR WINDOWS FUNDAMENTALS

> **TIP** To change from Table view to Form view, you can click the Quick Form button on the SpeedBar or press the F7 key. (F7 toggles between Form view and Table view.)

Entering Data with Special Field Types

This section describes special data-entry techniques as they apply to each Paradox field type. Although most data-entry techniques apply to all Paradox field types, some field types have special features.

Entering Data in Date Fields

Date fields are different from ordinary alphanumeric or numeric fields. One difference is that date fields can accept only valid dates. This means that you cannot enter **99/48/72** in a date field. You also cannot enter an invalid date for a particular month, such as June 31 or February 30.

Several display formats are available for dates. You can use any Paradox date format when entering dates. The program automatically converts the date to the current display format. Table 3.5 shows six ways to enter Bastille Day (July 14, 1789). The formats that include only two digits for the year assume that the century is the twentieth (that is, 19*xx*).

Table 3.5. Paradox Data-Entry Date Formats

Format	Example
MM/DD/YYYY	07/14/1789
MM/DD/YY	07/14/89
DD-Mon-YYYY	14-Jul-1789
DD.MM.YY	14.07.89
DD.MM.YYYY	14.07.1789

Paradox offers a special feature to speed the entry of dates. To enter today's date in a date field, press the space bar three times. The first press enters the current month, the second press enters the current date, and the third press enters the current year.

> **TIP**
>
> Paradox for Windows calculates the current date from the system clock on your PC. Therefore, be sure to set the clock as necessary to ensure that the current date is correct.

Entering Data in Memo Fields

You can use a *memo field* to store lengthy text remarks along with the database record. Memo fields are different from ordinary alphanumeric fields because they are stored in files outside the table, with the file extension of MB. Up to 240 characters of the memo field may be stored in the table itself, with the rest in the MB file.

To enter data in a memo field, select the field and enter Field view (as described previously). A special memo field window opens (Paradox calls this memo view), and the table disappears. You then can enter as much information in the field as you want. Just like any other window, the memo window can be resized or moved, and the scroll bar can be used to move within the memo area. Figure 3.8 shows a sample memo field.

The Color and Font properties of memo fields enable you to change the background color and display font. The Complete Display property determines whether a memo field is displayed for all records or only the current record in Table view. Additional properties are available for formatted memo fields.

Paradox provides additional text-editing functions in memo view which are not available in alphanumeric fields. For instance, pressing Tab or Enter in an alphanumeric field advances you to the next field; pressing Tab while in memo view inserts a tab and pressing Enter inserts a blank line. Table 3.6 shows keyboard commands used in memo view.

I — PARADOX FOR WINDOWS FUNDAMENTALS

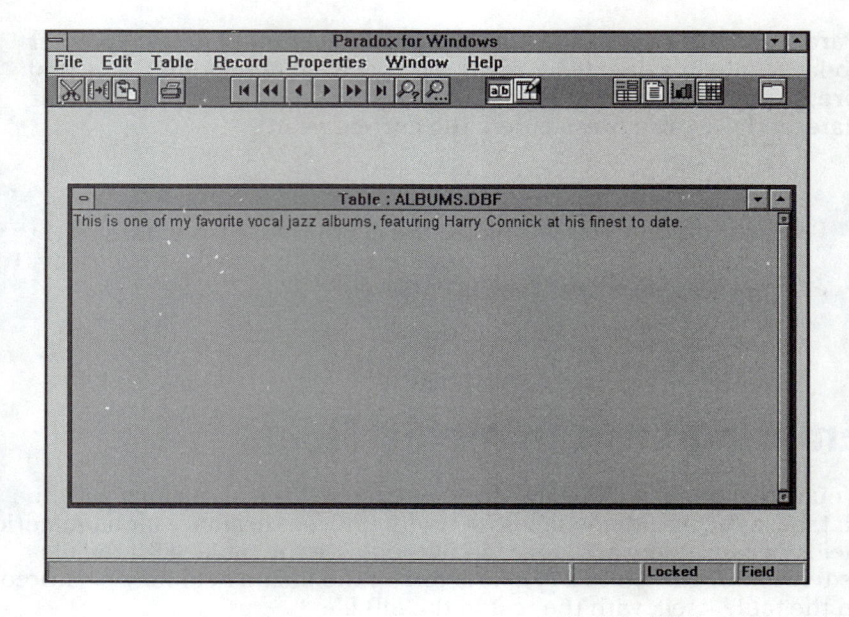

FIG. 3.8

Sample memo field.

Table 3.6. Keyboard Commands in Memo View

Key	Result
Cursor Movement	
PgUp	Up one screen
Ctrl+PgUp	Left one screen
PgDn	Down one screen
Ctrl+PgDn	Right one screen
Home	Beginning of line
Shift+Home	Select to beginning of line
Ctrl+Home	Beginning of memo field
End	End of line
Shift+End	Select to end of line
Left arrow	Left one character
Right arrow	Right one character
Up arrow	Up one line
Down arrow	Down one line

Key	Result
Ctrl+right arrow	Right one word
Ctrl+left arrow	Left one word
Block Operations	
Shift+up arrow	Select up one line
Shift+down arrow	Select down one line
Shift+Ins	Paste
Ctrl+Ins	Copy
Del	Delete selected block; delete character if no block is selected
Editing Commands	
Backspace	Delete previous character
Ctrl-Backspace	Delete previous word
Alt-Backspace	Undo edit
ESC	Undo edit
Tab	Tab
Enter	Insert carriage return/line feed and advance to next line

In a memo field, text automatically wraps to the next line as you reach the end of a line. If you change the size of the window, the word wrap is adjusted to fit.

When you finish entering the memo, double-click the Control box in the upper left corner of the window, or click once and choose Close. When you exit the memo field, Paradox automatically saves the data and brings back the table, displaying the first few characters of the memo field. If you click the Minimize button from the memo Edit window, the entire table will be minimized.

Memo view can be awkward to use because it may obscure some of the other fields in the table, making it difficult to tell which record you are editing. You can move the memo view window by clicking the title and dragging it to a new location to reveal more of the table. Persistent Field view does not apply to memo fields, so you must use one of the means listed earlier to switch to memo view.

I — PARADOX FOR WINDOWS FUNDAMENTALS

> **TIP** The Windows Clipboard is quite handy for editing memo fields. The Clipboard may be used to move text between Paradox and your word processor, so you may perform spelling or grammar checks or easily copy large sections of text from word processing documents. Use the Cut, Copy, and Paste options from the Edit menu, or consult your Windows documentation for additional details on moving text.

Entering Data in Formatted Memo Fields

A *formatted memo field* is the same as a memo field, except that you have more control over the appearance of a formatted memo field. You can use more than one font at a time in a formatted memo field. This is handy if you want a section of text to stand out from the rest of the screen, or you want to use a smaller font so that you can view more text at a glance.

To change the properties of the formatted memo field, go to memo view and press the right mouse button in the field to display the options. Table 3.7 shows the properties you can change and their options.

Table 3.7. Formatted Memo Field Properties in Memo View

Property	Description
Font	Typeface, size, style, and color
Alignment	Left, Center (horizontal), Right, Justify
Line Spacing	Single through triple spacing in half-space increments

Figure 3.9 shows a formatted memo field in the Albums table for storing your favorite lyrics from the album. Note that two different fonts were used to enter the text. To change the font in a formatted memo field, follow these steps:

1. Select the text by clicking and dragging the mouse.
2. Right-click to reveal the pop-up properties menu.
3. Change the font, color, and style of the text as desired. Your changes take effect immediately.

3 — ENTERING, EDITING, AND VIEWING DATA

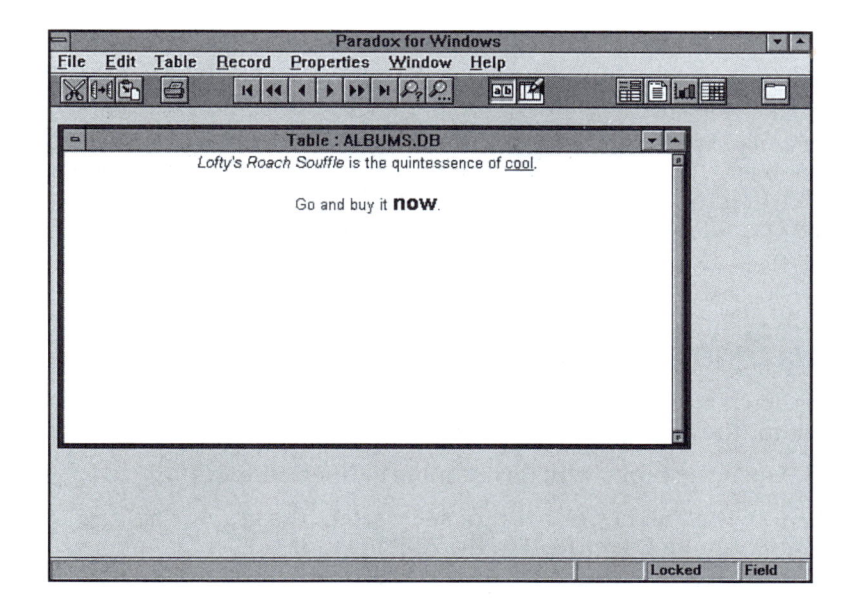

137

FIG. 3.9

Different fonts in a formatted memo field.

In addition to changing the properties of a formatted memo field, you can search and replace text as you would in a word processor. The search and replace feature is similar in memo fields and in tables, and is discussed later in this chapter, under "Using Search to Find Fields, Records, and Values."

> **NOTE** In essence, a formatted memo field has two sets of properties: one set available in Table view, and another set accessible only in Memo view. Formatted and unformatted memo fields have Complete Display, Color, and Font properties in Table view. In Memo view, however, formatted memo fields enjoy Font, Alignment, and Line Spacing properties; unformatted memo fields display no properties in Memo view.

Entering Data in Graphic Fields

Graphic fields contain bit-mapped images. These images are usually created by using graphics programs or by scanning images. Paradox for Windows supports BMP, GIF, EPS, TIF, and PCX graphics formats. If your graphics program uses another file format, convert the image to one of the supported formats before entering it in the Paradox for Windows database. (Many graphics software packages include a conversion option that produces one of the supported formats.)

You can enter graphics in Paradox for Windows in two ways. One approach is to type the DOS file name of the graphics file, including the path (directory name), such as \WINDOWS\LOGO.PCX. Another way to enter graphics in a Paradox for Windows field is to use the Windows Clipboard. Both of these techniques are explained in this section.

Specifying a Graphics File

Suppose that you have scanned a number of graphic images into files. To enter these graphics in a Paradox table, proceed as follows:

1. Open the table, which is Albums in the example.

2. Use the Tab key or the mouse to select the graphic field, which is the Album Cover field in the Albums table.

3. Press F9 or select the Edit Data button on the SpeedBar to switch to Edit mode.

4. Choose Edit, then select Paste From.

5. Use the Select File dialog box to choose the source graphics file. You may click the Browse button to scan through other directories. For instance, your Windows directory contains some BMP files used as wallpaper for the Desktop. Use one of these files to experiment with entering graphics.

6. Click OK to confirm your choice, and the graphic is inserted in the selected field.

Using the Windows Clipboard

You also can use the Windows Clipboard to insert graphics in a Paradox table. The advantage of the Clipboard is that you do not have to worry about the original file format of the graphic.

Follow these steps to move a graphic by using the Clipboard:

1. Use your graphics program to create or retrieve the object.

2. Select the object by using the appropriate tool for your program. In Microsoft Paintbrush, for instance, use the Cut tool. Click a corner of the graphic and drag to the opposite corner, as shown in figure 3.10.

3 — ENTERING, EDITING, AND VIEWING DATA

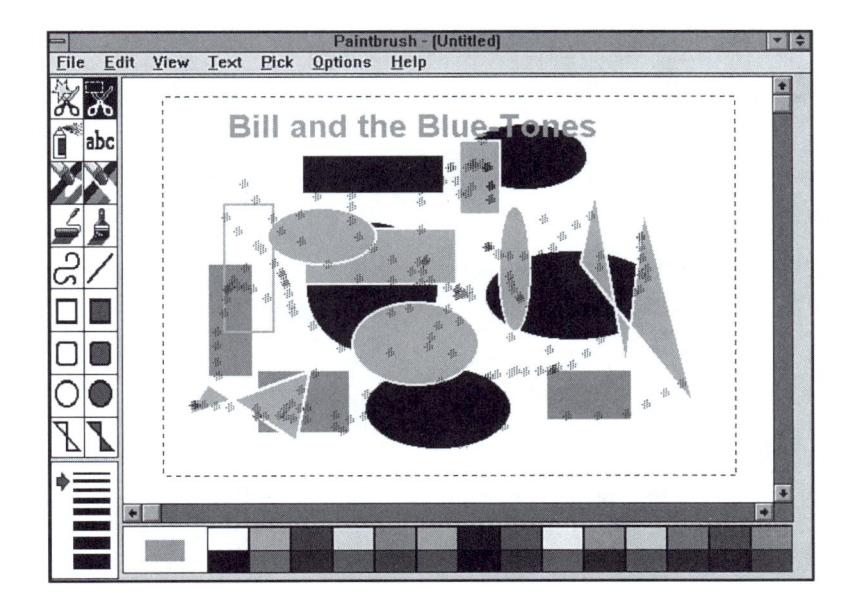

FIG. 3.10

A selected area in Microsoft Paintbrush.

3. Cut or copy the object to the Clipboard. In Microsoft Paintbrush, use the Edit menu to cut or copy.

4. Start Paradox for Windows and open the table in which you want to place the graphic.

5. Place the cursor in the field that will contain the graphic.

6. Press F9 or click the Edit Data button to switch to Edit mode.

7. Choose Edit and select Paste. The graphic appears in the field, as shown in figure 3.11.

You may not be able to see the entire graphic, especially in Table view. One way to see more of the graphic is to increase the width or the height of the column (see "Resizing a Column," later in this chapter). Another way to see more of the graphic is to zoom in on the field in Field view.

To switch to Field view, select the field with the mouse, Enter, or Tab. Then press F2, double-click, click the Field View button, or choose Table, Field View from the menu. The image is enlarged to fill the entire window, as shown in figure 3.12.

I — PARADOX FOR WINDOWS FUNDAMENTALS

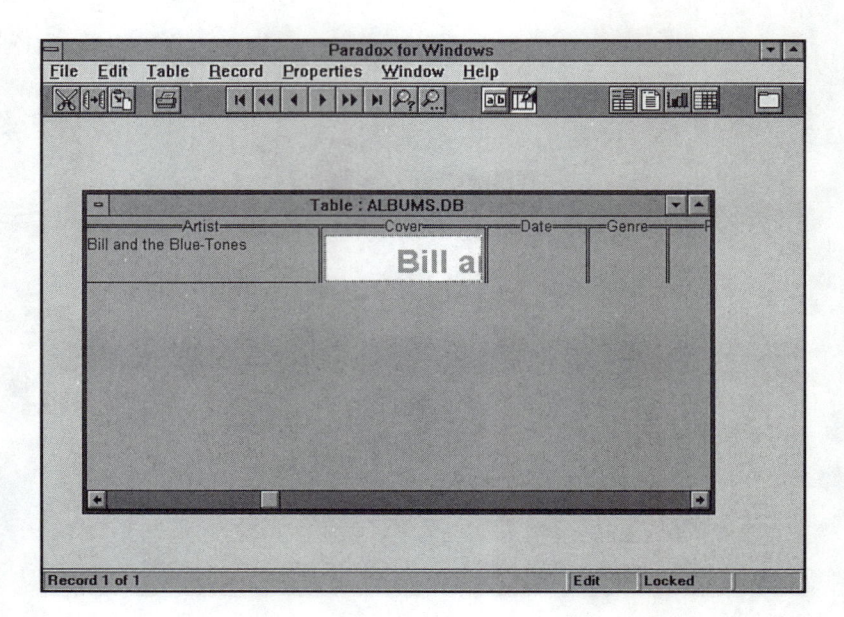

FIG. 3.11

A graphic pasted in a table.

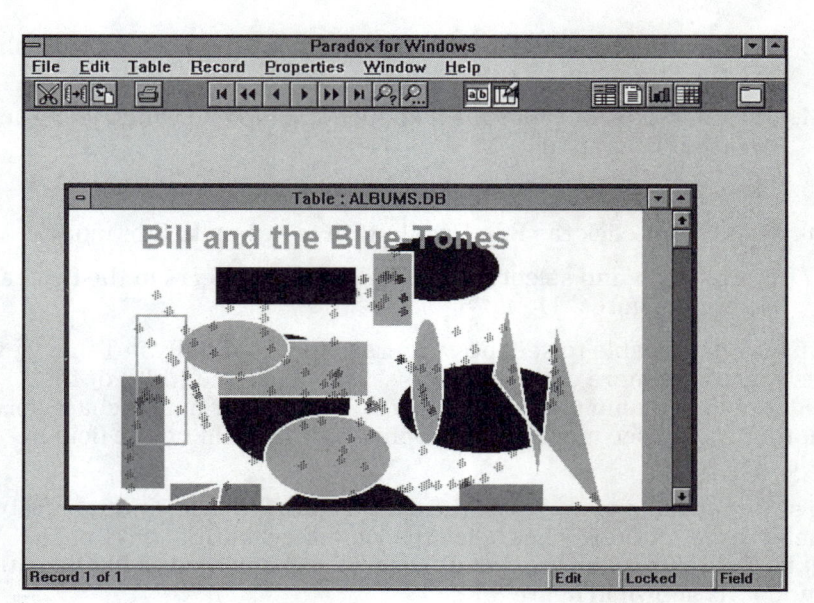

FIG. 3.12

A graphic in Field view.

You can return to Table view in several ways:

- Press F2
- Double-click

- Click the Control menu of the window and choose <u>C</u>lose
- Press Ctrl+F4 (the keyboard equivalent for close window)
- Click the Field View button in the SpeedBar

Changing Graphic Properties

Although graphic fields require special consideration, they are one of the most exciting reasons to use Windows and Paradox for Windows. You may want to customize the appearance of a graphic field. To access the field properties menu, select the field and right-click. You can change five properties of graphic fields, as shown in figure 3.13 and in the following list:

Field property	Function
Complete Display	Determines whether a graphic is displayed for all records or only the current record in Table view.
Magnification	Indicates the degree of magnification of a graphic image, from 25 percent through 400 percent. If you choose Best Fit, Paradox for Windows fits as much of the image as possible in the space allotted, even when the magnification is less than 25 percent or greater than 400 percent.
Alignment	Determines where the graphic is placed in the field. The graphic can align horizontally at the center, left, or right, or vertically at the center, top, or bottom.
Color	Uses the color palette to change the color of the field area behind the graphic. This property does not change the color of the graphic itself. All editing of the graphic image must be performed in the graphics software that produced the image.

NOTE Showing the graphic in Table view slows the screen display. To speed the display of the table, change the Render property from Always to Current. This displays the graphic only for the record you are currently viewing or editing.

I — PARADOX FOR WINDOWS FUNDAMENTALS

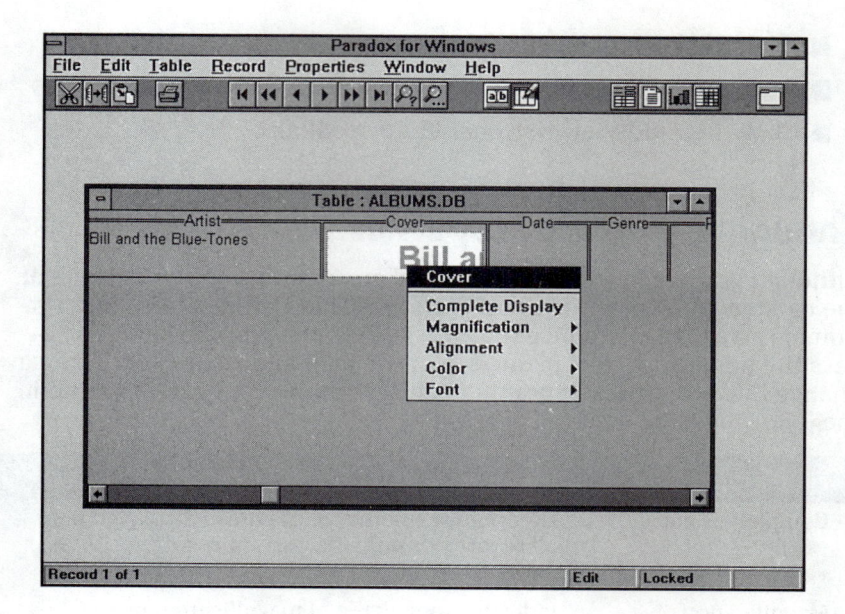

FIG. 3.13

Graphic field properties.

> **CAUTION:** Graphic fields use a great deal of disk space. Even a modest graphic file can be 100,000 bytes, and this adds up quickly as more records are entered.

Entering Data in OLE Fields

You can link a Paradox table to data stored in another Windows application (such as a spreadsheet) with OLE, or object linking and embedding. Using OLE is discussed in Chapter 7, "Using Advanced Form Techniques" and Chapter 11, "Exchanging Data with Other Applications."

Using Ditto To Repeat Entries

Another time saver is the Ditto keystroke command, Ctrl+D. If you place the cursor in a blank field and press Ctrl+D, Paradox for Windows fills in the value used in the same field in the preceding record. This feature works only for the second record and subsequent records in the table.

In addition to using Ditto for repeating the same information from record to record, you can use the Ditto feature to save time when entries are similar but not identical, especially for long fields. Press Ctrl+D to fill in the previous value, then edit the field.

Editing Data in Edit Mode

This section discusses some special features available in Edit mode. Many of these, such as cut and paste, may be familiar as standard Windows features. Others, such as Ditto, may be new to you.

Cutting, Copying, and Pasting Values

Sometimes, you may need repetitive values for a number of records or you may accidently transpose fields in a table. In these situations, Paradox's cut-and-paste capability can be useful. To perform a cut-and-paste, follow these steps:

1. Press F9 or click the Edit Data button to enter Edit mode.
2. Click the field to be cut or copied. This moves the cursor to the field. For this example, use the Title field in the Albums table.
3. Click again to enter Field view. The current status is displayed in the message area at the bottom of the window.
4. Click the starting location for the cut, and drag to the ending location. This marks the section of the field to be moved. Select the last word of the album title in this manner, as shown in figure 3.14.
5. Choose the Edit menu, and then choose Cut or press Shift+Del. If you do not want to remove the contents of the field, choose Copy instead of Cut.
6. Move the mouse pointer to the destination field in the next record and click. Then choose Edit, Paste (or press Shift+Ins). The last word of the album title is inserted in the field.

> **TIP**
> If you make a mistake performing a cut-and-paste operation, choose Edit and select Undo (or press Alt+Backspace).

FIG. 3.14

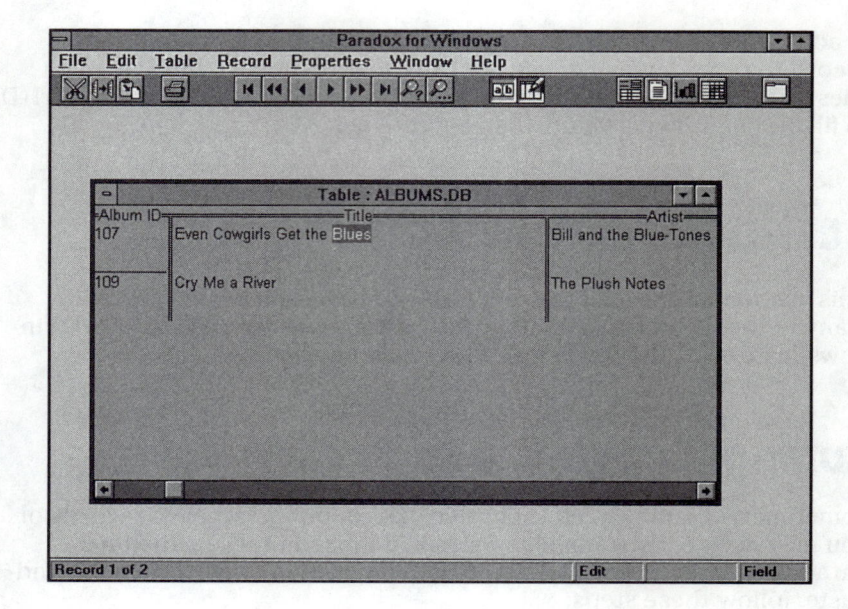

Selecting the last word of the Album title for cut and paste.

Using Undo

Even the most careful data-entry operators make mistakes. Paradox for Windows includes special features to limit the damage of heavy-handed typing. The quickest way to correct mistakes is to undo them before leaving the field. To undo a mistake, choose the Edit menu and select Undo. (Alt+Backspace is the keyboard shortcut.)

To try the Undo feature, enter a record for an album, with the title Bad. Next, edit the title, changing it from Bad to Worse. Now press Alt+Backspace to undo your change. The field returns to its original value. You also can undo a field edit by pressing Esc before you leave the field.

> **CAUTION:** The Undo feature works only while you are still in the field you changed. When you move to the next field or record, any changes are saved. Paradox Undo "remembers" only the previous field value until you leave the field. If you change a record twice, you can undo your second change but not your first change.

3 — ENTERING, EDITING, AND VIEWING DATA

Deleting Records

To delete a record, begin in Edit mode (press F9 to switch to Edit mode if necessary). Press Ctrl+Del to delete a record, or choose Record, Delete. The record is deleted, the table is adjusted to fill in the gap between the records, and the records are renumbered.

> **CAUTION:** Paradox for Windows does not ask for confirmation when records are deleted, and you cannot resurrect a record after it has been deleted. Use care when deleting records!

In Paradox and dBASE tables, records are tagged for deletion, but not immediately deleted from the table. To physically delete records, you must restructure the table by choosing the Pack Table option in the Restructure Paradox for Windows Table dialog box.

You can view deleted records in dBASE tables, although by default Paradox for Windows hides them from view. To view deleted records, choose Table, Show Deleted. Deleted records are indicated by a dark box on the left side of the deleted record. This option is not available for Paradox tables.

> **NOTE** You cannot delete more than one record at a time in record entry. If you highlight multiple records and press Ctrl-Del, nothing happens. You must delete records individually or create a query to delete multiple records.

For Related Information

◄◄ "Restructuring a Table," p. 111.

Using Search To Find Fields, Records, and Values

To edit a specific record or group of records, you could start at the top of the table and scroll through all the records one screen at a time until

I — PARADOX FOR WINDOWS FUNDAMENTALS

you find the ones you need. For a large table, however, this is not a practical approach.

Fortunately, Paradox for Windows provides several tools to help you locate a record quickly. You can move to a record by its record number (its sequence in a table) or by a field value. You may have an Employee file, for example, that contains records for everyone who works at your company. To find a particular employee's record, you may search by social security number or last name.

Paradox for Windows always starts its search at the beginning of the table, so you do not have to start the search from a particular cursor position. For the same reason, you cannot search backward, as you might find in a word processor.

You use the Locate menu to search in a table. The Locate options are accessed from the Record menu, as shown in figure 3.15. You can use keyboard shortcuts for Locate Value (Ctrl+Z) and Locate and Replace (Shift+Ctrl+Z).

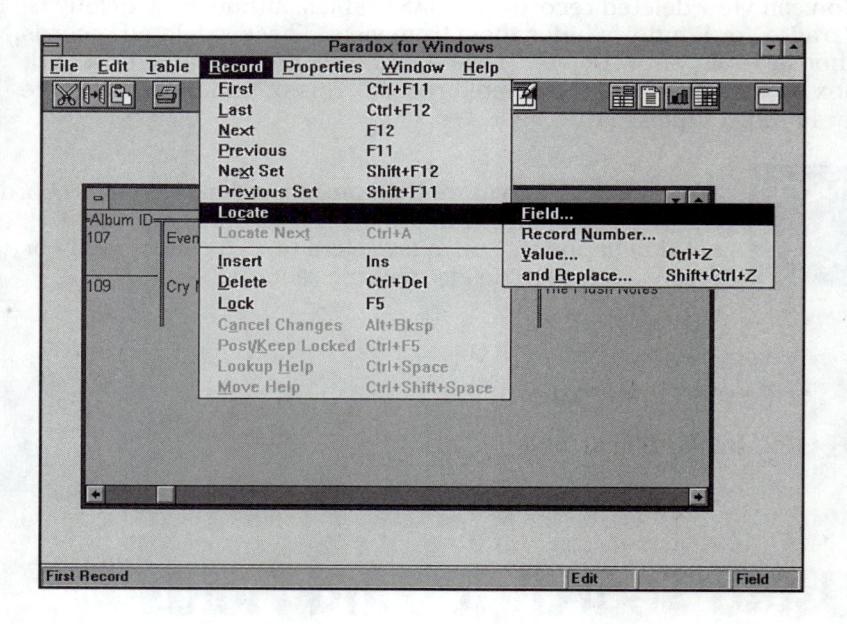

FIG. 3.15

The Record menu and the Locate submenu.

Searching for a Field

If you tire of moving the cursor from field to field one at a time, you can use a shortcut to jump directly to a field. First, choose Record, Locate, Field from the menu. The Locate Field dialog box appears (see fig. 3.16).

3 — ENTERING, EDITING, AND VIEWING DATA

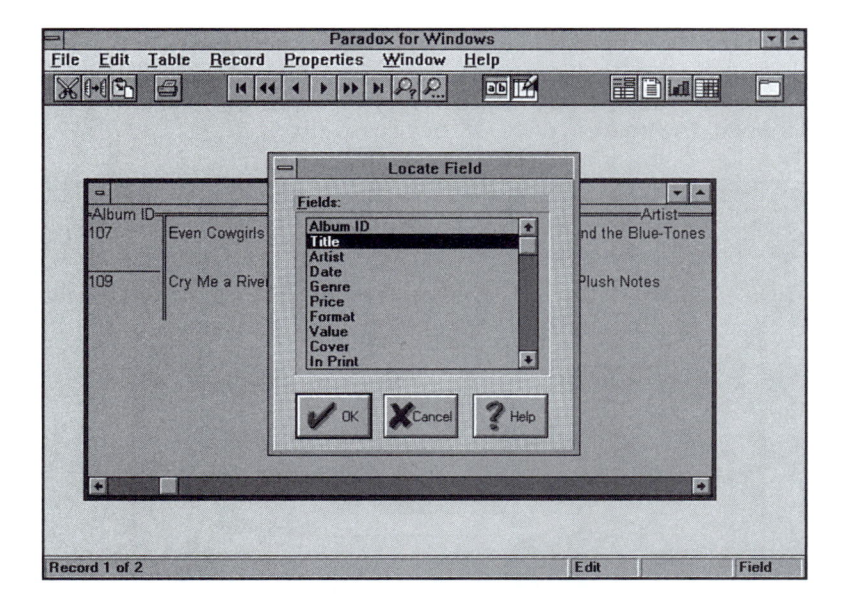

FIG. 3.16
The Locate Field dialog box.

Next, select the desired field from the list. Choose the Review field in the Albums table. Use the scroll bar to display additional fields if necessary. After you click Review and then click OK, the table returns to the screen and the cursor is in the Review field.

Searching for a field is most useful in tables with many fields. For short tables, you can just as easily move with the mouse or the standard cursor-movement keys.

You can combine a search for a field with a search for a value. First, search for the field; when you reach the correct field, you can search for a value as described in the next section.

Searching for a Value

The most effective way to search for a record is by *value*—what you entered into the field. To start a search for a value, click the Locate Field Value button (the magnifying glass icon with the question mark), or choose Locate from the Record menu, or press Ctrl+Z. When you place the mouse pointer on the button, the message line shows Locate Field Value. (In Paradox 3.5, this feature is known as Zoom.)

I — PARADOX FOR WINDOWS FUNDAMENTALS

A dialog box appears that lists all the fields in the table (see fig. 3.17). If you do not see the field you need, use the scroll bar to reveal additional fields. Click the field to search, then fill in the value you are searching for. To begin the search, click OK or press Enter.

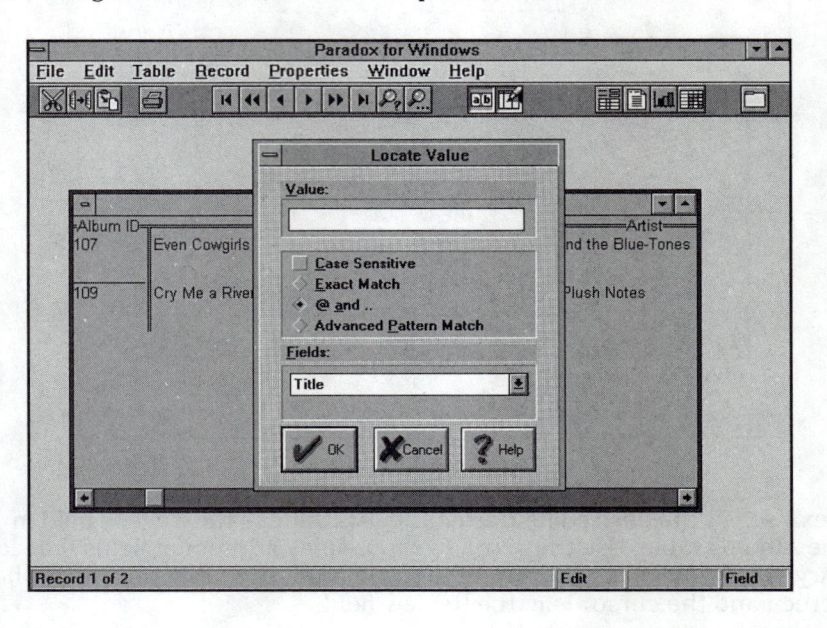

FIG. 3.17

The Locate Value dialog box.

If a matching record is found, the record is highlighted, and you can edit it. If a record is found but it is not the one you are looking for, you can continue the search by pulling down the Record menu and selecting Locate Next, pressing Ctrl+A, or clicking the Locate Next button (the magnifying glass with three dots) in the SpeedBar. Repeat this step as many times as necessary.

For instance, search the Albums table for all Rock albums by searching for Rock in the Genre field. Continue the search until you reach the end of the table. If Paradox for Windows cannot find a matching record, a message appears in the message area to tell you that the value was not found.

Paradox for Windows retains the search value used last, in case you want to perform the search again. You can erase or overwrite the search value for your next search. To perform the search again, click the Search Next button.

The search feature finds a match whenever your search string appears in a field. If you check the Advanced Pattern Match, you do not have to match the entire field. This means that a search in the last name field for Henry would find not only Henry, but also O'Henry and McHenry.

3 — ENTERING, EDITING, AND VIEWING DATA

If you choose the Exact Match box, Paradox for Windows searches for a value that exactly matches every character of your search expression.

You can choose to make your search case-sensitive or not by checking the Case Sensitive box. This means that uppercase and lowercase letters are treated differently. For instance, if you search for san francisco, you will not find San Francisco in the database.

> **NOTE** In a table, Paradox enables you to search for only one field at a time. To perform more complex searches, create a query. See Chapter 4, "Getting Started with Query By Example," for more information.

If you check the @ and .. box, you also can use wild cards, which are special characters that stand for missing characters, when you search by value. Paradox for Windows uses @ as the wild card for a single character. A search for J@n finds Jan and Jon, for instance.

The other Paradox wild card is .. which can stand for one or more missing characters. When you use the .. wild card, you do not have to type the entire field that you want to match. The search for J.. would yield Jane Eyre and Jonathan Swift, for example.

> **TIP** If you use wild cards in a search value, you can enter fewer characters, and you do not have to worry about the spelling of the portion of the value that the wild cards replace.

Searching for a Record Number

Paradox for Windows creates record numbers in every table. They are normally displayed in the leftmost column.

To search for a record number, click the Record menu, choose Locate, then specify Record Number. Paradox does not provide a keyboard shortcut to search by record number. The Locate Record Number dialog box appears, indicating the number of records in the table and asking you for the record number you are searching for (see fig. 3.18). Enter the record number and click OK to start the search. When the search is complete, the record whose number you specified and the neighboring records in the table are displayed.

I — PARADOX FOR WINDOWS FUNDAMENTALS

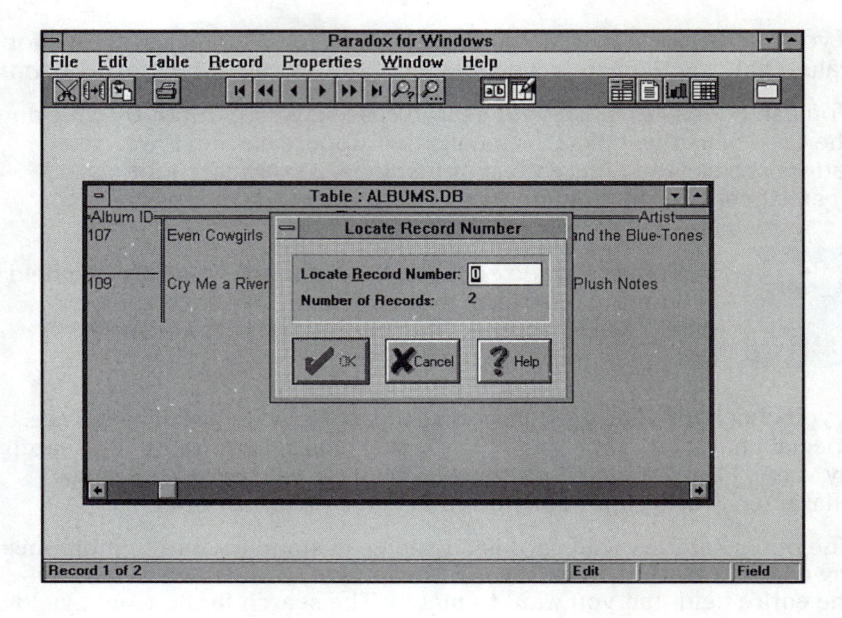

FIG. 3.18

The Locate Record Number dialog box.

Searching for a record number is handy when you remember the number, but it is a poor tool to rely on. In a keyed table, record numbers are constantly changing as records are added and deleted. Moreover, the record number is arbitrary and meaningless. You will get better results if you search for records by a value rather than by a record number.

Searching by record number is most useful when you are not looking for a particular record, but want to jump ahead in the table a number of screens. You could specify record 500, for example, to view the records stored 500 rows from the start of the table.

Searching and Replacing Values

Sometimes, you want to edit a large number of records at once. Suppose that you have a list of contacts in Moscow, and you want to change the country field from Soviet Union to Russia. Search-and-replace is just the tool you need.

Search-and-replace works like similar commands in word processing programs: it finds all occurrences of one value and replaces them with another value. To search and replace, make sure that you are in Edit mode, and then follow these steps:

1. Choose Locate from the Record menu, then select And Replace. As an alternative, you can press Ctrl+Shift+Z to skip directly to search-and-replace.

3 — ENTERING, EDITING, AND VIEWING DATA   **151**

2. The Locate And Replace dialog box appears (see fig. 3.19). This dialog box is similar to the Search dialog box. As in a search, choose the field and enter the target value. Next, fill in the value you want to use to replace the old value.

3. Suppose that you want to change all the albums you have entered as Blues to R&B. Enter **Blues** as the target value and **R&B** as the new value. To begin the operation, click OK.

4. If a record is found that matches your search, the cursor is positioned on that row and a dialog box appears to confirm that you want to make the change. Click Yes to make the change, No to skip the present record but continue the search, or Cancel to stop the operation. The search continues until all matches have been found or you cancel the operation.

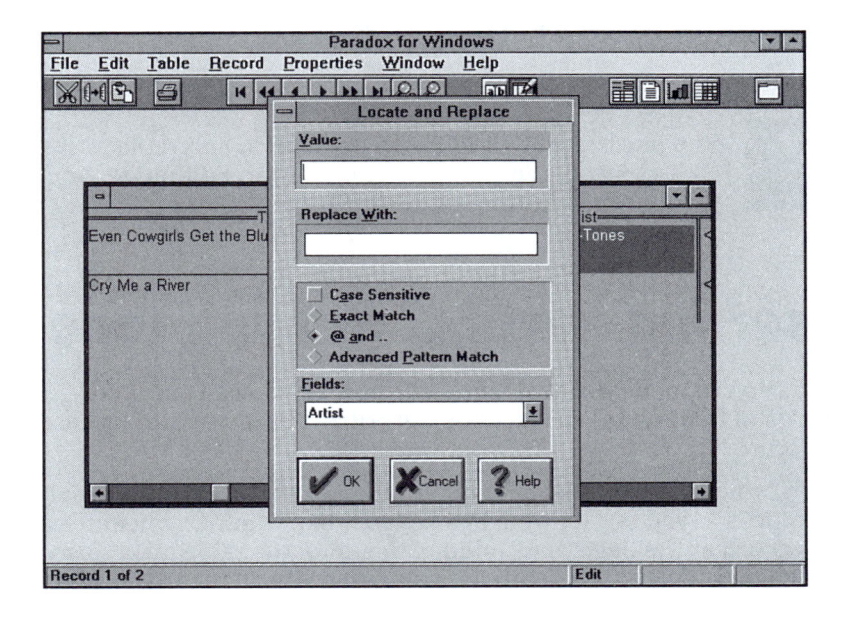

FIG. 3.19

The Locate and Replace dialog box.

TIP

The Confirm Replace dialog box can sometimes pop up in the wrong place, obscuring the change you are about to confirm. If this occurs, move the box to a better location on-screen by dragging the title bar.

Although search-and-replace can save you time, use it carefully to avoid unpleasant results. Search-and-replace sometimes replaces things you did not intend to change, because it finds partial matches based on your search criteria. For example, a search for book may also find cookbook and bookmaker and any other word that contains book.

Moreover, the replacement string you specify replaces the entire contents of the field, not just the string you are searching for. This means that if you replace book with novel, you will end up with three entries for novel where you once had book, bookmaker, and cookbook. Worst of all, the Undo feature does not work for search-and-replace, so your changes cannot be reversed.

TIP If you have a complex search-and-replace job, use a query rather than search-and-replace. A query offers more sophisticated search criteria and, more importantly, you can check the results of the changes before they are saved permanently. Queries do not ask for confirmation for each record changed, so they can be much quicker than locate-and-replace when you change many records. See Chapter 8, "Using Advanced Query By Example," for details.

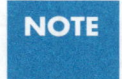

NOTE You must be in Edit mode to use search-and-replace. If you are in View mode, press F9 to change to Edit mode, or click the Edit Data button on the SpeedBar.

Inserting Records in Edit Mode

In addition to modifying existing records, you also can enter new records in Edit mode. This section describes the procedure for inserting records into a table.

How a table behaves when you enter new records depends on whether the table is keyed or unkeyed. In a keyed table, whether you enter a new record at the beginning, middle, or end of the table makes no difference because Paradox automatically reorders all records based on the key value. In an unkeyed table, you must insert a blank row to add a new record in a particular location.

The procedure for inserting a new record is the same for keyed and unkeyed tables, except in an unkeyed table you must move the cursor to the line below the desired location for the new record before you enter the data.

To insert a new record in a keyed or an unkeyed table, press the Ins key or choose Record, Insert from the menu. The program opens a blank row so that you can enter a new record.

Open the Albums table and enter a new record. After you finish, continue editing or press Ins again to enter more records. The location of the displayed record after it has been saved depends on whether the table is keyed or unkeyed. In the Albums table, the records are sorted by the primary key—Album ID. No matter where you insert the blank line and type the record, the table is displayed in primary key order. In an unkeyed table, the record remains where you inserted it.

Inserting records in an unkeyed table should be an infrequent event. Unkeyed tables are usually a symptom of poor database design, as discussed in Chapter 2. Keyed tables help prevent duplicate entries and are easier to browse through because the records are sorted in order by the key field value.

Entering and Editing Data with Multiuser Settings

Paradox can be used for single user, stand-alone systems, or on a network. To share data with other users, Paradox offers multiuser settings.

The principles for entering and editing records are the same on a stand-alone PC and on a network. A network, however, has additional safeguards to avoid conflicts when two or more people try to edit the same record.

A *local area network* (LAN) allows a number of PCs to share the same programs, data, and peripherals (such as modems and printers). In a networked database application, the data files are stored on the *file server*, a designated PC that contains shared files and sends them to each workstation when requested. Think of the file server as a hard disk drive shared by several users. When you are working at your computer and want to edit a file on the server, the file server transfers the file to your computer over the cables that connect the PCs on the network.

If two people had free access to the same data at the same time, disastrous data-entry errors could occur. Suppose that you attempted to correct the customer's balance at the same time another user was recording the payment. Whose changes would take precedence? How would you know that the balance had changed since you read the record? A network database must control multiuser access to tables to avoid this kind of difficulty.

Paradox for Windows provides features that handle multiuser access to network data files, so you don't have to worry about these kinds of questions. The primary tool for network security is *locking*. Locking can occur at several levels: the file level (a table), the page level (a group of records), or the record level (individual records). Locking means that one person takes temporary possession of a record (or page or file) to perform an action (updating, for example). When another user tries to access the record, the system returns a message that the file is locked and may prevent the second user from changing the record until the first person is finished.

Locking Options

Locking can be used to restrict all access or only certain kinds of access. If a lock is *read-only*, for instance, a second user can view the record but cannot change it.

Because the file server must send data files to each PC on a network, a time lag can occur between the time when one person views a file and another person retrieves it. One user could change a record while another user is viewing it on a different workstation. This time lag creates a need for *refreshing*. Refreshing is a process that redraws the table by looking at the file on the server again, including any changes that have been introduced by other users. Refreshing can be automatic or requested by a user. The problem with automatic refresh is that it takes time and network communications resources to constantly check for updates of each record.

Table 3.8 shows network locking options that users can access from the File, Multiuser menu from the Paradox Desktop.

Table 3.8. Network Locking Options

Option	Meaning
Display Locks	Displays the Table Locks dialog box so that you can set locking options for a table
Set Locks	Enables you to set and remove user locks
Set Retry	Makes another attempt to perform the update, in case a locking conflict prevents you from updating a record
Who	Lists current network users
User Name	Changes your username

3 — ENTERING, EDITING, AND VIEWING DATA

If you choose the Display Locks option, the Table Locks dialog box appears (see fig. 3.20). This dialog box enables you to set the locks for a table at one of four levels. No Lock removes your locks from the table. Read Lock prevents users from editing the table. Write Lock prevents others from reading or writing records in the table. Exclusive Lock is the most restrictive, combining read and write locks on the table.

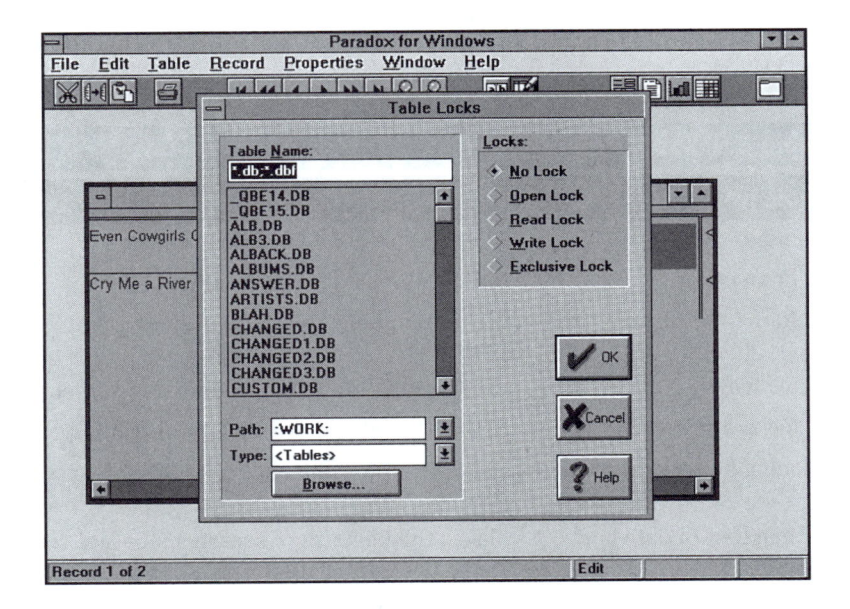

FIG. 3.20
The Table Locks dialog box.

Data-Entry Locks

You can lock the record you are currently editing. To lock a record, you must be in Edit mode. Choose Record, then select Lock or press F5. The message area indicates that the record is locked.

To unlock a record, choose Record, then select Unlock or press F5. Even if you do not explicitly unlock a record, it is unlocked after you finish editing and move to another record.

To keep a record locked for your entire editing session, choose Record, Post/Keep Locked or press Ctrl-F5.

If you are working on a stand-alone PC, record locking will not affect your tables.

Changing a Table's On-Screen Appearance

Paradox for Windows gives you many options for changing the way a table looks. These options enable you to create an attractive, customized table appearance. You can set the table properties listed in table 3.9.

Table 3.9. Table Properties

Table property	Purpose
Column width	Makes more columns visible on-screen
Column order	Shifts columns for easier editing
Field display format	Makes numbers and dates easier to interpret
Table length	Controls the number of records on-screen
Color and style of grid lines	Makes the table more visually appealing
Spacing between records	Provides more white space for easier reading
Screen font of data and column headers	Makes the best use of screen space and keeps data legible
Colors of foreground and background	Shows contrasting sections of the table

You can save a table's modified properties as defaults, and they will always be in effect when you view or edit records in that table. To save table properties, choose Properties and select Save Properties. If you change some properties of a table and want to revert to the previously saved properties, choose Properties, Restore Properties.

You can control some of these properties by manipulating screen objects with the mouse. For example, you can directly move or resize columns with the mouse. Other properties are changed through the properties menu of individual objects. To change the font or color of a field, you must right-click for the properties menu and make your selections.

> **TIP**
>
> To move a column using the mouse, drag the column header (the name of the column listed at the top of the table) to the new location. When you release the mouse button, the column is relocated.
>
> You can move columns also by using Ctrl+R, which rotates the column you select to the far right end of the table and advances all the other columns. You can repeat this action as many times as necessary to achieve the column order you want.

Resizing a Column

You can sometimes get a better view of the data by changing the width of the columns. This is especially true for short fields with long names, which Paradox for Windows automatically places in columns that accommodate the field names.

To change the width of a column, do the following:

1. Move the mouse pointer to the top of the right vertical border that separates the column you want to change from the next. The mouse pointer changes to a two-headed arrow.

2. Click and drag the border to the left or right to increase or decrease the width of the column.

3. Release the mouse button, and your change takes effect.

Making the columns narrower enables you to see more fields at one time. For example, the Paradox for Windows default setting for the first column, which shows the record number, is much too wide, unless you have hundreds of thousands of records (see fig. 3.21). By shortening the column to show only four or five digits, you can bring additional fields into view, as shown in figure 3.22.

You may want to shorten other columns. Suppose that you design a table with long fields for the first name and the last name to accommodate the longest possible entries. Most names, however, are shorter than the maximum length, so you may want to resize the column to the width of the average entry.

FIG. 3.21

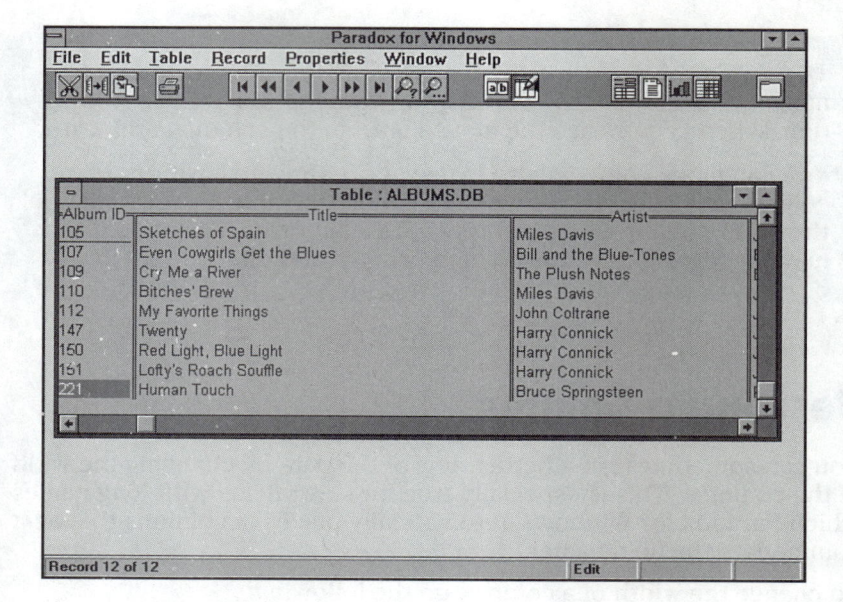

Records with a wide column width for the record number.

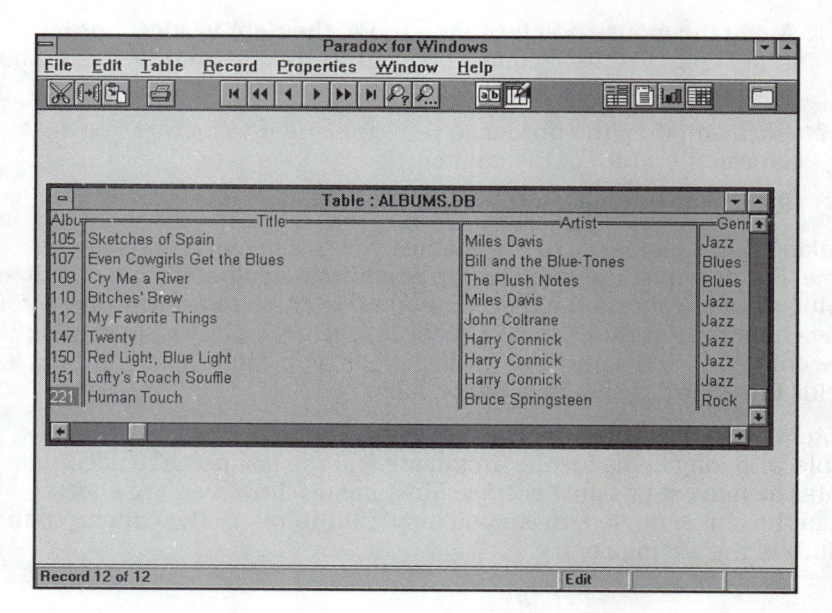

FIG. 3.22

Records with a narrowed column width for the record number.

> **TIP**
>
> Paradox makes the column width at least as wide as the field name, even if the field itself is short, as in a date field. If you work extensively in tables rather than forms, you may want to use a shorter (but still meaningful) field name so that the name won't be truncated when you narrow the column. For instance, you might want to call a field `InvDate` instead of `Date of Invoice`. The shorter field name more closely matches the length of the date field.

> **NOTE** If you make a column width narrower than the contents of the field, part of the field may not be visible. For alphanumeric and date fields, the field is simply cut off, even if doing so displays only part of a character. If a column for a number field is shorter than the value, the field is displayed as a series of asterisks (*).

Changing the Row Height

You also can adjust the space between rows to make the text easier to read. Resizing row height is particularly helpful when you need to view graphics in a table, because graphics are normally more than one line high.

To adjust the row height or the space between rows, follow these steps:

1. Place the mouse pointer on the line between the first and second rows in the record number column. The mouse pointer changes to an up/down arrow and the message area shows that you are resizing the row height.
2. Click the mouse, and drag the row to the desired height.
3. Release the mouse button, and your change takes effect.

Figure 3.23 shows the same table as figure 3.21, but with a larger row height.

Viewing Table Properties

Table properties control other display characteristics, including color, justification, font, and data formats. Tables consist of several smaller objects, such as column headers, fields, and the table grid. To view table properties, right-click the object you want to change.

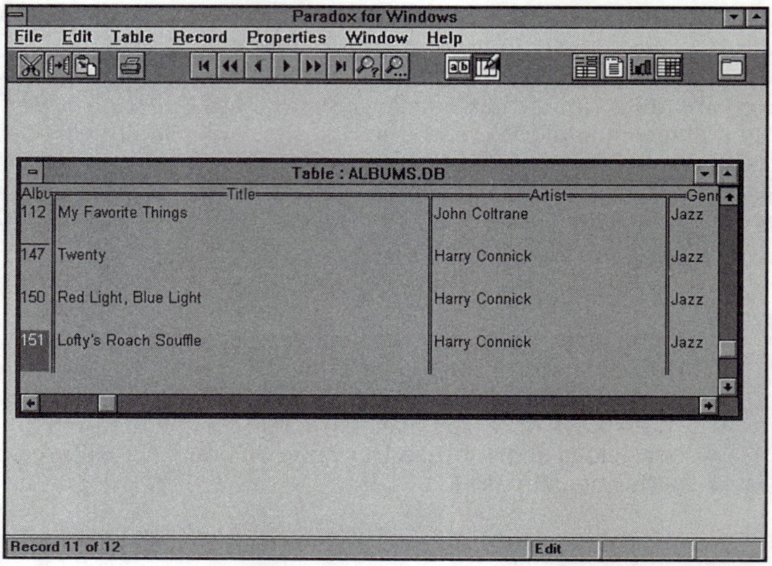

I — PARADOX FOR WINDOWS FUNDAMENTALS

FIG. 3.23

Records with a larger row height.

Another way you can inspect a table's properties is by using the keyboard, as follows:

Ctrl-M	Current data column
Ctrl-G	Grid properties
Ctrl-H	Current column header

The properties menu for each of these table areas contains controls for justification, color, and font.

Justification refers to the alignment of text in an area. Text can be left-aligned, centered, or right-aligned within a column. Vertical justification can be top, center, or bottom within a row.

To choose a *color* for a screen area, click the desired color on the Paradox for Windows palette (see fig. 3.24). You also can create custom colors.

The *font* is the character set used for screen text. Font consists of four elements: typeface, style, size, and color. You choose font characteristics from a special dialog box, the font palette (see fig. 3.25).

Click the circle at the top of the font palette to change to the floating font palette (see fig. 3.26). The floating palette enables you to change the typeface, size, and style from a single menu. The palette remains on-screen until you have finished your selections.

3 — ENTERING, EDITING, AND VIEWING DATA 161

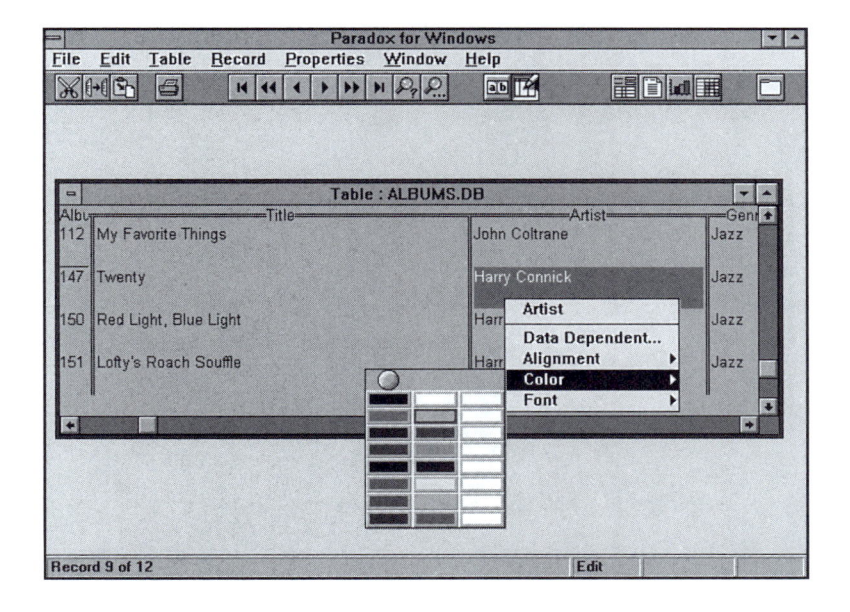

FIG. 3.24
The color palette.

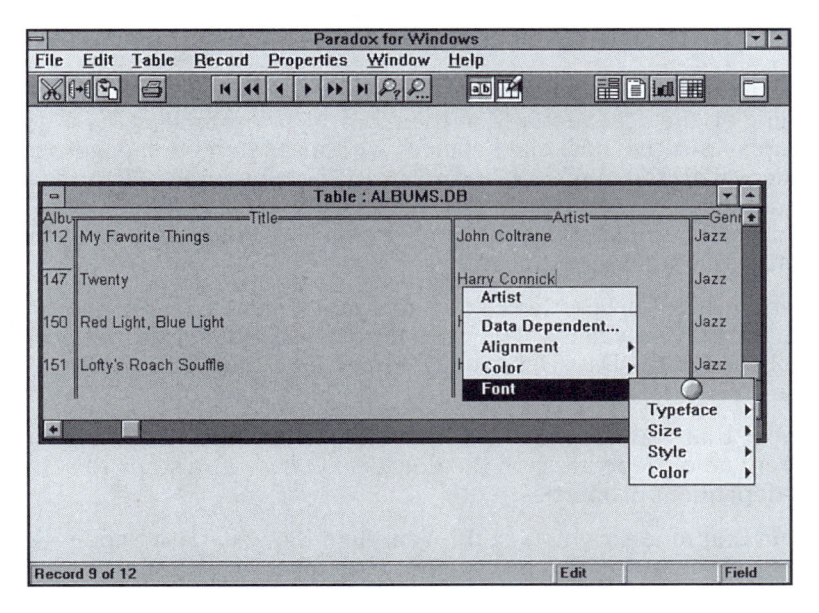

FIG. 3.25
The font palette.

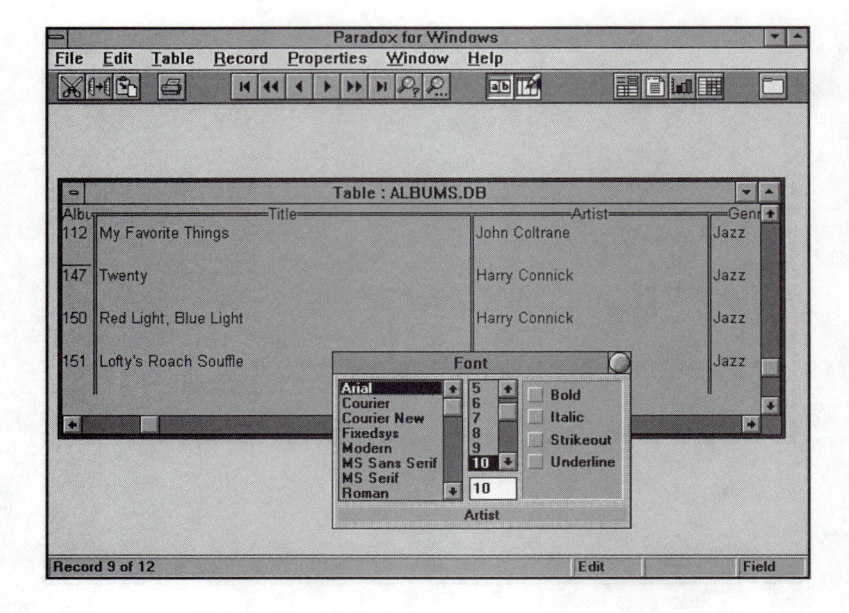

FIG. 3.26

The floating font palette.

Data-Dependent Properties

You can make the appearance of some types of data fields change, depending on the value entered in the record. For example, you may want to display positive financial balances with black numbers, negative balances with red numbers, and zeros with blue numbers. For an inventory database, you may want low inventory levels highlighted with bright colors. Data-dependent properties are attention-grabbers and can make an otherwise dull table come alive.

Data-dependent properties can be applied to alphanumeric, numeric, date, and currency fields. The rules for data-dependent properties are established in the Data Dependent Properties dialog box, shown in figure 3.27.

Suppose that you want to show the Year field in the Albums table in a different color depending on the decade. Follow these steps to activate data-dependent properties:

1. In Edit mode, right-click the Year field. Choose Data Dependent from the properties menu. The Data Dependent Properties dialog box is displayed (refer to fig. 3.27).

2. To declare the range, click the New Range button. The first line in the Ranges box darkens, and several choices in the menu become active.

3 — ENTERING, EDITING, AND VIEWING DATA

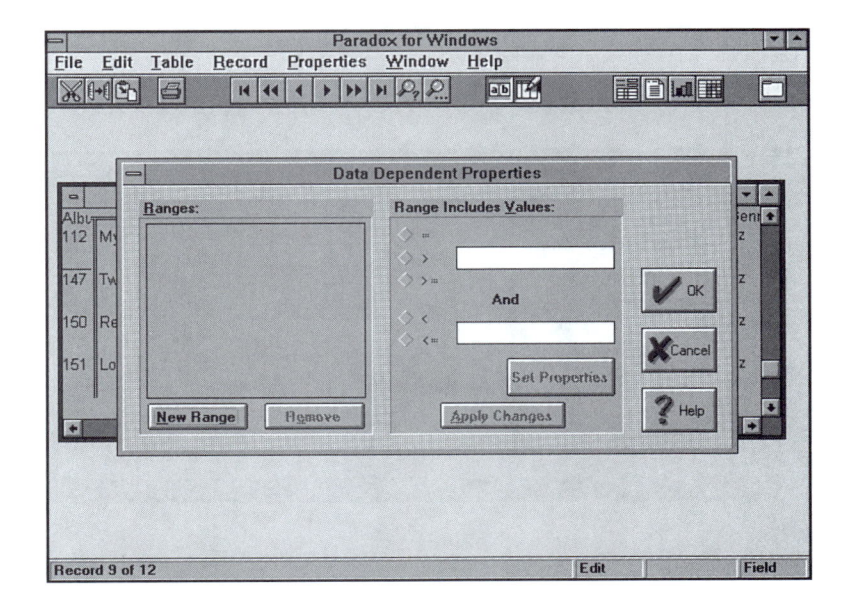

FIG. 3.27

The Data Dependent Properties dialog box.

3. Enter the low and high values for the first range by clicking the fields and typing in the numbers. Below the low and high values are choices for the comparison operator. Click the operator you want to use. For example, declare the first range to be between 50 and 59, inclusive, as shown in figure 3.28, using the >= and <= comparison operators.

4. Next, click the Set Properties button to modify the properties for this range. You can choose the text background color, style, and font (including text color). As you change the properties, the sample element to the left of the Set Properties button changes to show how a field in the range will look.

5. Click the Apply Changes button to accept the range you have defined.

6. Click the New Range button again to define the next range, and repeat steps 3–5 as many times as necessary to define the ranges for this field. For this example, define ranges for 60-69, 70-79, 80-89, and 90-99 to cover all the decades of your record collection. Choose contrasting colors or fonts for each range so that they will stand out from one another.

7. The Data Dependent Properties specification is now complete. Paradox automatically reorders your choices in order of the ranges, regardless of the order in which you define them. Click the OK button to save the Data Dependent properties.

I — PARADOX FOR WINDOWS FUNDAMENTALS

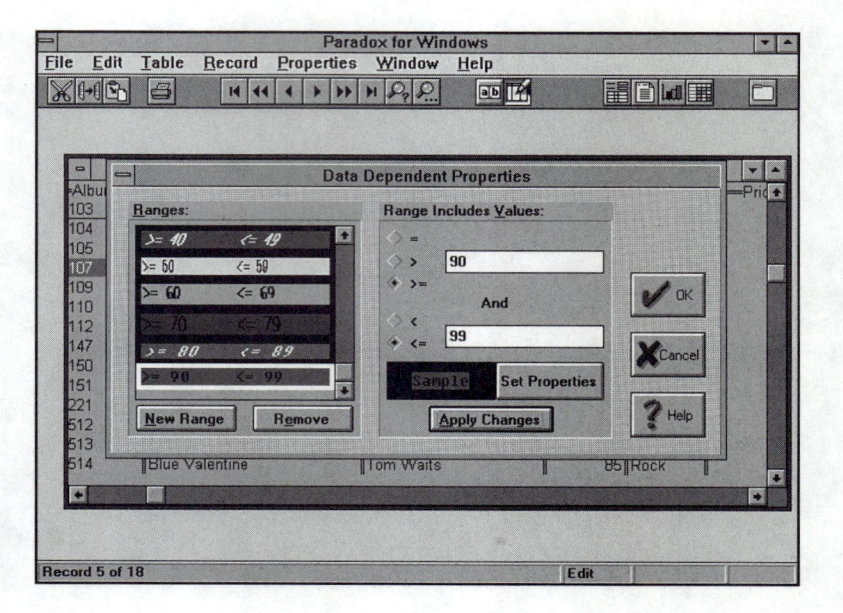

FIG. 3.28

Defining ranges for the Year field.

8. After you save your specifications, Paradox returns the table to the screen and changes the field display according to the data-dependent properties you have defined.

> **TIP** Be sure to use <= or >= in ranges. Otherwise, values that match your breakpoints are not affected by the range. For example, if you set one color for <100 and another for >100, an entry of 100 does not fall in either range and hence is not affected.

Data-dependent properties can be used with letters as well as numbers. For example, in an automobile sales database, you could use colors in the Color field so that the value Red is displayed in red letters and the value Blue is shown in blue letters. Sales staff could easily select a car's color by glancing at the data table. You can also use custom colors with data-dependent properties.

To achieve a more subtle effect with data-dependent properties, try using the same background color for each range but a different font color. You should also consider how the fields may appear on a monochrome monitor, as some color combinations are difficult to read without a color monitor.

Heading Properties

You can modify the way column headings are displayed in Table view by changing their properties. First, right-click the column name to reveal the Heading properties menu (see fig. 3.29). You can change three properties from this menu: the Alignment of the heading name (how it is centered above the column), the text Color (foreground and background), and the Font (typeface).

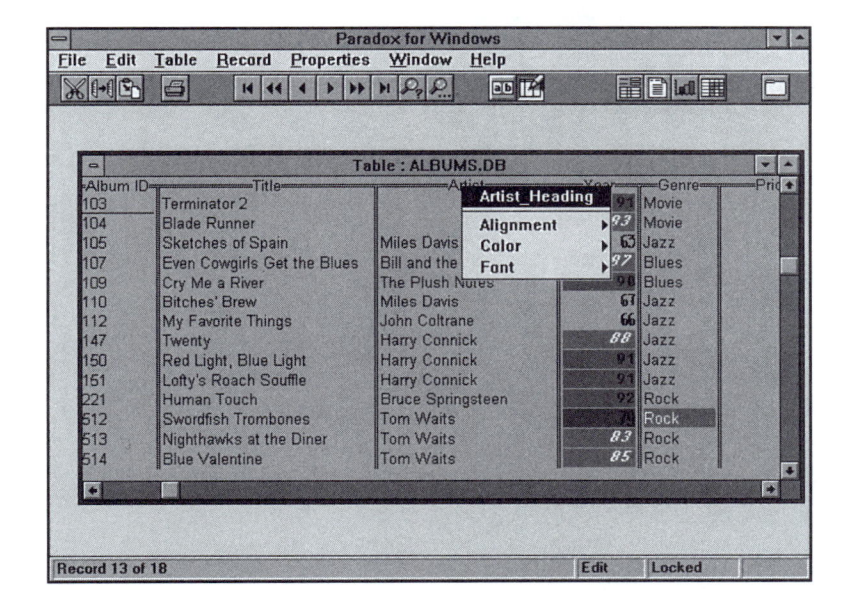

FIG. 3.29

The Heading properties menu.

Grid Properties

The *grid* consists of the lines that separate the rows and columns of a table. You can modify the color, line style, and current record marker of the grid.

The *current record marker* keeps track of the row and column where the cursor is positioned and is used to restore the correct cursor position when you move between tables (or other screen objects). To view the grid properties, position the mouse pointer on a grid line and right-click (see fig. 3.30).

I — PARADOX FOR WINDOWS FUNDAMENTALS

By default, Paradox includes Heading Lines and Column Lines in the grid. You also can choose Row Lines (between each record) by choosing Grid Lines, then Row Lines from the Grid properties menu. Remember that adding the Row Lines takes up extra space on-screen, so you will be able to see fewer records at a time.

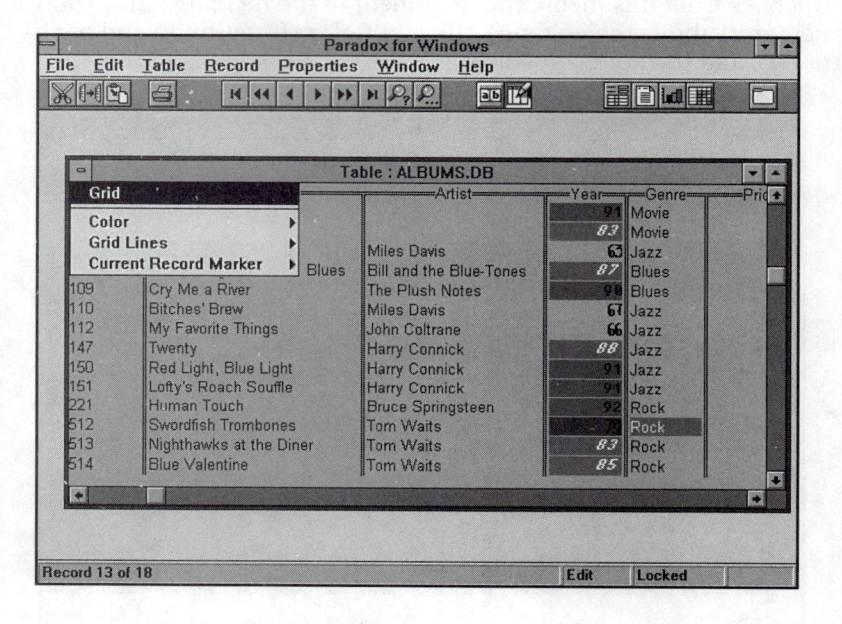

FIG. 3.30

Grid properties.

Data Properties

Columns have several properties you can customize. These data properties, such as color, font, justification, and display format are different for different field types. Text fields have the font property, for example, but graphic fields do not. To change data properties, place the mouse pointer on the data field and right-click. For a numeric field, the list of properties shown in figure 3.31 is displayed.

Saving Property Changes

Any changes you make to the properties of a table, such as formatting fields and changing colors, must be saved before you exit from the table. To save your changes for future use, do the following:

1. Choose the Properties menu.
2. Select View Properties, then Save.

    To restore the table to its default properties, select Restore from the Properties, View menu.

3 — ENTERING, EDITING, AND VIEWING DATA   167

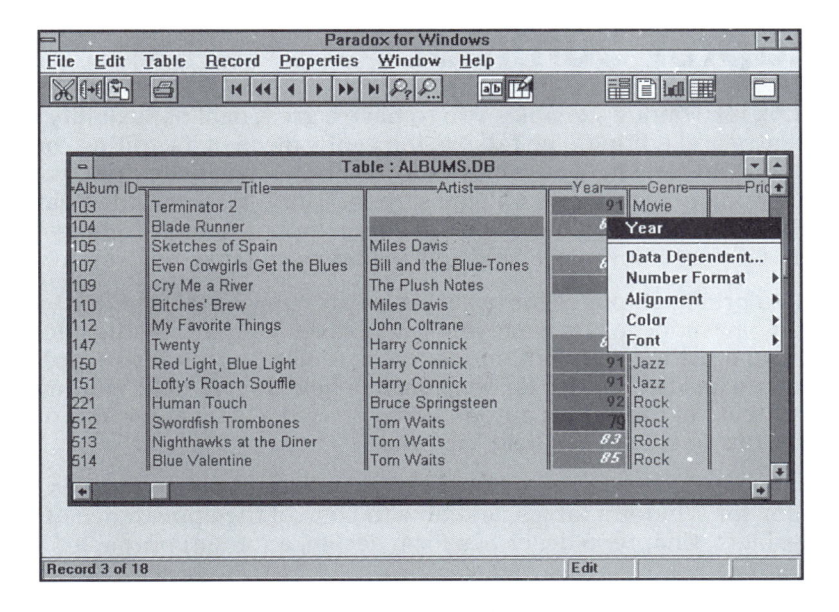

FIG. 3.31

Data properties for a numeric field.

When you exit a table after modifying its properties, you may see a dialog box asking whether you want to save the TV file associated with this table (see fig. 3.32). Choose Yes or press Enter to save your changes.

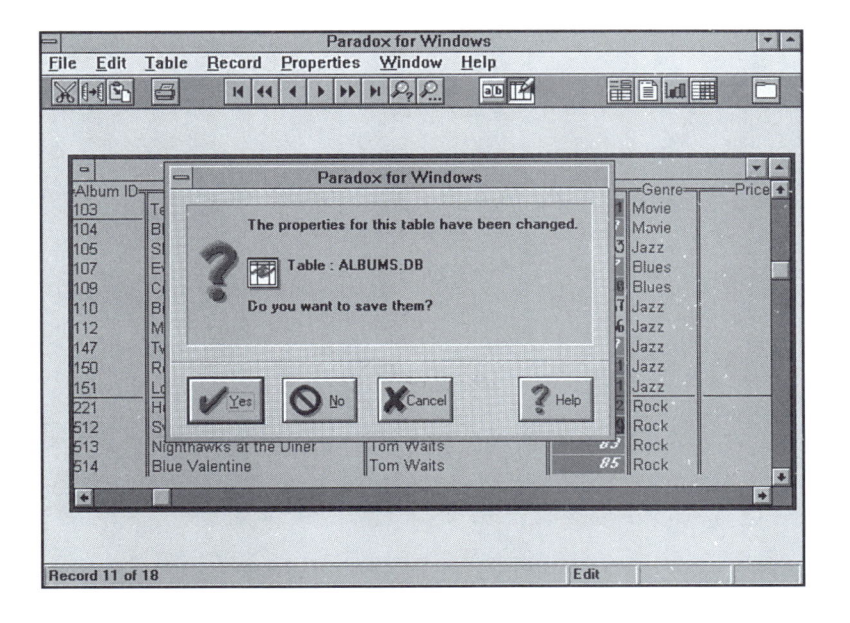

FIG. 3.32

Dialog box stating that the properties for this table have been changed.

Chapter Summary

Paradox for Windows enables you to have a great deal of flexibility in data entry and editing. The table is the centerpiece of its editing routine. You can view data as tables or forms. When you use tables, you can view many records on a single screen. Tables also provide built-in capabilities for moving quickly through the database or searching for records. Forms show more fields on a window, and can be customized.

The two principal modes for using tables are View mode and Edit mode. View mode, as its name implies, enables you to view the information. You must toggle to Edit mode to add, delete, or modify records. Edit mode has two modes for working in a field. In non-field View mode, the contents of the field is automatically erased as you enter new data. To edit text in a field, use field View mode.

This chapter has shown you how to enter, edit, and delete records in Paradox for Windows tables, and how to control the appearance of the table object. Chapter 5 describes form design, another approach to data entry.

CHAPTER 4

Getting Started with Query By Example

In Chapters 1, 2, and 3, you learned to navigate through Paradox and create database tables and records. Now you are ready to retrieve information from the database. In this chapter, you learn to extract data from Paradox using query by example (QBE).

For many users, learning a new computer language is an obstacle to making full use of a database. With QBE, you do not have to use a language at all. Instead, QBE offers a visual approach for retrieval, based on the familiar data table. In Paradox queries, you simply check the fields to be retrieved and offer an example to show your search criteria.

If Paradox for Windows is your first database, you probably will find its check mark and example techniques simple to understand and use. If you are familiar with more procedural, programming-oriented retrieval techniques, you may find QBE disarmingly simple at first. QBE is capable of performing sophisticated searches, however, supporting set operations well beyond the powers of dBASE and dBASE-compatible programs.

Queries can be used for more than just retrieving fields from database tables. A query can perform calculations, such as totals and averages, on your data. For example, you can calculate the sales tax your company owes by multiplying the amount of taxable sales by the tax rate, or calculate the average shipping cost for all orders to European destinations.

You also can insert, delete, or modify records based on a query. For example, a query can automatically add a late fee to past-due invoices or delete inactive customer records. Queries to modify data are discussed in Chapter 8, "Using Advanced Query By Example."

QBE supports single-table and multi-table queries. You can link up to 24 tables in a single query. This chapter deals with single-table queries. Multi-table queries are discussed in Chapter 8.

As you read this chapter, try the techniques it describes. To make your queries more interesting, you may want to add more test data to your tables.

The Benefits of Query By Example

Database management systems (DBMS) have always used programs to retrieve information. Traditionally, these programs have been written in programming languages that require months or years to master. These languages demand special syntax for queries and knowledge of dozens of commands. Forgetting to add a comma or a period can throw the entire query awry, resulting in an unsuccessful query and an error message.

One way to make information retrieval easier for users is to make programming languages resemble natural languages such as English. This approach is taken by Symantec's Q&A. Using a natural-language program, a user types a question such as "Which sales representatives are at least 10 percent above quota this month?" The program interprets this statement and formulates a query in a programming language. The problem with natural-language approaches is that English (and other human languages as well) can be ambiguous and misleading. Also, the same query can be phrased in many ways, so a natural-language program must have a large vocabulary to understand all variations.

Another approach to simplifying queries, pioneered by M. M. Zloof and others at IBM's Research Laboratory in Yorktown Heights, New York, is query by example. Instead of asking the user for sentences (in a computer language or a natural language), the QBE approach displays a form that resembles the data-entry table. The user simply fills in the parts of the data to be matched. The DBMS then interprets the QBE and generates a program to perform the retrieval. This is the approach adopted by the authors of Paradox for DOS, Richard Schwartz and Robert Shostak.

This chapter shows you how to build queries and manipulate Answer tables, which hold the results of a query. Using QBE, you can retrieve information from your Paradox for Windows database without writing a single line of program code.

Getting Started with Queries

To write a query, you first need a table that contains data. Figure 4.1 shows the Albums table with some sample records. See Chapter 2, "Designing Paradox Tables and Databases," for detailed instructions on creating this table. Copy some of the information listed here or enter data about your own music collection. If you enter your own data, be sure to change your search criteria in the examples offered here so that your queries will find records.

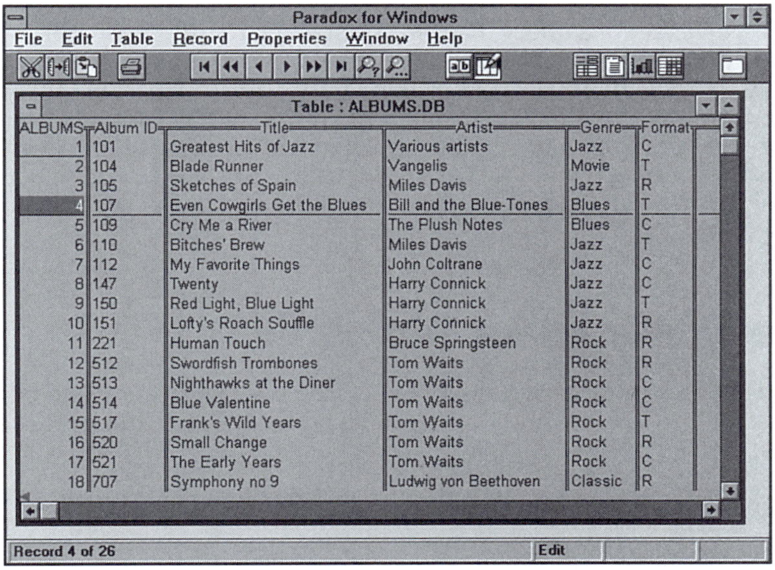

FIG. 4.1

Sample data in the Albums table.

Figure 4.2 is an example of a simple query. The Title and Artist fields are selected for all albums with a Genre of Jazz. The check marks in the Title and Artist fields indicate the fields to be retrieved.

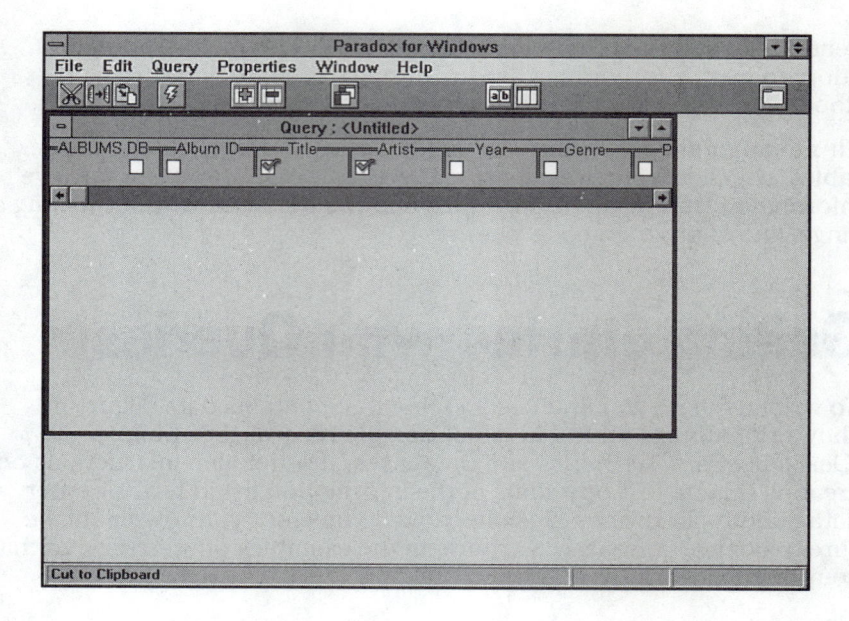

FIG. 4.2

A query to retrieve title and artist for all jazz albums.

When you execute a query, Paradox copies the records that match your criteria into a temporary table called Answer. The Answer table for the query in figure 4.2 is shown in figure 4.3. Note that the Answer table contains only the fields you checked when formulating the query. The records in the Answer table are listed in ascending alphabetical order by the selected fields (the album title in this case). At the bottom of the window, the message area displays the number of records in the Answer table and the cursor's position in the table.

The Query Editor Dialog Box

Now that you know what a query looks like, you are ready to examine all the features of the query window. To create a query, follow these steps:

1. Choose File, New, Query. The Select File dialog box appears (see fig. 4.4).

2. Click the table to use for the query, or click the Browse button to change to another directory. Click OK to confirm your selection.

3. The Query Editor window opens, as shown in figure 4.5.

4 — GETTING STARTED WITH QUERY BY EXAMPLE

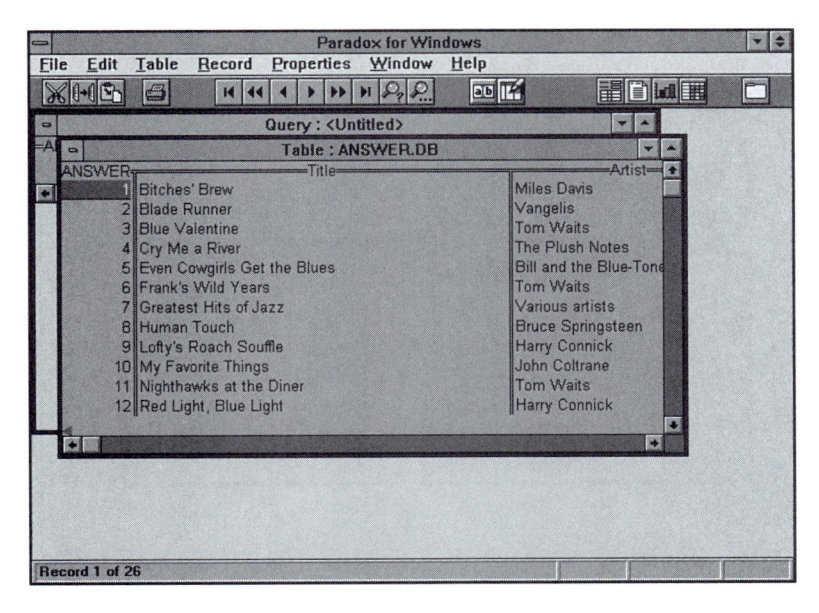

FIG. 4.3

The Answer table for the query in figure 4.2.

FIG. 4.4

The Select File dialog box.

I — PARADOX FOR WINDOWS FUNDAMENTALS

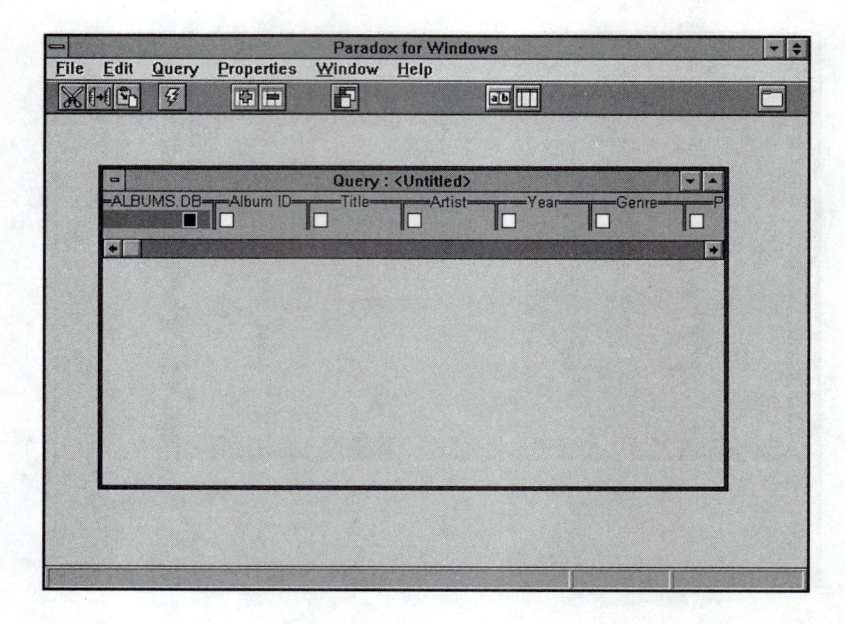

FIG. 4.5

The Query Editor window.

You use the Query Editor window to enter your search criteria and choose the fields to display in the query. The data table you are querying is displayed in a format that looks like the table but doesn't show the data itself. Instead, each column contains a check box and room to enter your search criteria.

You may retrieve data from more than one table in a query. Single-table queries are used for the examples in this chapter. For information on multi-table queries, see Chapter 8, "Using Advanced Query by Example."

Query tables can be manipulated, but not to the extent of data tables. To change the order of the fields, click and drag the column name. You can adjust the width of a column by clicking the right border and dragging it to the right or left. You cannot adjust column height, colors, or font in the query window.

Adding a Table to a Query

To add a second table to a query, choose Query, Add Table from the desktop menu, or click the Add Table button (a plus sign) in the SpeedBar. Choose the table from the Select File dialog box.

Removing a Table from a Query

If you add a table to the query by mistake, you can remove it by choosing Query, Remove Table or by clicking the Remove Table button (a minus sign) in the SpeedBar. The Remove Table dialog box appears (see fig. 4.6).

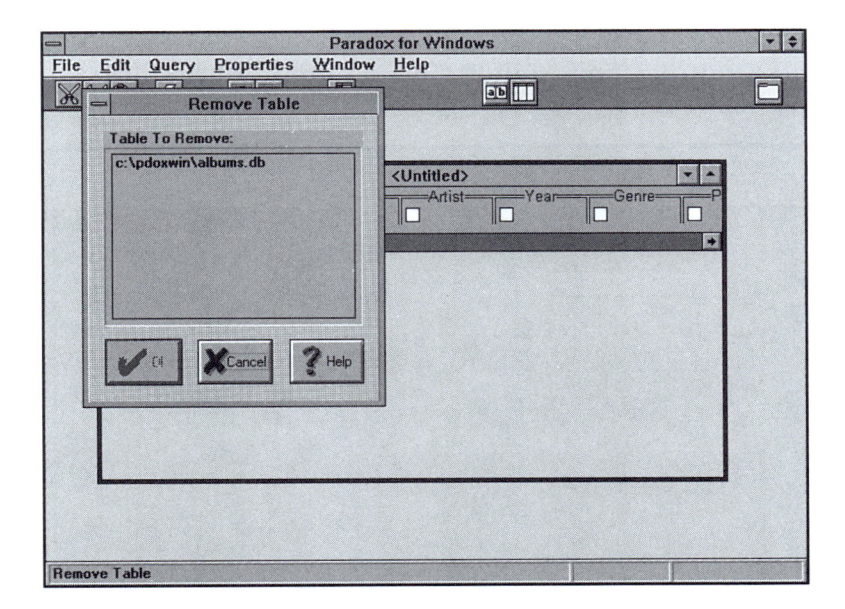

FIG. 4.6
The Remove Table dialog box.

Click to highlight the table to remove, then click OK or press Enter. Paradox removes the table from the query.

The Query Menu

The Query menu, shown in figure 4.7, is accessed from the menu bar or by pressing Alt+Q. A description of the options in the Query menu follows:

Option	Description
Add Table	Brings a new table into the Query Editor
Remove Table	Removes table from Query Editor

continues

I — PARADOX FOR WINDOWS FUNDAMENTALS

Option	Description
Field View (F2)	Enables you to edit the contents of a field in a query image (like Field view in record entry). By default, making a new entry in a query field erases the contents of the field. With Field view, you can move within the field and edit its contents.
Run (F8)	Executes a query
Wait for DDE	Waits for Dynamic Data Exchange to refresh the contents of an object. To learn how to set up DDE links, see Chapter 11.

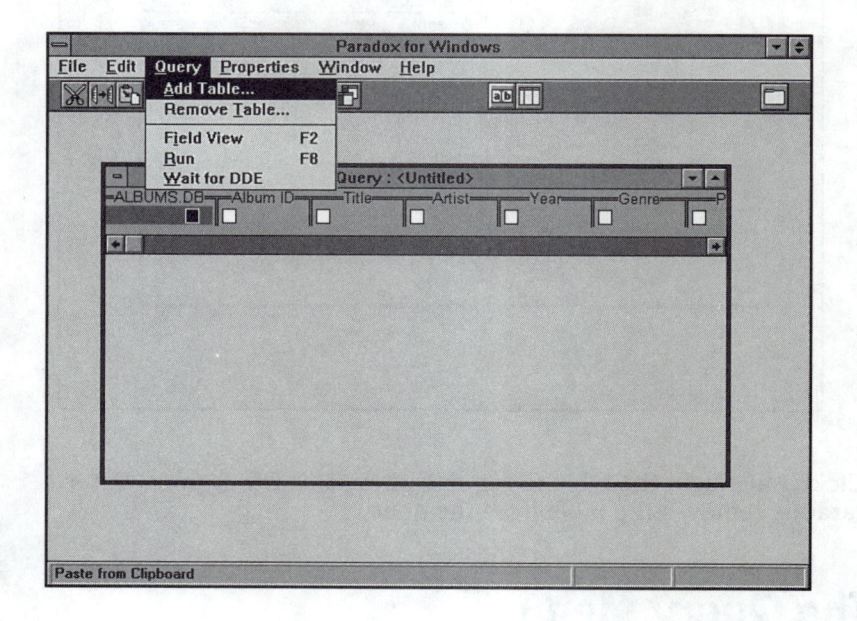

FIG. 4.7

The Query menu.

Handling Query Errors

If Paradox encounters an error in your query, the query is not processed. Instead, a dialog box appears, enabling you to correct the error and run the query again, as shown in figure 4.8.

In the example in figure 4.8, the error was caused by an attempt to run an empty query (with no fields checked). For some error messages, you can click the >> button to display more information on the error.

4 — GETTING STARTED WITH QUERY BY EXAMPLE   177

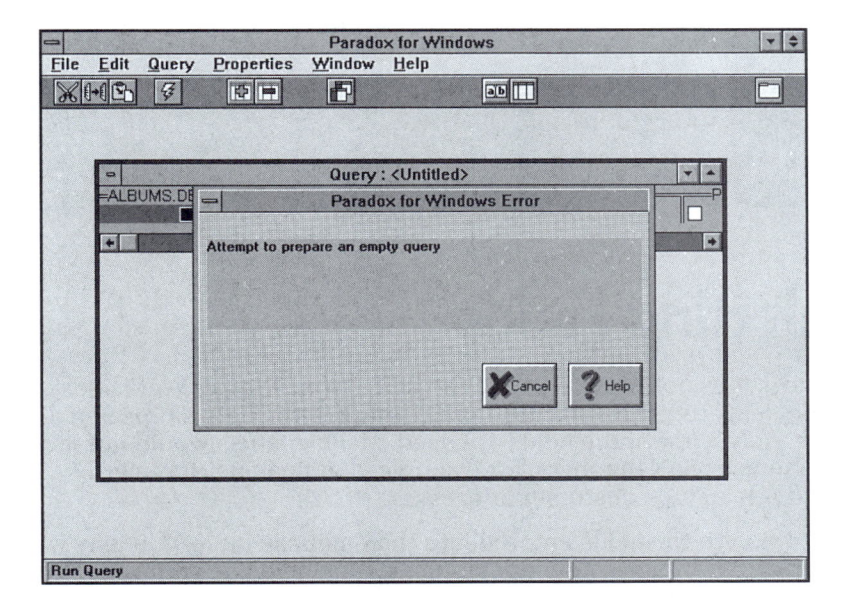

FIG. 4.8

The Paradox for Windows Error dialog box.

The Query SpeedBar

In the Query window, the SpeedBar displays ten buttons: Cut to Clipboard, Copy to Clipboard, Paste from Clipboard, Run Query, Add Table, Remove Table, Join Tables, Field View, Answer Table Properties, and Open Folder. These buttons provide an alternative to accessing functions from the menus or with function keys.

For now, you should learn the buttons for Add Table, Remove Table, and Run Query. Example elements are discussed in Chapter 8, "Using Advanced Query by Example." The Add Table button adds a table to the query window, and the Remove Table button removes a table. Run Query (the lightning bolt button) executes the query in the Query Editor dialog box. It replaces the Do It! command in Paradox for DOS.

NOTE When the Answer table is displayed, the SpeedBar buttons change to those used in the Edit table window. See Chapter 3, "Entering, Editing, and Viewing Data" for details.

For Related Information

▶▶ "Creating Multi-Table Queries," p. 366.

▶▶ "Using the File Browser," p. 474.

Selecting Fields

A query does not have to list all the fields from a table. You choose which fields to list by placing a check mark in the field's box. Sometimes, only a few of the fields are used. Mailing labels would not include telephone or FAX numbers, for example, and financial summaries would not include customer addresses.

In addition to the fields entered into the database table, you may want to create new fields by manipulating existing fields or performing calculations. For example, you could show the total price for an invoice or the total number of customers for each state.

The Check Mark

A check mark in the square box below the column name indicates that the field should be included in the Answer table. Four kinds of check marks are available in Paradox for Windows, as shown in figure 4.9, and each has a different effect on the Answer table (see table 4.1).

Table 4.1. Types of Check Marks

Check mark	Description
Check (F6)	Lists unique values from all records that meet the search, sorted in ascending order (for example, A to Z or 1 to 100)
Check Plus	Lists all values whether unique or not unique
Check Descending	Sorts values in reverse order from highest to lowest (for example, Z to A or 100 to 1)
GroupBy check	Specifies group of records for set query

4 — GETTING STARTED WITH QUERY BY EXAMPLE

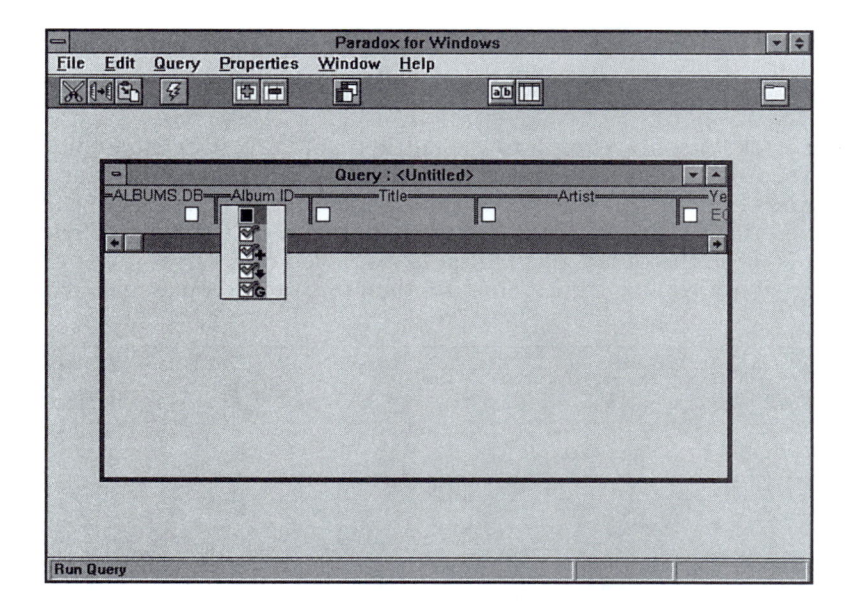

FIG. 4.9

Check mark types.

> **TIP** If you want to place a check mark in all fields in a table, place a check mark in the box below the table name.

You can enter a check mark by clicking the check box and choosing the type of check, or by pressing F6 and then Shift+F6 to scroll through the check mark types. If you click and hold down the mouse button on the check box, all the check types are displayed in a drop-down box, as shown in figure 4.9. Use the mouse to click the appropriate box. Click the empty box to remove a check mark.

Paradox defaults to a plain check mark if you click an empty check box and deletes the check mark if you click a filled check box. Therefore, you can quickly create a query by clicking the check boxes for each of the desired fields.

Displaying Duplicate Values

Because the Answer table normally displays only unique records, it could contain fewer records than the number of records in the database table that meet your search criteria. Suppose that a query retrieves only the City field from a list of clients. One entry for each unique city is displayed. The Answer table would contain only one record for New York, for example, even if the clients table contains 100 clients from New York.

With Check Plus, however, a row is entered in the Answer table for each record that meets the search criteria. A pair of simple queries illustrates the difference between Check and Check Plus. First, use the Albums table (ALBUMS.DB) and place a check on only the Artist field. When you run the query, each artist is displayed only once—even artists for whom you have entered more than one recording (see fig. 4.10).

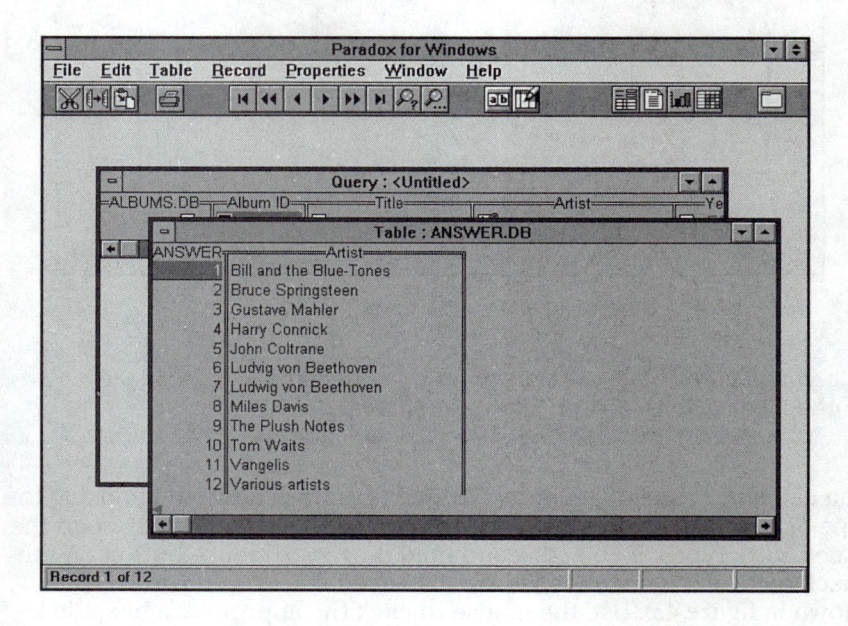

FIG. 4.10

Listing artists from the Albums table with the Check Mark.

Note that the artist names are sorted in alphabetical order. Because the artist name is stored first name first in a single field, the artists are not sorted by last name. You can correct this by entering the artist last name first or by creating a separate field to indicate the alpha sort order for the artist and filling in this new field with the alphabetic position for the entry. You may want to ignore an initial *The* for the London Philharmonic, or enter **John** as the sort order for Elton John.

Next, try the same query using Check Plus. Close the Answer table by double-clicking its Control menu, then click the check box in the Artist field and change the check to Check Plus. When you run the query, it produces an Answer table similar to that in figure 4.11.

This time, an artist is listed for each record in the table and repeated if more than one recording has been entered for that artist. The Answer

4 — GETTING STARTED WITH QUERY BY EXAMPLE

table also is no longer sorted. Instead, the Answer table appears in the same order as the original table (by Album ID). You can sort the Answer table in the same way as any other table, by choosing <u>T</u>able, <u>S</u>ort.

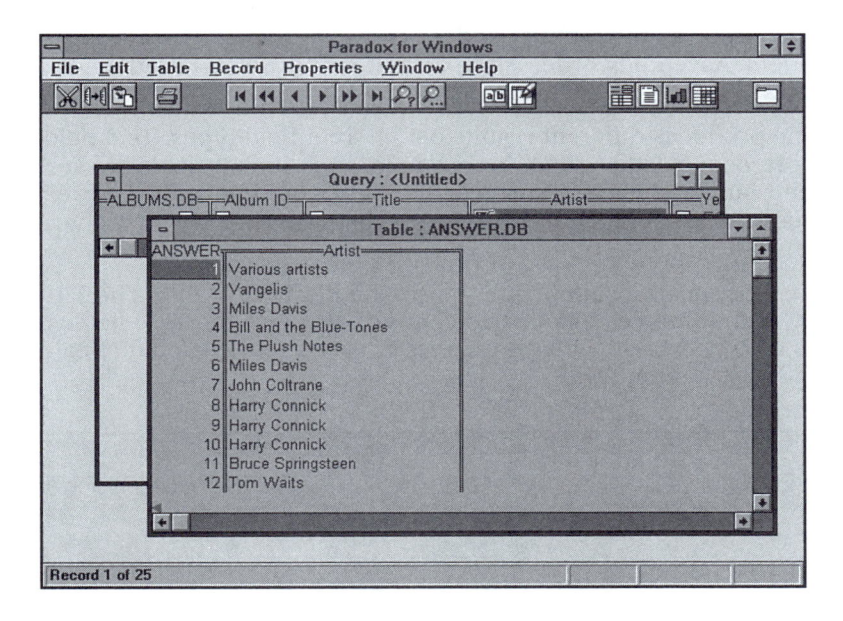

FIG. 4.11

Listing artists from the Albums table with the Check Plus.

The Answer table contains one record for each unique combination of fields requested in your query with plain check marks. If check marks placed in other fields make the records in the Answer table unique, the repeating value in the Artist field is listed for each record even without the use of Check Plus. For example, if you place a check in the Title field as well as in the Artist field, the Artist field is listed for each record in the Answer table. This occurs even if the same name occurs more than once because each record in the Answer table (the combination of title and artist) is unique. Check Plus does not sort the Answer table by the Artist field, but rather lists the artists in the same order as the Albums table.

Sorting

Sorting, also called *ordering*, determines the order in which records are printed. Most queries are more useful if the data is displayed in sorted order rather than random order. You might want to sort mailing labels, for example, by ZIP code for easier assembly of a bulk mailing. A class roster, on the other hand, would be sorted alphabetically by student name.

I — PARADOX FOR WINDOWS FUNDAMENTALS

Ascending sorts are used more often than descending sorts, especially for alphabetical listings. Descending sorts are useful when you want to show the most recent activities first (by sorting by a date field). You also can use descending sort to print a list of accounts receivable in reverse order by the number of days overdue, to highlight the worst offenders. Ascending order is the default sort order in Paradox for Windows.

Sorting produces different results on different field types. Text fields are sorted from left to right, for example, and number fields are sorted by their numeric value. A sort of a text field would put 1000 before 50 because the first character in 1000 (a 1) is lower than the first character of 50 (a 5).

Figure 4.12 shows a simple query from the RECORDS table. The Title, Artist, and Genre fields have been chosen. Because the Title field appears first in the table image, the records are listed in alphabetical order by the album title.

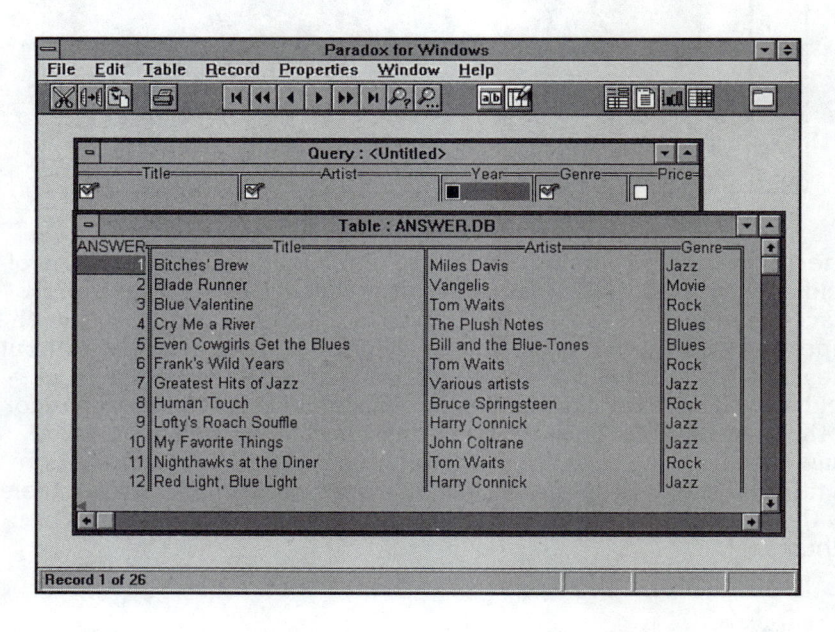

FIG. 4.12

The RECORDS.DB table sorted query for Title, Artist, and Genre.

To sort in reverse order, use Check Descending. Close the Answer table by double-clicking its Control menu. Then click the check box in the Title field and choose Check Descending (the check mark with the downward arrow). Run the query again. The resulting sort displays the same fields, but in descending alphabetical order (see fig. 4.13).

4 — GETTING STARTED WITH QUERY BY EXAMPLE

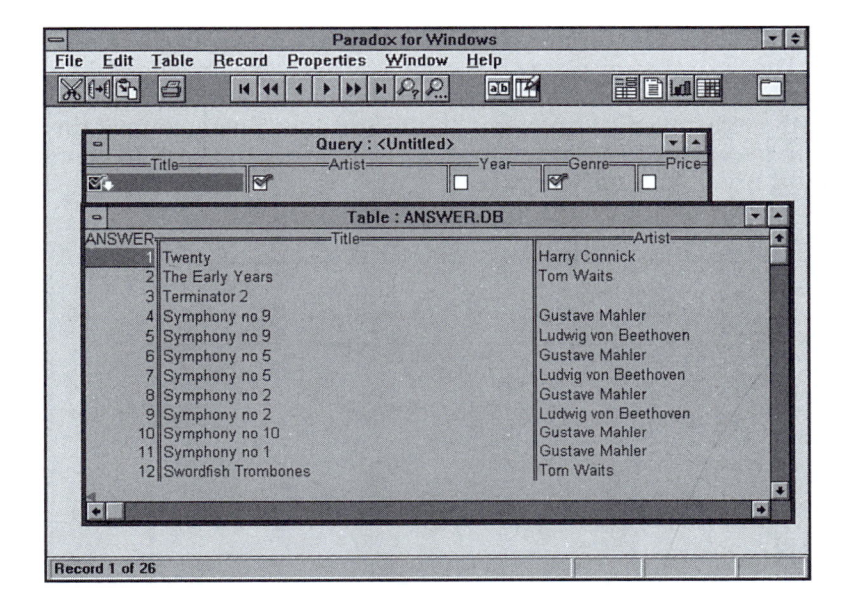

FIG. 4.13

RECORDS.DB table sorted in descending order by Title, Artist, and Genre.

If you instruct Paradox to select records based on more than one field, the Answer table will be sorted by each field checked, reading from left to right in the query editor. In figure 4.14, albums are sorted first by Artist, then by Title.

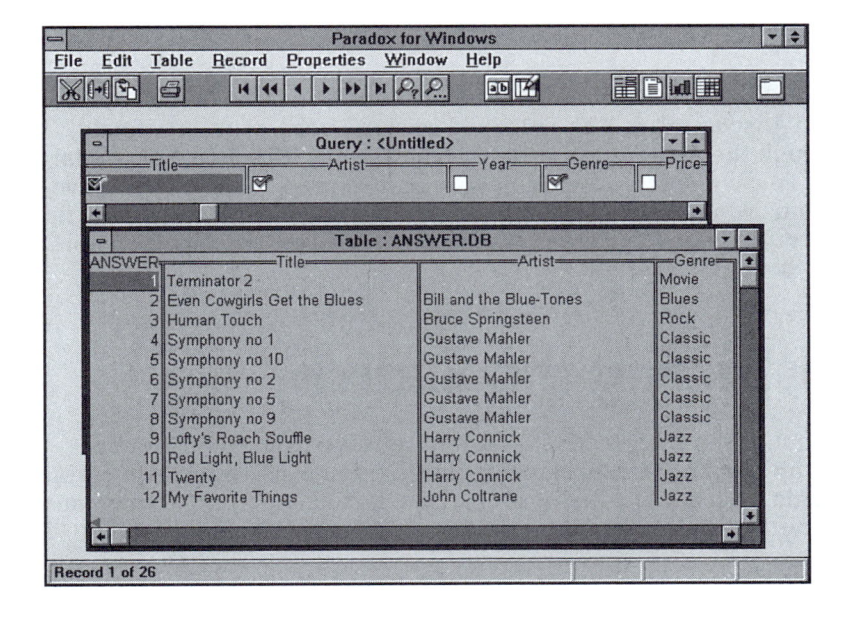

FIG. 4.14

The ALBUMS.DB query sorted by Artist (primary) and Title (secondary).

I — PARADOX FOR WINDOWS FUNDAMENTALS

To create a special sorting order, choose Properties, Answer Table, Sort. The Sort Answer dialog box appears, as shown in figure 4.15. Click the Artist field and then the right-arrow button to move the Artist field from the Available Fields column to the Sort By column. Repeat this step to move the Title field to the Sort By column. Click OK to confirm the sort order, and run the query.

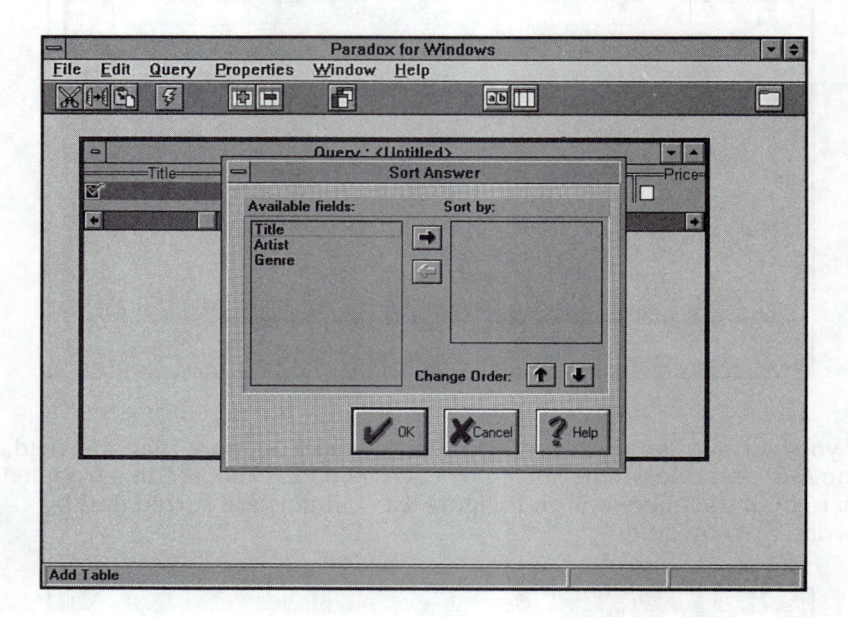

FIG. 4.15

The Sort Answer dialog box.

The sort order does not affect the order in which the fields appear in the Answer table. The Title field appears before the Artist field, although the Artist is the primary sort and the Title is the secondary sort. To change the order of fields in the Answer table, either move the columns when viewing the table or change the image of the table in the Answer table properties, as discussed in "Editing the Answer Table" later in this chapter.

Restricting the Search

The queries in the preceding section retrieved selected columns from all rows in a table. In many queries, you want to retrieve certain records from a table. Records can be selected according to any number of criteria, using one or more fields.

4 — GETTING STARTED WITH QUERY BY EXAMPLE

When planning your query, you may want to imagine that each record in a table is on an index card. You have a thick stack of these cards in your hand, each one representing a client, a student, an inventory item or, for this example, an album. A query enables you to specify which records will be listed, as if you were pulling out the desired cards from the stack. Using the check mark, you then can decide which fields from these selected records to list. To retrieve all jazz recordings from the Albums table, for example, enter **Jazz** as the Genre for the query, as shown in figure 4.16.

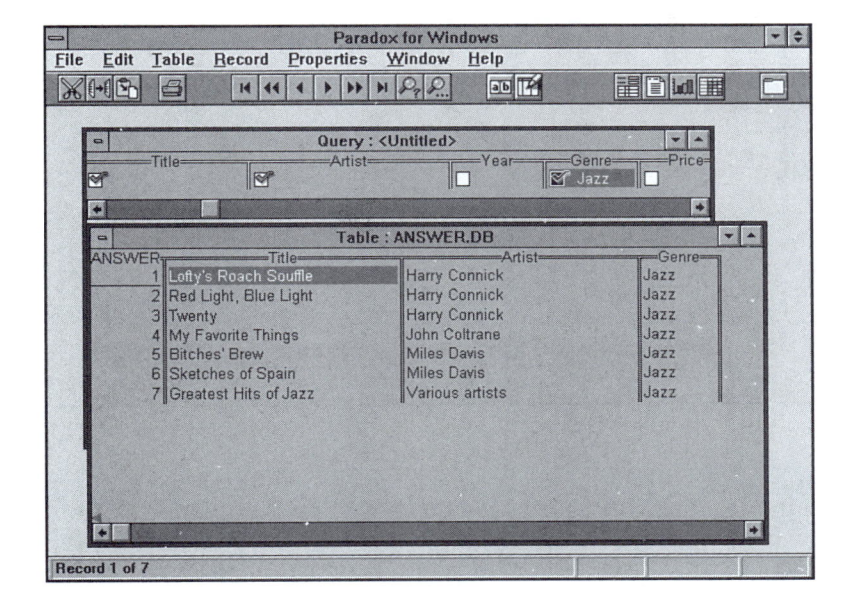

FIG. 4.16

Selecting all records where Genre = jazz.

You enter the search criteria in the region directly to the right of the check box. Paradox calls this the *statement area*. The statement area scrolls as necessary to accept your entry. When you move the cursor from the field, some of your entry may be hidden from view, but it will be visible if you return to the field.

Search criteria can compare your example to the database records in several ways. You can search for an exact match, for an inexact match, or with special operators such as greater than or less than.

Exact Match

By default, Paradox searches for an exact match of the value you enter as an example. In an exact match search, each letter must be the same (including capitalization), and all letters of the field value must be entered. For example, search the Albums table for all recordings by Harry Connick, as shown in figure 4.17.

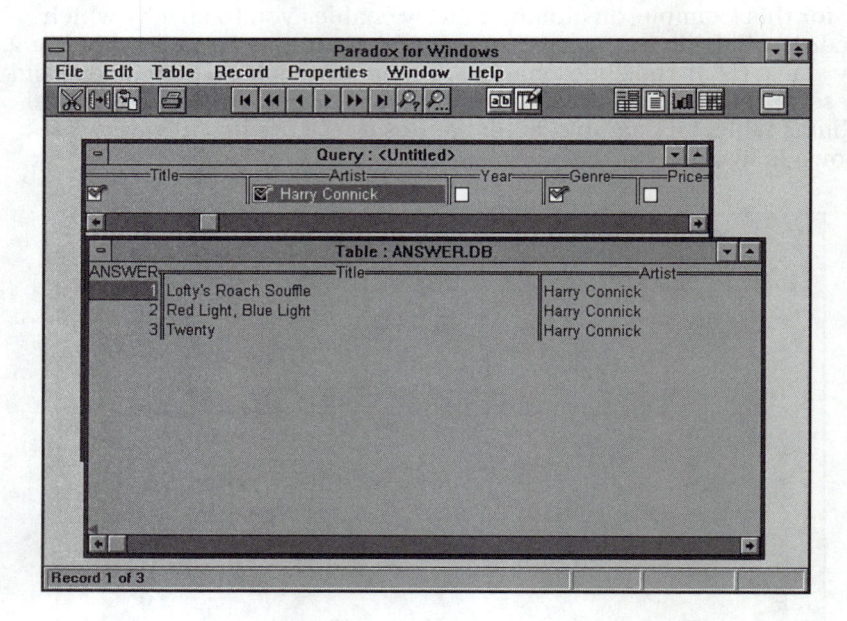

FIG. 4.17

Searching for an exact match.

> **TIP** Remember that when you use exact match in a query, capitalization counts. Be sure that all letters in your query exactly match the way they are entered in the table. For example, make sure that you enter 0, not the letter O, for zero and 1, not the letter l, for one.

When searching for a number, do not include punctuation marks such as dollar signs, commas, and periods. These characters are shown in the display of the table but are not stored in the field. For example, if you enter $2,500,999 to search for 2500999, the search will fail.

Approximate Match

Approximate matches are useful when you do not know all the information to use for a search. Perhaps you remember the street name but not the street number, or you cannot remember whether the address is Ocean Boulevard, Ocean Drive, or Ocean Street. This is where the LIKE operator and query wild cards are helpful.

The LIKE Operator

The *LIKE* operator enables you to search for a field value that sounds close to your entry. If you enter **LIKE SHKSPR** in a query, you can retrieve Shakespear, Shaekspeer, or Shakespeare because they contain many of the same letters in the same order. LIKE searches are not case-sensitive, so you do not have to worry about matching capitalization.

For example, you may not remember whether you have entered your Harry Connick records as Harry Connick or Harry Connick, Jr, or even misspelled the artist's name as Harry Conick or Harry Connack. To search for albums in which the artist name sounds like Harry Connick, use the LIKE operator, as shown in figure 4.18.

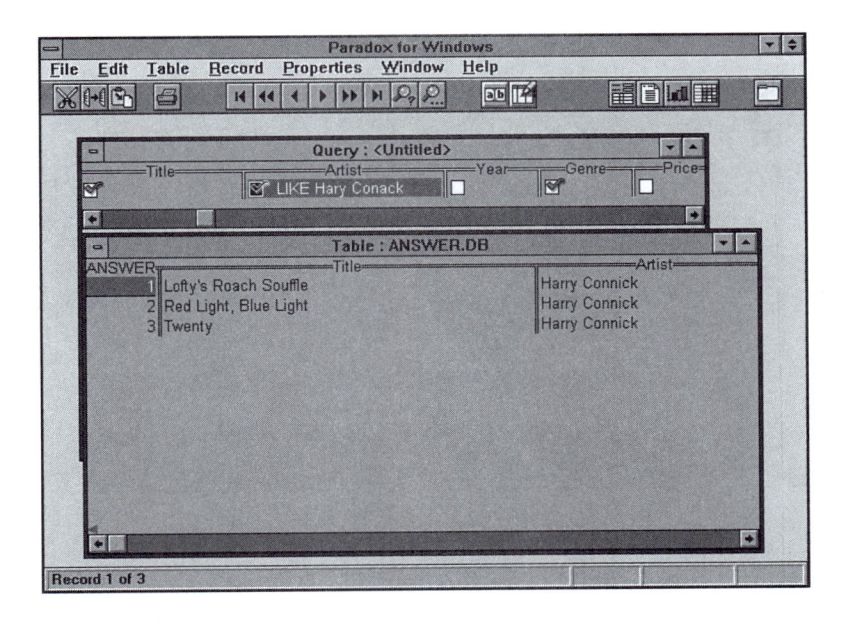

FIG. 4.18

Searching with the LIKE operator.

> **NOTE** The LIKE operator does not perform true phonetic searches for values that "sound like" the search example. Therefore, a search for LIKE fone will not find phone. The first character of the example must match exactly, so a search on pfone will find phone. The more letters you use, in the correct order, the closer you will get to the records you seek. If you strike out with a LIKE search, try using a wild-card search.

Wild-Card Operators

You can perform database searches to find partial matches by using *wild cards*—special characters used in queries that stand for one or more missing characters. For example, the Paradox for Windows @ wild card (for a single character) and .. wild card (for one or more unknown characters) can be used to find an inexact match. A search for S.. in the Title field, for example, could produce records such as "Sketches of Spain," "Small Change," and "Swordfish Trombones" (see fig. 4.19).

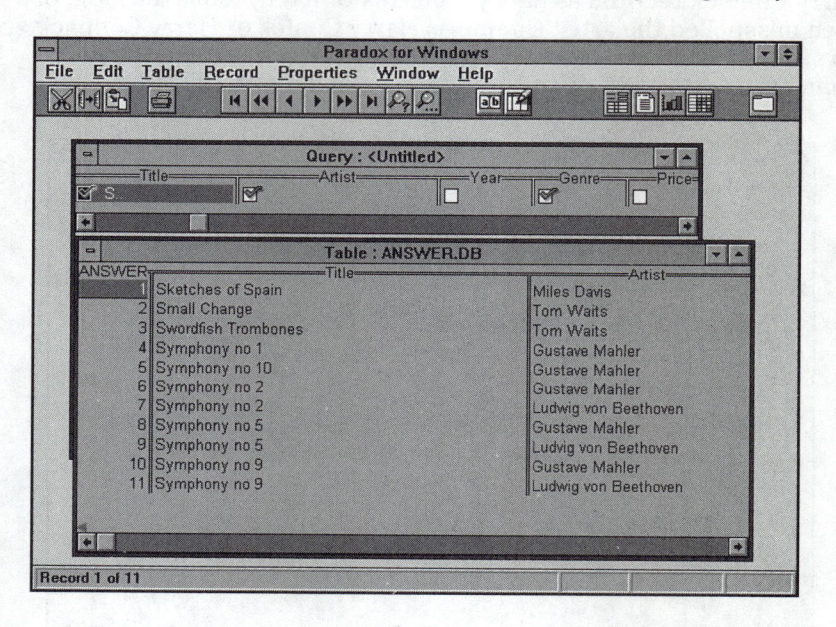

FIG. 4.19

Searching with the .. wild-card operator.

The @ wild card is similar but represents only one missing character. A search for J@n would find Jan and Jon, but not John or Jean because the search expression matches only three-letter words that begin with J and end with n. Table 4.2 shows how wild-card operators work in Paradox for Windows.

> **TIP**
>
> The Paradox @ wild card represents only one character and is similar to the DOS ? wild card. The Paradox .. wild card represents one or more missing characters and works in the same way as the DOS * wild card.

Table 4.2. Wild-Card Operators

Pattern	Matches
B..	Anything that starts with *B*, such as *Boise, By, By the bay*
b@t	Anything that starts with *b*, ends with *t*, and has one character in between, such as *bat, bit, but*. Would not match *boat* or *bought*.
b..s	Anything that starts with *b* and ends with *s*, such as *bags*, *big open spaces*
..T	Anything that ends with *T*, such as *point, hit, 100 Main Street*
..o..s	Anything that contains *o* and ends with *s*, such as *boats, formats, Open Systems*
6..9	Anything that starts with *6* and ends with *9*, such as *6789, 65 East Hampton #109*
12/../60	Any date that starts with *12* as the month and ends with *60* as the year, such as *12/01/60* or *12/14/60*

> **CAUTION:** If you mix the .. wild card with a decimal point or period in an example, use quotation marks to differentiate the single dots from the wild card. To search for a decimal number starting with 1, for example, you might type the following:
>
> 1"."..
>
> The period in quotation marks is the decimal point, and the second and third periods are the wild-card operator.

Range of Values

For some searches, you do not want an exact match or a partial match, but rather a range of possible values. For example, if you search your employee table for high commission sales representatives, you are not likely to know the exact amount of their commissions. Instead, you could search on a range. Using the > comparison operator, for example, you could search for commissions above $20,000. Figure 4.20 shows a search in the Albums table for all recordings made after 1970.

You also can search for values between two values. To retrieve monthly sales figures for May 1989, you would enter the following:

>= 05/01/89,<= 05/31/89

I — PARADOX FOR WINDOWS FUNDAMENTALS

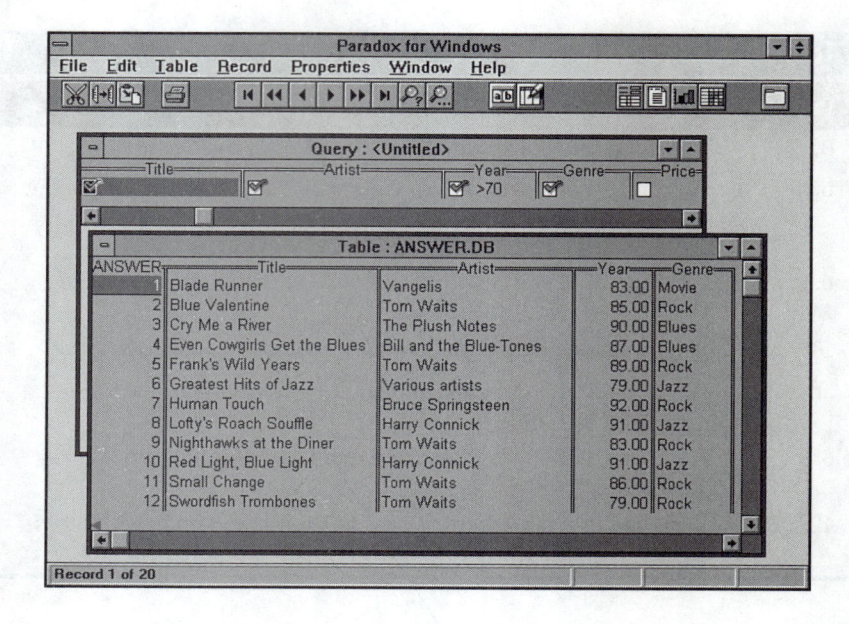

FIG. 4.20

Searching for a range of values using the > operator.

Note that a comma is used to connect the two criteria.

To facilitate searches for ranges, comparison operators are used. Table 4.3 lists the Paradox for Windows comparison operators.

Table 4.3. Table Comparison Operators

Operator	Meaning
=	equal to (optional)
>	greater than
<	less than
>=	greater than or equal to
<=	less than or equal to

Some searches require Paradox to perform various kinds of calculations. For some queries, Paradox for Windows uses special command operators. These operators are *reserved words* and thus have a special meaning to the query processor.

4 — GETTING STARTED WITH QUERY BY EXAMPLE

Special operators can be used to search for blank or nonmatching records, to change column names in the Answer table, for date arithmetic, and for other functions. You can search for all albums in which the Price field is blank, for example, to show albums for which you have not entered a price (see fig. 4.21).

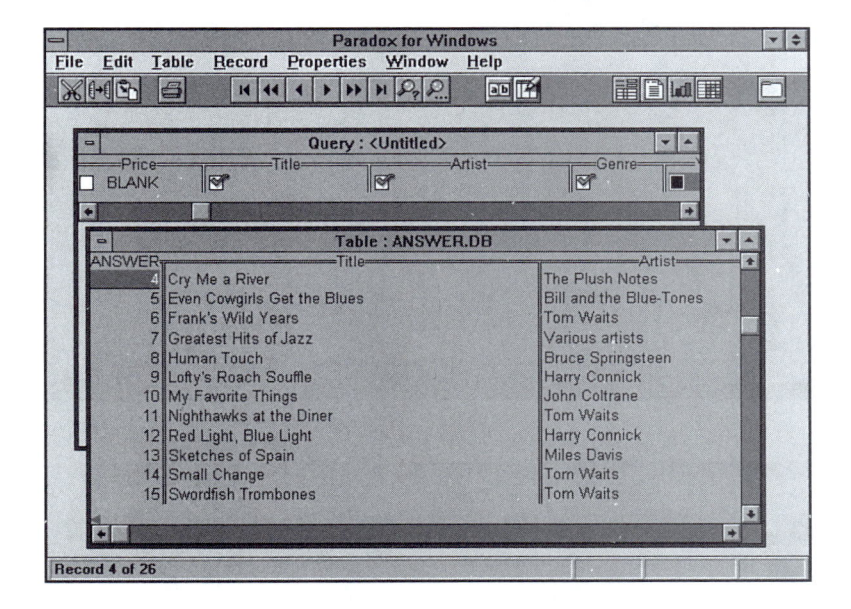

FIG. 4.21
Using the BLANK operator to search for missing values.

Intersection

You can use more than one search criterion to narrow your search. No special operators are used if the criteria are in two different fields. For example, you could find rock CDs by entering **C** in the Format field and **Rock** in the Genre field of the Albums table, as shown in figure 4.22.

If you need to use two criteria in the same field, and both criteria must be met for the search, separate the criteria with a comma, which represents the AND operator (see fig. 4.23). You can retrieve recordings from 1973, for example, by entering the following in the Recording Date field:

>=01/01/73,<=12/31/73

The first part of the example specifies that the date must be greater than or equal to January 1, 1973, and the second part stipulates that the date must be less than or equal to December 31, 1973.

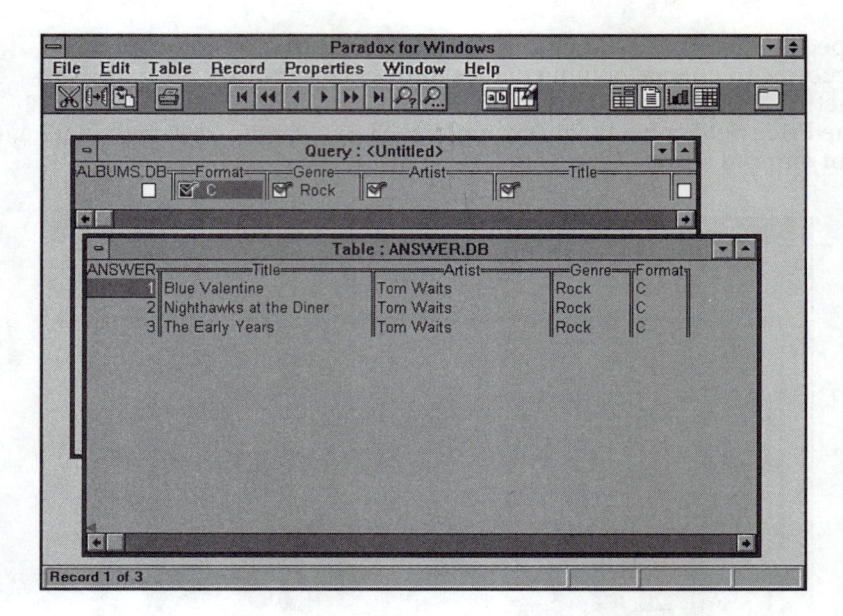

FIG. 4.22

Multiple criteria in different fields.

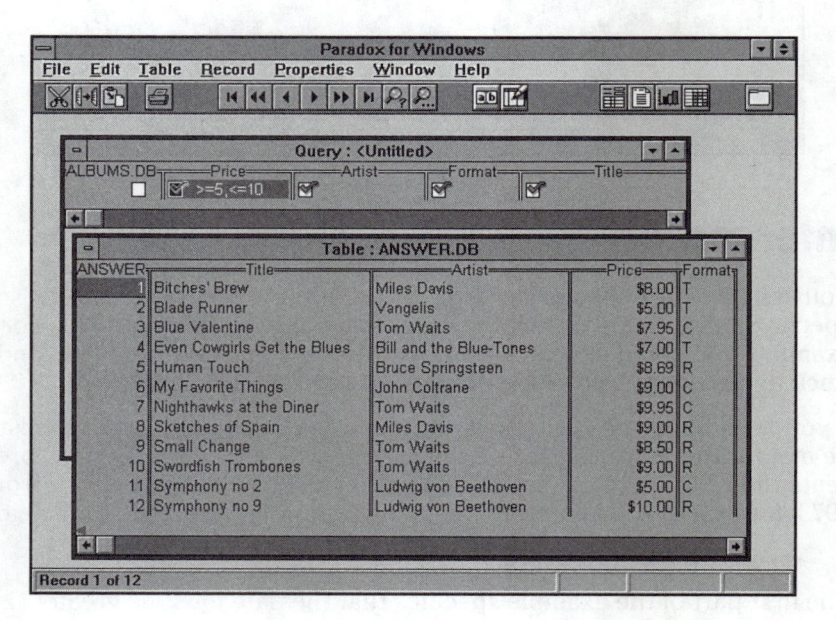

FIG. 4.23

Using the comma operator for multiple criteria.

> **TIP**
>
> Some queries can be written in more than one way. The query in the last example also could have been written as @@/@@/73 to match all dates with the year 1973. Try to become comfortable with using different expressions and operators in your queries.

Union

Sometimes multiple search criteria are required, but only one of the criteria must be met. For example, you might be looking for either rock or blues recordings. As with intersection, different approaches are used if your criteria are for one field or two fields.

If the criteria are in the same field, use the OR operator between the criteria. In the Genre field, for example, enter **Rock OR Jazz**. Paradox for Windows includes all the records that fit either category in the Answer table, as shown in figure 4.24. If you had used the AND operator to connect the search criteria—for example, Rock,Jazz—you would have found no records because a single record cannot have a Genre listed as both Rock and Jazz at the same time.

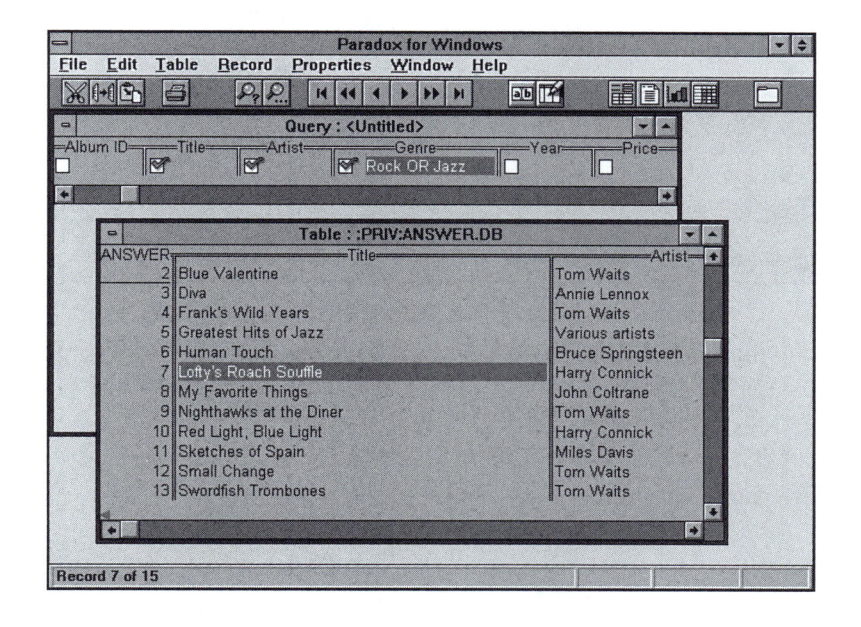

FIG. 4.24

An OR query and the resulting Answer table.

NOTE You may enter the OR operator in upper- or lowercase. Remember that Paradox is case-sensitive to the examples you offer unless you use wild cards or LIKE.

If multiple OR criteria are in different fields, enter them on the next line of the table, as shown in figure 4.25. You can retrieve all jazz records as well as all records by Tom Waits (whose music is hard to categorize), for example, by entering **Jazz** as the Genre, and **Tom Waits** as the Artist in the next line of the table. If both criteria are entered on the same line, they will retrieve the intersection—in other words, the records meeting both criteria. To add the second line to the query, simply press the down-arrow key.

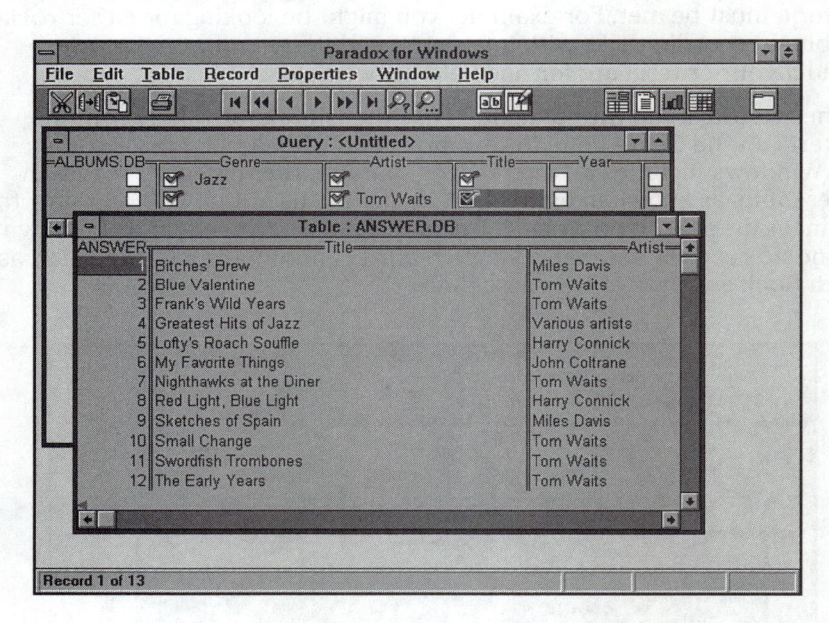

FIG. 4.25

OR criteria on multiple lines.

You can combine multiple intersection and union searches in a single query. You can restrict the preceding search, for example, to include only jazz albums (as opposed to compact discs and tapes).

Figure 4.26 shows a combination of intersection and union:

```
(Genre = Jazz AND Format = C) OR Artist = Tom Waits
```

TIP Choosing between the AND and OR operators can be confusing. If *both* criteria must be met, you should use AND. If *either* of the criteria should be met, you should use OR.

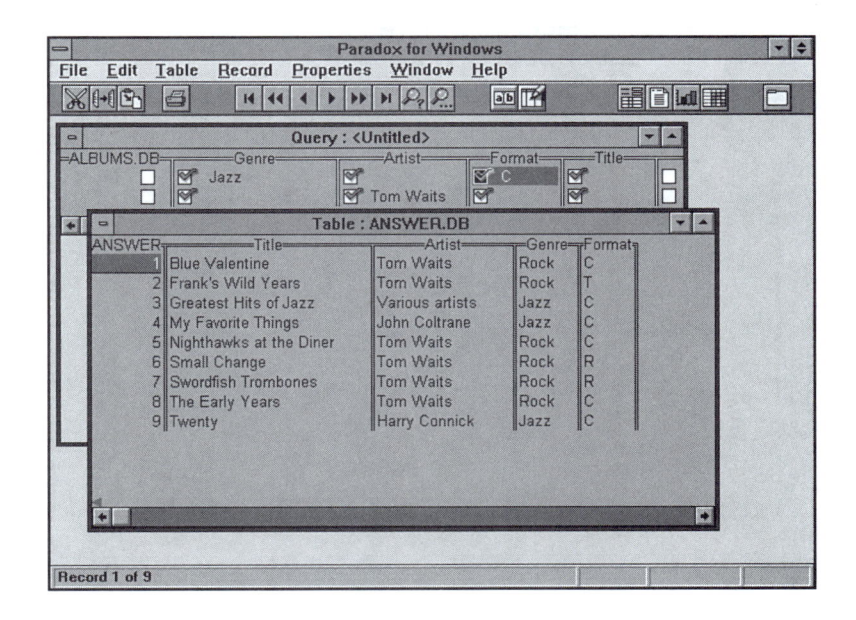

FIG. 4.26
Using intersection (AND) and union (OR) in a single query.

The AS Operator: Changing a Field Name

By default, the column headings in the Answer table are set to the field names from the source table. You may want to change the name of the column to make the query results easier to read or understand.

To change a column name, use the AS operator, as shown in figure 4.27. In the Albums table, for example, place a check in the Title and Artist fields. In the Artist field, you can enter **AS Performed by** to change the header of the Answer table to read Performed by instead of Artist.

> **T I P**
> One handy use for the AS operator is to convert the short field names of dBASE tables into the longer names supported by Paradox. Be sure to use AS to change any long field names or names containing spaces.

FIG. 4.27

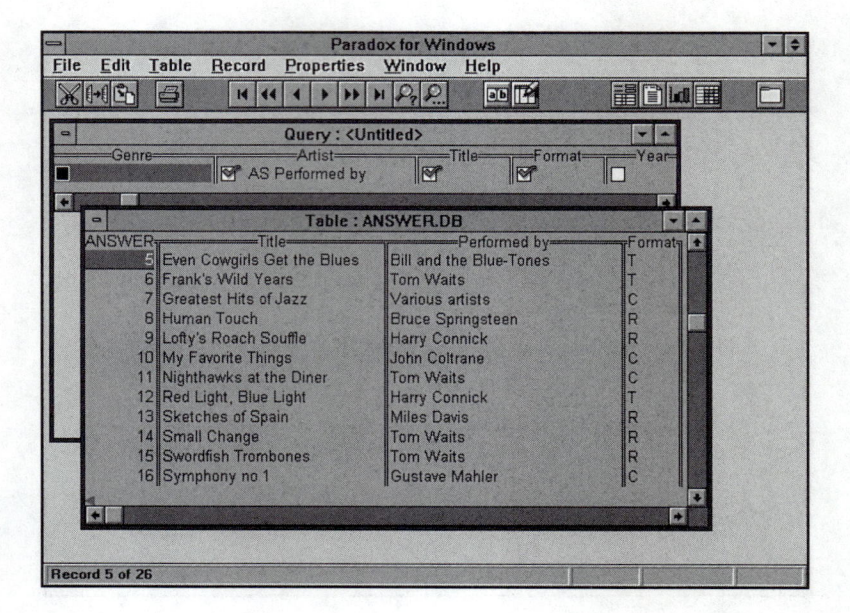

An example of the AS operator.

The NOT Operator: Finding Unmatching Values

The NOT operator is another powerful query tool. NOT enables you to find all records whose values are not the value you specify, as shown in figure 4.28. For example, if you want to lend your Jazz recordings to a friend who does not have a CD player but does have a turntable and a tape deck, you can enter **Jazz** in the Genre field and **NOT C** in the Format field.

The BLANK Operator: Finding Blank Values

Paradox for Windows even enables you to search for nothing—for records with blanks in specified fields. To search for blank values, you use the BLANK keyword. You can search for all employees who do not have middle initials, for example, by entering **BLANK** and the example in the MI field of the Employee table.

4 — GETTING STARTED WITH QUERY BY EXAMPLE

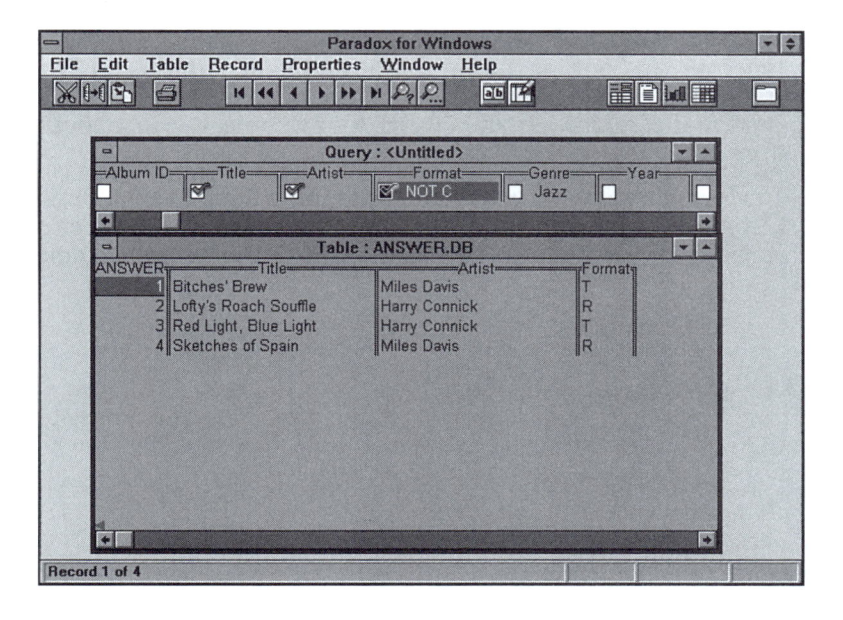

FIG. 4.28

An example of the NOT operator.

Leaving a field blank and using the BLANK operator produce very different results in QBE. If you leave a field blank in the query, *all* records are included in the Answer table—not just those records with blanks in that field. You must use the BLANK operator to search for records with blank field values.

> **T I P**
>
> When entering data, do not enter the word *blank* (or even *N/A* or some other abbreviation) in a field that has no value. These would be interpreted as entries in the field. Because BLANK is a reserved word, it has a special meaning in a query. Therefore, if you have a customer named Joe Blank, you will not find him if you search for a last name that equals Blank. To find the record, you must use quotation marks to search for "Blank" or LIKE "BLANK" so that Paradox for Windows recognize BLANK as a text value rather than an operator.

Searching in Exotic Field Types

Most of your queries will probably use traditional field types—alphanumeric, numeric, and date fields. You also can search for memo, graphic,

I — PARADOX FOR WINDOWS FUNDAMENTALS

and OLE object fields; you can search only for the existence of these fields, however, and not for the values they contain. Paradox for Windows provides no way to search for an image of a butterfly or for a memo field that contains a certain word, for example, because these fields store data outside the Paradox table.

To search for the existence of a memo or graphic field, use the BLANK or NOT BLANK operator. To find all albums with a memo field that contains a review, for example, enter **NOT BLANK** as the example element in the Review field.

> **TIP** Do not retrieve graphic or memo fields in your queries unless you absolutely must have them. The query table duplicates the contents of these fields and creates a large Answer table, dramatically slowing the query and consuming extra disk space.

> **CAUTION:** When designing a database, use memo fields only for the storage of extra information for which you will never need to search.

The TODAY Operator and Date Arithmetic

Many database applications call for the calculation of elapsed time. You may want to determine how many days it takes for a new order to be processed or how long it takes to collect your receivables. You use date arithmetic to perform these calculations.

Date fields can be used for date calculations. You can subtract the invoice date from the payment date, for example, to calculate the time between billing and payment. Examples of some common date arithmetic follow:

Date arithmetic	Description
<TODAY	Finds dates earlier than today's date
<TODAY - 90	Finds dates earlier than 90 days ago
TODAY + 30	Finds dates 30 days ahead of today's date

4 — GETTING STARTED WITH QUERY BY EXAMPLE

> **TIP**
>
> The value for the TODAY variable is determined by the system clock on your PC. Be sure to set the date properly with the DOS DATE command. If you do not leave your machine on all the time, be sure that the battery backup for the clock is working or reset the date each time you restart the computer.

Table 4.4 summarizes all Paradox query operators.

Table 4.4. Query Operators

Category	Operator	Meaning
Reserved symbols	Check mark	Displays unique field values in Answer
	Check plus	Displays field values, including duplicates, in Answer
	Check descending	Displays field values in descending order
	Check group	Specifies a group for set operations
Reserved words	CALC	Calculates a new field
	INSERT	Inserts records with specified values
	DELETE	Removes records with specified values
	CHANGETO	Changes specified values in fields
	FIND	Finds specified records in a table
	SET	Defines specific records as a set for comparisons
Arithmetic operators	+	Addition (number field) concatenation (alphanumeric field)
	–	Subtract
	*	Multiply
	/	Divide
	( )	Group operators in a query expression

continues

Table 4.4. Continued

Category	Operator	Meaning
Comparison operators	=	Equal to (optional)
	>	Greater than
	<	Less than
	>=	Greater than or equal to
	<=	Less than or equal to
Wild-card operators	..	Any series of characters
	@	Any single character
Special operators	LIKE	Similar to
	NOT	Does not match
	BLANK	No value
	TODAY	Today's date
	OR	Specifies OR conditions in a field
	,	Specifies AND conditions in a field
	AS	Specifies the name of a field in the Answer table
	!	Displays all values in a field regardless of matches

Understanding the Answer Table

During normal operation, Paradox creates various temporary tables to store the results of database actions. As you learned previously, the results of a query are placed in a temporary table called Answer. After you finish using a query, the Answer table is not deleted until you execute your next query or exit Paradox.

The Answer table can be manipulated in the same way as other Paradox tables. The Answer table can be renamed, sorted, or even used as the starting point for a new query.

> **CAUTION:** The Answer table is stored on your computer's hard disk, so be sure that you have enough free disk space to accommodate the rows you select. If you have a server-based application with large volumes of data, you could create queries whose results are so big that you cannot execute them. To prevent such a calamity, run a query to count the number of records that meet your criteria before you run the query itself. For instructions about using queries for counting and other aggregation processes, see Chapter 8, "Using Advanced Query By Example."

Sorting the Answer Table

By default, the Answer table is sorted in order of the source table for the query. You can change the sort order by using any of the fields in the Answer table.

You can sort in ascending or descending order. Ascending order is the default sort order for Paradox for Windows. It sorts from smallest to largest. Numbers are sorted in numerical order, but alphanumeric fields, even if they contain numbers, are sorted by the order of their characters as read from left to right.

In descending order, records are sorted from the largest to the smallest. Descending sorts can be useful to show the largest accounts, territories, or commissions at the top of a query, followed by smaller field values.

From the Properties menu, choose Answer Table, then Sort. The Sort Table dialog box appears (see fig. 4.29).

Click the first field to use for the sort and press the right-arrow button. The field appears in the Sort By box on the right side of the screen. To sort on more than one field, continue adding fields.

Editing the Answer Table

The Answer table produced by a query has the same properties as other Paradox for Windows tables: it can be edited, its columns can be shifted, and it can be saved or copied as a new table.

You can change the properties of the Answer table before you even run the query. Choose the Properties menu on the Query window. Select Answer Table, then Options. The Answer Table Properties dialog box appears (see fig. 4.30).

I — PARADOX FOR WINDOWS FUNDAMENTALS

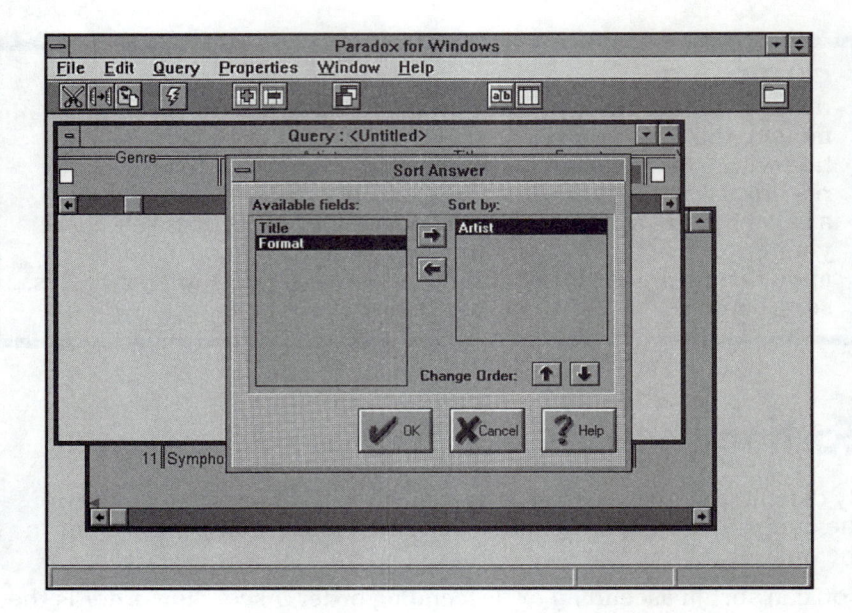

FIG. 4.29

The Sort Table dialog box.

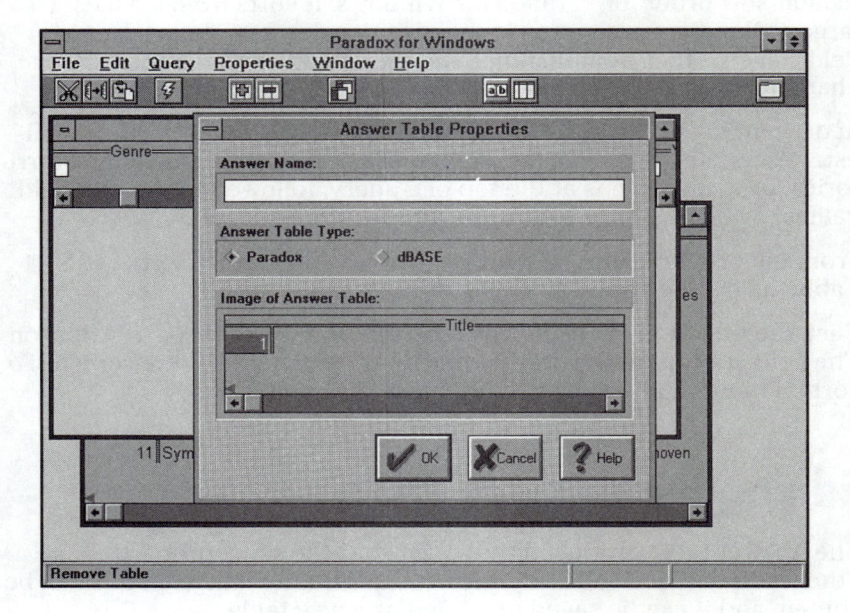

FIG. 4.30

The Answer Table Properties dialog box.

Using the Answer Table Properties dialog box, you can change the name, image, and table type of the Answer table. The supported table types are Paradox and dBASE. By default, a Paradox table type named

4 — GETTING STARTED WITH QUERY BY EXAMPLE

Answer is created and displayed. By changing the image of the Answer table, you control the order in which fields are displayed, color, fonts, and other properties.

> **TIP**
>
> To save the results of the query as a table, rename the Answer table before you run the query. Otherwise, the Answer table is deleted when the next query is run. If you decide to save the Answer table after you have run the query, choose Table, Restructure, then Save As to save the Answer table under another name. You also can use File, Table Utilities, Copy to copy the table or Rename.

> **TIP**
>
> You can use the Answer table as a shortcut for converting data from one table format to another. Just change the table type and name of the Answer table before running the query, and records selected in the query are written to the newly created table in the desired format. This technique is especially useful for extracting some of your records from a native Paradox table and transferring them to a dBASE table.

Printing the Answer Table

The Answer table can be printed like any other Paradox table. The simplest way to print the Answer table is to click the Instant Report button in the SpeedBar. For additional control over the format of printed output, you can create a report from the query as discussed in Chapter 6, "Getting Started with Reports."

Saving the Query

After you have gone to the trouble of writing a query, especially a complicated query, you probably will want to save it for future use. Paradox for Windows enables you to save a query as an object. To save the query, choose Save or Save As from the File menu. Name the query as you would name any Paradox object.

Chapter Summary

The capability to design and run queries is among the most valuable features of Paradox for Windows. Queries enable you to retrieve and sort data in nearly limitless ways, without writing a single line of programming code. If you want to retrieve information from a Paradox for Windows database, start by learning about queries.

Queries are also the basis for report writing and retrieving data with ObjectPAL. You cannot write good ObjectPAL programs without a solid understanding of interactive queries.

Queries have three aspects: field selection, record selection, and calculation. You select fields by entering check marks in the desired data columns. (You can use special check marks to group and sort fields.) You select records by furnishing an example of the values you are trying to find. Finally, queries can perform calculations based on fields in your data tables.

When a query is executed, the results are placed in the Answer table, a special temporary table created by Paradox for Windows. The Answer table can be manipulated (edited, sorted, and rearranged) in the same ways as any other Paradox for Windows table.

The next step in information retrieval is to get printed output from the database. This is the subject of the next chapter, "Getting Started with Forms."

CHAPTER 5

Getting Started with Forms

As you explored in Chapter 3, you can enter, modify, and delete records directly in Paradox tables. Table view is adequate for many tasks, but some tables do not lend themselves to direct access—particularly those with long fields, many fields, or field names that do not adequately guide the user. To make data in these tables more familiar and accessible, you can create customized Paradox forms.

Paradox for Windows uses forms to facilitate data entry and present information to the user. For users, forms are like windows into database tables. Forms can be used to change the order or formatting of fields. For example, users may prefer to see an address formatted like a mailing label rather than strung across the screen from left to right as a series of columns.

Forms and reports are called *design documents*, and they share many characteristics. They contain graphic display objects, such as lines, boxes, ellipses, text, and graphic images, as well as data. Special tools enable you to easily create and manipulate these objects on the form. You use many of the same techniques when creating all design documents, so the skills you learn for form design can be applied to reports.

This chapter shows how to create forms using a single data table. This chapter introduces all the form tools provided by Paradox and offers guidelines for effective form design. You learn how to create boxes, lines, ellipses, text, and graphics (such as a corporate logo) to accompany fields from a database table.

I — PARADOX FOR WINDOWS FUNDAMENTALS

You will find it easy to create simple forms in Paradox. The Instant Form feature gets you started with a basic form, and the tools in the SpeedBar are quickly mastered. Paradox forms are quick and easy, but they also can be powerful and sophisticated. For example, you could build a form for a dental office that records treatment, and also includes a drawing of the patient's mouth, indicating where the work was performed.

For coverage of advanced form techniques, including multi-table forms, calculations, crosstabs, graphs, and filters, see Chapter 7, "Using Advanced Form Techniques." Using ObjectPAL with forms is explained in Chapter 15.

What Is a Paradox Form?

A Paradox *form* is a special screen that enables access to one or more tables for entering, viewing, or editing data. Figure 5.1 shows a typical form. Forms give you more control over how data is displayed than Paradox tables. With forms, you can control the appearance and the order of the fields and add descriptive text labels and background text instructions. You can highlight important fields with a bright color, for example, or draw boxes around groups of fields. You can even add calculated fields that are not stored in the table, such as counts, totals, or today's date.

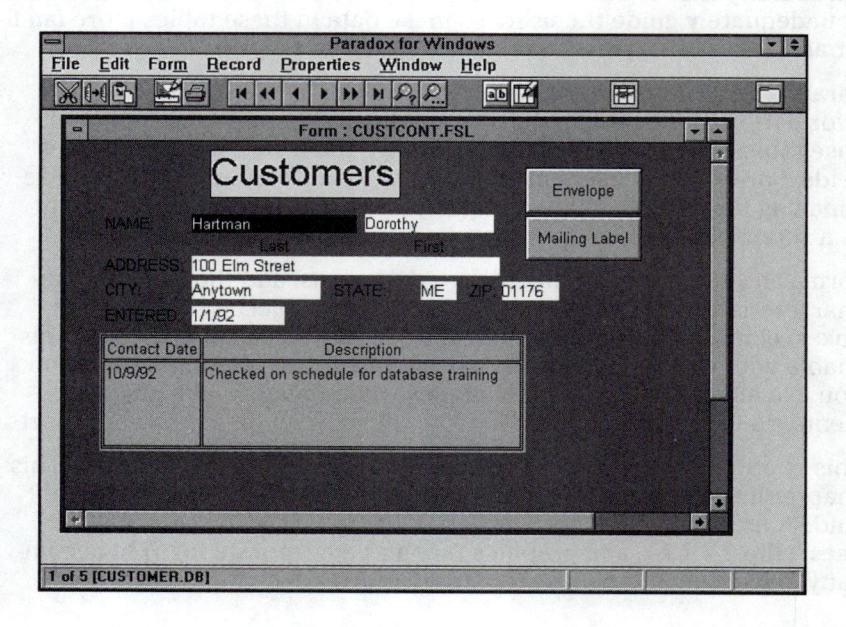

FIG. 5.1

A typical form.

Most users prefer forms to tables because forms are like the paperwork they use every day. A Paradox for Windows form can emulate the paper form so closely that users can enter data without looking up at the screen. Because you are working in Windows, you can use proportional typefaces and images to make database forms more realistic than character-based programs such as Paradox for DOS.

The next section briefly discusses the goals of form design. The middle of the chapter is devoted to the details of handling each type of form object. The chapter concludes with guidelines and tips for form design.

What Is Form Design?

The two keystones of form *design* (and report design) are appearance and consistency. Clear, easy-to-follow forms guide users to quicker and more accurate data entry. Important fields can be highlighted by position and color, and explanatory field labels in English can be used instead of cryptic field names.

Consistency helps users navigate your application. A consistent style makes a database easier to learn because the forms all resemble one another. Consistency also is valuable to you as a developer because you can save a great deal of time if you eliminate many routine decisions about each element you arrange on-screen (such as color, size, and font).

In most cases, the order of fields should match the order of the printed form or the order in which questions are answered for in-person or telephone data collection. You may want to cluster numeric fields—touch typists are proficient with the numeric keypad, and going back and forth from text to numbers slows the data-entry process.

Creating a New Form

If you have read this book from the beginning, you already created a Paradox for Windows form in Quick Start 1. When you enter data in a table, you can switch to a form by pressing F7 or clicking the Instant Form button. The default format created in the instant form is one field per line, with each field preceded by the field name.

NOTE Remember, you must create the Paradox table before you create the form to go along with the table. See Chapter 2 for instructions on creating tables.

To create a new form, choose File, New from the Paradox for Windows main menu, then select Form. This calls up the Data Model dialog box (see fig. 5.2). Use the Data Model dialog box to specify the name of the table or tables to be accessed by the form.

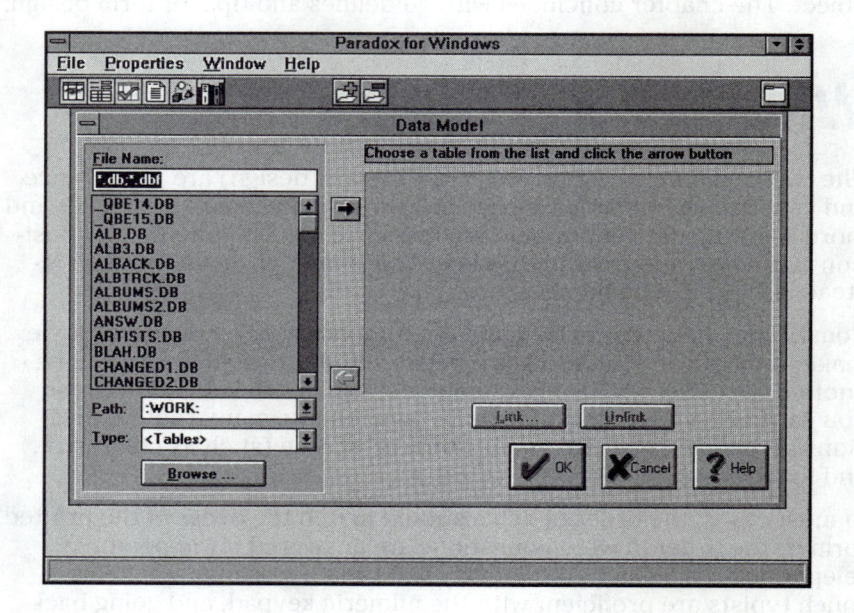

FIG. 5.2
The Data Model dialog box.

The Data Model dialog box contains a list on the left side of the screen of all the tables in your current work directory. You may scroll through the list with the scroll bar if there are more files than can be displayed in the window. On the right is the empty data model.

If you want to choose a table that is not listed in the current work directory, you can change the directory by clicking the Path pull-down menu. The Path menu lists the directory aliases you and the system have defined for Paradox. (An *alias* is a shorthand way to refer to a full DOS directory path.) The Type pull-down menu indicates what type of file is being listed; for form definition it reads <Tables>. To use the Browser, click the Browse button. The Browser is similar to the Windows File Manager and is explained in detail in Chapter 12.

Click the desired table to highlight it, then click the right-arrow symbol. As you select tables, they are shown in the data model area of the dialog box. If you choose the wrong table, click the left-arrow symbol to remove it from the data model. For a single table form, you only need to click the table name to highlight it and click the OK button rather than move the table to the data model area of the dialog box. Although you can design a form that doesn't use a table, in most cases you will want to use fields from a table. In this chapter, you use a single-table form.

NOTE From the Form Design window, you can display the Data Model dialog box by choosing For_m_ from the menu, then selecting Data _M_odel.

For this example, choose the Albums table, and click OK. Next, the Design Layout dialog box appears. You use this dialog box to choose the way that fields are laid out on the form. Figure 5.3 shows the Design Layout dialog box with the default settings for the Albums table.

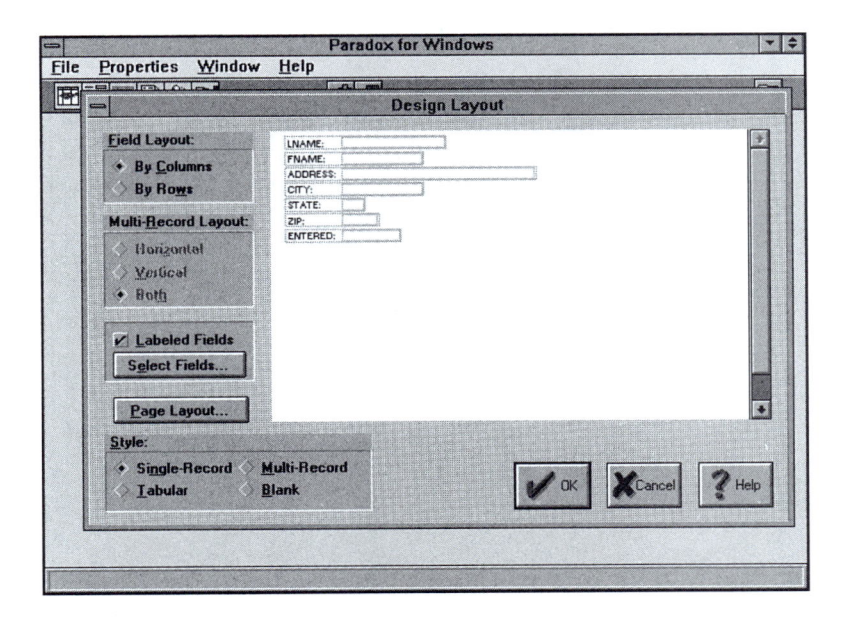

FIG. 5.3

The Design Layout dialog box.

NOTE If you are already in the Form Design window, you can display the Design Layout dialog box by choosing _D_esign from the menu, and then Design _L_ayout.

Choosing Design Layout for Fields

The first decision you should make in the Design Layout dialog box is whether fields should be listed from top to bottom or left to right. If you choose the By Columns option, one field is displayed per line, starting on the first line of the form. The By Rows option places fields after one another on a line until the line is full, then moves to the next line.

The Labeled Fields check box turns field labels on and off. The default setting is on. This option is not allowed in the tabular layout, in which field labels are always turned on.

The Select Fields button enables you to choose which fields from the table are shown on the form. Click the Select Fields button to display the Select Fields dialog box, as shown in figure 5.4.

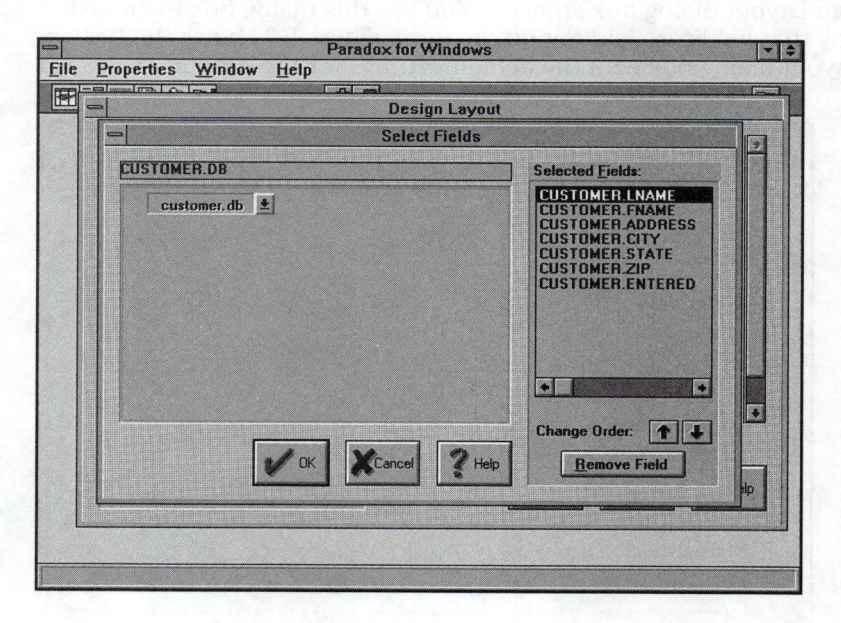

FIG. 5.4

The Select Fields dialog box.

On the left side of the Select Fields dialog box is the table (or tables) chosen for the form. On the right side of the dialog box is a list of all the fields included in the form. By default, all fields in the table are included in the list. To remove a field, click the field name to highlight it, then click the Remove Field button.

To change the order of the fields, highlight the field you want to move and click the arrow buttons next to Change Order to move the field up or down the list. To add a field to the form, click the pull-down menu

5 — GETTING STARTED WITH FORMS

next to the table name to reveal the list of fields, then click the desired field. When you have completed your choices, click OK to return to the Design Layout dialog box.

Page Layout is the next button on the Design Layout dialog box. Paradox defaults to screen design for forms and examines your Windows configuration for the screen size. If you choose Printer, you have many more options to change the printer orientation, paper size, and units of measure. If you choose to design a form for the printer, Paradox will restrict you to the fonts available for the printer you have selected in Windows.

You use the set of buttons in the lower-left corner of the Design Layout dialog box to choose the layout style of the form. This is the starting point for your custom design.

Selecting a Style

As shown at the bottom of the Design Layout dialog box (refer to fig. 5.3), Paradox for Windows offers four style options:

Single-Record. Displays one record at a time in the same layout as an instant form, with each field on a separate line following the field name (see fig. 5.5).

Multi-Record. Displays more than one record at a time, in a fashion similar to the single-record format. Displays more than one record by replicating the single-record format for as many records as will fit on-screen. A sample multi-record format is shown in figure 5.6.

Tabular. Displays the rows and columns as if you were working directly with the table (see fig. 5.7). If the table extends beyond the edge of the screen, you can scroll to reveal the rest of the table.

Blank. Displays an empty form. You must position each of the fields.

> **TIP**
>
> Even if you plan to make major changes to a form design, start with the single-record layout rather than the blank layout. Moving fields around the form is often easier than placing them one at a time on a blank form. When you start with all the fields displayed, you can easily judge how much space they occupy.

FIG. 5.5

An example of single-record style.

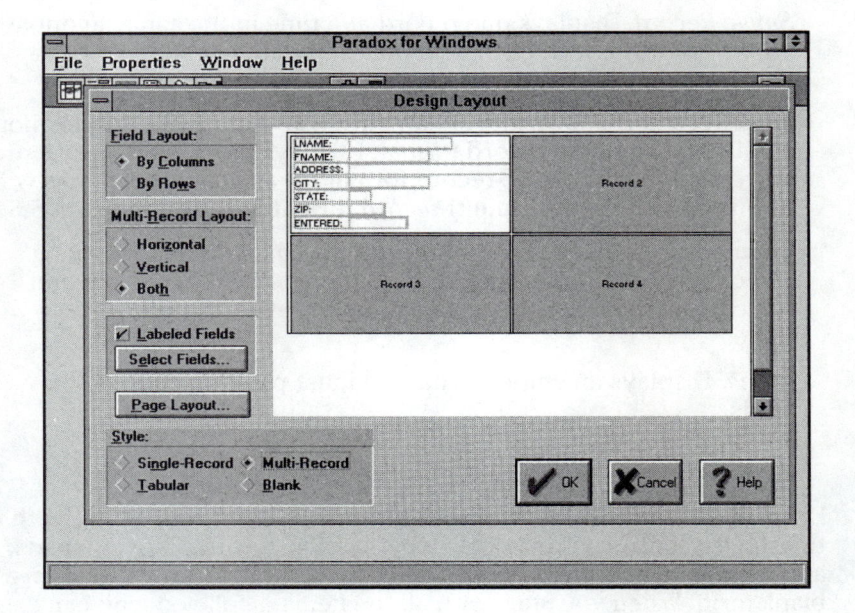

FIG. 5.6

An example of multi-record style, both horizontal and vertical.

For the Multi-Record style, you must choose whether multiple records are listed horizontally, vertically, or both horizontally and vertically (the default) as much as space allows (refer to fig. 5.6). If you choose Horizontal, a block containing all the fields is repeated from left to right

5 — GETTING STARTED WITH FORMS

in a single row, as shown in figure 5.8. If you choose Vertical, the records repeat in a column, as shown in figure 5.9. In the Both option, records are repeated in rows and columns, similar to mailing labels printed several labels across, as shown in figure 5.6.

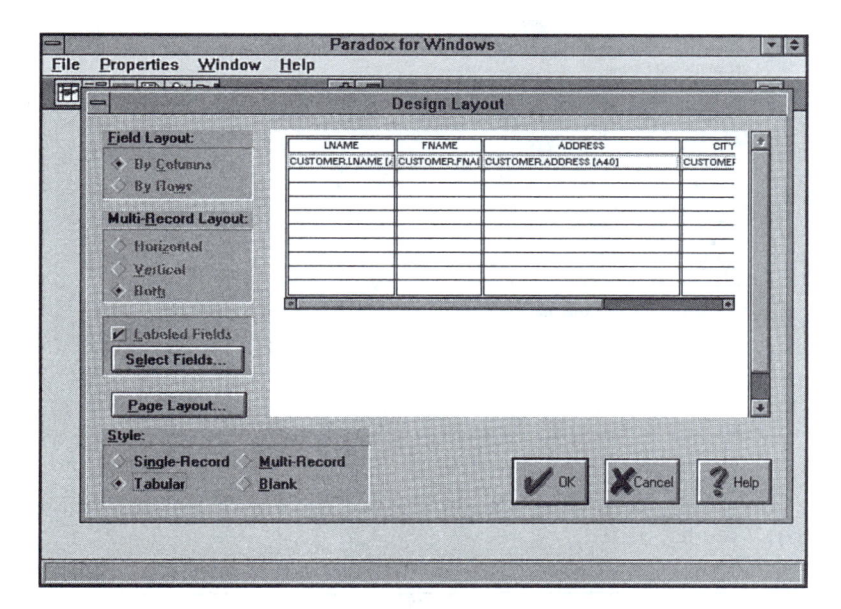

FIG. 5.7

An example of tabular style.

FIG. 5.8

An example of multi-record style, Horizontal layout.

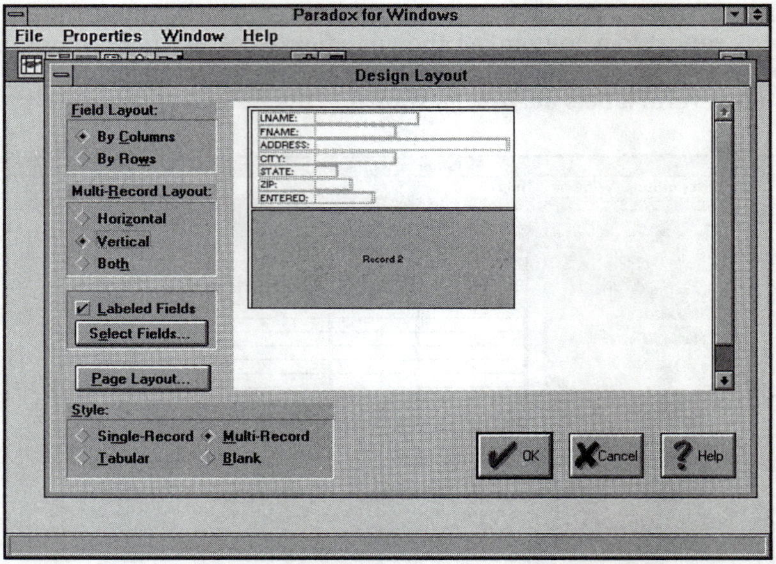

I — PARADOX FOR WINDOWS FUNDAMENTALS

FIG. 5.9

An example of multi-record style, Vertical layout.

After you set the layout style and click OK, the Form Design window appears (see fig. 5.10).

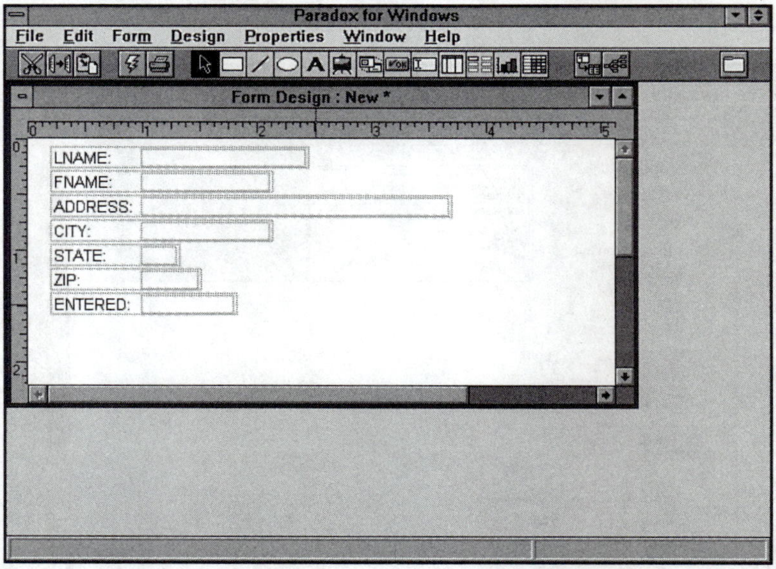

FIG. 5.10

The Form Design window.

5 — GETTING STARTED WITH FORMS

The Form Design window is where you design the form. This window consists of the title and menu bars, the SpeedBar, and the work area. The following section explains each of the tools in the SpeedBar.

For Related Information
▶▶ "Creating a Multi-Table Form," p. 324.

▶▶ "Creating Multi-Table Forms," p. 336.

FROM HERE...

Working in the Form Design Window

The Form Design window is where you perform most of your design work, including adding, deleting, moving, and modifying all screen objects. You can add elements such as boxes, ellipses, lines, and bit-mapped graphic images to spice up the appearance of a form and complement database fields.

Before manipulating objects on-screen, however, you must learn how to select them. This is the purpose of the first tool in the SpeedBar, the Selection Arrow. This tool is discussed under "Selecting Objects."

Paradox provides specialized tools for handling different types of screen objects. The twelve form design buttons in the SpeedBar (to the right of the selection arrow) are specialized tools for handling different types of screen objects (see fig. 5.11). Each of these tools is listed in table 5.1 and discussed in order of its appearance in the sections that follow.

Table 5.1. Design Tools in the Forms SpeedBar

Button	Name
▢	Selection Arrow tool
▭	Box tool
╱	Line tool

continues

Table 5.1. Continued

Button	Name
	Ellipse tool
	Text tool
	Graphic tool
	OLE tool
	Button tool
	Field tool
	Table tool
	Multi-record tool
	Graph tool
	Crosstab tool

FIG. 5.11

Form design tools in the SpeedBar.

Each screen object has a set of characteristics called *properties*. Each type of object contains a different set of properties. Some properties, such as color, are common to nearly every object. When you create an object, it has standard, or default, properties, which you can change by inspecting the object and choosing from its properties menu. The following sections explain the properties offered for each type of form object.

Selecting Objects

To create, move, or modify objects in a form, you must select them. You can select objects with the Selection Arrow tool (the first button in the SpeedBar) or from the keyboard. When you click the Selection Arrow to activate it, the mouse pointer becomes an arrow. The Selection Arrow is the default tool for this window, so the mouse pointer may already be an arrow.

When you select an object, small squares called *handles* appear around the object. You use the handles to drag the object in the workspace and to change the size or shape of the object. To stretch a box, for example, click a handle in the middle of one of its sides and drag it to the desired size. Click a handle on the corner of a box and drag to change both its height and width.

To move an object, click inside the object (not on its handles) and drag it to the desired location.

To select objects from the keyboard, press Tab to move the selection handles from the currently selected object to the next object in the form. To back up to the previous object, press Shift+Tab.

You can select one object or several objects at a time. To select multiple objects, press Shift while clicking the first object, then move to the next object and Shift+click again. Repeat this until you have selected all the objects you need. This is called the *Shift+click technique*.

Another way to select multiple objects is to define a rectangle on-screen and select all objects inside it. Paradox calls this the *Shift+drag technique*. First position the mouse pointer in a corner of the area to be selected. Then press Shift while holding down the left mouse button. Next, drag the mouse pointer to the diagonal corner. A dotted line shows the shape of the rectangle as you drag it. When you release the mouse button, all the objects in the rectangle are selected.

Finally, you can select all the objects in the window by choosing Select All from the Edit menu.

To deselect an object, place the mouse pointer on the selected object and press Shift+click again. The handles disappear. When two objects are close together, pressing Shift+click may select the second object rather than deselect the first object. Try Shift+click again until the object is deselected.

After you have selected one or more objects, you can manipulate them in several ways. You can move the objects by clicking and dragging, or use the Edit menu to cut, paste, or copy selected objects. The Edit menu commands have keyboard equivalents, which you may find quicker to use. These keyboard shortcuts are Shift+Del for Cut, Ctrl+Ins for Copy, Shift+Ins for Paste, and Del for Delete.

Displaying Object Properties

All Paradox objects have a set of characteristics, or properties, that you can control. To display the properties of an object, right-click the selected object, press Shift+F8, or choose Properties, Current Object from the Form Design window. Paradox calls this action *inspecting* an object.

Displaying Tool Properties

The SpeedBar tools have their own set of properties as well. You can define standard properties for all the objects you define. To display the properties of a tool, right-click the tool's icon in the SpeedBar. A properties menu appears with the heading PROTO, indicating that you are defining a prototype object (see fig. 5.12).

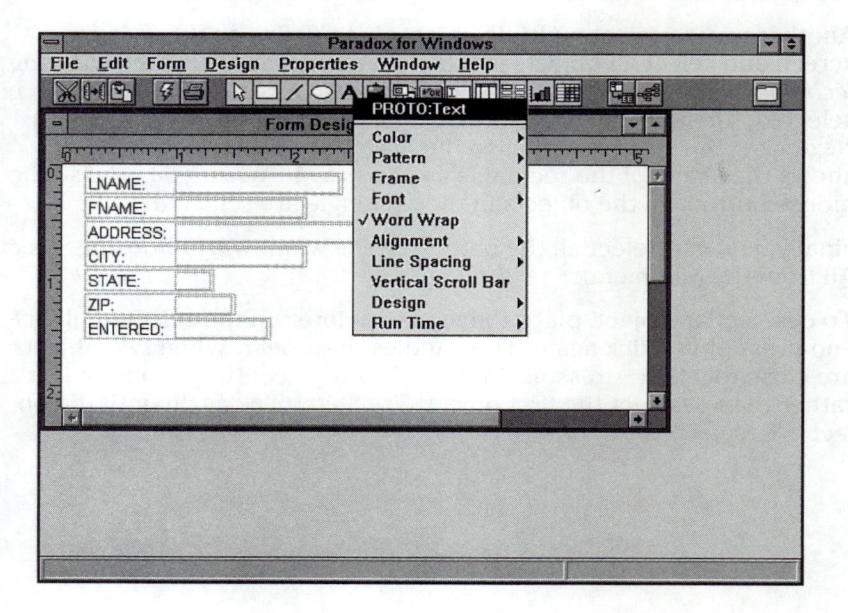

FIG. 5.12

The Text tool properties menu.

5 — GETTING STARTED WITH FORMS

For example, you may want to change all text from black (the default) to gray. Right-click the Text tool, then click Font from its properties menu. Click Color from the Font menu and choose the desired color from the color palette. Create a text object and enter some text to verify the color change.

> **NOTE** Changing the properties of a tool affects only the objects you create subsequently with that tool. Objects already on the form retain their original properties.

Drawing Boxes, Ellipses, and Lines

Paradox for Windows includes basic drawing capabilities for embellishing your forms. The Box, Line, and Ellipse tools in the SpeedBar work in much the same way as the tools in paint programs such as Microsoft Windows Paintbrush. Figure 5.13 shows a form with a box, a line, and an ellipse.

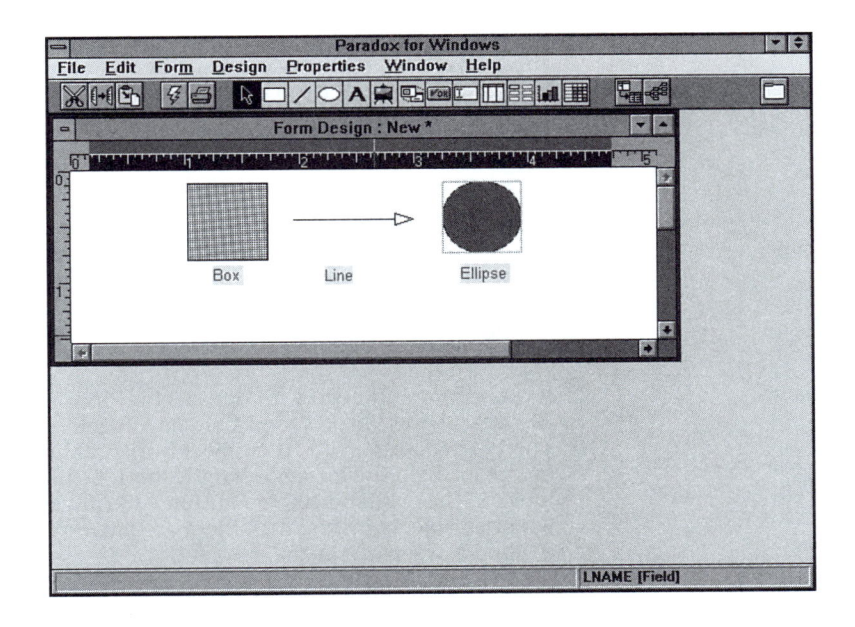

FIG. 5.13

A form with a box, a line, and an ellipse.

The Box tool, Line tool, and Ellipse tool all work in the same way. To use any of these tools, follow these steps:

1. In the SpeedBar, click the tool you want to use.

2. Move the mouse pointer to the starting point for the line, for the corner of the box, or for the edge of the ellipse.

I — PARADOX FOR WINDOWS FUNDAMENTALS

If you choose the Line tool, the mouse pointer changes from an arrow to a pencil. For the Box tool, the mouse pointer is a box under a crosshair. For the Ellipse tool, the mouse pointer is shown as a circle under a crosshair.

3. Click the mouse button to mark the starting point and drag the mouse to the desired length or shape of the object. When you release the mouse button, the object is drawn. If you do not like its shape, you can stretch or shrink the object by clicking its handles and dragging it until the desired dimensions.

These drawn objects have their own list of properties you can modify to change their appearance. Boxes and ellipses have essentially the same properties:

Property	Description
Color	Controls the fill color inside the object. For more information on colors, see "Setting Field Colors" later in this chapter.
Line	In an ellipse, controls the style, color, and thickness of the line that defines the outside of the object. This property displays a palette showing all the frame styles available. Note that for boxes this property is called Frame.
Pattern	Controls the color and style of the fill pattern inside the object (such as crosshair or dots). Paradox provides a palette that shows all the available patterns.
Frame	In a box, controls the style, color, and thickness of the line that defines the outside of the object. This property displays a palette showing all the frame styles available. Note that this property is called Line for an ellipse.
Design	A properties submenu with options for Pin Horizontal, Pin Vertical, and Contain Objects. The Pin properties affix the object horizontally or vertically in the form so that it cannot be moved. The Contain Objects option determines whether objects inside this object are moved or deleted along with the main object.
Run Time	Determines whether objects will be displayed or hidden when the form is used. Visible is the default setting, but invisible objects may be used as containers for other form objects.
Methods	Controls the behavior of the object in different situations. This option is used with ObjectPAL. Part III is devoted to ObjectPAL programming techniques.

5 — GETTING STARTED WITH FORMS

To change the properties of the object, click the list of properties and choose from the options for each property. The property changes take effect immediately so that you can see your results.

Lines offer a slightly different set of properties, as shown in the following table:

Property	Description
Color	Controls the color of the line. For more information on colors, see "Setting Field Colors" later in this chapter.
Line Style	Offers invisible, solid, and four different patterns of broken lines. When you choose Line style, a palette is displayed, showing each line style.
Line Type	Enables you to draw straight or curved lines. To draw a curved line, create it as a straight line and then change the line type property to Curved. To straighten a curved line, inspect its properties and change the Line Type to Normal.
Line Ends	Enables you to attach arrows to neither, either, or both ends of a line. No Arrow is the default for this property. If you choose On One End, the arrow is attached to the end of the line as you drew it—the end where you released the mouse button. To change the direction of the arrow, you must redraw the line. If you choose On Both Ends, arrows are attached to both ends of the line.
Thickness	Changes the thickness of the line, with seven degrees of thickness available. The default is a thin line. Like the Line Style property, Thickness enables you to choose from a palette of line widths.
Design	A properties submenu with options for Pin Horizontal and Pin Vertical. The Pin properties affix the line horizontally or vertically in the form so that it cannot be moved.
Run Time	Determines whether objects will be displayed or hidden when the form is used. Visible is the default setting, but invisible lines may be used as to control the movement of other form objects.
Methods	Controls the behavior of the line in different situations. This option is used with ObjectPAL.

The properties chosen from palettes (color, pattern, frame, font, line style, and line thickness) offer a special feature. If you click the round button at the top of the palette, it becomes a floating palette. This means that the palette remains on-screen while you are working with objects. This is useful if you are modifying the same property on several objects. Some floating palettes display extra features as well or offer a button to access a related dialog box (such as the custom color dialog box).

To change a line's properties, select the object and right-click to reveal the line properties menu. Use the mouse to choose from the properties listed.

NOTE The Elliptical line type is not compatible with arrows using Line Ends. Therefore, you may place arrows only on straight lines.

TIP If you want to use the same object more than once, select the object by clicking it and then choose Edit, Copy. Click on the page to indicate where you want the copy to appear, and then click the Paste tool to place the copy on the form. Repeat the positioning and pasting operations as many times as needed to complete your use of the object.

Adding Text

The next icon in the SpeedBar, the one with the letter A, is the Text tool. The Text tool is used to create screen objects that contain one or more lines of text. You can use text objects as titles for the form, or to provide on-screen help to explain how the form works. Text in Paradox for Windows can be manipulated in ways that ordinary text in a character-based application (such as Paradox for DOS) cannot be manipulated, such as controlling the type font and size.

To create a text object, follow these steps:

1. Click the Text tool. The mouse pointer changes to an A under a crosshair.

2. Position the mouse pointer in one corner of the box where the text should appear, then click and drag diagonally to make the text object the desired length and width. Don't worry about guessing the exact size of the text; you can adjust the box after you enter the text.

When you release the mouse button, the outline of the text object appears, with the mouse pointer in the upper-left corner. (If you choose center or right alignment for the text object, the cursor is placed in the center or on the right side of the line.)

3. Click again so that the mouse pointer changes to indicate you are in text edit mode (the insertion point looks like][).
4. Practice entering some text. The text wraps automatically in the text object. If you fill the entire box, the text scrolls up so that you can enter more.

The finished text object will look something like figure 5.14.

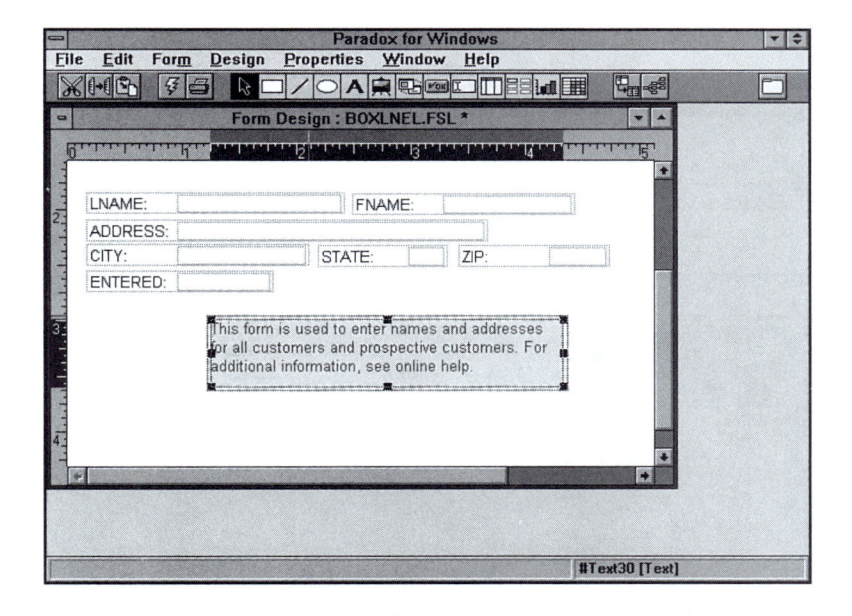

FIG. 5.14

A text object in a form.

The text object has thirteen properties, not counting submenus. To view the properties of the text object, place the mouse pointer in the box and right-click. The properties are displayed as shown in figure 5.15.

Many of the properties of a text object are the same as those for other objects. An unusual property is Search Text. This is not really a property, but rather a feature to help you correct errors in text. When you select Search Text, the Search & Replace dialog box appears, as shown in figure 5.16.

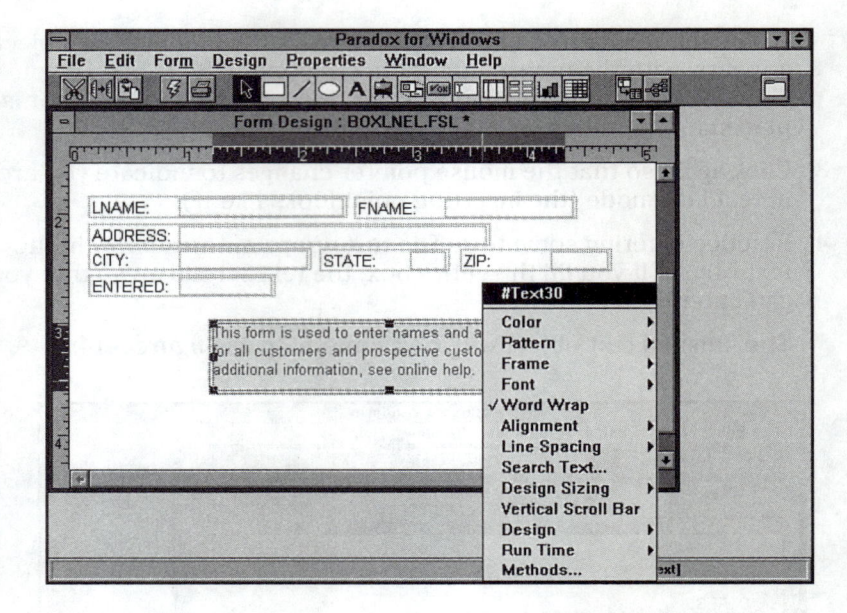

FIG. 5.15

The properties of a text object.

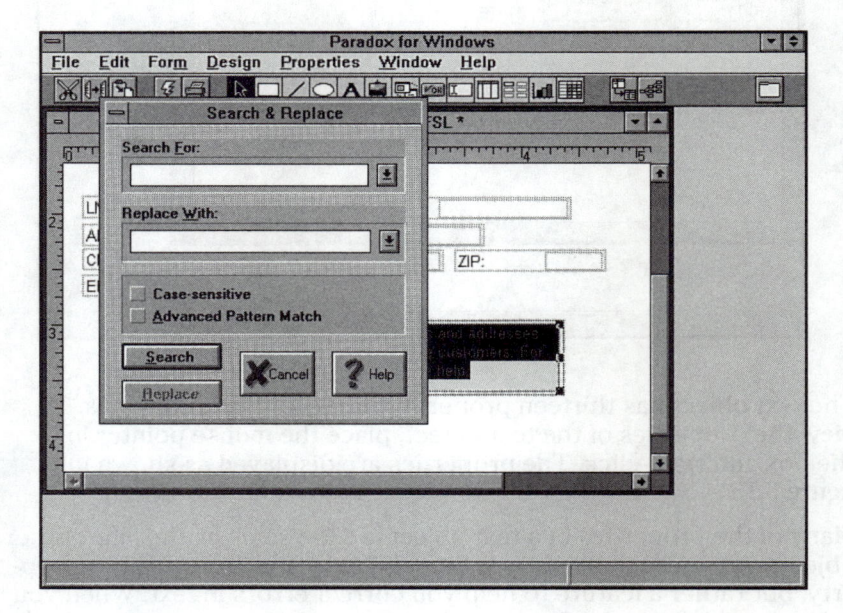

FIG. 5.16

The text object's Search & Replace dialog box.

Search & Replace works only in the text object you have selected. You can search forward or backward, search with case (capitalization) sensitivity or not, and replace all occurrences (globally) or a single occurrence.

5 — GETTING STARTED WITH FORMS

Another text property, Design Sizing, has to do with the ways in which the text object accommodates entries longer than the box. You can choose the default of Fixed size (which allows scrolling), Fit Text, or Grow Only (which grows as large as necessary so that all the text can be viewed at one time). Fit Text works in two different ways. With Word Wrap on, the box grows or shrinks vertically, adding new lines to accommodate long text entries. With Word Wrap turned off, the line can expand or shrink horizontally to show all the text. This property is more important in reports than in forms. The size of text may vary in reports, but in a form, you know how much space to allocate for a text object.

The Word Wrap property controls the behavior of text when it reaches the end of a line. With Word Wrap selected (a check mark is displayed), a word that is too large to fit at the end of a line advances automatically to the beginning of the next line. Without Word Wrap, text continues beyond the edge of the text object, so all the text may not be visible.

You can set the alignment of text in the text object to Left (the default), Right, Centered, or Justify. Left alignment starts each line of text in the leftmost column, with a ragged right margin. Right alignment lines up all lines on the right with a ragged left margin. The Centered option centers each line independently, so both margins may be ragged. Justify inserts spaces in the text so that the text aligns on both left and right sides. Unless all the text lines are close to the same length, justified alignment can produce unpleasant results. Figure 5.17 shows samples of each form of alignment.

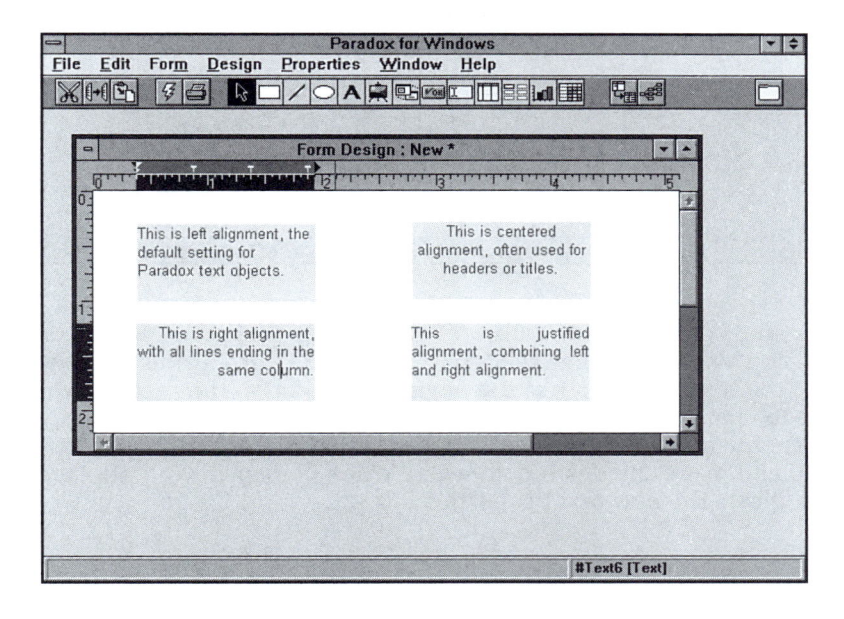

FIG. 5.17

Different text object alignments.

I — PARADOX FOR WINDOWS FUNDAMENTALS

Line spacing can be set to 1 line, 1.5 lines, 2 lines, 2.5 lines, and 3 lines. Single spacing is usually the most effective because it conserves screen space, which is often in short supply in your form.

The Font property enables you to change the font of the text. This property calls up a submenu that offers options for the typeface, size, style, and color of the text. The size is expressed in points. Type styles are normal, bold, italic, strikeout, underline, double underline, and word underline. The color option displays a color palette offering 25 colors, including 8 custom colors and a transparent color.

As an alternative to selecting these submenu options separately, you can click the round button at the top of the Font menu to use the floating Font menu. The floating Font menu, shown in figure 5.18, is similar to the floating color palette; it gives a list of the available typefaces and styles.

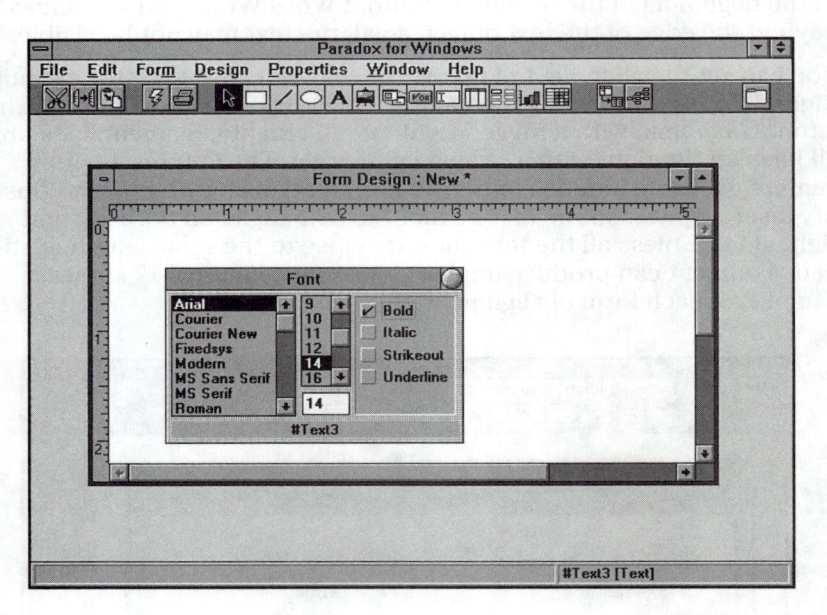

FIG. 5.18

The floating Font menu.

You can mix fonts in a text object by changing the font as you enter the text. You also can change the font (or other text properties) after you enter the text. First, click at the beginning or end of the section you want to change and drag the mouse so that the text is highlighted, then release the mouse button. Next, right-click to reveal the properties menu and make any desired changes. When you make your choice, the form shows the new text properties.

When all the text cannot be displayed at the same time in a text object, you should include a scroll bar. The scroll bar indicates how much of the text is hidden and provides a simple means for moving the text in the box. Clicking the Vert Scrollbar property places a scroll bar on the side of the text object, as shown in figure 5.19.

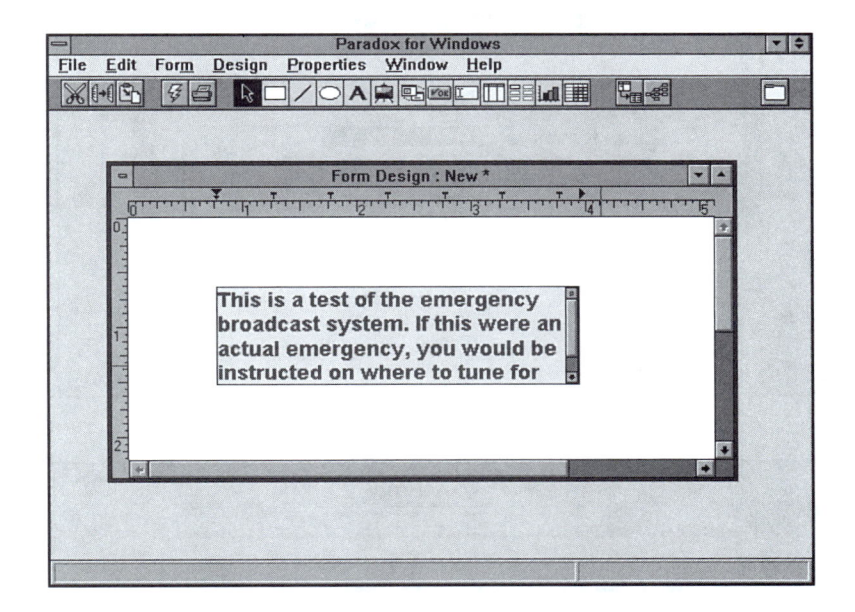

FIG. 5.19

A text object with a scroll bar.

The Color property controls the background color of the text object, using the same palette that controls the color of all objects. Figure 5.20 shows the color palette.

If using a bold color doesn't highlight the text enough, you can use patterns to highlight the background of a text object. You can choose from two dozen patterns, such as diagonal lines, crosshatching, and the popular brick wall motif. These patterns are especially effective for users with monochrome monitors, who cannot take advantage of Windows in color. If you do use color, be sparing with patterns. See figure 5.21 for the Pattern, Style property options available in Paradox for Windows.

To separate the text object from the rest of the form, you can surround the object with a frame or border. The Frame property has several line styles, and you can choose a thick or thin line in any palette color.

I — PARADOX FOR WINDOWS FUNDAMENTALS

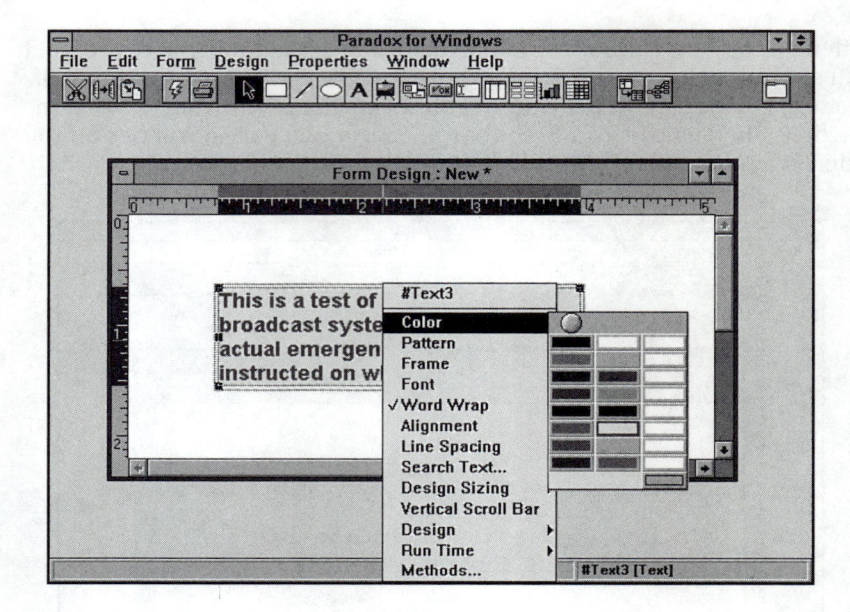

FIG. 5.20

The text object's Color palette.

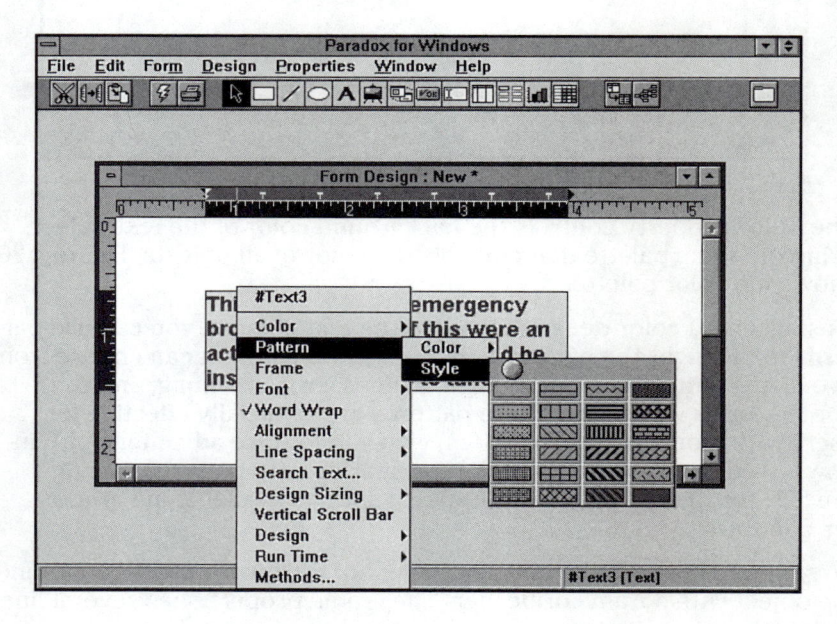

FIG. 5.21

The text object's Pattern, Style property.

The text object's Design property brings up a submenu with choices for Pin Horizontal, Pin Vertical, and Contain Objects. The Pin options affix a screen element in a position on the form so that the user cannot move it. A text object can be affixed vertically, horizontally, or both, by checking the Pin Horizontal and Pin Vertical options in the Design property. With Contain Objects checked (the default) Paradox enables you to handle all objects within this text object as a unit (for moving or deleting for instance).

The Methods property is used with ObjectPAL to attach code to a graphic. Methods are discussed at length in Part III of this book.

> **TIP**
>
> Be careful about using large fonts for forms because they occupy more screen space and may be more difficult to read than smaller fonts. The default Courier font, for example, is too large for many field labels, and is thin and difficult to read. You may also want to avoid fancy fonts such as script, because they are more difficult to read than plainer fonts. The display and printer fonts available to you depend on which fonts you have installed in Windows.

Adding a Graphic

Graphics on forms instantly let you know that you are looking at a Windows database instead of its DOS predecessor. A *graphic* is a bit-mapped image, such as a digitized photograph, a button, or a symbol. Do not confuse a graphic with a Paradox graph, such as a bar graph or pie chart, although both graphs and graphics may be placed in forms. Paradox has separate tools for graphics and graphs.

You define a graphic for a Paradox for Windows form in three steps. First, you create a bit-mapped image file using a scanner or a drawing program. Paradox for Windows accepts images from the Windows Clipboard or those saved as BMP, PCX, TIF, GIF, and EPS files. Most Windows graphics programs, including Microsoft Paintbrush (which comes with Windows), save images as BMP files. Microsoft Paintbrush also converts files from other graphics formats, such as MSO and PCX, to BMP files.

The second step is to define the area on the form where you want the graphic to appear. Select the Graphic tool, a button with a painter's easel, which is in the SpeedBar at the top of the Form Design window.

I — PARADOX FOR WINDOWS FUNDAMENTALS

After you choose the Graphic tool, the mouse pointer changes to resemble the graphic icon. Click one corner of the desired location of the graphic and drag to the opposite corner. A box stretches to show where the graphic is located (see fig. 5.22).

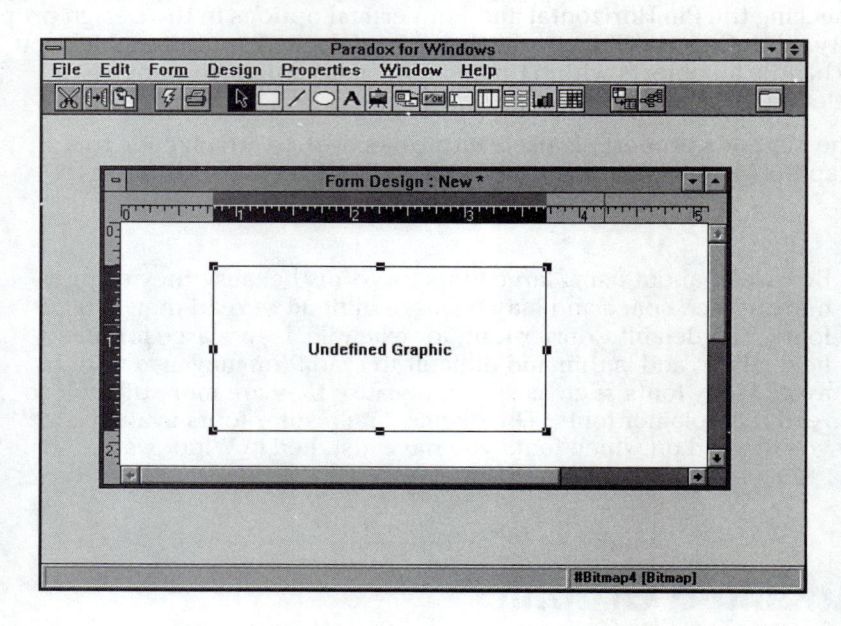

FIG. 5.22

An undefined graphic object.

The third step is to connect the object to the graphic file it will display. Place the mouse pointer on the graphic area and right-click to reveal the object properties menu, as shown in figure 5.23. You can view properties also by choosing Properties from the Options menu or by pressing Shift+F8.

To specify the graphics file, choose Define Graphic, then Paste From. The Paste From Graphic File dialog box appears (see fig. 5.24). You can use images from the Clipboard or any files in BMP format. For this example, use BMP files furnished with Windows.

If the graphic is not in the current directory path, click the Browse button at the bottom of the Paste From Graphic File dialog box. The Browser dialog box is displayed (see fig. 5.25). You can use the Browser to navigate all the directories on your computer. If you know the directory path, you can enter it in the directory field in the dialog box.

5 — GETTING STARTED WITH FORMS

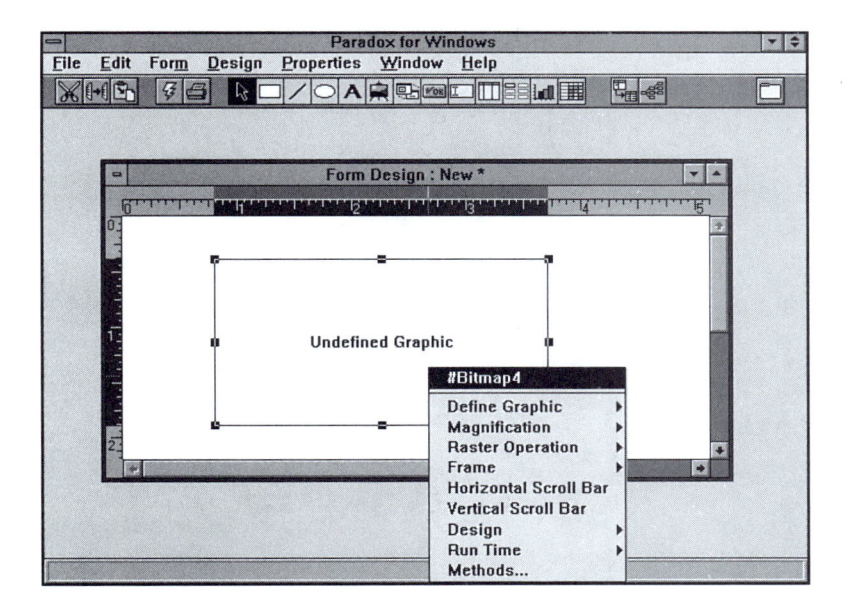

FIG. 5.23

The graphic object properties menu.

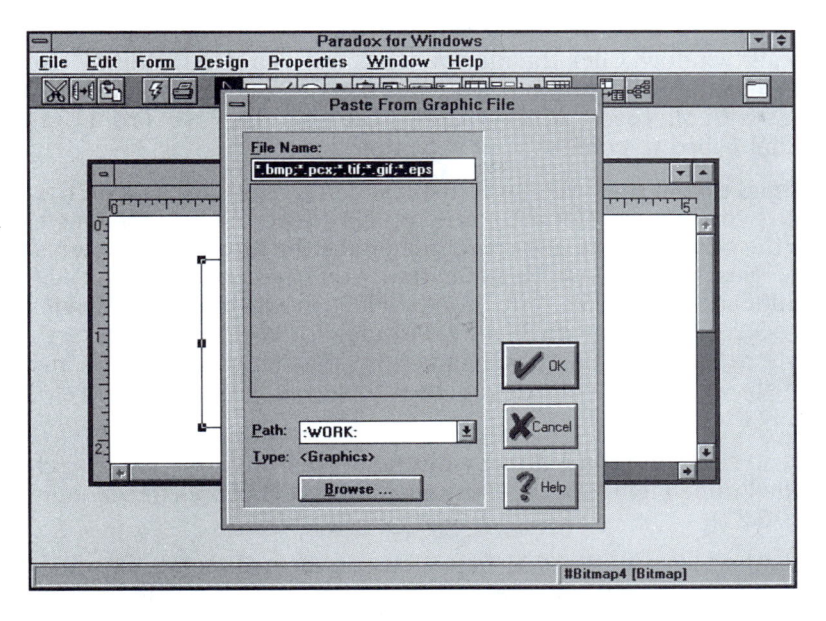

FIG. 5.24

The Paste From Graphic File dialog box.

I — PARADOX FOR WINDOWS FUNDAMENTALS

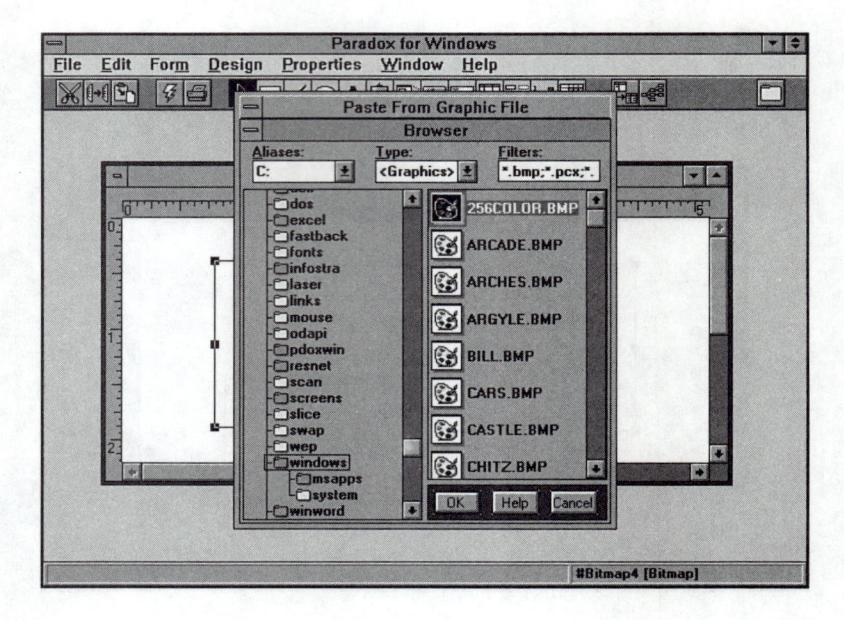

FIG. 5.25

The Browser dialog box.

When you choose a directory, the BMP files are displayed in the Browser window. Click the file you want, such as HARLQN.BMP used for this example. If you want, you may use one of the graphics files that comes with Microsoft Windows. Click OK from the Paste From Graphic File dialog box to confirm your selection.

The image from the BMP file is displayed in the graphic box on the form. If you choose a large image, you may need to scale the image to fit in the box. To scale a graphic, right-click the graphic to show its properties, then choose Magnification. You can choose a degree of magnification from 25% reduction to 400% enlargement, as shown in figure 5.26. If you choose Best Fit, Paradox for Windows chooses the magnification, which may go beyond the 25% minimum or 400% maximum shown on the menu. If you want to see all of the image, Best Fit is usually the right choice.

You can surround the graphic with the border of your choice by choosing the Frame menu option in the graphic object properties menu (refer to fig. 5.23).

The Embed Surrounded Object option connects objects within the graphic to the graphic so that they can be moved or deleted as a single unit. The default setting is ON, indicated by a check mark.

If the image is too big to be viewed in the graphic window, you can attach horizontal and vertical scroll bars to allow users to move the image in the window. Select either Horizontal Scrollbar or Vertical ScrollBar from the object properties menu to attach scroll bars.

FIG. 5.26

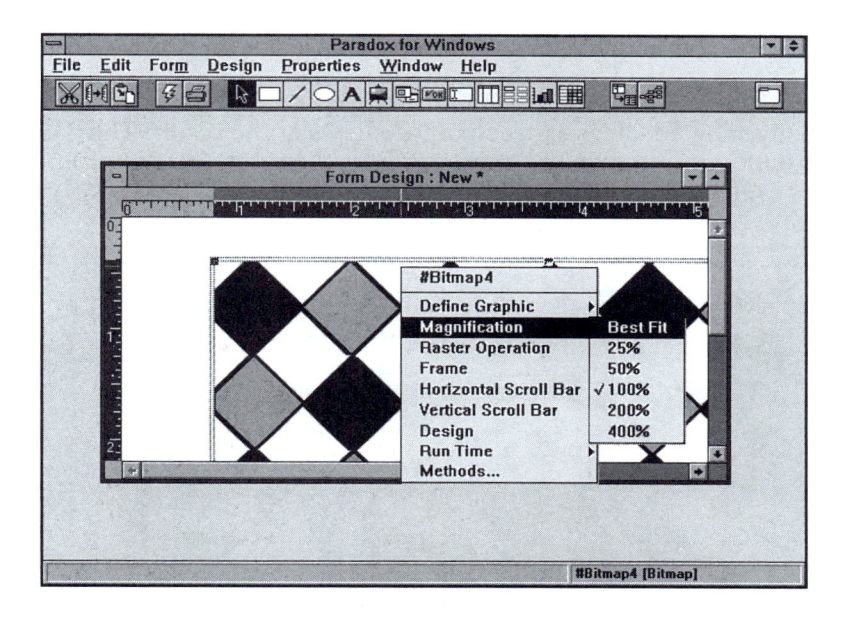

Graphic magnification options.

The Design option on the graphic object properties menu controls how the graphic is positioned on the form at run time. The Pin Horizontal and Pin Vertical options affix the graphic on the form, either horizontally, vertically, or both. The Contain Object option controls other objects placed within the graphic. The Size To Fit option allows the object to be adjusted for the best fit in the form.

Finally, the Methods menu item enables you to attach ObjectPAL code to the graphic so that the object can respond to events triggered by the user. See Chapter 13 for a discussion on using graphic fields with ObjectPAL.

TIP

You can easily overuse graphic images, especially when you are new to Windows. Be sure that graphics add to the usefulness of the form and are not there just because they are possible. The frequent use of a corporate logo may be good for business presentations, for example, but is not necessary for data-entry screens used by people who know all too well where they are working each day.

If you are a newcomer to graphical user interfaces such as Windows, you may be skeptical about the value of graphics in database applications. Soon, however, you will come up with intriguing uses for graphics.

I — PARADOX FOR WINDOWS FUNDAMENTALS

The following example uses graphics to enliven a boring form. A ski resort keeps track of the snow depth on each of its slopes to help customers choose where to make their runs (see fig. 5.27). A table stores the daily snow readings for each of the slopes at the resort. The data is superimposed on a map of the mountain, rather than presented as mere text (the slope names) and numbers (the snow depth).

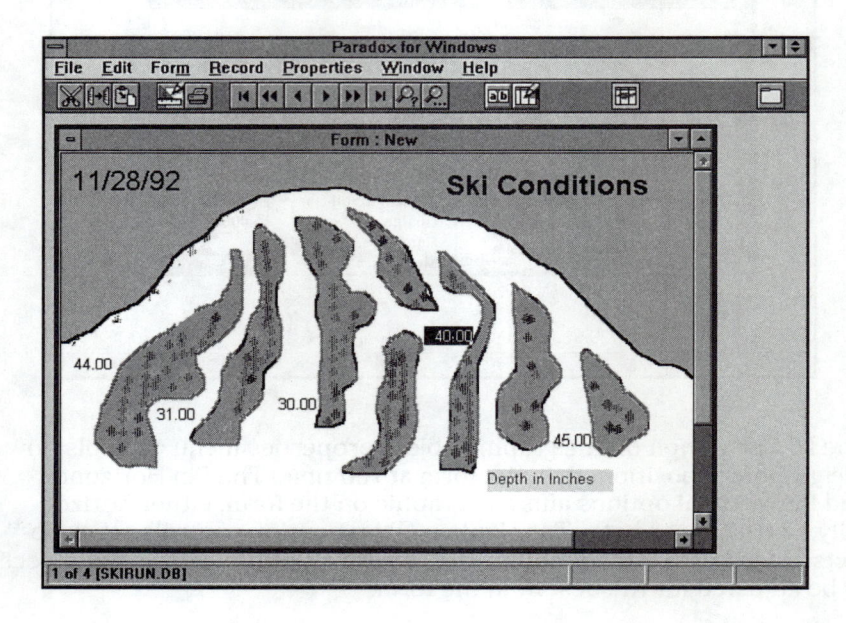

FIG. 5.27

The finished ski slope map form.

To create this form, you first must build the table to store the data. From the Paradox Main menu, choose File, New, Table. Create a new table called SKIRUN. Copy the field definitions from figure 5.28.

After you have created the table, enter a few sample records, such as those shown in the table in figure 5.29. See Chapter 3, "Entering, Editing, and Viewing Data," for detailed instructions on record entry.

Next, you must have a file containing the graphic you plan to use. In many cases, you will use graphics you have purchased or downloaded from bulletin boards. For this example, create a ski map by drawing it in Paintbrush or another drawing program. Use the freehand brush to create the outline of the map, then fill regions with the paint roller. The Spray Paint tool was used to add highlights to the trees between slopes, as shown in figure 5.30. To make the map more detailed, you could add symbols to denote the difficulty of the slope or lines to show ski lifts.

5 — GETTING STARTED WITH FORMS

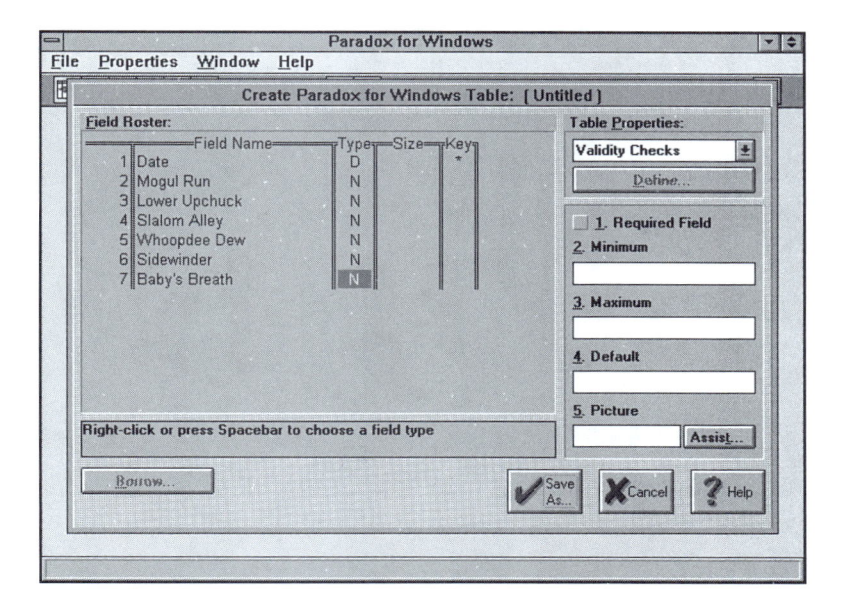

FIG. 5.28
The field definitions for the SKIRUN table.

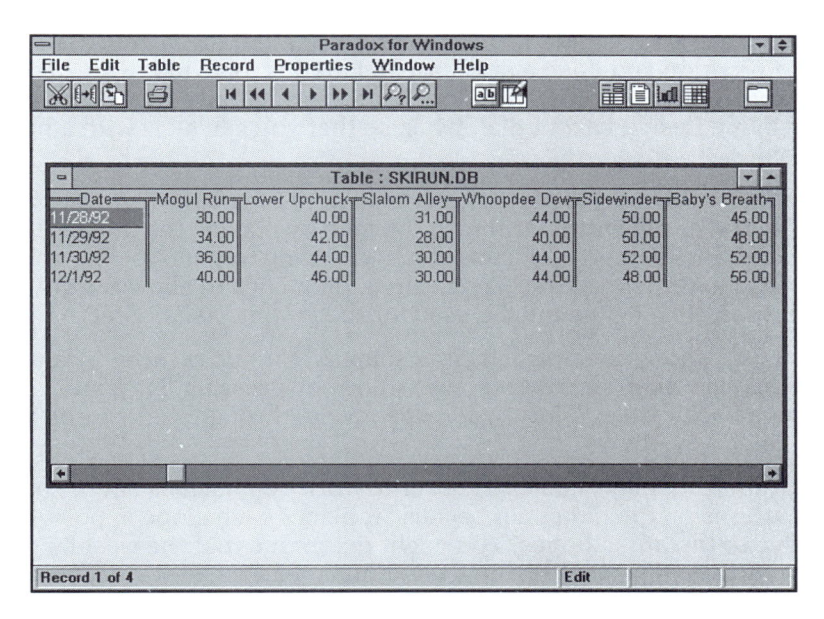

FIG. 5.29
The SKIRUN table with some data entered.

FIG. 5.30

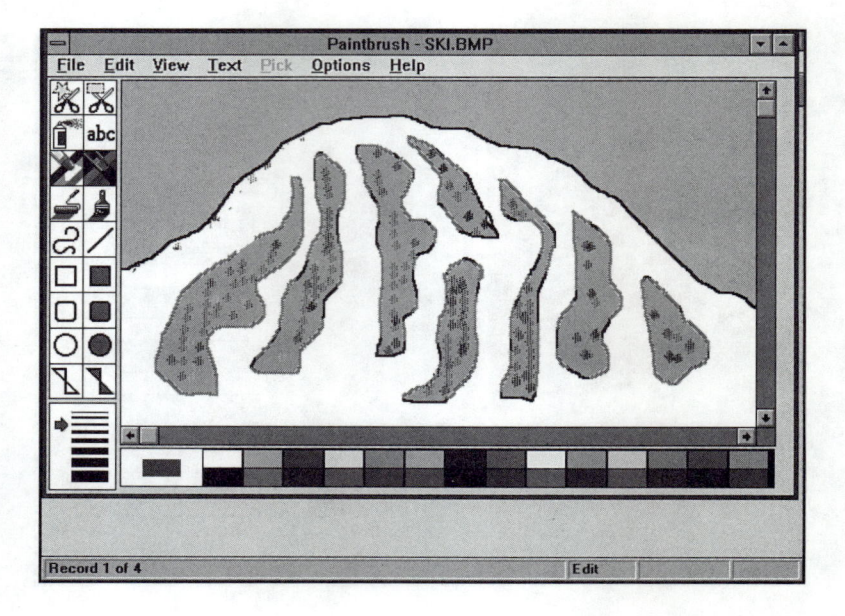

A ski slope map drawn in Paintbrush.

Next, save the file in BMP format, calling it SKI.BMP. Exit from the Paintbrush program and open a new form in Paradox for Windows. Choose the table that contains the ski slope data. Next, choose Blank as the Style in the Design Layout dialog box so that you can start with a blank screen.

Use the Graphic tool to place a graphic where the map will be displayed. Cover the entire form with the map by placing the mouse pointer in one corner, and clicking and dragging to the opposite corner. After you have defined the graphic area, right-click to show the graphic properties, then define the file used for the graphic as SKI.BMP.

Figure 5.27 shows the finished slope map as it would be seen by a user. You can view another day's snow readings by pressing PgUp and PgDn to move backward and forward, respectively, through the records in the table.

The graphic display enables the user to draw conclusions about snowfall patterns on the mountain because it places each slope in position relative to the other slopes. You might determine that the west face of the mountain has better snow conditions than the east side, for example, or that the steeper runs are accumulating less snow.

This type of graphic form could be used in more sophisticated applications. You could create a weather map with fields for the temperature in various cities, for example, as well as graphics to show high and low pressure, the sun, clouds, rain, and snow.

> **For Related Information**
> ▸▸ "Working with Table Objects," p. 361.

Adding OLE Objects

OLE, or object linking and embedding, is a Windows technique for moving data from one program to another. The OLE feature can be used with Paradox forms, as discussed in Chapter 11, "Exchanging Data with Other Applications."

Adding Buttons

Windows uses buttons to interact with the user, such as the OK button used to confirm when you leave a Windows session. Paradox enables you to define buttons of your own for forms. These may be used to trigger ObjectPAL scripts or choose from choices to enter data in a table. The types and uses of buttons are discussed in Chapter 7, "Using Advanced Form Techniques," and in Chapter 13, "Getting Started with ObjectPAL."

Buttons are used to interact with the user, so they are not available for reports.

Adding Fields

Because the main purpose of a form is to access data in Paradox tables, fields are perhaps the most important objects in a form. You use the Field tool to create and place fields on a form. In addition to using fields from tables, Paradox offers several special kinds of fields, including Read Only fields, calculated fields, and system-derived fields. The same basic techniques are used for all field types, as discussed in this section.

Placing Regular Fields

To place regular fields (that is, fields from database tables), use the Field tool to define the box where the field will be placed. Right-click the new field to reveal the properties menu and choose Define Field. A list of all the fields in the table or tables you are using is displayed. Click the name of the field you want, and the new field is assigned. You also can edit any of the other field properties at this time.

Placing Read Only Fields

Read Only fields are the same as regular fields, except the user may not enter data in a Read Only field. Read Only fields are useful for showing the results of calculations or for repeating important fields on pages after the first page of a form. For instance, if you have a multi-page form for entering customers, you may want to repeat the customer name at the top of each page so that users can keep track of whose record they are entering. By making these fields read-only, the user cannot enter or edit data in such fields.

To designate a field as Read Only, create the field as you would a normal field. Right-click to display the object properties and click Run Time. Choose Read Only from the Run Time submenu. To change a field from read-only to data entry, click this property again.

> **TIP** Be sure to make Read Only fields stand out from fields that allow data entry. Use a different font or text color so that the user does not confuse the two kinds of fields or grow frustrated trying to maneuver the cursor into a Read Only field.

Placing Calculated Fields

Forms can contain fields that are calculated based on other fields or other records in the database. These fields are for display only, and are not to be entered by the user.

Paradox forms offer seven summary functions accessed from the Define Field Object dialog box, as follows:

Sum	Total of all values
Count	Number of occurrences of a value
Min	Minimum value for all records
Max	Maximum value for all records
Std	Standard deviation, a statistical measure

5 — GETTING STARTED WITH FORMS

Var   Variance, another statistical function

Avg   Mean of non-null values

You may find summary functions more useful in reports than in forms.

You might use the Count summary function to display the total number of sales in a retail store so that you could present an award to the millionth customer. The Sum function could be used to keep a running total of all your real estate sales commissions.

To define a summary field, follow these steps:

1. Use the Field tool to place the field on the form.
2. Right-click to reveal the properties menu, and choose Define Field.

   A list of all the fields in the form or forms you are using is displayed.
3. Do not click any of these form names; instead, click the first line of the list labeled .... The Define Field Object dialog box is displayed (see fig. 5.31). This dialog box is used to define new fields.
4. Select a field from the field list.
5. Choose a summary type from the Summary drop-down list.
6. Click OK.

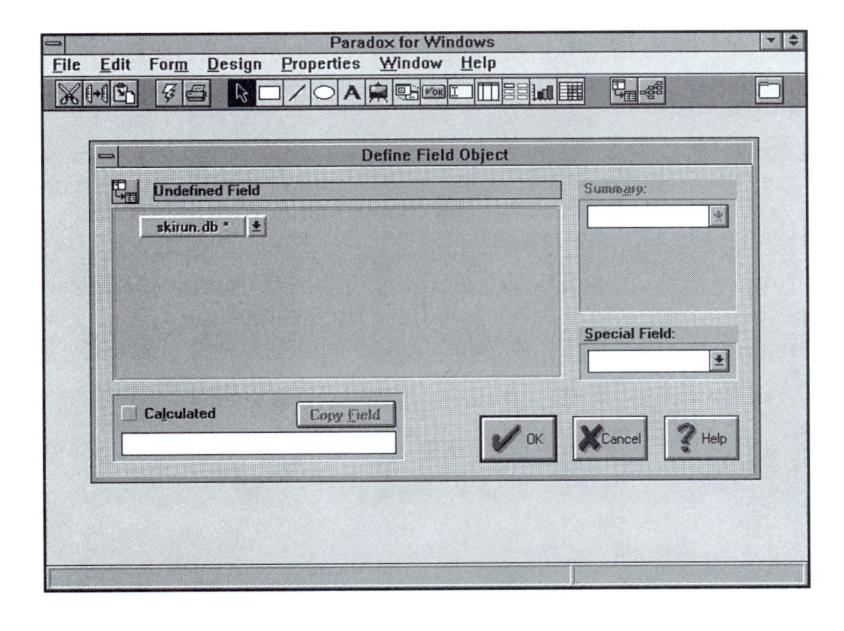

FIG. 5.31

The Define Field Object dialog box.

Placing the Record-Number and Other System Fields

In addition to the fields that you define, each table contains system fields that may be displayed on a form. Click the pull-down menu on the table in the Define Field Object dialog box, and scroll to the bottom of the list. The following system fields are listed:

<Table Name>

<Record Number>

<N of Records>

<N of Fields>

The *N* stands for number, as in the number of records and the number of fields. Again, these fields are not entered by users. If you want to display them, however, just choose the appropriate field name from the pull-down menu.

Placing Special Fields

In addition to the system fields that accompany each table, Paradox contains special fields calculated outside database tables. To use a special field, click the Special Field pull-down menu on the Define Field Object dialog box (refer to fig. 5.31). The menu expands to reveal the following fields:

Today	The current date, as stored in the system clock of your PC. The format of the Today field may be changed to any standard Paradox date format.
Now	The current time in hours, minutes, and seconds, again from the system clock.
Page Number	The current page number
N of Pages	The total number of pages

The Page Number and N of Pages options are more useful for reports than for forms.

TIP

If you choose to display the current time with the Now special field, you may want to change the display type so that seconds are not shown. Users may want to know the time, but some find it annoying to watch the seconds tick by on their data-entry forms.

To suppress seconds, you must create a new time display format. Define a new field as Now, then examine its properties and choose Format. Click Time Format to reveal the list of standard time formats. Next, click the option labeled ... to open the Select Time Format dialog box. This box enables you to define your own display formats for a time value (see fig. 5.32). You can choose 12-hour or 24-hour clocks for the field format.

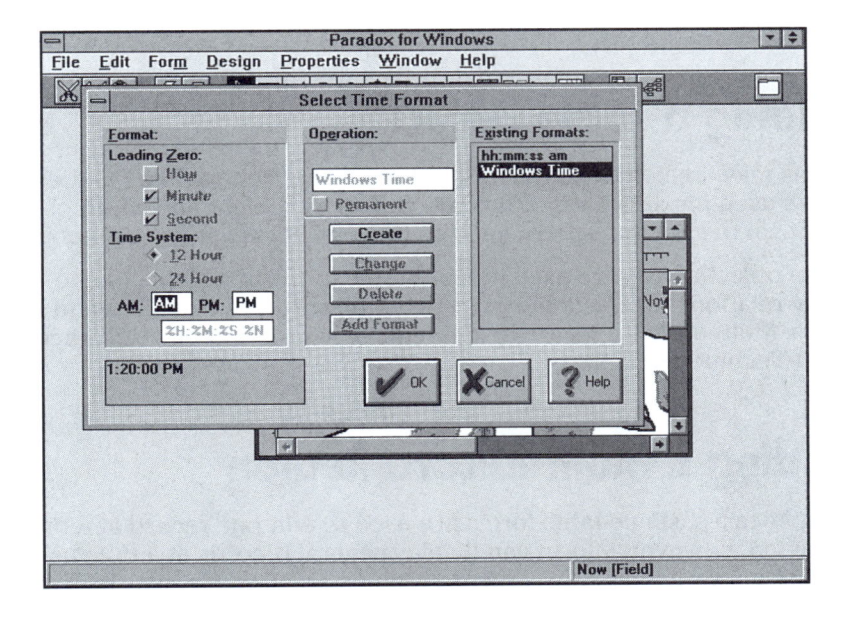

FIG. 5.32

The Select Time Format dialog box.

Erasing Fields from the Form

To erase fields, simply select one or more fields (just as you would select any other screen object) and choose Cut from the Edit menu. If you delete a field by mistake and catch your mistake immediately, choose Edit, Paste to replace it.

Reformatting a Field

Paradox for Windows offers a number of special display formats to simplify data entry in forms. Display formats are different from field types (such as alphanumeric or date) because they do not affect what is stored in the table, only the way it is displayed. For instance, you may want to display the date for Bastille Day as July 14, 1789, rather than 7/14/1789 or 14-Jul-1789.

To change the display type of the field, choose Format from the field properties menu. Different display types are available for different field types.

Paradox also offers advanced display types such as drop-down edit fields and radio buttons, which are explained in Chapter 7, "Using Advanced Form Techniques."

Adding a Table Object

Forms may include table objects. Table objects behave like Paradox tables used for data entry. You can control the height and width of columns, the column labels, and the order of fields within table objects.

Table objects often are used in multi-table forms in which a one-to-many relationship exists between two tables, such as invoices and line items. Multi-table forms are discussed in Chapter 7, "Using Advanced Form Techniques."

Adding a Multi-Record Region

In most cases, single-table forms are used to edit one record at a time. If needed, however, a form can display several records at a time using multi-record regions. (Multi-record regions are used frequently in reports and mail-merge documents.) In essence, a multi-record region is just a copy of a form for a single record. Multi-record regions can repeat horizontally, vertically, or in both directions.

One way to create multi-record regions is to choose Multi-Record from the Design Layout dialog box, as discussed previously in this chapter. You also can define a multi-record region with the Multi-Record tool. Multi-Record regions are explored in Chapter 7.

Adding a Graph

Paradox has the built-in capability to generate a wide range of business graphs, such as bar graphs, line graphs, and pie charts. Graphs may be placed on forms or reports. Building Paradox graphs is discussed in Chapter 7.

Adding a Crosstab

Crosstab, which stands for cross tabulation, is a special way to look at data by building a matrix that correlates records by two or more values at the same time. The columns of the crosstab show the possible values for a field, and the rows show the values for a second field. You could create a crosstab, for example, to show total sales by product by region. Crosstabs may be placed in forms but not in reports. Crosstabs are discussed in Chapter 7.

The Data Model Tool

To the right of the design tools in the SpeedBar are two additional tools: the Data Model tool and the Object Tree. The Data Model is used to define the tables used for a form, as shown earlier in figure 5.2. (To reveal the dialog box in fig. 5.2, click the Data Model tool.)

The Object Tree

The Object Tree displays a window that shows all the objects defined for a form. The Object Tree is used for writing scripts with ObjectPAL, or for selecting objects in a complex form. See Part III for tips on using the Object Tree.

For Related Information
▶▶ "Working with Fields," p. 287.
▶▶ "Working with Table Objects," p. 361.

FROM HERE...

General Design Considerations

This section provides tips and techniques for applying the form design tools you have just learned. These guidelines can help you develop style standards for the database applications you develop.

Paradox for Windows enables you to control the color of many form objects. This is particularly useful for customizing field colors in a form. Although the aesthetic value of color should not be undervalued, you should use colors conservatively and strategically.

You can use color to highlight certain field characteristics. You could make all required fields white on a red background, for example; this could remind the user to fill each of these fields before attempting to save a record. Other types of fields that might benefit from highlighting include key fields and calculated fields.

Colors can emphasize screen text. Bright colors can get the user's attention and warn of impending danger, such as hazardous procedures that delete data. You can choose from many pleasing color combinations and a few hideous ones as well. Keep in mind the user who must sit through extensive data-entry sessions with the colors you choose. Do not go overboard with wild color combinations that may tire the user.

Do not forget that many users work with monochrome monitors, so test your color combinations on monochrome monitors to make sure that your form has the proper highlighting and contrast without the use of colors. This testing is particularly important if you are building an application for distribution and don't know the monitors on which it will be displayed. Users can change their screen colors through Windows, but you want to find color combinations that work on both color and monochrome systems without modification.

Paradox for Windows also offers the amazing capability to change the color of a field depending on the value it contains. This feature, called data-dependent properties, can create impressive effects. Data-dependent properties are discussed in Chapter 7.

As with all screen elements, be consistent with colors. When you find a pleasing palette, use it throughout the application (and all your applications, if possible). Do not use different colors for two screens that perform similar functions. For instance, all menus should use the same color scheme, as should all data-entry forms and views.

Color is a property of nearly every screen element. To inspect the properties of an object, place the mouse pointer on the object and click the right mouse button. Choose Color from the list of properties and the color palette is displayed (see fig. 5.33).

5 — GETTING STARTED WITH FORMS

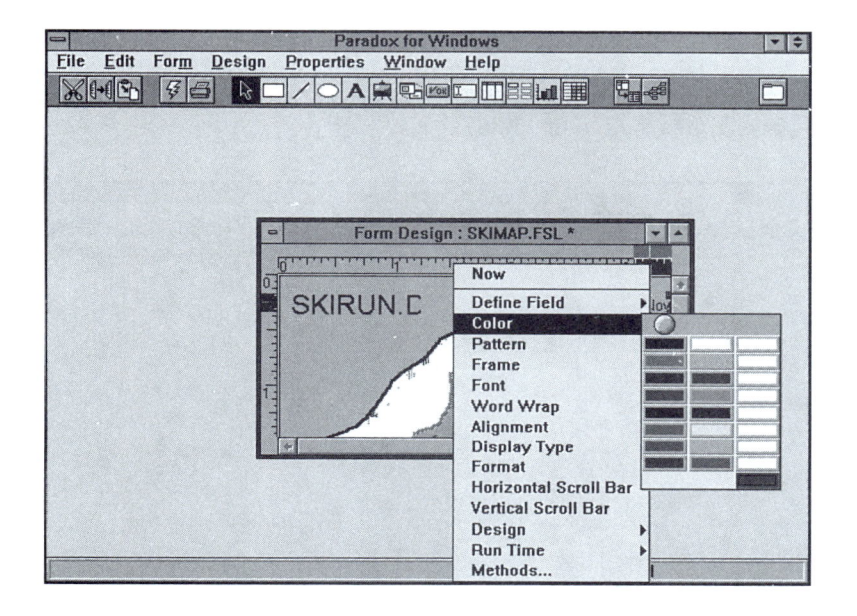

FIG. 5.33

A color palette.

To change the color of a screen element, click the desired color combination. A few choices on the palette are blank so that you can mix your favorite colors.

To create a custom color, click the button at the top of the color palette to access the floating palette. The palette appears as a dialog box with the colors divided into three columns (see fig. 5.34).

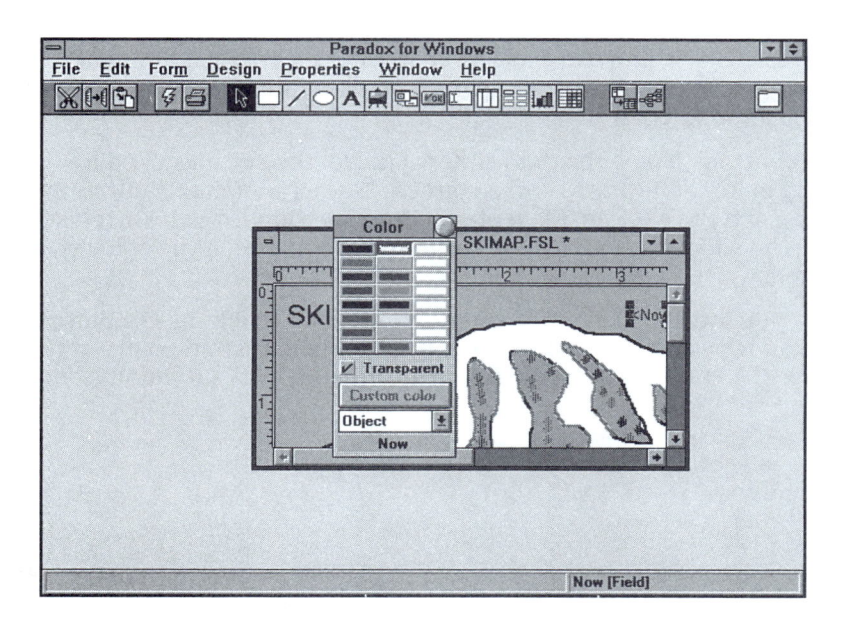

FIG. 5.34

The floating color palette.

I — PARADOX FOR WINDOWS FUNDAMENTALS

Click one of the blank custom colors in the right column. The Custom color button label changes from gray to blank to show that the button is operational. Click the Custom Color button, and the Custom Color dialog box appears (see fig. 5.35).

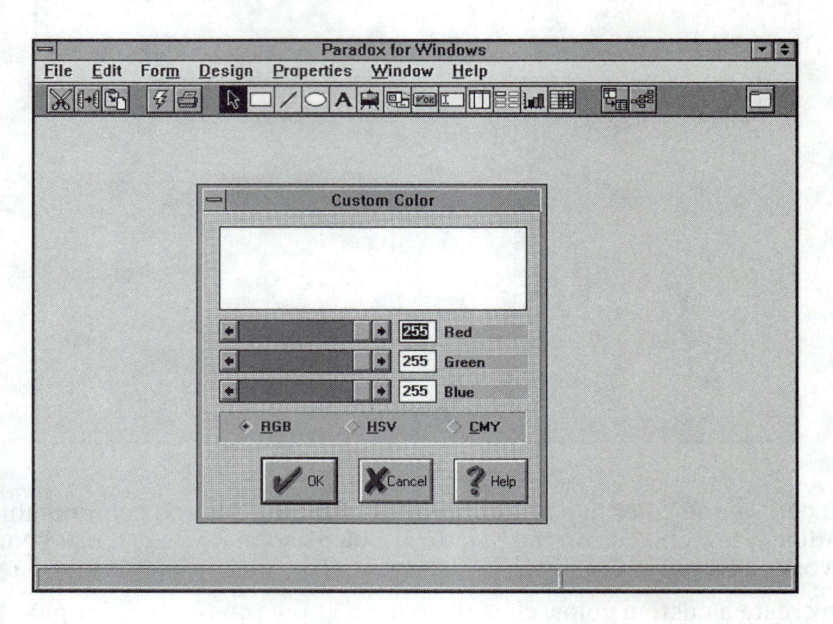

FIG. 5.35

The Custom Color dialog box.

Use the data sliders labeled red, green, and blue to set the custom color. Click the slider button and drag it, releasing the mouse button at the desired position. Sliders to the right produce white, those to the left create black, and those in the center create gray. Experiment to find out how to create other colors. Some combinations produce textures as well as solid colors.

Radio buttons below the data sliders control the settings used for mixing colors, offering RGB (red, green, blue), HSV (Hue, Saturation, Value), and CMY (Cyan, Magenta, Yellow) methods. If you switch settings, the sliders automatically recalibrate to maintain the color you created.

When you are satisfied with your color creation, click the OK button. You can repeat these steps to define up to eight custom colors in the palette. To make the floating palette disappear, click its round button again.

Working with Multiple Objects

So far in this chapter, you have edited the properties of one object at a time. This can be tedious, however, if you must change the characteristics of several objects. You may want to change the font for all the field labels, for example, to the same style and size.

This section describes several Paradox tools and techniques for working with multiple objects. Shared property menus, for example, can modify the properties of multiple selected objects. Object embedding moves or deletes several objects in a larger container object. Object groups may be defined to treat several objects as one. Paradox can reset the size or alignment of several objects to make them uniform. Finally, you can customize Designer Properties to reflect your preferences for how objects are manipulated.

Using Shared Property Menus

Fortunately, Paradox anticipated the need to edit the properties of multiple objects at a time by providing a feature called *shared menus*. To use shared menus, follow these steps:

1. Select all the objects you want to modify. The objects do not have to be the same object type to use this feature. (See "Selecting Objects" earlier in this chapter for instructions on selecting multiple objects.)

2. Right-click one of the selected objects. The properties menu of the object is displayed.

3. As you change a property, the property is changed in all the other selected objects that share the property. If you select a text object, an ellipse, and a table, and you change the color of the text object to red, the ellipse and table also change to red.

Understanding Embedding

An *embedded* object is contained in another object and is moved or deleted along with the object that contains it. This feature can save you quite a bit of work when moving complex objects around the workspace.

By default, larger objects embed all smaller objects that fit within their boundaries. If you want to place an object on top of a larger one but not embed it, you must change the Embed Surrounded Object option on the properties menu of the larger (container) object. To break an embedded object from its container, either change the Embed Surrounded Object option as just described, or select the embedded object and move it (or part of it) beyond the boundaries of the container object.

When you delete a container object, all the objects within it are automatically deleted. If you delete the embedded object, the container object is not deleted.

Grouping Objects

You can work with several objects as a unit without surrounding them with a container object. To define a group of objects, select all the objects using the Shift+click technique, then choose Design, Group from the Paradox menu (see fig. 5.36). The handles from the individual objects disappear, and handles appear around the perimeter of the entire group. Now the group can be moved or deleted as a unit.

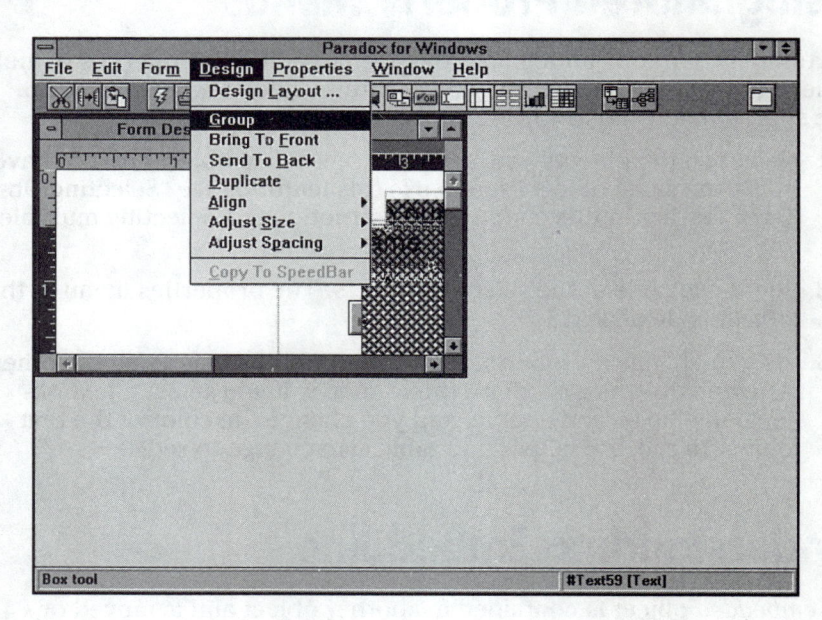

FIG. 5.36

The Design menu in the Form Design window.

NOTE A group contains only the objects you select prior to using the Group option. Although the program draws a line around the perimeter of the group, other objects that happen to fall within this line are not automatically part of the group.

5 — GETTING STARTED WITH FORMS

249

After you define a group, you may treat it as a single object, copying, deleting, or moving with a single operation. You can use the Bring To Front or Send To Back options on the Design menu, for example, to move all the objects in the group to the foreground or background of the form.

To remove the group, select Ungroup from the Design menu. Now the objects are treated individually again. Note that the Group option is dimmed if no objects are selected, and Ungroup appears only when a group is selected.

Adjusting Alignment, Size, and Spacing

You can change the shape and size of individual objects one at a time using the object's properties. Paradox goes a step further, however, enabling you to adjust the alignment, size, or spacing of several objects with a single command. Each of these three commands is performed independently and is accessed from the Design menu. You can quickly sketch in objects without worrying about their exact size or position, and correct them later.

For this example, start by drawing three squares of different sizes, roughly lined up diagonally, as shown in figure 5.37. Select all three squares, using the Shift+click technique.

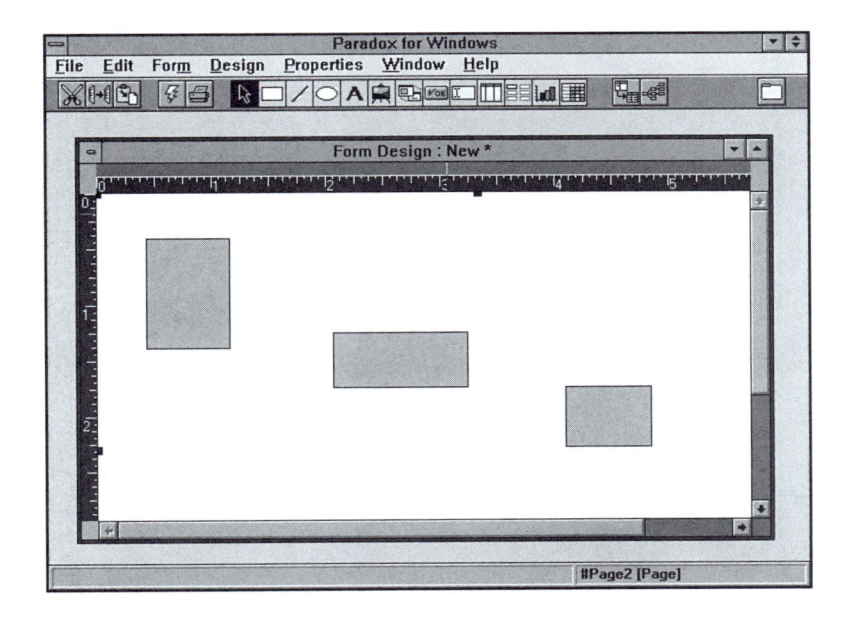

FIG. 5.37

Three squares before modification.

Choose <u>D</u>esign, <u>A</u>lign. The Align menu displays the following six choices:

Align <u>L</u>eft	Aligns all the boxes along a vertical line, even with the leftmost box
Align <u>R</u>ight	Aligns all the boxes along a vertical line, even with the rightmost box
Align <u>C</u>enter	Aligns all the boxes along a vertical line, even with the center box
Align <u>T</u>op	Aligns all the boxes along a horizontal line, even with the top box
Align <u>B</u>ottom	Aligns all the boxes along a horizontal line, even with the bottom box
Align <u>M</u>iddle	Aligns all the boxes along a horizontal line, even with the middle box (see fig. 5.38)

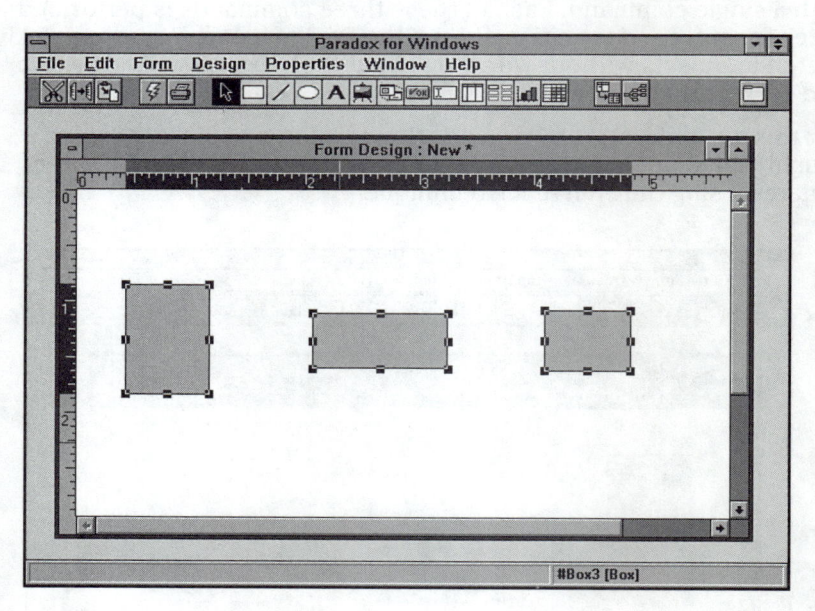

FIG. 5.38

Three squares after Middle alignment.

Next, adjust the size of the objects. Choose <u>D</u>esign, Adjust <u>S</u>ize. You can adjust the height and width of the objects independently, to either the size of the smallest or the largest object selected, as follows:

Minimum **W**idth	Adjusts the width of all objects to the width of the smallest object
Ma**x**imum Width	Adjusts the width of all objects to the width of the largest object
Minimum **H**eight	Adjusts the height of all objects to the height of the smallest object
M**a**ximum Height	Adjusts the height of all objects to the height of the largest object.

Adjusting the width and height to the maximum size results in the form shown in figure 5.39. You may have to use the Align **M**iddle command a second time to realign the resized objects.

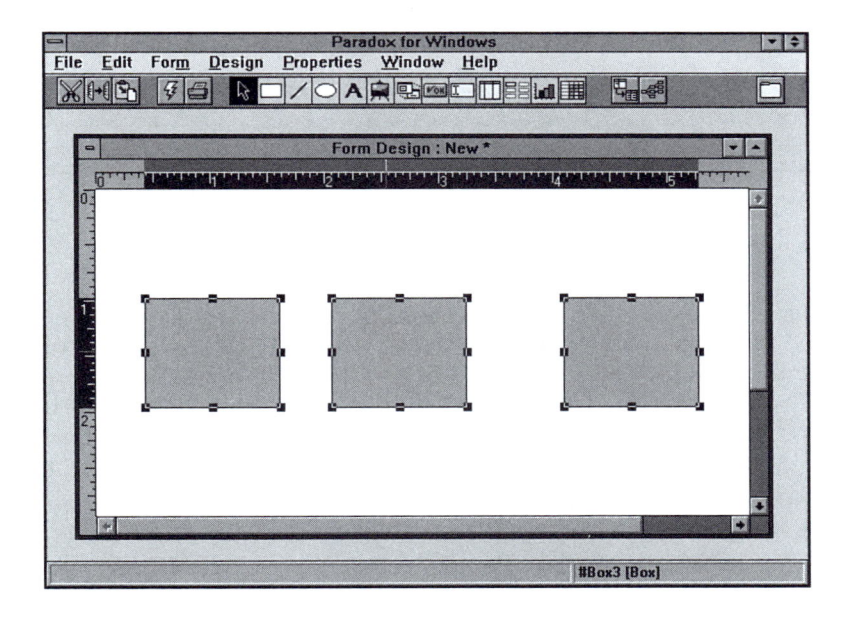

FIG. 5.39

Three squares after adjusting the width and height.

The third means of adjusting objects is Spacing, which is the space between the objects. To adjust spacing, choose **D**esign, Adjust S**p**acing, and select Horizontal or Vertical. Choosing Horizontal evens out the space between the objects as measured from left to right. Choosing Vertical evens out the space between the objects as measured from top to bottom. Figure 5.40 has been adjusted horizontally.

FIG. 5.40

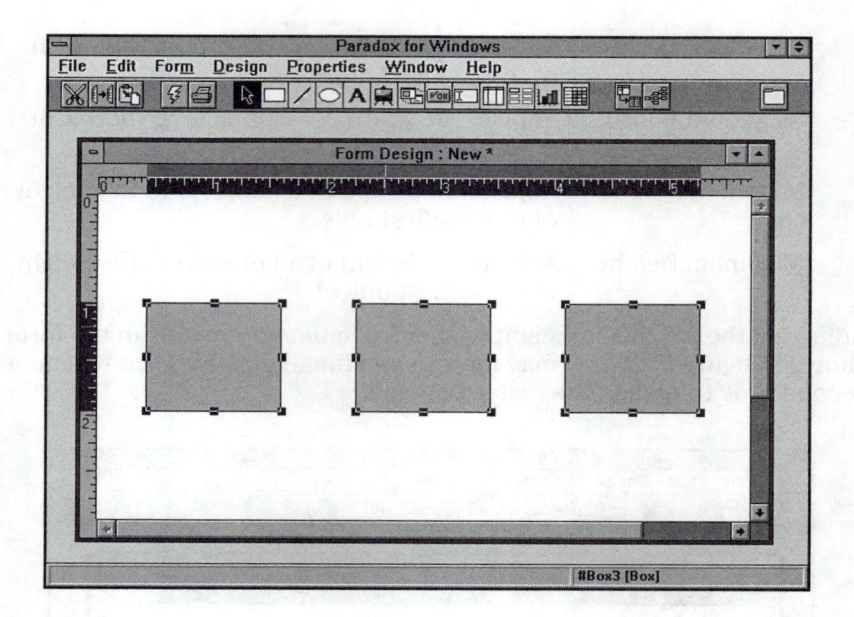

Three squares after using Adjust Spacing (horizontal).

Designer Properties

You can define certain preferences for how objects are displayed and moved in design documents, as well as create a set of standard properties called *prototype objects*. Select Properties from the Paradox menu and choose Designer. The Designer Properties dialog box appears (see fig. 5.41).

Settings in the Designer Properties dialog box affect both types of design documents: forms and reports. Explanations of each of the choices in the Designer Properties dialog box follow.

Under Design Preferences, the Select From Inside option enables you to choose from two methods of selecting composite objects (objects nested within one another). If you turn off Select From Inside, clicking to select an object within a larger, container object automatically selects the larger object. This enables you to move a composite object more easily. With Select From Inside activated (the default), clicking a composite object selects the innermost object. If you click again, the outer object is selected.

The Frame Objects option displays a frame as a dotted line around each screen object. If you turn this option off, frames are displayed only for objects whose frame properties you have changed from the default style or color.

FIG. 5.41

The Designer Properties dialog box.

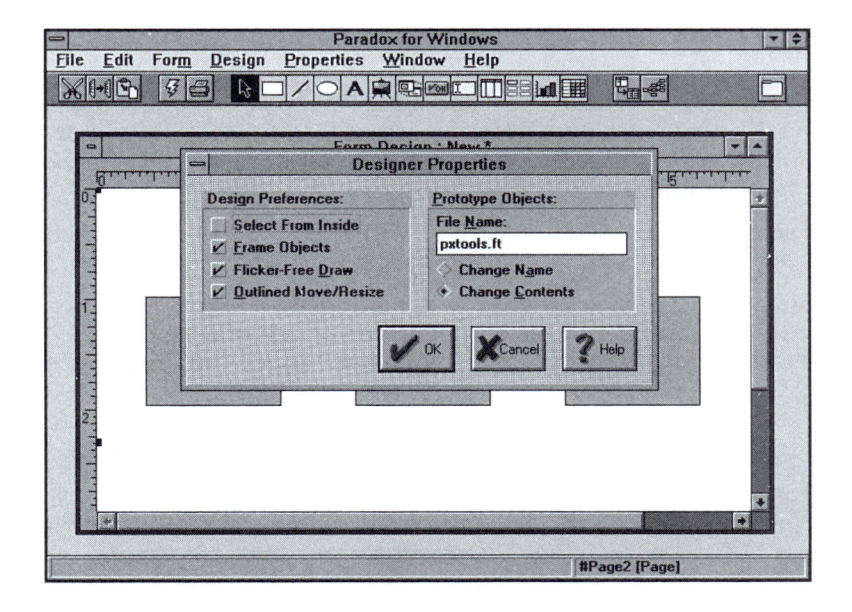

Flicker-Free Draw changes the display mode to prevent the occasional flickering you may observe when moving or resizing screen objects. Using this option may slow down these screen operations.

Outlined Move/Resize offers options for what you see when you move or resize an object. With the setting off, the object itself is displayed when you move or resize it. If you check Outlined Move/Resize, the outline of the object is displayed when you move or resize it. Displaying the outline rather than the object speeds screen redrawing as you manipulate the object, so checking this option can make movement and resizing faster.

After you check your choices from the Designer Properties dialog box, click OK to save them.

Using Rulers and Grids

Paradox for Windows provides rulers and grids to help you position screen elements accurately and evenly on the form. These tools are handy for form design, but are even more important in writing reports, when aligning text is crucial.

The Rulers

The rulers measure the vertical and horizontal position of the mouse pointer. By showing a mark that corresponds to the mouse pointer location, the rulers enable you to see the exact position of the mouse pointer at all times.

You can turn off either or both rulers with the Properties menu. Hiding the ruler gives you a bit more room to view the form.

By default, the ruler uses inches as the unit of measure, with marks for every 1, 1/2, 1/4, and 1/16 inch. To change the unit of measure, choose Properties, Grid Settings from the menu bar to open the Grid Settings dialog box (see fig. 5.42).

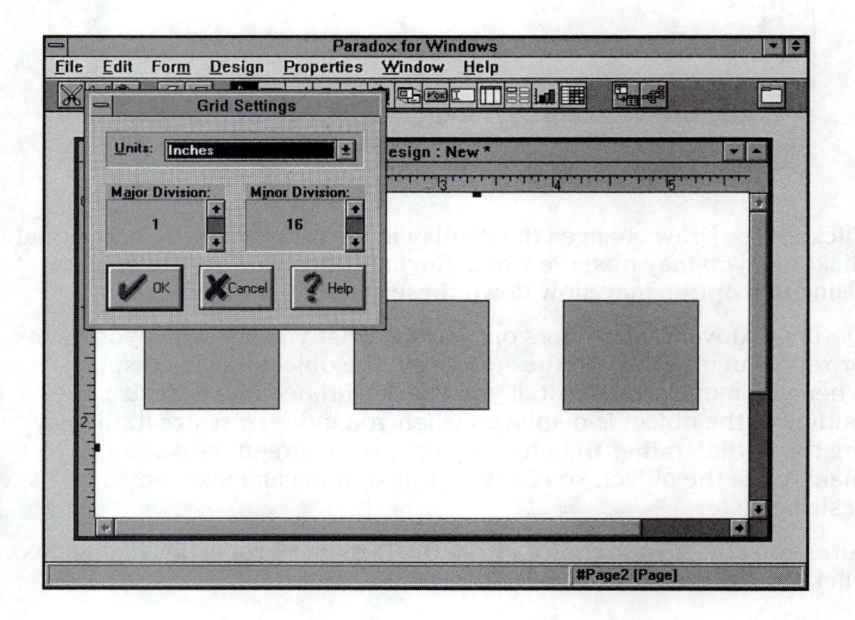

FIG. 5.42

The Grid Settings dialog box.

The Grid Settings dialog box controls the unit of measure (inches or centimeters) and the number of subdivisions on the ruler. You can make a ruler with marks every half centimeter, for example, by choosing centimeter for the units, 1 for the major division, and 2 as the minor division.

The Expanded Ruler

For enhanced control of text, you can choose the expanded ruler. In addition to displaying the location of the mouse pointer, the expanded ruler controls margins, tabs, line spacing, and the alignment of text. Its features are similar to those of rulers found in word processors. Although you can use the Expanded Ruler in creating forms, it is used more commonly for reports in which long text passages are needed.

To display the expanded ruler, choose Properties, then choose Expanded Ruler. The expanded ruler appears at the top of the form workspace, as shown in figure 5.43. The top of the expanded ruler, just before the upper border of the Form Design Window, contains three groups of buttons.

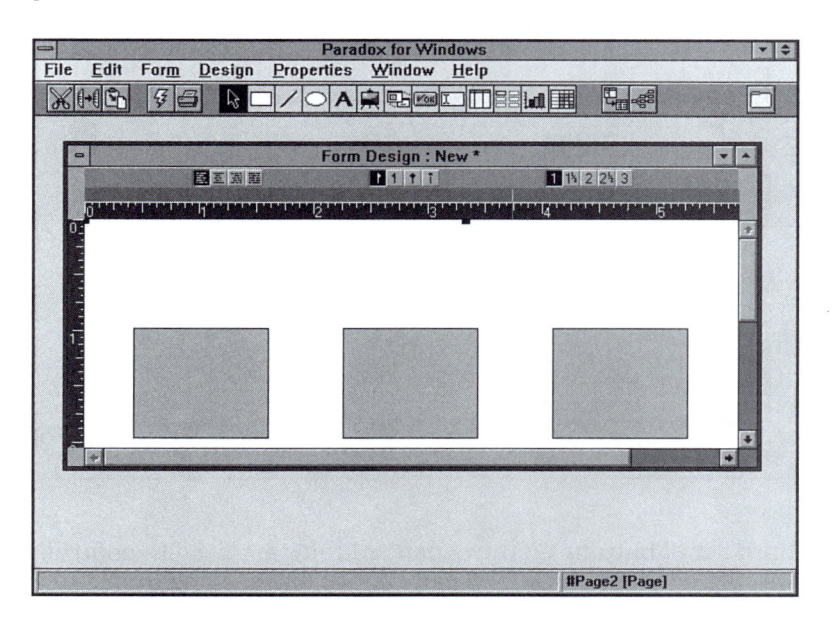

FIG. 5.43

The Expanded Ruler.

The first group of buttons, on the left, control text alignment or justification in a text object. The buttons have little jagged lines that simulate text on a form. The first button (reading from left to right) depicts the default of left justification, the second button represents centered justification, the third button shows right justification, and the fourth button shows full justification. Whichever justification you choose, try to be consistent in all your forms. Of all these, the riskiest is usually full justification, which can stretch short lines of text almost beyond recognition.

I — PARADOX FOR WINDOWS FUNDAMENTALS

The second group of buttons enables you to place tabs in the horizontal ruler. Paradox for Windows supports four types of tabs: right, left, center, and decimal tabs (see fig. 5.44). *Right tabs* are the standard tabs used in word processors and typewriters. Text following a right tab is lined up to the right of the tab marker. This means that the first character of all text after right tabs starts at the same horizontal position. *Left tabs* place the text to the left of the tab marker. They align all the last letters of the words before the tab. *Center tabs* center the text around the tab mark. Finally, *decimal tabs* are used to line up the decimal points of numeric entries.

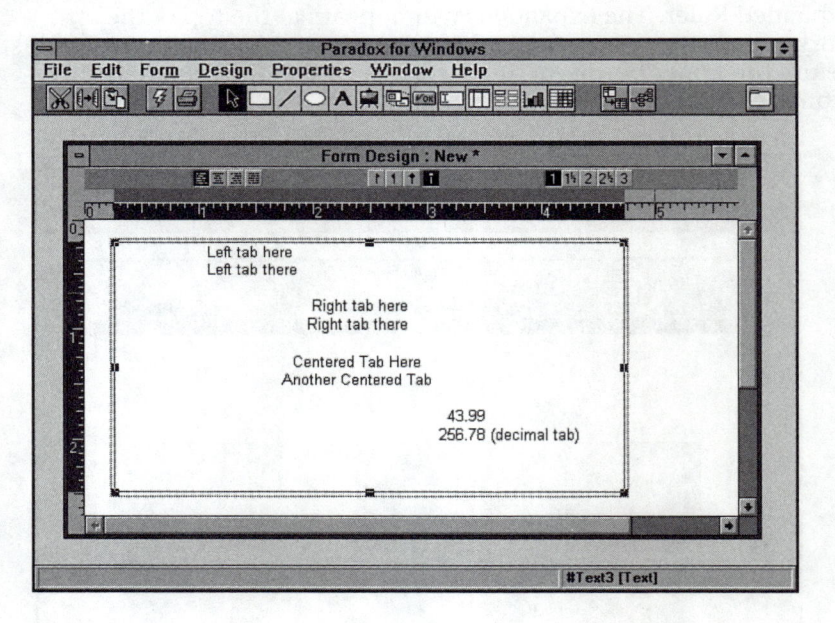

FIG. 5.44

The types of tabs.

The third set of buttons on the expanded ruler are used to control the line spacing of a text block. You can choose line spacing from 1 to 3, in half line steps. Text in the selected text object is resized to reflect the line spacing, and the next text object you create will use the line spacing currently selected. The default is single-spaced text lines.

A special tool similar to tabs is the indent marker, shown in figure 5.45. This tool is shown just below the text alignment buttons, between the left and right margin markers. The indent aligns a paragraph to the right or left of the margin marker. To place an indent marker, drag it with the mouse.

5 — GETTING STARTED WITH FORMS   257

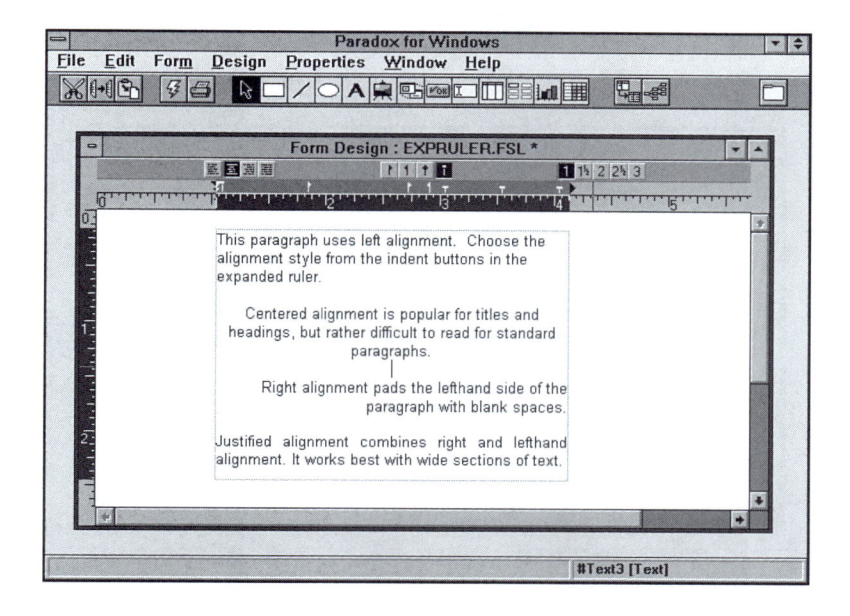

FIG. 5.45

Types of indentation.

The Grid

The *grid* consists of vertical and horizontal lines that cover the entire surface of the form, dividing it into squares. Grids are commonly used in business graphics and drawing programs.

To activate the grid, choose Show Grid from the Properties menu. The grid covers the entire work area (see fig. 5.46). The grid shows lines for the major divisions (inches in this case) and dots for the minor divisions (sixteenth inches here).

To enjoy the full benefit of the grid for aligning objects, choose Properties, Snap to Grid. Objects automatically align with the nearest grid mark whenever they are placed, resized, or moved. Instead of moving smoothly across the form surface, the objects jump from one grid mark to the next; with Snap to Grid, objects cannot be positioned midway between grid marks.

You may want to use coarser units of measure with Snap to Grid. If the unit is too fine, you may have difficulty seeing whether objects are lined up with one another. With a coarser grid setting, you notice any misalignment easily.

I — PARADOX FOR WINDOWS FUNDAMENTALS

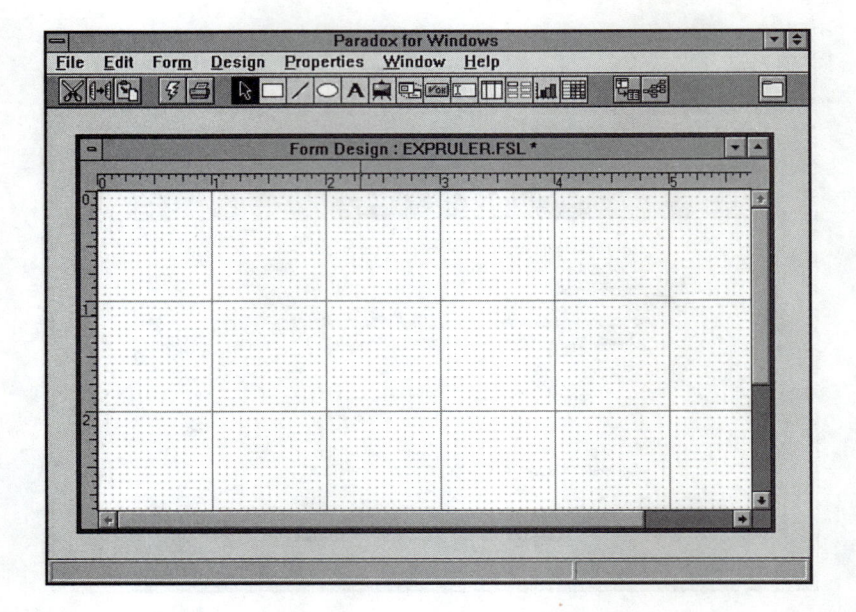

FIG. 5.46

A grid displayed in the Form Design window.

Using Zoom

Even when you maximize the Form Design window, you may not be able to see small objects closely enough to work with them easily. The Zoom option enables you to change the scale of the form display to magnify or reduce the objects on the workspace.

To zoom, choose Properties, then select Zoom. Standard zoom magnifications are provided from 25% (one-fourth normal size) to 400% (four times normal size). Three automatic zoom options enable you to maximize the width of the window, maximize the height of the window, or resize both the width and the height for the best fit. These zoom options may exceed the magnification or reduction provided by the zoom percentage choices.

NOTE The Zoom command in Paradox for Windows bears no resemblance to the Zoom command in Paradox for DOS, which is used to locate data.

Figure 5.47 shows a form at 50 percent magnification. Zooming out from a form is helpful to see the "big picture," especially for large or complex forms.

5 — GETTING STARTED WITH FORMS

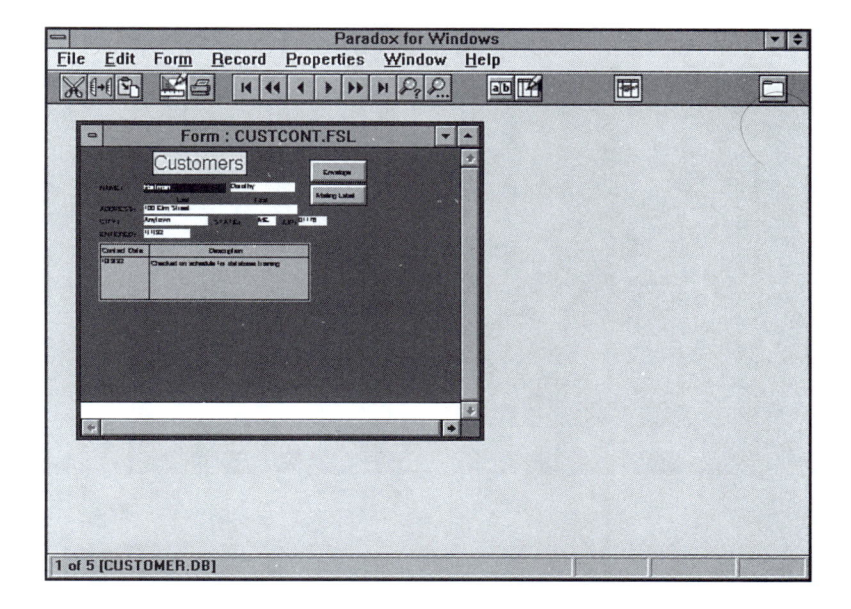

FIG. 5.47

A form displayed at 50 percent magnification.

Saving the Form Design

You can save the form you have designed in several ways. At any time, you can save the file by choosing Save from the File menu. The Save As option enables you to rename the form you are working on and save it under the new name. The changes you have made are not reflected in the original form.

If you do not save the form, a save form dialog box appears when you close the Form Design window (see fig. 5.48). This box reminds you that changes have been made to the form and asks whether you want to save these changes.

If you choose Yes, the changes are saved and the form design window closes. If you choose No, the changes are discarded. This is the option you should choose if you have made mistakes in the form design and want to start with the version of the form as you last saved it. The Cancel option returns you to the Form Design window and the Help button displays appropriate Paradox for Windows help.

I — PARADOX FOR WINDOWS FUNDAMENTALS

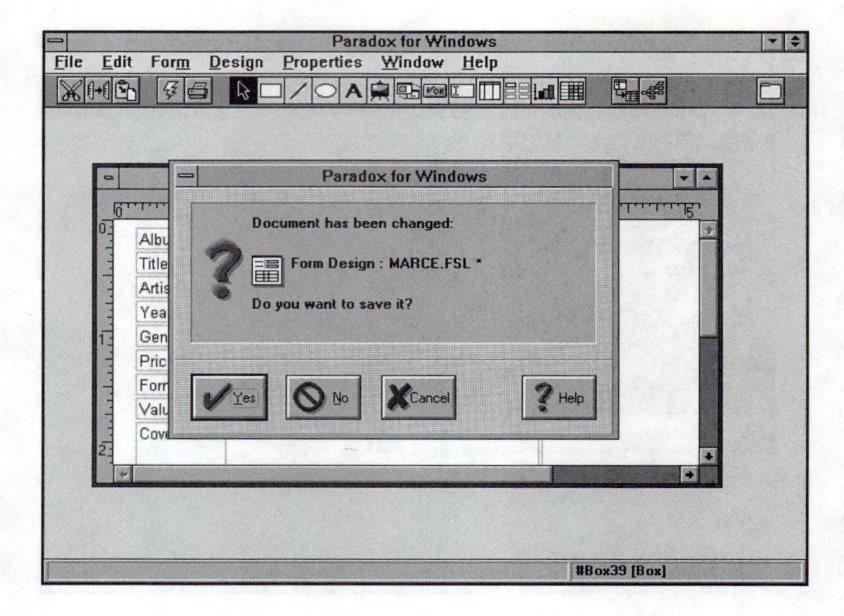

FIG. 5.48

The save form dialog box.

Testing the Form

A form, like all other database elements, is not complete until you test it. After you build a form, try entering a few sample records. Make sure that the field lengths accommodate your data and that the flow of the form and the field colors are pleasing. Also, watch for any error messages that pop up during record entry.

You can go directly from form design to testing by pressing the View Data button (it looks like a lightning bolt) in the SpeedBar, by choosing Form, View from the menu, or by pressing F8.

Use the form you have created to enter records in Albums. Find out whether you like the order and position of the fields, as well as their display types and lengths.

From the Form window, you can quickly navigate through all the records in a table. As usual, you can invoke navigational commands in several ways. One quick approach is to use the navigational buttons on the SpeedBar.

5 — GETTING STARTED WITH FORMS

The Form view navigational buttons, shown in figure 5.49, resemble the controls of a tape recorder. They move the cursor as follows:

◀◀ (first)	First record in the table
◀◀	Backward a screenful of records
◀	Backward one record
▶	Forward one record
▶▶	Forward a screenful of records
▶▶ (last)	Last record in the table

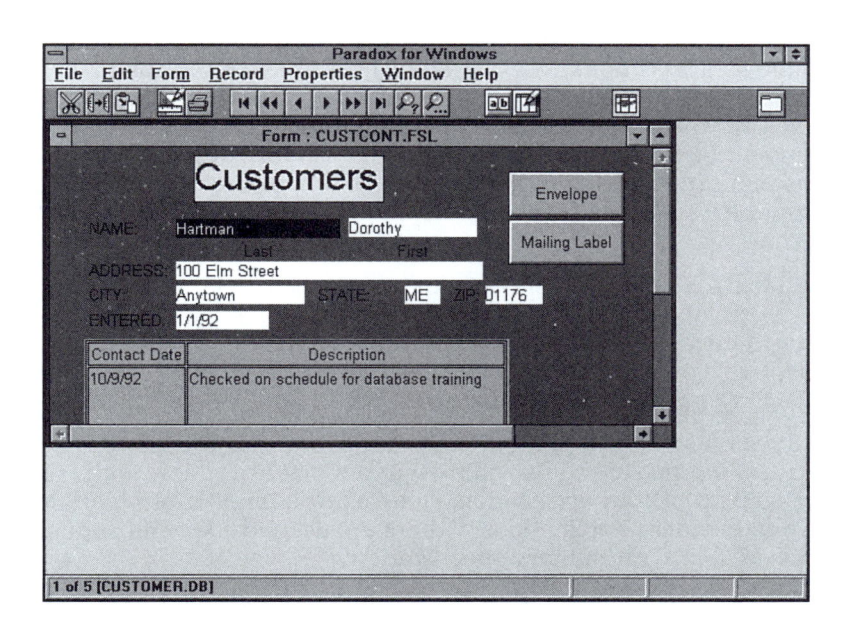

FIG. 5.49

Form view navigational buttons.

Some navigational buttons have menu and function key equivalents. From the Record menu, you can select First, Last, Next, Previous, Next set, and Previous set. The function key commands are F12 for the next record, F11 for the previous record, Ctrl+F12 for the last record, and Ctrl+F11 for the first record. (No function key is available to move a screen of records at a time.) These function key commands may seem familiar because they are the same navigational options available in table view.

Guidelines for Text and Field Labels

As stressed throughout this chapter, extra text makes forms easier to use than tables. In particular, long field labels on the form help the user fill in fields correctly. Background text to explain a form can also provide help.

You should make the wording of field labels as understandable as possible. Avoid using ambiguous words for labels and choices. A label such as Name usually is not specific enough. Does it mean the customer name, the product name, or your name? The label Name also does not tell the user the proper format for entering the name. A better field label might be Name (Last, First MI), which is more descriptive and shows that the name should be entered last name first. Similarly, Year may not be a sufficient label for a field that stores the fiscal year or the academic year.

Remember that a field label does not have to be the same as the field name. Field labels are not limited to a few characters and may include spaces to improve readability. If your field names are too short to be descriptive, you can use the field label to explain the field. A label such as Last Order is much better than LSTORDT.

Abbreviations can be helpful in form design because they save space on-screen, but be sure to use abbreviations that are widely understood in the context of your application. Quite a few abbreviations work in nearly all business applications. Others are used in a specific industry, such as MILSPEC for military specification.

You do not need labels for all fields. Often, the meaning of a system-derived field is obvious, such as customer address fields displayed automatically on an invoice when the customer number is entered.

Capitalize labels consistently. Choose either all uppercase letters or mixed case. All lowercase usually is not recommended. Whatever you choose, use the same style for every form. Microsoft Windows and Paradox for Windows use mixed uppercase and lowercase.

Use the same label to refer to the same field in different forms. You create unnecessary confusion when you change a field label—for example, from Customer ID in one form to Customer Code in another.

Do not embed numbers or punctuation in the labels unless this makes them more meaningful, even if the field name contains numbers and punctuation (for example, REC_DTE3). Labels should be long enough to be meaningful but concise to conserve screen space. For example, you seldom need to label a field ADDRESS2 when it is situated unambiguously in an address block.

Punctuation can help set off a label from its field. If you choose to use a colon between the field label and the field, use the colon with every field and use consistent spacing. Dollar signs are useful for highlighting fields in which dollar amounts are entered. If you want to draw special attention to screen text, use characters such as < or *, as in <<< WARN- ING: DO NOT PROCEED >>>. In addition to the alphabet, you can use graphics or boxes with bold colors.

Screen Layout

All the form design possibilities offered by Paradox for Windows are wasted if you do not employ them properly. This section offers guides for honing your form design skills.

Screen layout demands a fine eye for graphic design. Users spend far more time staring at the data-entry screens than you spend building the entire database, so give them something they will not become tired of. Strive to make screens not only easy to use but as interesting as possible.

The advent of Windows has changed the prevailing taste in PC database screens. Windows copies the paper form more closely than character-based DOS applications by using dark letters on a light background and various sizes of text labels.

You can use the following general guidelines for Paradox form design. Consider these a starting point rather than rigid rules.

- Use color conservatively. Rather than change the color of the background, keep most of the background white or light and use colored text or graphics.

- Choose a small, proportionally spaced font (such as Roman or Modern) for field labels and a larger, fixed space font (such as Courier) for the fields. This simulates typing information into a paper form because a proportionally spaced font looks typeset and a fixed space font looks like a typewriter's characters.

- Use boxes to surround groups of fields, making each box the same length. Boxes can tie together related fields, such as the fields for a shipping address, and make the form easier to understand. This makes your form resemble the paper forms used to gather information for data entry. Place the field name in the upper left corner of each box.

- Use mixed upper- and lowercase letters rather than all uppercase. Mixed case is in keeping with Windows style and does not seem as harsh as all caps.

Feel free to experiment with your own design ideas. One of the strengths of Paradox for Windows is that you can make your forms look and behave just about any way you want.

Chapter Summary

Forms in Paradox for Windows are used to enter, edit, and display information stored in data tables. You can use a wide range of text and graphic tools to tailor the form to your special requirements. Forms can be simple or complex, and can contain multiple tables, text objects, geometric shapes, graphs, crosstabs, and bit-mapped graphic images.

If you follow the basic rules of form design, your forms will be readable and consistent. Remember, you don't have to use all the features that Paradox for Windows offers in every form you create.

Now that you know how to create forms, you can make the second type of Paradox design document—reports. Nearly all the techniques of form design also are used in report writing, so you will be putting the knowledge gained in this chapter to work once again.

CHAPTER 6

Getting Started with Reports

Entering information into a database is of little use if you have no way to retrieve it. This is where reports come in. Reports enable you to retrieve any or all information in the database. A report may contain any combination of fields and draw on information from one table or several tables. Reports often produce paper forms such as invoices, order forms, or mailing labels that previously were prepared by hand.

Reports are the flip side of data-entry forms. Whereas forms are used to get information into the database, reports are used to get it out. Like forms, reports are highly visible to database users. Many principles of form design apply equally to report writing.

Like forms, reports are Paradox design documents. Many of the same objects, commands, and techniques are used in both types of design documents. Therefore, this chapter covers some of the same material in Chapter 5, "Getting Started with Forms," as it relates to reports.

The first part of this chapter discusses the major steps in report writing. The second part presents some examples and descriptions of the tools and techniques used to create different report formats.

NOTE If you are new to Paradox, you may find it strange that report writing does not include any provisions for specifying record selection criteria. In essence, Paradox separates the report into two parts. You first write a query to select the records (and their order), and then you create a report to define the format.

Examining Types of Reports

Several types of reports exist, some of which you probably have encountered outside the computer world. Other reports—such as invoices, packing lists, and bills of lading—are commonly used in order processing. Summary reports are used to calculate totals and averages from large numbers of records, such as monthly or quarterly financial reports and the expense summary you receive from your credit card company.

Graphs are another form of reporting. Capabilities for business graphics are increasingly popular in database software. Paradox for Windows includes integrated business graphics so that you can create professional quality graphs without using another program. Paradox for Windows graphs are introduced in Chapter 10, "Creating Crosstabs and Graphs." You may include graphs in Paradox reports.

Reports usually are printed, but they can also be displayed on-screen or printed to a disk file. This chapter deals with all reports, regardless of where or how they are displayed.

Understanding Paradox Reports

A Paradox for Windows report is a special kind of object. As a design document, it has much in common with a Paradox for Windows form. With few exceptions, the same tools are used for designing forms and reports. Therefore, you may get a sense of déjà vu as you read the instructions for report tools.

Printing a Quick Report

Any time you are viewing a Paradox table, including the Answer table created by a Paradox query, a report is only a mouse click away. An instant report, introduced in Quick Start 1, is a "quick and dirty" way to get output from a data table. By clicking the Quick Report button, a default format is created and all records in the table are sent to the printer. You may specify the page size and number of pages to include in the instant report.

If you have already defined one or more reports for a table, you can use the Quick Report button to print your preferred report. To set your preferences, choose Properties, Preferred, and Report from the menu. The choose file dialog box appears, labeled Choose Preferred Report. Choose the report you want to associate with the Quick Report button.

For example, you may want to make an invoice the preferred report for an order-entry form. You also can define a preferred form, graph, and crosstab for a table.

NOTE The Quick Report in Paradox for Windows is similar to the Instant Report in Paradox for DOS.

Quick reports are sent automatically to the printer. To send a report to the screen, you must open a report rather than use the default quick report.

Creating a Report

This section describes the mechanics of report writing in Paradox for Windows. From the Paradox Desktop, choose File, New, Report (or right-click the Report button in the SpeedBar and choose New). The Data Model dialog box appears (see fig. 6.1).

Choose the main table for the report from the list on the left side of the dialog box. For this example, start with a single table report. (Multi-table reports are covered later in this chapter.) Click ALBUMS.DB and click the OK button. ALBUMS.DB is the table you created in Chapter 2, "Designing Paradox Tables and Databases." The Design Layout dialog box appears (see fig. 6.2).

Selecting a Report Layout

Paradox offers several standard report layouts. The standard layouts may be used as is or modified for your special requirements.

After you choose the table or tables for the report, the next step in report design is to fill in the Design Layout dialog box, as shown in

I — PARADOX FOR WINDOWS FUNDAMENTALS

figure 6.2. This dialog box is similar to the one used to create a data-entry form. The default setting is tabular style, which places the table fields in the record band and includes column headers and borders. The result resembles view mode in the table window.

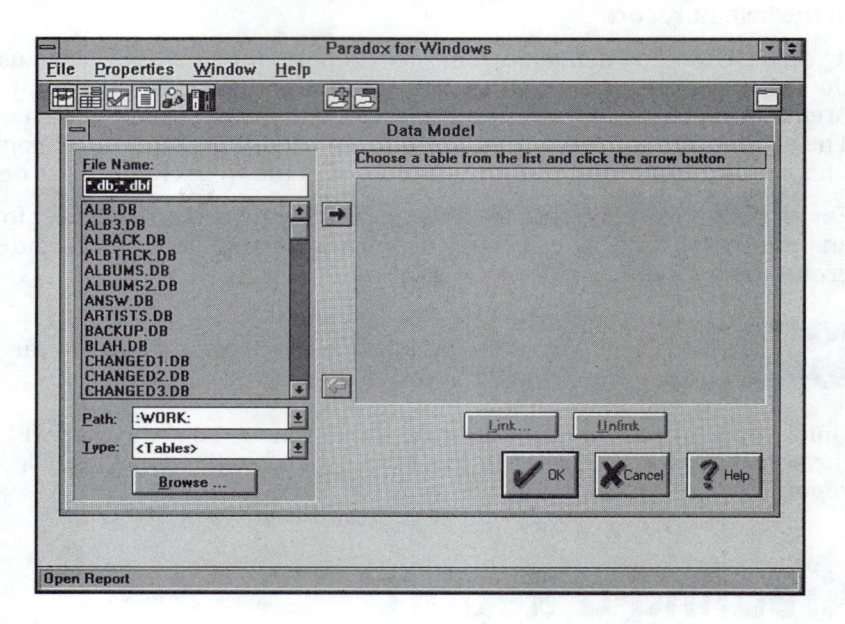

FIG. 6.1

The Data Model dialog box.

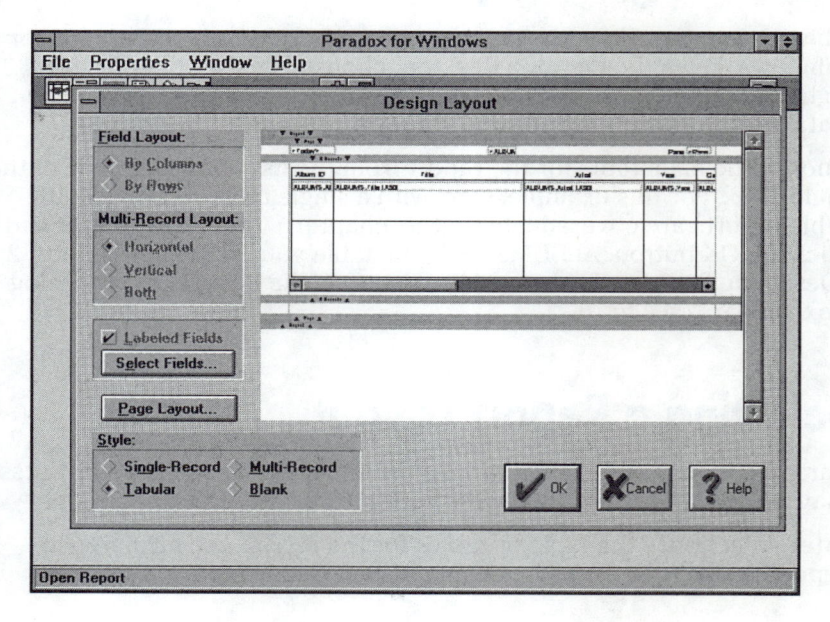

FIG. 6.2

The Design Layout dialog box.

6 — GETTING STARTED WITH REPORTS

Options in this dialog box enable you to set the layout characteristics, such as how the fields are arranged in the report format. The box in the upper right corner of the window shows a preview of the layout.

The Field Layout box controls the order of the fields in the record band. Fields can be laid out from top to bottom, with each field on a separate line, or from left to right to fill the space available on each line. In the default tabular style, fields are arranged in columns with field labels at the top of each column (the Field Layout options are not active with the Tabular style selection).

The next set of options in the Design Layout dialog box concerns multi-record layout. The Multi-Record option is active only when the Multi-Record style is chosen. This option enables you to repeat records in the record band across (horizontally), down (vertically), or both. Figure 6.3 show the Design Layout dialog box with both horizontal and vertical multi-records. The first record shows the positioning of each field, with subsequent boxes (record 2, and so on) showing the position of additional records.

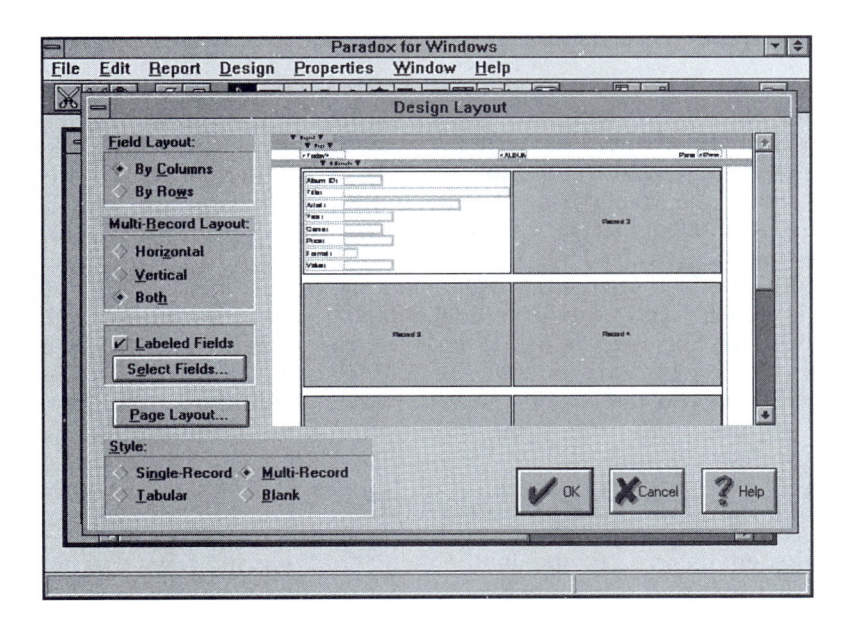

FIG. 6.3

A Multi-Record report layout style.

The Labeled check box enables you to turn the field names on and off. In the default tabular style, field names are displayed in column headers, so this option is not active.

To select which fields to include in the report, click the Select Fields button. The Select Fields dialog box appears (see fig. 6.4). By default, all fields in the selected table are included in the report.

I — PARADOX FOR WINDOWS FUNDAMENTALS

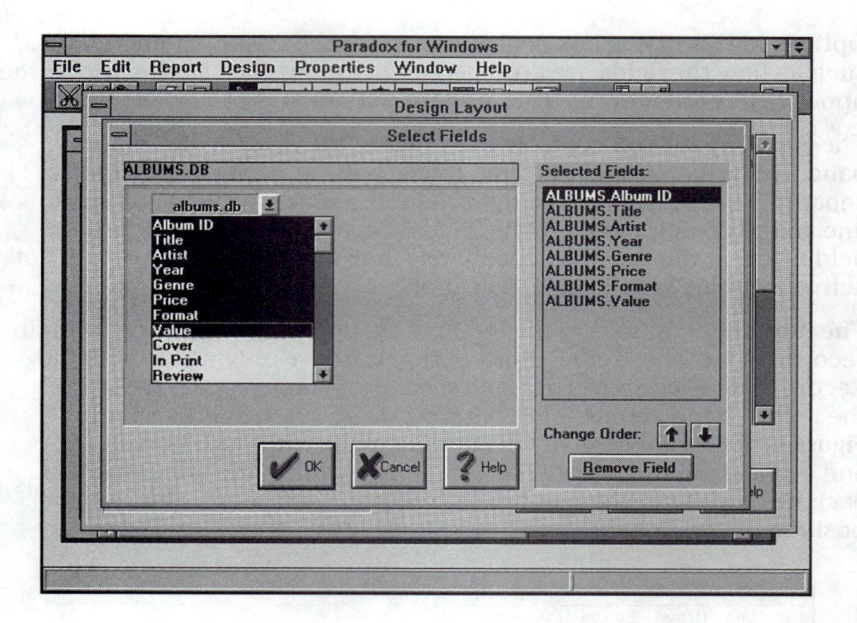

FIG. 6.4

The Select Fields dialog box.

The left side of the dialog box contains a data model containing all the tables you are using for the report. To see the fields in a table, click the pull-down menu next to the table name as shown in figure 6.4. On the right side of the screen is a list of the fields included in the report. To remove a field from the report, highlight the field by clicking it, and then click the Remove Field button. To add a field to the report, pull down the field list for the table and click the desired field name. The field is transferred to the Selected Fields list. To reorder a field, highlight it in the Selected Fields list and click the Change Order fields' up- or down-arrow buttons to move the field to the desired position. Remember that you can always move the fields within the format later.

Setting the Page Layout

Paradox enables you to specify the format of the printed page to be used by the report. Click the Page Layout button in the Design Layout dialog box. The Page Layout dialog box appears (see fig. 6.5).

You can choose page sizes from standard Paradox options or define a custom paper size. In addition, you can designate top, bottom, left, and right margins. The default settings are for letter size (8 1/2- by 11-inch) paper, with half-inch top, bottom, left and right margins. Paradox also defaults to portrait orientation. Choose Landscape to change the printer orientation. Paradox displays an icon showing how the page orientation will look.

6 — GETTING STARTED WITH REPORTS

If you are planning to send the report to the screen, choose Scree̱n from the ̱Design For option. Click OK to return to the Design Layout dialog box.

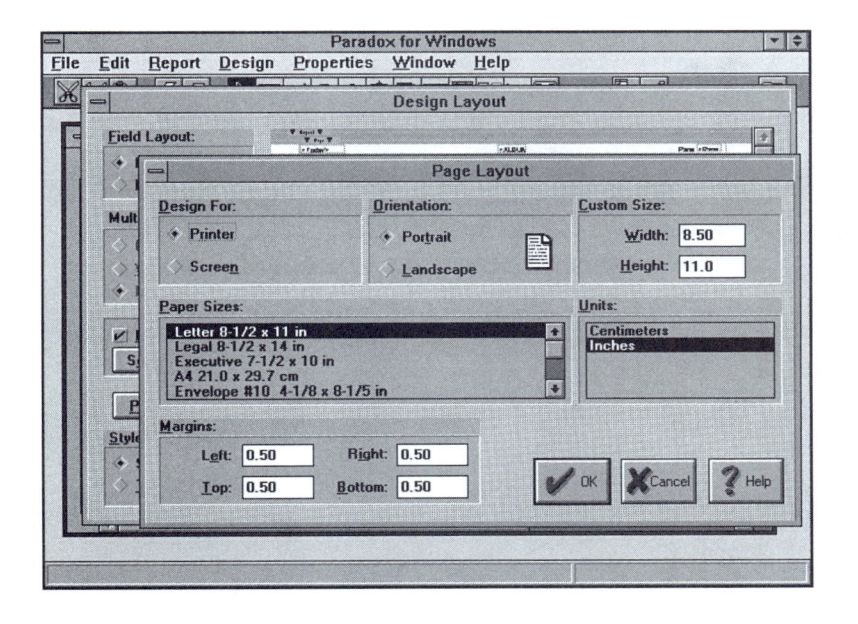

FIG. 6.5

The Page Layout dialog box.

Choosing the Layout Style

Next, choose the layout style for the report from the ̱Style options in the Design Layout dialog box. You can use the default layout settings as the starting point for your report, then modify the format for your needs. You can choose from the following ̱Style options:

Option	Description
Single-Record	One record is printed at a time. This layout is handy for tables with a large number of fields.
Multi-record	Prints several records, with fields repeating either vertically or horizontally in the record band. You can use multi-record style for formatting mailing labels, for instance.
Tabular	The default setting. It resembles table view in the table window. Tabular layout inserts a table object in the record band of the report format.
Blank	Any empty format that requires you to place all the fields manually. This layout is handy when you need only a small number of fields from the table, or when the field order must be altered drastically for the report.

I — PARADOX FOR WINDOWS FUNDAMENTALS

Try to choose the layout closest to the finished format of the report. When you are finished with the layout style, click the OK button. The Report Design window appears (see fig. 6.6). This is where the real work begins.

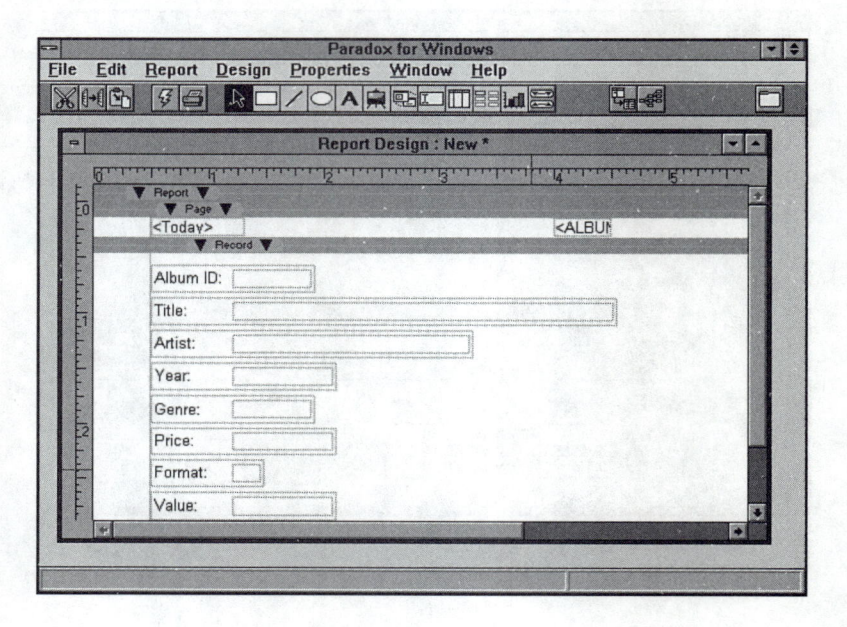

FIG. 6.6

The Report Design window.

> **NOTE** The difference between tabular and multi-record styles is that the multi-record style creates separate objects for fields and field labels, whereas the tabular style creates a single table object that contains the fields and labels. Table objects enable you to easily change the column width or reorder columns in a single step. You must move several objects in a multi-record layout to make the same change.

Working in the Report Design Window

The Report Design window is similar to the Form Design window. The window displays the format of the report you are working on, along with special formatting tools and options. Figure 6.7 shows the SpeedBar tools in the Report Design window.

6 — GETTING STARTED WITH REPORTS

FIG. 6.7
The Report design SpeedBar.

The SpeedBar in the Report Design window contains one button not found in the Form Design window—the Add Band button—and is missing the Button tool and Crosstab tool. The SpeedBar buttons specific to form design are discussed in the following table, starting with the View Data button, which resembles a lightning bolt.

Button	Name	Description
	View Data	Displays the report on-screen
	Print Report	Sends the current report to the printer
	Selection Arrow	Selects objects for moving, resizing, deleting, or editing
	Box tool	Draws boxes in report format
	Line tool	Draws lines in report format
	Ellipse tool	Draws ellipses (including circles) in report format
	Text tool	Adds text objects to report format
	Graphic tool	Adds bit-mapped graphic to report format
	OLE tool	Adds object linking and embedding (OLE) objects to report format
	Field tool	Adds fields to report format
	Table tool	Adds table objects to report format
	Multi-record tool	Adds multi-table objects to report format

continues

I — PARADOX FOR WINDOWS FUNDAMENTALS

Button	Name	Description
	Graph tool	Adds graph (bar graph, pie graph, and so on) to report format
	Add Band	Adds an optional group band to the report format
	Data Model	Shows the relationships of tables used in the report
	Object Tree	Shows related objects, used in ObjectPAL

Each report object has a set of characteristics called *properties*. Some properties, such as color, are common to nearly every object. When you create an object, it comes with standard or default properties, which you can change by examining the object and selecting from the properties menu. The following sections explain in detail the properties offered for each kind of form object.

Selecting Objects

To create, move, or modify objects in a report, you must select them with the Selection Arrow tool or the keyboard. When you click the Selection Arrow to activate it, the mouse pointer becomes an arrow. The Selection Arrow is the default tool for this window, so the mouse pointer may already be an arrow.

When you select an object, handles appear around the object. You use the handles to drag the object in the workspace and to change the size or shape of the object. To stretch a box, for example, click on a handle in the middle of one of its sides and drag it to the desired size. Click on a handle on the corner of a box and drag to change both its height and width. To move an object, click inside the object (*not* on its handles) and drag it to the desired location.

To select objects from the keyboard, press Tab to move the selection handles from the currently selected object to the next object in the form. To back up to the previous object, press Shift+Tab.

You can select one object or several objects at a time. To select multiple objects, press Shift while clicking the first object, then move to the next object and press Shift+click again. Repeat these steps until you have selected all the objects you need. This is called the *Shift+click technique*.

Another way to select multiple objects is to define a rectangle on-screen and select all objects inside it. Paradox calls this the *Shift+drag technique*. First position the mouse pointer in a corner of the area to be selected. Then press Shift while holding down the left mouse button. Next, drag the mouse pointer to the diagonal corner. A dotted line shows the shape of the rectangle as you drag it. When you release the mouse button, all the objects in the rectangle are selected.

Finally, you can select all the objects in the currently selected object by choosing Select All from the Edit menu.

To deselect an object, place the mouse pointer on the selected object and press Shift+click again. The handles disappear. When two objects are close together, pressing Shift+click may select the second object rather than deselect the first object. Try Shift+click again until the object is deselected.

After you have selected one or more objects, you can manipulate them in several ways. You can move the objects by clicking and dragging, or you can use the Edit menu to move selected objects. The Edit menu commands have keyboard equivalents as well, which you may find quicker than choosing from the menu. These keyboard shortcuts are Shift+Del for Cut, Ctrl+Ins for Copy, Shift+Ins for Paste, and Del for Delete.

Displaying Object Properties

Like form objects, report objects have properties that you control. To display the properties of an object, right-click the selected object, press Shift+F8, or choose Properties, Current Object from the Create Form window.

Displaying Tool Properties

The SpeedBar tools have their own set of properties as well. You can define standard properties for all the objects you define. To display the properties of a tool, right-click the icon for the tool in the SpeedBar. For instance, you may want to change the font of all text objects in a report. Right-click the Text tool, then click Font from its properties menu. Click Font from the Font menu and choose the desired typeface. Create a text object and enter some text to verify the font change.

> **NOTE** When you change the properties of a tool, the change affects only the objects you subsequently create with that tool. Objects already on the report retain their original properties.

Drawing Boxes, Ellipses, and Lines

Paradox for Windows includes basic drawing capabilities for embellishing your reports. The box, line, and ellipse tools in the SpeedBar work in much the same way as the tools in paint programs such as Microsoft Windows Paintbrush.

The Box tool, Line tool, and Ellipse tool all work in the same way. See Chapter 5, "Getting Started with Forms," for additional information. To use the Box, Line, or Ellipse tool, follow these steps:

1. Click the tool you want to use on the SpeedBar.

2. Move the mouse pointer to the starting point for the line, the corner of the box, or the edge of the ellipse. If you choose the Line tool, the mouse pointer changes from an arrow to a pencil. For the Box tool, the mouse pointer is a box under a crosshatch. For the Ellipse tool, the mouse pointer is shown as a circle under a crosshatch.

3. Click the mouse button to mark the starting point and drag the mouse to the desired length or shape of the object. When you release the mouse button, the object is drawn. If you do not like its shape, you can stretch it or shrink it by clicking its handles and dragging it until it has the desired dimensions.

These drawn objects have their own list of properties that you can modify to change their appearance. Boxes and ellipses have the same properties:

Property	Description
Color	Controls the fill color inside the object. For more information on colors, see "Setting Field Colors" later in this chapter.
Frame	Controls the style, color, and thickness of the line that defines the outside of the object. This property displays a palette showing all the frame styles available.
Pattern	Controls the color and style of the fill pattern (such as crosshatch or dots) inside the object. Paradox provides a palette that shows all the available patterns.
Contain Objects	Treats objects inside the box or the ellipse as part of the box or ellipse for movement or deletion.
Pin	Affixes the object either horizontally or vertically in the form so that it cannot be moved.

Property	Description
Methods	Controls the behavior of the object in different situations. This option is used with ObjectPAL. Part III is devoted to ObjectPAL programming techniques.

To change the properties of the object, click on the list of properties and choose from the options for each property. The property changes take effect immediately, so you can see your results.

Lines have a slightly different set of properties, as follows:

Property	Description
Color	Controls the color of the line. For more information on colors, see "Setting Field Colors" later in this chapter.
Line style	Offers invisible, solid, and four different patterns of broken lines. When you choose Line style, a palette is displayed, showing each line style.
Line type	Enables you to draw Normal (straight) or Elliptical (curved) lines. To draw an elliptical line, create it as a straight line and then change the line type property to Elliptical. To straighten a curved line, inspect its properties and change the Line type to Normal.
Line extremity	Enables you to attach arrows to neither end, either end, or both ends (extremities) of a line. No Arrow is the default for this property. If you choose On One End, the arrow is attached to the end of the line as you drew it, that is, the end where you released the mouse button. To change the direction of the arrow, you must redraw the line. If you choose On Both Ends, arrows are attached to both ends of the line.
Thickness	Changes the thickness of the line, with four degrees of thickness available. The default is a thin line. Like the Line style property, Thickness lets you choose from a palette of line widths.
Pin	Affixes the line either horizontally or vertically in the form so that it cannot be moved.
Methods	Controls the behavior of the line in different situations. This option is used with ObjectPAL.

The properties chosen from palettes (color, pattern, frame, font, line style, and line thickness) offer special features. If you click the round button at the top of the palette, it becomes a floating palette. This means that the palette remains on-screen while you are working with objects, which is useful if you are modifying the same property on several objects. The floating palettes may display more features as well, or offer buttons to access related dialog boxes such as the custom color dialog box.

To change a line's properties, select the object and right-click to reveal the line properties menu. Use the mouse to choose from the properties listed.

Adding Text

The Text icon in the SpeedBar is used to create screen objects that contain one or more lines of text. You can use text objects as titles, text labels, or background text for a report.

To create a text object, click the Text tool. The mouse pointer changes to an *A* under a crosshatch. Position the mouse pointer in one corner of the box where the text appears, then click and drag diagonally to make the text object the desired length and width. Don't worry about guessing the exact size of the box, because you can adjust the box after you enter the text.

When you release the mouse button, the outline of the text object appears, with the mouse pointer in the upper-left corner. (If you choose center or right alignment for the text object, the cursor is placed in the center or on the right side of the line.) Click again so that the mouse pointer changes to indicate that you are in text edit mode (the pointer looks like][). Practice entering some text. Note that text wraps automatically in the text object. If you fill the entire box, the text scrolls upward so that you can enter more.

To view the properties of the text object, place the mouse pointer in the box and click the right mouse button (see fig. 6.8). See Chapter 5, "Getting Started with Forms," for an explanation of text object properties.

Adding a Graphic

A graphic in a report lets you know instantly that you are looking at a Windows database instead of a DOS database. A graphic is a bit-mapped image, such as a digitized photograph, an icon, or a symbol.

Do not confuse a graphic with a Paradox graph, such as a bar graph or a pie chart. (Both graphs and graphics, however, can be placed in a report.) Paradox has separate tools for graphics and graphs. See Chapter 5 for a discussion of graphic objects. You use the same steps to insert a graphic in a report or in a form.

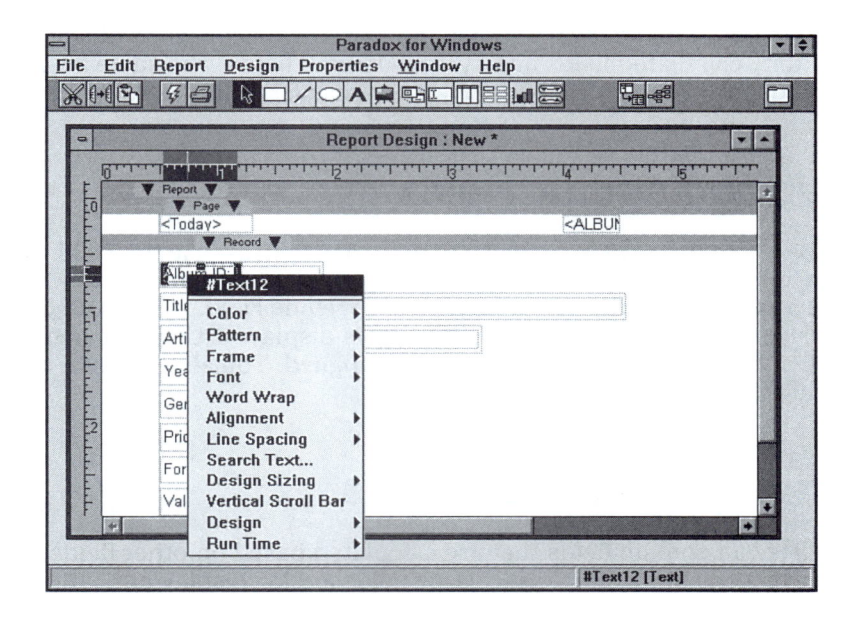

FIG. 6.8

The properties of a text object.

For Related Information

◄◄ "Working in the Form Design Window," p. 215.

Adding OLE Objects

As mentioned, OLE (object linking and embedding) is a Windows technique for moving data from one program to another. The OLE feature may be used with Paradox reports so that Paradox pulls data from other applications such as spreadsheets or graphics. OLE is discussed in Chapter 11, "Exchanging Data with Other Applications."

Adding Fields

Because the main purpose of a report is to access data in Paradox tables, fields are perhaps the most important objects in a form. The Field tool is used to create and place fields on a form. In addition to using fields from tables, Paradox offers several special kinds of fields, including calculated fields and system-derived fields. The same basic techniques are used for all field types, as discussed in this section.

Placing Regular Fields

To place regular fields—fields from database tables—use the Field tool to define the box where the field will be placed. Right-click the new field to reveal the properties menu and choose Define Field. A list of all the fields in the table or tables you are using is displayed. Click the name of the field you want, and the new field is assigned. You also can edit any of the other field properties at this time.

Placing Calculated Fields

Reports can contain fields that are calculated based on other fields or other records in the database. These fields are for display only; the user cannot enter them.

Paradox reports offer seven summary functions:

Sum	The total of all values
Count	The number of occurrences of a value
Min	The minimum value for all records
Max	The maximum value for all records
Avg	The mean of non-null values
Std	The standard deviation, a statistical measure
Var	Variance, another statistical function

In addition to summary functions, you may use the first, last, and previous navigation buttons to display values from the first, last, and previous records in the table. You may find summary functions more useful in reports than in forms.

You can use the Avg summary function, for example, to display the average sales by sales representative in order to compare the performance of each sales representative to the average. The Sum function is used frequently in reports to show group subtotals, such as sales amounts by product code or by date, as well as in calculating the grand total for a report.

To define a summary field, follow these steps:

1. Use the Field tool to place the field on the report.
2. Right-click the field to reveal the properties menu, and choose Define Field. A list of all the fields you are using is displayed.
3. Do not click any of these field names; instead, click ..., which is the first line in the list.

   The Define Field Object dialog box appears (see fig. 6.9). This dialog box is used to define new fields.
4. Use the pull-down menu on the table name to choose the field, then select from the summary function pull-down menu.
5. Click OK when you complete your choice.

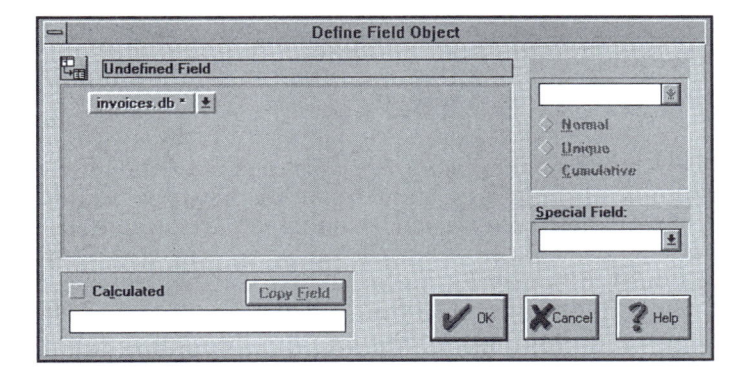

FIG. 6.9

The Define Field Object dialog box.

Placing the Record-Number and Other Special Fields

In addition to the fields that you define, each table contains system fields that can be displayed on a report. Click the pull-down menu on the table in the Define Field Object dialog box and scroll to the bottom of the list. The following system fields are listed:

    <Table Name>
    <Record Number>
    <N of Records>
    <N of Fields>

The *N* stands for number, as in the number of records and number of fields.

In addition to the system fields that accompany each table, Paradox contains special fields calculated outside database tables. To use a special field, click the Special Field pull-down menu on the Define Field Object dialog box. The menu expands to reveal the following fields:

Field	Description
Today	Displays the current date, as stored in the system clock of your PC. The format of the Today field may be changed to any of the standard Paradox date formats.
Now	The current time in hours, minutes, and seconds, again from the system clock
Page Number	Displays the current page number
N of Pages	Shows the total number of pages

Reformatting a Field

Paradox for Windows offers two properties to control the format of a field in a report—Display Type and Format. Display types and formats are different from field types (such as alphanumeric or date) because they do not affect what is stored in the table, only the way it is displayed. Options for Display Type are Labeled, Unlabeled, Drop-Down Edit, List, Radio Buttons, and Check Box. The Labeled and Unlabeled options enable you to include or remove the field label. List, Radio Buttons, and Check Box display the field as a list, radio button, or check box. The Drop-Down Edit option is not available for reports.

To change the display type of the field, choose Display Type from the field properties menu. Number and date fields have a property called format. For example, you may want to display the date for Independence Day as July 4, 1776 (Windows Long) rather than 7/4/1776 or 4-Jul-1776. Standard Paradox number field formats are Windows $, Windows #, Fixed, Scientific, General, Comma, Percent and Integer. You also may define your own number and date display formats.

Adding a Table Object

Reports may include table objects, which behave like Paradox tables used for data entry. You can control the height and width of columns, the column labels, and the order of fields in table objects.

Table objects often are used in multi-table reports that have a one-to-many relationship between two tables, such as invoices and line items.

Adding a Multi-Record Region

In most cases, single-table reports list one record per line. If needed, however, a report can display several records at a time using multi-record regions. In essence, a multi-record region is just a copy of a format for a single record. Multi-record regions may repeat horizontally, vertically, or in both directions.

One way to create multi-record regions is to choose Multi-Record from the Design Layout dialog box, as discussed previously in this chapter. You also can define a multi-record region with the Multi-record tool.

Adding a Graph

Paradox has the built-in capability to generate a wide range of business graphs, such as bar graphs, line graphs, and pie charts. Building Paradox graphs is discussed in Chapter 10.

Using the Data Model Tool

To the right of the design tools in the SpeedBar are two additional tools: the Data Model tool and the Object Tree. The Data Model is used to define the tables used for a report. Click the Data Model button to reveal the Data Model dialog box.

Using the Object Tree

The Object Tree displays a window that shows all the objects defined for a form. The Object Tree is used for writing scripts with ObjectPAL. See Part III for tips on using the Object Tree.

For Related Information
▶▶ "Creating Graphs," p. 436.

Understanding Bands

Paradox for Windows, like many database packages, divides the format of a report into several areas, or *bands*, as shown in figure 6.10. The bands are like concentric layers that repeat at specified intervals. Paradox for Windows has four types of bands, and each contains a header and a footer section:

Band	Description
Report band	Prints at the beginning (first page) and end (last page) of the report. A report footer could contain grand totals for the entire report, for example.
Page band	Prints at the top (header) and bottom (footer) of each page. This is where the report title, the date, and the page number are usually placed.
Group band	Prints at the beginning and end of each group of records, if a group is defined in the report. You might use a group band to show clients by state, for example, with subtotals and counts listed at the bottom of each state.
Record band	Prints once for each record that is printed. This is where the detail from the table prints, usually in tabular format. Summary reports do not have a record band; they print only the group and report totals.

FIG. 6.10

Types of report bands.

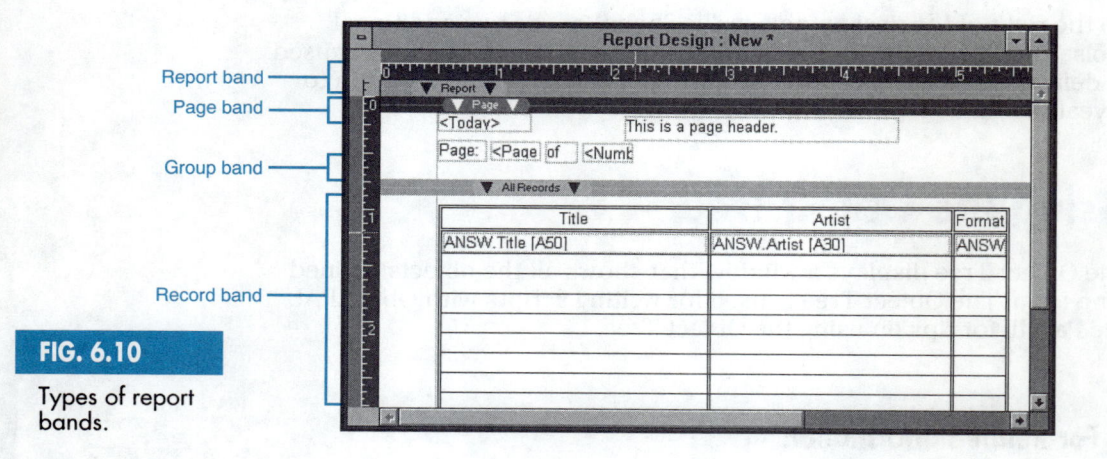

Figure 6.11 shows the way that the report bands print on the finished report.

FIG. 6.11

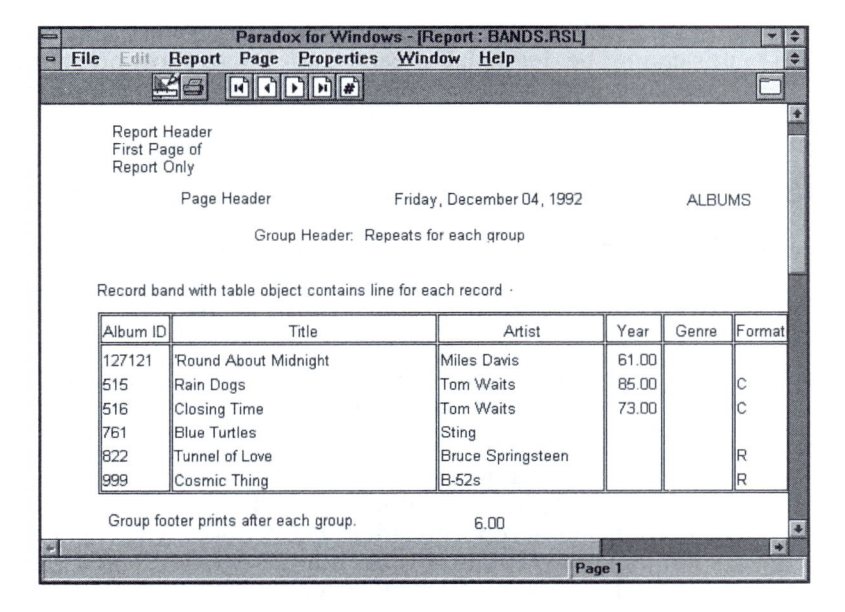

Sample output.

Resizing Bands

When you create a report format, Paradox for Windows automatically generates the default page, report, and record bands. You can make each band as large as you want, or condense it to no lines so that it does not appear on the report.

To resize a report band, select it by clicking the band. The selected band is highlighted in the bar along the left border of the window. Drag the top or bottom band up or down until the band is the desired size.

You may turn the band labels off and on by choosing Properties, Band Labels. Turning the band labels off will save a few lines on the screen, which will help you see more of a lengthy report design.

Use the mouse to drag the band to the desired length. When you place the mouse pointer on the edge of a selected band, the pointer changes to a two-headed arrow, indicating that you can move or resize the band. No keyboard method exists for resizing a report band.

Deleting a Band

To delete a band, select it by clicking the band label. Next, choose Delete from the Edit menu or press the Del key. The band disappears from the report. You can add or delete group bands. Page, report, and record bands cannot be deleted, but can be shrunk to show no lines so that they are not printed.

Specifying Report Headers and Footers

The report header and footer print only once for the entire report. The report header prints on the first page of the report, and the report footer appears on the last page of the report before the page footer for that page.

To specify the contents of the report header and footer, simply place objects such as fields, text, or graphics in the header or footer band.

Any objects can be placed in the header and footer bands. Typically, the report header contains a description of the report, a memorandum or letter to preface the report, or routing instructions. By default, Paradox includes nothing in the report header of any report. The report footer might contain grand totals or other summary fields, and a line indicating that the report is finished, such as

```
***END OF REPORT***
```

> **TIP** Use the report header to identify your report and show the date it was printed. You also may want to include graphics in a report header, such as your corporate logo; including graphics on each record would slow down printing.

Specifying Page Headers and Footers

The page band prints on the header and footer of each page in a report. Nearly every report should repeat the report name either in the report header or the page header so that you can identify the report. The page header band is the logical place for page numbers, either in the header or the footer section. For reports that cover a specified range of records, the page header should explain which records are included. For instance, you might have a page header that looks like the one in figure 6.10.

See the instructions for placing special fields to learn how to place page numbers in the page bands. By default, Paradox places the table name, report date, and page number in the page header band.

At a glance, you can tell what the report is about, the page number, and additional information (such as the period of time the information covers).

Working with Fields

Nearly every report contains one or more fields from the database. You also can create new fields based on calculations. Regardless of where the field comes from, Paradox for Windows gives you a great deal of control over its appearance and behavior.

Placing a Regular Field

To add a field from a database table to the report format, follow these steps:

1. Get to the Report Design window by choosing File, New, Report from the Paradox Desktop or by right-clicking the Report button and choosing New.
2. Choose ALBUMS.DB as the table for the report.
3. Click OK in the Report Layout dialog box to accept the default layout.
4. Click the Field tool in the SpeedBar. The mouse pointer changes to look like the Field tool icon, with a right angle above it.
5. Move the mouse pointer to the desired location of the field.
6. Click one corner of the field and drag the mouse pointer to the opposite corner.
7. Release the mouse button and the new field is shown on the report layout. A new field, labeled Undefined field, is created.
8. To designate the field name, right-click the new field to inspect its properties. You will see the field properties, as shown in figure 6.12.
9. Choose Define Field, then choose the desired field from the list provided.

    You can change the field properties to alter the way the field is displayed in the report.

I — PARADOX FOR WINDOWS FUNDAMENTALS

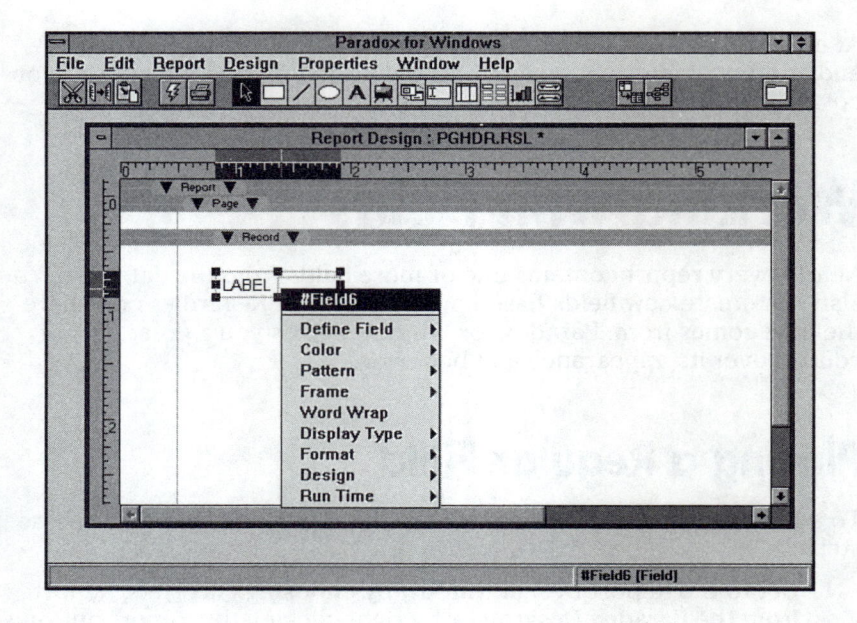

FIG. 6.12

The field properties menu.

Deleting a Field

To remove a field from a report, click the field. Press the Del key, or choose Edit, Delete from the menu. The field disappears from the report design.

If you delete a field by mistake, you can retrieve it by choosing Edit, then selecting Undo. If you delete and Undo does not appear on the Edit menu, you must either re-create the deleted objects or discard your changes by exiting without saving the report. The Undo command works only if you have not performed another editing function, so try to catch mistakes as early as possible.

Manipulating the Table Object

Table objects are used in the record band of tabular style reports. With few exceptions, the same controls are used to manipulate the table object in the Report Design window as in the Table Edit menu. Therefore, the following commands (and their explanations) are similar to those discussed in Chapter 3, "Entering, Editing, and Viewing Data."

Just as you can change the way a table is displayed for editing data, you can customize the table object for a report. For instance, you may want to delete certain columns, change the column order, resize columns, or change the fonts in a table object.

Resizing the Table Object

You can adjust the size or position of the entire table object. Select the table object by clicking the object. Handles appear around the entire table object to indicate that it has been selected.

Next, use the handles to drag the object and change its location or size. Release the mouse button when you have completed your changes.

Resizing a Column

To change the column width, use the Selection Arrow tool on the SpeedBar. Click the top of the right border of the column you want to change. The mouse pointer changes to a two-sided arrow and the message area displays `Resizing column width`. Drag the border to the left or right to increase or decrease the width of the column. When you release the mouse button, the column is resized. The field names are followed by their types (indicated by the one-letter abbreviation) and their lengths to give you an idea of how much space is needed.

If you resize the column to a length of zero spaces, the column is deleted. The message area indicates that the column will be deleted when you move the right column border all the way to the left of the column.

> **NOTE** You must use the right side of the border to resize a column. If you move the left border of a column, you will resize the previous column.

Moving, Adding, and Deleting a Column

To move a column, click the record object or move to top of the table until the "mailbox" appears. The message area displays `Moving column`. Next, drag the column to the desired position. When you release the mouse button, the column is moved.

To add a column to a table object, select the table object in the Report Design window and press Ins.

To delete a column, select the table object, then place the mouse pointer on the vertical border on the right side of the column, as if you were resizing the column. Click the border, then move the border to the left or right until the mouse pointer touches the next column. The message line reminds you that you are deleting a column. When you release the mouse button, the column disappears. You also can delete a column by selecting the column and pressing the Del key.

Changing the Row Height

You can adjust the space between two rows to make the text easier to read. Place the mouse pointer on the border between the first and second rows (the message area shows that you are resizing the row height), click the mouse, and drag the row to the desired spacing. When you release the mouse button, your change takes effect.

Viewing Report Table Properties

To view report table properties, select the table object and click the right mouse button. The table properties menu appears (see fig. 6.13). The following list of properties is displayed:

Property	Description
Define Table	Chooses the table for the report. The Define Table Object dialog box (see fig. 6.14) is displayed if you click this property.
Color	Controls the background color of the table.
Pattern	Controls the color and style of the fill pattern (such as crosshatch or dots) of the background inside the table.
Grid	Sets characteristics for the lines separating rows and columns. Single, double, triple, and simulated three-dimensional grids are available in every color.
Repeat Header	Repeats the header on each page or prints it only once. The default setting is repeated.
Detach Header	Sets the header text apart from the data rows.
Horizontal Scroll Bar	A horizontal scroll bar for use when the table extends beyond the edge of the screen.
Design	Options are Pin Horizontal, Pin Vertical, and Size to Fit. Pin Horizontal and Pin Vertical prevent the object from being moved either horizontally or vertically when another object in the report expands or contracts. Size to Fit automatically rescales the object to fit.

6 — GETTING STARTED WITH REPORTS

Property	Description
Run Time	Options are Pin Horizontal, Pin Vertical, Show All Columns, Show All Records, and Breakable. Breakable means that the table object can be split over more than one page if it does not fit on a single page.
Delete When Empty	Suppresses display of the table frame object if the table it based on is empty.

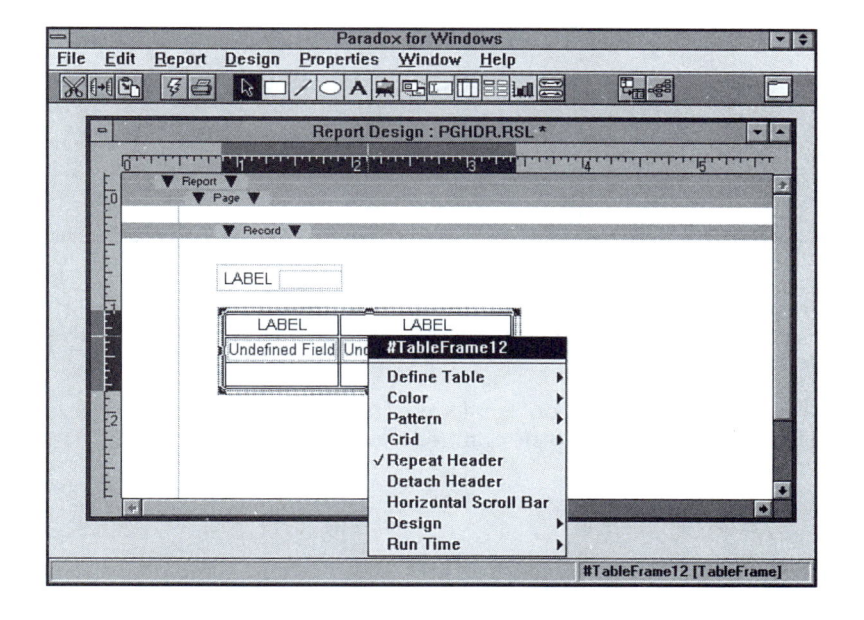

FIG. 6.13

Table Object properties.

Previewing and Saving a Report

To see how the report will look before you print it, you can preview the output on-screen. Click the View Data tool (the lightning bolt) in the SpeedBar, and the report is displayed on-screen. If the report is too wide to fit on-screen, use the scroll bars to move the cursor horizontally and vertically in the report. Use the buttons in the SpeedBar to move between pages of the report. You also can preview a report by choosing Preview from the Report menu or by pressing F8.

I — PARADOX FOR WINDOWS FUNDAMENTALS

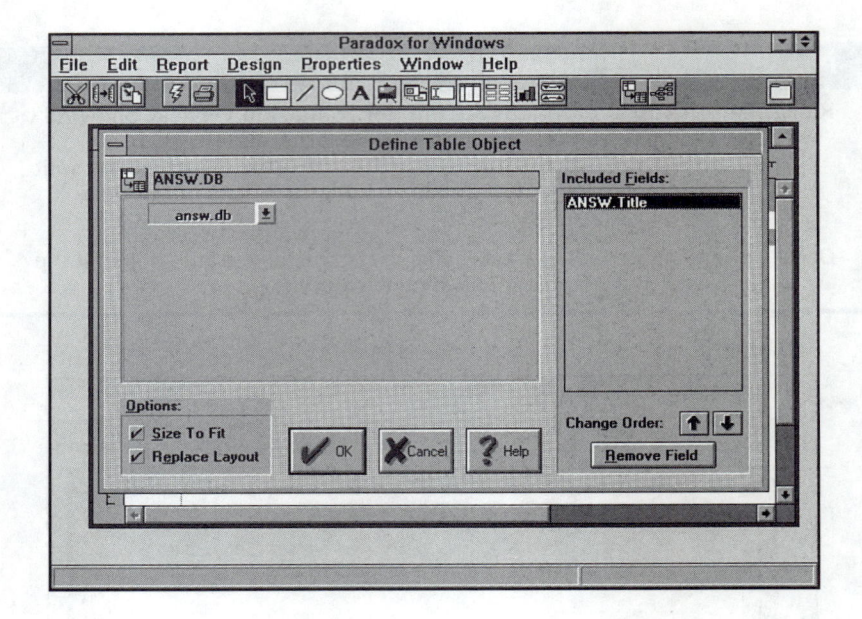

FIG. 6.14

The Define Table Object dialog box.

When you have finished previewing the report, you can return to the Report Design window by clicking the Design button (or choose Report, Design from the menu).

To preserve your work, you must save the report. Choose File, Save. To save the report under another name, choose Save As and specify the new report name.

Printing a Report

To print a report, simply click the Print button in the SpeedBar from the Report Design window or the report preview window. The Print File dialog box appears (see fig. 6.15).

Use the Print File dialog box to select the page range and the number of copies to be printed. The default setting is to print one copy of all pages.

Controlling the Printer

In Windows applications such as Paradox for Windows, the printer is controlled by Windows rather than by printer drivers in the application software. This means that you can use any of the hundreds of printers supported by Microsoft Windows.

To view your printer settings, choose P_rinter Setup from the Paradox F_ile menu. The Printer Setup dialog box appears (see fig. 6.16). This dialog box lists all the printers currently installed for Windows, with the selected printer highlighted. Click the printer name to change the printer selection. To change printer options, click the M_odify Printer Setup button to reveal the setup dialog box for your printer (see fig. 6.17).

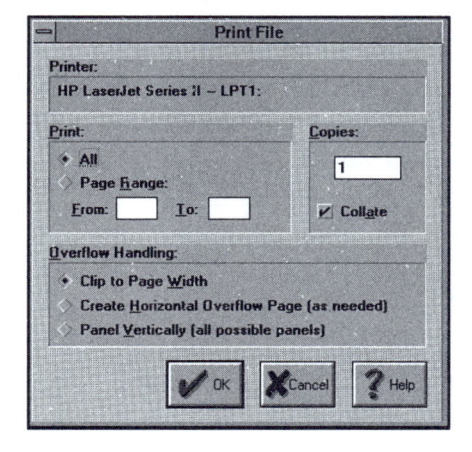

FIG. 6.15
The Print File dialog box.

Use the pull-down menus to adjust setting for R_esolution, Paper Si_ze, Paper S_ource, and M_emory. Additional options for fonts and cartridges may be available. Consult your Windows documentation for additional help on configuring printers.

> **TIP**
> The lower the printer resolution, the faster your reports will print. For draft output on a laser printer, reduce the resolution from 300 to 150 or 75 dots per inch.

I — PARADOX FOR WINDOWS FUNDAMENTALS

FIG. 6.16

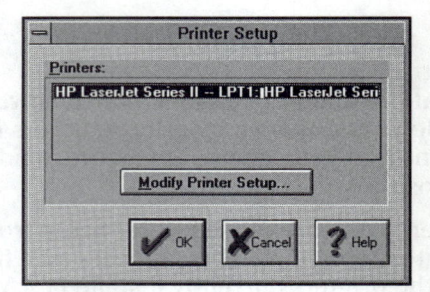

The Printer Setup dialog box.

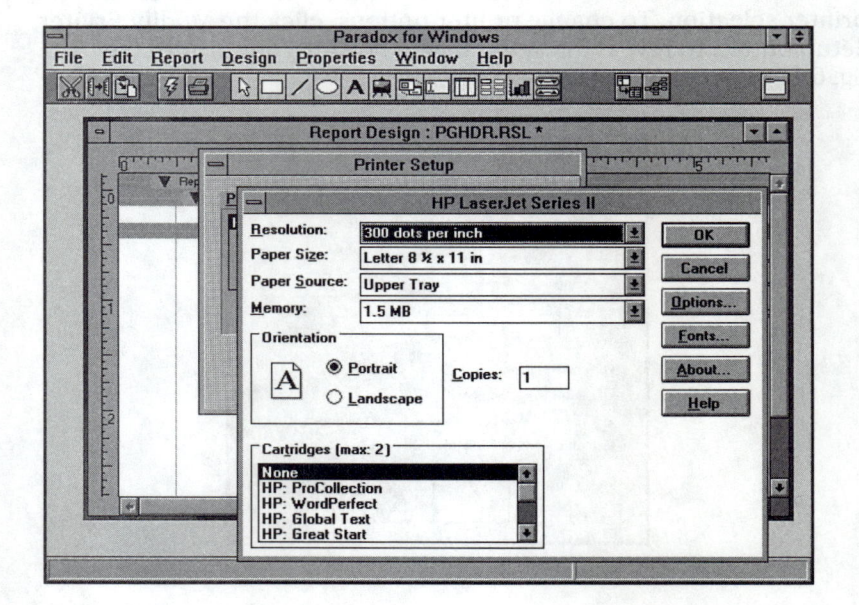

FIG. 6.17

The printer settings for the HP LaserJet Series II printer.

Printer Orientation

Another printer choice involves the way the report prints on the paper. Many printers, especially laser printers and ink-jet printers, can print vertically (portrait orientation) or horizontally (landscape orientation). You can change the printer orientation from the Printer Setup dialog box.

Examining Some Typical Paradox Reports

Some types of reports are found in nearly every database application. If you build a number of applications, you will find yourself creating reports similar to these time and time again. This section offers prototypes along with hints for each type of report.

Mailing Labels

Many databases contain information on people, and such databases are often used to generate mailing labels. This example shows how to create three-across labels for a laser printer.

1. Start with a table that contains address information. If you followed Quick Start 1, you can use the Customer table; or you can create a Customer table with fields similar to the following:

Field Name	Type	Length	Key
LNAME	A	20	Yes
FNAME	A	15	Yes
ADDRESS	A	40	No
CITY	A	15	No
STATE	A	2	No
ZIP	A	5	No
ENTERED	D	-	No

2. Choose New, Report from the Paradox File menu or right-click the Report button and choose New.

3. Choose Customer from the File Selection dialog box. The Design Layout dialog box appears.

4. In the Design Layout dialog box, choose the Multi-Record style, and turn field labels off. Turn off field labels by clicking the Labeled Fields check box. The finished Design Layout is shown in figure 6.18. Click OK and the Report Design window appears.

5. In the Report Design window, move the fields into the proper arrangement for mailing labels, as shown in figure 6.19. Move the first and last names to the same line, for example, and then place

the city, state, and ZIP together, inserting a comma (use the Text tool) between city and state. Adjust the size of the record area by clicking and dragging to eliminate unneeded blank space in the format.

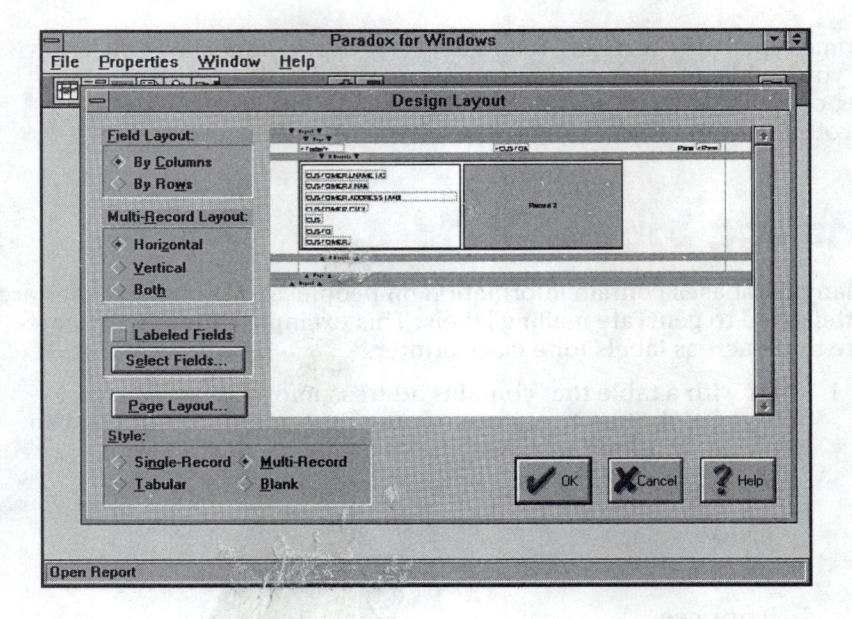

FIG. 6.18

The Design Layout for mailing labels.

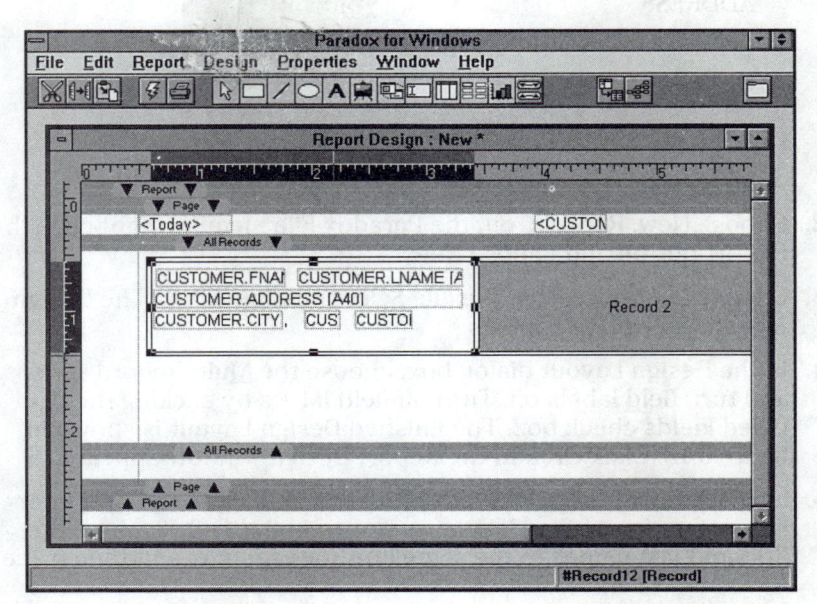

FIG. 6.19

Report Design for mailing labels.

6 — GETTING STARTED WITH REPORTS

6. Turn off the frame around each record by viewing the record properties and changing the frame style to blank (see fig. 6.20).

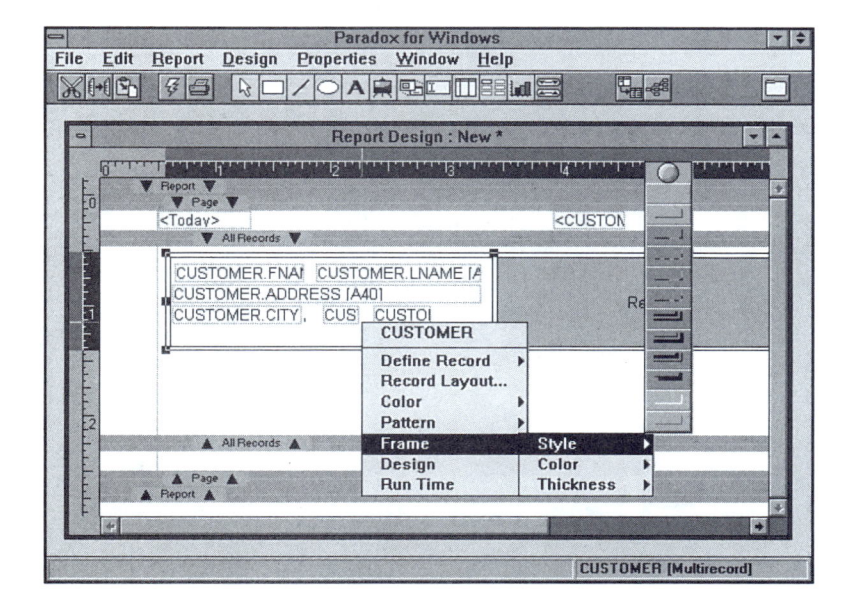

FIG. 6.20

Record Frame Style properties menu.

7. By default, Paradox displays the entire field up to its maximum length, padding any extra spaces with blanks. For lines with more than one field (such as first and last name on the first line of the label), this creates unpleasant gaps in the report. To trim the spaces, select the last name field, inspect its properties (right-click), and uncheck Run Time, Pin Horizontal. Repeat this step for all fields that are not the first fields in a line—the State and ZIP fields.

8. To change the number of labels printed on each row, select the record band and right-click to reveal its properties menu. Choose Record Layout to reveal the Record Layout dialog box (see fig. 6.21).

9. Enter the correct settings for your label stock—for this example, 2 across and 1 down. The Record Layout dialog box also enables you to choose the order in which records are printed, either from left to right, then down, or sorted down one column and then the next.

10. Choose File, Save to save the report. To view the report, click the View button in the SpeedBar. To return to Design mode, click the Design button in the SpeedBar. After you are happy with the

I — PARADOX FOR WINDOWS FUNDAMENTALS

format, click the Print button to print the labels. If you make any changes to the report, be sure to save them by saving the report again.

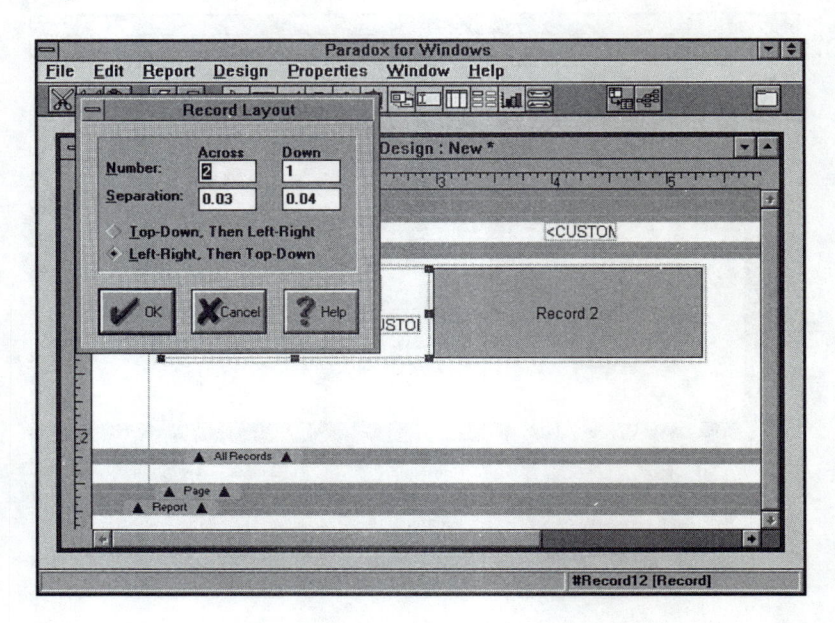

FIG. 6.21

The Record Layout dialog box.

The finished report is shown in figure 6.22. Depending on the label stock you are using, you may have to fine-tune the fonts and dimensions so that each label is positioned correctly.

> **TIP** The grid is an excellent tool for aligning fields in report design. Choose Show Grid and Snap to Grid from the Properties menu to ensure perfect alignment.

Many other reports use a format similar to mailing labels. Attendee rosters, for example, may resemble mailing labels. All you need to add are a report title, date, and other header information. If you add the text of a form letter to the format, the report can be converted from a label into a form letter. Use Save As to save the modified report under a new name. In this way, you can use the label report as the basis for other reports.

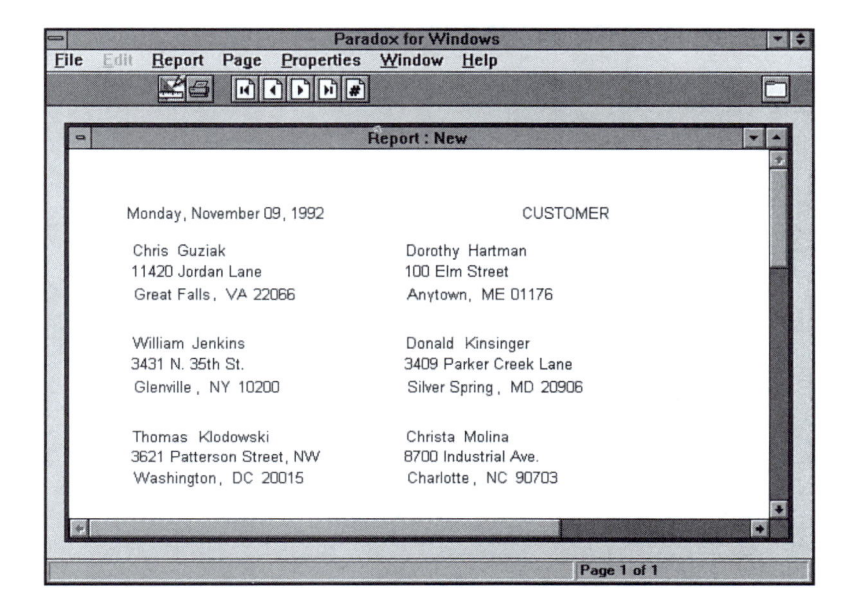

FIG. 6.22 Mailing label example.

Items in Groups

Another common reporting requirement is to divide records into groups. In the album database, you may want to group your holdings by genre (classical, rock, jazz, and so on). By setting up group bands, you can make each group stand out from the next, as shown in figure 6.23.

Follow these steps to create a report with grouping:

1. Create the report by choosing File, New, Report from the menu. Choose the table (ALBUMS.DB) and the report layout (tabular style), as described in previous examples in this chapter.

2. In the Report Design window, click the Add Band button in the SpeedBar to add a group band to the format.

   The Define Group dialog box appears (see fig. 6.24).

3. Specify the field to be grouped in the Define Group dialog box. Click the Genre field, then OK. The Report Design window appears, with a new band containing the genre field (see fig. 6.25).

FIG. 6.23

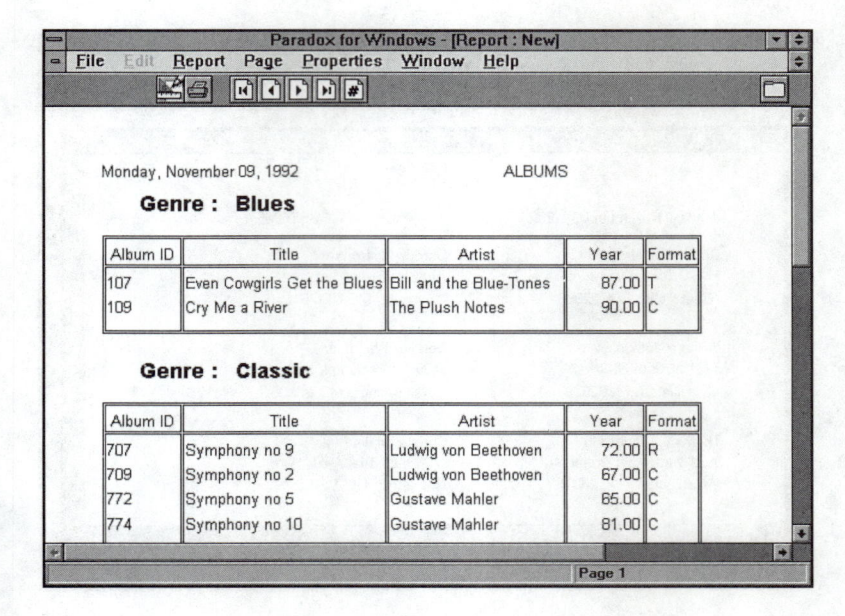

Albums grouped by Genre.

FIG. 6.24

The Define Group dialog box.

You may want to move or modify the field placed for you. You could omit the field label, for example, because the meaning of the field is obvious in the context of the report, or you could change the size or style of the field to make it stand out from other data.

You can even set up multiple levels of grouping. The bands of a report format with multiple levels of grouping should be read from the outside in, as if you were peeling an onion. In other words, the outside group

6 — GETTING STARTED WITH REPORTS

band contains the highest level of grouping, followed by progressively lower levels of grouping. Figure 6.26, for example, shows a report with grouping for both genre and format so that albums are divided by genre and within each genre by format.

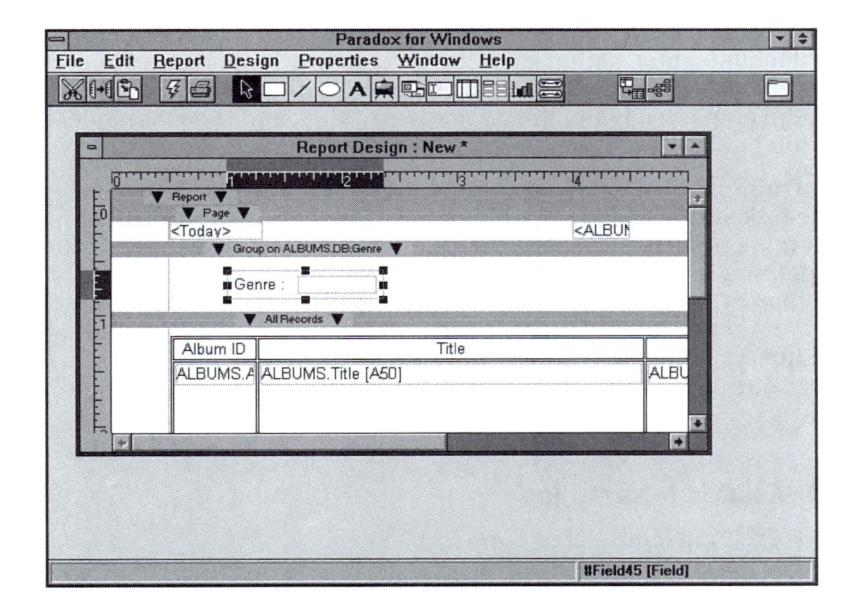

FIG. 6.25

The Report Design window showing a group band.

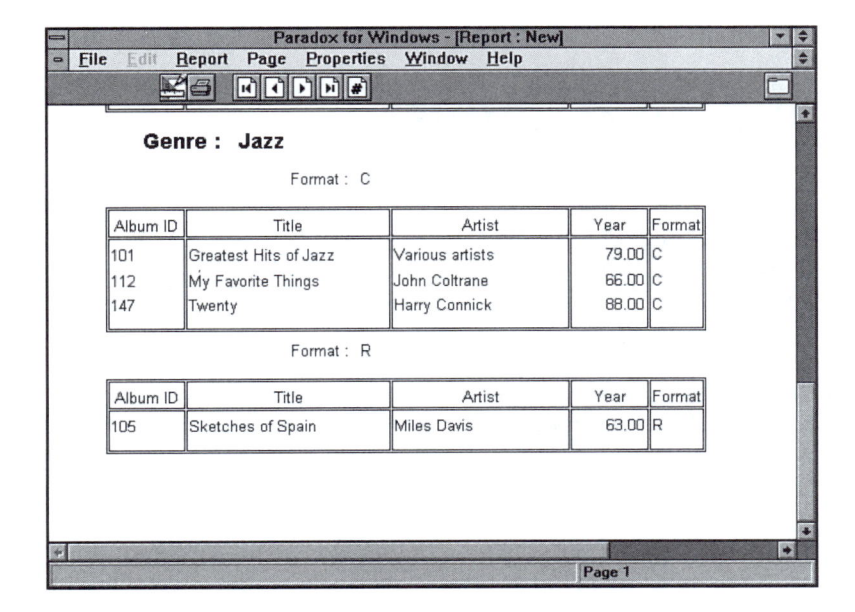

FIG. 6.26

Albums by Genre and Format (two levels of grouping).

Creating Multi-Table Reports

So far in this chapter, you have learned how to create reports that draw data from a single database table. Many times, however, a report should contain data from more than one table. For example, an invoice would include information from the invoice header table, the line items table, and the customer table. An employee listing might include data from the employee table, the dependents table, and the insurance benefits table.

With Paradox for Windows, multi-table reports are nearly as easy as single-table reports. Paradox offers two different ways to approach multi-table reports: using the data model in the Define Report window and defining a report based on a multi-table query. The simpler approach is to use a query to retrieve information from multiple tables into the Answer table, then create a report to list that information. Using a query as the basis for a report is also preferable because you can easily control the order of records in a query.

For Related Information
▶▶ "Creating Multi-Table Forms," p. 336.
▶▶ "Creating Multi-Table Queries," p. 366.

Planning a Report

Some general principles can help you design more effective reports in Paradox. Before delving into the details of creating a report, you should step back and think about how the report will be used. Throughout the design process, keep in mind the purpose of the report and its audience. You may want to start with a rough sketch of the report format.

Several characteristics separate good reports from inferior ones. Good reports help the reader get straight to the point, with a minimum of distraction. They are pleasant to look at and easy to read. Good reports are immediately understandable, even to someone who is not familiar with your database.

Although Paradox for Windows offers the intrepid report writer tremendous power and flexibility, it also contains its share of pitfalls. The sheer variety of objects that can be displayed on the screen or sent to the printer is mind-boggling at first. If overused, some special features (especially graphics) can be annoying gimmicks rather than tools for communication. Although this book covers all Paradox report features, you should not feel compelled to use them all in each report.

As a starting point to planning a report, look at the reports around you. For financial reporting, check the tables in the back of corporate annual reports. For database reports, use preprinted business forms (such as invoices, shipping lists, and form letters) as models. Look at other printed tables for inspiration, such as the baseball box scores in the newspaper. All these can teach the principles of sound report design.

Easy on the Eyes

To ensure that your reports make a good first impression, follow the principles of graphic design. Use some discipline in organizing words on paper, leaving ample white space (blank spaces and lines) to provide a place for the eye to rest.

Use the right size of paper to accommodate your information, and take advantage of special printer features such as boldface, underscore, and special typefaces (fonts) to set off important information. If a report is too wide to fit on standard (8 1/2- by 11-inch) paper in portrait orientation, even using fine print, switch to landscape orientation.

Clear and Concise

In reports, less can be more. A concise report is much easier to read and understand than one cluttered with needless detail. Include only the fields necessary to understand the report.

Figure 6.27 is an example of a report with unnecessary field labels. Although the field labels (title, artist, genre, format, and so on) are necessary to guide the user performing data entry, they are superfluous and even distracting on a report. A label is needed only when the meaning of the field is unclear, as in the credit limit and year-to-date purchases of each customer.

Figure 6.28 shows a streamlined version of the same report. Note that a short line is inserted between each record to improve legibility.

The report in figure 6.28 illustrates another good reporting standard: most reports should contain a header with the name of the report and the date it was produced. Without report names, you may not be able to tell which report you are reading. Repeat the header on every page. By default, Paradox for Windows includes the table name and today's date in the report header.

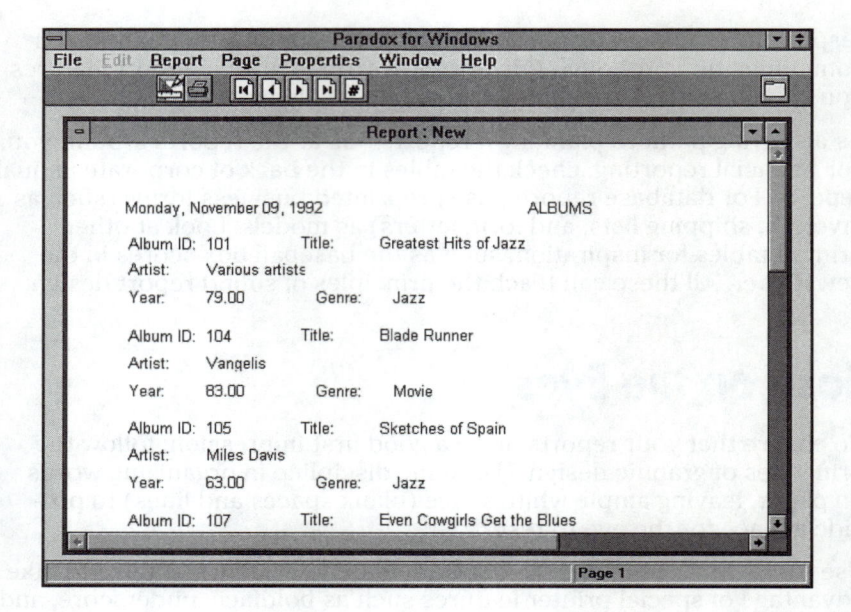

FIG. 6.27

Report with unnecessary field labels.

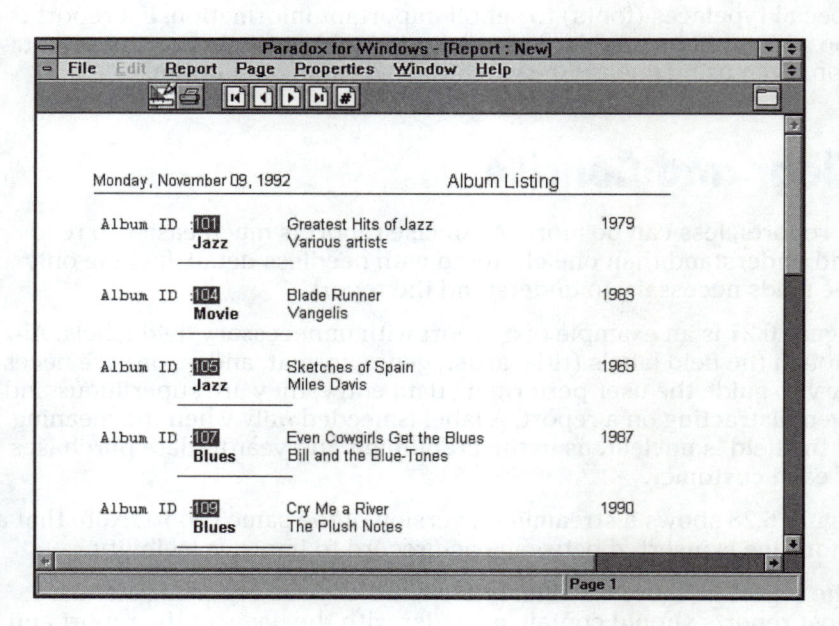

FIG. 6.28

A better report format.

For columnar reports, the header should show the meaning of each column of data. If the report does not include all records in the database, the header should include details of the selection criteria. For example, a sales report header should have something like "From 01/01/92 through 06/30/92" to indicate which transactions are included.

Meaningful

As you are creating reports, try to remember the business need filled by the report. Should it convey detailed information on each item or summary information for the big picture? Will the meaning of each of the rows or columns be evident? How would the reader expect the information to be sorted?

Do not take shortcuts if they reduce the clarity of the report. Avoid abbreviations unless they are universally understood, and try to use fields that the user does not have to struggle to translate. If a marketing report grouped by region shows customers by ZIP code, for example, it also should list the customer's state.

Be sure to indicate the units of measure (for example, dollars or gallons) for numeric fields. You commonly see reports in which you cannot tell millions of dollars from dollars, or units from dollars. Repeat headings for columns of numbers on each page, and for any column whose meaning is not obvious.

Examining Report Style

After you have learned the mechanics of creating and manipulating objects in Paradox for Windows reports, you can concentrate on the more important job: creating documents for effective business communication. All the rules of graphic design for data-entry screens—as well as additional considerations—apply to report design.

In most professions, people use printers and photocopiers that print in black and white. This means that your palette is reduced to shades of gray for printed output. Try to use the layout, fonts, and special effects to distinguish your reports.

Be sure to use a blank line (white space) to separate one group from the next, and a combination of single and double lines (or other graphic elements) to show totals. This kind of layout is easier to read than plain single-spaced formatting, and it highlights the key information, such as group and grand totals.

Consistency is important in report writing. Consistency not only improves your reports, but also saves you time by eliminating routine layout decisions for each new report.

Using different fonts or typefaces helps make your reports look more polished and professional. After you are accustomed to proportional fonts such as Times Roman and Helvetica, you will never want to go back to boring typewriter fonts such as Courier again.

I — PARADOX FOR WINDOWS FUNDAMENTALS

Be conservative with your use of fonts. One typeface in two or three sizes is usually sufficient. Using more than one typeface on a page may make your report look more like a ransom note than a business document (see fig. 6.29). You may want to use the same fonts in all of your reports.

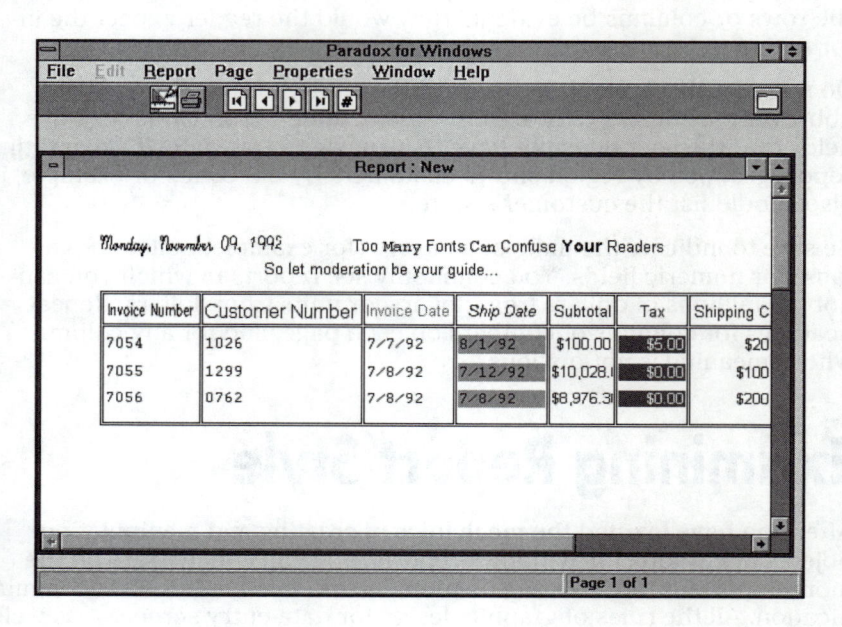

FIG. 6.29

Use of excessive fonts in a report.

Write down your personal style preferences as you go along. For example, do you prefer your page numbers at the top or bottom of the page? Centered, flush right, or flush left? Do you use the number by itself, or with # or the word *Page* before it? These small touches make a difference in the overall appearance of an application and make the output more professional than mix and match reports. Again, consistency is the key to successful reports.

Chapter Summary

Reports are used to present information from the database. They are especially useful for presenting summary information that cannot be viewed directly in the table. A variety of report formats are available, including listings, summaries, mailing labels, invoices, shipping lists, receipts, and even bar code labels for inventory tracking.

To make your report writing easier, you should adopt style standards for reports, including the following elements:

- Header layout (report title, date, and page number)
- Standard abbreviations (for example, *p.* for page)
- Display of selection criteria on the report
- Format conventions (for example, letter or legal size)

Above all, make your reports pleasing to the eye and easy to understand. Reports usually reach a wider audience than the users of your database, so be sure to make your reports as useful as possible.

PART II

Paradox for Windows Power Techniques

OUTLINE

Quick Start 2: Exploring Advanced Paradox Features

Using Advanced Form Techniques

Using Advanced Query By Example

Using Power Entry and Editing Features

Creating Crosstabs and Graphs

Exchanging Data with Other Applications

Working with Your Files

QUICK START 2

Exploring Advanced Paradox Features

This chapter, which is the second of two quick-start chapters in this book, introduces you to advanced Paradox for Windows features. This quick start offers instructions on how to use secondary indexes, multi-table forms and queries, validation checks, crosstabs, and graphs but does not delve deeply into each feature or option. For detailed information, turn to the other chapters in Part II.

Many advanced Paradox features are quite easy to learn. Although Paradox offers a long list of features for designing business graphs, for example, creating a basic graph is simple.

Creating Sample Tables

To follow along with the exercises in this chapter, you need the tables that the first quick-start chapter described. If you have not already done so, create the Customer table, shown in figure QS2.1. You may borrow the structure of the table you created in Quick Start 1. Be sure to add the new fields for Customer ID (the key field) and Sales Rep.

II — PARADOX FOR WINDOWS POWER TECHNIQUES

FIG. QS2.1
The Customer table.

Next, create the Orders and Line Items tables, shown in figures QS2.2 and QS2.3. Be sure to specify the key fields shown in these figures.

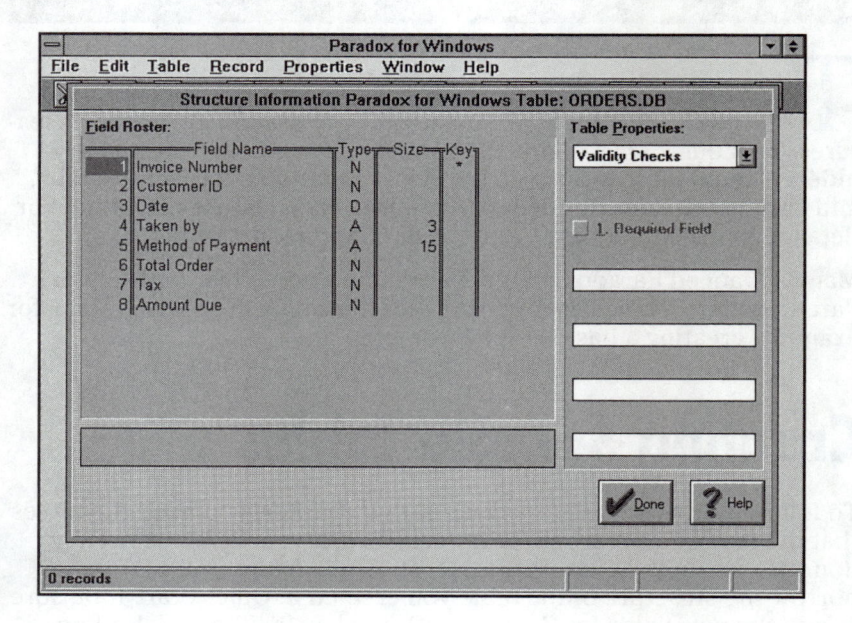

FIG. QS2.2
The Orders table.

FIG. QS2.3

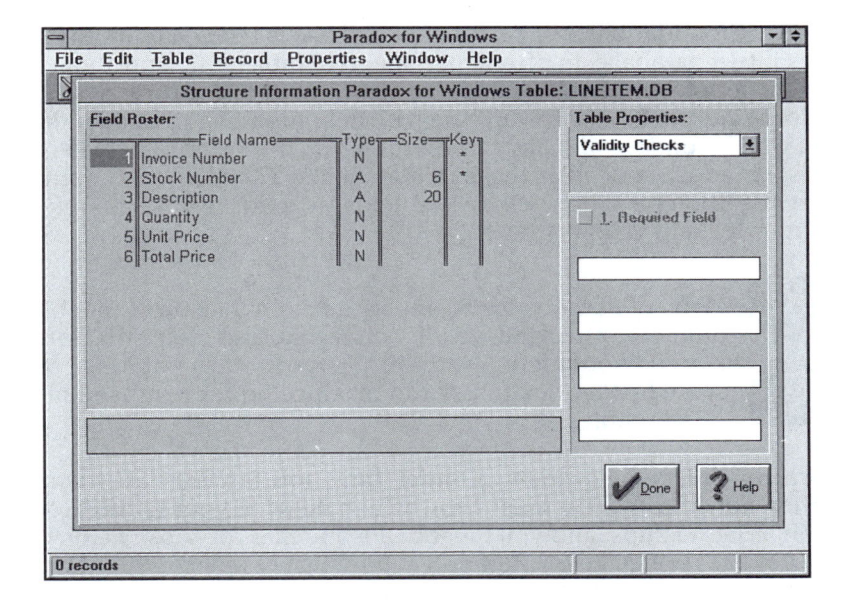

The Line Items table.

Because of the DOS eight-character file-name limit, name these tables CUSTOMER, ORDERS, and LINEITEM, respectively.

To make the exercises more interesting, enter some sample data—at least six records in each table. Sample data enables you to determine whether your database is working properly when you view data or run queries.

The examples offered in this chapter are simplified to illustrate important Paradox features. You could expand these examples further by adding tables for inventory, shipping methods, and sales-tax rates. No matter how complex the database's structure, you use the same basic techniques to relate Paradox tables to one another.

Linking Tables as a Database

As the introduction to this book notes, Paradox for Windows is a more "relational" database-management system than Paradox for DOS or, for that matter, than Xbase (dBASE compatible) products such as dBASE, FoxPro, and Clipper. Paradox for Windows contains more of the features of the relational model. Although many users may not appreciate the value of relational fidelity, these features, which safeguard the integrity of the database and simplify database administration, are of paramount importance.

One of the foundations of a relational database is its capability to link tables into a database. In dBASE parlance, "database" meant "table," so the concept of a multi-table database was foreign to the program. Paradox for Windows moves toward the true definition of a relational database, which consists of many tables. After you create links between tables, Paradox recognizes these relationships. The features that make this recognition possible include key fields, secondary indexes, referential integrity, and validity checks.

> **NOTE** Many of Paradox for Windows' relational features (such as duplicate checking, validity checking, and referential integrity) do not function with dBASE-type tables—another reason why Paradox tables can produce better results than dBASE tables.

Before you link tables, you must understand how tables relate to one another. Specifically, you must know which fields in your tables are used in relationships, and you must define indexes for those fields (primary keys or foreign keys). Paradox automatically indexes all primary keys; you may designate secondary indexes for foreign keys.

What Is a Secondary Index?

An *index* is a special file designed to retrieve or sort records quickly, based on the value of one or more fields. The index file enables the database management system (DBMS) to find a specific record without reading each record in a table from the beginning to the end of the file (a *sequential search*). With indexes, Paradox can find records much faster than performing a sequential search. Paradox for Windows, like its DOS predecessor, automatically defines an index for each table's key field. The program also enables you to create *secondary indexes* for additional fields.

In many cases, you want to define a secondary index for a *foreign key*—a field that serves as the key field for a different table—because a secondary index speeds operations that involve two tables. For example, you might have a Personnel table in which the Social Security number field is the key field and a Department table in which the Department field is the key field. Creating a secondary index for the Department field in the Personnel table would speed certain operations, such as grouping employees by departments.

In the Orders table, you might want to define a secondary index for the Customer ID field, because this field links the table to the Customers table, which contains customer addresses and other information. To define this secondary index, follow these steps:

QUICK START 2 — EXPLORING ADVANCED PARADOX FEATURES

1. Open the Orders table and then choose Re_s_tructure from the _T_able menu. The Restructure Table dialog box appears (see fig. QS2.4). (This dialog box is similar to the Define Table dialog box.)

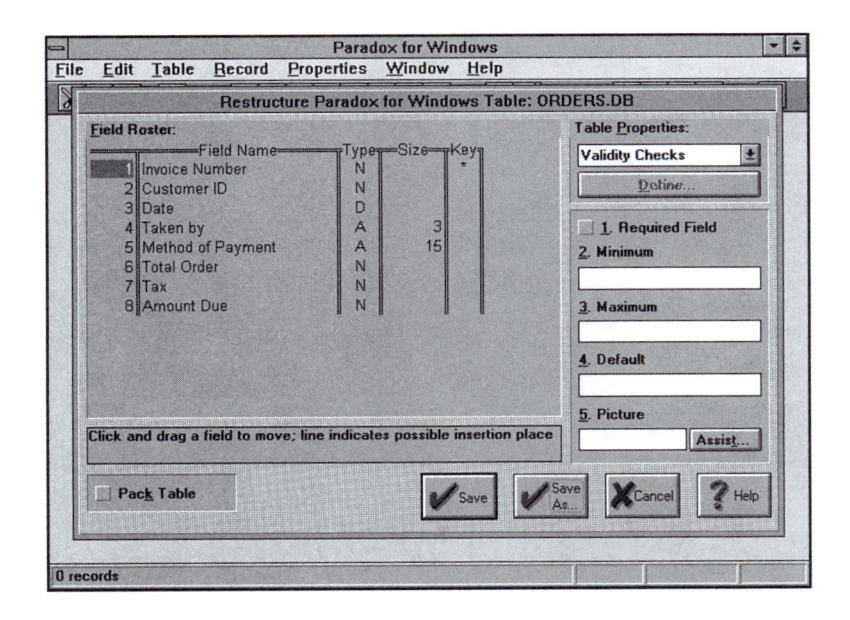

FIG. QS2.4

The Restructure Table dialog box.

2. Pull down the menu under Table _P_roperties by clicking the box next to Validity Checks; (see fig. QS2.5) then choose Secondary Indexes.

3. Click the _D_efine button to reveal the Define Index dialog box.

4. Define a new secondary index for the Customer ID field. Click the field name to highlight it and then click the right-arrow button to move the field name from the Fields list to the Indexed Fields list.

5. Click the OK button to save this new index.

6. Click the Save button in the Restructure Table dialog box to save your changes.

The performance benefits of secondary indexes become greater as the size and complexity of a table grows. If you have only a dozen employees, for example, you might not notice any difference in performance between indexed and unindexed tables, but you would if your table contained 10,000 names.

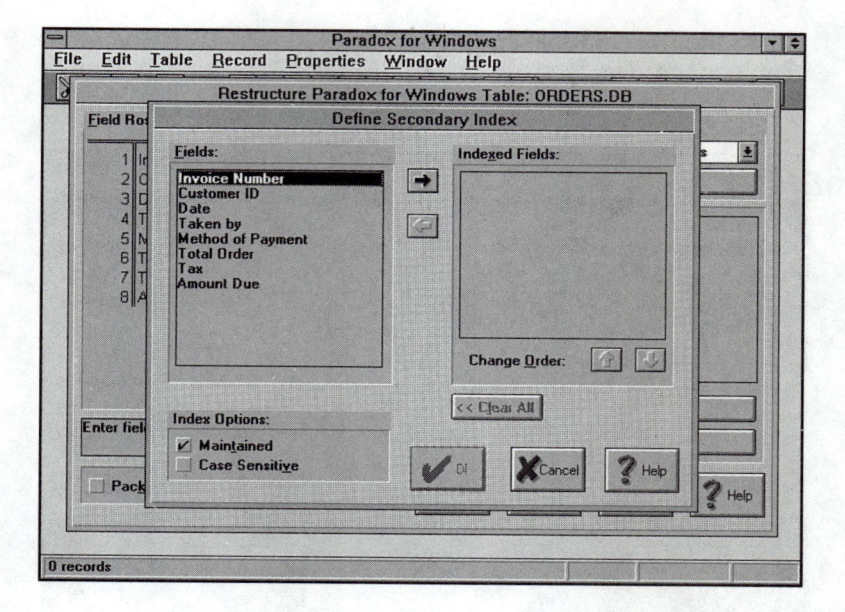

FIG. QS2.5
The Define Index dialog box.

What Is Referential Integrity?

Referential integrity refers to a database's capability to prevent data anomalies when a record that affects data in other tables is entered, modified, or deleted.

Suppose that you maintain tables of clients and their stock portfolios. What would happen if a client changed her name? If the tables were linked by client names and you did not change the name in the stock-portfolio table, you might lose that client's stock-portfolio records, which would no longer relate to a valid record in the other table.

Referential integrity, however, prevents such a loss of data by automatically changing related records and by preventing changes that would adversely affect another table. You would not want to lose the records of clients, for example, who maintain active portfolios. After you define how your tables are related, Paradox for Windows takes care of many cases of referential integrity.

In the sample database used in this chapter, you would not want users to enter line items for invalid invoice numbers. To prevent this problem, define referential integrity between the Orders and Line Items tables by following these steps:

1. Open the Line Items table and then choose Restructure from the Table menu. The Restructure Table dialog box appears (see fig. QS2.6).

QUICK START 2 — EXPLORING ADVANCED PARADOX FEATURES

2. Pull down the menu under Table Properties by clicking the box next to Validity Checks, and then choose Referential Integrity.
3. Click the Define button to reveal the Referential Integrity dialog box (see fig. QS2.7).

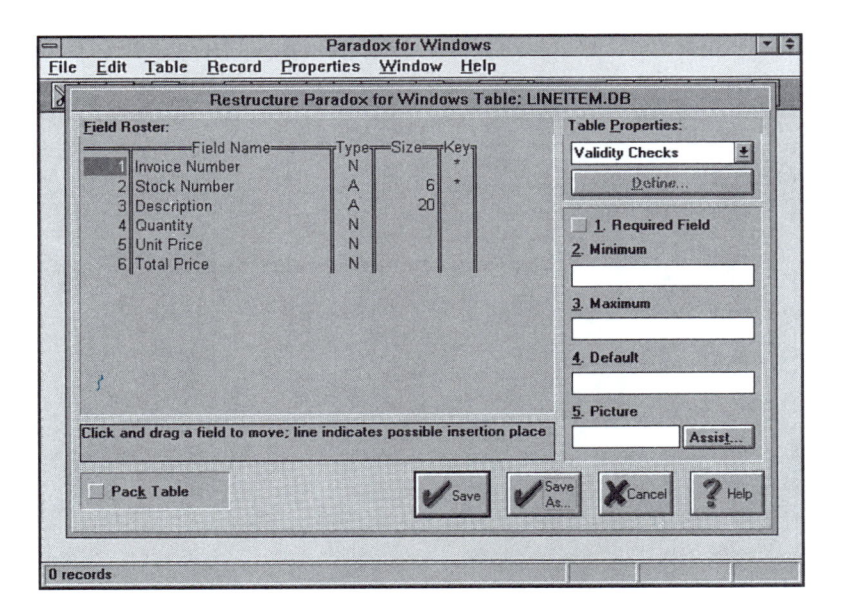

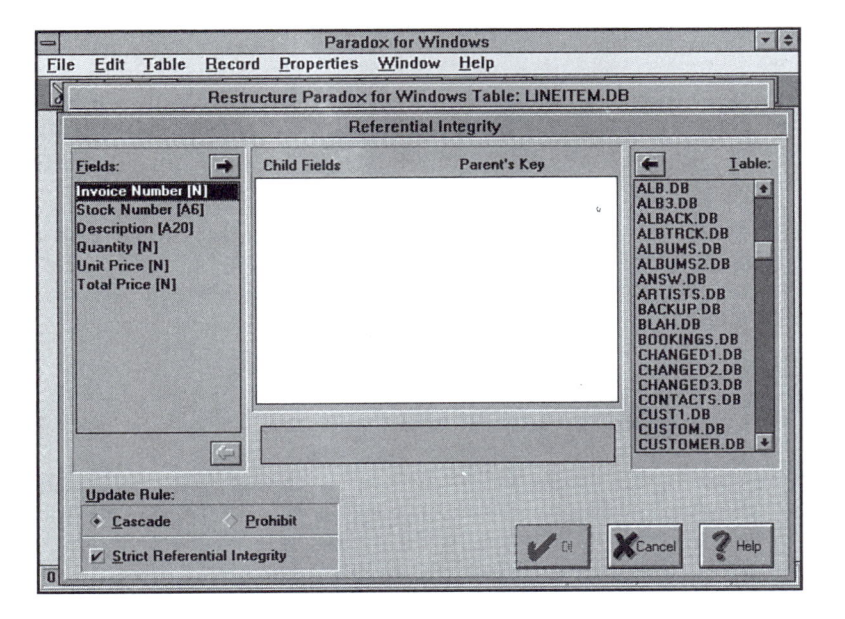

FIG. QS2.6

The Restructure Table dialog box.

FIG. QS2.7

The Referential Integrity dialog box.

4. Select Orders in the Table list on the right side of the dialog box.

5. Click the INVNO field name to highlight it, and then click the right-arrow button to move the field name from the Fields list to the Child Fields list.

6. Click the OK button to save your referential-integrity rule. The Save Referential Integrity As dialog box appears (see fig. QS2.8).

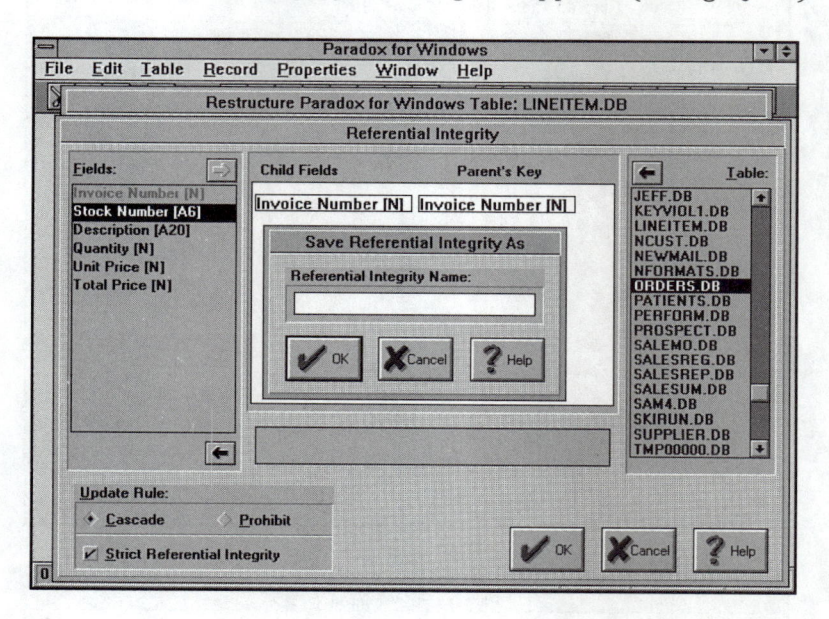

FIG. QS2.8

The Save Referential Integrity As dialog box.

7. Because you can define more than one referential-integrity rule for a table, you must give each rule a unique name. Type **"ORDERS"** as the name of the referential-integrity rule. Click the OK button to save.

8. The referential-integrity rule (ORDERS) appears in a list below table properties. If you defined more referential integrity rules, these also would be listed here. Click the Save button to save your changes to the table.

What Is Table Lookup?

Often you want to limit the values that are acceptable in a field. *Table lookup* enables you to define a reference table that contains all the valid entries for a field. When you enter data in the field, Paradox checks the entry against the lookup table and accepts the entry only if it appears in the lookup table. You also can use table lookup in conjunction with referential integrity; seeing records from a related table helps you enter valid information.

Lookup tables enable you to define a list of values and retain the option of adding values later, without reprogramming. For example, you might want to assign a sales representative to each customer by entering the initials of the sales representative in the Customer table. Table lookup prevents users from entering invalid initials in the Sales Rep field by checking entries against the Salesrep table. It also provides help by displaying a list of all sales representatives as needed. You also can add new sales representatives to the Salesrep table as they are hired so that the list of valid entries is kept up to date.

To create a lookup table, follow these steps:

1. Create the main table (Customer) and lookup table (Salesrep) by choosing File, New, Table from the Paradox Desktop. If you followed the examples earlier in this chapter, you have already created the Customer table (refer to fig. QS2.1). Be sure to designate Rep ID as the key field for the lookup table, as shown in figure QS2.9.

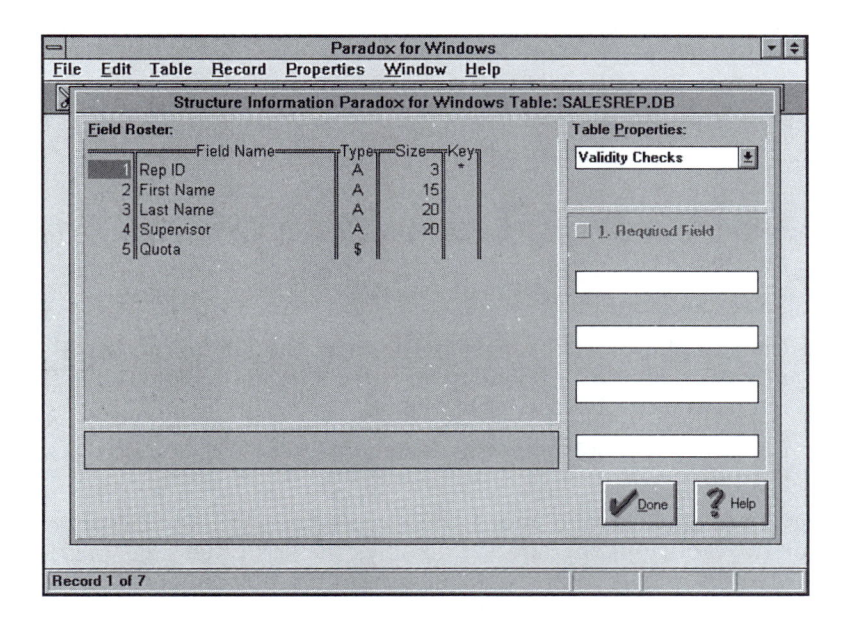

FIG. QS2.9

The Salesrep Table.

2. Open the Customer table, and choose Table, Restructure from the menu. The Restructure Table dialog box appears, as shown in figure QS2.10. Move the pointer to the Sales Rep field, which you want to use for the lookup, and click the Validity Checks box. A menu of validity-check options appears.

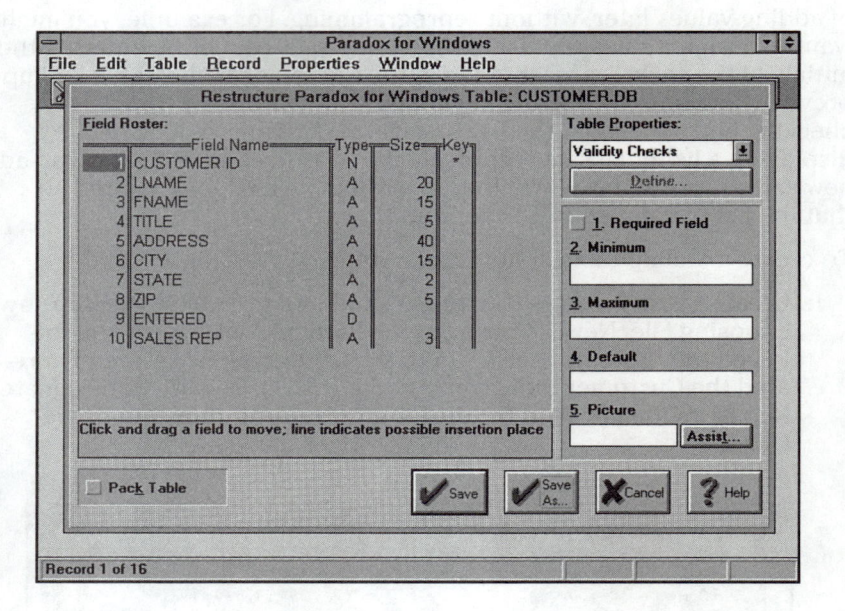

FIG. QS2.10

The Restructure Table dialog box.

3. Select Table Lookup. The Table Lookup dialog box appears (see fig. QS2.11).

4. Select SALESREP.DB.

5. Click to place a check mark in the Help And Fill box so that Paradox will provide help when you enter data in the field. Click the OK button to save the table lookup.

6. Click the Save button at the Restructure Table dialog box to save the table.

If you try to enter invalid information in the Sales Rep field after you define the table lookup, Paradox displays the error message `Unable to find lookup value` in the message area at the bottom of the screen, indicating that the field lookup failed to find a matching value in the related table (see fig. QS2.12). To view a list of valid entries, press Ctrl+Space. The lookup table is displayed (see fig. QS2.13).

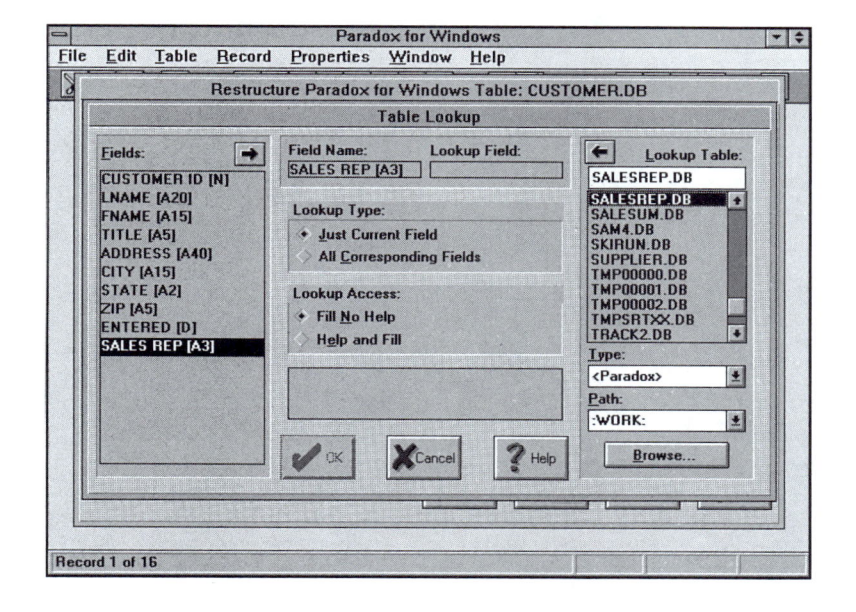

QUICK START 2 — EXPLORING ADVANCED PARADOX FEATURES

FIG. QS2.11

The Table Lookup dialog box.

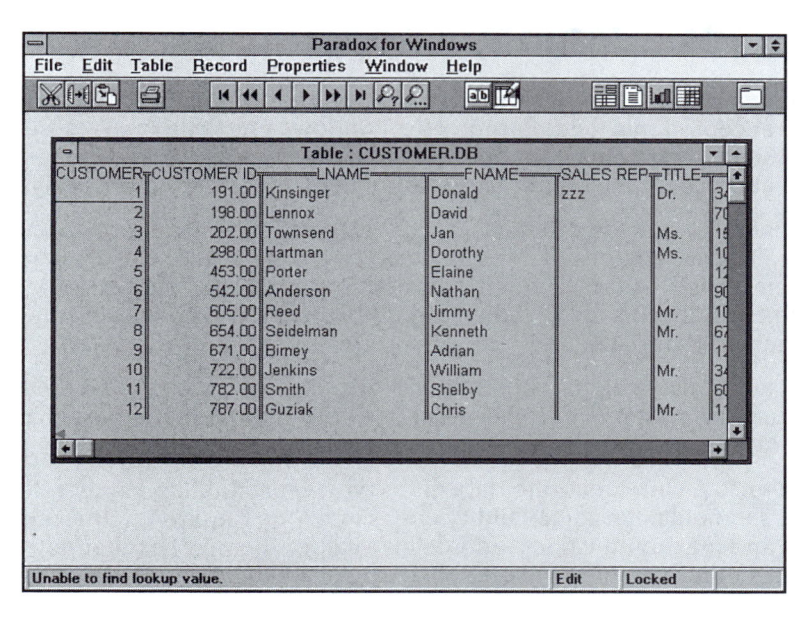

FIG. QS2.12

Validity-check error message.

FIG. QS2.13

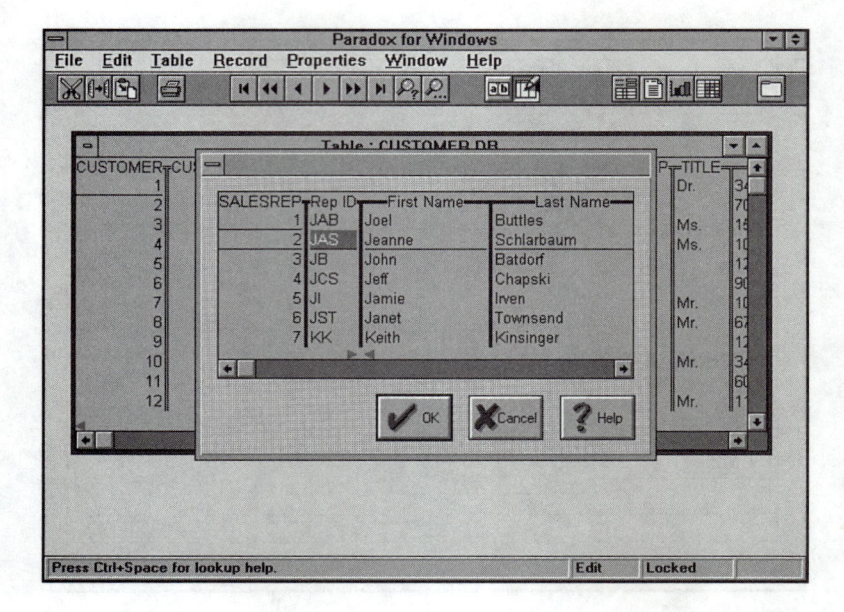

Getting help for table lookup.

What Is a Validity Check?

A *validity check* is a series of criteria that an entry must meet in order to be accepted in a field. Paradox for Windows checks to make sure that the field contains data, that the data falls between allowable minimum and maximum values, and that the data is formatted properly.

The default value for a field also may be specified in a validity check. One of the advantages of Paradox validity checks is that the checks are associated with a table rather than tied to a particular data entry form or ObjectPAL program. Validity checks protect data, no matter how you access that data.

You cannot use validity checks in graphic, memo, binary, or OLE fields, because the contents of those fields are stored outside the Paradox for Windows table.

In order to ensure accurate data entry, you can establish validity checks in fields. Paradox validity checks include required fields, minimum and maximum values, and default values. Remember that you can define a different set of validity checks for each field in a table.

Required Fields

If a table contains required fields, you cannot enter a record without entering data in those fields. To designate a field as required, place the pointer on the field in the Restructure Table dialog box. Click the check box next to Required Field in the Validity Checks section of the Define/Restructure Table dialog box (see fig. QS2.14).

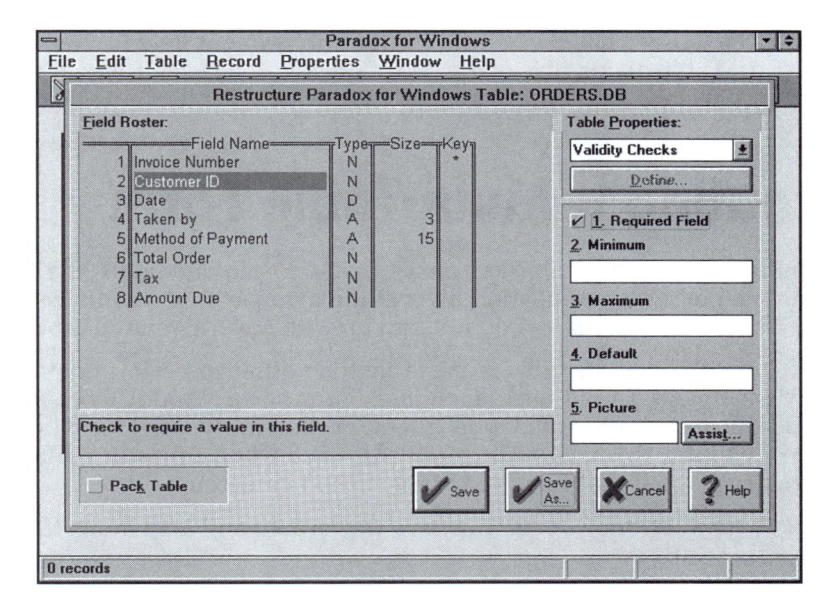

FIG. QS2.14

Making the customer number required in the Orders table.

Next, try to enter a new record in the Orders table without filling in the Customer ID. The error message `Field value required` appears in the message area at the bottom of the screen.

Minimum and Maximum Values

You can define minimum and maximum values for data in a field by typing those values in the Minimum and Maximum boxes in the Validity Checks section of the Define/Restructure Table dialog box.

For example, you might set a lower limit of 0 for Order Amount in the Orders table so that no order with a negative amount can be entered. Similarly, you might place an upper limit of 99,999 to prevent users from inadvertently typing in extra digits, assuming that orders never exceed 99,999.

Default Values

If you choose the Default option, Paradox automatically enters the default value you specify in a field that you leave blank. A school system in Houston might use TX, for example, as the default value for the State field in a student-addresses database. Any students who live outside Texas would be a minority.

To make Check the default payment method in the Payment Method field of the Orders table, click the Method of Payment field in the Restructure Table dialog box. Next, type **Check** in the Default box in the Validity Checks section of the Define/Restructure Table dialog box.

Creating a Multi-Table Form

All but the simplest databases consist of more than one table. In a relational-database application like Paradox, you should scrutinize your design carefully if you do not end up with several related tables.

Unfortunately, switching from one table to another to perform data entry is confusing and time-consuming. Paradox for Windows provides multi-table forms into which you can enter data designated for more than one table. This feature commonly is used when a master table is related to a detail table, such as Invoices and Line Items.

To create a multi-table form that uses the Orders and Line Items tables, follow these steps:

1. From the Paradox for Windows desktop, choose File, New, Form. The Data Model dialog box appears (see fig. QS2.15).

2. Click ORDERS.DB, then click the right-arrow button to add that table to the data-model diagram area. The Orders table will be the master table for the multi-table form.

3. Click LINEITEM.DB, then click the right-arrow button to add that table to the data model (see fig. QS2.16).

4. Place the mouse pointer on the master table (Orders). The mouse pointer changes to the linker shape.

5. Click and hold down the mouse button, and drag the mouse to draw a line that connects the master table to the detail table. A line with a double arrowhead connects the table. The double arrowhead indicates a one-to-many relationship between Orders and Lineitems. This means that each record in Orders can have multiple related records in Lineitems.

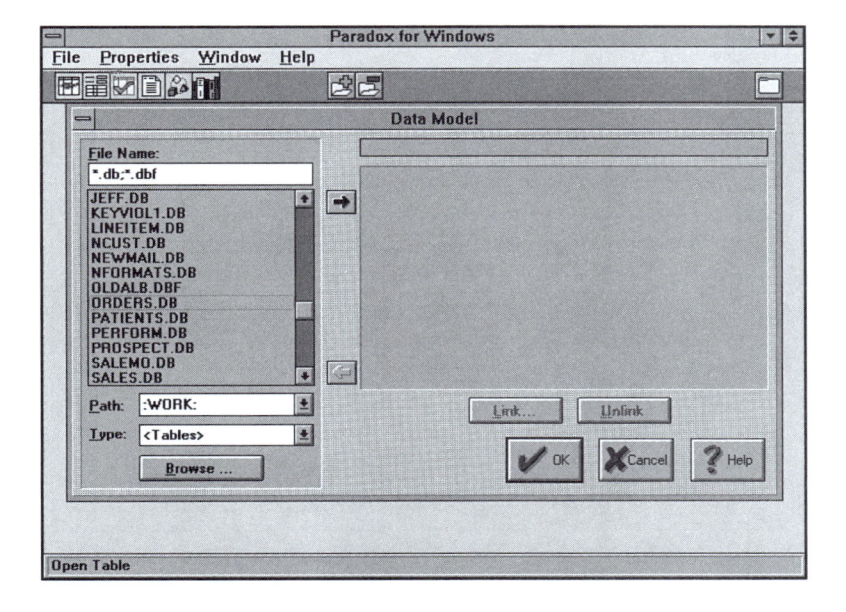

QUICK START 2 — EXPLORING ADVANCED PARADOX FEATURES

FIG. QS2.15

The Data Model dialog box.

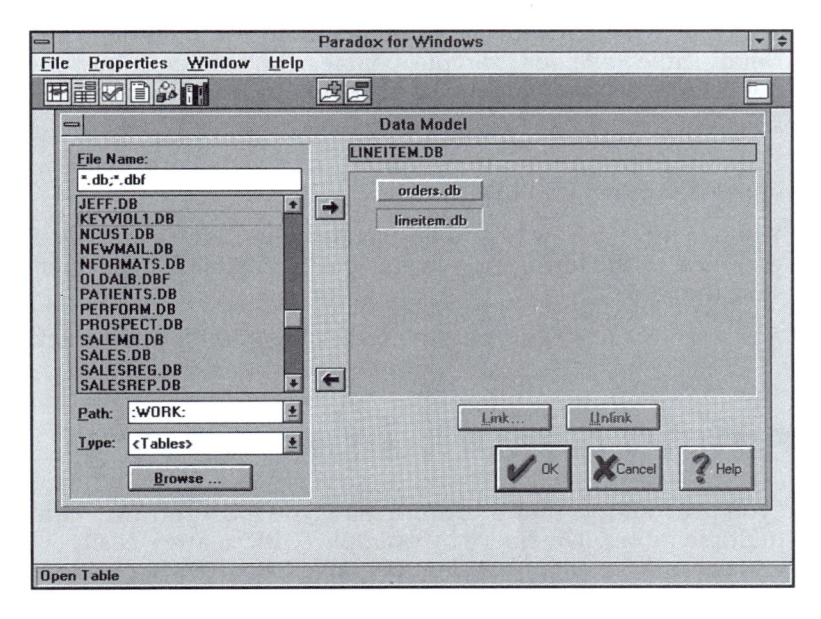

FIG. QS2.16

Orders and Lineitem data model.

6. Click OK or press Enter to continue. The Design Layout dialog box appears (see fig. QS2.17).

FIG. QS2.17

The Design Layout dialog box.

This dialog box contains additional options for multi-table forms. Detail Table Style, for example, enables you to specify how the detail record should be displayed. For now, leave the default choices.

7. Click OK or press Enter to continue. The Create Form window appears (see fig. QS2.18).

8. You use this window to add design elements, such as text and graphics, to the form. For now, choose Save from the File menu to save the form.

After you learn these steps, you can create a multi-table form quickly.

Creating a Multi-Table Query

When you use multiple tables to store data, you must retrieve data from multiple tables. The query by example (QBE) feature easily handles requests for data from multiple tables. In order to perform the search, you first must define the relationship between the tables.

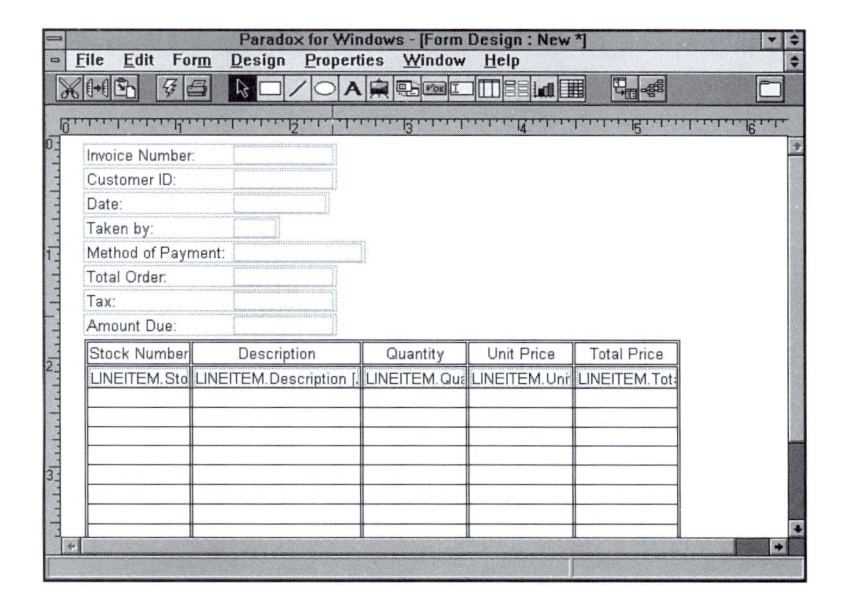

FIG. QS2.18
The Create Form window.

Using Example Elements To Link Tables

You can create a multi-table query that joins the Customers and Orders tables, using the Customer ID field as the link between the tables.

To create a multi-table query with example elements, follow these steps:

1. From the Paradox Desktop, choose File, New, Query from the menu. The Select File dialog box appears (see fig. QS2.19).

2. Click CUSTOMER.DB to use the Customers table for the query. The Query Editor window appears (see fig. QS2.20).

3. Click the Add Table button in the SpeedBar (the plus sign). Choose ORDERS.DB from the Select Table dialog box and click OK to add the Orders table to the query. The Orders table appears in the query editor below the Customer table (see fig. QS2.21).

4. Click the Join Tables tool in the SpeedBar. This tool uses common fields to link tables. The field used to link the Customer and Orders tables is the Customer ID.

FIG. QS2.19

The Select Table dialog box.

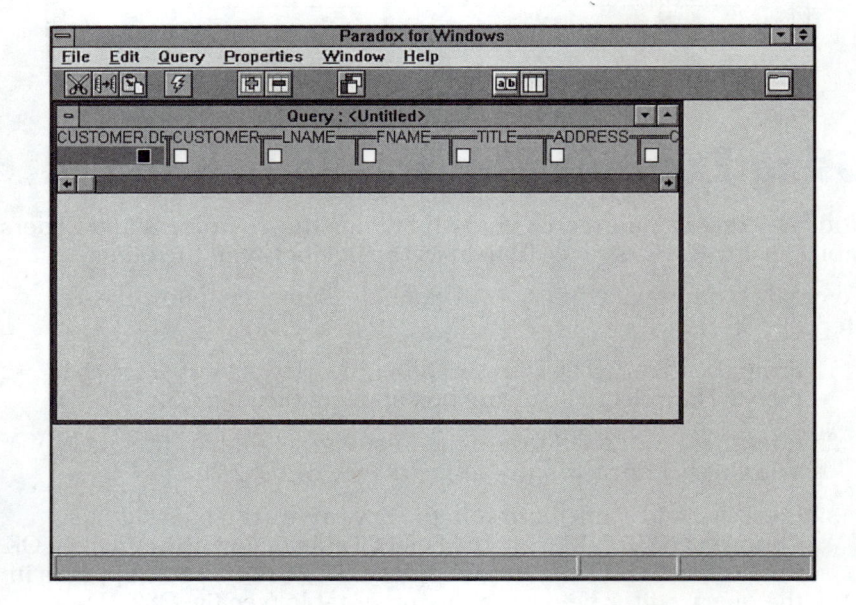

FIG. QS2.20

The Query Editor window.

5. Place the Join Tables cursor in the Customer ID field of the Orders table image and click. Paradox places the example image (EG01) in the field.

6. Click in the Customer ID field of the Orders table.

7. Click the check boxes of the fields you want to retrieve in the query, as shown in figure QS2.22.

QUICK START 2 — EXPLORING ADVANCED PARADOX FEATURES

8. Save the query by selecting File, Save from the menu. Close the Query Editor window by double-clicking the control menu in the Query Editor.

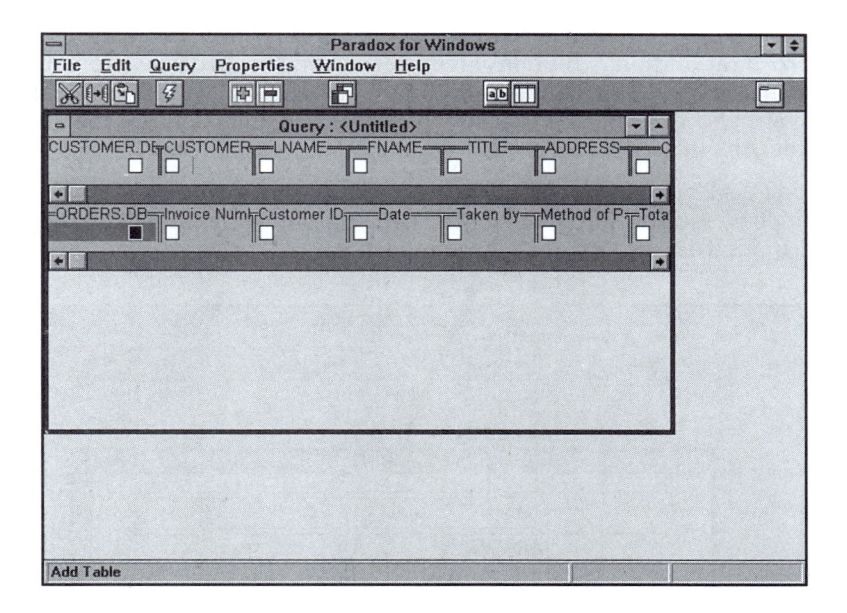

FIG. QS2.21

The Customer and Orders tables in the query editor.

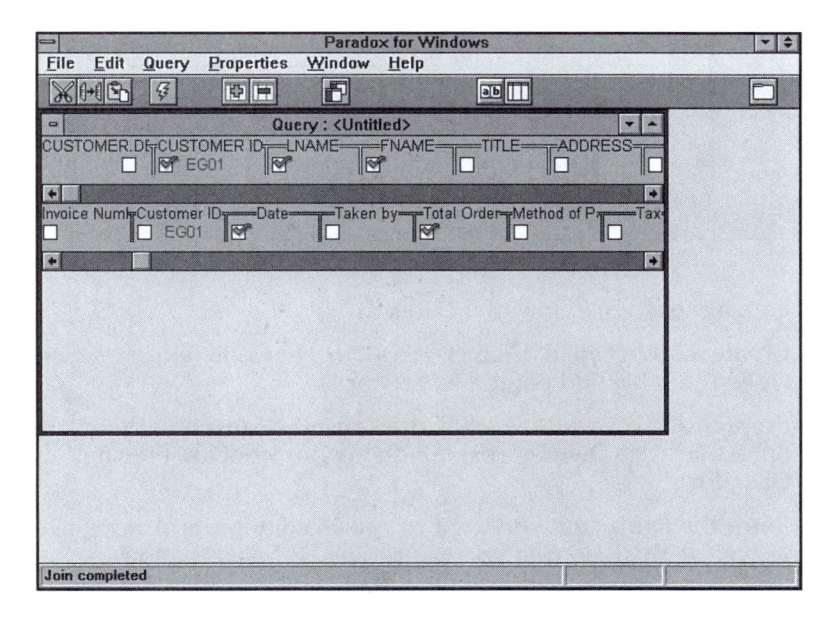

FIG. QS2.22

Using example elements for multi-table query.

Creating a Crosstab

In addition to standard report formats, Paradox provides two powerful ways to display numerical data: crosstabs and graphs. *Crosstab* stands for cross tabulation, which involves correlating records by two values at the same time. The columns of the crosstab show values in one field; the rows show the values in a second field. The cells contain the sum of the records in the intersecting columns and rows.

Figure QS2.23, for example, shows a crosstab that displays sales by product by month. The products appear on the horizontal axis; the month numbers appear on the vertical axis.

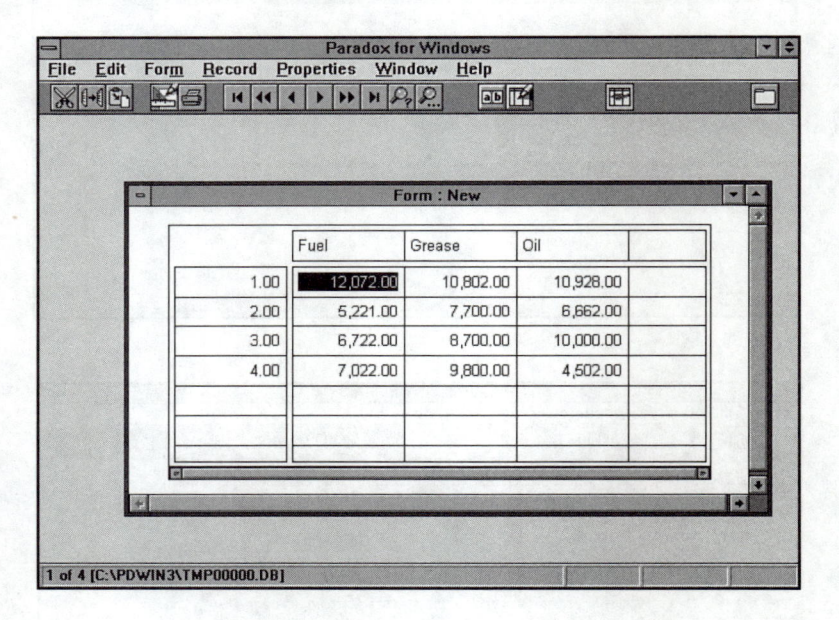

FIG. QS2.23

Crosstab for sales by product by month.

To create a crosstab, follow these steps:

1. Create a table called SALESTOT.DB, as shown in figure QS2.24. Open the table and enter a few records.

2. From the Table window, click the Crosstab button in the SpeedBar. The Define Crosstab dialog box appears (see fig. QS2.25).

3. Enter the fields that you want to use as columns and categories, as well as the field that you want to use for aggregation.

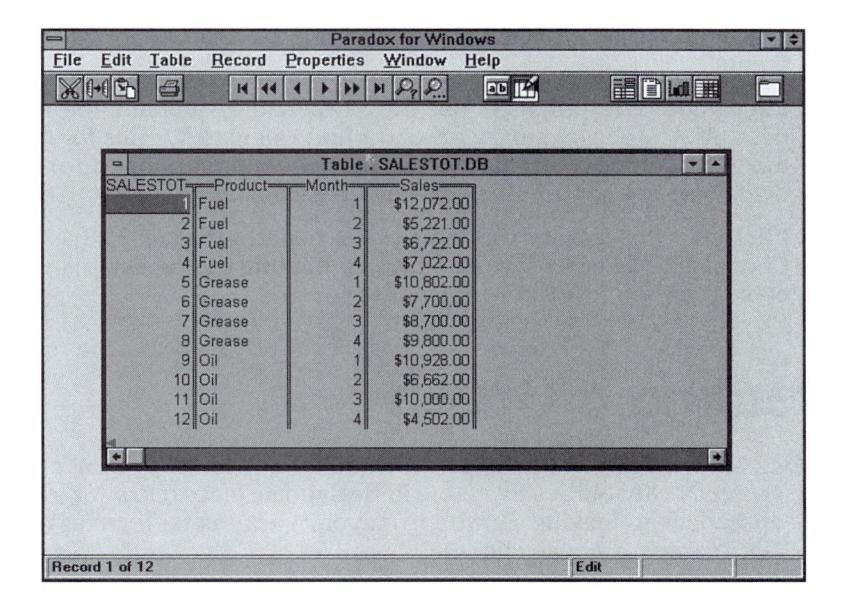

QUICK START 2 — EXPLORING ADVANCED PARADOX FEATURES

FIG. QS2.24

The SALESTOT table.

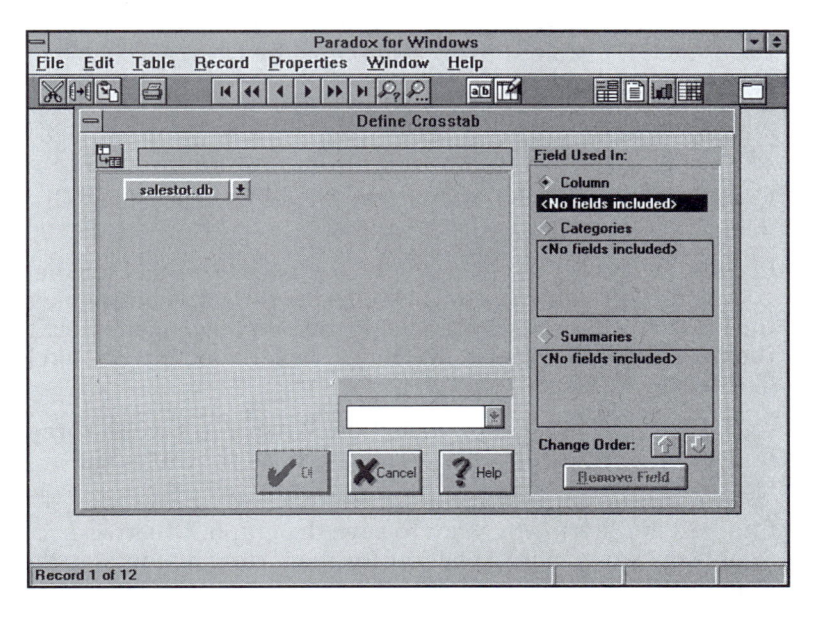

FIG. QS2.25

The Define Crosstab dialog box.

To view a list of fields in the table, click the pull-down menu next to the table name. Click the box labeled Column, then pull down the menu next to the table name in the data model area of the dialog box. Click Product to select product name as the column.

4. Click Categories, then select Month from the field pull-down menu.

5. Click Summaries, then choose the Sales field. By default, Paradox uses SUM as the summary operator and calculates totals for the field listed under Summaries. Use of other summary operators is discussed in Chapter 10, "Creating Crosstabs and Graphs."

6. Click OK. The crosstab appears (refer to earlier fig. QS2.23). Choose File, Save to save the form containing the crosstab, or close the form if you do not want to save it.

Creating a Graph

Paradox for Windows contains powerful built-in business graphics—the same graphics capabilities available in Borland's Quattro Pro for Windows spreadsheet. Making a graph from your Paradox table takes only a few keystrokes or mouse clicks.

To create a graph, follow these steps:

1. Create a table that contains numeric data suitable for a graph, as the SALESTOT table shown earlier in figure QS2.24.

2. Open the table that contains the data for the graph by choosing File, Open, Table from the Paradox Desktop menu or clicking the Table button in the SpeedBar.

3. Click the Quick Graph button in the SpeedBar. The Define Graph dialog box appears (see fig. QS2.26).

4. Click 1-D Summary as the graph type. Choose Product for the x-axis and Sales for the y-axis by clicking the radio button next to the axis value label, and then using the pull-down menu next to the table name. The finished Define Graph dialog box should look like figure QS2.27.

5. Click OK to save the graph definition. When you save the graph definition, the data appears in the graph, as shown in figure QS2.28.

6. Choose File, Save if you want to save the graph. Otherwise, double-click the control window for the form that contains the graph to close it.

You can change the properties of the graph to create many types of graphs.

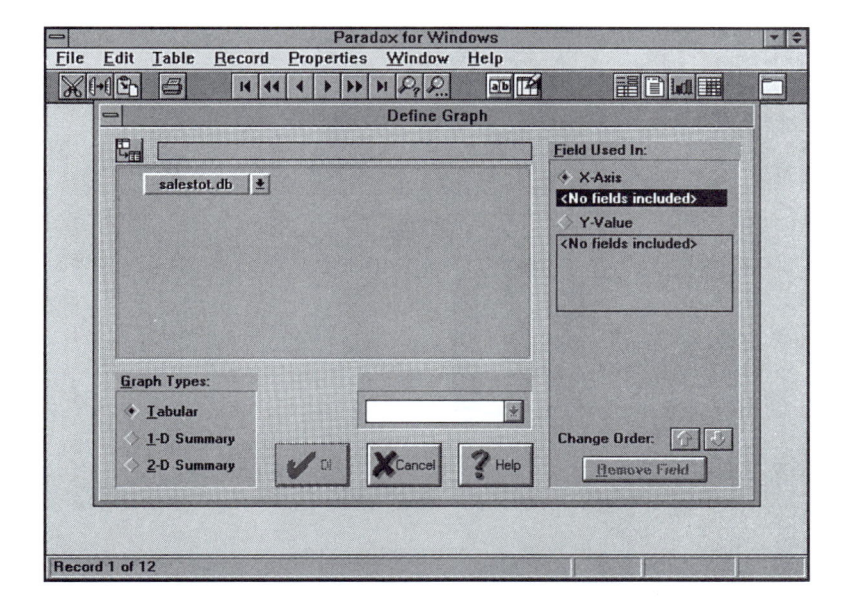

QUICK START 2 — EXPLORING ADVANCED PARADOX FEATURES

FIG. QS2.26

The Define Graph dialog box.

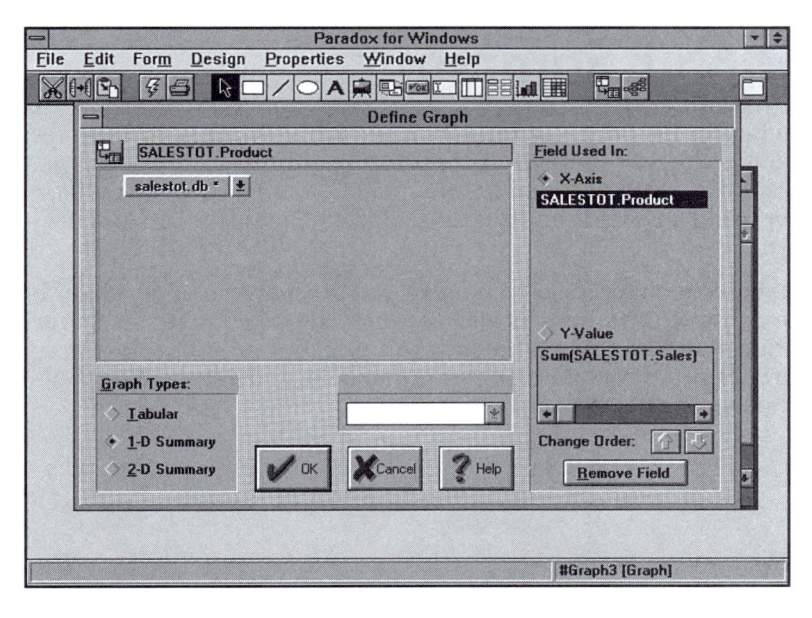

FIG. QS2.27

The completed Define Graph dialog box.

FIG. QS2.28

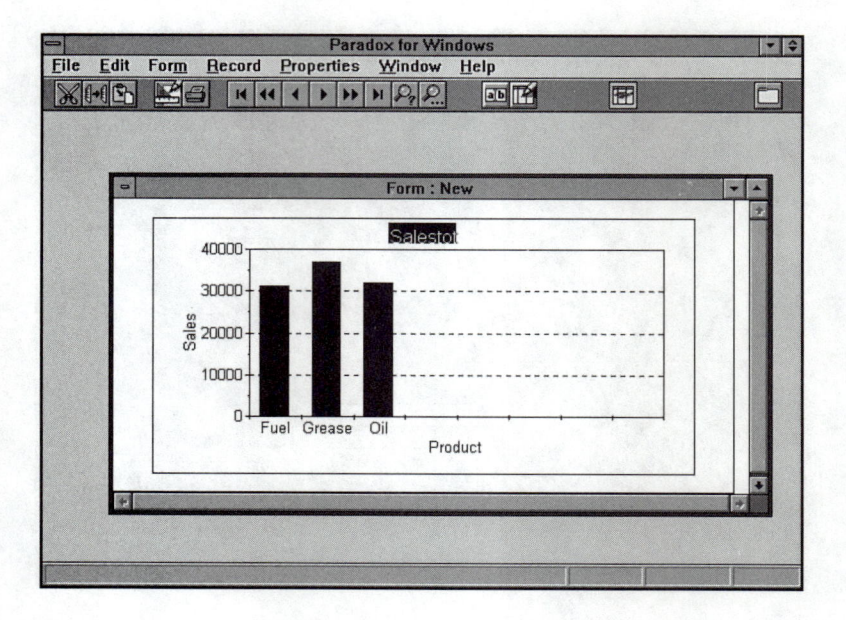

Sales by product.

Chapter Summary

This chapter introduced a few advanced Paradox for Windows features: validation checks; referential-integrity rules; multi-table forms, queries, and reports; crosstabs; and graphs. You learned how to link tables together using key fields and set up referential integrity and lookup tables.

The following chapters, which make up Part II of this book, cover new features introduced here as well as some advanced hints for features introduced in Part I. You should take advantage of all the advanced features in order to round out your database and get the most out of Paradox for Windows.

CHAPTER 7

Using Advanced Form Techniques

In Chapter 5, "Getting Started with Forms," you learned how to create customized forms to simplify data entry. In addition to the form features introduced in that chapter, Paradox for Windows offers a number of advanced features to make your forms more powerful and useful. While many advanced form features require little or no programming, they do require a solid understanding of relational database theory and of the data structure for your application. Some form tools, such as buttons, require a working knowledge of ObjectPAL. See Part III of this book to learn how to program in ObjectPAL.

This chapter shows you how to perform the following advanced techniques:

- Access multiple tables in a form
- Use subforms to show a one-to-many relationship between two tables (such as invoices to line items)
- Use nested subforms (subforms within subforms) for two one-to-many relationships
- Create buttons and pull-menus for data entry tasks
- Embed table objects and graphs within forms

Creating Multi-Table Forms

In a relational database such as Paradox, you can divide data among a number of tables to protect the integrity of the data and to minimize redundant data entry. Unfortunately, going from one table to another to view or edit related data is distracting.

Multi-table forms enable users to view and edit from a single screen information stored in more than one table. In many cases, working from a single screen is more convenient than having to move from one table to another to view bits of related data. A personnel application, for example, may have separate tables for employee names, benefits, dependents, pay history, and vacation allowances. You can create a separate form for each of these tables, but then the user must view several forms to see all the information about an employee.

Most users would prefer the one-stop shopping of a multi-table form—especially when the related tables do not contain enough information to make them easy to understand. In a personnel application, for example, you may use the employee social security number rather than the employee name as a primary key. To look up vacation days in the vacation table, you then must know the social security number of the employee or go to the personnel table and look it up. The multi-table form solves these problems by displaying all the data the user needs on one form, as illustrated in figure 7.1.

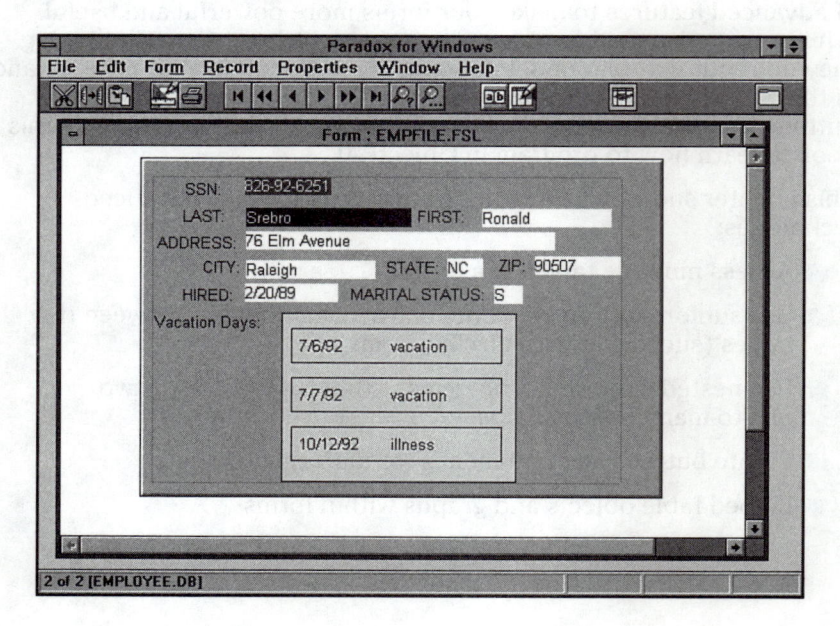

FIG. 7.1

A sample multi-table form.

In order to create a multi-table form, you first must create the tables themselves. In the following examples, the main table is known as the *master table*, and the related tables are the *detail tables*. In many cases, the master table displays a single record while the detail table displays several records at one time; for example, the master table displays an invoice and the detail table displays invoice line items.

The examples in this chapter use the Albums table introduced in Chapter 2, along with new tables for Tracks and Performances, as shown in figures 7.2 through 7.4.

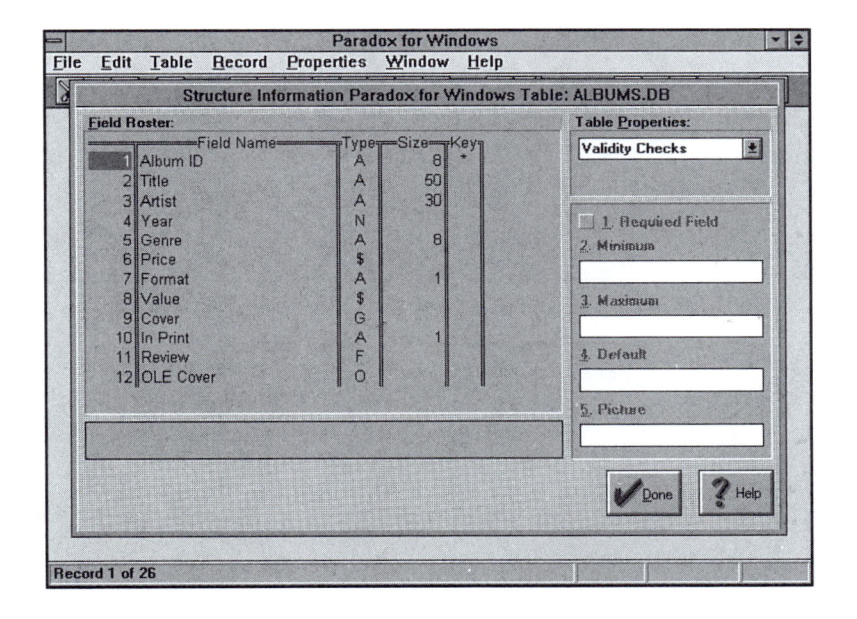

FIG. 7.2

The structure for the Albums table.

Paradox requires indexes on fields used for relationships. If you have designated a field as a key field, Paradox automatically builds an index. If the field is a foreign key (the primary key of a related table), you must establish a secondary index in order to create a table link. The fields you use in the relationship do not have to have the same name, but they should be of the same type and length. See Chapter 2, "Designing Paradox Tables and Databases," for the basics of table design, including a discussion of primary keys.

In the following sections, you gain an understanding of the relationships that can exist among databases, and you learn about secondary indexes.

II — PARADOX FOR WINDOWS POWER TECHNIQUES

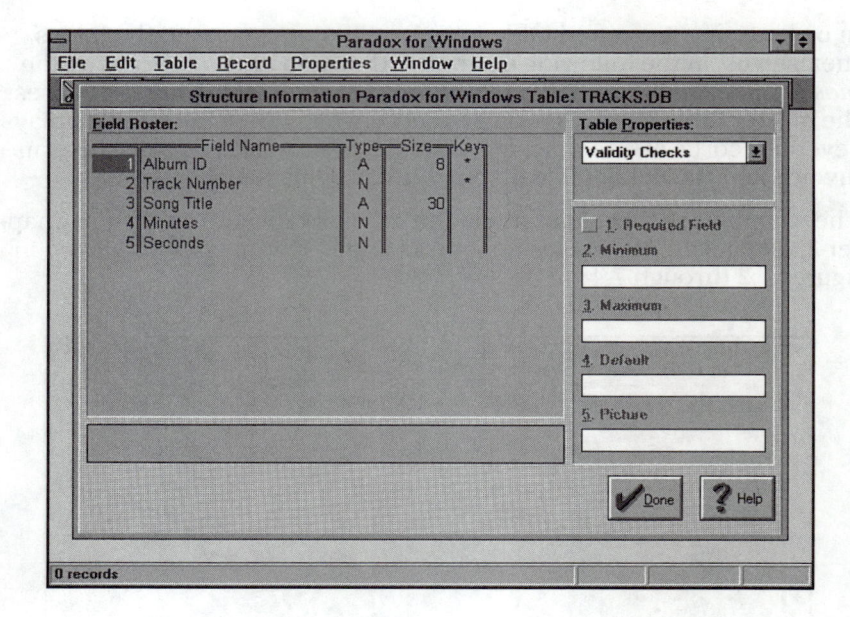

FIG. 7.3

The structure for the Tracks table.

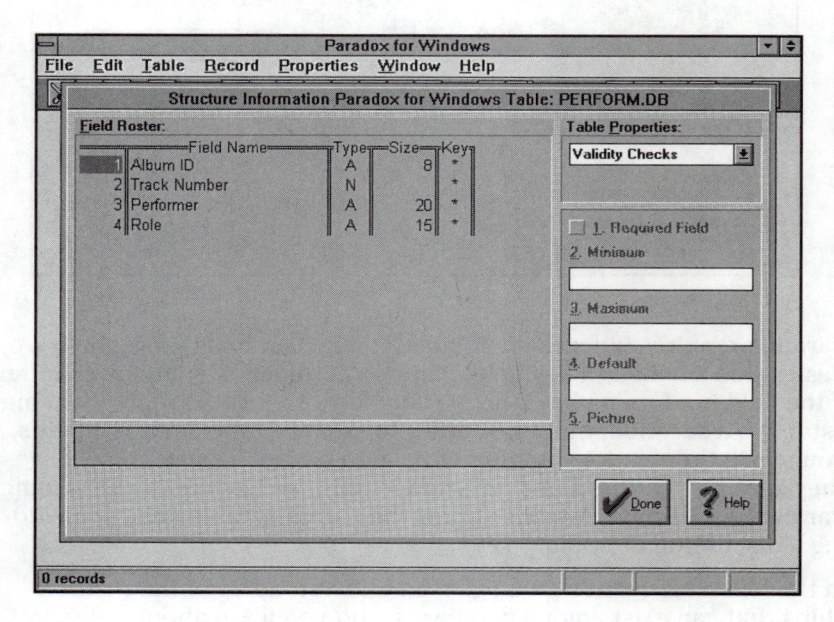

Fig. 7.4

The structure for the Performances table.

Understanding Relationships

Database relationships can be confusing. Three types of relationships can exist among records within a relational database: one-to-one, one-to-many, and many-to-many. The number of records that relate to each other on each side of the relationship determines the relationship type.

Defining Relationships

The first type of database relationship is a *one-to-one relationship*. In a one-to-one relationship, one and only one record in a table relates to one and only one record in a second table. You can create, for example, separate tables for each customer and each credit account. Assuming that you allow a customer only one account and that an account is assigned to only one customer, this relationship is a one-to-one relationship.

The second type of relationship is a *one-to-many relationship*. A one-to-many relationship occurs when a record in one table has one or more related records in a second table, but each record in the second table relates to only one record in the first. To borrow a time-honored example, customers can have more than one invoice, but you write each invoice to only one customer. If you look at the relationship as starting in the second table, this relationship is a many-to-one relationship, but this term means the same as a one-to-many relationship.

Finally, each record in one table can have multiple records in a second, related table, and each record in the second table can have multiple, related records in the first table. This relationship is a *many-to-many relationship*. Orders and inventory can have a many-to-many relationship, for example, with each order containing multiple inventory items and each inventory record relating to multiple orders.

In practice, the many-to-many relationship is difficult to deal with in relational databases, so you usually convert it by analytic sleight of hand into two one-to-many relationships. In the orders/inventory example, you can add a new entity of line items between orders and inventory. Consequently, each order can have multiple line items, but each line item belongs to a single order (a one-to-many relationship). Each inventory record can have multiple line items, but each line item calls for a single inventory item (another one-to-many relationship).

Drawing a Data Model

One of the best ways to sort out relationships is to draw a data model. A *data model* is a diagram that identifies the database's major entities and the relationships among these entities. The entities are what you track in the database and are represented in Paradox tables. Paradox for Windows generates a data model after you have specified the relationships among the tables, but drawing out your own data model beforehand—on paper or on the computer—is better because it helps you understand how to design multi-table forms and queries. If you identify a one-to-many relationship, for example, you may want to add a multi-record area to your form to show both tables.

You can depict a data model in many ways. For this chapter, a simple data model is sufficient. You can represent each entity by a box with the table name written inside. You can make the boxes large enough to enter the field names inside the boxes as well.

Use any drawing tools with which you feel comfortable. The Windows Paintbrush program works well, as does any word processing program that enables you to draw lines and boxes. You can even draw the data model in a Paradox form with the box and line tools.

To show the relationships between the tables, draw a line to connect the related tables. The lines can be single or forked to indicate the type of relationship. A single line indicates a one-to-one relationship; a forked line indicates a one-to-many relationship. (The fork is on the many side of the relationship.) The data model in figure 7.5 illustrates the relationships between the Artists, Albums, and Tracks tables in the Albums tracking database.

As you can see from figure 7.5, the relationship between artists and albums is one-to-many because each artist may have one or more albums, but each album is made by one artist. Similarly, each album can have several tracks, but a track belongs to only one recording.

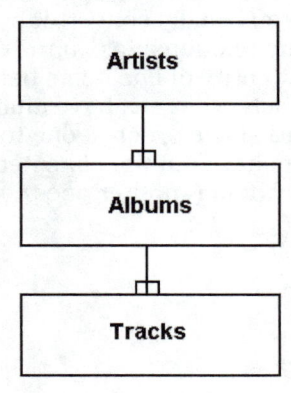

FIG. 7.5

The album tracking data model, one-to-many relationship.

7 — USING ADVANCED FORM TECHNIQUES

If you change the assumptions for the database, however, you also must modify the data model. The structure shown in figure 7.5, for example, does not allow a recording to be related to multiple artists, as may be the case for some collaborative efforts. Who would you enter for the artist if the album were made by Thelonius Monk and John Coltrane, for example? To meet this new requirement, you must change the relationship to many-to-many, as shown in figure 7.6.

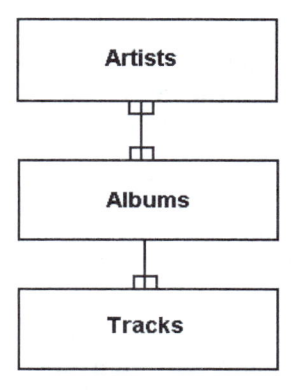

FIG. 7.6

The album tracking data model, many-to-many relationship.

The data model in figure 7.6 allows for multiple artists to be associated with a single recording. But what if the artists were different from one track to another on the same recording? How would you account for anthologies, soundtracks, and other compilations? If you use the data model in figure 7.6, each song on the album appears as though each of the artists associated with the album recorded it, which may lead to disappointing searches. The data model, therefore, can be further refined, as in figure 7.7.

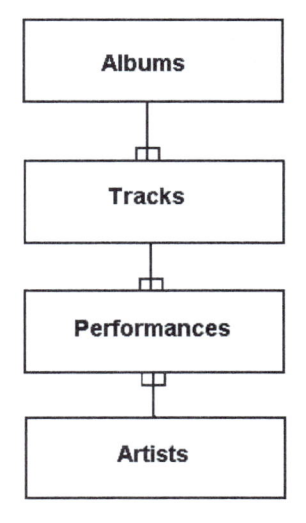

FIG. 7.7

The album tracking data model, two one-to-many relationships.

In figure 7.7, the artists now relate to the individual track rather than to the recording as a whole. This arrangement would be handy when searching for tracks made, for example, by the Miles Davis Quartet with Bill Evans as pianist. A new entity, Performances (called PERFORM in Paradox due to the eight-character table name limit), depicts the instance in which an artist performs on a particular track.

This kind of entity is sometimes called a *weak entity* because it is more conceptual than concrete. It serves the purpose of breaking the many-to-many relationship of tracks and artists into two one-to-many relationships. Each track can have multiple performances, and in turn each artist can have multiple performances. The track "Come Talk to Me" from Peter Gabriel's album *Us*, for example, has Manu Katche on drums, Tony Levin on bass, David Rhodes on guitar, Chris Ormston on bagpipes, Sinead O'Connor on vocals, and Peter Gabriel on vocals, programming, triangle, keyboard bass, and keyboards. In this data model, each recording can have multiple tracks, each track can have multiple performers, and each artist can perform on multiple tracks.

> **TIP** Most databases do not handle many-to-many relationships well, and Paradox is no exception. You can convert many-to-many relationships into two one-to-many relationships by inserting an intermediate entity. Invoices and Inventory, for example, have a many-to-many relationship. Inserting a Line Items table would change this to two one-to-many relationships (from Line Items to Invoices and from Line Items to Inventory).

You also can use Performances to show multiple composers for a song rather than trying to fit them into a single composer field in the Tracks table. This arrangement also leads to more accurate searches because you do not have to use wild cards to find, for example, Paul McCartney as composer. You don't have to search for "Lennon and McCartney," or "Lennon, Harrison, McCartney." If you use the Performance table for composers, you may want to change its name to something broader; the table then can be used to show the producer, arranger, and other personnel.

A full-blown Paradox database is likely to have dozens or even hundreds of related tables; thus, the data model can be quite complex. No matter how large the database, the principles for defining relationships remain the same.

> **TIP**
>
> One clue that a one-to-one relationship exists is when the key fields for two tables are identical. You may have, for example, a table for customer addresses and another table for customer demographics. Each of these tables uses a customer number as a primary key. The two tables with a one-to-one relationship are good candidates to combine into a single table.

Building a Data Model

To design multi-table forms, you must build a data model to illustrate the relationships. The data model shows the entities (things) that are tracked in the database and the links (relationships) among these entities.

To build a data model follow these steps:

1. From the Paradox Desktop, choose File, New, Form. The Data Model dialog box appears (see fig. 7.8).

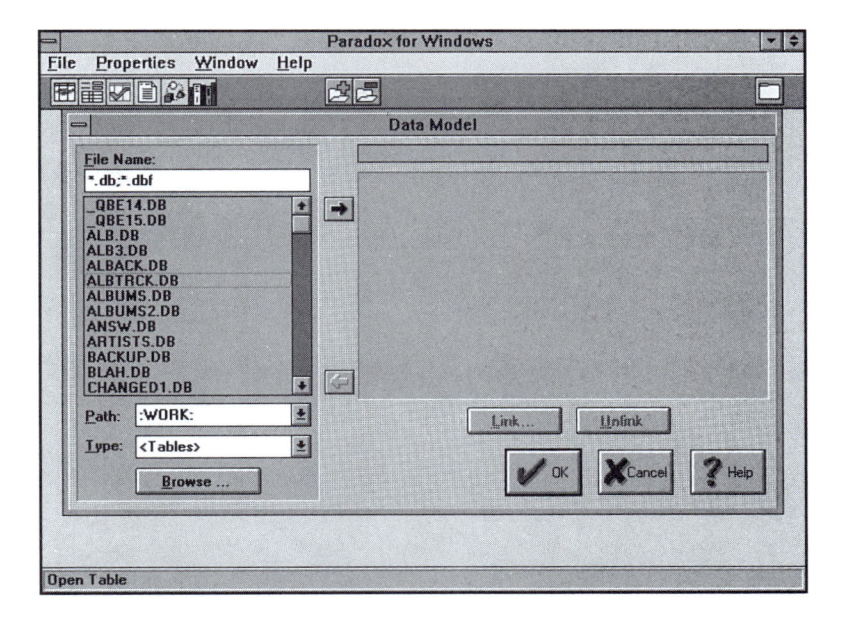

FIG. 7.8

The Data Model dialog box.

2. To move a table to the data model area on the right side of the dialog box, double-click the table name or click once to select the table and click the Add Table arrow to the right of the table list. Add the Albums and Tracks tables to the data model. You also can select tables with the keyboard by moving the cursor to the field name and pressing Alt+A.

3. If you accidentally choose the wrong table, you can remove it by clicking the table name in the data model area and then clicking the Remove Table arrow (pointing to the left).

4. Next, draw the relationship, or link, between the tables. You must set up the links one at a time. To link two tables, click the master table, which in this example is Albums. When you click the master table, the mouse pointer changes to the data-model icon. Drag the icon to the detail table Tracks.

When you release the mouse button, the Define Link dialog box appears (see fig. 7.9). Don't worry if other tables are between the tables you link; Paradox rearranges the tables after you link them.

Paradox attempts to link the tables for you and determine the type of relationship based on the key fields for each table. If Paradox cannot determine how the link should be created, you can enter the specifications in the Define Link dialog box.

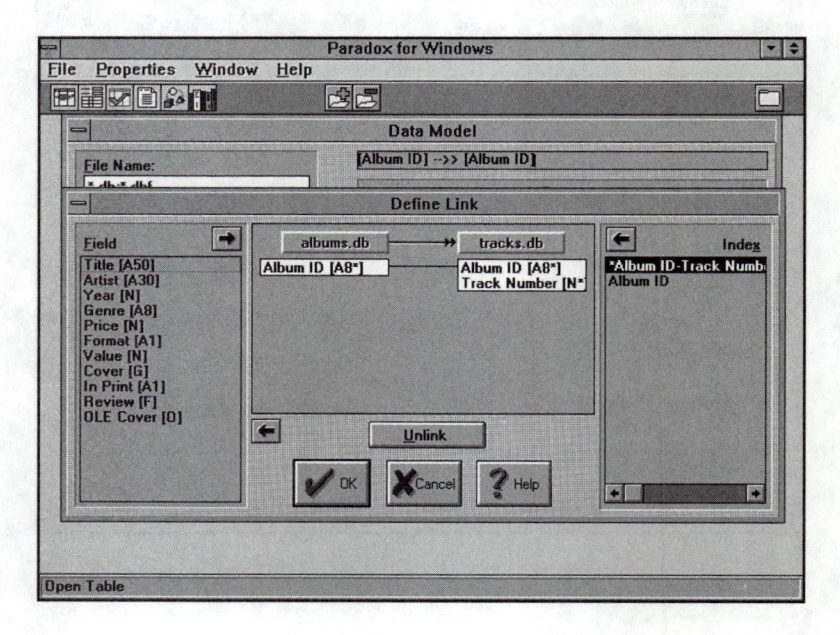

FIG. 7.9

The Define Link dialog box.

7 — USING ADVANCED FORM TECHNIQUES

5. Select the fields you want to link in the Define Link dialog box. Paradox indicates the primary and secondary keys available from each table with an asterisk next to the primary keys. If you have not designated a key field or a secondary index, no field names are listed, and it is impossible to link the tables. In this example, the Album ID field links the tables.

   After you choose the fields to link, Paradox shows the type of relationship between the tables. A double-headed arrow is drawn from ALBUMS.DB to TRACKS.DB, indicating that these tables have a one-to-many relationship. One-to-one relationships are indicated by placing one table atop the other with a single arrowhead pointing to the detail table.

6. Click OK to save the link. You are returned to the Data Model dialog box.

7. Click the OK button in the Data Model dialog box to continue. The Design Layout dialog box appears (see fig. 7.10).

   The Design Layout dialog box is the same one you use for single-table forms, but three new options for multi-table forms are now active. Fields Before Tables determines whether the fields from the master table will appear before (the default) or after the detail table. The Detail Table Style determines whether detail records are displayed as tables (the default) or records. The Number of Master Records option determines whether one master record is displayed (the default), multiple records are displayed, or no master records are displayed. For this example, use a Single Record master record and Table detail records.

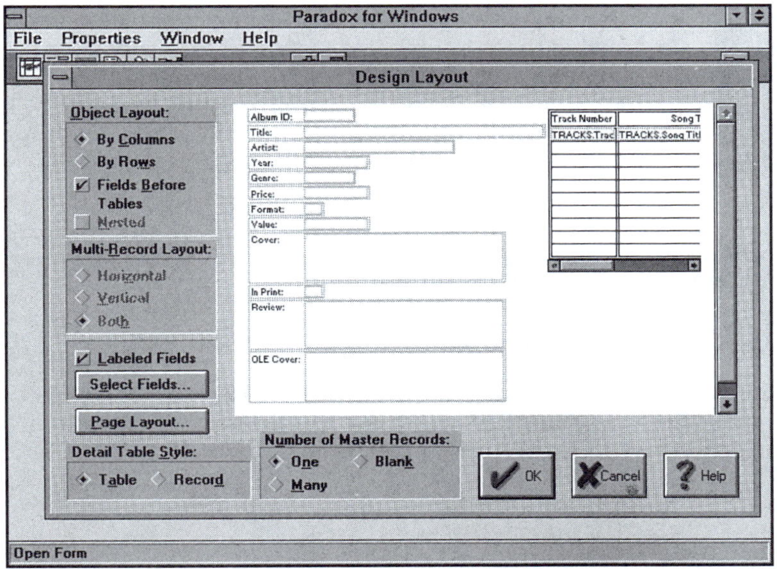

FIG. 7.10

The Design Layout dialog box.

8. Edit the form, using color and fonts to improve the appearance of the screen. Save the new form and test it by entering sample data. Using the multi-table form, you can view and enter albums along with their related tracks. Figure 7.11 shows the finished multi-table form.

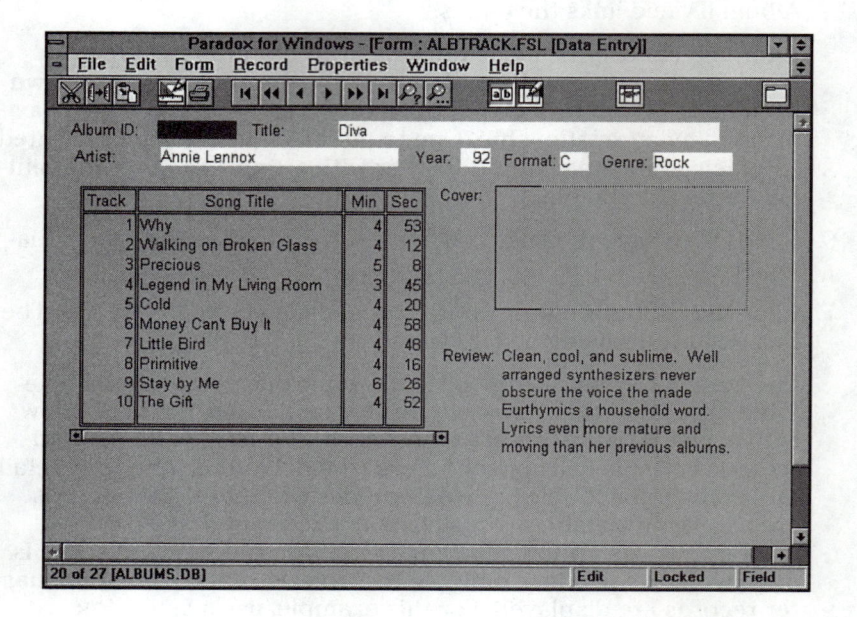

FIG. 7.11

The Albums/Tracks Multi-Table form.

> **NOTE** When drawing the relationships in the data model, start with the master table and draw the line to the detail table. By drawing the relationships in this way, Paradox for Windows detects a one-to-many relationship because of the compound key you used in the detail table. If you draw the link starting in the detail table, Paradox erroneously assumes that you are creating a one-to-one relationship.

Defining and Modifying a Secondary Index

As discussed in Chapter 2, Paradox automatically creates and maintains indexes for primary key fields. For some data models, you must define secondary indexes to establish table links.

Defining a secondary index is as simple as defining other optional field characteristics, such as validity checks and table lookup. To define a secondary index, follow these steps:

1. From the Create Table or the Restructure Table dialog box, click the Table Properties button in the upper-right corner of the dialog box, and choose Secondary Indexes from the pull-down menu.

2. Click the Define button below the menu. The Define Secondary Index dialog box appears (see fig. 7.12).

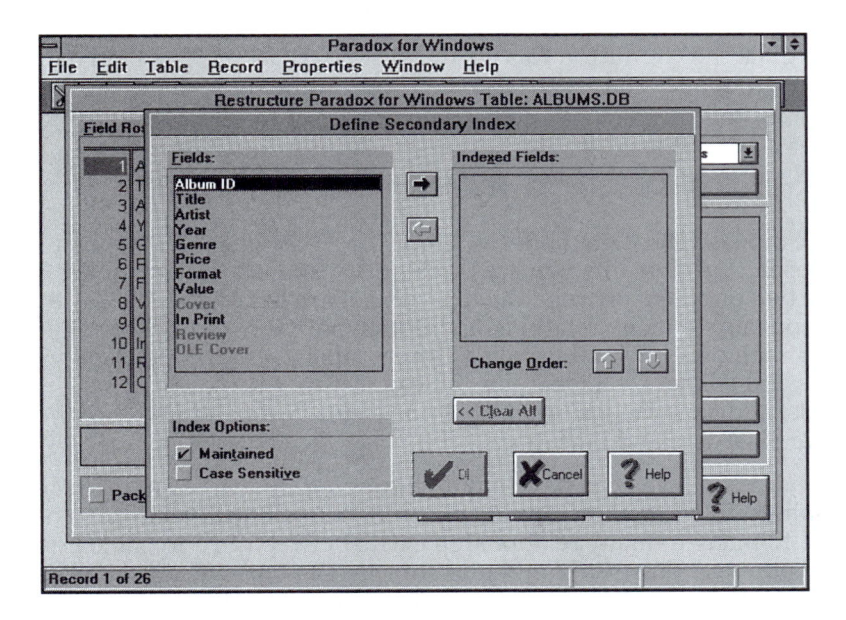

FIG. 7.12

The Define Secondary Index dialog box.

3. At the bottom of the dialog box are general options for the secondary index.

    Choose the Maintained check box if you want to maintain the index automatically—in other words, if you want Paradox to update the secondary index when you change records in the table.

    The Case Sensitive option means that the index will differentiate between upper- and lowercase letters. Case-sensitive indexes are used in dBASE tables. By default, secondary indexes are not case sensitive.

> **TIP**
>
> Be selective in creating secondary indexes because maintained indexes require extra processing time each time you add or delete a record or modify the index field. Only build maintained secondary indexes for indexes you use frequently or those required for referential integrity.

  4. Choose the field or fields to build the index. A secondary index can use more than one field at a time.

  5. Click the OK button to save the secondary index. The field name now appears under the Table Properties field.

Creating Nested Multi-Table Forms

You can make the data model as simple or as complex as you want to represent the elements you are tracking. One common data model contains two one-to-many relationships, which are linked together as a one-to-many-to-many relationship. A pizza parlor, for example, may enter each order in a table called Orders, along with the customer name and address. A Line Items table can store the pizzas, drinks, salads, and sandwiches ordered. A one-to-many relationship exists between Orders and Line Items.

Because each pizza can have multiple toppings, you need a third table, Toppings, to show each topping ordered. If you look at all three tables, a one-to-many-to-many relationship exists between Orders, Line Items, and Toppings. This kind of relationship is sometimes abbreviated as 1->M->M. Paradox allows you to create a "nested" subform—a subform within a subform—to show a 1->M->M relationship.

The Albums tracking system has a 1->M->M relationship between Albums, Tracks, and Performances. Each Album has multiple tracks, and each track can have multiple performances.

As an exercise, build a nested multi-table form to show all three tables on a single form by following these steps:

  1. From the Paradox Desktop, choose File, New, Form. The Data Model dialog box appears (refer to earlier fig. 7.8).

  2. Add the Albums, Perform, and Tracks tables to the data model by clicking the table name and clicking the Add Table arrow.

3. Next, draw the relationship, or link, between the tables. Click the Albums table and drag the Define Link icon to the detail table Tracks. When you release the mouse button, the tables are linked.

4. Repeat step 3 to draw the link between Tracks and Perform. If the Define Link dialog box appears, click OK to accept the fields that Paradox chooses for the link.

   The data model is now complete, as shown in figure 7.13.

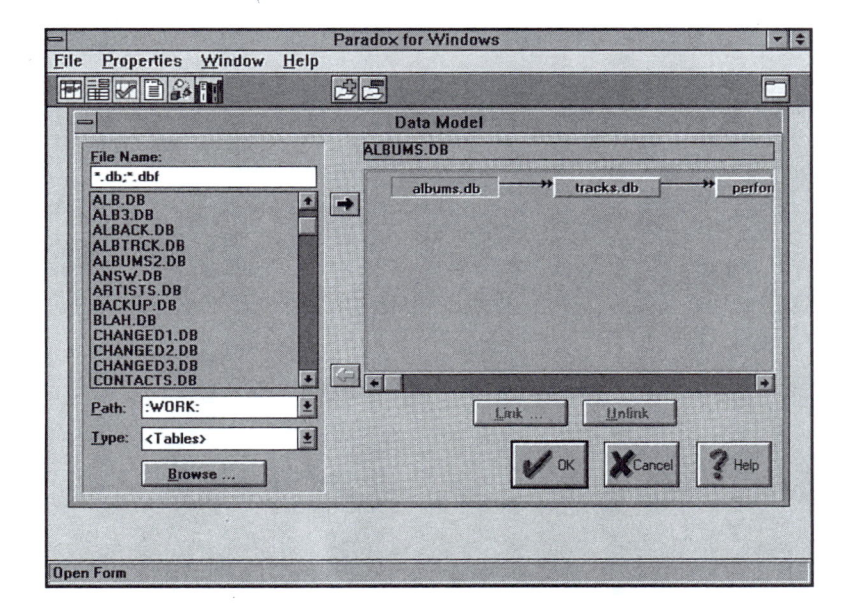

FIG. 7.13

A 1->M->M relationship in the Album Tracking System.

5. Click the OK button in the Data Model dialog box to continue. The Design Layout dialog box appears (see fig. 7.14).

6. Uncheck the Labeled Fields box to make extra room on the form. You can add labels later.

7. The Nested option is now active, so click it. This will nest the PERFORM.DB table within the TRACKS.DB table in the form.

8. Click OK. The Form Design window appears.

9. Edit the form as needed to improve its appearance. Save the new form and test it by entering sample data. You now can enter data into three related tables from the same form (see fig. 7.15).

FIG. 7.14

The Design Layout dialog box for a nested multi-table form.

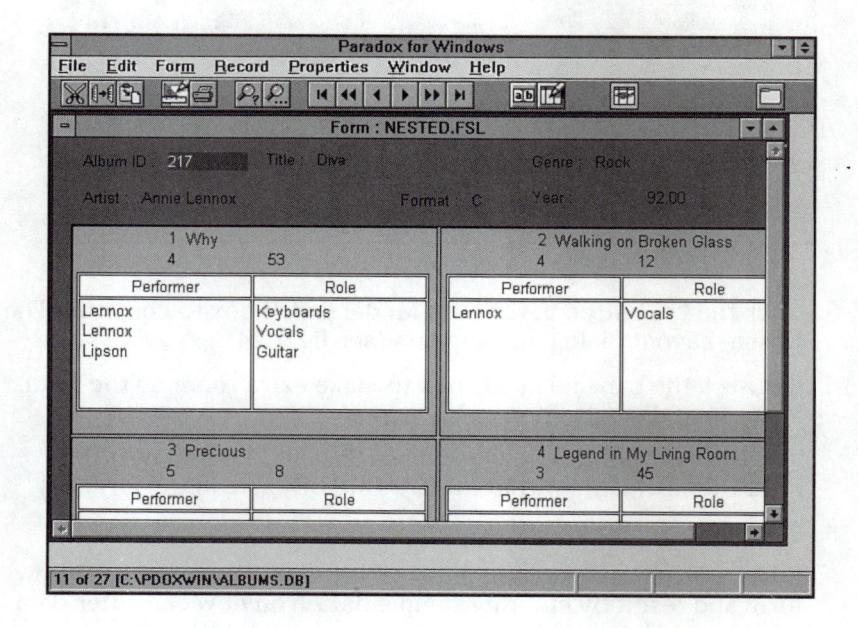

FIG. 7.15

The nested multi-table form Albums, Tracks, Performances.

Defining Special Form Fields

Paradox for Windows offers a number of special field display types to simplify data entry in forms. These field types are not field types in the sense that data is a field type. Instead, they provide help to the user and then fill the data in the table fields as usual. To illustrate, a drop-down edit field or radio button to choose a shipping method enters *Mail* in the invoices table, although the user is simply clicking a menu or button.

The display type does not affect the contents of the field for reporting or other purposes. The purpose of the display type is to make entering or understanding data in the field easier. In the following sections, you learn how to create a drop-down edit field, a list field, radio buttons, and a check box. This section also explains how to create special field display options for drop-down menus, radio buttons, and check boxes.

Creating a Drop-Down Edit Field

A drop-down edit field is a menu of choices that appears when the user clicks a small box (called the drop-down arrow) to the right of the menu name. You already used drop-down menus in Paradox for Windows, which uses a drop-down edit field on the table definition dialog box for validity checks. The advantage of the drop-down edit field is that it takes up less space than displaying the same menu at all times, but the user can view it when necessary. The user also can enter the data directly in the field rather than choose from the menu.

Use a drop-down edit field only when you can enter a finite list of values in a field. The cooking time for a steak, for example, has a finite list of values—rare, medium rare, medium, medium well, and well done. On the other hand, do not use a drop-down edit field for customer name, because it would be impossible to define all the possible names in advance.

A drop-down edit field also is appropriate for the Genre field (Rock, Jazz, and so on) in the Albums table because you can choose from only a few genres. To create a drop-down menu for a field, follow these steps:

1. From the Paradox menu, choose File, New, Form. The Data Model dialog appears.

2. Choose Albums and click OK. The Design Layout dialog box appears.

3. Click OK to accept the default form layout. The Form Design window appears.

4. In the Define Form window, select the Genre field (by clicking it).

5. Inspect the Genre field properties by right-clicking. The Genre properties pop-up menu appears (see fig. 7.16).

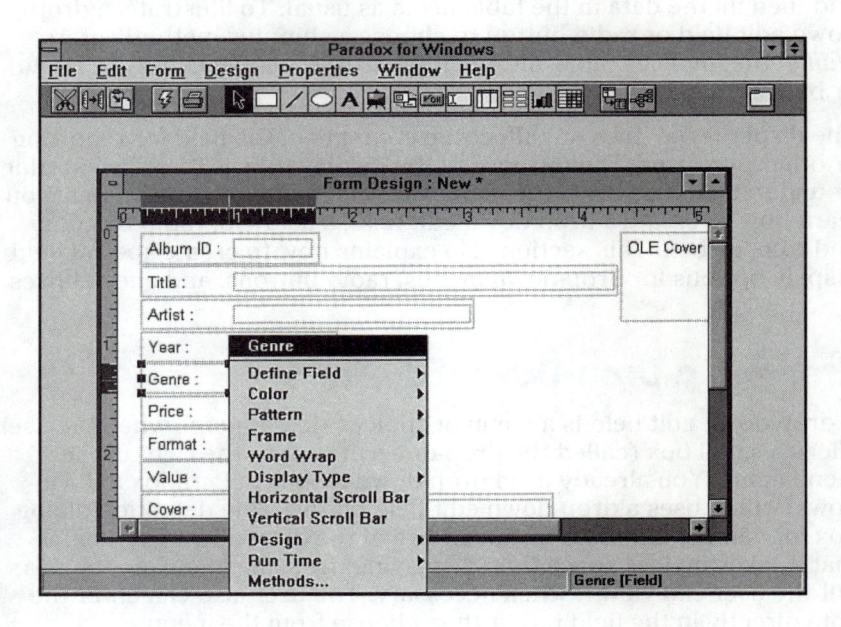

FIG. 7.16

The Genre properties menu.

6. Choose Display Type and then Drop-Down Edit. The Define List dialog box appears (see fig. 7.17).

7. Type in the list of valid entries for the field exactly as they should be entered in the table. You can include, for example, Country, Rock, Jazz, Blues, or other categories.

8. Sort the choices in alphabetical order by clicking the Sort List button. You also can change the order of the menu choices in the Item List by selecting a choice and using the Change Order arrow buttons to move it within the list.

9. After you are happy with the contents and order of the menu choices, click OK. The drop-down edit field appears as a box, as shown in figure 7.18.

7 — USING ADVANCED FORM TECHNIQUES

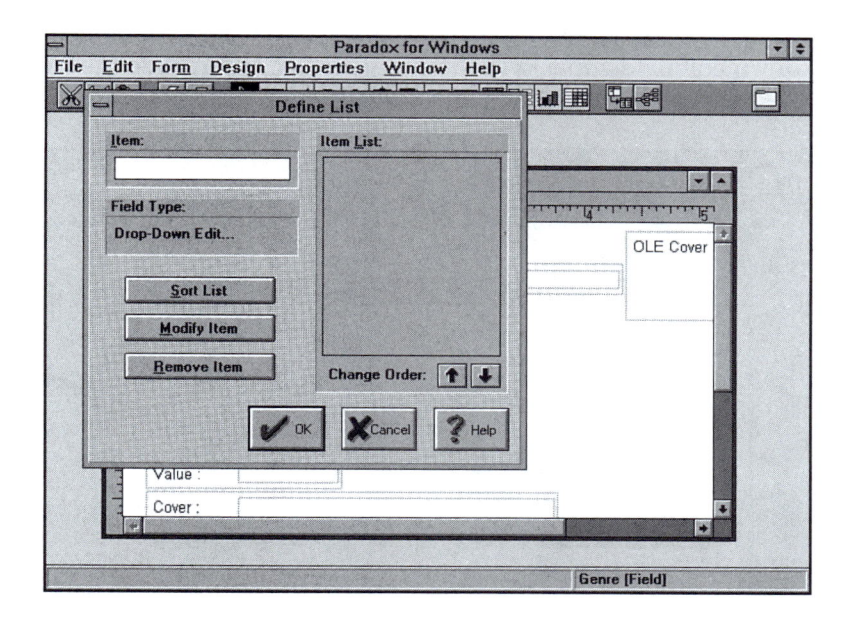

FIG. 7.17
The Define List dialog box.

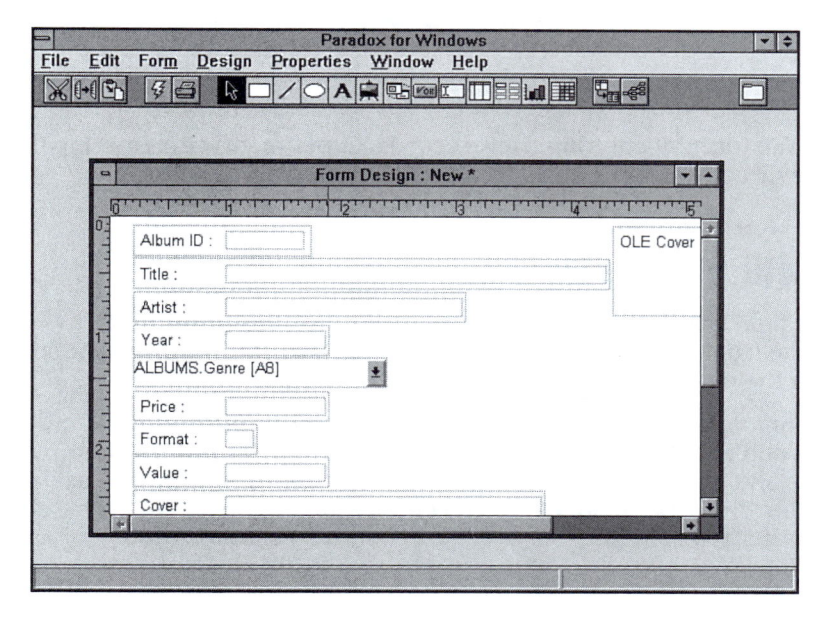

FIG. 7.18
The Genre drop-down edit field in form design.

II — PARADOX FOR WINDOWS POWER TECHNIQUES

10. Save the form, and then run it. Now you can see how the drop-down edit field appears to the user (see fig. 7.19). When the user clicks the field, the list of choices is displayed.

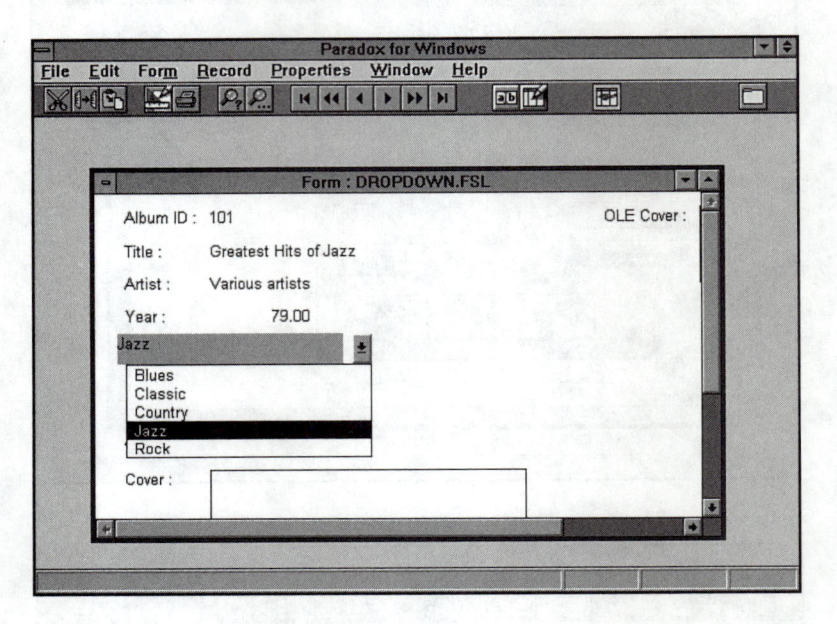

FIG. 7.19

The Genre drop-down edit field in data entry.

Test the form by entering a few records. Experiment with entering the value directly and choosing from the menu.

Creating a List Field

A list field is similar to a drop-down menu, but it requires users to choose from a list rather than enter a value directly. Again, use it only when the choices are finite and relatively stable.

A common use for a list field is for payment terms such as cash, credit card, and net 30. You probably don't want users to make up their own terms and enter them into a field. In the Albums table, you can use a list field for the Genre field. Users can choose among Rock, Country, Jazz, and other types of music.

7 — USING ADVANCED FORM TECHNIQUES

To create a list field, follow these steps:

1. From the Create Form window, select the Genre field by clicking it. Be sure to select the field itself rather than the box containing the label and the field.
2. Inspect the field properties by right-clicking. The properties menu appears.
3. Choose Display Type, and then List. The Define List dialog box appears (see fig. 7.20).

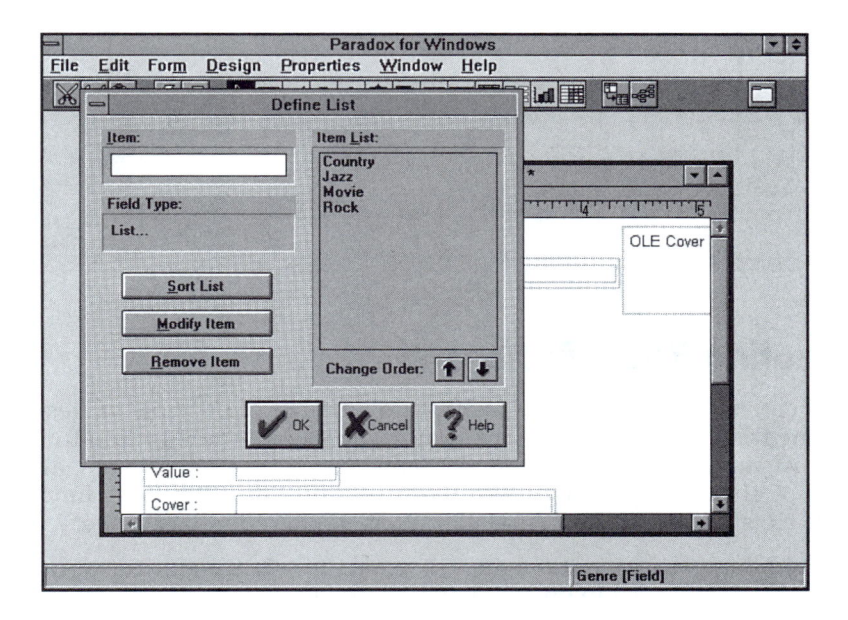

FIG. 7.20
The Define List dialog box.

4. Type in the list of valid entries for the field exactly as you want them to appear in the table. As with a drop-down edit field, you can arrange the choices in whatever order you prefer.
5. Choose OK to save the field. Save the form as usual and run it. The finished list field is shown in figure 7.21. Note that Paradox highlights the choice you have made for each record as you scroll through the table.

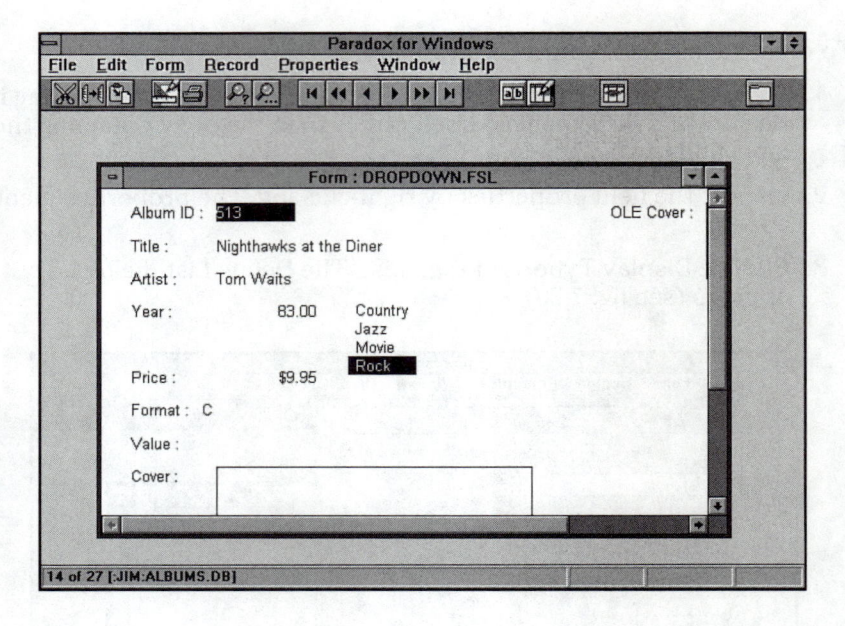

FIG. 7.21

A list field for Format in the Albums table.

Creating Radio Buttons

You can restrict some fields to a limited number of possible values. An airline reservation system, for example, may use a radio button to choose among first class, business, and coach seats. The system allows for no other choices in this field. The radio button is similar in function to the List field display format, but it has a different appearance.

In the Albums table, you may opt to use a radio button for the Format field. To create a radio button field, follow these steps:

1. Select the field by clicking it.

2. Inspect the field properties by right-clicking. The properties menu appears.

3. Choose DisplayType and then Radio Buttons. The Define List dialog box appears (see fig. 7.22).

4. Type in the list of valid entries for the field exactly as you want them to appear in the table. In this case, they should be C, R, and T to stand for Compact Disc, Record, and Tape.

5. Choose OK.

6. You can edit the text labels for the button. For this example, change C to CD, R to Record, and T to Tape. The finished radio button is shown in figure 7.23.

7 — USING ADVANCED FORM TECHNIQUES

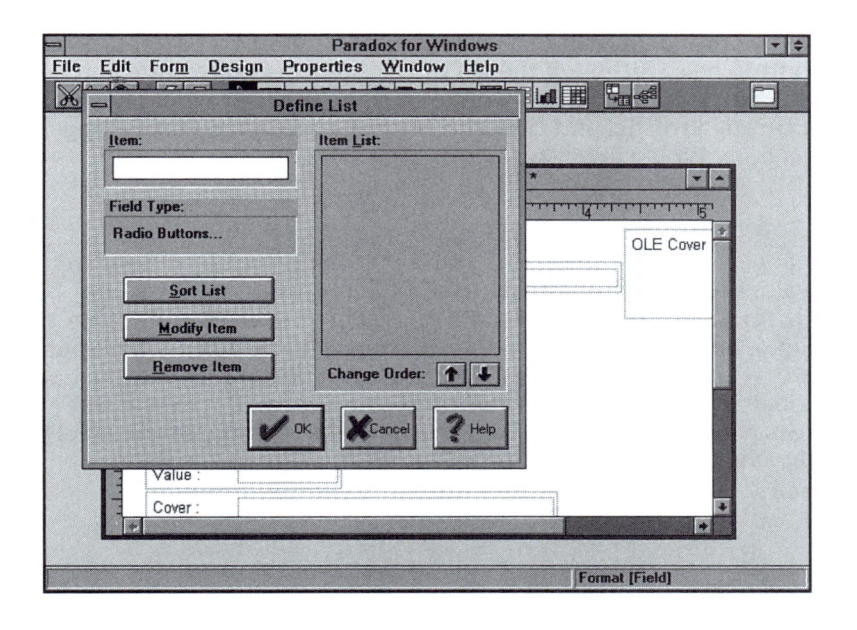

FIG. 7.22
The Define List dialog box.

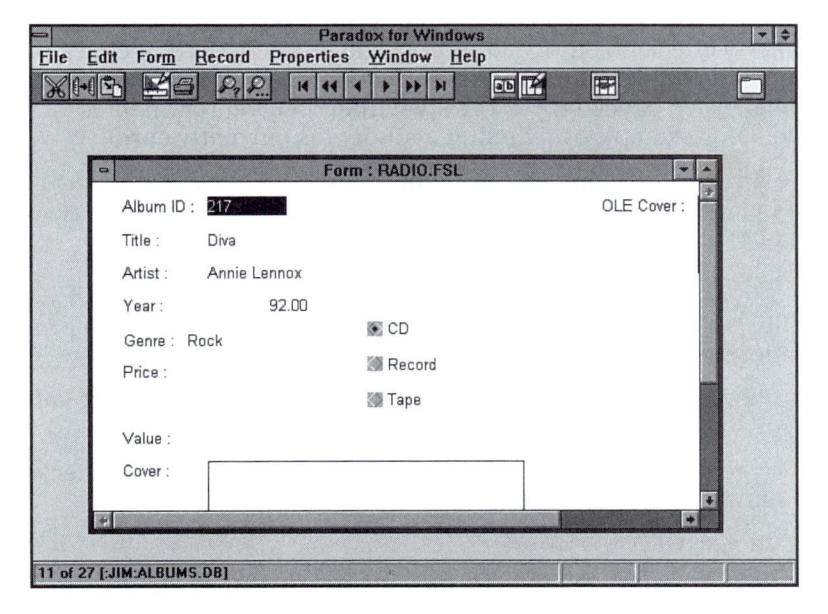

FIG. 7.23
A radio button field for Format in the Albums table.

There is a practical limit to the number of choices you can put in a radio button field. Although the list of U.S. states is finite, for example, it still may be too large to use a radio button. The user would have to hunt through the list and click the correct state, which takes longer than simply typing in the two-letter abbreviation.

> **TIP** The labels for check boxes and radio buttons do not have to match the values entered in the table itself. You may want to use a one-character abbreviation for source of lead in a telemarketing table, for example, but enable users to choose from a check box or radio button with the choices *phone*, *direct mail*, or *trade show* listed. To make the labels different from the values to be entered, first define the choices as they should be entered in the table. Next, edit the labels for the choices to appear the way you want users to see them.

Creating a Check Box

A check-box field is similar to a radio button, but it contains only one button—a check box that can be checked or unchecked. A check box, therefore, is only suitable for fields that have two possible responses. You may use a check box to show whether an inventory item is stocked, for example, or whether a student is currently enrolled.

In the Albums table, for example, you can use a check box for the In Print field to indicate whether the title is or is not in print. To create a check-box field, follow these steps:

1. Select the In Print field by clicking it.
2. Inspect the field properties by right-clicking the field. The properties menu appears.
3. Choose Display Type and then Check Box. The Check Box Values dialog box appears (see fig. 7.24).
4. Type in the values to be entered when the check box is checked and when it is left blank.
5. Choose OK.

    As with radio buttons, you can edit the text that appears on a check box. For this example, the text should read `In print?`. The finished check box field is shown in figure 7.25.

7 — USING ADVANCED FORM TECHNIQUES

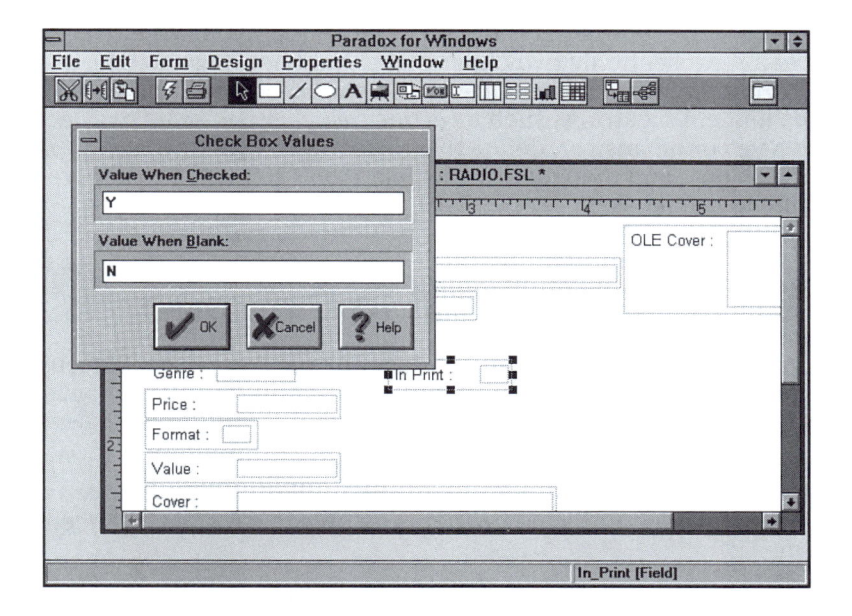

FIG. 7.24
The Check Box Values dialog box.

FIG. 7.25
A check box for the In Print field.

II — PARADOX FOR WINDOWS POWER TECHNIQUES

The table field stores what is entered in a check box. Because the table field can represent only two choices, it should be a logical field, or a single-character field such as Y or N. You waste space in the table if it stores longer text strings such as *active customer* and *sales prospect*. To store a yes or no answer, define the values as 1 and 0 or Y and N, save the check box, and then modify the field labels to make them more meaningful to the user.

Using the Button Tool To Define Forms

You can place buttons in forms to trigger database actions. Buttons are similar to the tool icons in the SpeedBar. You have extensive control over the appearance and function of buttons.

In order to use a button, you must attach an ObjectPAL method. Programming with ObjectPAL is covered in Part III of this book. If you do not write an ObjectPAL method, a button object is just an ornament in a form.

Use the Button tool in the SpeedBar to place buttons in your form design. To change the properties of a button, select the button and right-click to display the properties menu, as shown in figure 7.26.

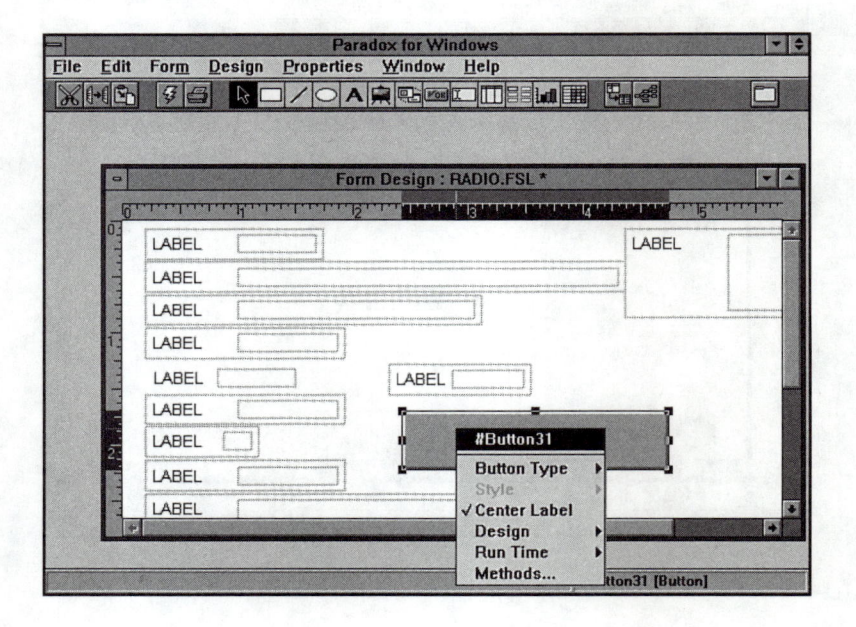

FIG. 7.26

The list of button properties.

7 — USING ADVANCED FORM TECHNIQUES

In essence, a button actually consists of two objects: the button itself and the button label. The label can be selected by clicking the button twice. Button labels have the same properties as other text objects, as shown in figure 7.27. For example, you can change the size, typeface, and color of the button label.

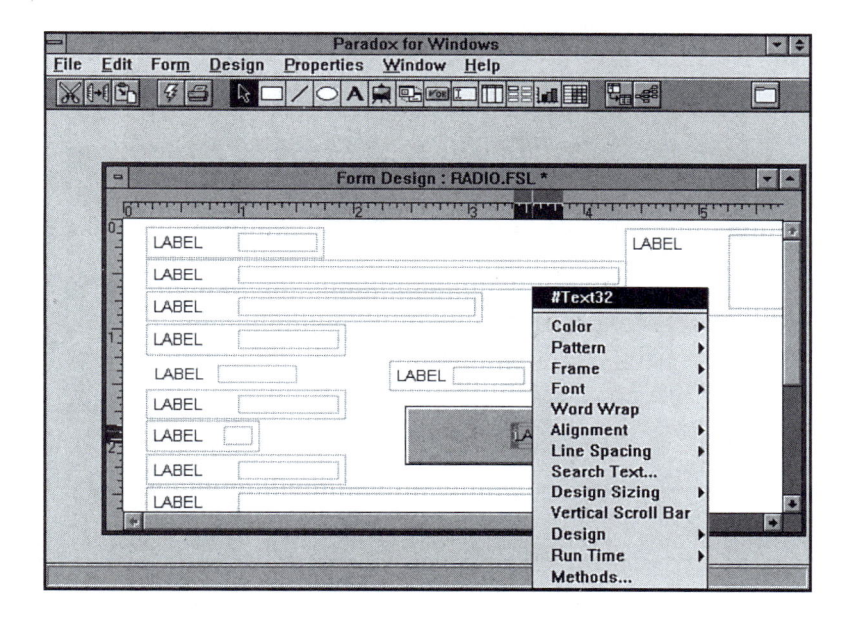

FIG. 7.27

The list of button label properties.

> **TIP**
> The OLE tool in the SpeedBar enables you to create objects and link them to other Windows applications. The OLE feature is described in Chapter 10, "Exchanging Data with Other Applications."

Working with Table Objects

Table objects with reports appear to be much the same as the tables themselves, but they have slightly different characteristics.

In some ways, you have greater control over the appearance of a table object within a form than you do over the table itself. You can modify the components individually—the fields themselves, the text objects, and the grid—that make up a field object. You can place more than one field in a column to save space, for example, and add new fields to perform calculations. Finally, you can add new design elements such as graphics, other tables, graphs, crosstabs, lines, boxes, and ellipses. The properties of a table object are shown in figure 7.28.

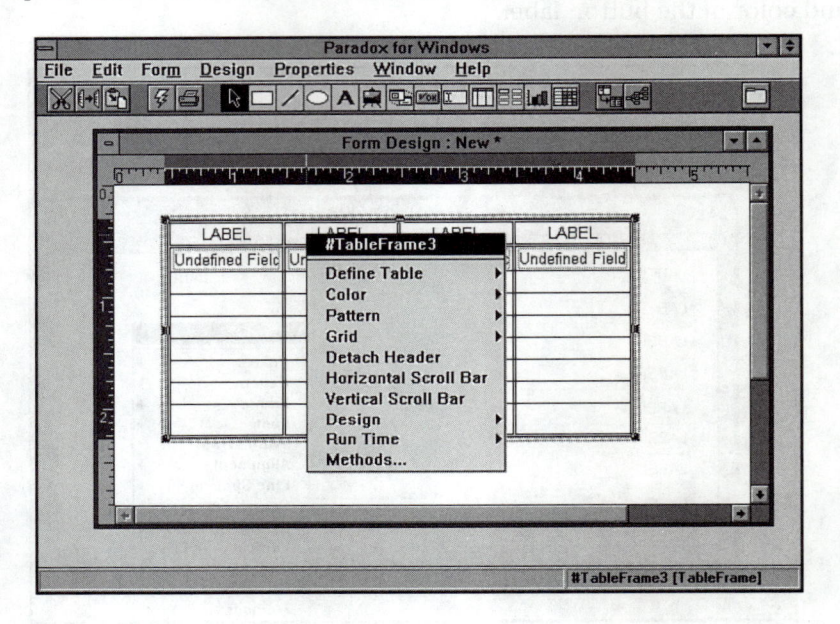

FIG. 7.28

The Table Object properties menu.

Try to use a table object by creating a tabular form from the Albums table. Resize the column width or row height by clicking and dragging the grid line. Insert a new column by selecting the column to the right of where you want the new column to appear and pressing the Ins key. Delete a column by selecting the column to delete and pressing the Del key.

Setting Filters

During data entry, you may want to restrict the records a table displays or use an alternate sort order to display the records. Either of these options is possible by setting a *filter*. Choose Form and then select Order/Range. The Order/Range dialog box appears (see fig. 7.29).

7 — USING ADVANCED FORM TECHNIQUES

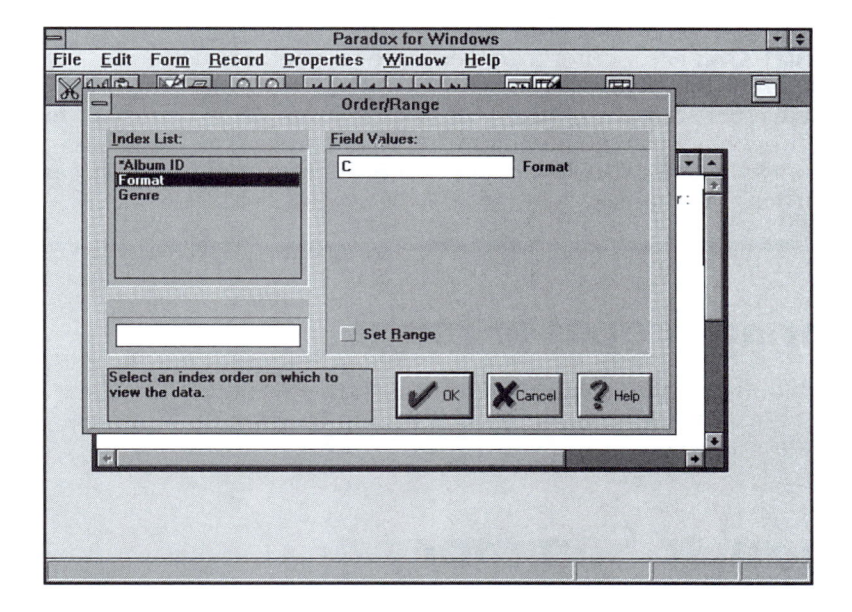

FIG. 7.29
The Order/Range dialog box.

The box lists the available keys for sorting the table. These keys are the primary keys you defined, as well as any secondary keys. To choose an existing key, click the desired key, and then choose OK or press Enter. The table instantly appears in the new sort order.

You also can restrict the records based on a range of values in the key field you use to sort. Enter a value in Field Values for the records you want to display. When you click OK, the table appears with only those records that meet your filter criteria.

Using filter criteria is a handy way to avoid multiple searches when working on a select group of records. If you are processing orders for a given period of time, for example, you can use a secondary key on the date field and filter the table so you only see the records from that time period. When you leave the table, the filter conditions disappear, and sorting reverts to the primary key. Figure 7.29, for example, is set to display only compact discs from the Albums table by choosing the Format field and entering a value of **C**.

> **CAUTION:** Filter criteria are sensitive to whether a letter is upper- or lowercase. If you want to work with records only from states that start with the letters A–F, for example, you must enter **A** (uppercase) as the minimum and **F** (uppercase) as the maximum values because lowercase letters fail to match the uppercase entries in the table.

Placing Graphs in Forms

Graph objects can be placed in forms with the Graph tool. You learn about creating graphs from Paradox data in Chapter 10, "Creating Crosstabs and Graphs."

Chapter Summary

Although you can create a Paradox form instantly with the Quick Form button and easily with standard layout options, Paradox for Windows offers a number of advanced form design features.

Some form techniques affect only the appearance of the form and not the underlying data in Paradox tables. You can use, for example, advanced field display types such as pull-down lists and check boxes to make data entry simpler and more accurate. You can even define buttons in forms to trigger ObjectPAL programs.

Multi-table forms enable you to view and edit information in multiple tables from a single form. Paradox for Windows supports not only side-by-side, multi-table regions (like Paradox for DOS) but also nested subforms that represent one-to-many-to-many relationships among three tables. The data model graphically represents table relationships and prompts you to establish links using the appropriate fields.

Combined with what you learned in Chapter 5, "Getting Started with Forms," the advanced form features introduced in this chapter give you full control over how data appears to the user.

CHAPTER 8

Using Advanced Query By Example

In Chapter 4, "Getting Started with Query By Example," you learned how to retrieve information from single Paradox tables by checking the desired fields and filling in example elements. In this chapter, you learn to use query by example (QBE) for more advanced operations. In particular, you learn how to perform multi-table queries and set operations.

The advanced query operations you learn in this chapter include the following:

- Retrieving data from more than one table by using multi-table queries
- Specifying search criteria from one table to retrieve data from a second table.
- Performing calculations within a record and on groups of records
- Using set operations to compare groups of records
- Inserting, deleting, and modifying records

Creating Multi-Table Queries

In a well-designed relational database, data is spread across several tables to protect the integrity of the data and to eliminate redundant data entry. In such a database, a single table contains only a portion of the data you are tracking; therefore, a query that involves only a single table cannot provide you with a complete answer. Multi-table queries are necessary to obtain many of the queries you ask your database.

A sales application, for example, draws information from many tables, including tables for customers, invoices, line items, inventory, suppliers, employees, reorders, and reorder items. To find a list of all customers ordering inventory items on back order, therefore, you must use a multi-table query that includes the customers, invoices, line items, and inventory tables.

With Paradox for Windows, a normalized data structure (as described in Chapter 2) with many tables is no obstacle to easy data retrieval. Queries can pull data from multiple tables as easily as from single tables. In fact, Paradox can handle up to 24 tables in a single query. The same basic query operators used in single-table queries are used in multi-table queries but with a slight twist: you first must establish a relationship between the tables.

In a relational database, tables are related when a record in one table corresponds to one or more records in another table. Usually, the tables share a common field, so records with the same value in these fields are related to one another. In the Album tracking database, the Album ID field relates the Albums and Tracks tables, and the Album ID and Track Number fields (the composite key for Tracks) relate the Tracks and Performances tables. A doctor's office, for example, tracks patient immunizations by using a Visits table. The same doctor's office stores billing information in a Patients table. Both include a patient ID field (the social security number), which has the same value in both tables (see fig. 8.1). If patient Billy Archer has a patient ID of 123-45-6789 and a visit is recorded for patient 123-45-6789, then that visit belongs to Billy Archer. Therefore, the patient ID field links the two tables.

Figure 8.2 shows an example of a multi-table query showing medical patients and their office visits. The query contains the patients' first name and last name from the Patients table along with the date of the visit and diagnosis from the Visits table.

Paradox for Windows uses example elements to designate links between tables. In order to set up these links, you must understand the relationships between your tables.

8 — USING ADVANCED QUERY BY EXAMPLE

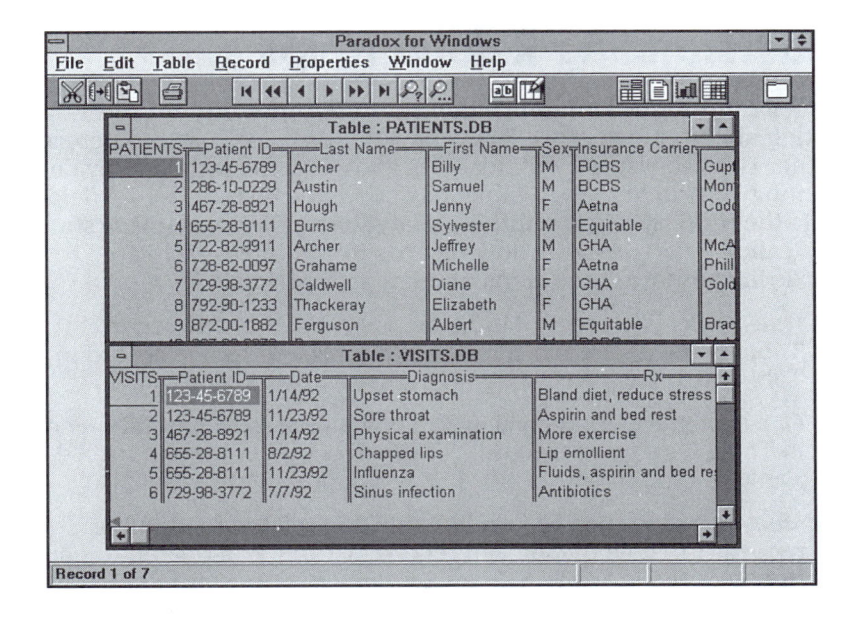

FIG. 8.1

The Patients and Visits tables.

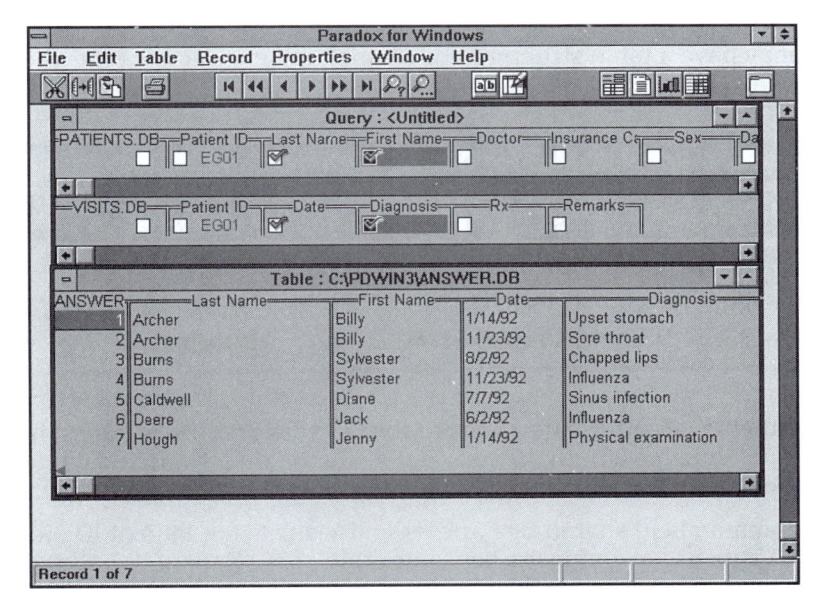

FIG. 8.2

A multi-table query for patients and visits.

Understanding Relationships

Chapter 2 introduced relational database concepts that are essential to creating multi-table queries. First, the field (or fields) used to determine whether two records are duplicates is known as the primary key. In addition to a primary key, a table may contain a foreign key—a field that is the primary key in another, related table. Relationships (sometimes called links) describe how records in one table are related to records in another. Three kinds of relationships exist:

- *One-to-one*. Each record in Table A is related to one record in Table B and each record in Table B is related to one record in Table A.

- *One-to-many*. Each record in Table A is related to multiple records in Table B and each record in Table B is related to one record in Table A.

- *Many-to-many*. Each record in Table A is related to multiple records in Table B and each record in Table B is related to multiple records in Table A. Many-to-many relationships should be broken into two one-to-many relationships by creating an intermediate table.

You may have a table structure, for example, that resembles the one in table 8.1.

Table 8.1. Relationships for Doctors, Patients, and Visits

Table	Key	Foreign key
Doctors	Last Name	None
Patients	Patient ID	Doctor
Visits	Patient ID + Date	Patient ID

The Patients table is related to both the Doctors and Visits tables, because patients have both doctors and visits. No direct relationship exists between the Doctors and Visits tables in this example.

The common field shared by Patients and Visits is the Patient ID. Because Visits has a composite key consisting of the Patient ID and the Date, you can enter more than one visit for each patient.

Similarly, customers and invoices share the Customer # field. The fact that Customer # is a foreign key under invoices implies that the relationship between customers and invoices is one-to-many; each customer can have many related invoice records. If the Customer # field were the primary key in Invoices, each customer would be allowed to have only one invoice, which would severely limit the growth of your business.

Using Example Elements

Paradox uses example elements in two quite different ways. First, you learn how to use example elements to link tables together. Second, you learn to use example elements to represent field values to perform calculations and other functions.

Using Example Elements To Join Tables

The way to link tables in Paradox queries is to tell Paradox which fields define the relationship between tables. Paradox for Windows enables you to establish the relationships yourself by using example elements. Example elements are special characters (such as EG01) that are identical in fields of one or more query forms.

To create a multi-table query and to define the example elements, use the Albums example created in Chapter 2 and follow these steps:

1. To open the query editor, right-click the Open Query icon on the SpeedBar of the Paradox Desktop and choose **N**ew. The Select File dialog box appears (see fig. 8.3).

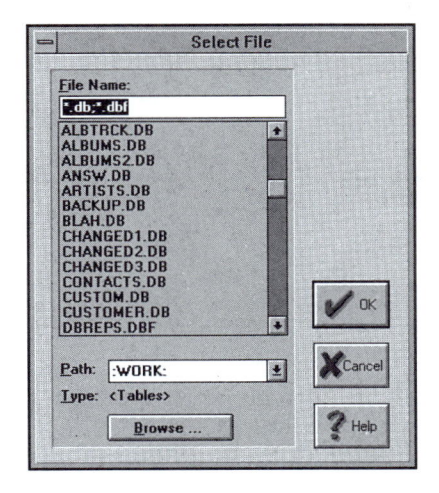

FIG. 8.3

The Select File dialog box.

2. Add the Albums table to the query editor by clicking the table name ALBUMS.DB, and then choosing OK.

3. Add the Tracks table by clicking the Add Table button in the SpeedBar of the Query window. Choose TRACKS.DB from the Select File dialog box.

4. Select the fields to appear in the Answer table by clicking the check box in the Title and Artist fields in the Albums table and Song Title in the Tracks table. A check mark appears in the check boxes.

5. Next, establish the relationship between the tables by providing an example element in the related fields. Click the Join Tables tool on the SpeedBar. The message area says `Performing Join` and the mouse pointer changes to `EG` to show that you are placing an example element. Click the Album ID field in the Albums table and again in the Tracks table. `EG01` appears in these fields to show that you have placed an example element (see fig. 8.4).

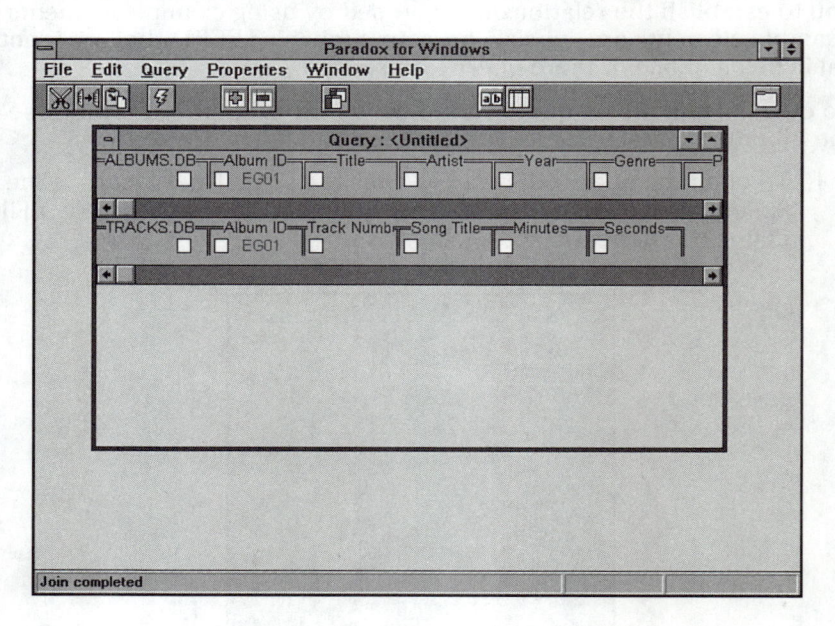

FIG. 8.4
Using the Example Element to join the Albums and Tracks tables.

6. Select the fields from both tables to appear in the Answer table by clicking the check box below the field names. For this example, choose Title and Artist from the Albums table and Song Title from the Tracks table.

7. Run the query by clicking the Run Query button (the lightning bolt button), choosing **R**un Query from the **Q**uery menu, or pressing F8. The Answer table appears.

If you are relating more than two tables, use a different example element for each of the relationships. You can use EG00 to relate Albums to Tracks, for example, EG01 to relate Tracks to Performances, and EG02 to relate Performances to Artists. Each time you click the Join Tables button, the example element is increased by one.

> **NOTE** A column (field) in a query may contain search criteria, calculations, and example elements.

You may not be able to see the entire contents of a column until you edit it. To view the remaining characters, place the cursor in the field and move to the right to reveal the rest of the characters.

Using Example Elements To Represent Values

In addition to their role in multi-table queries, you can use example elements for queries within a single table to represent values found in a search. In essence, using example elements to represent values enables you to combine two queries into one.

Suppose that you want to identify all the Tom Waits albums you own that were recorded after *Blue Valentine*. First, you write a query to determine the year that *Blue Valentine* was recorded (see fig. 8.5). You discover that it was recorded in 1978. Next, you write a query to show albums by Tom Waits with a recording date greater than 78 (see fig. 8.6).

Although this two-step approach works, it is a bit cumbersome. Using the example element combines these two steps into a single query. First, define an example element for the Year field, and enter **"Blue Valentine"** in the Title field as your search criterion. Next, press the down arrow to insert a new row in the query. Place the example element in the Year field and insert a < symbol before it. Figure 8.7 shows the finished query, which uses example elements to link the result of the first query (78) to the search in the second query.

Note that the greater than (>) comparison operator is used in the second line of the query. You can use other comparison operators with example elements just as you use constant values. If you omitted the comparison operator, the query would find only albums recorded in 1978 (an exact match of the example element).

II — PARADOX FOR WINDOWS POWER TECHNIQUES

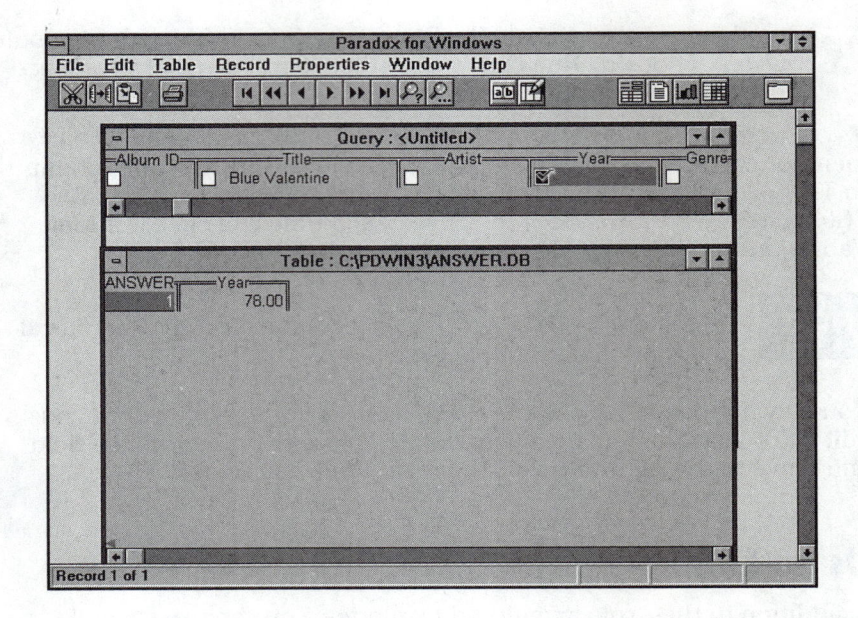

FIG. 8.5
Query to find year of *Blue Valentine*.

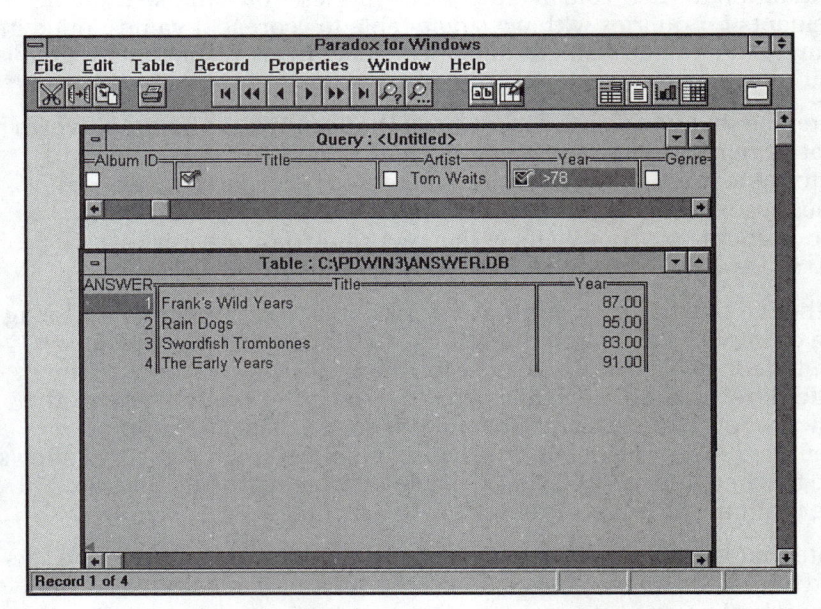

FIG. 8.6
Query for all albums by Tom Waits after 1978.

8 — USING ADVANCED QUERY BY EXAMPLE   373

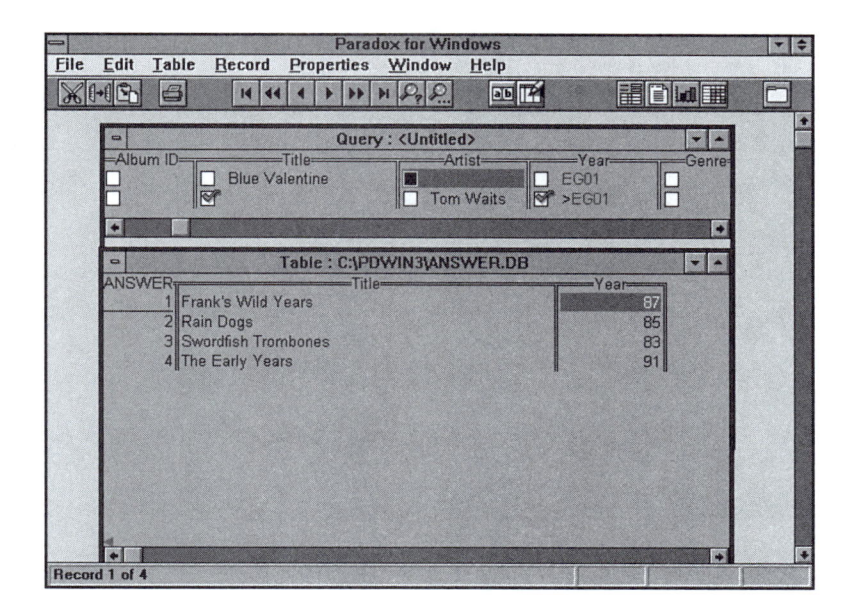

FIG. 8.7

Searching for all Tom Waits albums recorded after *Blue Valentine* in a single query.

> **TIP**
>
> If you have used other database software, you may find that the use of example elements to represent a value is similar to the use of variables in algebra or memory variables in programs such as dBASE. Think of the example element as a temporary holding place for the result of a query.

Specifying Multiple Conditions in Multi-Table Queries

In multi-table queries, you can use search criteria just as you do in single-table queries. You can enter the selection conditions in any or all of the tables as long as the tables are linked to one another with example elements. The following sections show how to use multiple criteria from different tables. These criteria may be exclusive (the AND operator) or inclusive (the OR operator). You also can combine AND and OR operators in a query. Figure 8.8 shows an advanced query to find all jazz or rock Albums that contain songs over 5 minutes in length.

FIG. 8.8

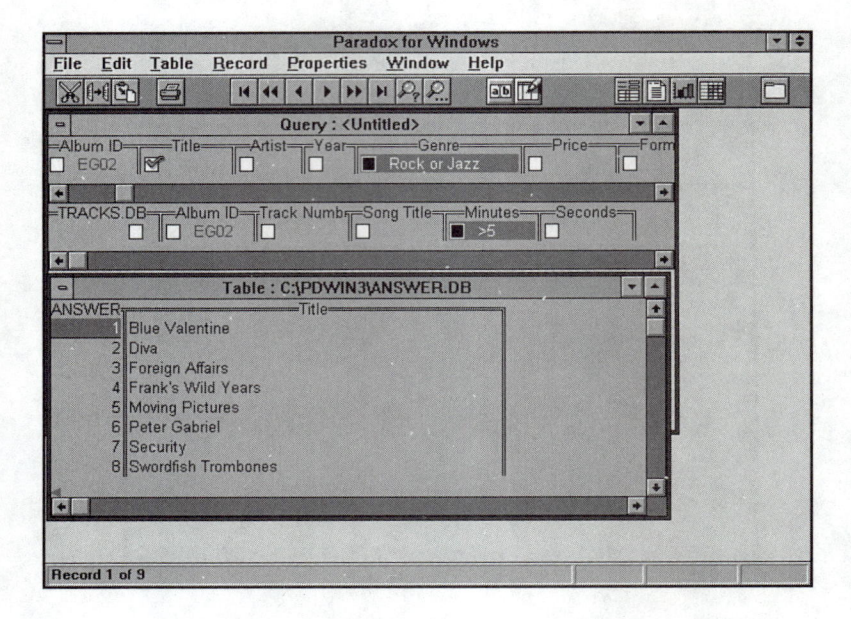

A multi-table query with AND and OR conditions.

Creating AND Conditions

To make a search narrower, you can use the AND condition. This means that the record must meet both search conditions in order to be included in the Answer table. First, use the Join Tables tool in the SpeedBar to link the two tables. Next, fill in the desired values in the appropriate fields from the joined tables. You can include search conditions in the same field used as an example element. The query in figure 8.9, for example, searches for albums by Miles Davis which contain the track entitled "'Round About Midnight."

Creating OR Conditions

You can use the OR operator to widen the scope of your search by allowing a match with multiple values. For example, you might want to search for all customers from California OR Illinois. Within a single field, use the OR operator as you do in a single-table query. For OR conditions across multiple fields, use separate lines in the query image, as shown in figure 8.10.

You cannot use OR conditions in example element fields. The OR condition creates ambiguous links between the tables and, therefore, returns invalid results. In other words, example elements link all records in the

8 — USING ADVANCED QUERY BY EXAMPLE

two tables as long as their field values match. You might want to list all album titles in which the artist is Harry Connick or that contain the word *love* in any of their song titles (whether or not they are by Harry Connick), as shown in figure 8.10.

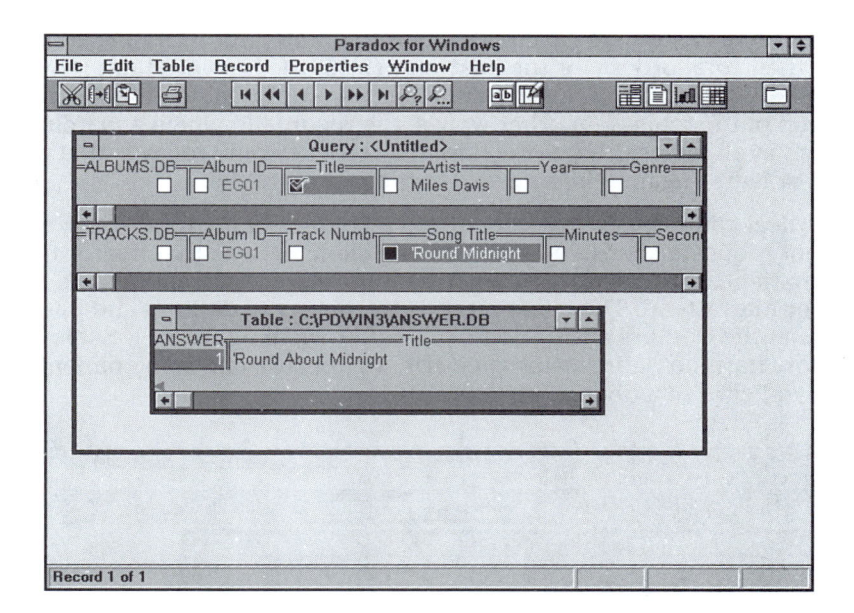

FIG. 8.9
A query with multiple AND conditions.

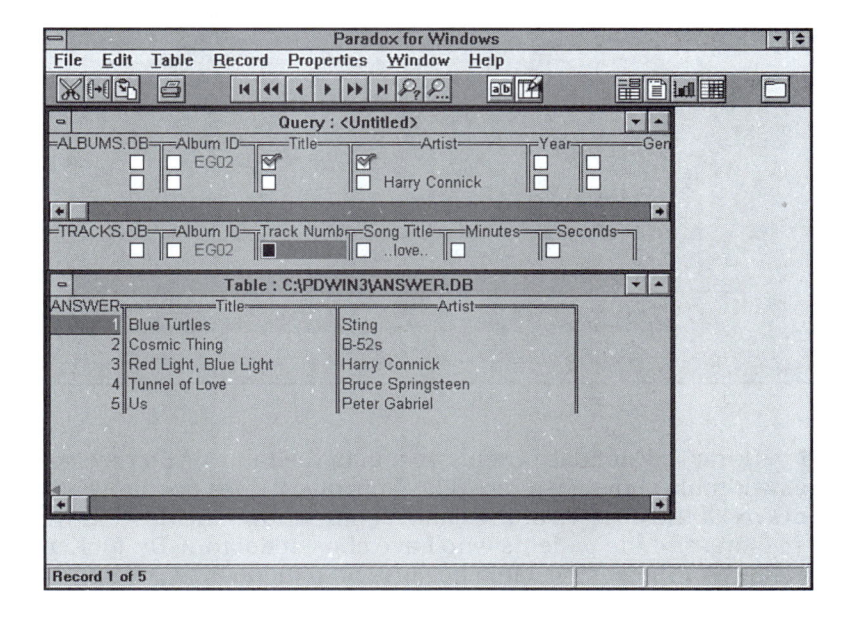

FIG. 8.10
A query with multiple OR conditions.

Creating Inner and Outer Joins

All multi-table operations are called *joins* in relational database parlance because they join two or more tables. A query might list the names of all customers (from the Customer table), for example, along with their total orders for the past year (from the Invoices table). By default, multi-table queries in Paradox for Windows yield only the intersection of the tables—in other words, the records in which a match occurs in all tables. Therefore, Paradox retrieves only records that have at least one matching record in the related table.

A medical clinic, for example, employs a number of doctors. When a patient requests a particular doctor, the clinic assigns that doctor to that patient. For patients who express no preference, any available doctor may attend. The clinic records the names of doctors and patients in the Doctors and Patients tables shown in figure 8.11. Some doctors have no patients assigned (Dr. McKenzie), and some patients have not chosen a doctor (Mr. Burns).

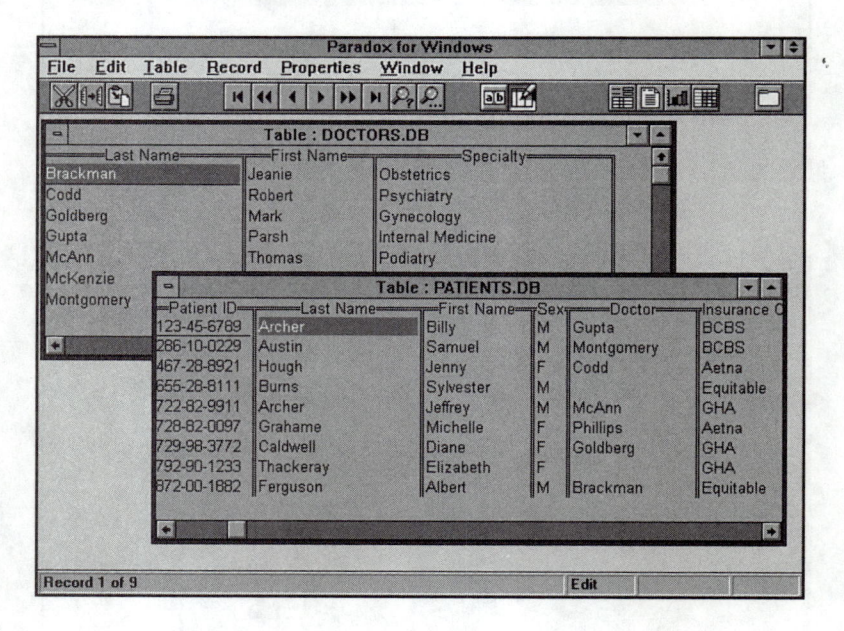

FIG. 8.11

Doctors and Patients tables.

If you perform the standard exclusive join of the tables, you receive the answer table shown in figure 8.12. This query does not show all the patients or all the doctors at the clinic. It only shows the doctors who have patients and the patients who have chosen doctors. Dr. McKenzie is not shown in the answer table because no patients have been

8 — USING ADVANCED QUERY BY EXAMPLE   377

assigned to him. Mr. Burns is not shown because he has not yet been assigned a doctor. The AS query operator was used in this query to distinguish between the name of the doctor and the name of the patient in the answer table. To include the doctors or patients missing from this query, you must use an outer join.

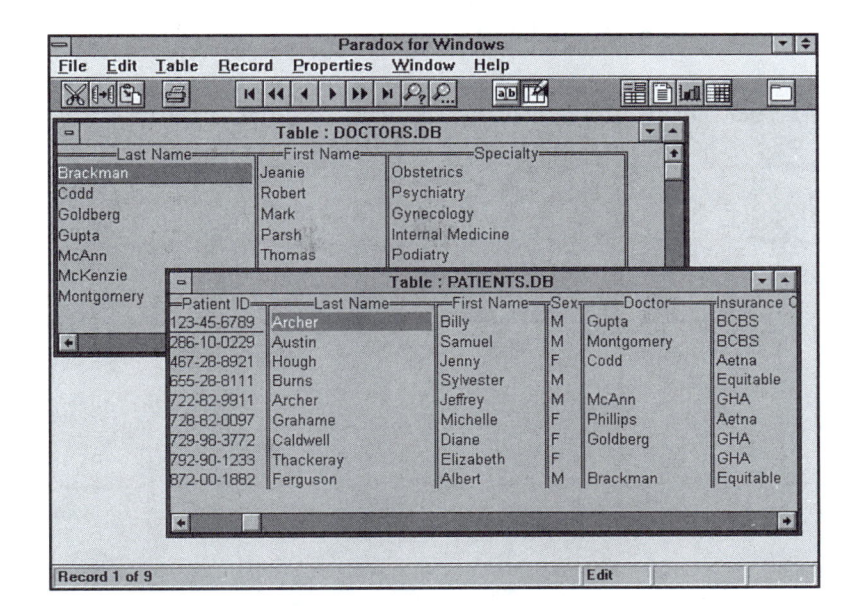

FIG. 8.12

The Answer table for an exclusive join query.

Paradox supports other types of joins that will produce different results. Table 8.2 lists the type of joins permitted by Paradox.

Table 8.2. Relational Table Joins in Paradox

Join type	Description
Inner (exclusive)	All records with a matching record in another table (the default)
Outer (inclusive)	
Asymmetrical	All records from one table and only matching records from the second table
Symmetrical	All records from both tables regardless of whether they have matching records in the second table

II — PARADOX FOR WINDOWS POWER TECHNIQUES

In addition to the default exclusive join, Paradox supports an inclusive join that enables you to retrieve the union of two tables—records from either or both tables regardless of whether they have any related records. To broaden the search to show all doctors, simply add an exclamation point (!) to the example element in the table from which you want to list all records (whether or not a matching record is in the related table), as shown in figure 8.13.

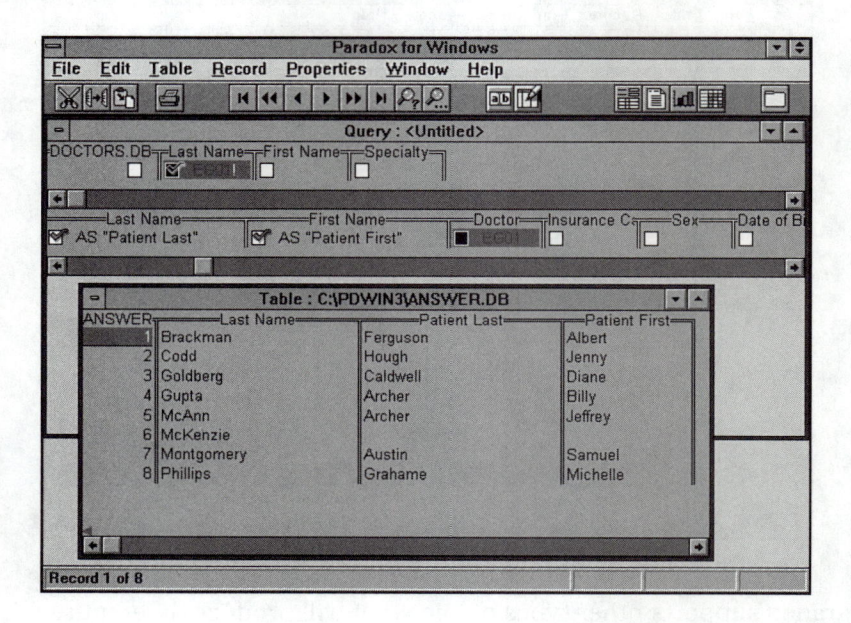

FIG. 8.13

The Answer table for an asymmetrical, outer join query.

This inclusive join of the tables is called an outer join because it contains some records that fall outside the intersection of the two sets. In this case, the outer join is asymmetrical because all records are included from the table on one side of the relationship (the Doctors table) but not on both sides. Therefore, Dr. McKenzie is included in the answer table although he has no patients.

To make the outer join symmetrical, use exclamation points on the example elements on both sides of the relationship. Now, as shown in figure 8.14, the Answer table includes all patients and all doctors. Burns and Thackeray appear along with the other patients, although they have not been assigned doctors.

NOTE You may use only one inclusive link per line, up to a maximum of two inclusive links in a query. Therefore, a query with three tables may use an inclusive link between two of the tables but not for all three, if they are related on only one field.

8 — USING ADVANCED QUERY BY EXAMPLE

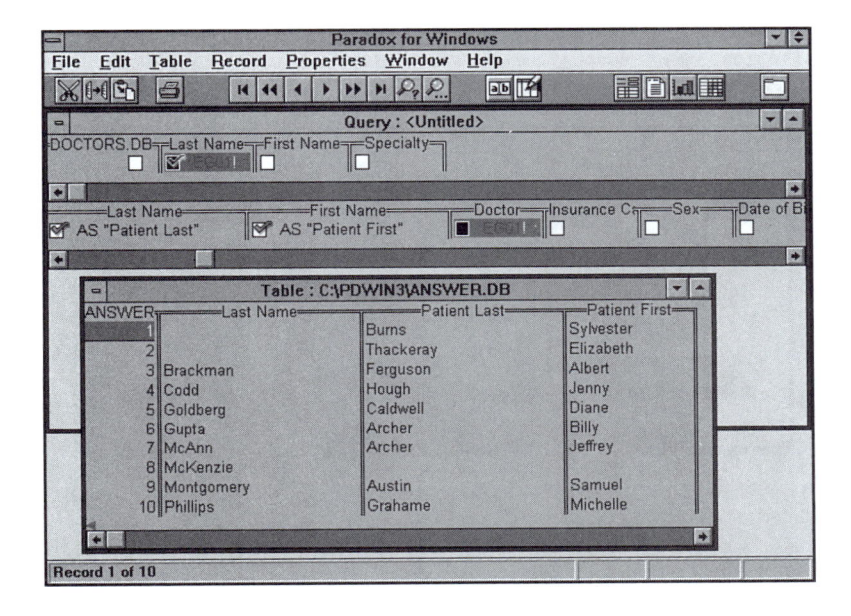

FIG. 8.14

The Answer table for a symmetrical, outer join query.

Try these three kinds of joins (exclusive, inclusive asymmetrical, and inclusive symmetrical) on the Albums and Tracks tables. If you have entered some albums without entering any tracks, those albums do not appear in an exclusive join. To list all albums along with their tracks (even albums with no tracks entered), you must use an outer join.

Performing Calculations in Queries

Many PC database users cling to spreadsheets to perform calculations. They export their data to a spreadsheet and then use the mathematical functions of the spreadsheet to manipulate numeric data. The built-in mathematical functions and business graphics of Paradox for Windows takes care of these needs without having to resort to a spreadsheet. When you add in the power of Paradox graphs, you may never need to use your spreadsheet again. Figure 8.15 shows a query to produce statistics based on the Albums table.

In QBE, Paradox for Windows provides two kinds of calculations: calculations within a record, using one or more fields from the record; and summary calculations, which count multiple records.

II — PARADOX FOR WINDOWS POWER TECHNIQUES

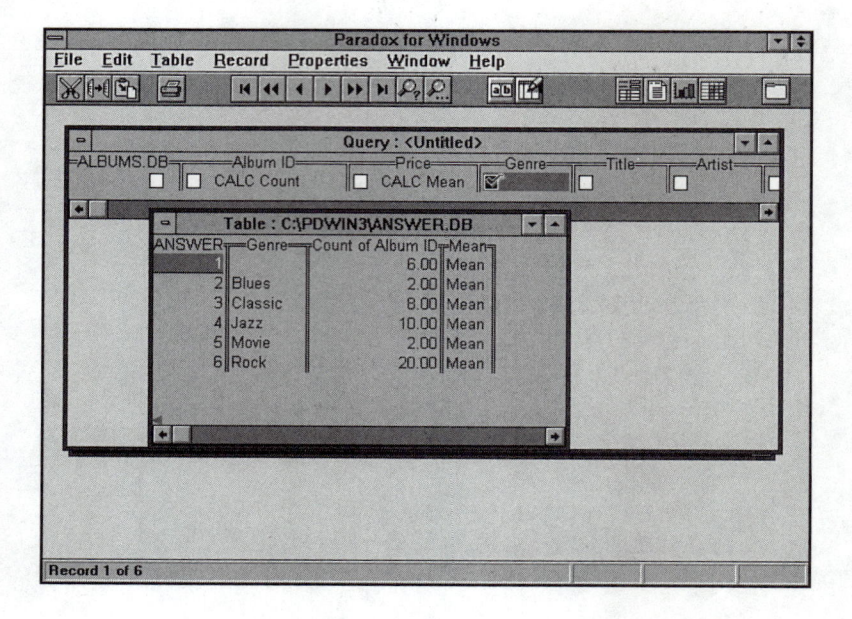

FIG. 8.15

A query that produces counts and averages for the Albums table.

Performing Calculations within a Record

In most queries, you list the values contained in the fields. Using the CALC operator, you can perform calculations on field values. The results of the calculation appear as new fields in the Answer table. Calculated fields within a record use field values (represented by example elements), numeric and alphanumeric constants, and the arithmetic operators shown in table 8.3.

Table 8.3. Query Arithmetic Operators

Function	Operator
Addition	+
Subtraction	–
Multiplication	*
Division	/
Grouping	( )

The CALC operator adds a new column to the Answer table, labeled with the CALC expression you use in the query. CALC is a keyword

8 — USING ADVANCED QUERY BY EXAMPLE

indicating that there is a calculation to perform within a query. The CALC operator is used to join fields together as well as for mathematical calculations. To change the name of the Answer table column, use the AS operator described in Chapter 4, "Getting Started with Query by Example."

> **TIP**
>
> The CALC operator is not case-sensitive, so you need not worry about capitalization.

The following sections describe different ways that the CALC operator may be used in a query.

Performing Numeric Calculations

To perform calculations on numeric fields, use example elements to identify the field for the calculation and then create a query similar to that shown in figure 8.16.

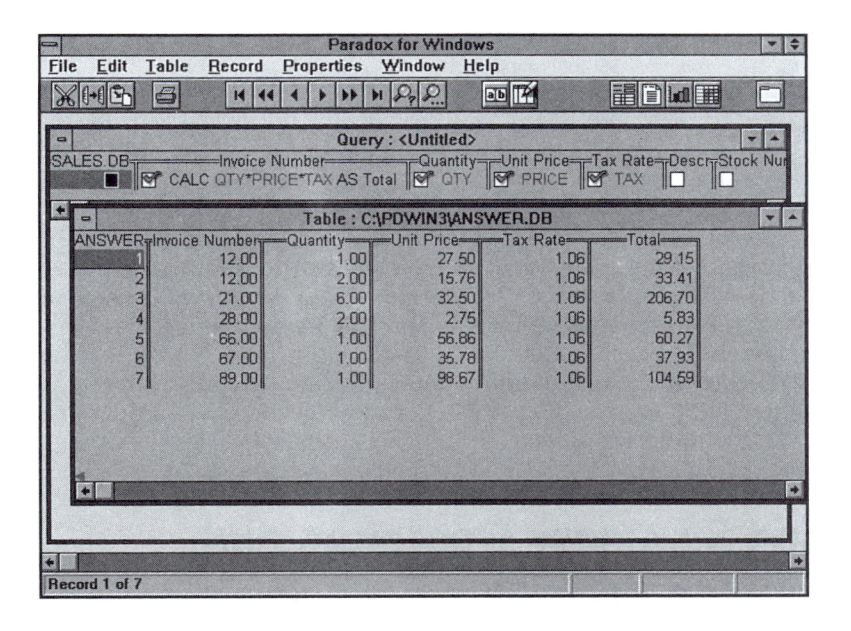

FIG. 8.16

A numeric calculation query where quant * price * tax = total price.

Combining Alphanumeric Values

You also can use the CALC operator to join two or more alphanumeric fields. You may want to join a person's title—Mr. or Ms., for example—with his or her last name to use as a salutation in a letter. The CALC expression uses the + to combine example elements or alphanumeric constants.

To combine the TITLE and LNAME fields in the CUSTOMER table, follow these steps:

1. In the query editor, define the example element for the LNAME field by placing the cursor in the field, pressing F5, and entering **"LNAME"**. The example element is highlighted to show that it is different from a standard search criterion.

2. Define the example element for the TITLE field by placing the cursor in the field, pressing F5, and entering **"TITLE"**. Press F5 again to exit from example mode.

3. Enter a comma to separate the example element from the CALC statement. Enter the CALC statement (**CALC TITLE+" "+LNAME**), pressing F5 to enter example mode when entering the two example elements.

4. Enter **AS Salutation** to rename the calculated field in the answer table.

NOTE You may use any names you choose when defining example elements. You may find that using field names makes the example elements easier to remember and identify.

This expression actually joins three elements: the title field, the Lastname field, and a space. Paradox for Windows normally removes (truncates) leading and trailing spaces from fields that are combined (concatenated), so you must use " " to insert the space between the fields. The final AS expression renames the calculated field in the Answer table to Salutation. Figure 8.17 shows an example of a query combining alphanumeric values.

Using Summary Operators and Grouping Records

You can use summary operators to calculate statistics that encompass a number of records. You may want to determine, for example, the average monthly commission for your sales staff or total taxable sales by state. To determine such statistics, you must look at many records. Paradox summary operators, as shown in table 8.4, enable you to calculate sum, average, maximum, minimum, and number of values for all records in a table or for groups of records. The table also shows the default for each grouping operator where applicable. If the grouping operator is ALL, then all records are counted in the calculation. If the grouping operator is UNIQUE, only unique instances of each value are calculated.

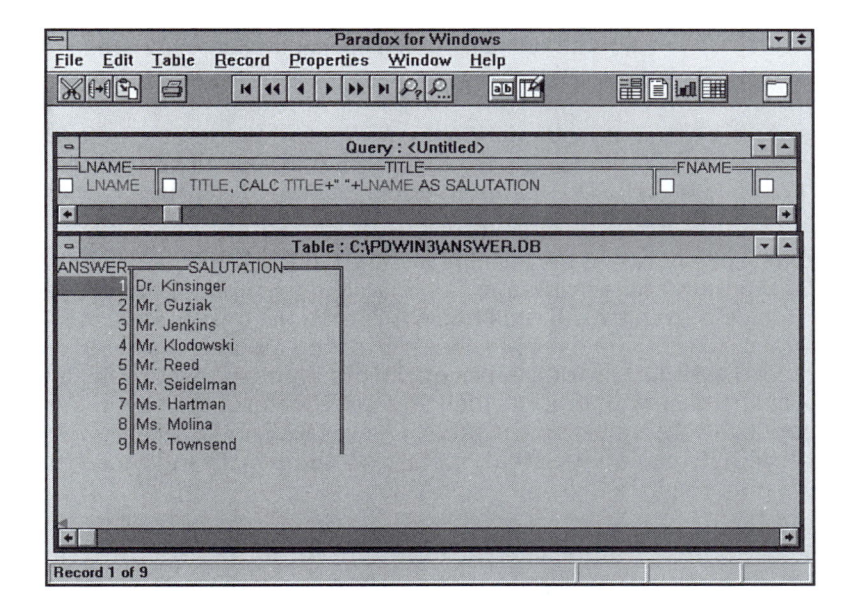

FIG. 8.17

Using CALC to combine alphanumeric values.

Table 8.4. Query Summary Operators

Operator	Description	Field types	Default grouping
Summary Operators			
AVERAGE	Averages of values in a field	N,D,$	All
COUNT	Number of values in a unique field	A,N,D,$	
MIN	Lowest value in a field	A,N,D,$,T	Unique
MAX	Highest value in a field	A,N,D,$,T	Unique

continues

Table 8.4. Continued

Operator	Description	Field types	Default grouping
SUM	Total of all values in a field	N,$	All

Grouping Operators

ALL	Calculate summary based on all values in a group, including duplicates		
UNIQUE	Calculate summary based on unique values in a group		

To perform a summary calculation, place the CALC operator in the field to be summarized followed by the summary operator of your choice (such as SUM or COUNT). If you do not check any other field, Paradox for Windows performs the computation for all records in the table.

The difference between performing a standard Paradox query and a summary operation is evident in the following example. If you retrieve the Price field from the Albums table, for example, only unique values are shown. Even if you have purchased a dozen albums at $10.99, only one record with $10.99 for the price appears in the Answer table. If you perform a summary operation such as a sum or mean, however, Paradox counts all the values in the table. Figures 8.18 and 8.19 show the difference between queries that operate on all records and those that include only a selected group of records.

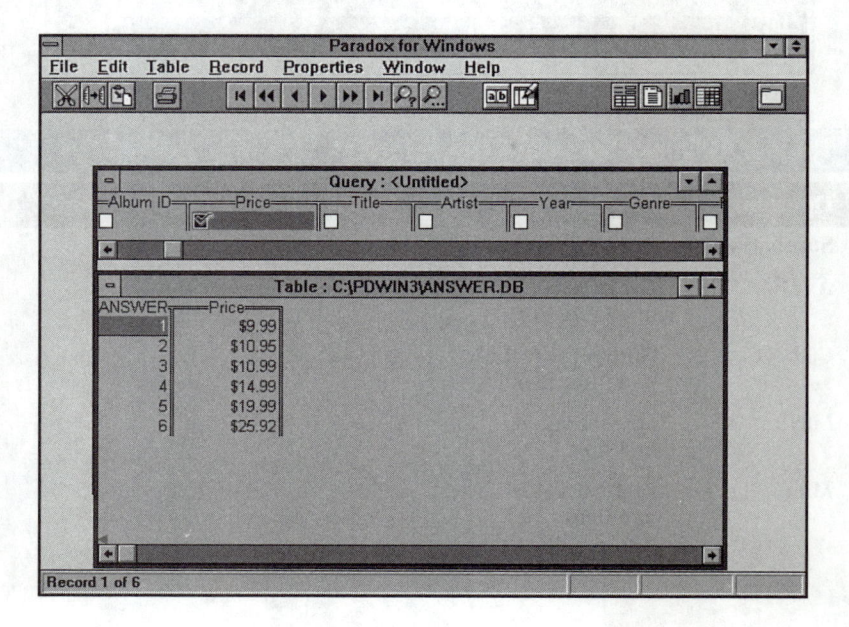

FIG. 8.18

A query listing price for all records.

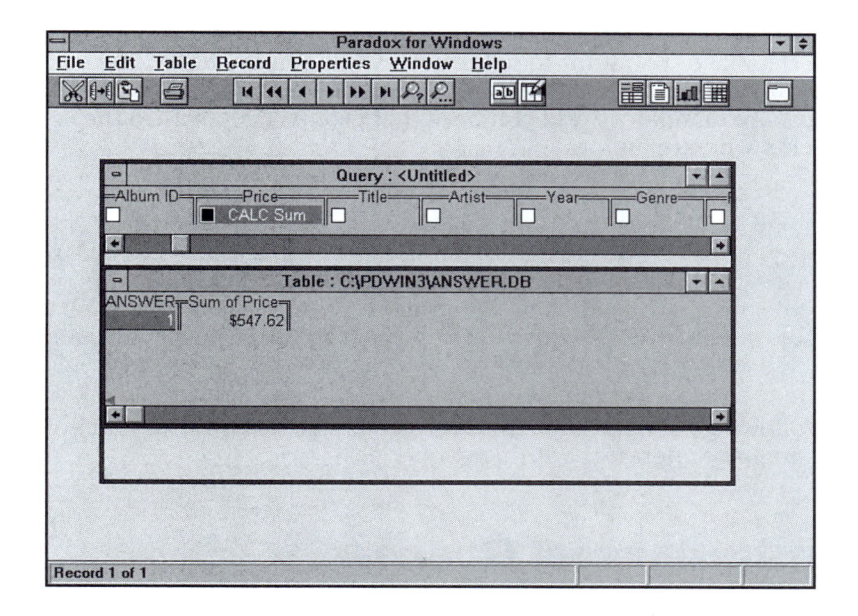

FIG. 8.19

A summary query listing total price for all recordings.

Unlike standard Paradox queries, the summary operators include by default duplicate records in the Answer table. If you place a check in the genre field of Albums, for example, the Answer table shows only one record for each unique genre that you enter. If you use a summary operator, however, Paradox includes the values from each record in the query and not just those unique in the Answer table. The use of unique records does not affect the outcome of MIN and MAX but can change the result of COUNT. To exclude duplicate records, enter **UNIQUE** after the summary operator—for example, enter **CALC COUNT UNIQUE**.

> **NOTE** Although COUNT, MAX, and MIN work on most field types (except exotic field types including graphics, binary, and memo fields), average and sum are only meaningful for number and date fields. You cannot calculate the average or sum of an alphanumeric field.

Comparing Sets of Records

In addition to retrieving records and performing summary calculations on groups of records, Paradox for Windows enables you to compare groups of records to one another. These special queries are known as *set operations*. To illustrate a set operation, consider a college enrollment database. You want to determine which juniors have fulfilled the mandatory classes. To answer this question, you must know which classes are mandatory and compare that group of records to the set of students who are juniors.

> **TIP** Set operations can be much more confusing than standard Paradox queries. Drawing a set diagram of the query before you write it is one of the best ways to keep your set straight. Be sure to take the time to test set operations to ensure that you retrieve the records you want.

The following sections explain how to construct set queries and how to use summary operators within set queries.

Constructing Set Queries

Paradox for Windows can accomplish set operations in a surprisingly simple fashion. To define a set operation, follow these steps:

1. Type the selection criteria for the records that constitute the first set.

2. In the first column used to define the set, enter SET by clicking in the first column and choosing **S**et from the drop-down list.

3. Add other tables and use example elements to link tables if you are performing a multi-table query.

4. Enter the desired set operator before the example element in the field used to define the set.

5. Place a check mark in all the fields you want to appear in the Answer table.

> **NOTE** Do not use the check marks or summary operators in the fields used to define a set. The check marks are used only for the records to be compared to the set.

Special operators used with set queries are listed in table 8.5.

Table 8.5. Set Comparison Operators

Operator	Description
ONLY	Displays records that match only members of the defined set
NO	Displays records that match no members of the defined set
EVERY	Displays records that match every member of the defined set
EXACTLY	Displays records that match all members of the defined set and no others

To illustrate, a travel agency maintains a table of all vacation bookings for its customers (BOOKINGS) and a table of all trip packages (TRIPS), as shown in figure 8.20. You can define a set of all cruises and compare a list of customer purchases to this set. If you use the ONLY operator, you retrieve customers who have taken cruises but no other kind of vacation, as shown in figure 8.21. If you use the NO operator, you retrieve customers who had never taken a cruise. The EVERY operator retrieves those customers who have taken every cruise offered by the agency. The EXACTLY operator combines ONLY and EVERY, retrieving customers who have taken each and every cruise but no other types of vacations.

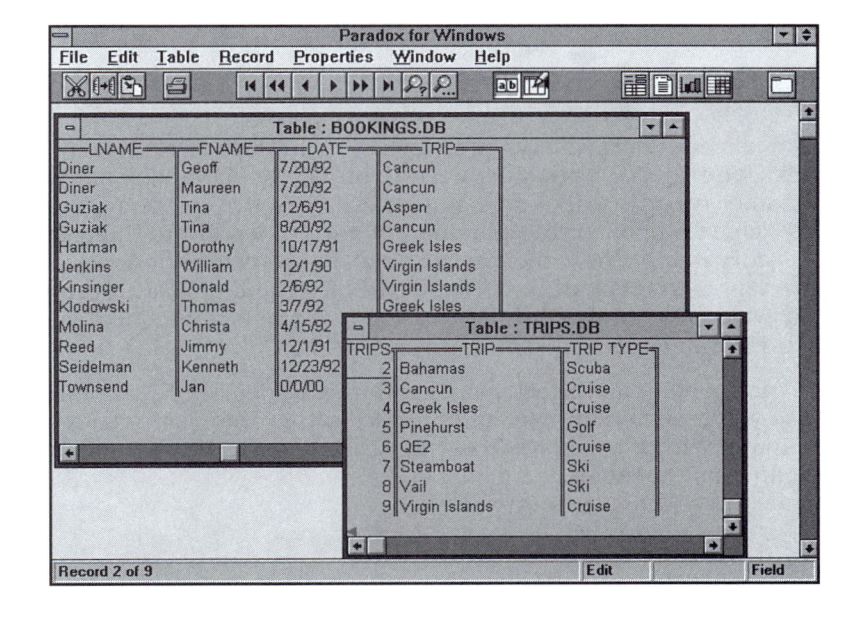

FIG. 8.20

The Bookings and Trips tables.

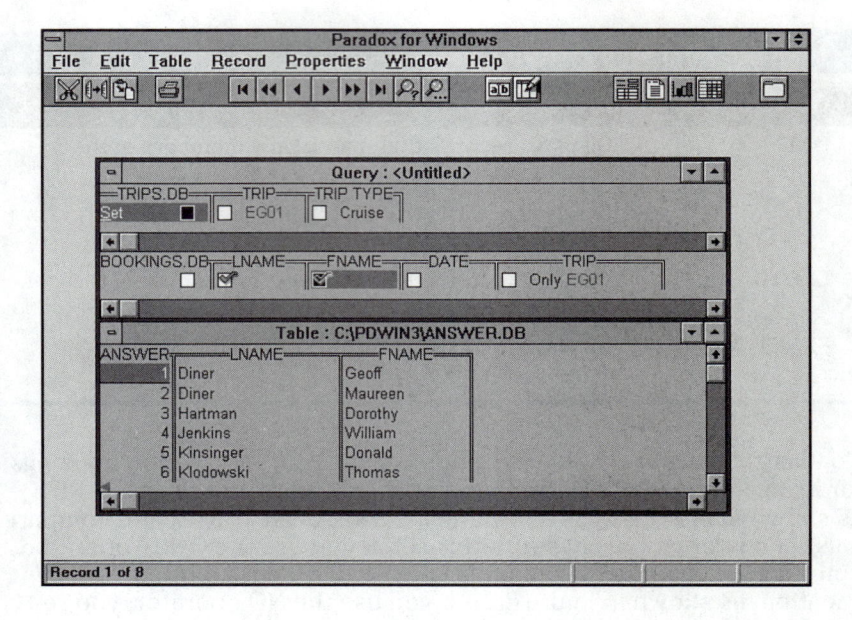

FIG. 8.21
Using ONLY to find customers who have taken only cruises.

NOTE The GroupBy check allows you to group records by values in a field without displaying that field in the Answer table. The GroupBy check works only with set queries.

Changing Tables with Queries

You can use queries not only to retrieve data but also to change records. For example, you might want to update the company name for all customer records from Acme Industrials when the company is renamed Acme Conglomerate Unlimited, or add 10 percent to the price of all inventory items after a fuel tax increase. Paradox for Windows uses the special reserved operators INSERT, DELETE, and CHANGETO for this purpose. In addition, the FIND operator enables you to locate records in a table based on QBE search criteria.

You do not need to use check marks with these special QBE operators because you are affecting the entire record rather than just retrieving one column. With the exception of the FIND operator, these queries do not create Answer tables.

8 — USING ADVANCED QUERY BY EXAMPLE

> **CAUTION:** Note that the INSERT, DELETE, and CHANGETO operators directly and permanently change the contents of your tables. Although some ways exist to recover from errors, exercise extra care with these powerful operations.

> **TIP**
>
> Before you run a query that changes records, use the same criteria to retrieve them. The Answer table displays the records to be changed. This procedure helps you avoid damaging the database by using the wrong search criteria.

The following sections explain how to insert, delete, change, and find records.

Inserting Records

Although most records are added to database tables manually, you may find times when you want to transfer data from one table to another for a number of records. If the tables have identical structures, you can use the Add option from the File, utility menu. In many cases, however, the structures of the tables are different.

The INSERT operator matches the fields of the source table to the fields of the destination table. When you execute an INSERT query, Paradox copies all the records from the source table and adds them to the destination table.

To illustrate, say that you purchase a mailing list for a promotion, and you want to merge the file into your customer mailing list before you create form letters and mailing labels. You receive a dBASE table called NEWMAIL with the field structure found in table 8.6.

Table 8.6. Purchased Mailing List

Field name	Type	Length
TITLE	Alphanumeric	5
LNAME	Alphanumeric	15
FNAME	Alphanumeric	10
STREET	Alphanumeric	30

continues

Table 8.6. Continued

Field name	Type	Length
STREET2	Alphanumeric	30
CITY	Alphanumeric	15
STATE	Alphanumeric	2
ZIP	Alphanumeric	5
BUSPHONE	Alphanumeric	10

Your Customer table (NCUST.DB) has the structure found in table 8.7. Note that the field types in the two tables are the same, but the field names and lengths are different in some cases.

Table 8.7. Your Customer Table Structure

Field name	Type	Length
TITLE	Alphanumeric	5
LAST NAME	Alphanumeric	15
FIRST NAME	Alphanumeric	10
ADDRESS	Alphanumeric	40
ADDRESS2	Alphanumeric	40
CITY	Alphanumeric	15
STATE	Alphanumeric	2
ZIP	Alphanumeric	9
TELEPHONE	Alphanumeric	10
LEAD SOURCE	Alphanumeric	8

The INSERT query enables you to specify the mapping of the fields and transfer the data from one table to another. To create an INSERT query, follow these steps:

1. Add both the source and destination tables to the query editor.
2. Use example elements to connect each field in the source table to the destination table, as shown in figure 8.22. Be sure to use a different example element for each field. To change the example element, click the Join Tables button on the SpeedBar. If you want to combine two fields from the source table into one field in the

destination table, use + to connect the example elements in the destination field.

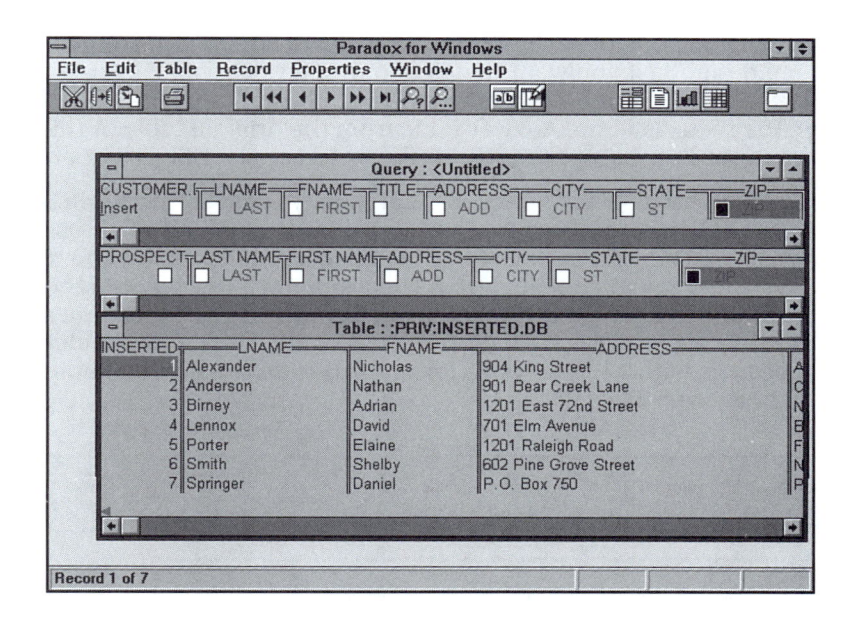

FIG. 8.22
An example of an INSERT query.

3. After you have entered the example elements, fill in INSERT in the leftmost column of the destination table (below the table name) by clicking and choosing from the drop-down list of query operators, which is displayed just below this field.
4. Run the query by clicking the Run Query button on the SpeedBar.
5. A temporary table named Inserted appears showing the new records Paradox has inserted into the destination table.

Use CALC operators to fill in fields with calculation values. To fill in constant values for all new records, enter the value directly in the field on the destination form of the query. You may want to identify all these new prospects with a code such as ACMELIST in the Lead Source field to show how you entered the name.

TIP

INSERT queries are handy for transferring data from an existing table into a newly created reference table. If you wanted to create a reference table which listed all the cities for customers (or another address list), for example, you could create the Cities table and then write an INSERT query to transfer all the cities from the mailing list table to the Cities table.

Deleting Records

When you discover that records are inaccurate or obsolete, you can remove them in one of several ways. You can delete records one at a time in Edit mode if you want to delete only a few. Or you can create an Answer table with query, and then use the Subtract table option to delete the records in the Answer table from the original table. A third approach, and probably the most direct, is to use the DELETE operator.

A DELETE query deletes all records that meet your search criteria. To perform a deletion, enter your search criteria as usual but don't use check marks. Then, fill in Delete in the leftmost column below the table name by clicking and choosing from the drop-down list. If your record player finally gives out, for example, you may decide to contribute all your LP albums to your public library. You could use a query to delete all recordings with a format of R (for record) from the Albums table, as shown in figure 8.23.

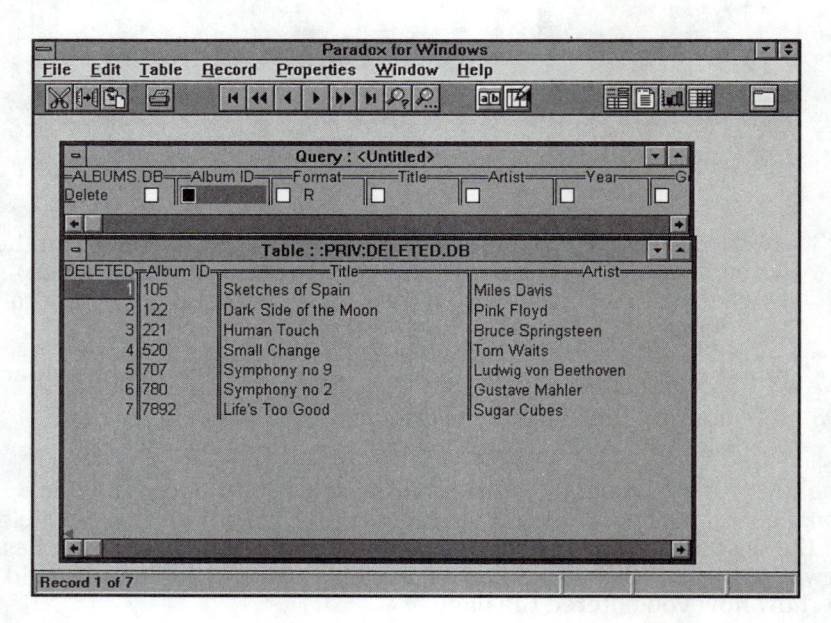

FIG. 8.23

Using a query to delete all albums from your collection.

When you run the query, a temporary table called Deleted appears. This table contains all the records deleted from the original table.

To recover from mistakes made while using DELETE, you can use INSERT to add the deleted records back to the original table. Like it does with other temporary tables, Paradox erases the Deleted table the next time you perform the same operation. Therefore, be sure to check the results of a DELETE operation before performing another deletion. If you want to keep the records in the Deleted table for archiving or other purposes, rename the Deleted table or copy the table to a permanent table, as the Deleted table will be overwritten by the next DELETE operation.

> **CAUTION:** Entering no search criteria selects ALL records; therefore, a DELETE operation removes all records in a table. Be sure to enter search criteria if you want to delete only a few records.

Changing Records

So far, you have learned how to change records by editing the data using a table or a form. For wholesale changes, however, this approach can be quite time-consuming and tedious. Say, for example, that a new telephone area code is created for all your customers in Baltimore or Beverly Hills or your company decides to raise the credit limits of all its customers by 10 percent? In cases such as these, the CHANGETO operator comes to the rescue.

To modify records with CHANGETO, follow these steps:

1. Add to the query editor the desired table or tables.
2. Type the search criteria for the records you want to change.
3. In the field to be changed, type the old value, a comma, and then CHANGETO, followed by the new value. Do not place quotation marks around the values.
4. Run the query.

You can use CHANGETO with constants or calculations. The query shown in figure 8.24, for example, changes the genre in the Albums table from Rock to Pop.

If you want to change records to several different values based on different criteria, enter each CHANGETO on a separate line in the query.

CHANGETO produces a temporary table called Changed instead of an Answer table. The Changed table contains the records as they were before the CHANGETO operation. If you make a mistake in a CHANGETO query, you can delete the changed records in the original table and add the Changed table records. You also can reverse your mistake by writing another CHANGETO query to switch the field back to its previous value. Be careful that your query does not affect records which do not need to be changed.

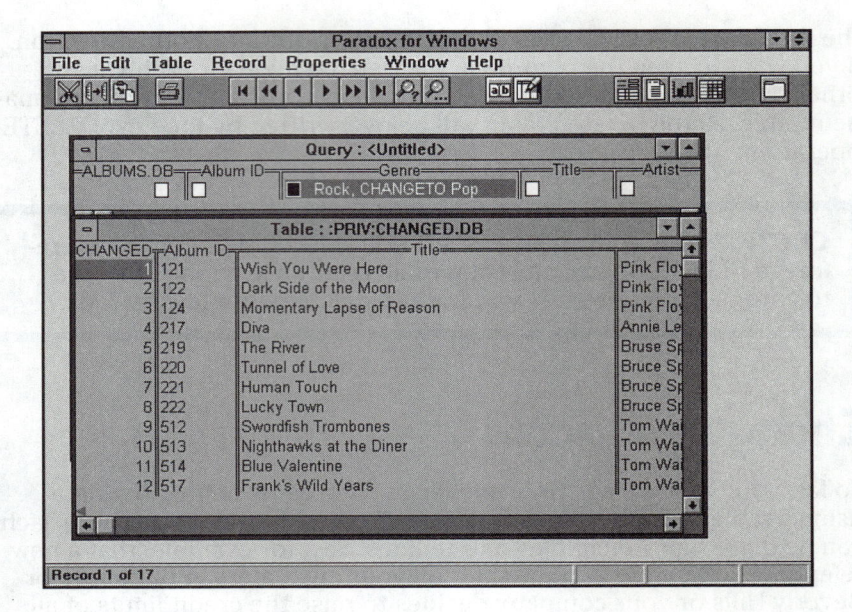

FIG. 8.24

An example of a CHANGETO query.

You can use example elements and arithmetic operators in conjunction with CHANGETO. You could give all employees a ten percent raise, for example, by entering **Salary, CHANGETO Salary * 1.1** in the Salary field.

Chapter Summary

In this chapter, you learned how to perform multi-table queries and set operations, to use example elements to indicate relationships between tables, and to perform queries that add, delete, and modify records. Combined, these features give you great control over your data through queries.

With set operations, you can create sophisticated queries that compare sets of records to one another. To achieve the same results without set operations, you would have to write several queries. For example, you could write a query to show all the customers who have purchased each and every unique item in your inventory.

Paradox for Windows enables you to link up to 24 tables in a single query. By linking tables, you can include fields that come from several different tables in the same query. For example, you may need customer information, order totals, and inventory availability on the same report. By using a multi-table query, you can gather these fields even though they are stored in separate tables.

You also have used QBE to add, delete, and modify groups of records with a single query. This allows you to save a great deal of time compared with the tedious task of editing one record at a time.

CHAPTER 9

Using Power Entry and Editing Features

Safeguarding the quality of your data requires eternal vigilance. To assist in this task, Paradox provides you with several features that detect errors during data-entry, including validity checks, table lookup, and referential integrity. Password protection prevents unauthorized users from accessing information in your database. By using the powerful features described in this chapter, you can prevent many common data-entry errors.

Compared to its DOS predecessor, Paradox for Windows gives the database designer much more control over the values accepted in each field (*domain* in relational database jargon) and the way that changes in one table are reflected in related tables (*referential integrity*). Moreover, many integrity checks can be established without any programming at all.

> **NOTE** Most of the features discussed in this chapter apply only to Paradox tables. For dBASE tables, extensive programming is required to enforce integrity checks, and these programs can be circumvented by accessing the table directly. Therefore, integrity checks are another reason to choose Paradox rather than dBASE tables for your application.

When planning your database tables, write down a list of the password protection, validity checks, and referential integrity rules that will apply. You may end up with a list such as the following:

- Addresses must contain valid postal abbreviations for states (table lookup).
- ZIP codes must fall within the range of legitimate entries for each state (minimum and maximum values). They must conform to the standard format for U.S. ZIP codes, with five or nine digits and must consist of numbers only (no letters).
- Customers may not be deleted if they have an outstanding invoice (referential integrity).
- Changes in stock numbers must be reflected in all warranty registration records (referential integrity).
- All customers must have a telephone number.
- Only department managers can view employee salary information (password protection).

As you will see, some rules may be implemented in several different ways.

Paradox attaches integrity checks to the table itself. They are in effect whenever data is entered in tables or manipulated through queries. Integrity checks therefore are created in the Create or Restructure Table dialog box. On the right side of the dialog box is the Table Properties pull-down menu, which accesses Validity Checks, Table Lookup, Secondary Indexes, Referential Integrity, and Password Security (see fig. 9.1).

This chapter begins with an examination of each of these table properties in turn, with the exception of secondary indexes, which are covered in Chapter 7, "Using Advanced Form Techniques."

Using Validity Checks

Validity checks can make your database easier to use and more reliable. They help reduce the training time for new users by quickly pointing out common entry errors. Paradox validity checks enable you to designate fields as required, set up minimum and maximum values for a field, create default entries, and define the format of a field with a picture.

9 — USING POWER ENTRY AND EDITING FEATURES

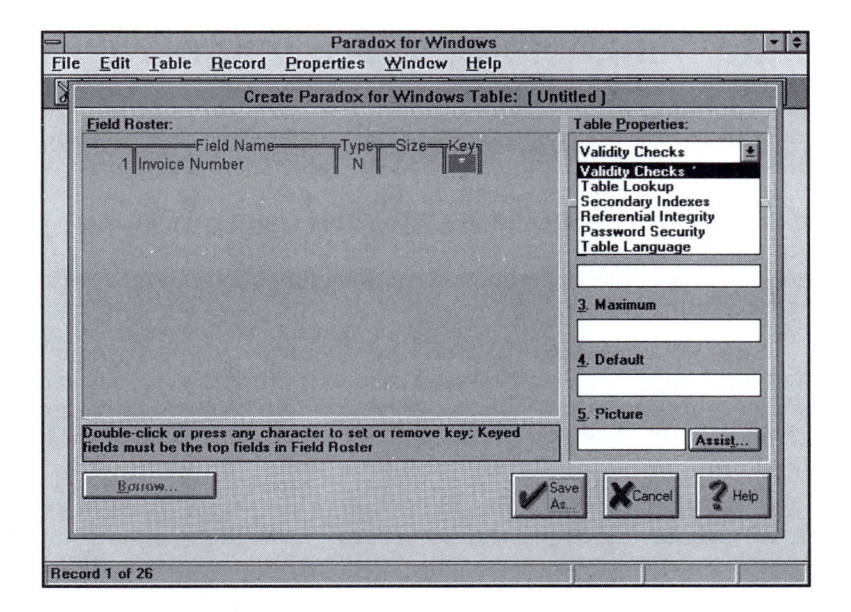

FIG. 9.1

The Table Properties menu in the Create (or Restructure) Table dialog box.

For minimum, maximum, and default values, you can enter constants or use special Paradox functions, such as Today for the current date on the computer clock.

Entering Values in Required Fields

You can designate fields that must be filled before a record can be saved in a table. Key fields should always be required fields because two records with blank key fields are considered duplicates. An invoice line items table, for example, should have Stock Number and Quantity As Required fields because no purchase is valid without this information.

Be careful not to designate fields as required if a legitimate entry may not have a value for that field. If you make stock numbers required, be sure to have stock numbers for all merchandise that may be sold, or at least a catchall stock number for miscellaneous items.

TIP

If you have a large number of required fields, you may want to wait to designate them until after you have built the table and entered some sample data. Having to enter a large number of fields to test the table during the development process will take more time.

Setting Minimum and Maximum Values

If you do not have a finite list of choices that are acceptable for a field, you may still know the range of allowable entries. Paradox for Windows enables you to create a range check at the table level. Thereafter, any entry in the table is checked against the allowable range, whether entered directly into the table or in a form. This check is much more reliable than similar constraints provided in dBASE products, which depend on the user accessing the data through special forms for data entry and editing.

You can protect some fields against invalid entries by specifying minimum and maximum values. You may place a minimum value of zero for an invoice amount, for example, so that sales can be made only for positive amounts of money (assuming that you do not use invoices for refunds).

You also can specify minimum and maximum values for dates. You can catch outrageous errors in entry by making 1/1/80 the minimum value for a truck purchase date in a vehicle tracking table, assuming that you have no trucks purchased before 1980. If you do not create such a limitation, users may transpose the numbers of a year, entering 07/20/19 instead of 07/20/91. Such an error may dramatically change the results of a report listing the average age of your vehicles.

Maximum values are created in the same way as minimum value range checks and serve the same purpose. For example, you may make 1/1/75 the maximum value for a birth date field in an employee table, assuming that no workers are younger than 18 years.

> **TIP** If you use a field to show a percentage for allocation purposes (such as splitting budget items among departments), make 100 the maximum value allowed in order to prevent accidental entry of 900 rather than 90 percent. Obviously, this practice does not apply to percentages that may legitimately exceed 100, such as grow rates.

To designate range limits, enter the minimum and maximum values on the Create Table or Restructure Table dialog box.

Accepting or Changing a Default Value

You can save time and prevent errors by assigning default values for fields in each table. For example, you might make 1 the default quantity for an invoice line items table if most purchases are for a single item.

9 — USING POWER ENTRY AND EDITING FEATURES

As with minimum and maximum values, Paradox accepts only constants or the Today operator as default values. You cannot use field names, mathematical symbols, or other operators to calculate the default. Thus, you cannot use `today + 1` as the default for a date field in order to fill in the tomorrow's date or `price * qty` to multiply the price times quantity for an invoice line item.

> **TIP**
>
> To fill in today's date in a date field, press the space bar three times. Paradox fills in the month, then the date, then the year.

> **For Related Information**
>
> ◂◂ "Specifying Validity Checks," p. 99.
>
> **FROM HERE...**

Assisting Data Entry with Pictures

Pictures enable you to control the format of the field value as it is entered. A picture defines the type of character for each position of a field. Many fields, such as ZIP codes and telephone numbers, have special formats. Picture functions simplify the data-entry process by filling in literal formatting characters as needed and generating error messages when incorrect entries are attempted. Table 9.1 lists Paradox picture characters.

Table 9.1. Picture Characters

Character	Use
#	Number digit
?	Any letter (upper- or lowercase)
&	Any character (convert to uppercase)
@	Any character (convert to lowercase)
;	Following character is a literal, not a picture string character

continues

Table 9.1. Continued

Character	Use
*	Following character may be repeated any number of times
[ ]	Optional items enclosed in brackets
{ }	Grouping operators
,	Alternative values

Characters that are not special picture characters are interpreted as constants.

Pictures also can be used to check against a short list of valid responses. If you use {P,S,M,L,XL} as the picture function for a size field, for example, only these letters are allowed. This practice prevents a user from entering **9** or **SM** as the size. This type of integrity control can be helpful if you need to search or sort on a field because it leads to more consistent data entry. If you do not control the range of possible entries, you have to guess all the synonyms that may have been entered for your search value.

You may want to add a field for sex to the Artists table as follows:

1. Define a table to contain the artist ID, first name, last name, birth date, and sex, as shown in figure 9.2. Make the Sex field alphanumeric, one character in length.

2. Place the cursor on the Sex field and click Validity Checks to set validity checks.

3. Make the Sex field required by checking the Required Field box.

4. Establish a default of F (assuming that you have more records by female artists than men in your collection) by entering **F** in the Default box.

5. In the Picture option, enter **{M,F}** to indicate that M and F are the only legitimate entries for this field.

6. Save the table.

Enter a few records in the table to test it. Be sure to try some invalid characters in the Sex field. You should hear a beep until you enter a valid character in the field. No error message is displayed when you enter an invalid character, and Paradox does not display the list of valid characters. Be sure to explain such fields to users before they perform data entry, or list the options as background text on a data-entry form.

9 — USING POWER ENTRY AND EDITING FEATURES

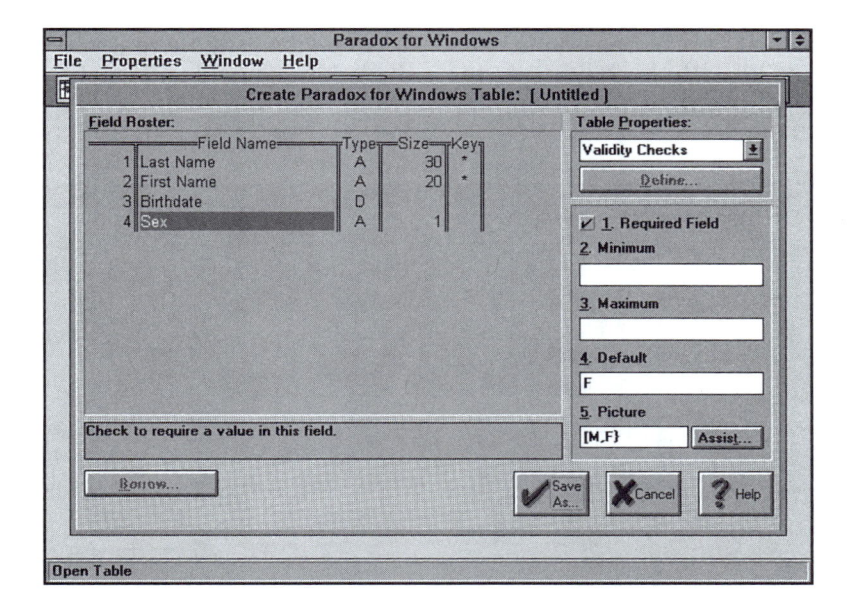

FIG. 9.2

Required, Default, and Picture for Sex field.

If you forget how to define picture patterns, Paradox reminds you. Just click the Assist button next to the Picture field in the Define Table dialog box. The Picture Assist dialog box appears (see fig. 9.3). Fill in your picture pattern and click the Verify Syntax button to make sure it is correct. If you want, you can borrow one of the sample picture patterns that comes with Paradox. Click the pull-down menu next to Examples to view the sample picture patterns.

Using Table Lookup

On many occasions, restricting the choices of the data-entry operator to a list of valid entries is advisable. You may have a Shipping Method field, for example, in an Invoices table. The valid shipping methods in your company are Regular Mail, Parcel Post, Overnight, and Special Courier. You do not want the operator to enter **Mail** for regular mail or **Express** for overnight, nor do you want the operator to create a new method called **Slow Boat**.

At the same time, these options may change in the future, and you don't want to have to rewrite programs just because the possible entries change. The best way to control data-entry choices while leaving

II — PARADOX FOR WINDOWS POWER TECHNIQUES

room for future expansion is to use a *lookup table*, a table that you create and fill with the valid options for the field. The field you want to verify should be the key field of the lookup table and should occur first in the table.

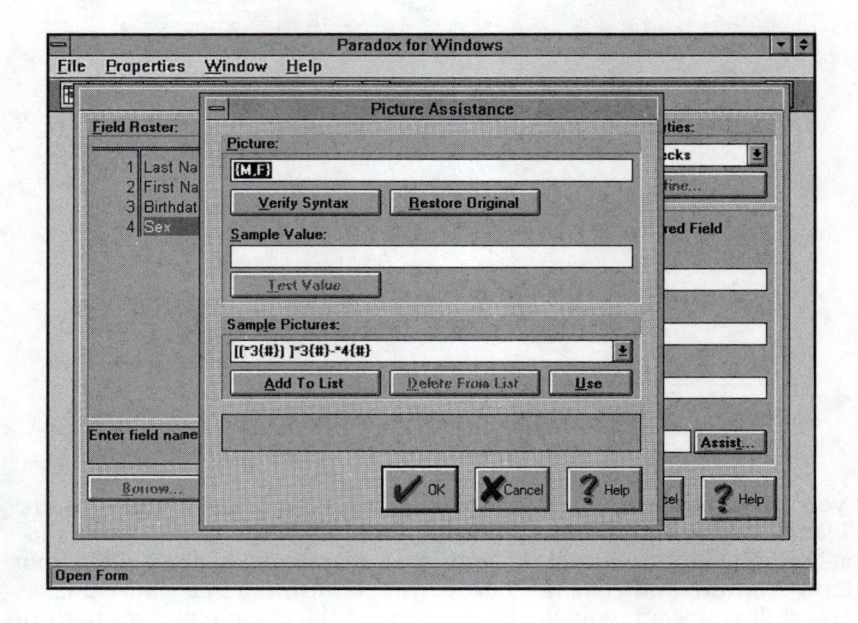

FIG. 9.3

The Picture Assistance dialog box.

Suppose that you have been using a one-letter code to indicate the Format in the Albums table (A for album, C for compact disc, and so on). A user may unwittingly enter an invalid format code such as Q or Z in the table, harming the integrity of the database. By using a table lookup, you can prevent this problem and still allow for new album formats as needed. Just follow these steps:

1. Create a reference table (FORMATS.DB) that contains two fields: Format (one character alphanumeric) and Description (12 character alphanumeric. The description reminds the user what the code stands for and may be used on reports. See figure 9.4 for the table definition.

2. Make the Format field the key field for the reference table so that no letter can be entered twice. Using a key field causes the reference table to display alphabetically by format code. Add the records in table 9.2 to the reference table now.

9 — USING POWER ENTRY AND EDITING FEATURES

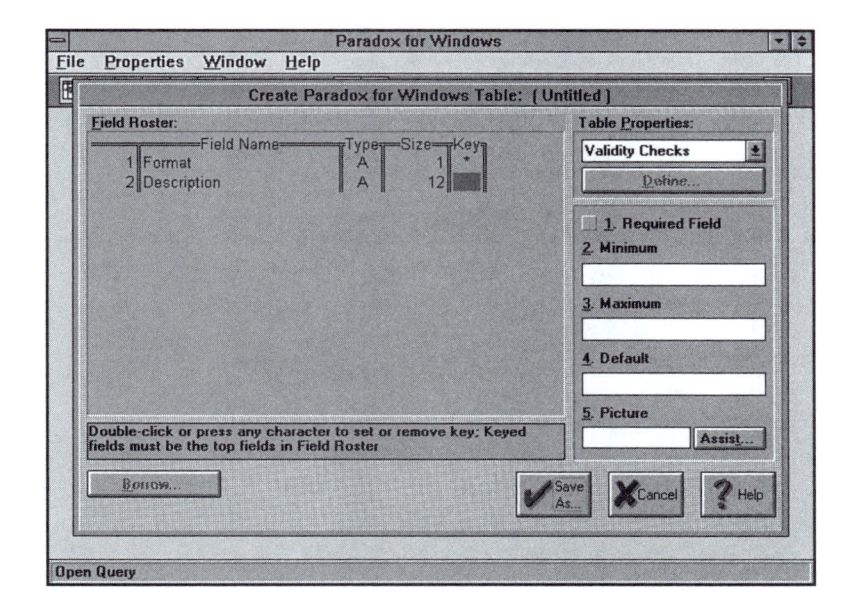

FIG. 9.4

The Table Definition for the Formats table.

Table 9.2. Reference Table for Format Codes

Format	Description
A	Album
C	Compact Disk
R	Record
T	Tape

3. Restructure the Albums table by opening the table and choosing Restructure from the Table menu.
4. Click the Format field in the table definition.
5. Pull down the menu for Table Properties by clicking the pull-down menu box; choose Table Lookup.
6. Click the Define button below the Table Properties menu or press Alt-D.
7. The Table Lookup dialog box appears, as shown in figure 9.5.

II — PARADOX FOR WINDOWS POWER TECHNIQUES

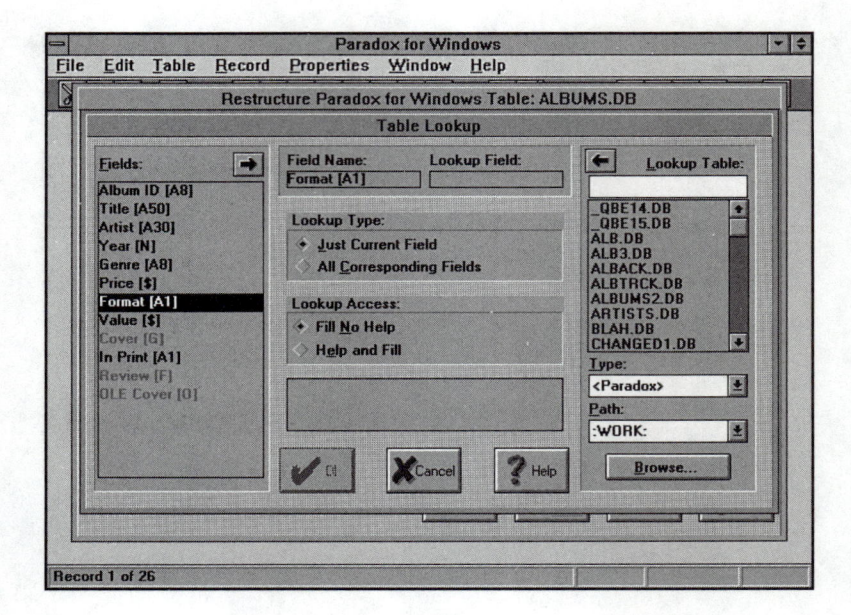

FIG. 9.5
The Table Lookup dialog box.

8. Click FORMATS.DB to select the Lookup Table. Click the left arrow button to move the lookup fields from the Lookup Table column to the Lookup Field field.

9. For this example, click the Help And Fill option under Lookup Access. Other table lookup options are explained later.

10. Click the OK button to save the table lookup.

11. Click the Save button to save your changes to the Albums table. If you have already entered data in the table, Paradox will ask you whether to enforce the new rule on existing data (see fig. 9.6). For this example, click OK on the Restructure Warning dialog box.

After you have defined the table lookup, open the Albums table and enter some new records. If you enter an invalid format code in the format field, you receive the error message `Unable to find lookup value`, and you are not allowed to leave the field without providing a valid value. Note that you cannot leave the field blank because a blank value also fails the lookup. Press Ctrl+space bar to display the lookup table. The dialog box shown in figure 9.7 appears.

To fill in the field from the table lookup, click your choice and then click the OK button. The field is automatically filled, and you are returned to Edit mode in the Albums table.

9 — USING POWER ENTRY AND EDITING FEATURES   407

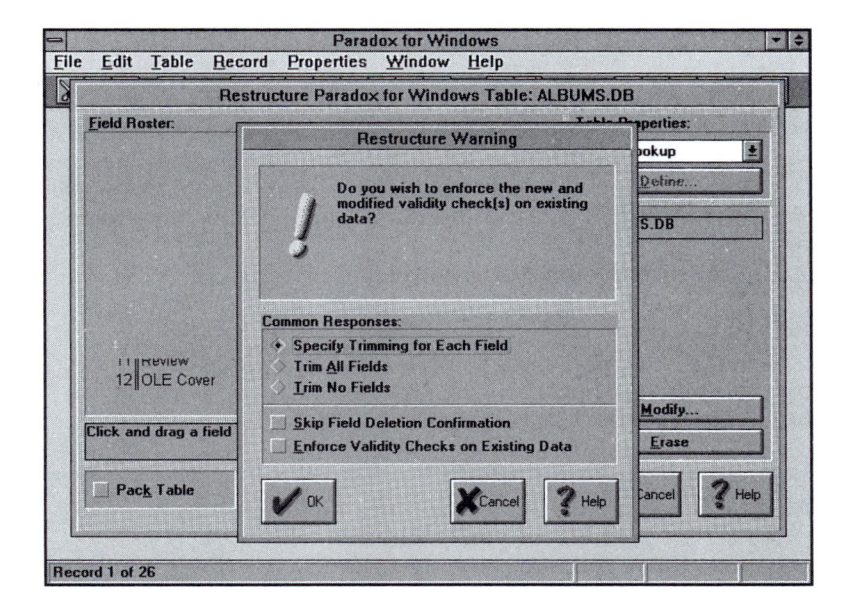

FIG. 9.6

The Restructure Warning dialog box.

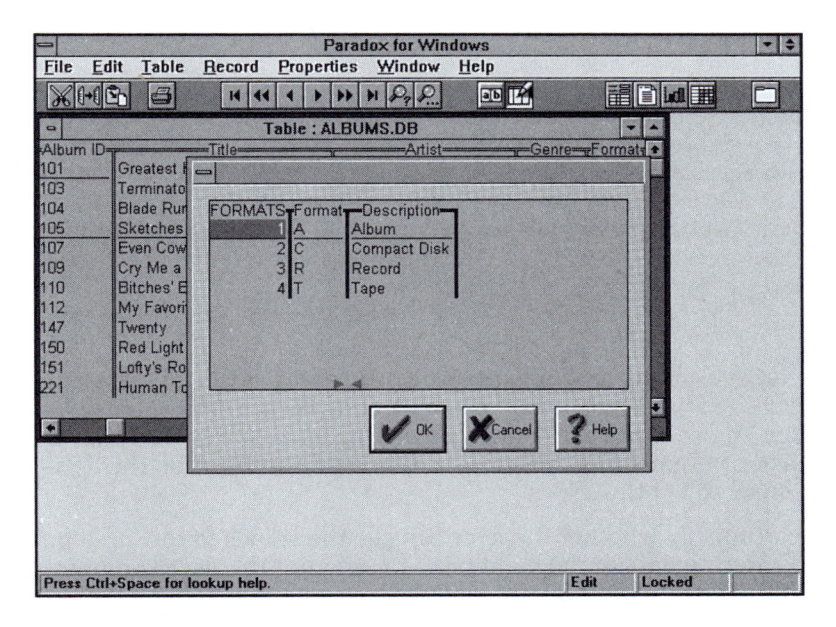

FIG. 9.7

The lookup table displayed during data entry.

> **TIP**
>
> Although you are not required to use the same field name in the source table as the key field of the lookup table, using the same field name can help you remember how the tables are related. Also, be sure to use the same field type and length (for field types where length is specified) on both sides of the lookup. You receive no warning when you change the structure of the lookup table, but you see the message `First field of lookup table is not of the appropriate type` when you try to open it.

If you need a new option in the lookup table, you simply open the lookup table and add new records. The next time you perform the lookup, the new records are displayed.

> **CAUTION:** Be sure that your reference table contains all valid entries for the field before you establish a table lookup. Otherwise, the records you have already entered in the table could be rejected and placed in the Keyviol (key violations) table.

> **TIP**
>
> If you choose Help And Fill, Paradox displays the message `Press Ctrl+Space for lookup help` as the user enters the field for the table lookup. Unfortunately, this message disappears as soon as a value is entered. You may want to place a note on the form to remind the user to press Ctrl+space bar to display the lookup table. Also be sure to mention the table lookup feature in any user documentation you prepare for the database.

You can use a code, as shown here, or the entire description for the choice. The advantage of using a short code is that data entry is quicker. Try to make the codes as meaningful as possible so that they are easier to remember. You also may want to add text on the data-entry form to list the codes.

You can specify whether the user can see the values in the lookup table while entering data in the main table or whether the user is required to match the lookup table's entries without seeing them. In most cases, viewing the lookup table makes entry easier. Sometimes, however, a long lookup table can clutter the screen, so experienced users often prefer to bypass the display of the lookup table and enter the values directly.

9 — USING POWER ENTRY AND EDITING FEATURES

You have two main options for which fields should be filled, as well as suboptions for displaying the lookup table or not, as shown earlier in figure 9.5.

- *Just Current Field.* Fills only the field on which the lookup is defined.

- *All Corresponding Fields.* Fills the lookup field as well as any other fields in the source table that match those of the lookup table.

- *Fill No Help.* Looks at lookup table while you are performing data entry but does not display lookup table. This option can frustrate users who do not know the permissible values for a field. The only way to escape from the record is to guess a valid entry or delete the record.

- *Fill No Help.* Does not display lookup table. As with Private Lookup, this option is rather unfriendly.

- *Help and Fill.* Reminds user to press Ctrl+space bar to display lookup table. Displays lookup table when you are entering data and fills field automatically.

The options for All Corresponding Fields enable you to enter more than one field based on the table lookup. You can look up the Artist from the Albums table (based on the Album ID in both tables), for example, and store this field in Tracks. A common use of this feature is to look up the customer name from the Customers table and store it in the Invoices or Orders table. Remember, however, that performing such a lookup is a violation of the rules of normalization. It results in wasted space from redundant data storage and possible data anomalies if the information is changed in one place and not the other.

After you try lookups, you will find many uses for them. Table 9.3 shows some typical uses for lookup tables.

Table 9.3. Examples of Lookup Tables

Source	Lookup Table
Addresses	States
Membership	Member Type
Registration	Sessions
Line Items	Invoices
Line Items	Inventory
Benefits	Personnel
Timesheets	Personnel

> **CAUTION:** Using a table lookup causes Paradox to open the primary table and the reference table when you are performing data entry. For this reason, you cannot restructure the reference table as long as the primary table is open because the primary table uses the reference table to perform the table lookup.
>
> Deleting a lookup table is dangerous. Paradox does not warn you when you delete a lookup table, but after you have done so, you cannot open the primary table. You receive the error message `Lookup table is corrupt or missing`, and you must re-create the lookup table in order to access the primary table.

Understanding Referential Integrity

Table lookup is designed primarily as an aid to data entry; it does not automatically reflect changes in the lookup table to related tables. You may have a customer table, for example, that refers to a lookup table containing country codes. If you change the country code for the United Kingdom from GB to UK, the customer table still has fields that contain the old value. You must run a query or edit them to correct the discrepancy.

Referential integrity is a more powerful vaccine against data inconsistency. If you establish referential integrity, a change in one table will *cascade*, or ripple, to affect all related records in other tables. In order to use referential integrity, you must start with a sound database design, and you must understand the relationships among the tables. Again, a database schema showing the tables and their relationships can be quite useful.

You must meet the following conditions in order to establish referential integrity:

- Fields must be the same type and length (the field names may be different).
- Tables must be in the same directory.
- Table type must be Paradox.
- Primary keys must be defined for the tables.

9 — USING POWER ENTRY AND EDITING FEATURES   411

For non-Paradox type tables, availability of referential integrity differs. For dBASE tables, referential integrity must be provided by each program that accesses the tables, and users must be prevented from using BROWSE or other commands to access data tables directly.

To define referential integrity, follow these steps:

1. Open the *child table* (the table that needs to verify its field against the master table), and then choose Table, Restructure from the menu. For this example, choose the Tracks table.

2. Click the pull-down menu for Table Properties and choose Referential Integrity.

3. Click the Define button to reveal the Referential Integrity dialog box (see fig. 9.8).

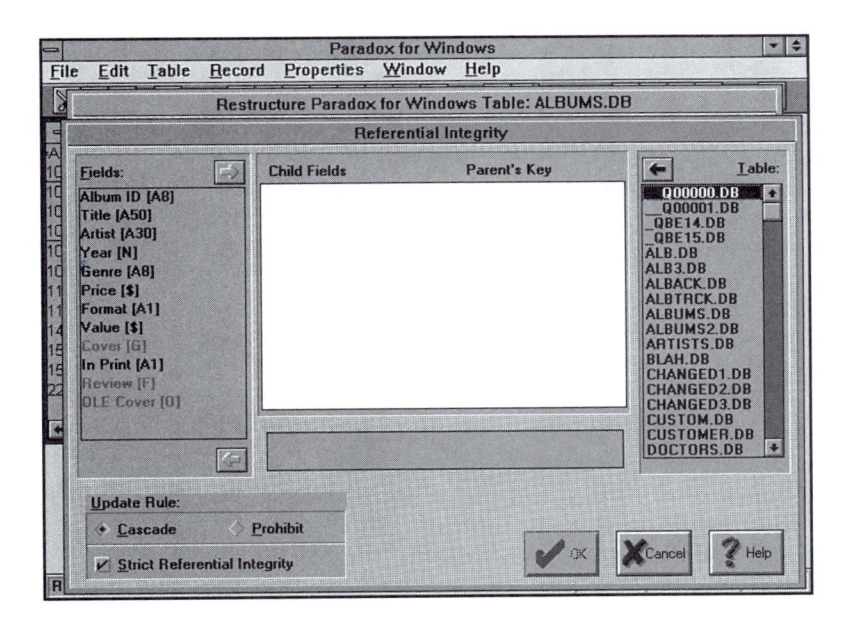

FIG. 9.8

The Referential Integrity dialog box.

4. Choose Albums as the parent table by double-clicking the table name or clicking the table name and then the left-arrow button.

5. Choose the field to relate the tables, in this case Album ID, by clicking the field name and then the right-arrow button.

6. Click the OK button to save your referential integrity definition.

7. Enter a name (up to eight characters, no spaces) for the Referential Integrity rule you have created (see fig. 9.9). Use ALBTRACK to

name this rule. The name is required in case you need to define more than one set of referential integrity rules for the same table.

8. You are returned to the Restructure Table dialog box, and the referential integrity rule is added to the box below Table Properties.

9. Save the table by clicking the Save button.

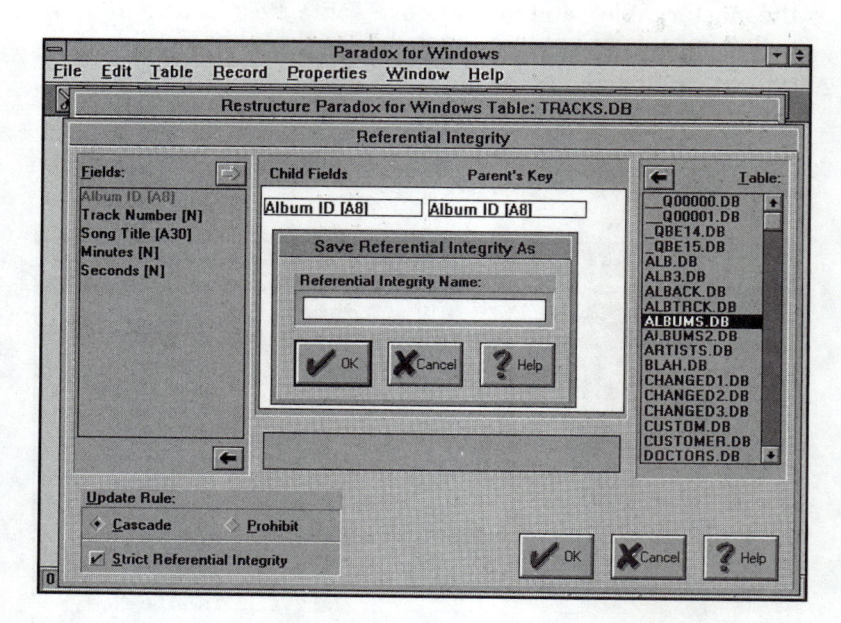

FIG. 9.9

The Save Referential Integrity As dialog box.

> **TIP** When naming referential integrity rules, use a name that reminds you which tables are linked, such as ALBTRACK to link Albums and Tracks or TRKPERF to link Tracks and Performances.

> **NOTE** Paradox does not allow you to define some complex types of referential integrity. For instance, you cannot define referential integrity rules for nested one-to-many relationships.

Updating across Linked Tables

You can choose between two update options for handling edits that affect referential integrity. Choose the option you want by clicking the appropriate box in the Update Rule area of the Referential Integrity dialog box.

The first Update Rule option is Cascade, which causes changes in the primary table to be reflected in the related table. If you change an Album ID in Albums, for example, the Album ID is changed in the appropriate records in the Tracks table as well.

The second Update Rule option is Prohibit. If you choose Prohibit, you cannot change the key field as long as records in related tables are dependent on the record you are editing. If you try to change the Album ID of "Kind of Blue" and you have already entered Tracks for this album, for example, you receive an error message and you cannot save your changes. If no related records are dependent on the record you are modifying, you can change the record even though the Prohibit option is active.

Cascade is more useful than Prohibit in many situations because Prohibit forces the user to contact the database administrator to modify the table. Prohibit is the correct option when you want to enable a user to enter new records but not modify the key field of existing records. In a sales application, for example, you may want to prevent a user from changing the customer ID after an order has been entered.

> **NOTE** Cascade requires group lock on the parent and the child tables. If either of the tables is locked by another user, you cannot save your changes.

Deleting Referential Integrity

To remove referential integrity from a table, choose Referential Integrity from the Table Properties in the Restructure Table dialog box. A list of the referential integrity rules is displayed on the right side of the dialog box. Click the name of the referential integrity rule to highlight it; then click the Erase button to remove it.

II — PARADOX FOR WINDOWS POWER TECHNIQUES

Modifying Referential Integrity

To modify referential integrity in a table, choose Referential Integrity from Table Properties in the Restructure Table dialog box. A list of the referential integrity rules is displayed on the right side of the dialog box. Click the name of the referential integrity rule to highlight it; then click the Modify button to edit it. The Referential Integrity dialog box displays, and you can change your selections as though you were creating a new referential integrity rule.

Defining Password Protection

You may define passwords for database tables to prevent access or modification of data by unauthorized users. Paradox for Windows offers several levels of access, or *rights*, for each table. The following section applies only to Paradox tables. Other table types may or may not support password protection or other security schemes. dBASE tables, for example, do not support password protection.

To create a password, click the drop-down menu in the Table Properties area of the Create/Restructure Table dialog box; then select Password Security from the menu. Click the Define button, and the Password Protection dialog box appears (see fig. 9.10).

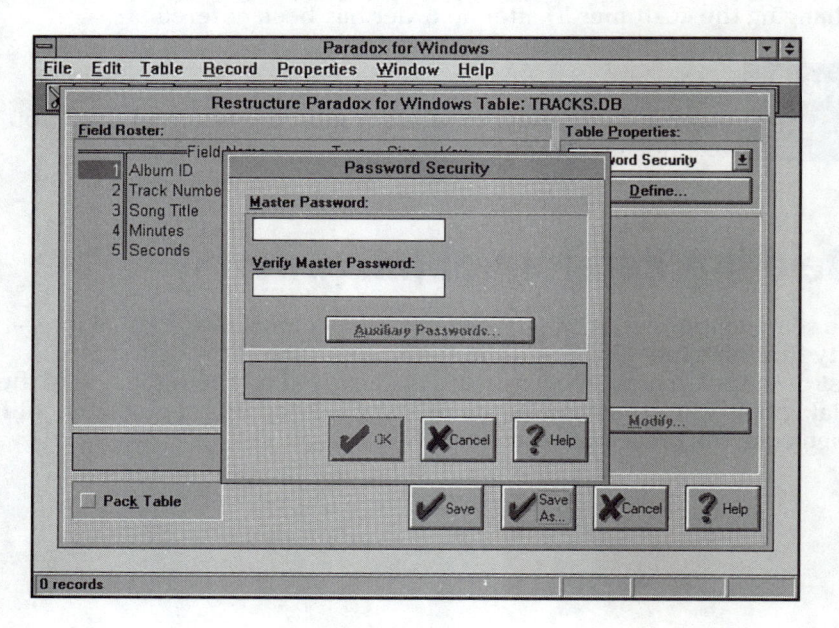

FIG. 9.10

The Password Protection dialog box.

Type the password for the table in the Master Password field. For extra security, the password is represented by asterisks as you type it. Enter the password again in the Confirm Master Password field. If you do not type the same password, Paradox for Windows displays an error message and enables you to try again. Click OK to save the password, and then save the table by clicking the Save button in the Restructure Table dialog box.

Open the table by choosing File, Open, Table from the Paradox Desktop. Figure 9.11 shows how you are prompted for a password in data entry with the Enter Password(s) dialog box. If you know the password, you may also remove it at this dialog box so that you are not prompted for a password the next time you open the table.

FIG. 9.11
The password prompt.

The master password gives you all rights to the table, including the right to restructure or delete it. If you want to allow limited access to other users, you can create auxiliary passwords and determine which rights each password is assigned.

To add even greater flexibility, password access may be granted on three levels within a table. *Table rights* apply to the entire table. *Field rights* offer the most detailed security control by granting access to a particular field.

Table Rights

To grant more detailed security rights, click the Auxiliary Passwords button on the Password Protection dialog box. The Auxiliary Passwords dialog box appears, as shown in figure 9.12.

To assign auxiliary passwords, start by filling in the password in the Current Password field. Next, choose the Table Rights and Field Rights to be assigned to this password. Table 9.4 lists the types of table rights, from greatest to least access. When you are finished, click the Add button and proceed to enter as many passwords as you need. Click the OK

II — PARADOX FOR WINDOWS POWER TECHNIQUES

button when you have finished defining auxiliary passwords. You are returned to the Password Security dialog box. Click OK to return to the Restructure Table dialog box and Save to save your changes.

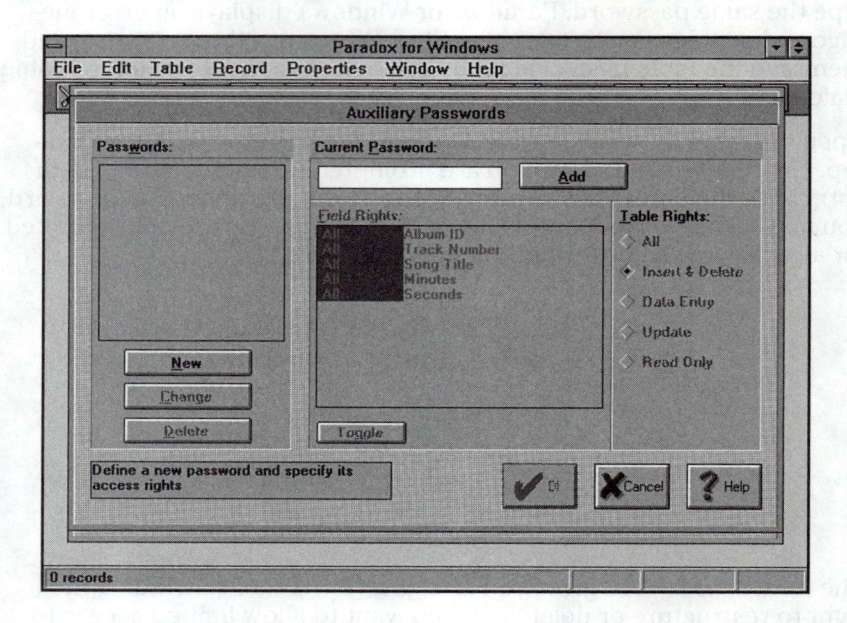

FIG. 9.12

The Auxiliary Passwords dialog box.

Table 9.4. Levels of Password Access

Level	Description
All	Same as master password; may perform all actions, including restructuring or deleting table.
Insert & Delete	May add or delete records but cannot restructure table.
Data Entry	May enter new records but cannot delete records.
Update	May modify existing records but cannot add or delete records. May not modify key fields because modification may constitute new entry.
Read Only	May view data but cannot add, modify, or delete records.

Field Rights

You can set field rights for each field within a table. You may want to grant a user access to the Invoices table, for example, but hide the Sales Commission field from view. Field rights have three levels:

Level	Description
All	View or modify
ReadOnly	View but not modify
None	Neither view nor modify

The default field security is All. To change the field security, double-click the field name. Each time you double-click or click the Toggle button, the next security option is displayed.

Denying a user access to a field does not make the column disappear in the table; only the values are hidden. If you want to prevent a user from learning that a column exists, you may want to use a custom data-entry form that excludes the column.

> **NOTE** Paradox for Windows does not support password security based on the contents of the record. For example, you may not allow a user to see some but not all records in a table. This level of password protection is available in some database servers (Oracle and Sybase, for example) that you can use in conjunction with Paradox for Windows.

> **CAUTION:** Be sure to remember your passwords. If you lose them, recovering your data may be difficult or impossible.

Handling Key Violations

When you designate a primary key in a Paradox table, duplicate entries are not allowed. If you make changes to the database that violate this rule, Paradox for Windows creates a temporary table called Keyviol to temporarily store the offending records. If more than one key violation table is present, Paradox sometimes numbers the key violation table Keyviol2, Keyviol3, and so on.

II — PARADOX FOR WINDOWS POWER TECHNIQUES

To restore the records in Keyviol records to the table, you must edit the Keyviol table so that the records no longer break the rules of the table. You must change key fields, for example, to values that do not duplicate existing records in the table.

After you have cleaned up the data, choose File, Utilities, Add. The Table Add dialog box appears (see fig. 9.13). Choose Keyviol as the table to transfer from and the original table as the table to transfer data to. Click the Add button to transfer the records.

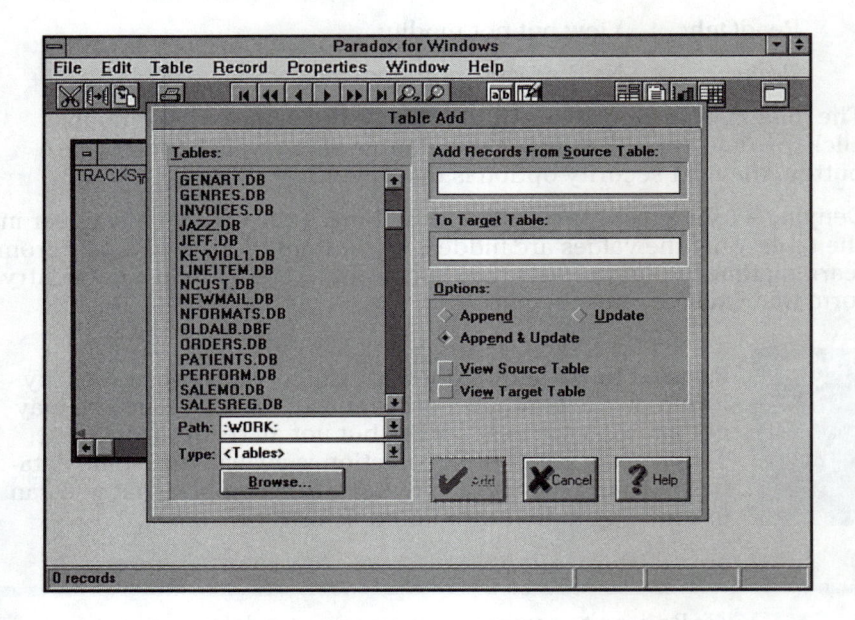

FIG. 9.13
The Table Add dialog box.

Chapter Summary

This chapter showed how to take advantage of advanced Paradox for Windows features to help maintain data integrity. Using validation checks, table lookups, referential integrity, and password protection, you can protect your database against common data-entry errors and unauthorized access to data.

As you develop the requirements for a database, be sure to make a note of the integrity checks and security needed. Consider all the data-entry pitfalls that users must avoid and plan for the worst to achieve the best results. Then use the techniques you learned in this chapter to safeguard the database from inconsistency.

Chapter 10 shows how to use crosstabs and graphs to present your data to users. You will learn how to add graphs to forms and reports to make statistical information more meaningful.

CHAPTER 10

Creating Crosstabs and Graphs

In addition to representing your data with words and numbers, Paradox for Windows provides tools so that you can get your point across visually. These tools include crosstabs and graphs, which you can generate quickly and easily in Paradox.

Crosstabs and graphs represent numerical data rather than text; in other words, you must have a statistic to show to use crosstabs and graphs. You can base the statistic on the values in a number field or an aggregation based on the value in another type of field (such as date or alphanumeric). You can graph, for example, total sales (a number field) or count your customers by state (an alphanumeric field).

The best way to learn graphs is to start with crosstabs, because crosstabs create the numbers used in the creation of graphs. The following section shows how to create crosstabs in the Paradox form window.

Creating Crosstabs

Crosstabs present summary information from database tables. A crosstab is a raw form of a graph; it contains the numbers that are converted into visual elements such as lines or other shapes in a graph. Understanding crosstabs provides essential background for learning how to create Paradox for Windows graphs.

Defining a Crosstab

Crosstab stands for *cross tabulation*, which is a special way of analyzing data by building a matrix that correlates records by one or more values at the same time. The columns of the crosstab show the possible values for one field, and the rows show the values for a second field. Each of the cells where a column and row intersect contain a count or sum from the records that meet both criteria. For example, you could use a crosstab to show the breakdown of your customers by age and state, showing the number of customers in each age range for each state.

A crosstab resembles a spreadsheet in that it contains summary information rather than details on each record. A crosstab is much better than a spreadsheet, however, because you do not have to fill each cell individually. Instead, the summary values are calculated from values stored in your database tables.

Understanding Types of Crosstabs

Paradox offers two types of crosstabs: one-dimensional and two-dimensional. Before you create a crosstab, you must choose the type that best represents your data.

One-Dimensional Crosstabs

Paradox for Windows calls the simplest crosstabs *one-dimensional*. A one-dimensional crosstab analyzes one statistic broken down by values in another field. To illustrate, you can create a crosstab showing by genre the number of albums in the Albums table (see fig. 10.1).

> **NOTE** The Crosstab tool is available only in Paradox forms; you cannot include crosstabs in reports. To print a crosstab, choose File, Print when viewing the form.

10 — CREATING CROSSTABS AND GRAPHS   423

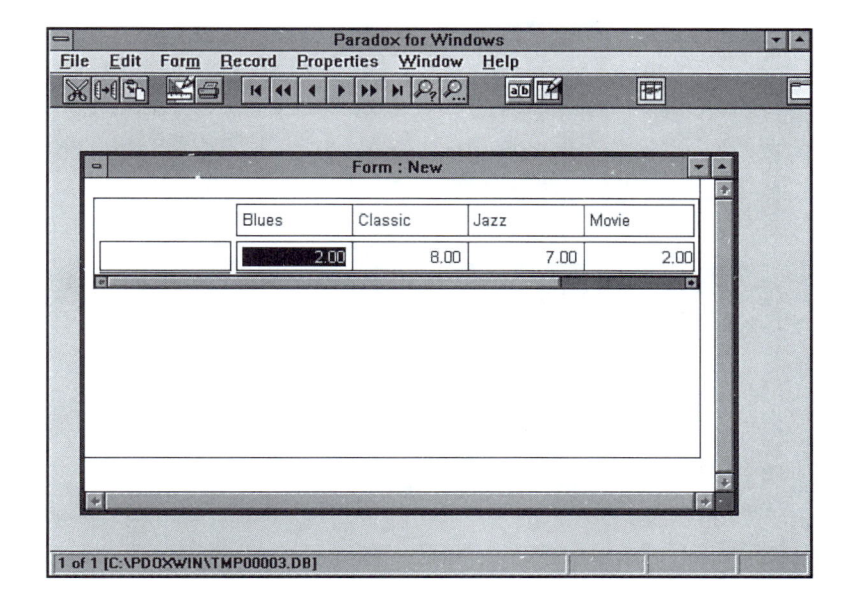

FIG. 10.1

A crosstab for album showing count by genre.

The easiest way to create a one-dimensional crosstab is to start in the Table Edit window, as in the following steps:

1. Choose File, Open, Table from the Paradox Desktop or click the Open Table button in the SpeedBar. Choose ALBUMS.DB as the table name. The Albums Table appears.

2. Click the Quick Crosstab button in the SpeedBar. This button is second from the right and looks like a spreadsheet with cells of various colors. The Define Crosstab dialog box appears (see fig. 10.2).

3. To generate a crosstab, you must specify the fields which will be used for the horizontal and vertical axes of the matrix. Click the pull-down menu next to the table name ALBUMS.DB to reveal a list of fields.

4. Choose Genre by clicking it. ALBUMS.Genre appears in the Column field of the dialog box.

5. Check the box to the left of Summaries to specify which field will be counted for the crosstab. Click the ALBUMS.DB pull-down menu and choose Album ID. The expression Count(ALBUMS.Album ID) appears in the Summaries field (see fig. 10.3). The Count operator is the default for a text field in a crosstab; Sum is the default for number fields. Other summary functions are discussed later in this chapter.

II — PARADOX FOR WINDOWS POWER TECHNIQUES

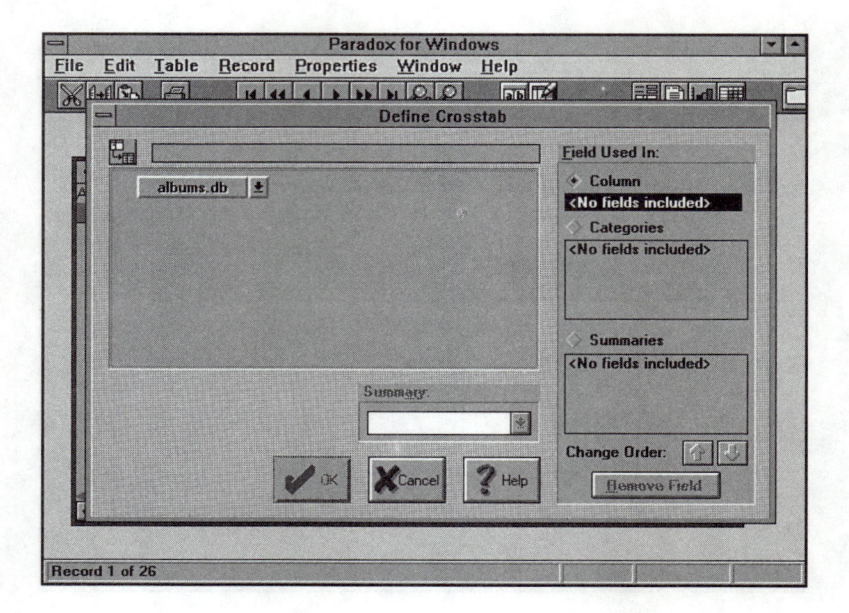

FIG. 10.2
The Define Crosstab dialog box.

6. Click OK to run the crosstab. The finished crosstab appears, as shown in figure 10.4.

7. Save the crosstab by clicking the Design button in the SpeedBar, then choose File, Save (or Save As).

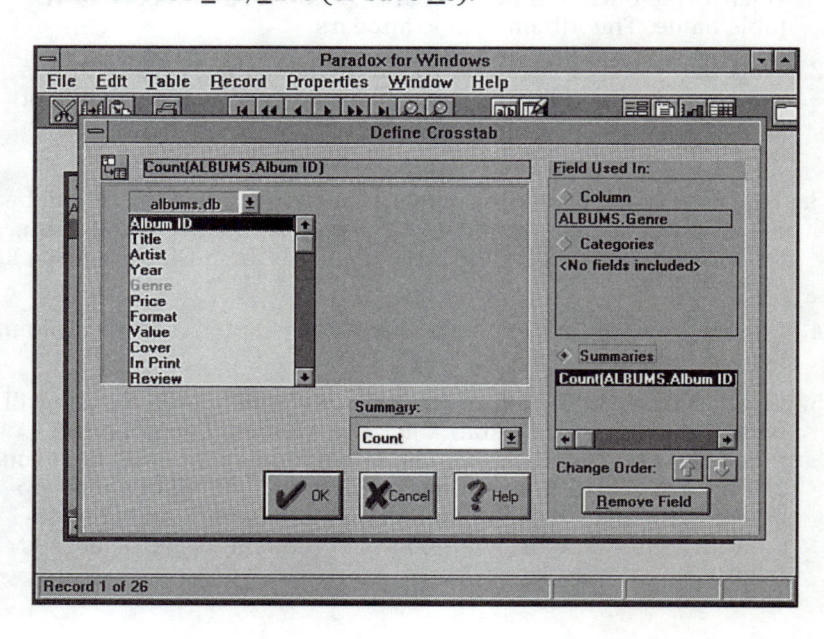

FIG. 10.3
Choosing a Summary for the crosstab.

10 — CREATING CROSSTABS AND GRAPHS

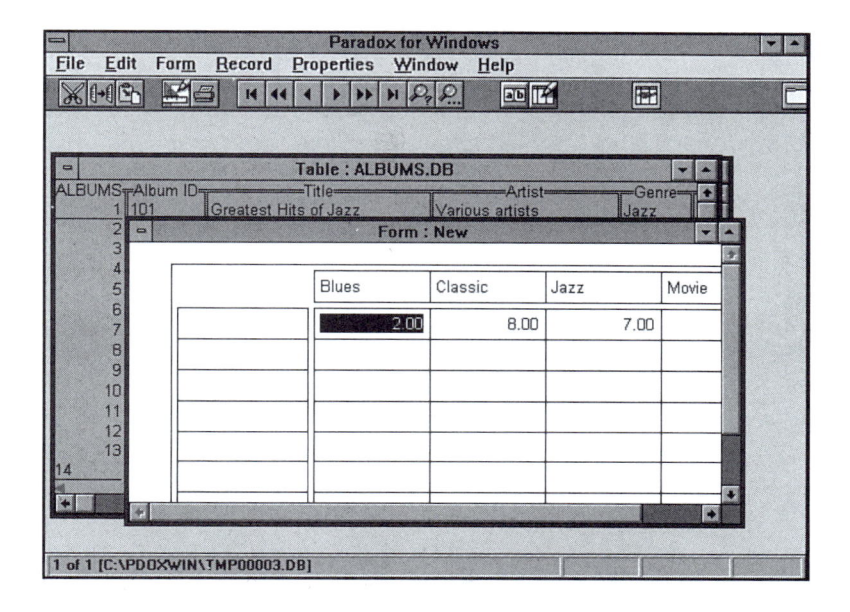

FIG. 10.4
The finished Quick Crosstab.

The following steps provide an alternative way to create a crosstab:

1. From the Paradox desktop, choose File, New, Form.
2. Choose Albums in the Data Model File dialog box.
3. In the Design Layout dialog box, click the Blank layout style option and OK to open the Form Design window.
4. Click the Crosstab button on the SpeedBar from data entry in a table. The mouse pointer changes to a miniature crosstab.
5. Click in the form work area to establish a corner of the crosstab object. Drag the mouse pointer to the opposite corner and release. Don't worry about the exact size of the crosstab; you can adjust it later. A blank crosstab object appears (see fig. 10.5).
6. Right-click the crosstab object to display its pop-up properties menu (figure 10.6).
7. Click Define Crosstab from the properties menu and choose ... from the menu. The Define Crosstab Object dialog box appears (see fig. 10.7).
8. Enter the fields you want to appear as columns and categories, as well as the field to use for aggregation. Using the Albums table as an example, click the pull-down menu next to the table name to view a list of fields in the Album table. Then choose Genre as the column and Album ID as the summary field.

II — PARADOX FOR WINDOWS POWER TECHNIQUES

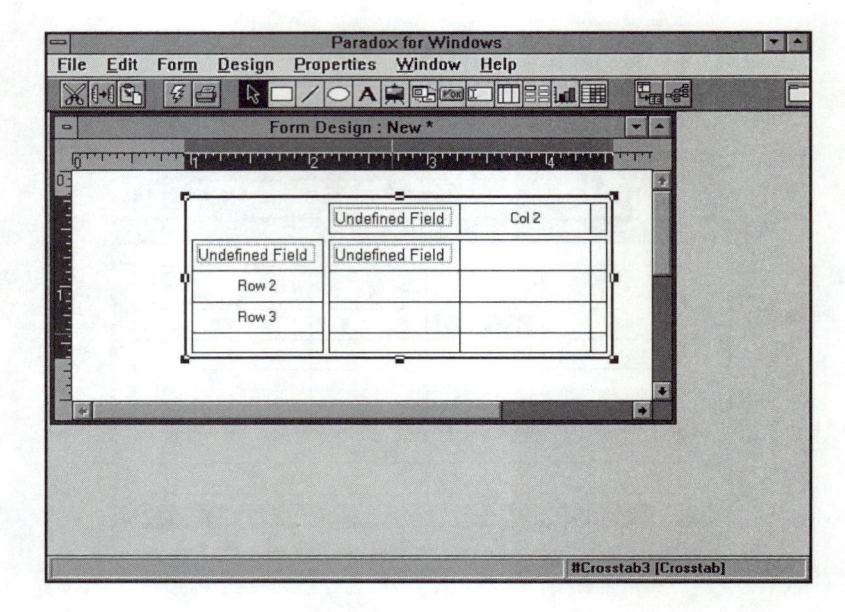

FIG. 10.5

An undefined crosstab object.

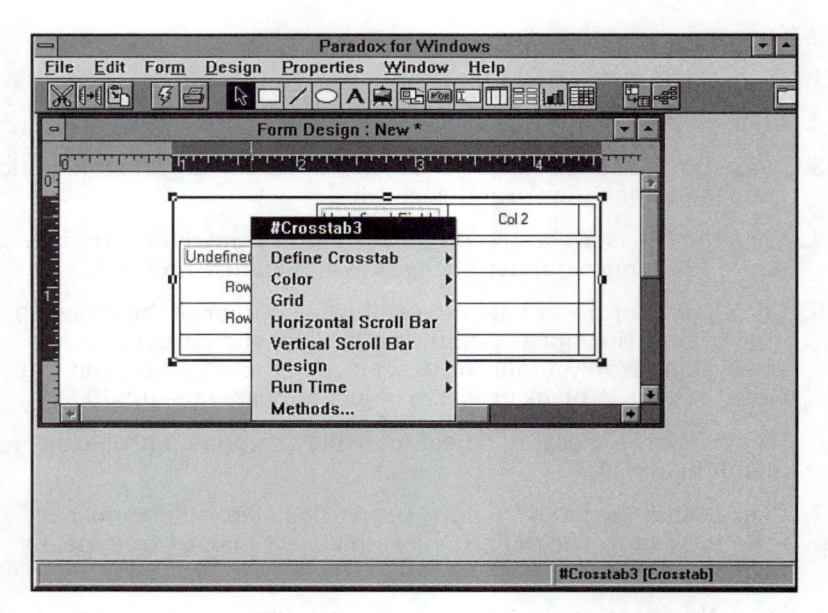

FIG. 10.6

Crosstab properties menu.

9. Click OK to save the crosstab definition. The finished crosstab definition shows the field names used for the rows and columns (see fig. 10.8).

10 — CREATING CROSSTABS AND GRAPHS

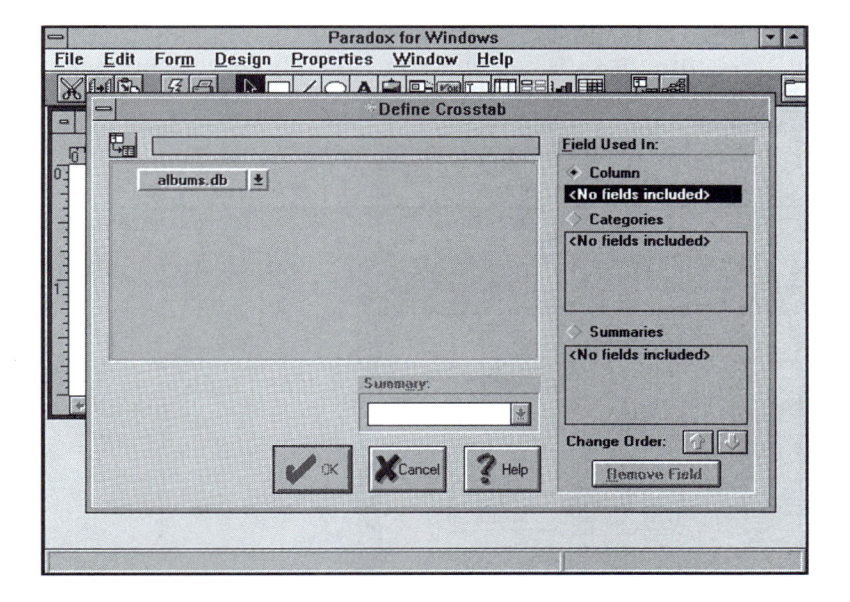

FIG. 10.7
The Define Crosstab dialog box.

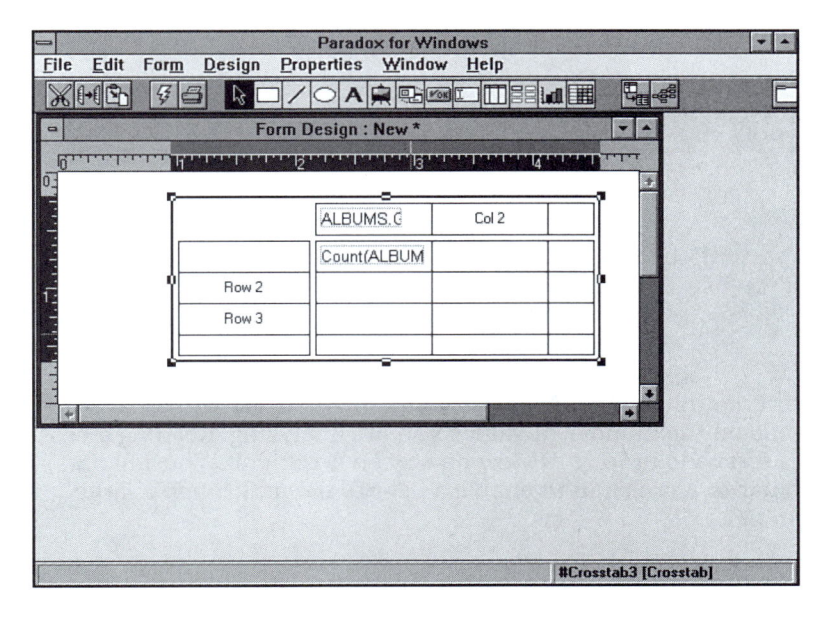

FIG. 10.8
The finished crosstab definition.

To view the crosstab with data, click the View Data button (the lightning bolt) on the SpeedBar.

You can display the same crosstab by turning it on its side (see fig. 10.9). To turn the crosstab on its side, simply enter Genre under Categories rather than under Columns in the Define Crosstab dialog box. You may want to adjust the size of the crosstab, as only one column is needed for a one-dimensional crosstab.

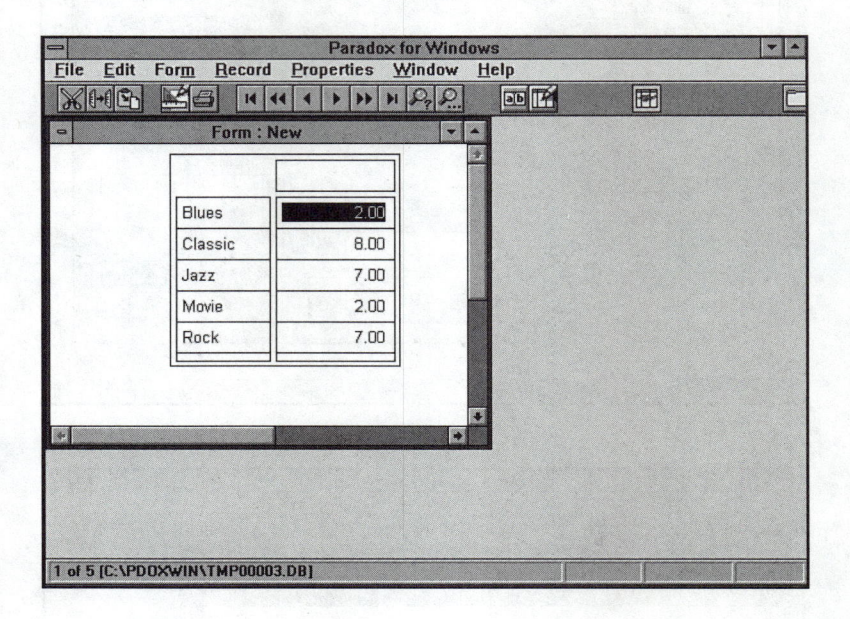

FIG. 10.9

A one-dimensional cross-tab, turned 90 degrees.

> **TIP**
>
> You may notice that a one-dimensional crosstab resembles a report with group subtotals. In fact, you can obtain the same result in a report as with a one-dimensional crosstab.

The orientation you choose (horizontal or vertical) for the crosstab depends on the number of values you are analyzing. Reading a crosstab that is too wide or long to view on-screen is difficult. You can add a scroll bar to a crosstab to enable a user to move through a large crosstab.

Two-Dimensional Crosstabs

A *two-dimensional* crosstab uses two ranges of values to analyze data and produces a matrix with multiple rows and columns. You may have, for example, a membership table that contains the names, addresses, and professional degrees of all your members. Perhaps you want to analyze the geographic breakdown and the highest academic degree earned by each member.

This type of comparison is tedious to compile by hand and, without the crosstab feature, would even take awhile to create on the computer because you must run separate reports grouped by state and by degree. Paradox for Windows, however, can accomplish this analysis with crosstabs in a few mouse movements and keystrokes. To create a crosstab for Albums by genre and format, for example, follow these steps:

1. In the Form Design window (using the Albums table), click the Crosstab tool and place a crosstab object in the work area.

2. Right-click the object to display the properties menu; then choose Define Crosstab and click ... to display the Define Crosstab dialog box.

3. Choose Genre as the column and Format as the category. For the summary, choose Album ID (Paradox uses this field to count the records). The completed crosstab definition is shown in figure 10.10.

4. Save the crosstab and then run it with the Display Data button in the SpeedBar. The crosstab that appears is similar to the one in figure 10.11.

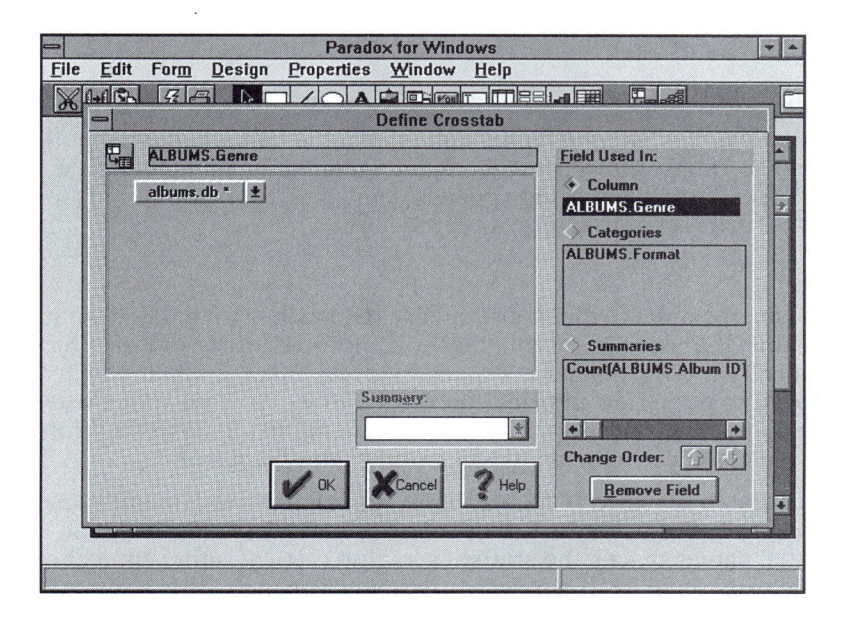

FIG. 10.10

Crosstab definition for a two-dimensional crosstab for genre and format in Albums.

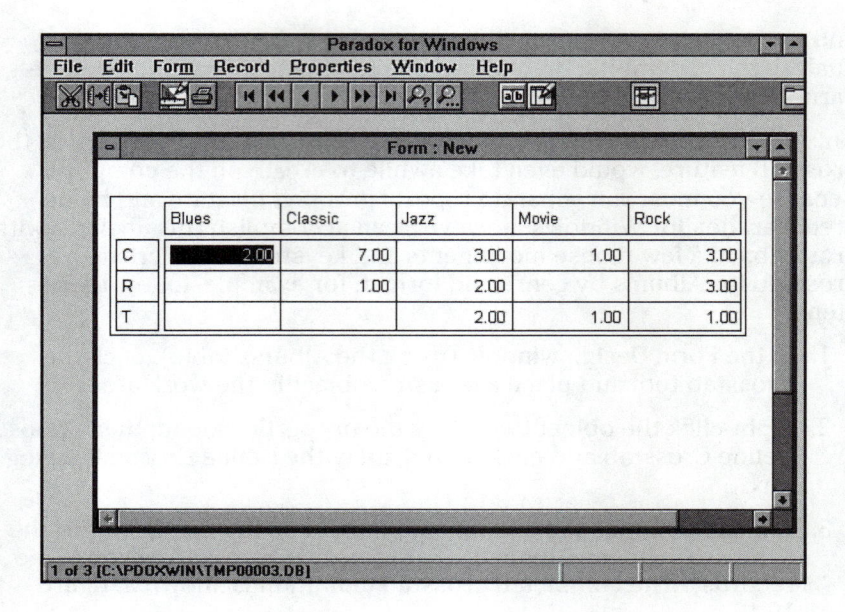

FIG. 10.11

A two-dimensional crosstab for genre and format in Albums.

Using these steps, you can easily create your own two-dimensional crosstabs. Simply choose Column for the field values to list at the top of the crosstab, Categories for a second field to show on the left side of the crosstab, and Summaries for the field to count (or sum, min, max, avg) in each cell of the matrix.

> **TIP**
> Another way to generate a crosstab is with the Quick Crosstab button in the Table Edit window. Click the Crosstab button to display the Crosstab dialog box and proceed according to the directions for building a crosstab that appear in the Form window.

You use crosstabs to display summary data rather than detail from individual records. Be careful, however, not to distort your data as you summarize it. This danger is especially acute when summarizing text as opposed to numerical information. To illustrate, you may start with a table containing sales totals by month (see fig. 10.12). What is wrong with the crosstab in figure 10.13 showing sales by month?

The crosstab in figure 10.13 also analyzes sales by month, but it uses the names for the months rather than the numbers 1-12. Using the months' names places the statistics in alphabetical rather than chronological order, making the upward trend in sales much less apparent. A better crosstab would use the month number so that the table is shown in chronological order (see fig. 10.14).

10 — CREATING CROSSTABS AND GRAPHS

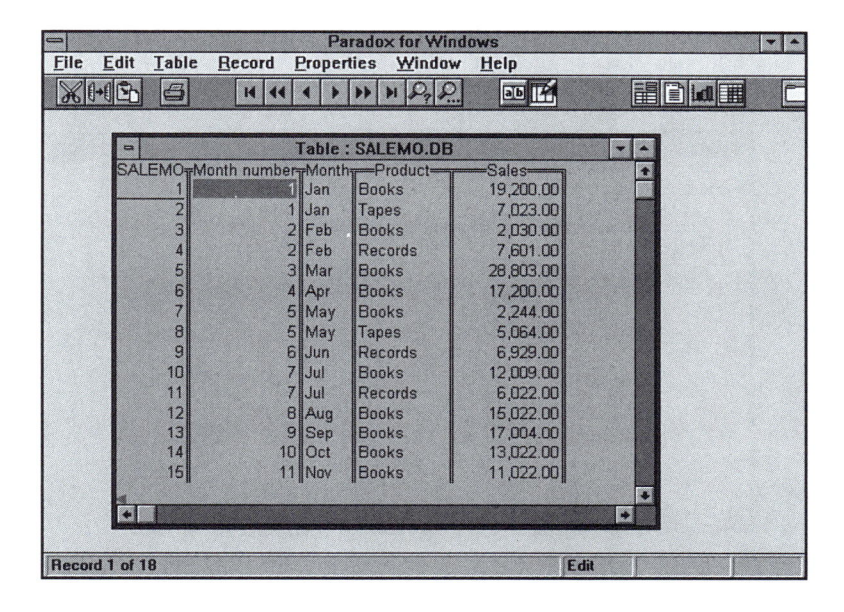

FIG. 10.12

The Sales Totals by Month table.

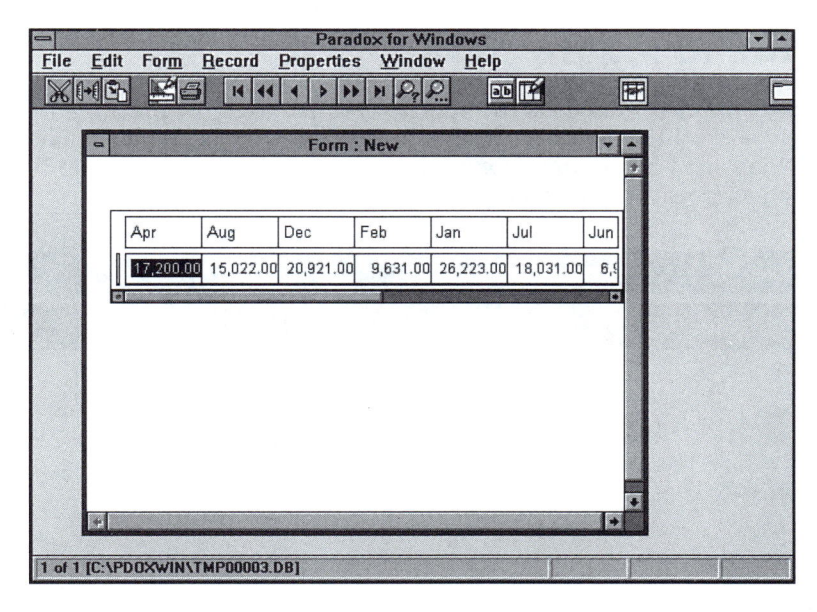

FIG. 10.13

Sales Totals by Month crosstab by month name.

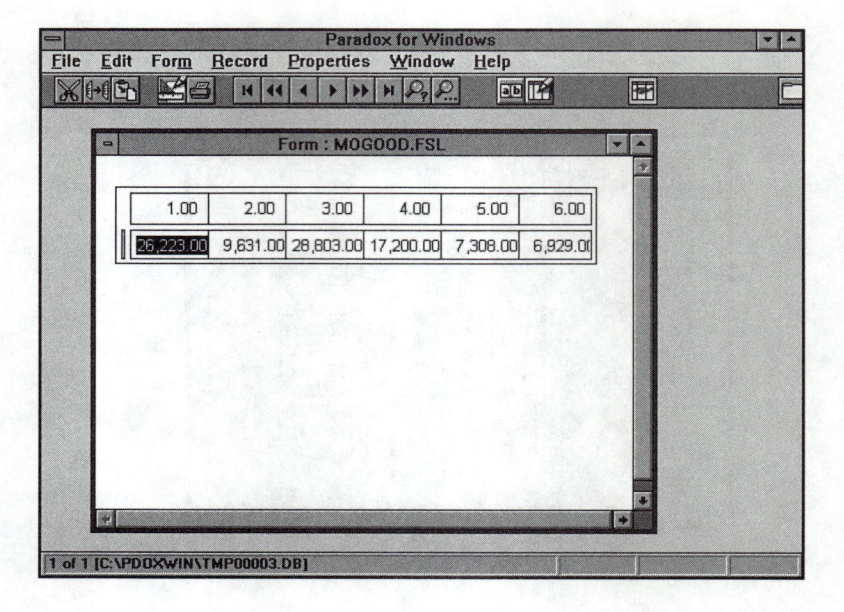

FIG. 10.14
A better crosstab.

Defining Aggregators

Paradox for Windows calls the special variable used for producing counts and other totals an *aggregator*. You may have used a similar function called an *accumulator* in other database packages. Table 10.1 lists all aggregators for crosstabs.

Table 10.1. Crosstab Aggregators

Aggregator	Explanation
Sum	Total for a field or expression
Count	Number of occurrences of a field or expression
Min	Lowest value in a set
Max	Highest value in a set
Avg	Average (mean) value

You must specify whether the aggregator is normal, unique, or cumulative. This characteristic determines which records in the set are counted by the aggregator. *Normal* aggregators count all records in which the field is non-null (not blank). Thus, Paradox does not include blank test scores (for example, when a student is absent for a test) when calculating the average test score for students. It counts duplicate values, however. Therefore, the scores of all students who score 95, for example, are taken into account.

A *unique* aggregator also ignores null values but rejects duplicates. Paradox counts each unique value for a field once and only once. The most common application for unique aggregators is to count the number of different values in a field.

Cumulative aggregators maintain a running total on a field throughout a set of data. The aggregator is initially set to zero and then increased by each record processed. Unique and cumulative aggregators are used in reports but not in forms.

Customizing Crosstab Settings

The elements that make up a crosstab are the crosstab itself, fields, field labels, and the grid. Like other Paradox objects, you can change the properties of the elements that make up a crosstab. To change the property of a crosstab object, choose the object and right-click to reveal the properties menu. Table 10.2 summarizes crosstab element properties, grouped by object.

Table 10.2. Crosstab Element Properties

Element	Properties	Description
Crosstab	Define crosstab	Defines crosstab dialog box
	Color	Specifies background color
	Grid	Grid line style and color
	Horizontal scroll bar	Horizontal scrolling
	Vertical scroll bar	Vertical scrolling
	Design	Affixes crosstab in form horizontally or vertically
	Run Time	Displays/hides crosstab
	Methods	Attaches an ObjectPAL method
Summaries	Add a Summary	
	Color	Specifies background color
	Grid	Grid line style and color
	Horizontal scroll bar	Horizontal scrolling
	Vertical scroll bar	Vertical scrolling
	Methods	Attaches an ObjectPAL method

continues

Table 10.2. Continued

Element	Properties	Description
Column	Define Column Field	
	Color	Specifies background color
	Grid	Grid line style and color
	Horizontal scroll bar	Horizontal scrolling
	Vertical scroll bar	Vertical scrolling
	Methods	Attaches an ObjectPAL method

Fields placed in a crosstab have the same properties as all fields in Paradox forms. Likewise, grid properties in crosstabs are similar to those for grids in tables.

In addition to changing the properties of crosstab elements, you can change the format of the crosstab. The default crosstab Paradox creates for you may not be the right height or width to suit your data (fig. 10.15 shows a default crosstab). Often, a default crosstab format includes extra (empty) rows and columns. In the Form Design window, simply click and drag to shrink or enlarge the overall crosstab size, column width, or row height.

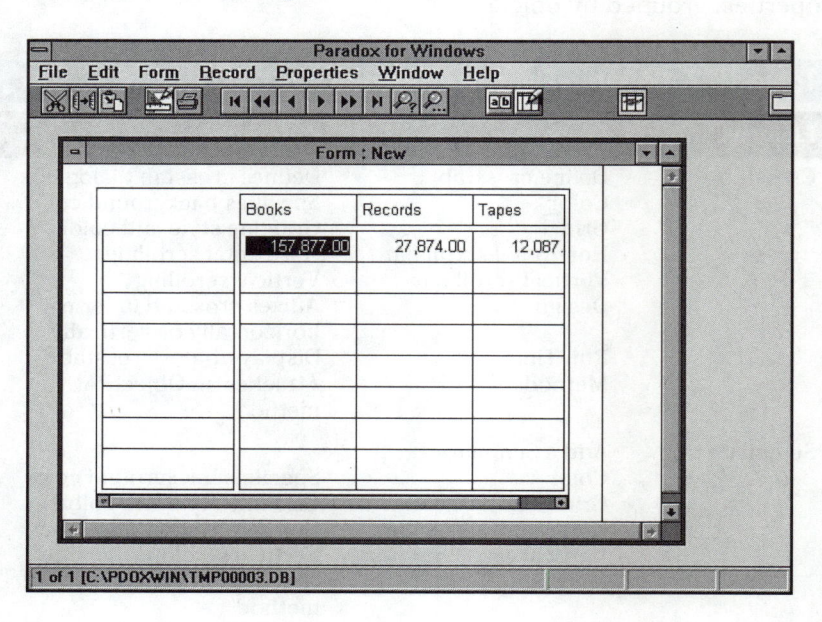

FIG. 10.15

A default crosstab.

On the left side of the default crosstab is a cell that contains the field name for each row. In some cases, this label wastes space and distracts from the crosstab. Although you cannot remove this label completely, you can reduce it to a thin black line by clicking and dragging the right side of the cell to the left as far as possible. See figure 10.16 for an improved, reformatted crosstab.

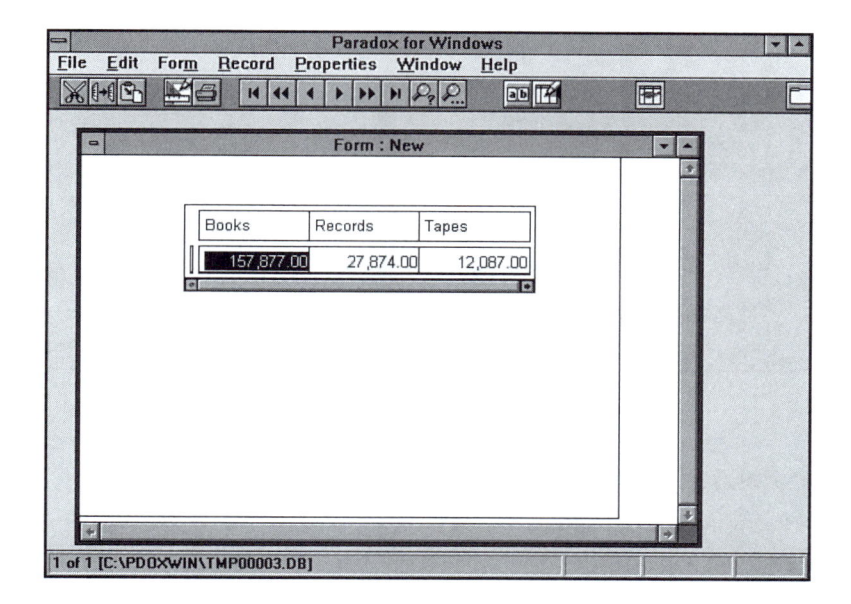

FIG. 10.16

A reformatted crosstab.

Using the Data Model

Multi-table crosstabs enable you to analyze data drawn from more than one table. To create a multi-table crosstab, add all the tables you want to the data model. The data model shows the relationships among tables in your database (see fig 10.17). After you have established the links between the tables, you can choose fields from either table for the crosstab. In effect, Paradox is combining both tables into a single table.

NOTE Multi-table crosstabs only work for tables with a one-to-one or many-to-one relationship. For one-to-many relationships, you can create a query that summarizes information from the two tables and generates the crosstab from the resulting Answer table.

FIG. 10.17

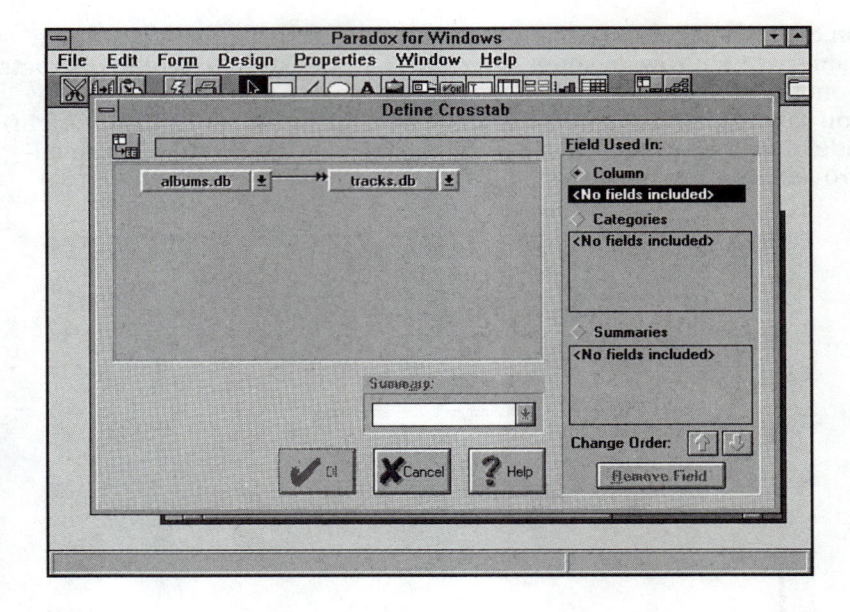

A multi-table crosstab definition using the data model.

For Related Information

◂◂ "Adding a Crosstab," p. 243.

◂◂ "Creating Multi-Table Forms," p. 336.

Creating Graphs

Graphs can be a powerful means of communication. They can simplify complex data and highlight important trends in more dramatic ways than mere text and numbers on a page. Imagining today's annual reports, corporate briefings, and other business documents without pie graphs, bar graphs, and line graphs is difficult. Computer magazines are peppered with fancy three-dimensional graphs to compare performance, hardware, and software.

CAUTION: Graphs, like the statistics they represent, can be misleading. Summary data can distort the truth and draw the user to erroneous conclusions. You must be careful to choose graphs appropriate to the information you are communicating to ensure that the correct numbers find their way into your graphs.

You can create graphs in two ways from your Paradox for Windows tables. One way is to use another graphics program—such as Microsoft Powerpoint, Lotus Freelance, or Harvard Graphics—to draw a chart. Using object linking and embedding (OLE) and dynamic data exchange (DDE), you can move the numbers from Paradox for Windows to any graphics package that supports these capabilities. See Chapter 11, "Exchanging Data with Other Applications," for information on using OLE and DDE to communicate with other programs.

The second way to create a graph—and the subject of this chapter—is to use Paradox for Windows' built-in graphics. The graphics engine has been completely overhauled from Paradox for DOS and is the same as that used for Borland's Quattro Pro for Windows. Paradox for Windows offers better control over all graph elements and a number of new graph types.

> **NOTE** You can use graphs only with numeric data. You cannot graph other field types, such as text, unless you somehow convert them into numbers by counting or otherwise aggregating them.

Before you create a Paradox graph, you should learn some special graph terminology. The following section is an overview of the anatomy of a graph, highlighting graph features you can control in Paradox.

Understanding the Parts of a Graph

The art of graphing uses special terminology to describe the parts of a graph. These terms may differ from one graphics program or spreadsheet to another. They are defined in this chapter using Paradox for Windows terminology, along with synonyms used in other packages. Figure 10.18 shows the elements of a typical graph and table 10.3 describes these graph elements.

Table 10.3. Descriptions of Graph Elements

Elements	Description
Axes	For bar, line, and scatter charts, the vertical (y-axis) and horizontal (x-axis) lines that show units of measure. Three-dimensional charts use a third axis—the z-axis—to indicate depth.
Bars	Solid or shaded rectangles that represent data points. Bars can be horizontal or vertical and can be stacked on top of one another, clustered, or separate.

continues

Table 10.3. Continued

Elements	Description
Frame	A box around the graph area, usually a thin line, that separates the graph from surrounding titles and other text.
Graph area	The area where the data is represented by lines, bars, pies, or other means. This area excludes the title, legends, and other text on the graph.
Grid lines	Lines drawn perpendicular to the axes across the graph area to make measurements easier to read.
Labels	Text that explains the meaning of data points in the graph.
Legend	Explanation of the various series of data represented in the graph by shading or color. Usually appears at the side or bottom of the graph.
Scale	The unit of measure for the x- and y-axes. Graphs are usually scaled so that all values to be charted fall within the range of the axes, and the axes are divided into equal units.
Series	A set of data to be graphed. A graph representing annual sales, for example, can contain a series of data for each sales region. This data comes from Paradox for Windows tables.
Tick marks	Small lines or other symbols, along with axes that indicate units, that make the graph easier to read.
Titles	Text surrounding the graph area, including the graph title and information such as source or date.

Understanding Types of Graphs

Paradox for Windows offers several types of graphs, each suitable for particular purposes. Some of the graph types are essentially the same but have different visual impact.

Bar graphs represent each value in a series with a bar that connects the size of the value on the y-axis to the x-axis. Figure 10.19 shows the types of bar graphs Paradox for Windows supports.

10 — CREATING CROSSTABS AND GRAPHS

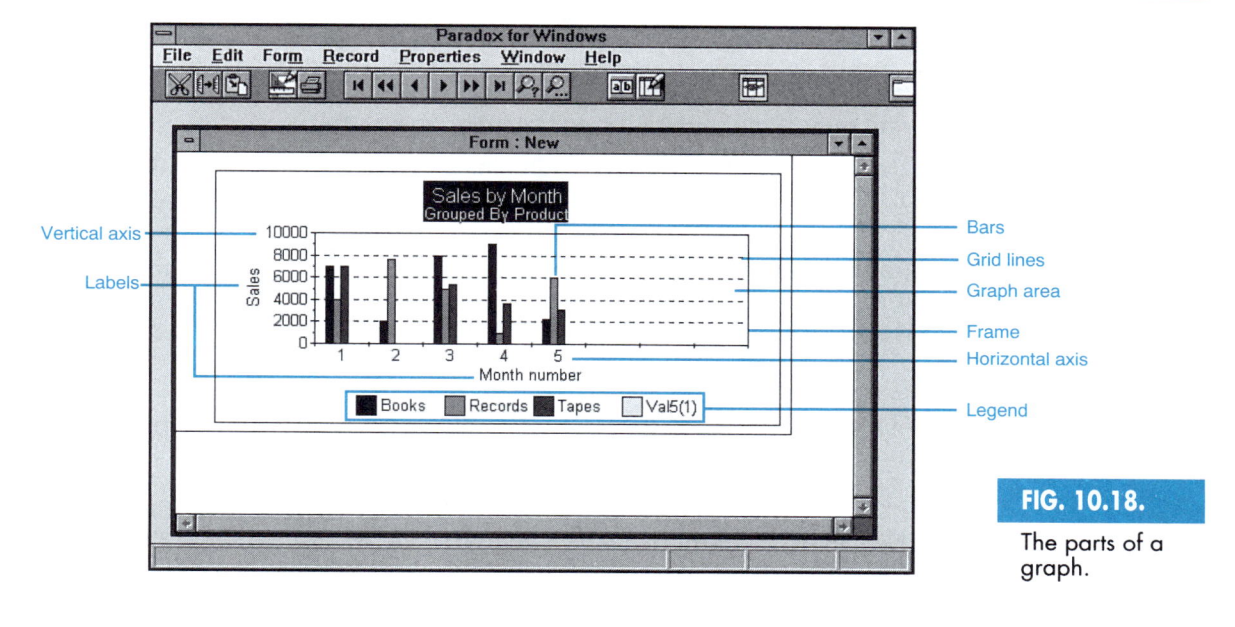

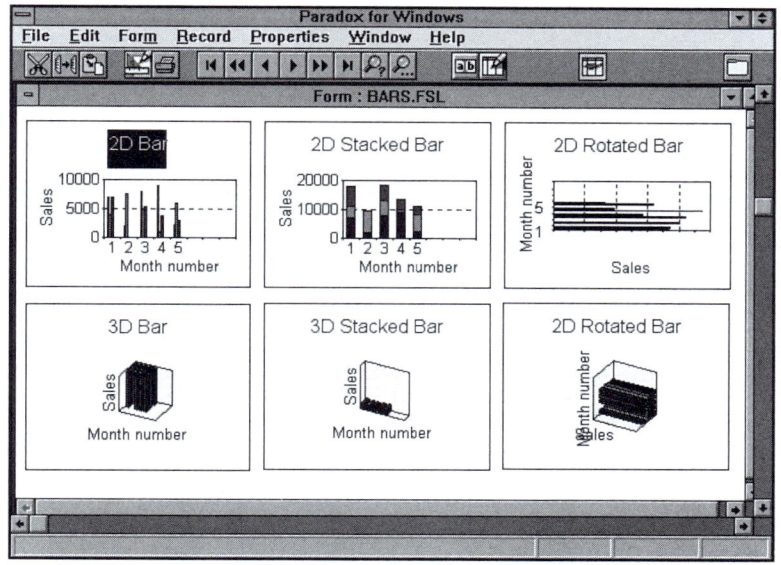

FIG. 10.18.

The parts of a graph.

FIG. 10.19

Bar graphs supported by Paradox for Windows.

If more than one series is graphed, you can place each series next to each other in a *clustered* bar graph or leave each one separate. Instead of placing the bars for multiple series next to one another, the *stacked-bar* graph combines them into one bar, providing both the size of the total data and the relative size of segments within the total.

Three-dimensional bar graphs give the illusion of depth to a graph by using a shadow effect on the bar, pie, or surface. Paradox does not support true three-dimensional graphs, which correlate three factors showing their relationships along the x-, y-, and z-axes.

You can rotate the two- and three-dimensional bar graphs so that their bars run horizontally or vertically; however, you cannot rotate stacked-bar graphs.

One of the most appetizing business graph types, the *pie graph*, shows the proportion of parts to the whole. You can use a pie graph, for example, to show the installed base of computer operating systems, with a pie segment assigned to each operating system based on its percentage of the user base.

By definition, a pie graph can contain only one set of data for one point in time. Sometimes when multiple pie graphs are used side-by-side, the size of the pie is proportional to the total size of the population represented by the graph. Sometimes special effects are used to enhance the appearance of a pie graph, such as pulling out a pie segment to highlight it or using a three-dimensional shadowing effect. Figure 10.20 shows the pie graphs Paradox for Windows supports.

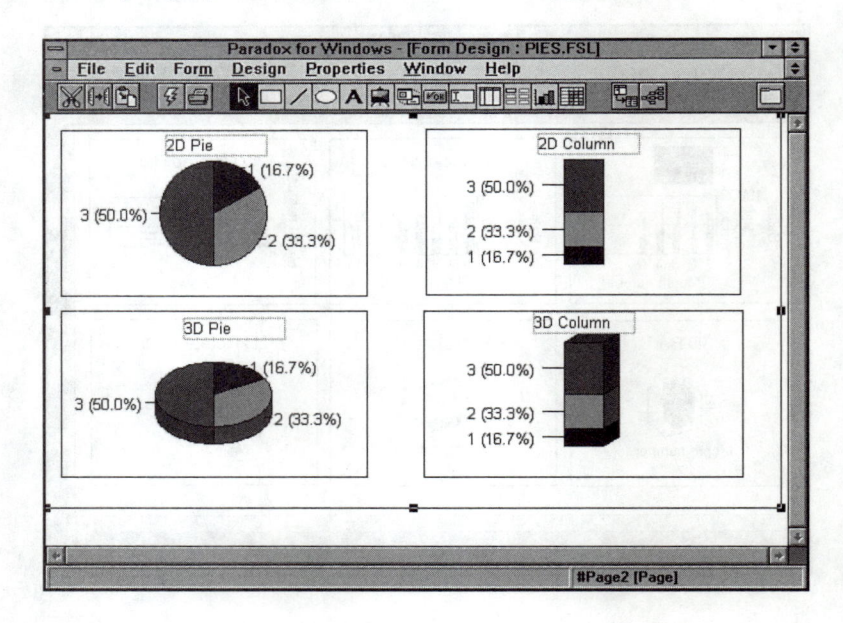

FIG. 10.20

Pie graphs supported by Paradox for Windows.

Although bar and pie graphs are the most popular, Paradox offers a number of other business graph types (see fig. 10.21). A *line graph* connects data points in a series to show change over time. Multiple series often are used in the same graph as lines using the same unit of measure. In this way, the series can be compared directly to one another. Similar to a line graph, the *marker graph* uses symbols other than a line to represent its data points. Punctuation marks and geometric shapes often are used as markers, with a different marker for each series on the graph.

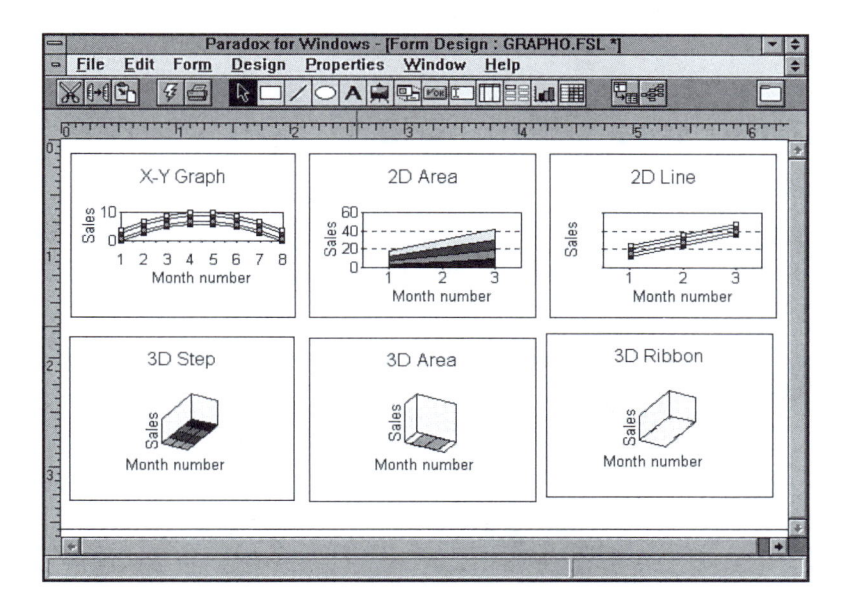

FIG. 10.21 Other types of Paradox graphs.

The *x-y graph* compares two series of numeric data to one another, showing whether the two are correlated. This type of graph also is called a *scatter graph*.

An *area graph* simultaneously shows an overall trend along with the relationship of its constituent parts to the whole. You can use, for example, an area graph to show sales trends of PC processors, comparing 286, 386, and 486 sales over a period of time. The overall line would shift as total sales grew, and the area underneath the line would shift to show the proportion of the market each processor gained or lost. An area graph can be looked at as a combination of a stacked-bar graph and a line graph. You also can create a three-dimensional area graph to show a surface rather than just a line.

Paradox *columns* graphs are a square version of pie graphs. Instead of dividing a circle into wedges, you can divide two- or three-dimensional columns and label each section, or *slice*. As with pie graphs, you can explode one or more sections from a columns graph.

> **T I P**
>
> You can build graphs based on any table, including temporary tables. Therefore, you can use a query to generate the numbers for the graph and then build the graph based on the answer table. You may want to rename the Answer table so that the graph name is more descriptive than the default name, Answer.

Placing and Defining a Graph Object

In the form and report design windows, you can use the graph tool to create graph objects. You also can create a graph by using the Quick Graph button in the SpeedBar of the Edit Table window. This Quick Graph tool creates a default graph in the form design window and instantly shows your data.

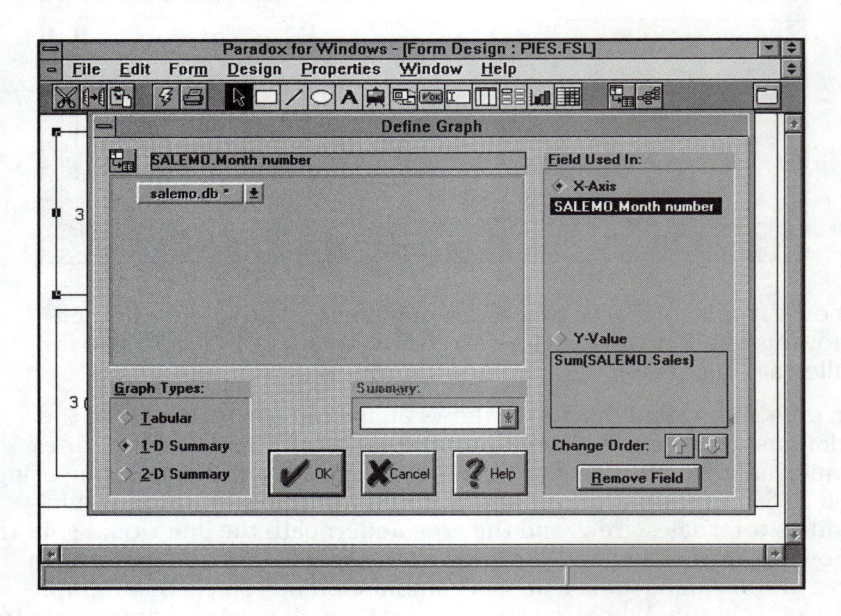

FIG. 10.22

The Define Graph dialog box.

The Define Graph dialog box gives you three choices under Graph Types: Tabular, 1-D Summary, and 2-D Summary. This field does not mean what you might expect; another graph property, called Graph Type, enables you to choose among bar graphs, pie graphs, and other graph types. The choices here in the Define Graph dialog box have to do with how graph values will be calculated. A Tabular graph uses the numbers directly from the table, without performing any aggregation for you. The 1-D Summary aggregates one field from the table and shows it in the graph. The 2-D Summary correlates two fields from the table with one another and aggregates one of the fields. A 1-D Summary graph is similar to a one-dimensional crosstab; a 2-D Summary graph is similar to a two-dimensional crosstab. Table 10.4 summarizes Paradox graph types.

Table 10.4. Graph Types in the Define Graph Dialog Box

Type	Description
Tabular	Graphs the contents of a field directly without performing any summary calculations. Commonly used with an answer table that already has calculated summary data. A tabular graph displays the series in order by its y-axis values.
1-D Summary	Summarizes a field based on grouping by the value in another field. This graph uses the results of a one-dimensional crosstab. The series are listed in order by the x-axis value.
2-D Summary	Summarizes multiple sub-groups of data within a group (refer to fig. 10.17). A two-dimensional crosstab is the underlying analysis for a two-dimensional Data type.

> **TIP**
>
> The Ctrl+F7 command used to create an instant graph in Paradox for DOS has been translated to Paradox for Windows, and it can be used instead of clicking the Quick Graph button.

Customizing Graph Settings

As with crosstabs, the best way to work with graphs is to use default Paradox settings, then change the properties of the object to suit your needs. You have a great deal of control over how a graph looks. You can change, for example, the color and style of most elements of a graph. To view the properties of a graph element, right-click the desired part of the graph. Table 10.5 shows the separate properties for parts of a graph.

Table 10.5. Paradox Graph Properties

Element	Properties	Description
Entire graph	Define Graph	The Define Graph dialog box
	Color	The color palette (background)
	Pattern	Submenus for background color and style
	Frame	Submenus for style, color, and thickness
	Data type	Tabular, 1-D Summary, 2-D Summary
	Graph type	17 types (bar, pie, and so on)
	Min x-values	Minimum value for x-axis
	Max x-values	Maximum value for x-axis
	Options	Show or hide title, legend, grid, axes, and labels. Options vary for different graph types.
	Design	Pin Horizontal, Pin Vertical, or Contain Object
	Run Time	Visible to display when form is run, Tab Stop for user's cursor to stop on graph in form
	Methods	Attach ObjectPAL methods to graph
Background	Color	The color palette (background)
	Pattern	Submenus for background color and style
Legend box	Color	Color for legend box background
	Pattern	Submenus for background color and style
	Font	Typeface, size, and style
	Legend Pos	Place legend on bottom or to right of graph

10 — CREATING CROSSTABS AND GRAPHS

Element	Properties	Description
X-Axis	Define X-value	Choose fields for x-axis
	Title	Up to 18 characters for axis title
	Ticks	Control font and interval of axis tick marks
Y-Axis	Define Y-value	Choose fields for y-axis
	Title	Up to 18 characters for axis title
	Scale	Choose scale from Auto-Scale (the default), Logarithmic, Low Value, High Value, and Increment
	Ticks	Control font and interval of axis tick marks
Title Box	Title	First line of graph title
	Subtitle	Second line of graph title
	Color	Background color for graph title
	Pattern	Background pattern for graph title
1st Series	Define Y-Value	Choose field for y-value
	Color	Background color for series
	Pattern	Background pattern for series
	Remove This Y-Value	Delete this series
	Type override	Change display type for series from default type to alternate type (choices depend on graph type you are using)

Figures 10.23 through 10.29 show the properties menus for all graph elements.

FIG. 10.23

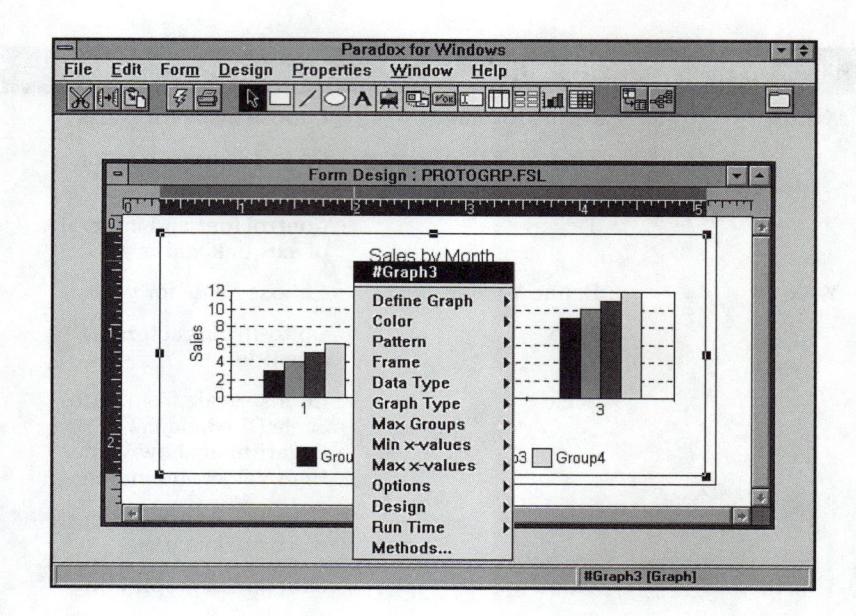

Entire graph properties menu.

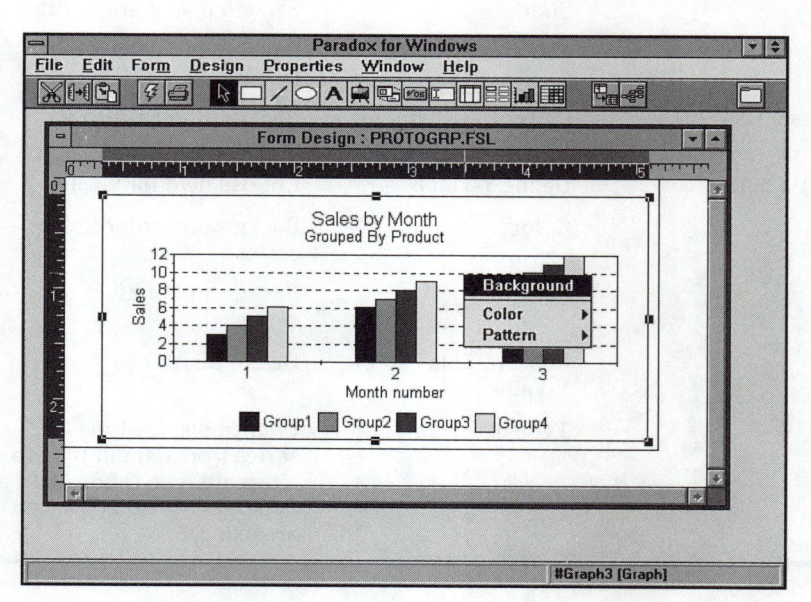

FIG. 10.24

Graph Background properties menu.

10 — CREATING CROSSTABS AND GRAPHS   447

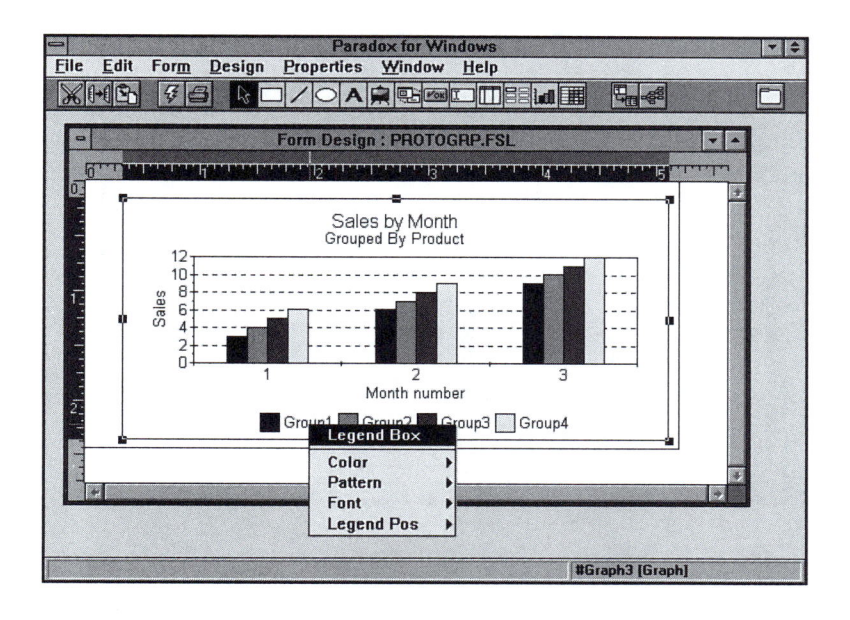

FIG. 10.25

Graph Legend Box properties menu.

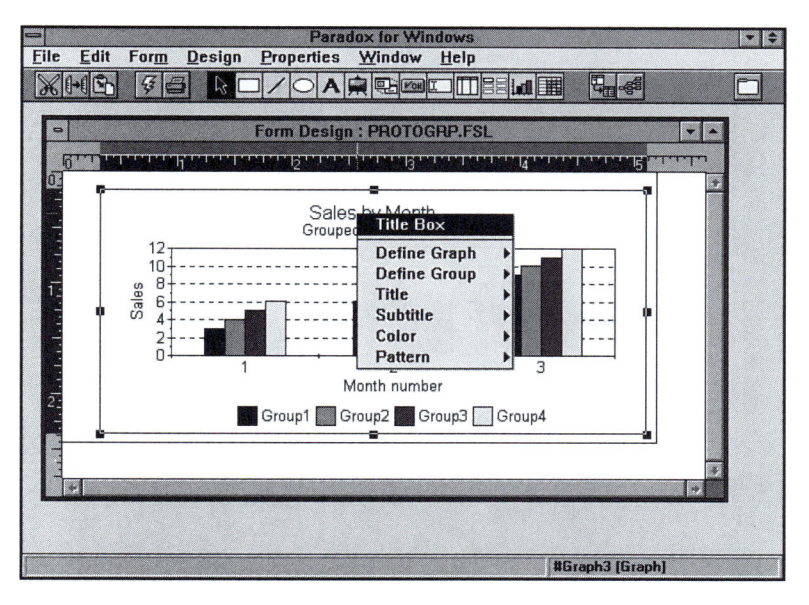

FIG. 10.26

Graph Title Box properties menu.

II — PARADOX FOR WINDOWS POWER TECHNIQUES

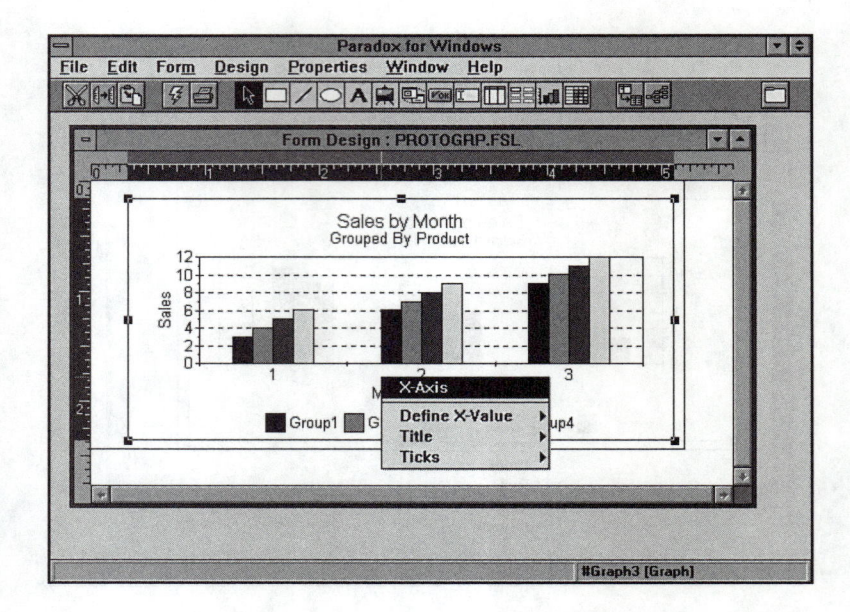

FIG. 10.27

Graph X-Axis properties menu.

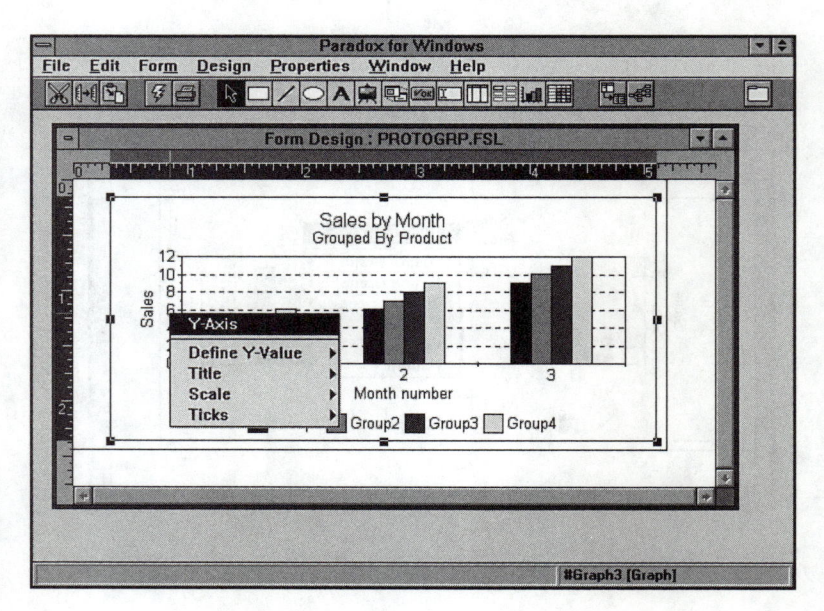

FIG. 10.28

Graph Y-Axis properties menu.

10 — CREATING CROSSTABS AND GRAPHS

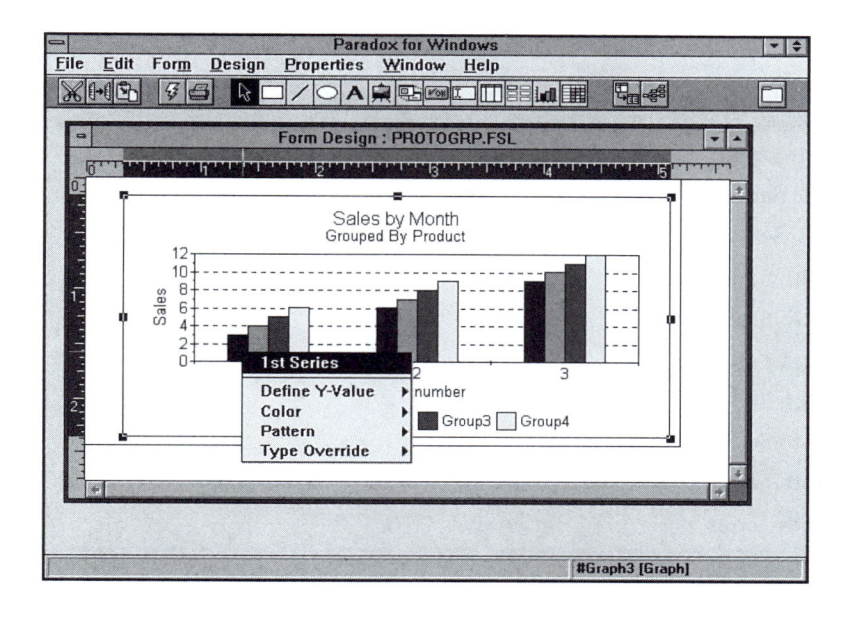

FIG. 10.29

Graph Series properties menu.

Table 10.6 shows the default colors and patterns for Paradox graphs. To change the color of an object, inspect the object and change the color (or pattern) property.

Table 10.6. Default Graph Settings—Colors and Patterns

Setting	Color
Background	White
Main title	Black
Subtitle	Black
X-axis title	Black
Y-axis title	Black
1st Series	Red
2nd Series	Green
3rd Series	Blue
4th Series	Yellow
5th Series	Orange
6th Series	Reddish brown

continues

Table 10.6. Continued

Setting	Color
7th Series	Khaki
8th Series	Medium green
9th Series	Cyan
10th Series	Dark blue
11th Series	Pink
12th Series	Pale yellow
13th Series	Pale green
14th Series	Pale cyan
15th Series	Pale yellow
16th Series	Burgundy

In a pie graph, the 17th series (pie slice) is red, and subsequent slices repeat the colors of the first 16 slices. You may want to avoid a pie graph with 17 slices, therefore, as the first and last slices appear the same color.

Although all graph types use color, some graph types have different properties. The following sections show how to customize graph settings for particular graph types.

Customizing Series Settings

Depending on the type of graph you choose, you have several options for changing the way that each series of data appears. In a bar graph, for example, you can change the value represented, remove the series entirely, override the display type, and change the title, color, and pattern of the series. Remember that your changes affect all the data points for the series, not just the one you choose in order to change a series property.

Customizing Pie and Bar Settings

The default design for the pie or bar graph shows eight bars or pie slices. When you view data with the graph, however, the proper number of data elements appears.

Another option with pie graphs is to create separate pies for each group, as shown in figure 10.30. This graph shows sales by month, grouped by product.

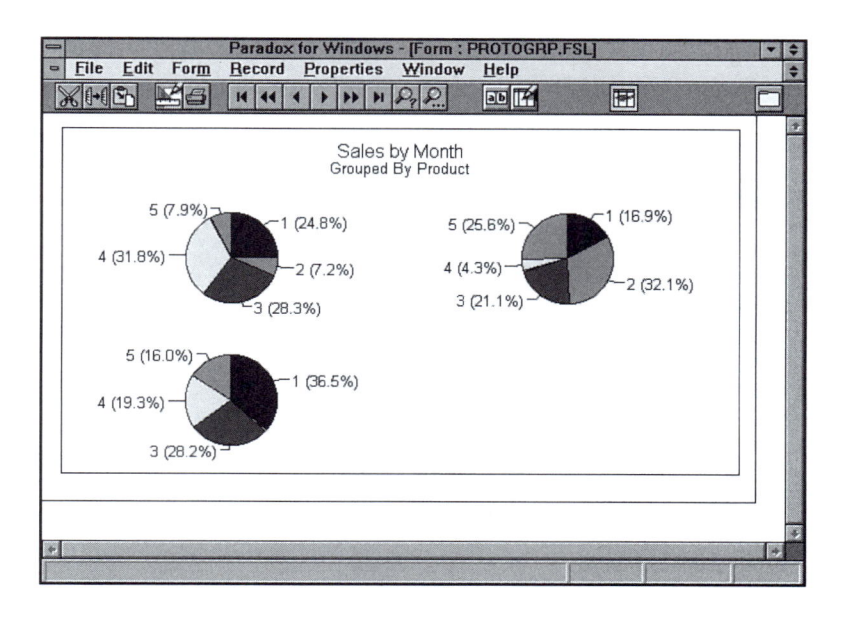

FIG. 10.30

Multiple pie graphs.

To explode a pie section from a pie or columns graph, click the desired section and choose Explode from the properties menu of the pie section. The pie section is pulled away from the rest of the graph, as shown in figure 10.31. You can explode as many pie sections as you want.

For Related Information

◂◂ "Adding a Graph," p. 243.

Printing a Graph

To print a graph, simply choose File, Print from any Paradox menu. The Print File dialog box appears. Choose the page range and number of copies you want, and click OK to begin printing. Be sure to make the graph large enough. Choose Properties, Zoom, and then choose 50% to display a larger area of the form or report. Stretch the graph to fill the space available. You also may need to enlarge the font size of the titles and labels to pleasing proportions.

Depending on the configuration of your computer, graphs can take significantly longer to print than text reports.

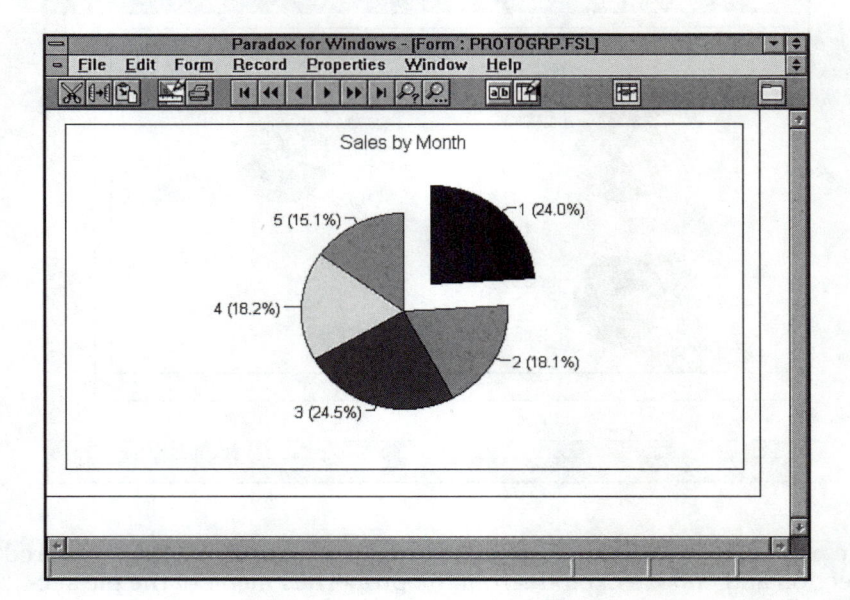

FIG. 10.31

An exploded pie section.

TIP Unless you are producing color printouts or slides, be sure to use color combinations that are attractive and readable when converted to black-and-white. Avoid a dark background color with dark letters, for example, because the letters are difficult to read if you convert them to black-and-white.

To print a graph in landscape orientation, choose File, Printer Setup from the menu to display the Printer Setup dialog box. Click the Modify Printer Setup button and the setup for your printer appears. To change to landscape printing, click the Landscape button in the box labeled Orientation, or press Alt+L.

Chapter Summary

Graphs and crosstabs are powerful ways of expressing summary information from your Paradox for Windows database, and they are fast and easy to create. Just the same, you should take time to plan that the graph or crosstab adds to your presentation and accurately reflects your data.

You can embed graphs in forms or reports. Sometimes, you may want to create a form that contains nothing but a graph. For example, you may want to present data to managers as a graph rather than have them look at the raw data in the table by using a form which consists of a graph.

Now that you have mastered presenting data in Paradox, the next chapter shows you how to share information with other applications. You learn how to link your Paradox tables, forms, and reports with Windows word processors, graphics programs, and databases.

CHAPTER 11

Exchanging Data with Other Applications

Paradox for Windows may be your primary source of business data, but it may not be your only source. You may rely on spreadsheets or other database programs for some information. Although you could enter (or import) this information into Paradox for Windows tables, Windows enables you to link Paradox and the other application directly so that data in Paradox is refreshed automatically. For example, you can transfer an Excel or Quattro Pro graph to a Paradox form, or access documents created in your favorite word processing program.

Paradox for Windows supports two methods of accessing data from other Windows applications: Dynamic Data Exchange (DDE) and Object Linking and Embedding (OLE). Each method has its strengths and weaknesses.

In DDE and OLE, an application (Paradox for Windows, a spreadsheet, a word processor, or another program) can be either the source or the recipient of data. The source is called the *server*; the recipient is called the *client*. Paradox for Windows can be either the server or the client in DDE but only the client in OLE.

To use DDE or OLE effectively, you must be proficient in both the client and the server application.

The DDE and OLE methods are different from exporting or importing data. When you import data into Paradox tables, you are copying information from another file. DDE and OLE, on the other hand, maintain links, or *channels*, with the application in which the data was created. You have to import again to reflect any changes in the external data. When you use DDE or OLE, however, changes made by other programs are communicated to Paradox for Windows through DDE or OLE.

> **T I P** Not all applications support DDE and OLE, although most popular Windows databases, spreadsheets, and word processors have this feature. Check your program before you attempt to link it to Paradox for Windows.

> **CAUTION:** Creating links to other applications makes your Paradox database vulnerable to changes in data sources. For example, a link to a spreadsheet cell is disrupted if the file is renamed or deleted, or if the cell is moved from one location in a spreadsheet to another. Because OLE and DDE data are not part of Paradox, you do not have as much control of data integrity as if all the data were stored inside Paradox. For instance, you cannot define referential integrity so that Paradox updates external data.

What Is DDE?

Dynamic Data Exchange is a feature of Windows applications that enables you to transfer values from one application to another. You can use DDE to transfer a spreadsheet cell to a Paradox table, for example, or an address from a Paradox table to a document in your word processor.

Many popular Windows databases, spreadsheets, and word processors support DDE, including Microsoft Excel, Word for Windows, Ami Pro, Q+E, Lotus 1-2-3 for Windows, Quattro Pro, and Superbase 4.

11 — EXCHANGING DATA WITH OTHER APPLICATIONS

> **TIP**
>
> One way to tell whether an application supports DDE is to look at its Edit menu. If you see a Paste Special, Paste Link, or Link option, the application probably supports DDE.

Using DDE To Get Values

To use Paradox as a DDE client, follow these steps:

1. Open the DDE server application from the Windows Program Manager. For this example, use Microsoft Excel. If you do not have Excel, use another Windows spreadsheet.

2. Open the spreadsheet EXPENSES.XLS, which comes with Excel as a sample file (see fig. 11.1), or create your own spreadsheet. Consult your spreadsheet documentation for instructions on opening a spreadsheet.

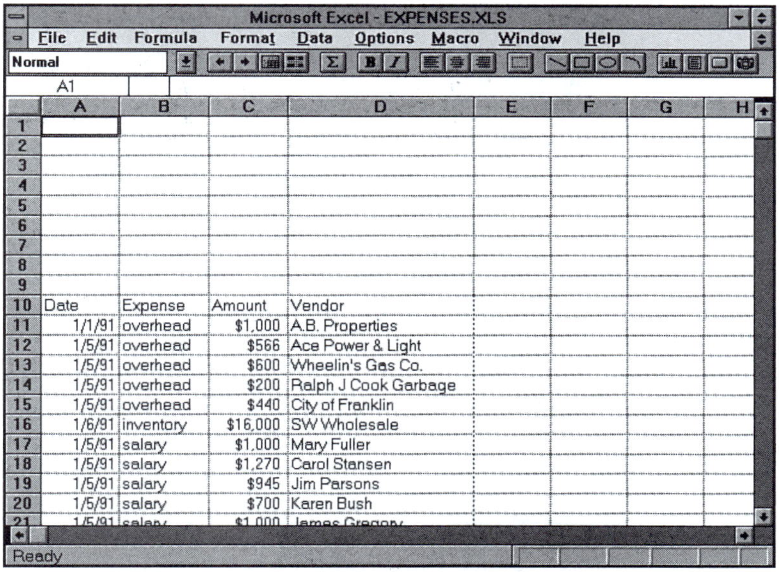

FIG. 11.1

An Excel spreadsheet EXPENSES.XLS.

3. Click one of the cells in the column labelled Vendor (the D column) to highlight it.

II — PARADOX FOR WINDOWS POWER TECHNIQUES

4. Choose Copy from the Edit menu. The cell is copied by Excel to the Windows Clipboard, as shown in figure 11.2.

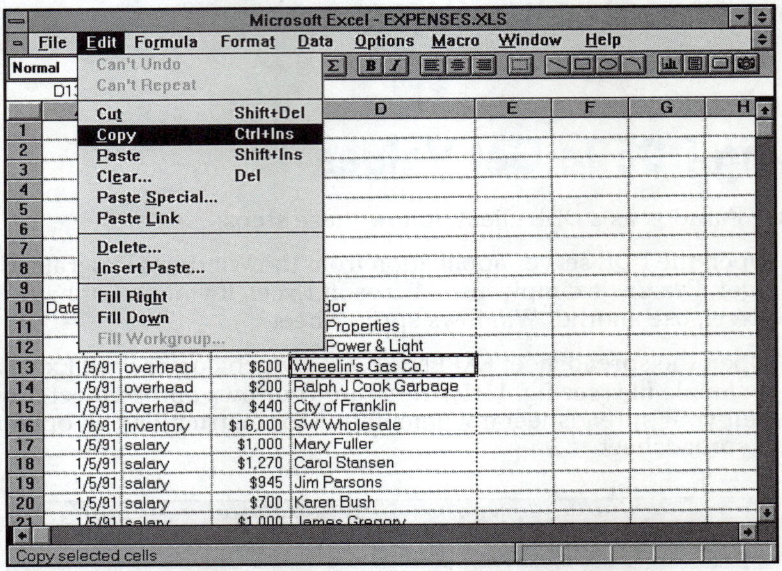

FIG. 11.2

Using the Excel copy command to copy a spreadsheet cell (or range) to the clipboard.

5. Switch to Paradox for Windows with the Task Switcher by pressing Ctrl+Esc and then choosing Paradox for Windows from the Task List.

    If you have not already launched a session of Paradox for Windows, launch Paradox from the Program Manager.

6. Choose File, Open, Table to open the table that will receive the data. For this example, use the VENDORS.DB table furnished with Paradox (see fig. 11.3), or create your own similar table.

7. Press F9 or click the Edit button to switch to Edit mode. Press Insert to insert a blank row. Place the cursor in the Vendor Name field and then choose Paste Link from the Edit menu. A formula appears in the field, indicating the location of the value to be pasted (see fig. 11.4).

8. To view the spreadsheet, select the DDE field and press Shift+F2. Excel opens, displaying the spreadsheet you used for DDE.

11 — EXCHANGING DATA WITH OTHER APPLICATIONS

FIG. 11.3

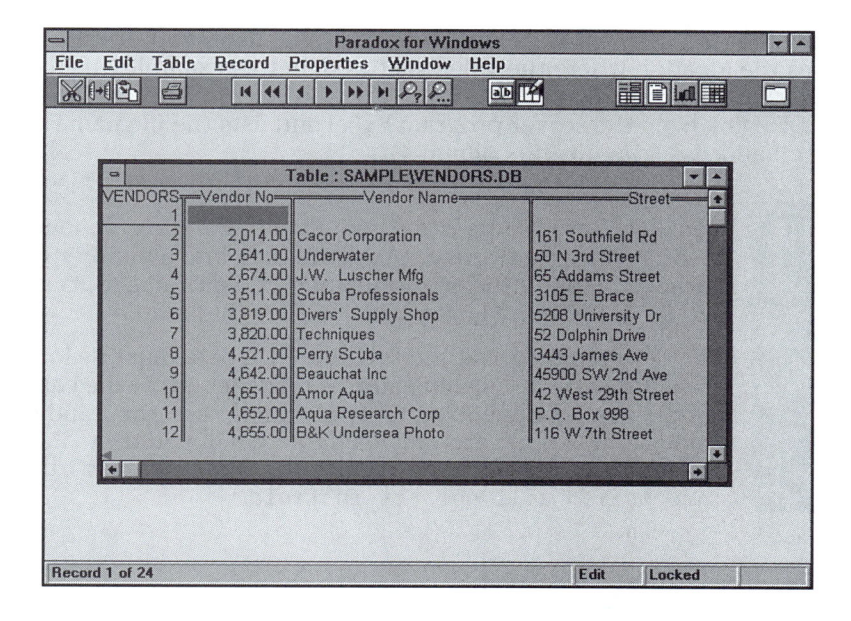

The VENDORS.DB table before using DDE.

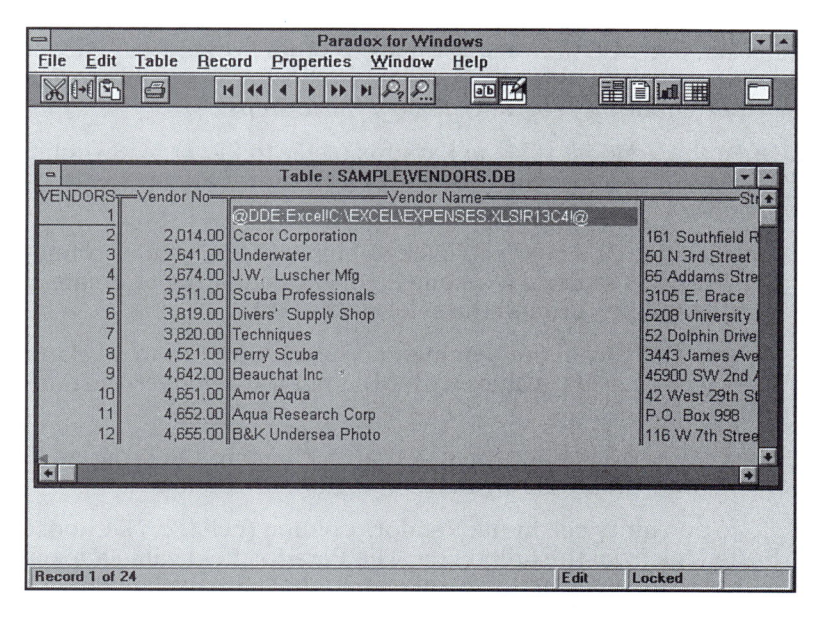

FIG. 11.4

A DDE formula linking a Paradox field to an Excel spreadsheet cell.

Notice that the DDE link does not store the value itself; rather, DDE stores the location where the value is stored. In this example, the formula @DDE:Excel!C:\EXCEL\EXPENSES.XLS!R13C4!@ identifies the link as a DDE link from the server program Excel and lists the file name and the cell address (row 13 and column 4).

> **NOTE** You can use DDE to paste data only into Paradox alphanumeric fields. If you attempt to paste data into a number field, Paradox displays the error message `Illegal character` and dims the Paste Link option on the Edit menu.
>
> The Paradox field that receives the DDE data must be long enough to hold the calling address. The length of the calling address varies depending on application, directory, and file names, but is often around 40 characters. If you try to Paste Link to a shorter field, you receive the error message `Link information will not fit in field`.

Using DDE To Send Values

Paradox can use DDE to transfer values to other Windows applications. Try the following example to move data from a Paradox table to Excel (or another Windows program). Follow these steps:

1. Open the Vendors table in Paradox (refer to fig. 11.3). Switch to Edit mode by pressing F9 or clicking the Edit Data button in the SpeedBar.

2. Move to the Title field and click to highlight the Vendor Name field. (To select more than one field, click and drag to create a highlighted box around the selected fields.)

3. Choose Copy from the Edit menu or press Ctrl+Ins. (You also can use Cut to transfer values with DDE, but Cut removes the data from the field.)

4. Use the Task Switcher (press Ctrl+Esc) to go to the Program Manager and open Excel (if you have not already done so).

5. Go to an empty cell in the Vendors column (cell D257). Choose Paste Link from the Edit menu. The Paradox field value appears, with the link information displayed in the message line directly above the spreadsheet (see fig. 11.5).

FIG. 11.5

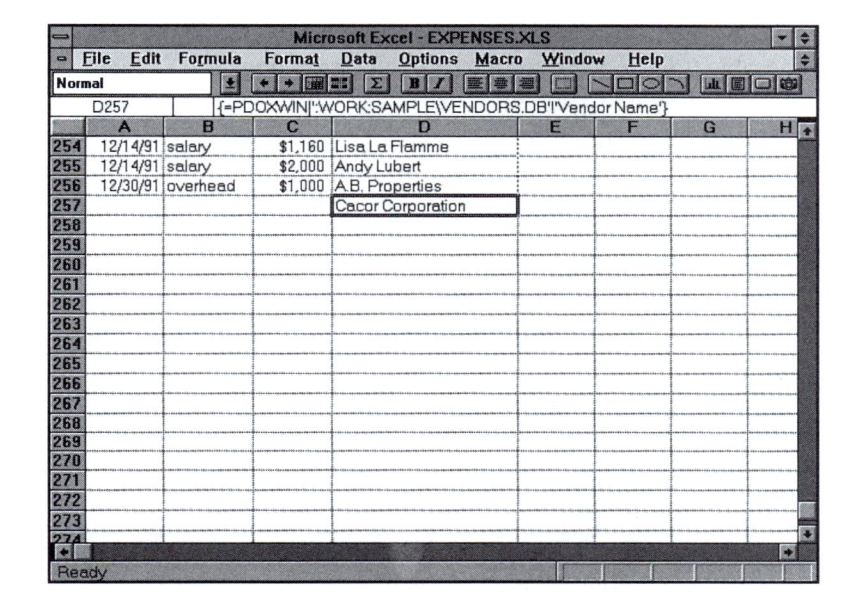

An Excel spreadsheet with a DDE link to a Paradox table.

6. Switch back to the Paradox window and move the cursor through the table. As you move through the table, the value displayed in the Excel spreadsheet changes. You now have linked the spreadsheet to the database.

> **NOTE** You can establish only one active DDE link between two applications at a time. After you open a Paradox table with a DDE link to a spreadsheet, for example, you cannot open another table and create a second DDE link to another application (even if the link is to the same spreadsheet). If you attempt to create a second link, Paradox dims the Paste Link option in the Edit menu.

What Is OLE?

As its name implies, *Object Linking and Embedding* enables you to embed an object in an application that is linked to another application. An *embedded* object includes, or encapsulates, the data needed to create it. You can open an embedded object and modify the underlying data.

When you leave the object by switching from the application that created the object to another application, your changes are saved and reflected in the object you embedded in the linked application.

OLE enables you to run other OLE-capable Windows software without leaving Paradox. For instance, you may want to use your favorite graphics program or word processor to create or modify files, and take advantage of OLE to access them from a Paradox database.

OLE objects are used in Paradox for Windows data tables and in Paradox design objects (forms and reports). Note that OLE fields are not available in dBASE or Paradox for DOS tables.

NOTE Although a graphic field is used for this example, OLE also can be used for other data types, such as text or numbers.

Placing OLE Objects in Design Documents

You may want to embellish a data-entry form with a clever graphic that indicates the current weather report. Rather than redefine the Paradox form every day, you can create an OLE object that references the graphic so that you can access the drawing by using the program that created it. As you change the graphic to show weather changes, the graphic will be displayed automatically on Paradox forms that contain the OLE object. An OLE object in a design document is different from an OLE field in a table, because the object is not entered by the user and does not change from one record to the next.

To create an OLE object in a design document, follow these steps:

1. Use the Windows Paintbrush program (or another OLE-capable program) to create a sunny graphic for a bright summer day, as shown in figure 11.6.

2. Save the file as WEATHER.BMP.

3. Select the contents of the graphic by clicking the Pick tool, clicking on one corner of the image, and then dragging the mouse pointer to the opposite corner of the graphic (see fig. 11.7).

4. Choose Copy from the Edit menu (see fig. 11.8) or press Ctrl+C to move the graphic to the paste buffer. (You also can use Cut to move OLE objects.) The paste buffer is a temporary holding place for data to be transferred between Windows applications.

11 — EXCHANGING DATA WITH OTHER APPLICATIONS   463

FIG. 11.6

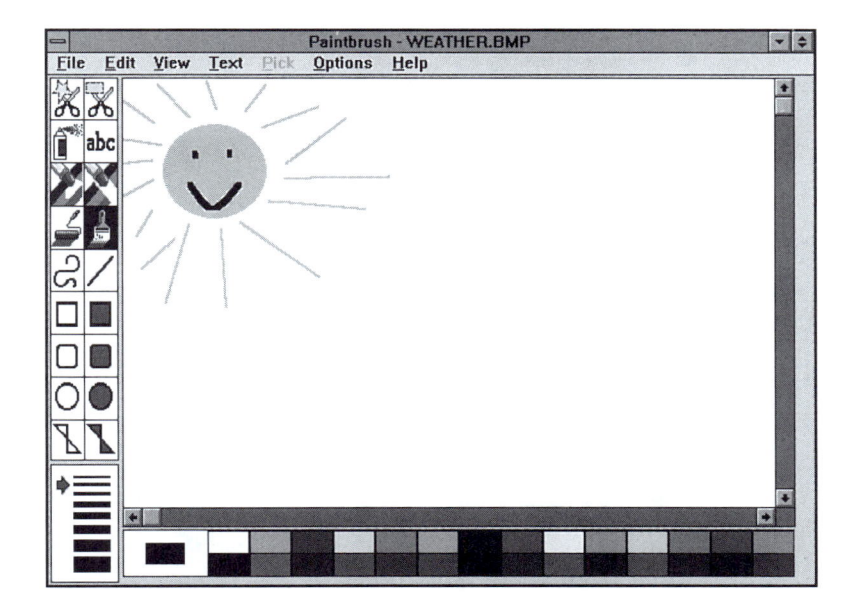

Summer graphic in Microsoft Paintbrush (WEATHER.BMP).

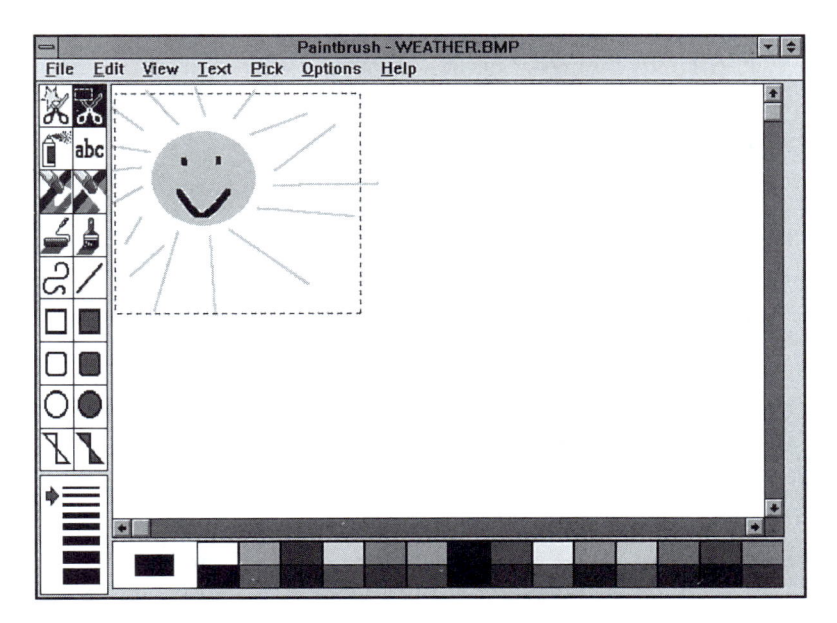

FIG. 11.7

Selecting the graphic in Paintbrush to paste into Paradox.

II — PARADOX FOR WINDOWS POWER TECHNIQUES

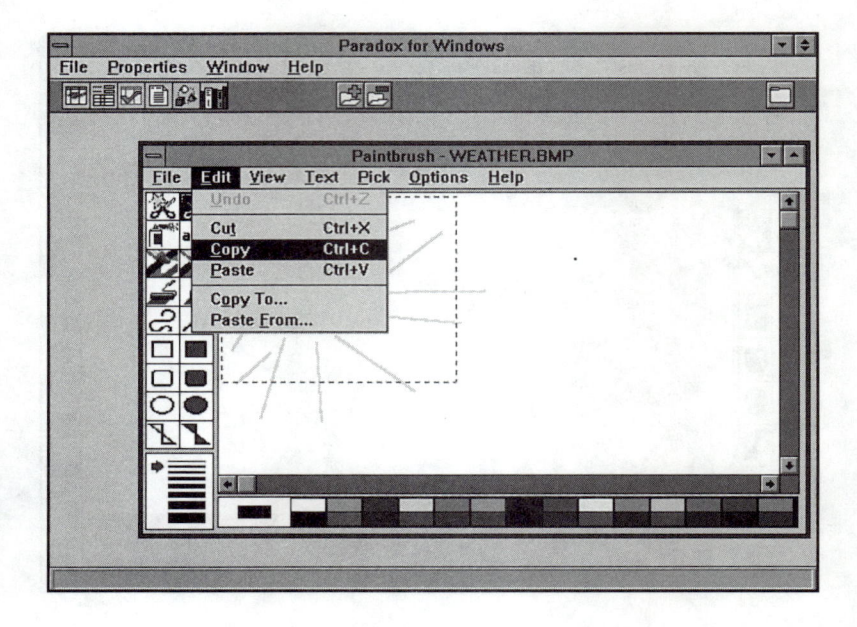

FIG. 11.8

The Windows Paintbrush Edit menu.

5. Switch to Paradox by clicking the Control menu and selecting S<u>w</u>itch To, or by pressing Ctrl+Esc.

6. Choose the Program Manager and start Paradox or choose Paradox from the Task List if you are already running Paradox.

7. Create a new Paradox form by choosing <u>N</u>ew, <u>F</u>orm from the <u>F</u>ile menu. Choose the Albums table and the default layout. The Form Design window appears, as shown in figure 11.9.

8. In the Form Design window, click the OLE tool. Then place the OLE object where you want it to appear in the form. A box labeled Undefined OLE appears (see fig. 11.10).

9. Right-click to display the properties menu for the OLE object. Choose Define OLE and then Paste Paintbrush. The graphic appears in the Paradox form (see fig. 11.11).

10. Click the Run button (the lightning bolt) to see how the form looks.

11. Switch back to the Paintbrush program and change the drawing. When you go back to the Paradox form, after choosing <u>F</u>ile, <u>U</u>pdate from Paintbrush, your changes appear in the form.

FIG. 11.9

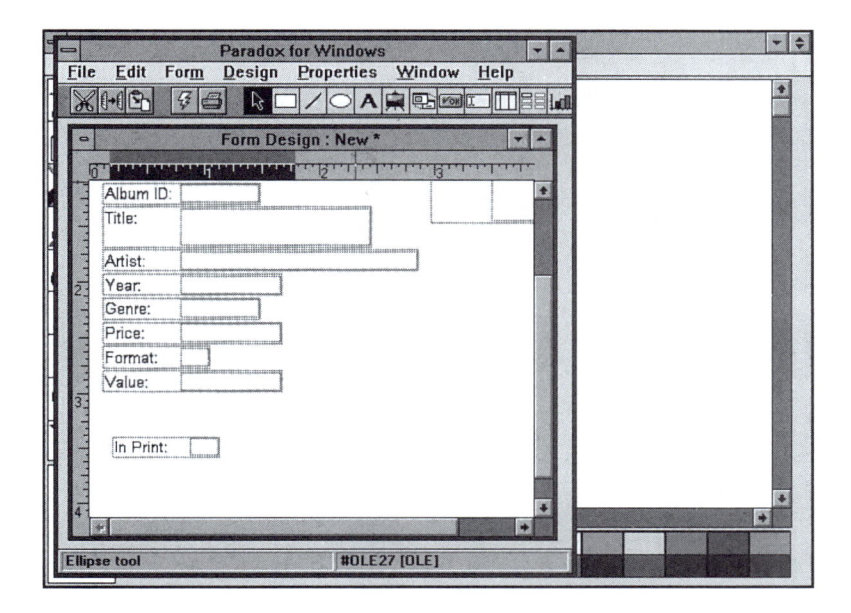

The Paradox Form Design window.

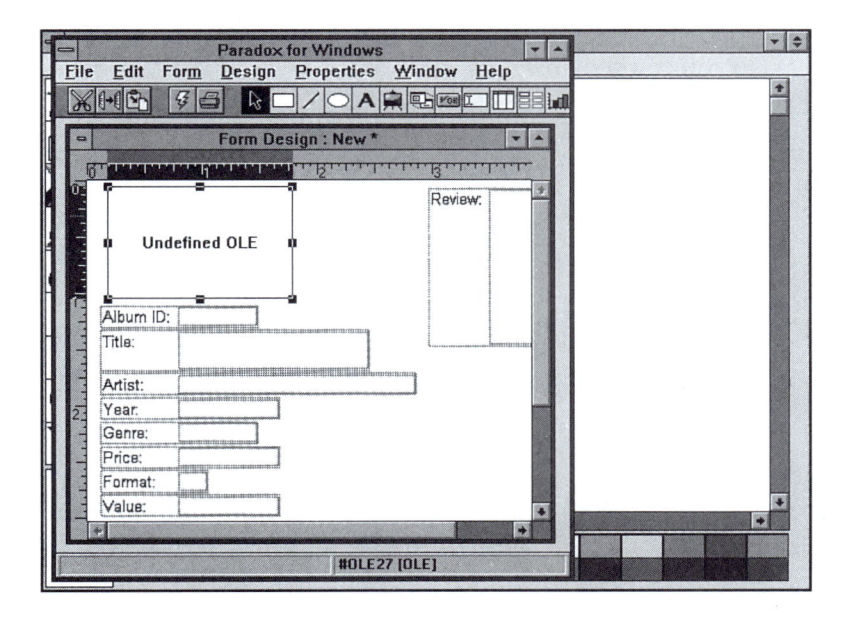

FIG. 11.10

Undefined OLE object in the Paradox form design window.

II — PARADOX FOR WINDOWS POWER TECHNIQUES

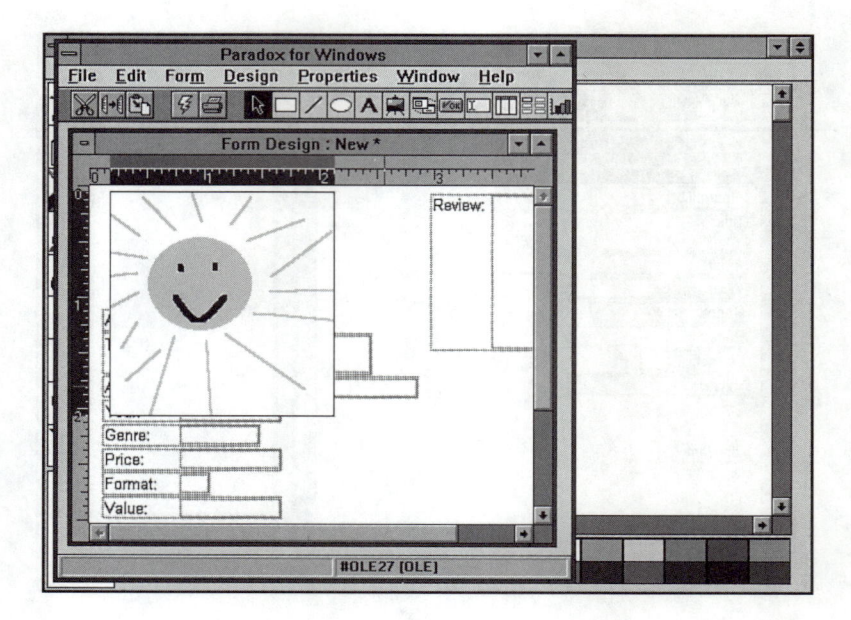

FIG. 11.11

The OLE graphic in the form design window.

Figure 11.12 shows both the Paradox and Paintbrush windows on-screen, so you can see how your edits of the WEATHER.BMP file affect the Paradox form.

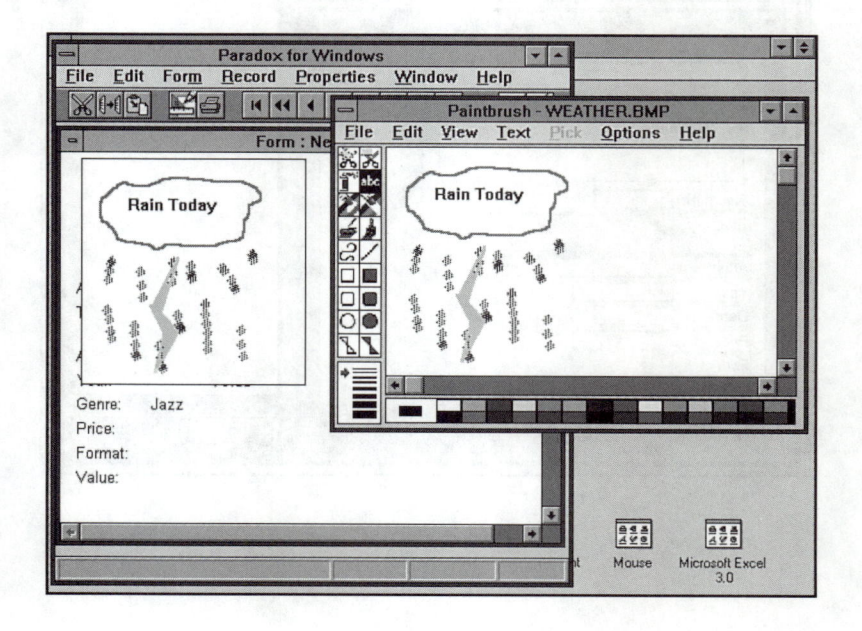

FIG. 11.12

Editing the OLE graphic and viewing the Paradox form.

Placing OLE Fields in Tables

Another way to use OLE with Paradox is to place an OLE field in a Paradox table. This means that your data table will reference a file created by another program. This OLE file could be a graphic, text, sound, or other file.

To define an OLE field, follow these steps:

1. Define a field in a Paradox table with the field type of OLE. For this example, add a field called OLE Album Cover in the Albums table.

2. Use the graphic created in the previous example (WEATHER.BMP). Press Ctrl+Esc and use the Task Switcher to run the Windows Paintbrush program and open the file, as shown earlier in figure 11.6.

3. Select the contents of the field by clicking the Cut tool, clicking on one corner of the image, and then dragging the mouse pointer to the opposite corner of the graphic.

4. Choose Copy from the Edit menu or press Ctrl+C to move the graphic to the paste buffer.

5. Switch to Paradox by clicking the Control menu and selecting Switch To or by pressing Ctrl+Esc.

6. Open ALBUMS.DB by choosing File, Open, Table from the Paradox Desktop. The Table Edit window appears (see fig. 11.13).

7. Press F9 or click the Edit button to switch to Edit mode. Choose Edit, Paste Link. The graphic appears in the Paradox form (see fig. 11.14).

> **TIP**
>
> OLE enables you to create databases that let users access other applications without ever leaving Paradox. For example, you could set up a database to track all office correspondence, using an OLE field to store a copy of each letter sent. To view or edit the letter, you could simply double-click the field or press Shift+F2 and instantly you would open the source application and the correct file.

FIG. 11.13

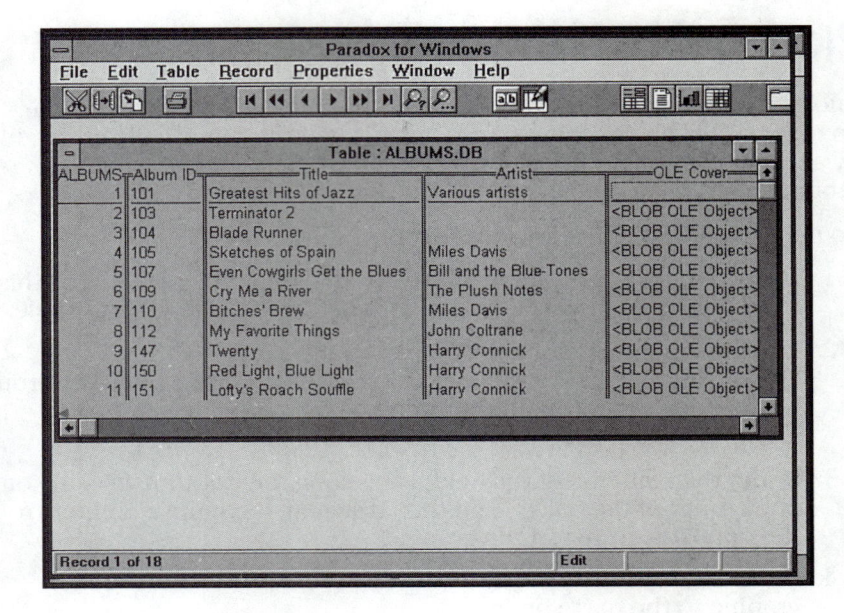

The Table Edit window showing ALBUMS.DB.

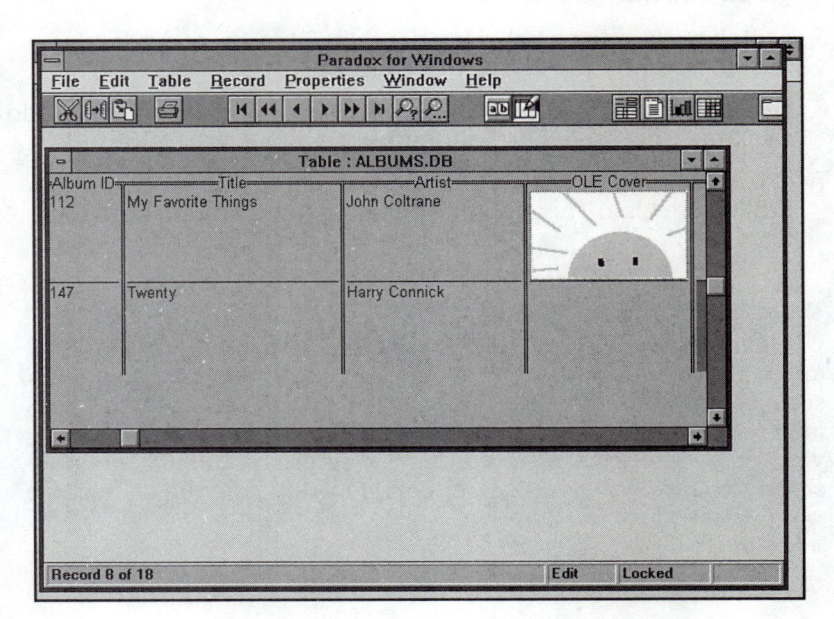

FIG. 11.14

OLE data pasted into ALBUMS.DB.

Changing an OLE Object's Properties

Like all Paradox objects, OLE objects have a set of properties that you can control through the properties menu (see fig. 11.15). To display the properties menu, select the OLE object and right-click.

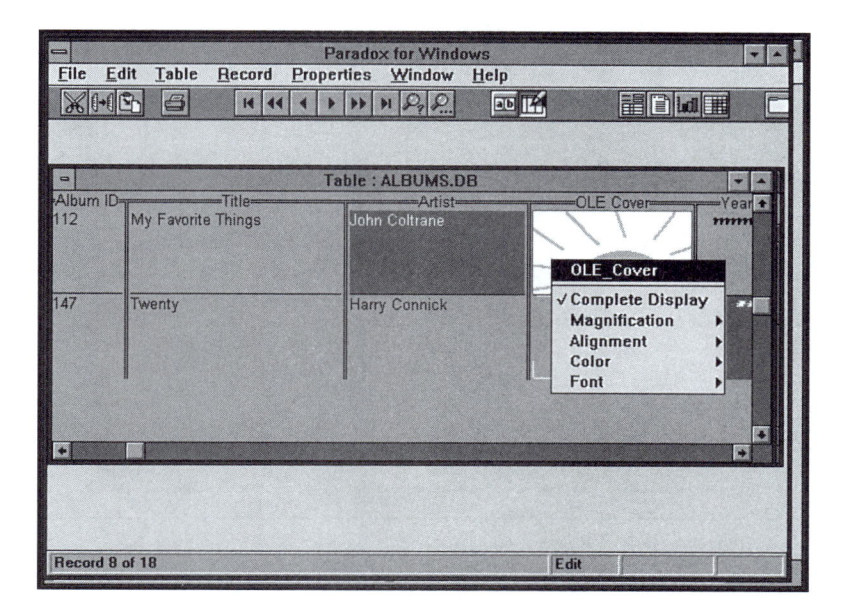

FIG. 11.15

OLE data field object properties menu.

The properties available for an OLE data field are similar to the properties for graphic fields. For example, you can change the magnification of an image, include vertical or horizontal scroll bars, place a frame around the object, glue the object in place on the form, and attach ObjectPAL methods. ObjectPAL is discussed in Part III.

An OLE object in a design document has a property that ordinary graphic objects do not possess—Define OLE. To see these properties, right-click the OLE object to display the properties menu and then choose Define OLE. Two choices appear in the Define OLE submenu: Paste and Edit (see fig. 11.16).

- *Paste.* Establishes a link between the OLE server and client, copying an object from the server application and pasting that object in the client application. If you later change the original object, however, the linked object does not reflect those changes. This is called a *cold link.*

II — PARADOX FOR WINDOWS POWER TECHNIQUES

- *Edit.* Opens an object's source application when the object is opened. For example, if you created an object in Windows Paintbrush, Edit activates Paintbrush and opens the object.

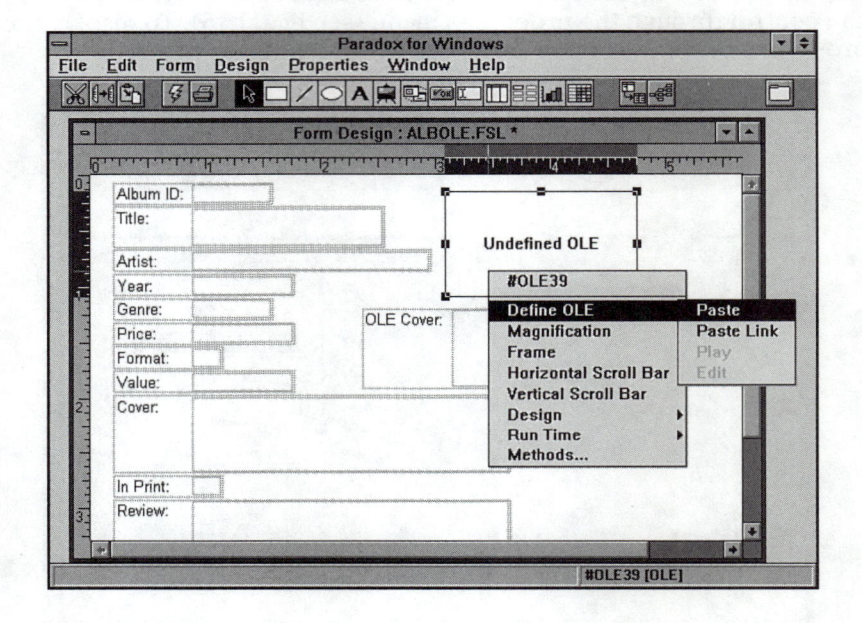

FIG. 11.16

OLE object in a design document properties menu.

Now that you know how to use DDE and OLE, how do you decide which to use? In general, you should use DDE to transfer small, discrete pieces of data into Paradox, or if you need to link data originating in Paradox. OLE is used when you need to access larger data elements from Paradox, or if you want to be able to run the server program from Paradox. Table 11.1 summarizes the features of each.

Table 11.1. Feature Comparison of DDE and OLE

Feature	DDE	OLE
Automatic link	Optional	Mandatory
Speed	Faster	Slower
Memory requirements	Lower	Higher
Storage requirements	Lower	Higher
Capacity	Small	Large
Client support	Yes	Yes
Server support	Yes	No

For Related Information

◂◂ "Entering Data in OLE Fields," p. 142.

◂◂ "Adding OLE Objects," p. 237.

Chapter Summary

Paradox for Windows opens up new opportunities to connect to other data on your PC or network. By using Dynamic Data Exchange (DDE) and Object Linking and Embedding (OLE), you can link Paradox tables and forms to files created and maintained in other software programs. These data-exchange methods make data storage simpler because they enable you to store data in only one place.

Both DDE and OLE have limitations. If you need maximum control of data integrity, you are much better off to store all your data in Paradox so that you can enforce referential integrity, range checks, and other relational database rules. Moreover, if your Paradox database depends on values from foreign spreadsheet or documents, unforeseen changes in those data sources can threaten your Paradox data.

Now that you have learned how to use Paradox links to other applications, you are ready to explore the files that make up a Paradox database and the techniques used to handle these files. Chapter 12 shows how to use file utilities, folders, and the Paradox File Browser.

CHAPTER 12

Working with Your Files

While you build your database application, Paradox creates files. Even a small database is likely to consist of several dozen files, and for each Paradox for Windows object you create, you may be making several files. A table, for example, uses a file for the data itself and other files for such things as indexes and validation checks.

If you have completed the exercises in the previous chapters of this book, you have created a table called ALBUMS. If you browse through your working directory, you should find files with a file name of ALBUMS and extensions of DB, MB, PX, TV, VAL, and others. This chapter explains the file types that Paradox for Windows creates and describes the utilities that help you manage your Paradox files.

Paradox does not maintain a catalog of the files that make up your database. In fact, the concept of a database application consisting of tables and related objects does not truly exist in Paradox. The good news is that where the database files are located doesn't matter; an application can use files spread across many directories on local or network drives, and multiple applications may coexist in a single directory. In addition, tables and other objects may be shared by multiple applications. The bad news is that you must work hard to keep track of where you place files and of the possible implications of renaming or deleting Paradox objects. You also must go to special lengths to devise strategies for backing up and restoring your databases, because Paradox lacks its own backup capabilities.

Before you can access your database files, you must find them. One way to sort through your hard disk is to use DOS commands such as TREE and DIR. You also can use commercial directory utility programs. If you prefer to view the directory structure graphically, you can use the Windows File Manager. Finally, Paradox for Windows has its own data-access feature: the File Browser. The next section explains how to use the File Browser.

> **TIP** Keep each database application in a subdirectory of its own. This practice simplifies backing up or moving the database.

> **CAUTION:** Never place an application in a DOS root directory. DOS allows fewer files in a root directory than in a subdirectory and you can easily run out of files in a root directory.

Using the File Browser

The File Browser feature gives you a mouse-driven method of navigating through the directories on your disk or network. This feature is similar to the Windows File Manager, in that File Browser also shows directories and files graphically. The File Browser is more convenient than the File Manager, however, because you can access it directly by clicking a button in dialog boxes that ask you for the name of a file.

For example, choose File, Open, Form from the Paradox desktop. The Open Document dialog box appears (see fig. 12.1). To use the File Browser, press the Browse button at the bottom of the dialog box. The Browser window opens (see fig. 12.2).

The Browser also can be accessed from other dialog boxes where you choose file names, as shown in Table 12.1.

Table 12.1. Dialog Boxes Offering the File Browser

Dialog Box	File Type
Add Table	Table
File Export	Various export formats
File Import	Various import formats

12 — WORKING WITH YOUR FILES

Dialog Box	File Type
Open Table	Table
Open Document	Form, Report
Select File	Query
Table Add	Table
Table Delete	Table
Table Empty	Table

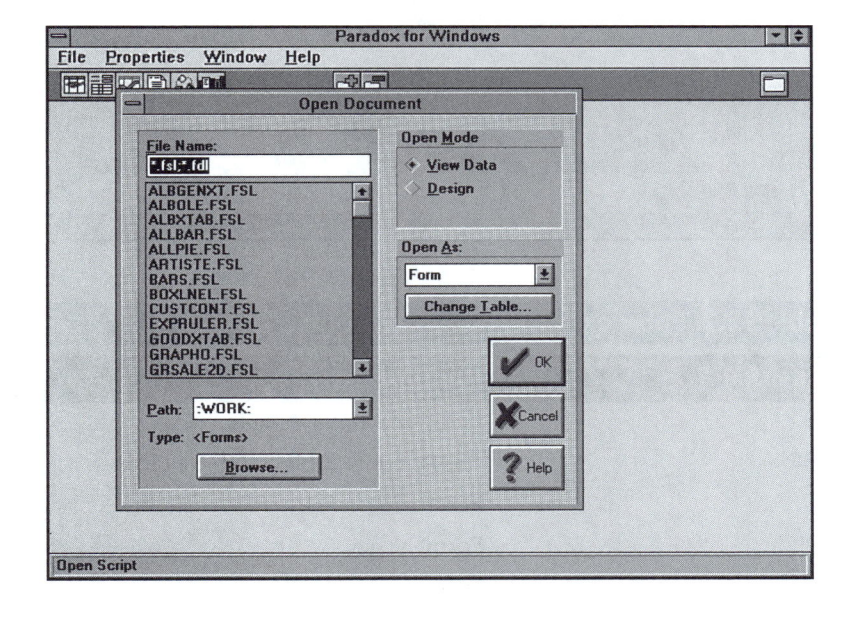

FIG. 12.1

The Open Document dialog box.

When you open the Browser, you see a top-level directory for the current disk drive. The Browser window lists subdirectories and files in alphabetical order so that you can easily find the file you need.

You can change the display to view any of the disk drives available to you. You can use the Aliases drop-down menu to switch drives. (You also can create aliases to represent directories, as discussed later in this chapter.)

The Browser window displays the contents of the current directory, using icons to show the type of file you are viewing. Files with extensions that Paradox cannot recognize are displayed as binary files.

Table 12.2 lists Paradox for Windows file types.

II — PARADOX FOR WINDOWS POWER TECHNIQUES

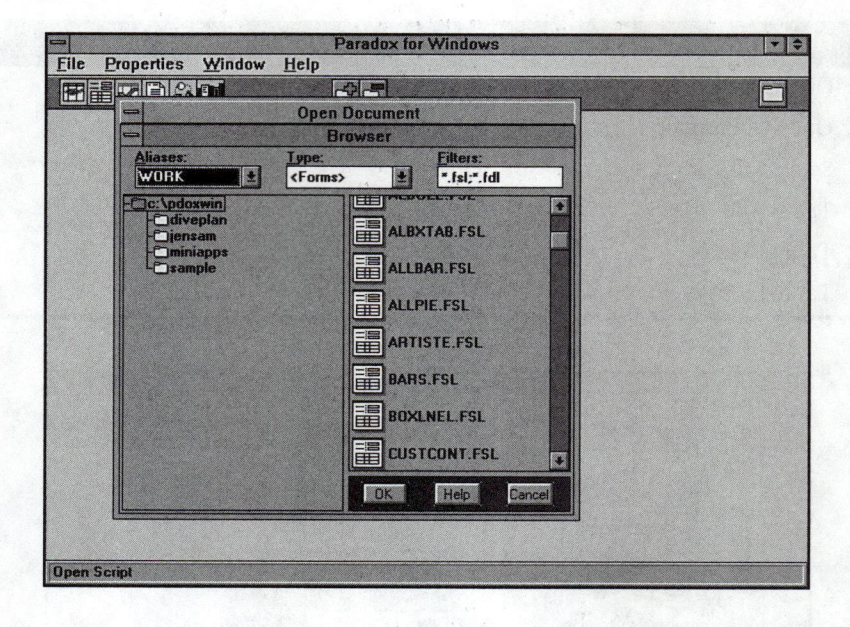

FIG. 12.2

The Browser Window.

Table 12.2. Paradox for Windows File Types

Extension	File Type
DB	Paradox database table
DBF	dBASE-compatible database table
F	Form
FDL	Form
FSL	Form
FTL	Compiled Form
MB	Memo/BLOB data associated with table
PX	Primary Index
QBE	Query by Example
RSL	Report
RDL	Report
SDL	Script
SSL	Script
SQL	SQL query

Extension	File Type
TV	Table View Settings
VAL	Validation checks associated with table
X01	Table index, with last two numbers incremented
Y01	Table index, with last two numbers incremented

The File Browser does not display all types of files in a directory. It restricts the files to the type you need in two ways: by restricting the file type and by using filters.

The Type pull-down menu at the top of the Browser window shows the type of file to be opened and is filled in by Paradox, depending on which dialog box you were using when you pressed the Browse button.

A filter gives you even greater control. By default, Paradox fills in filters to match the file type. You can specify all or part of the target file type. For example, you could specify *.NDX to show only dBASE index files or ALBUMS.* to show all files associated with the Albums table. The asterisk is the DOS wild card, which stands for one or more missing characters.

To change the filter, simply type the filter expression in the Filters field. If you want to use more than one filter expression, separate each expression with a semicolon, as in *.FSL;*.F.

Table Utilities

You already have learned how to create new Paradox objects and edit existing Paradox objects, using the File, New and the File, Open menu commands discussed in earlier chapters. Paradox also supplies special utilities to move data to and from tables; to delete, rename, and copy objects; and to perform other database administrative functions.

To access Paradox utilities, choose Utilities from the File menu of the Paradox desktop. The Paradox Utilities menu appears (see fig. 12.3).

The following sections group Utilities together by function and include references to other methods for accomplishing the same tasks from other Paradox menus.

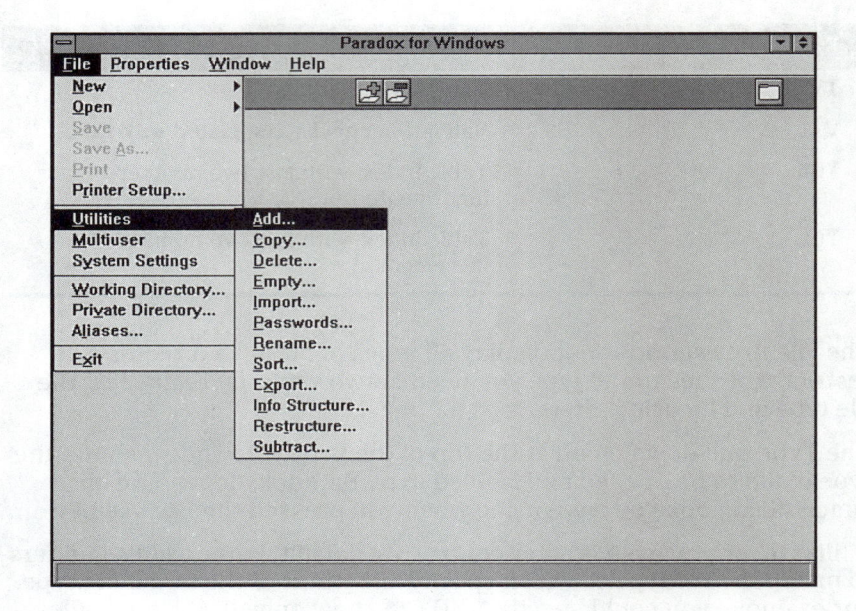

FIG. 12.3

The Utilities menu.

Transferring Records from One Table to Another

To transfer records from one table to another, use the Utilities, Add option by following these steps:

1. Choose File, Utilities, Add. The Table Add dialog box appears (see fig. 12.4).

2. Select the name of the source table in the Tables list box, or type the file name in the Add Records From Source Table text box. If the table is not in the current directory, type the entire DOS file name, including the directory path.

3. Select the name of the destination table in the Tables list box, or type the file name in the To Target Table text box. If the table is not in the current directory, type the entire DOS file name, including the directory path.

NOTE To view tables in other directories, click the Browse button and use the File Browser (described earlier in this chapter).

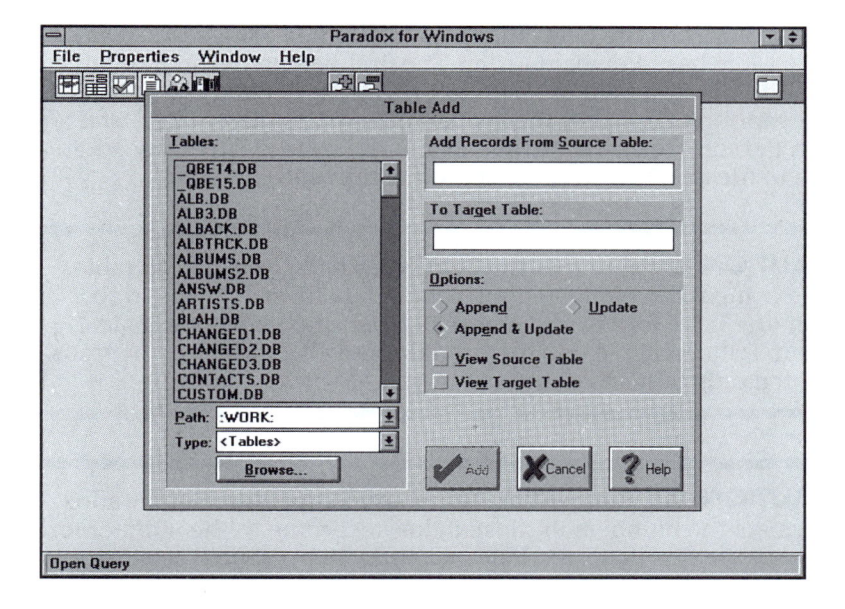

FIG. 12.4

The Table Add dialog box.

4. Choose one of the following Options by clicking the appropriate check box:

   Append. Choose this option to add all nonmatching records to the destination table. Paradox places duplicate records in the Keyviol (key violation) table, where you can edit or discard them.

   Update. Choose this option to replace duplicate records in the destination table with records from the source table. Paradox copies the replaced records to the Changed temporary table and discards nonmatching records.

   Append & Update. Choose this option to replace duplicate records with records from the source table and add nonmatching records to the destination table. Paradox writes records to the Keyviol and Changed tables as described in the preceding paragraphs.

   In keyed tables, Paradox determines duplicate records by the values in the key fields. In unkeyed tables, including dBASE-type tables, records are never considered duplicates.

5. To view the source table or the destination table, click the View Source Table or View Target Table check box. To view both tables, click both check boxes.

6. Click the Add button. Paradox transfers records from the source table to the destination table.

Paradox matches the fields in the source table to the fields in the destination table based on field order. The first field in the source table is copied to the first field of the target table, the second field of the source table is copied to the second field of the target table, and so on. When Paradox reaches the last field of the source table, any additional fields in the destination table are left blank (null).

> **CAUTION:** Be sure that the field types and sizes in both tables are compatible. You cannot transfer data from a date field to a number field, for example, or data from a text field to a logical field. Data in memo, binary, graphic, and OLE fields can be transferred only to fields of the same type.

> **CAUTION:** All number-field types are compatible, but Paradox formats the numbers in those fields according to the number format of the destination table. If an alphanumeric field is shorter in the destination table than in the source table, Paradox truncates the field, and you may lose data.

Subtracting Records in One Table from Another

Just as you can transfer records from one table to another, you can subtract the records in one table from another table. If two sales representatives maintain separate tables of customer names, for example, you may want to delete from one table the names that appear in both tables.

To subtract records, follow these steps:

1. Choose File, Utilities, Subtract. The Table Subtract dialog box appears (see fig. 12.5).

> **CAUTION:** The tables you use in a subtract operation must be the same table type and must have the same field types and field order. Paradox does not warn you that table structures are different before it attempts a subtract operation, so you may want to create a backup of the table first.

12 — WORKING WITH YOUR FILES

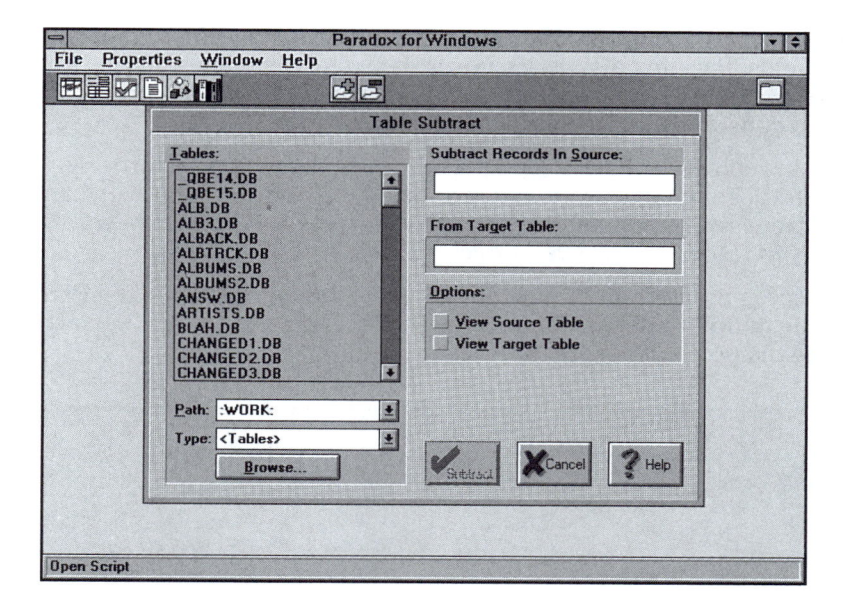

FIG. 12.5

The Table Subtract dialog box.

For Related Information
◄◄ "Restructuring a Table," p. 111.

FROM HERE...

Renaming Paradox Objects

You can rename any Paradox object (tables, forms, reports, and so on) that you create. In most cases, renaming an object is as simple as changing its DOS file name.

For tables, however, you must follow some special procedures. Changing a table name can affect many DOS files and Paradox objects.

Restructuring and Sorting Tables

In a relational database, the order of records within a table is usually irrelevant. After all, you can retrieve information in queries and reports in any desired sort order, or search for records by field values during record entry. Sometimes, however, you may want to control the order of records within a table.

II — PARADOX FOR WINDOWS POWER TECHNIQUES

The best way to sort a table is by designating a key field. In tables with key fields, Paradox displays records based on the values in the key fields. As new records are added or modified, the display order is updated constantly so that records are always in key order.

In unkeyed tables, Paradox displays records based on the order in which those records were entered. Using the Sort function, you can rearrange records in an unkeyed table, or you can create a new unkeyed table from a keyed table.

To access the Sort function, choose File, Utilities, Sort from the Paradox desktop or choose Table, Sort from the table window. The Sort Table dialog box appears (see fig. 12.6).

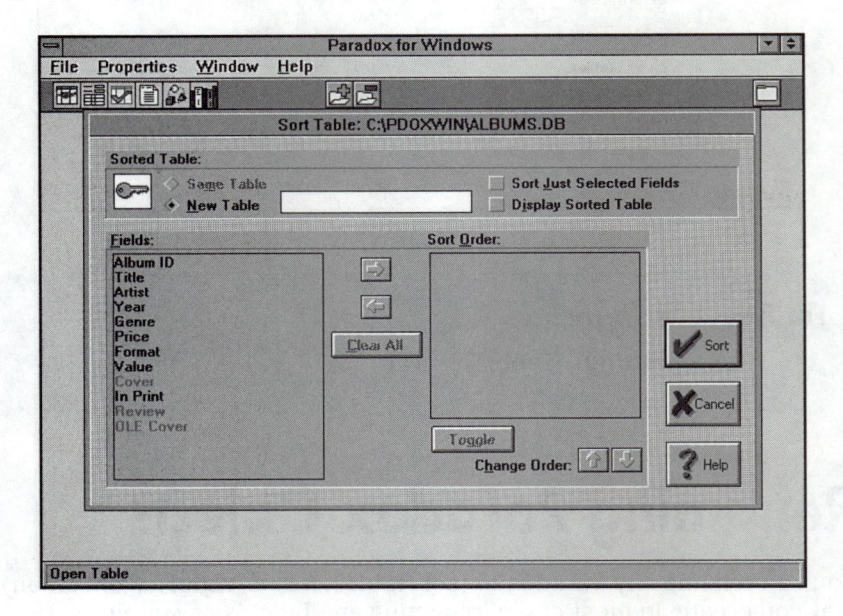

FIG. 12.6

Sort Table dialog box.

The top of the dialog box lists four sorting options. A key indicator is shown next to the key field of the table to remind you how the table is sorted by default. Indicate your choices by clicking on the appropriate check box. The sorting options are as follows:

- *Same Table*. Sorts to the current table. This choice is available only for unkeyed tables.

- *New Table*. Sorts to a new table. (If you are sorting to a new table, you must type a table name in the text box.) You must use this option if you are sorting a keyed table.

12 — WORKING WITH YOUR FILES

483

- *Sort Just Selected Fields.* Sorts only the fields listed in the Sort Order List box.

- *Display Sorted Table.* Displays the resulting table when the sort is complete. (Otherwise, Paradox returns to the point where you requested the sort.)

You cannot sort based on graphic, binary, memo, formatted memo, or OLE fields. Paradox for Windows dims the names of fields of these types in the Fields list box, indicating that you cannot choose those fields.

To specify the sort order for the table, you must choose each of the fields to be used in the sort. To choose a field, click the field name in the Fields list box and then click the right-arrow button. The field name appears in the Sort Order list box. If you use multiple fields for sorting, the order in which you choose the fields determines the result of the sort.

The Sort Table dialog box contains the right-arrow button for moving fields to the Sort Order list box, the left-arrow button for removing fields from the list, the Change Order up-and-down arrow buttons for moving a selected field up or down in the Sort Order list box, and the Toggle button to change the type of sort order selected. If you want to start over, click the Clear All button.

By default, Paradox uses ascending sort order (from lowest to highest values). A sort-order indicator appears before each field name in the Sort Order list box. To reverse the sort order, double-click the sort-order indicator (the 123... next to the field name), or press the Toggle button.

You can sort the Albums table by genre and artist into a new table GENART so that recordings are grouped by genre and within genres by artist names. To perform this sort operation, follow these steps:

1. Choose Utilities, Sort from the File menu or choose Table, Sort from the table window.

2. The Select File dialog box appears. Choose ALBUMS.DB and click OK. The Sort Table dialog box appears (refer to fig. 12.6). (If you choose to sort from the Table window, this step is unnecessary.)

3. Choose sort options and field names in the Sort Table dialog box. For this example, create a new table (GENART.DB) to hold the sorted data, and choose Genre and Artist as the sort fields, using ascending sort order (the default). You click Toggle to change to descending sort order.

4. Click the Sort button.

II — PARADOX FOR WINDOWS POWER TECHNIQUES

5. If you enter the name of an existing table as the sort destination, Paradox asks you to confirm whether the new sorted table will overwrite an existing table (see fig. 12.7).

Figure 12.8 shows the table before and after sorting.

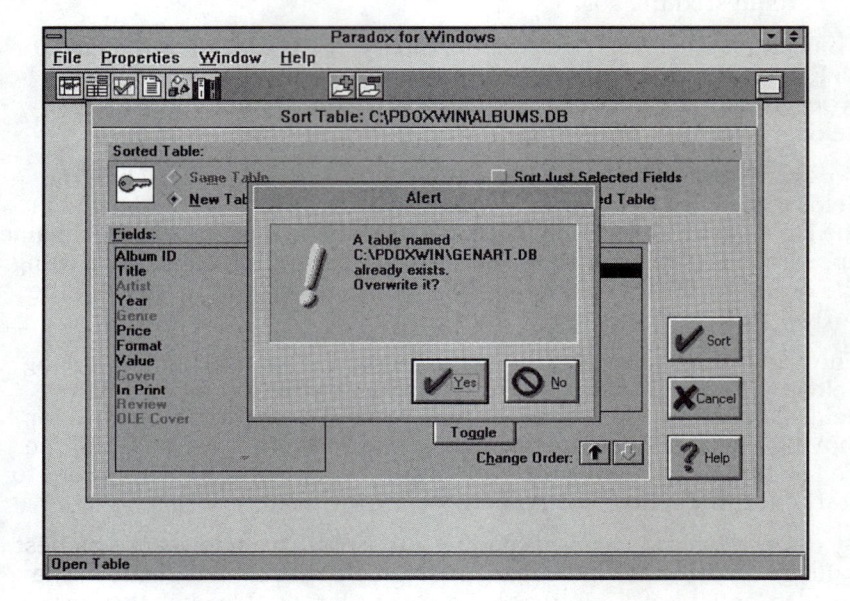

FIG. 12.7

Confirmation to overwrite existing file warning.

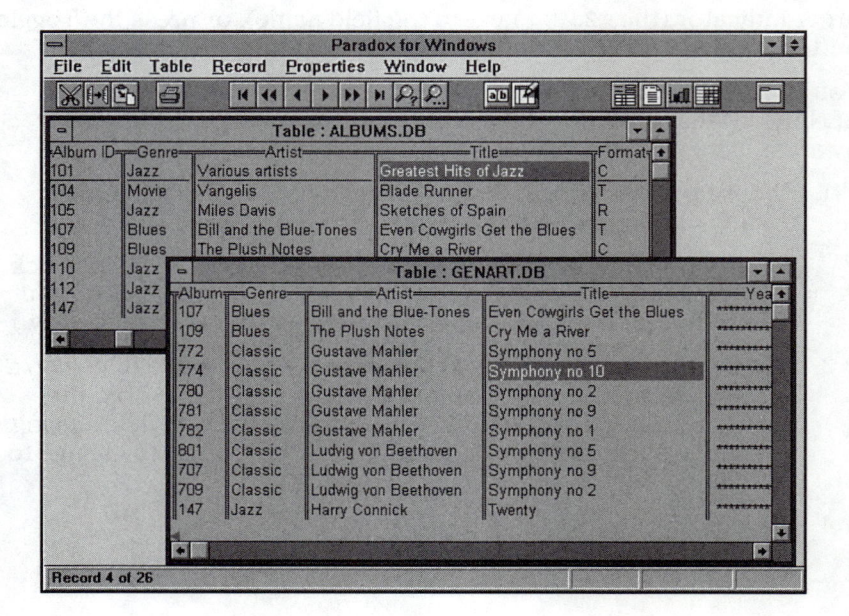

FIG. 12.8

Albums table sorted by genre and artist.

The Albums table is displayed in order by its key field (Album ID) and the sorted table is unkeyed (the Album IDs no longer are in order) and displayed in the sort order you chose in the Sort Table dialog box.

> **TIP**
>
> If you use keyed tables whenever possible, you do not have to sort your tables. If you use unkeyed tables, you must re-sort them whenever you add records. Another disadvantage of unkeyed tables is that they cannot detect duplicate entries.

> **CAUTION:** When you create new tables for sorted information, you are duplicating information in your database, wasting space, and threatening data integrity by permitting the same information to be updated in two different places.

For Related Information

◀◀ "Defining a Primary Key," p. 90.

Importing and Exporting Data

Although Paradox databases can directly access Paradox, dBASE, and SQL database server tables, from time to time you may need to incorporate files in other formats—for example, you may purchase a commercial mailing list or download a ZIP-code reference table from a bulletin board. Paradox for Windows enables you to import data in eight file formats, as shown in the following list:

Spreadsheet
  Quattro
  Quattro Pro for DOS
  Quattro Pro for Windows
  Lotus 1-2-3, Version 1.A
  Lotus 1-2-3, Version 2.x
  Excel

ASCII
  Fixed-length
  Delimited

Importing from a Spreadsheet

Paradox does not directly transfer spreadsheet data into an existing Paradox table. Instead, the program creates a new table whose structure copies the spreadsheet cells.

To import a spreadsheet, follow these steps:

1. Choose File, Utilities, Import. The File Import dialog box appears (see fig. 12.9).

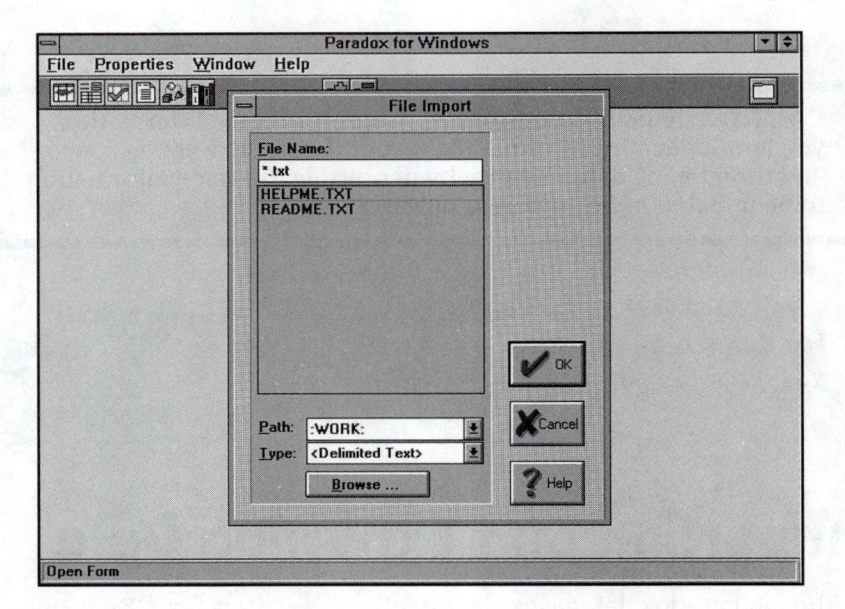

FIG. 12.9

The File Import dialog box.

2. Select the spreadsheet type by clicking the Type pull-down menu and clicking your choice (see fig. 12.10).

3. Choose the file name in the File Name box of the File Import dialog box. (If the file is not in the current directory, use Browse to change directories.) Click OK and the Spreadsheet Import dialog box appears (see fig. 12.11).

4. In the New Table Name box, type the file name of the table to be created.

5. Choose the table type for the new table by clicking the Paradox or dBASE check box. Paradox is the default table type.

12 — WORKING WITH YOUR FILES

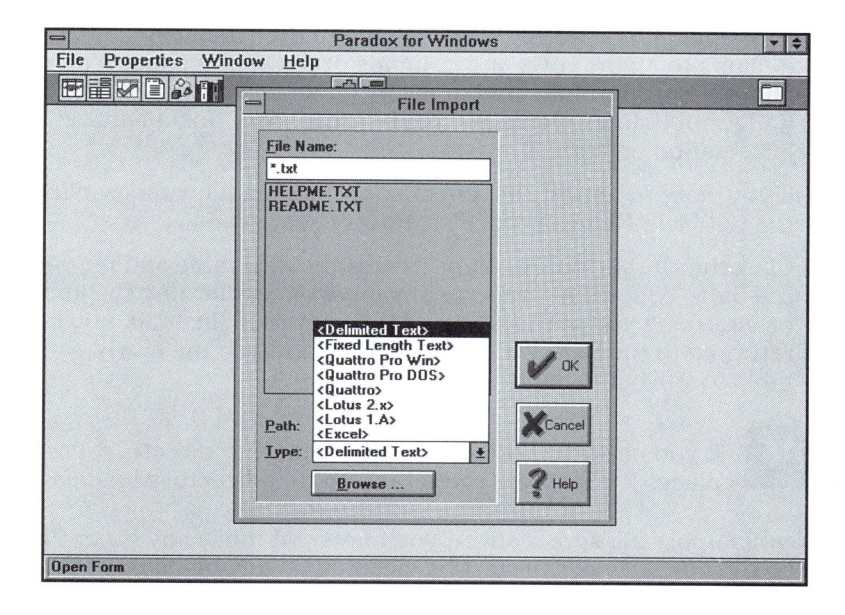

FIG. 12.10

The File Import dialog box with Type menu pulled down.

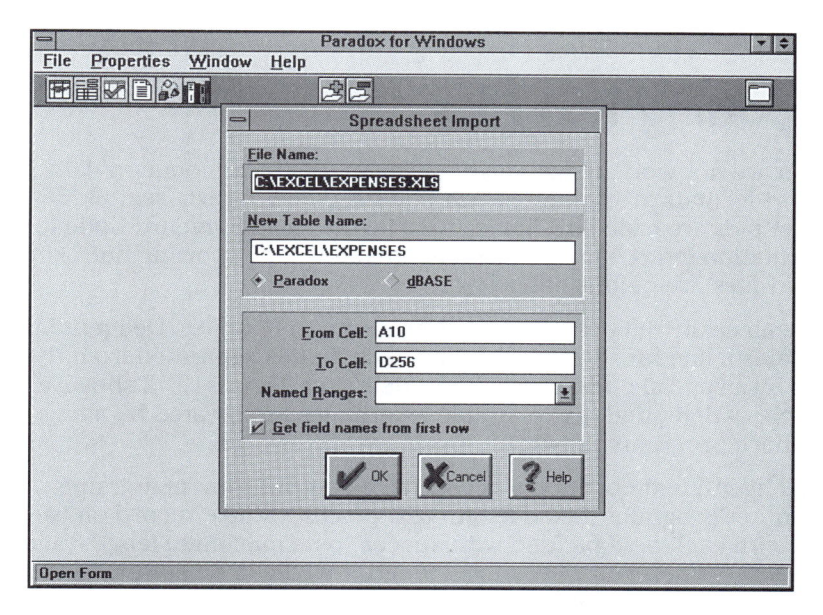

FIG. 12.11

The Spreadsheet Import dialog box.

6. Specify the range of spreadsheet cells to import. You can type the cell addresses in the From Cell and To Cell boxes, or you can type

the name of a range you have defined in the spreadsheet. Paradox defaults to all the rows and columns of the spreadsheet. You may choose to import a named range by choosing from the Named Ranges pull-down menu. See your spreadsheet documentation for information on named ranges.

7. If you want to import the spreadsheet's column headings, click the Get Field Names From First Row check box.

8. Click the OK button. Paradox creates the new table and imports the data. You will not receive any message confirming the import or informing you of the status of the operation. Instead, you are returned to the Paradox desktop. You can open the newly created table to verify the import.

NOTE If you import a spreadsheet from another directory, Paradox places the newly created table in that directory by default.

After you import the spreadsheet, you may treat it like any other Paradox table. You may want to start by cleaning up any blank rows that may have been imported and by adding a key field for the table. You also can change field names and lengths as needed.

Importing Text Files

If you are not working with a spreadsheet, the most common data import formats are delimited text and fixed-length text. Text files sometimes are called ASCII files for the American Standard Code for Information Interchange. The steps to follow for importing both kinds of text files are quite similar.

You can easily tell delimited from fixed-length text files. Delimited text contains a line for each record, and each field is separated from the next by a special character called a delimiter. Figure 12.12 shows a sample of delimited text. Variable length files are created by many database programs as output.

Fixed-length text commonly is created as output from mainframe computer programs. Fixed-length text places a single record on each line, with each field padded with spaces to its maximum length (see fig. 12.13). When you view a fixed-length text file in an editor, all the fields should line up as columns (be sure not to use a proportionally spaced font).

12 — WORKING WITH YOUR FILES

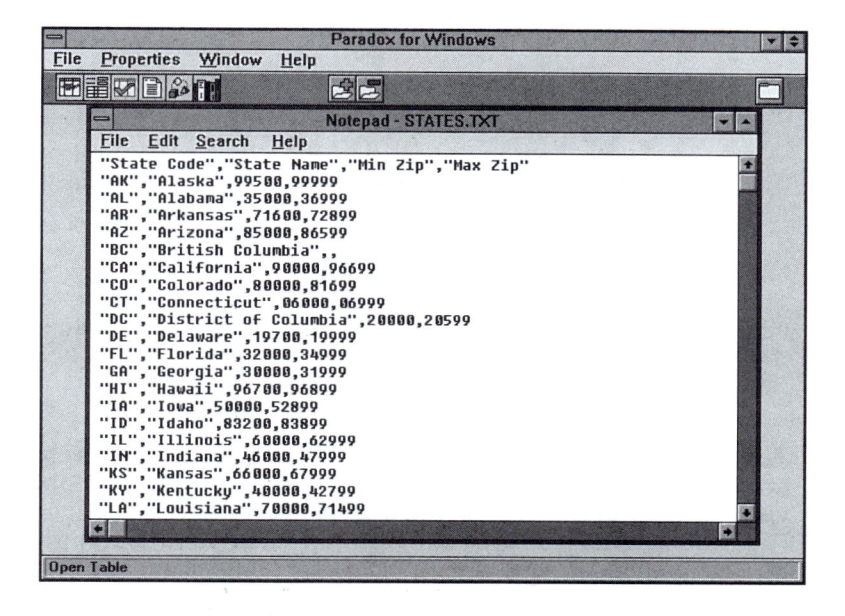

FIG. 12.12
A delimited text file.

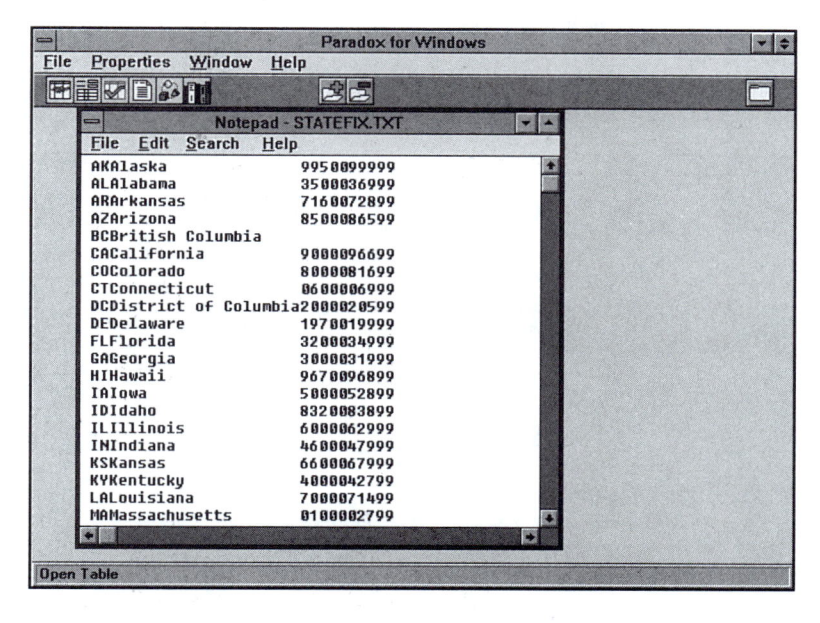

FIG. 12.13
A fixed-length text file.

II — PARADOX FOR WINDOWS POWER TECHNIQUES

To import from a delimited text file, follow these steps:

1. Choose File, Utilities, Import from the Paradox Desktop. The File Import dialog box appears (see fig. 12.14).

2. Select the source file from the list—STATES for this example. Click the Browse button to switch to another directory if necessary.

3. Click OK and the Delimited ASCII Import dialog box appears (see fig. 12.15).

4. The Delimited ASCII Import dialog box enables you to name the new table and choose the table type. The defaults are to name the table after the source file and create a Paradox table. Click the Options button to view or change import options. The Text Options dialog box appears (see fig. 12.16).

5. The Fields Separated By section enables you to specify the character used to separate one field from the next. For this example, choose Other and enter ^ in the field to the right of Other. The Fields Delimited By section indicates the character (if any) which is used to surround each field. Choose Nothing for this example.

6. The Delimited Fields check boxes offer to import Text Fields Only or All Fields. Click OK to return to the Delimited ASCII Import dialog box.

7. Click OK at the Delimited ASCII dialog box to perform the import.

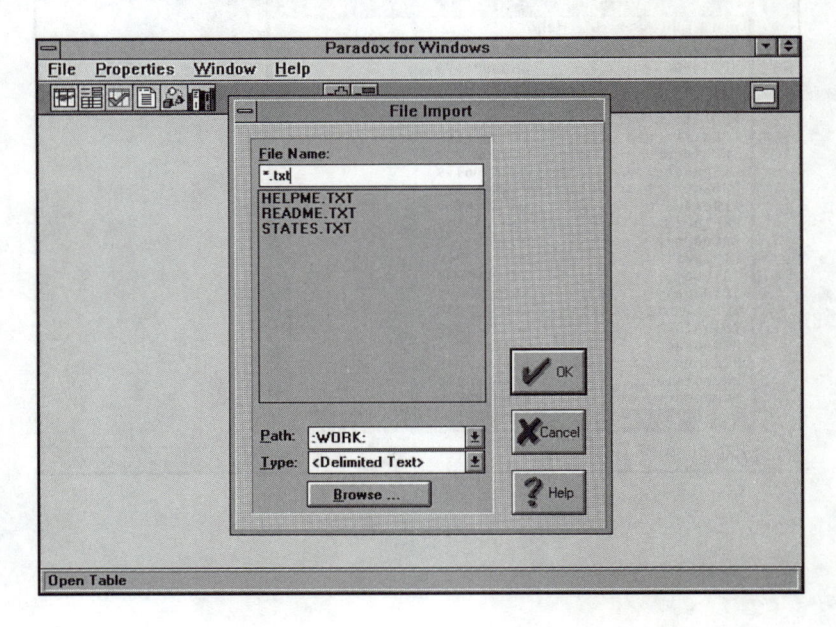

FIG. 12.14

The File Import dialog box.

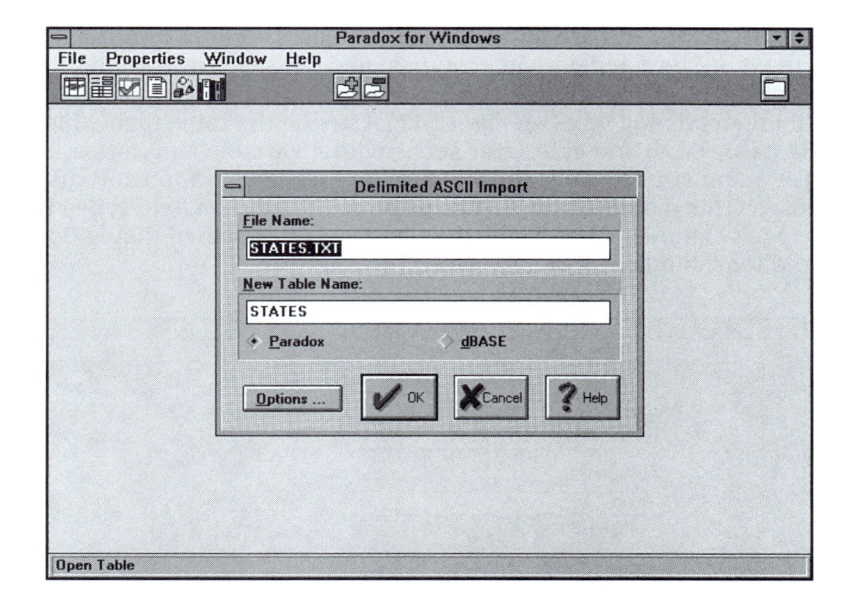

12 — WORKING WITH YOUR FILES

FIG. 12.15

The Delimited ASCII Import dialog box.

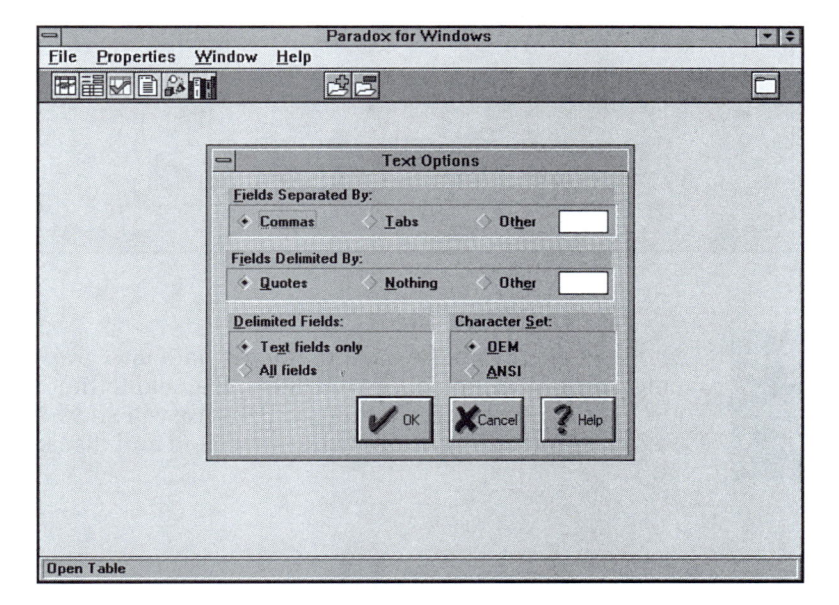

FIG. 12.16

The Text Options dialog box.

Fixed-length imports are quite similar to variable-length imports, but you must define the field names, types, and lengths explicitly before you perform the import. Fill in the table definition in the Fixed Length ASCII Import dialog box (see fig. 12.17). Choose the table name, file name, table type, and character set as with a variable-length text import. You must remember the valid field types for Paradox and dBASE tables, as this dialog box does not provide the help on field types that you receive in the Define Table dialog box. Your finished dialog box should look something like figure 12.18.

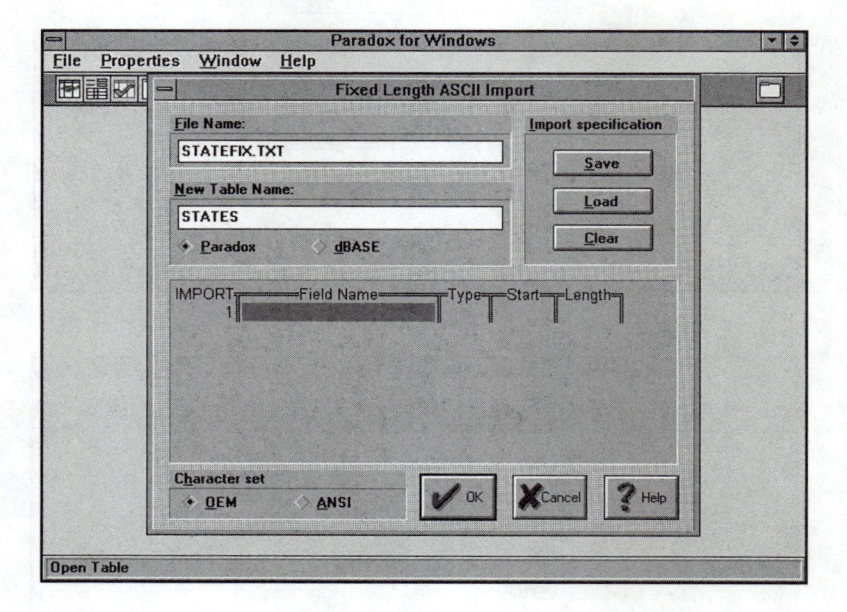

FIG. 12.17

The Fixed Length ASCII Import dialog box.

NOTE Text imports may not be used to import data into graphics, memo, formatted memo, or OLE fields. If a field in the source file exceeds 255 characters, Paradox will show the first 255 characters as an alphanumeric field and discard the rest.

Exporting Paradox Tables to Spreadsheets

Just as you can import from spreadsheets and text files, you can export to these files. Exporting enables you to share information with users who do not have a copy of Paradox for Windows.

FIG.12.18

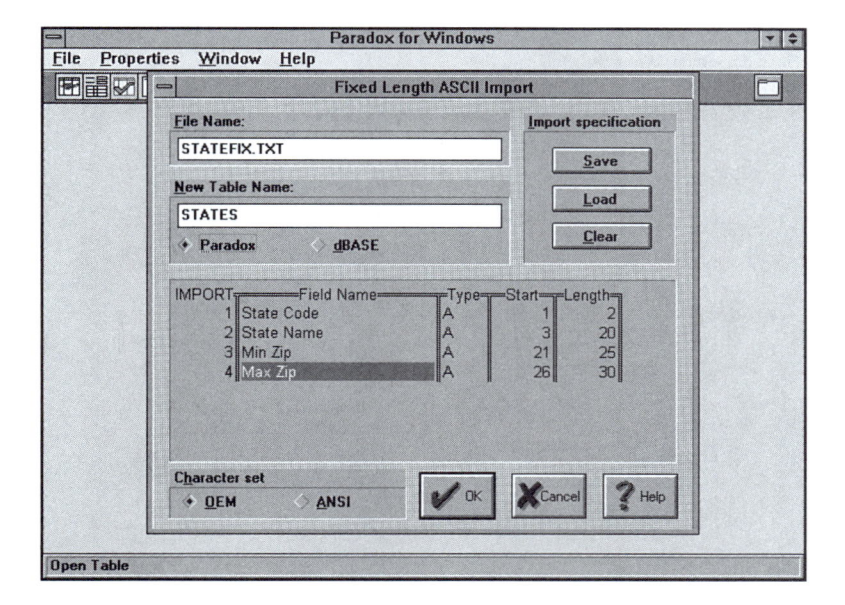

The Fixed Length ASCII Import dialog box with fields defined.

To export a Paradox table to a spreadsheet, follow these steps:

1. Choose File, Utilities, Export. The Table Export dialog box appears (see fig. 12.19).

2. Choose the source table for the export by typing the file name in the Table Name box, clicking the file name, or using the Browse button. For this example, choose the ALBUMS.DB table.

3. Choose the Export File Type by clicking your choice in the list. For this example, choose Quattro. Click OK and the Spreadsheet Export dialog box appears (see fig. 12.20).

4. In the New File Name box, type the file name of the spreadsheet you want to create.

   Paradox defaults to the table name.

5. If you want to export the table's column headings, click the Make Row Headers From Field Names check box (the default). Click OK to perform the export.

The steps are similar to export to fixed or delimited ASCII files. See the sections on importing from text files for information on choosing text file options.

II — PARADOX FOR WINDOWS POWER TECHNIQUES

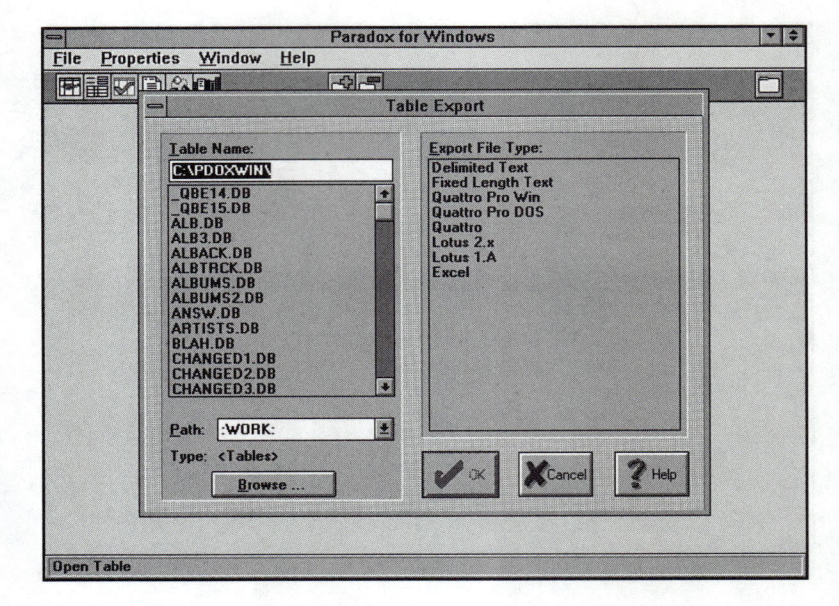

FIG. 12.19

The Table Export dialog box.

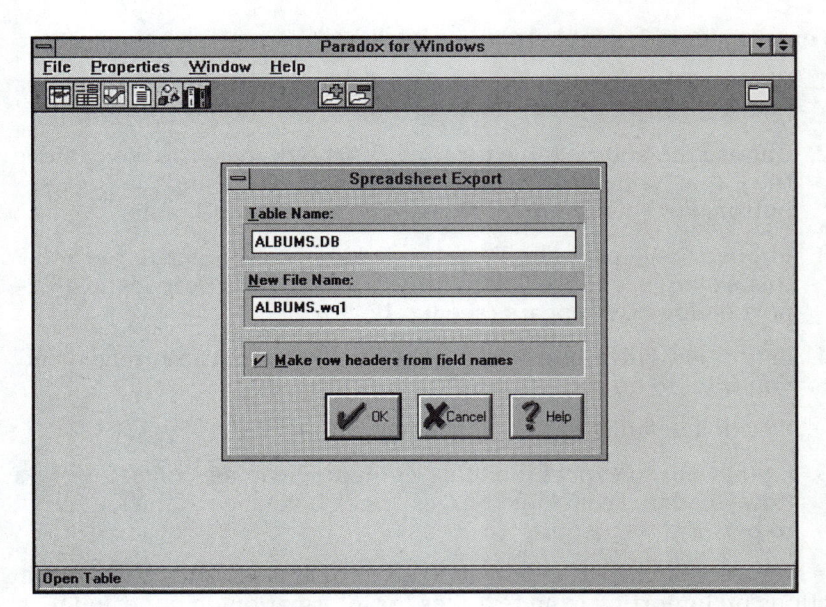

FIG. 12.20

The Spreadsheet Export dialog box.

Renaming Tables

From time to time you may realize that you have chosen an ambiguous or inappropriate name for a table. To change the name of a table in your Paradox database, follow these steps:

1. Choose File, Utilities, Rename. The Table Rename dialog box appears (see fig. 12.21).

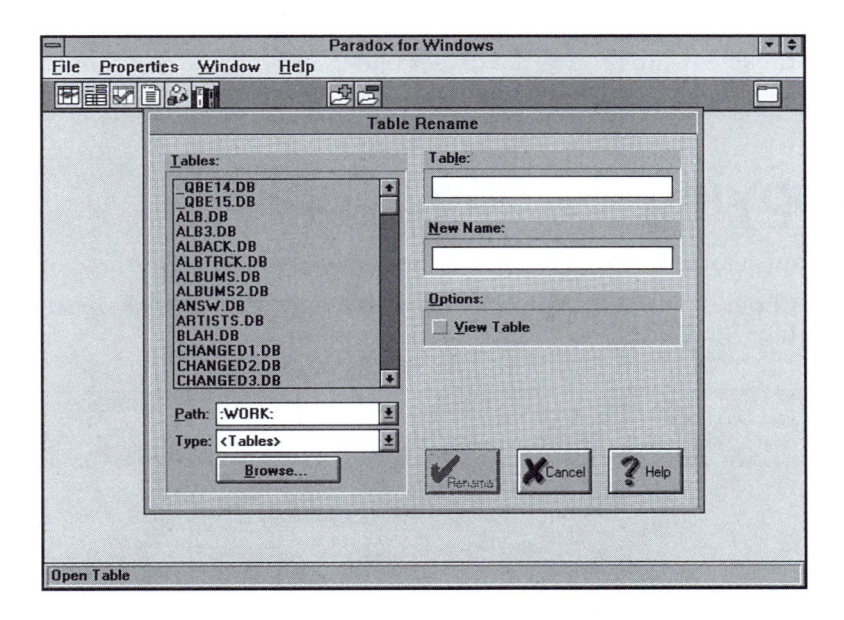

FIG. 12.21

The Table Rename dialog box.

2. Type the old table name in the Table box.
3. Type the new table name in the New Name box.
4. If you want to view the renamed table, click the View Table check box under Options.
5. Click the Rename button. Paradox renames the table.

> **CAUTION:** Do not rename tables with the DOS Rename (REN) command. If you do so, you will break the link between the table and other associated database objects such as forms, reports, queries, indexes, and validity checks. This can cause serious damage to your database.

Renaming Forms, Reports, Scripts, and Queries

Paradox does not provide a specific menu option for renaming objects other than tables. You can use the DOS rename command (REN) or the Windows File Manager to change DOS file names.

Another way to rename nontable objects is to open the object in design mode (click the Design button in the SpeedBar). Use the Save As option from the File menu to save the object under a new name and then delete the original copy of the object.

Copying Paradox Tables

To copy a table in your Paradox database, follow these steps:

1. Choose File, Utilities, Copy. The Table Copy dialog box appears (see fig. 12.22).

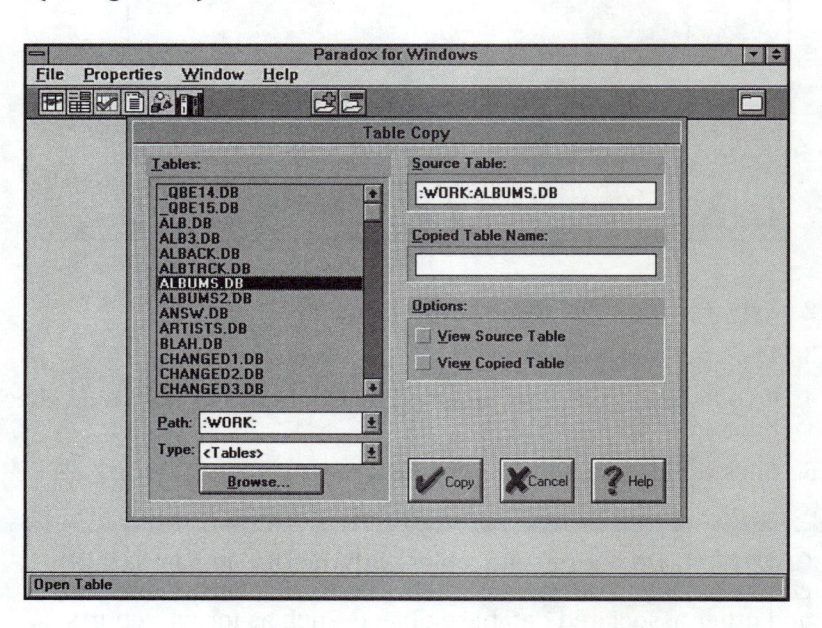

FIG. 12.22

The Table Copy dialog box.

2. Type the old table name in the Source Table text box.
3. Type the new table name in the Copied Table Name box.

4. To view the source table, click the View Source Table check box under Options. To view the copied table, choose View Copied Table. You may view both the source table and the copied table by checking both boxes.

5. Click the Copy button. Paradox copies the table.

> **CAUTION:** Although you can copy a table with the DOS COPY command, you risk losing the other files related to the DB or DBF file, such as validity checks, indexes, and table view settings.

Paradox has no menu option for copying objects other than tables (such as forms, reports, scripts, and queries). You can copy an object by opening the object in Design mode and using the Save As option from the File menu to save the object under a new name.

Deleting Objects and Emptying a Table

When you delete tables, be sure to use the File, Utilities, Delete command so that Paradox deletes all files associated with the table, such as validation checks and memo fields.

To delete a table, choose Utilities, Delete from the File menu. The Table Delete dialog box is displayed (see fig. 12.23). Choose the table to delete by clicking it in the Tables list or by entering the table name in the Table Name text box. Click the Delete button to complete the action.

If you want to delete all the data in a table but keep the table itself, choose the Empty option in the Utilities menu. The Table Empty dialog box appears (see fig. 12.24). You may view the table after it is emptied by clicking the View Table option. Fill in the table name and click the Empty button to delete all records.

> **NOTE** If you defined a password in the table, you must enter the password to delete the table. If you have forgotten the password, you can delete the table by deleting its DOS files, but be sure to delete all the files that relate to the table, including indexes, validation checks, and memo fields.

FIG. 12.23

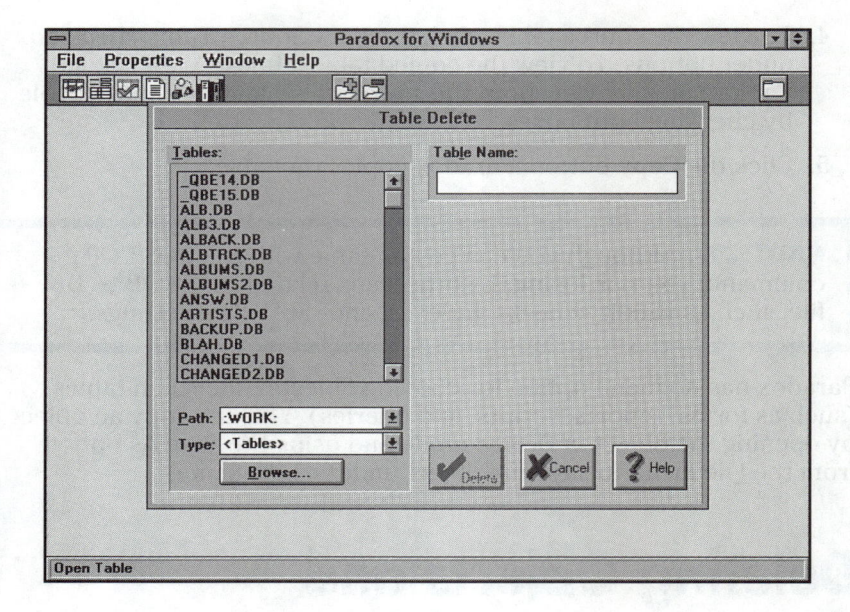

The Table Delete dialog box.

Defining Aliases

In Paradox, an *alias* is a shorthand way to refer to a DOS directory in lieu of typing the entire path name. You can use the alias INVENT, for example, to refer to files in C:\PDOXWIN\APPS\INVENT.

Using an alias rather than a DOS directory path enables you to install and move applications more easily. As long as the alias points to the correct directory, you do not have to know the full path name where the database is located.

To define an alias, follow these steps:

1. Choose File, Aliases. The Alias Manager dialog box appears (see fig. 12.25).

2. Click the New button to create a new alias.

3. Enter the new alias name—for example, Inventory.

4. Enter the DOS directory path where the alias should point (for example, C:\PDOXWIN\APPS\INVENT).

    The Driver Type is used with SQL database tables and requires the purchase of Borland's SQL Link. Leave this set to Standard.

5. Click OK to save the alias for the current session. You must use Save As to save the alias permanently.

12 — WORKING WITH YOUR FILES

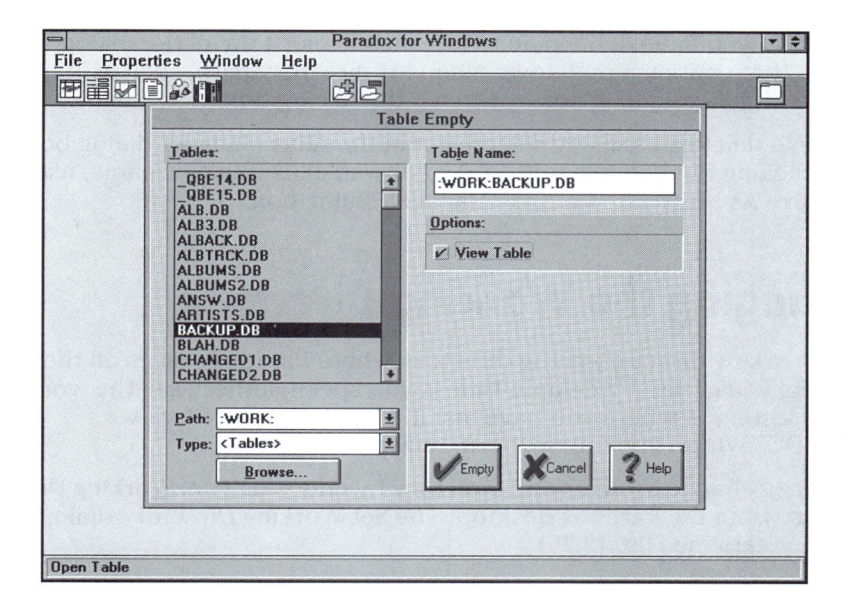

FIG. 12.24

The Table Empty dialog box.

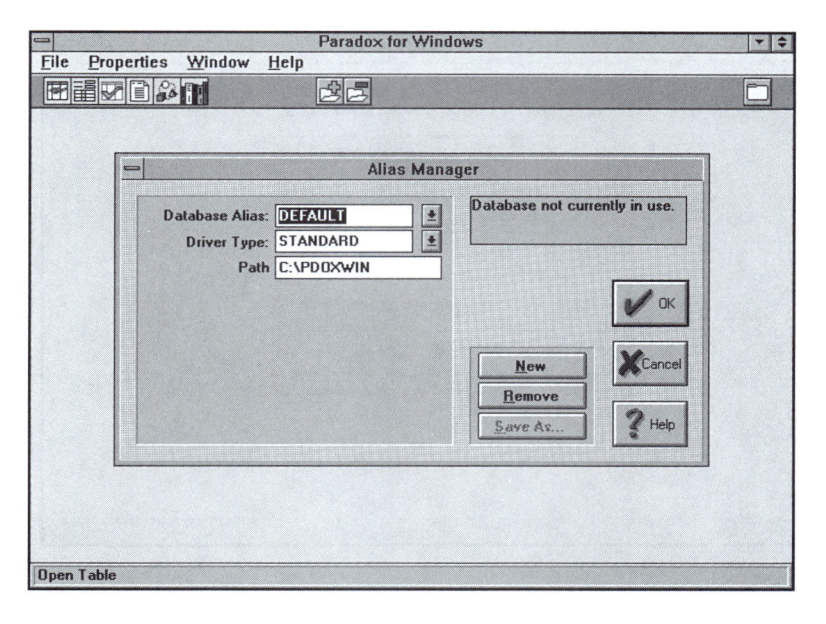

FIG. 12.25

The Alias Manager dialog box.

II — PARADOX FOR WINDOWS POWER TECHNIQUES

Now that you have defined an alias, you can use it on all the dialog boxes that contain a pull-down menu for directory path, such as the Open Document dialog box or Open Table dialog box.

You can delete an alias by selecting it in the Alias Manager dialog box and clicking the Remove button. To copy an alias to a new name, use the Save As button in the Alias Manager dialog box.

Changing the Working Directory

The Working directory is the directory where Paradox places all the objects you create by default. Unless you specify otherwise, the working directory is where you have installed Paradox for Windows (C:\PDOXWIN, if you follow the standard installation).

You may change the Working directory by choosing File, Working Directory from the Paradox desktop. The Set Working Directory dialog box appears (see fig. 12.26).

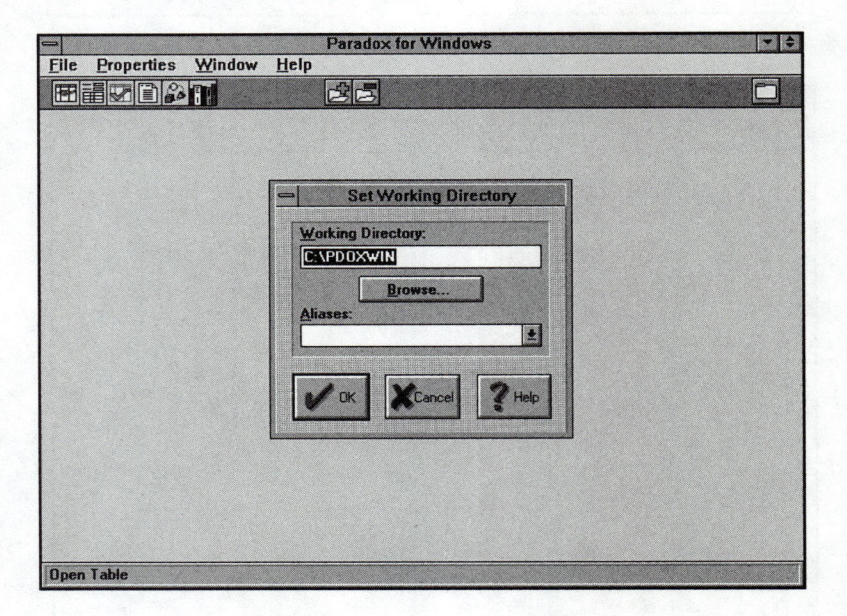

FIG. 12.26

The Set Working Directory dialog box.

Enter the directory path to serve as the working directory. You can change the working directory whenever you need to. Click OK to save your changes.

12 — WORKING WITH YOUR FILES

Creating Private Directories

You can designate a private directory for storage of temporary tables. Private directories, which should be different for each network user, can be on a network or on local disk drives.

To designate a private directory, follow these steps:

1. Choose File, Private Directory. The Private Directory dialog box appears (see fig. 12.27).

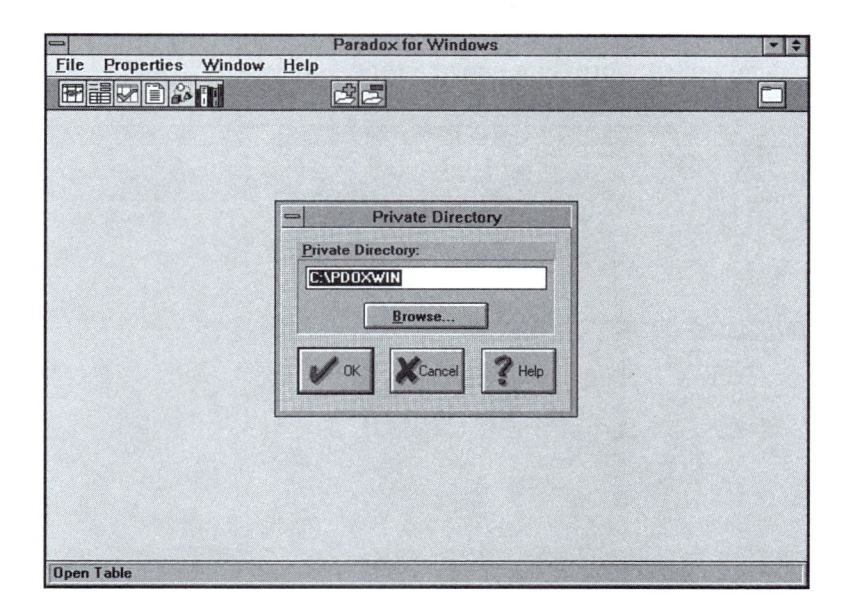

FIG. 12.27

The Private Directory dialog box.

2. Type the drive and directory path for the private directory, or use the File Browser to scan your directory tree. (The private directory you choose must already exist; Paradox does not create a new directory for you.) Use the DOS MAKEDIR command or the File Manager to create new directories.

Paradox uses the alias PRIV: to stand for your private directory. By default, the private directory is set to the directory where you installed Paradox for Windows.

Using Multiuser (Network) Features

Paradox provides a number of special features to control multiuser access to database objects. The following sections describe special utilities to manage multiuser features. Most of these features are available from the Multiuser submenu of the File menu (see fig. 12.28).

While multiuser features are most important to network Paradox users, they also apply to stand-alone systems because Windows enables you to open an object more than one at a time.

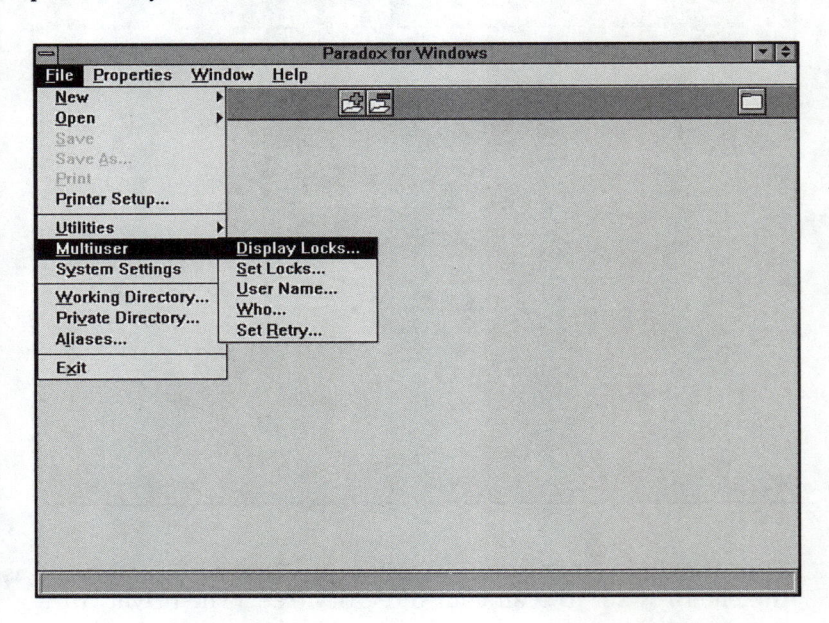

FIG. 12.28

The Multiuser submenu.

Viewing File Locks

In order to control access to files, Paradox uses *locks*, which grant permission to open a file. Locks are similar to checking out library books; they control access so that only one person at a time may "check out" an object. Luckily, much of the locking is handled automatically by Paradox for Windows.

Paradox stores information on all current locks in the system table LOCKS.DB. To view the locks table, choose File, Multiuser, Display Locks. The Select File dialog box is displayed. Choose a table and click OK. Paradox opens the LOCKS.DB table, as shown in figure 12.29.

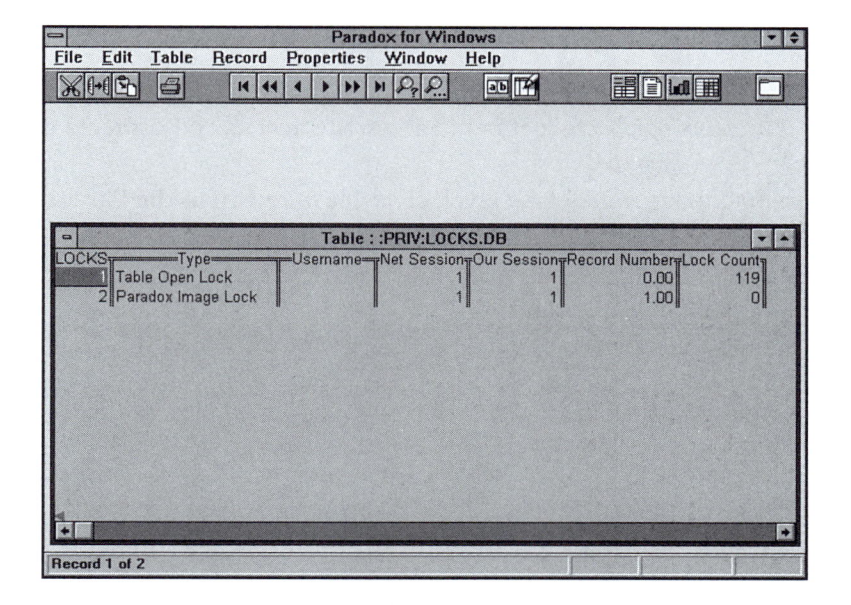

FIG. 12.29
The LOCKS.DB table.

Setting Locks on Tables

To facilitate multiuser access, Paradox controls locks on objects to prevent users from making simultaneous changes to the data that are incompatible. Although Paradox automatically places and removes most locks, you may want to control locking manually. You may want to deny access to a certain table, for example, whenever a user is editing that table.

To set user locks, follow these steps:

1. Choose File, Multiuser, Set Locks. The Table Locks dialog box appears (see fig. 12.30).

2. Select the table name in the Table Name box, or click the Browse button to access the File Browser.

3. Choose one of the following lock options:

    No Lock. The default. Removes all locks from the table. Paradox automatic locking remains in effect, and users can lock records during record entry.

    Open Lock. Prevents other users from putting an exclusive lock on a table, but allows them access to the table.

Read Lock. Permits read-only access for other users.

Write Lock. Prevents read or write access.

Exclusive Lock. Prevents read and write access and protects the table's name.

After you choose the locking level, click OK to return to the Paradox desktop and save your changes.

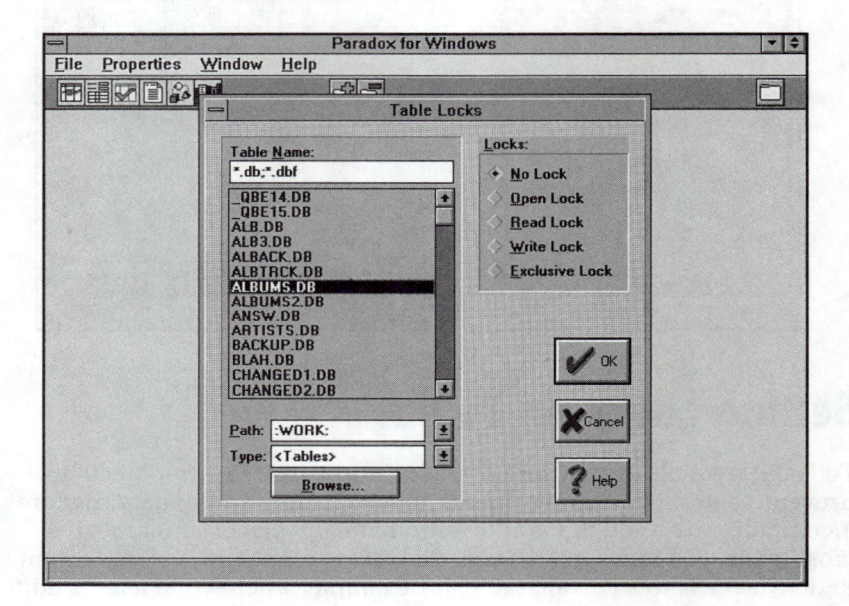

FIG. 12.30

The Table Locks dialog box.

> **NOTE** Even the tightest locking scheme does not provide complete protection of a table. Users still can delete the files used by the table at the DOS prompt or in the Windows File Manager, as long as they have the necessary network privileges.

Displaying Your User Name

You can display network user names within Paradox. To display your user name, follow these steps:

1. Choose File, Multiuser, User Name. The Network User Name dialog box appears, showing the user name you used to sign onto the network. If you are not connected to a network, the dialog box appears as shown in figure 12.31.

2. Click OK to return to the Paradox desktop.

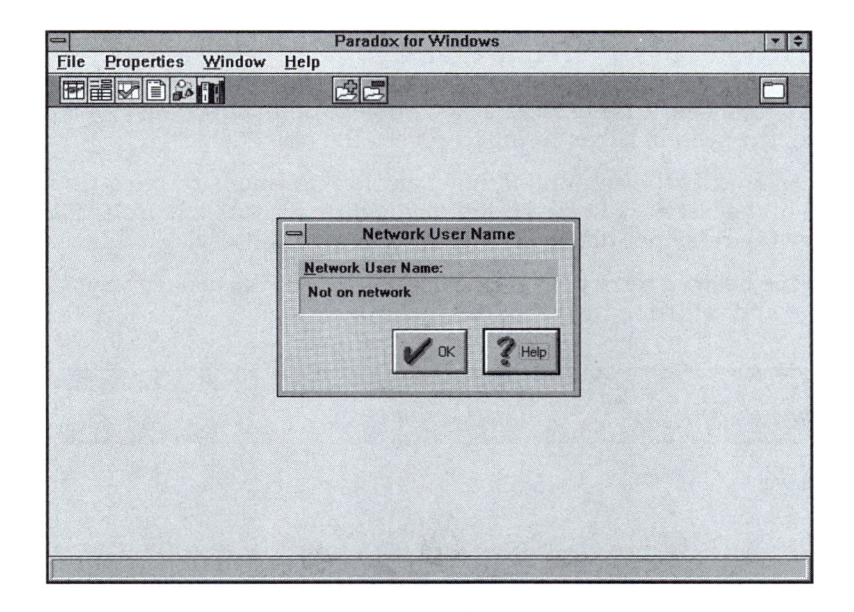

12 — WORKING WITH YOUR FILES

FIG. 12.31
The Network User Name dialog box.

Viewing User Names

To view a list of users who currently are logged into Paradox for Windows, choose File, Multiuser, Who to display the Current Users dialog box (see fig. 12.32). The list is blank if no other users are currently logged on. Click OK to return to the Paradox desktop.

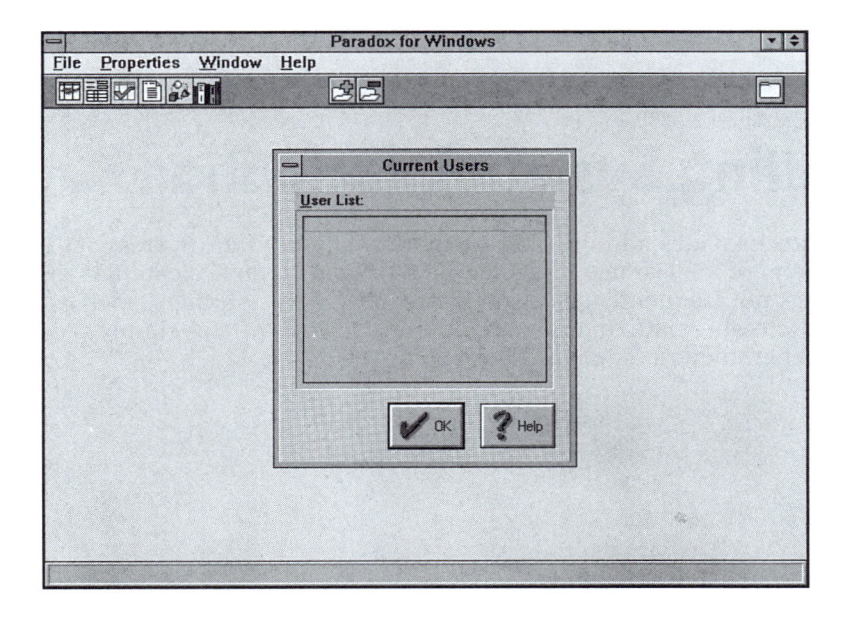

FIG. 12.32
The Current Users dialog box.

Setting Retry Intervals

When a user tries to access a Paradox object that another user has locked, the system keeps trying to access the object.

You can specify the amount of time Paradox continues retrying (in seconds) in the Network Retry Period dialog box, shown in figure 12.33. To change the retry period, select File, Multiuser, Set Retry.

Enter the desired retry period (in seconds). Click OK to save your change and return to the Paradox desktop.

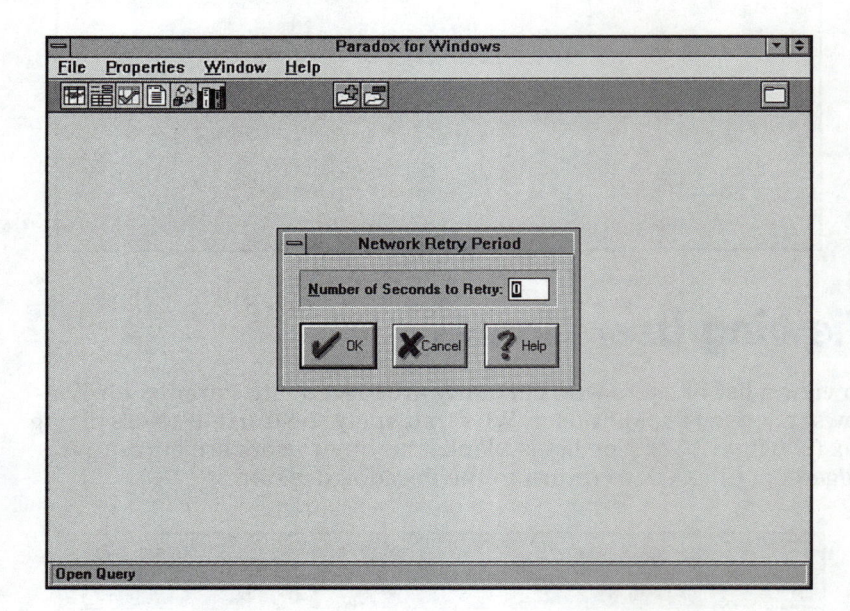

FIG. 12.33

The Network Retry Period dialog box.

Getting System Information

Paradox provides additional system information on the System Settings submenu of the File menu (see fig. 12.34). This menu is a catch-all of settings not frequently accessed by the user. Some settings, such as Auto Refresh, relate to multiuser operation, while others simply set global parameters (such as Blank as Zero).

12 — WORKING WITH YOUR FILES

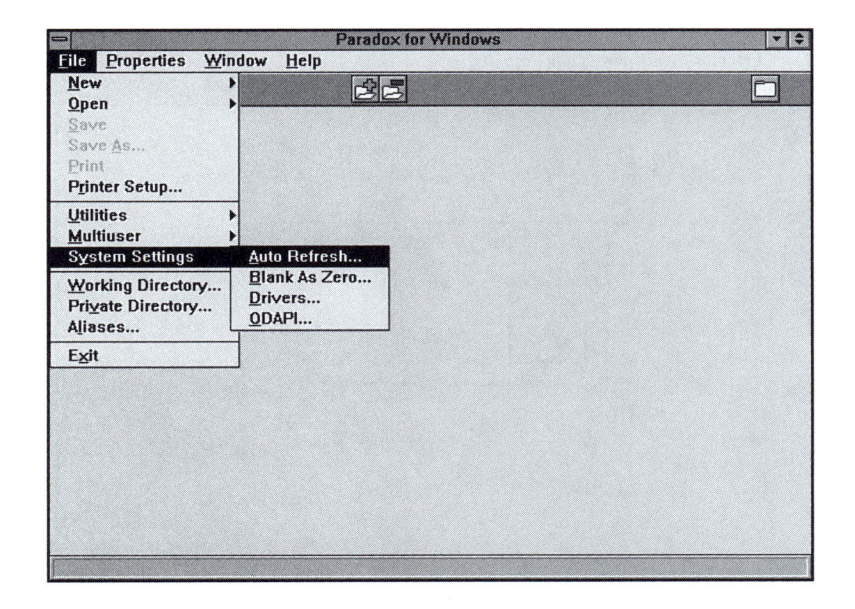

FIG. 12.34

The System Settings submenu.

Using Auto Refresh

In a multiuser environment, other users may change data even as you are viewing it. Consequently, the data you see on-screen may already be out of date before you edit it. Paradox uses the auto refresh (automatic refresh) feature to repaint the data screens periodically, showing the latest changes (if any).

By default, Paradox refreshes data screens at five-second intervals. You can change the auto refresh interval by choosing File, System Settings, Auto Refresh. The Network Refresh Rate dialog box appears (see fig. 12.35).

NOTE Setting more frequent refresh intervals increases network traffic because each refresh requires that information be sent from the server to workstations. With large numbers of users or large files, this slow-down can be noticeable; consult your network administrator for the best auto refresh settings.

FIG. 12.35

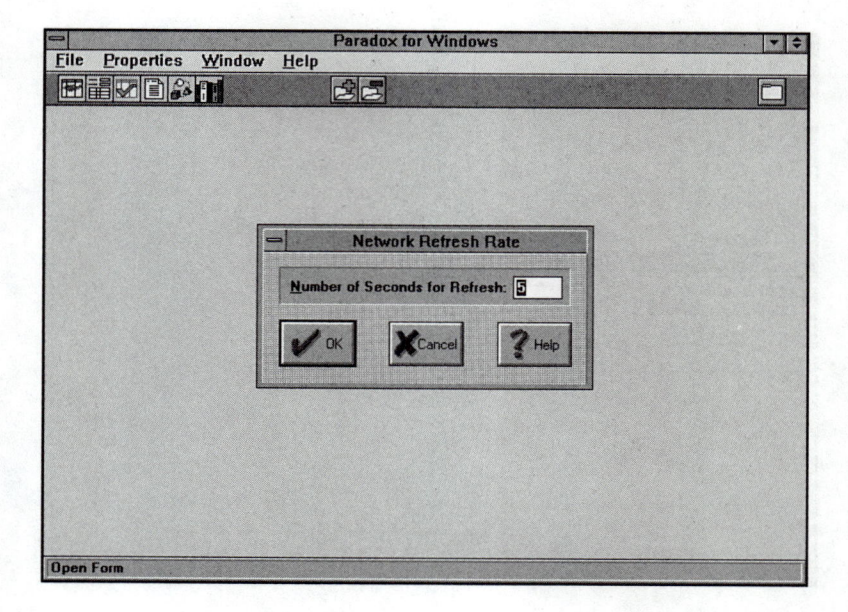

The Network Refresh Rate dialog box.

Blank as Zero

By default, Paradox treats blank number fields differently from those with a value of zero. For example, blank fields are not counted when calculating averages. If you choose Blank as Zero from the System Settings submenu, Paradox will treat blank fields as if they contained zeros.

Viewing Database Drivers

Just as a printer driver enables you to use different types of printers from Windows, a database driver is software that enables you to connect to another type of database. In the future, Borland will provide drivers to connect Paradox for Windows to support new database types.

Choose File, System Settings, Drivers to open the Current Drivers dialog box (see fig. 12.36).

12 — WORKING WITH YOUR FILES

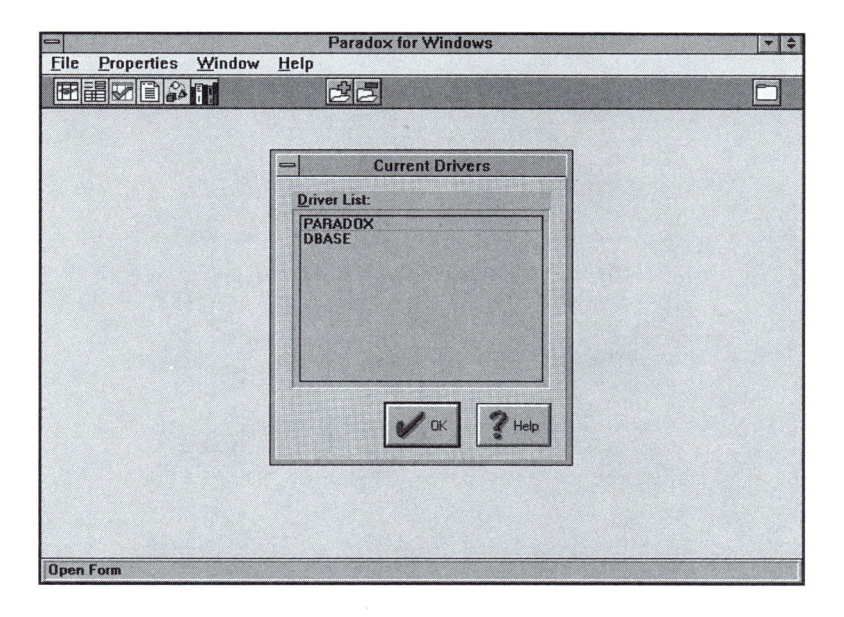

FIG. 12.36

The Current Drivers dialog box.

The Driver List shows the types of database drivers currently attached to Paradox for Windows. Straight out of the box, Paradox provides drivers for Paradox and dBASE type tables. You must purchase additional drivers (called SQL Link) for connections to additional database types, including SQL database servers, when they become available.

Viewing ODAPI Information

You can view or modify information on your current Paradox configuration. Choose File, System Settings, ODAPI to open the ODAPI System Information dialog box (see fig. 12.37). ODAPI stands for Object Database Application Programming Interface. This dialog box shows configuration information, such as language drivers and buffer size.

To change these settings, run the Configuration Utility (an icon in the Paradox for Windows program group).

The Local Share setting determines whether Paradox enforces its automatic locking rules. Local Share should be set to On for network use or if objects will be used by more than one application or Paradox session concurrently. Local Share should be set to Off for stand-alone databases. For locking purposes, however, you can choose On to treat a stand-alone system as if it were a network. When you finish viewing the settings, click OK to return to the Paradox desktop. If you set Local Share On, be sure to load SHARE.EXE before starting Windows.

FIG. 12.37

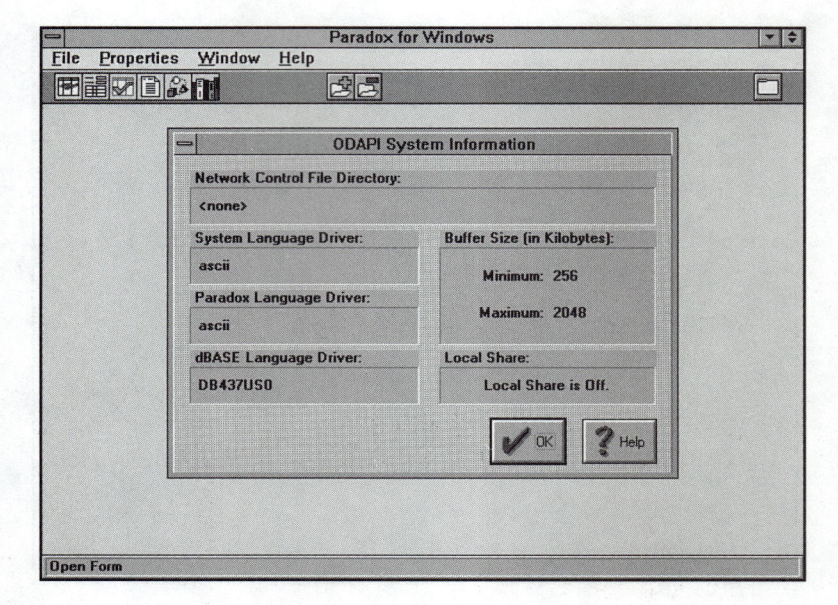

The System Information dialog box.

Chapter Summary

This chapter covered how to manage the many files that make up a Paradox database application. The File menu provides important functions to delete, rename, and copy database tables, to transfer data among Paradox tables, import and export data, and control the database environment for stand-alone and network workstations.

Although many Paradox objects can be copied, deleted, or renamed by directly manipulating the DOS files, Paradox tables may consist of several DOS files and are better handled using only the Paradox utilities.

Paradox also provides shortcuts to typing long DOS directory paths with its Aliases, Private Directories, and Working Directory. These features are particularly useful in administering databases at many sites in different hardware and network configurations.

PART III

Programming Paradox for Windows

OUTLINE

Getting Started with ObjectPAL

Understanding ObjectPAL Basics

Sample Application: Using ObjectPAL

Sample Application: Working with Multiple Forms

Sample Application: Working with Dialog Boxes and Tables

Sample Application: Adding Menus

13
CHAPTER

Getting Started with ObjectPAL

ObjectPAL is the integrated programming language for Paradox for Windows. You can use ObjectPAL to add new features to a Paradox application—features that you cannot add interactively.

If you are a new programmer, you will find that you can easily spruce up an interactive application with ObjectPAL, as in the following examples:

- You can add buttons that perform frequently repeated actions.
- If your database contains a large volume of data, you can build a dialog box that helps users get to the records they want to edit when something more sophisticated than a standard search is required.
- The success of your application may depend on a robust data-entry module. If so, you can create an editing routine that watches what users enter and responds to incorrect entries.
- On the frivolous side, if you're looking for a way to add a little pizzazz, you can create animation effects with ObjectPAL.

If you've never programmed before and aren't sure that you really want to learn ObjectPAL, you should glance through the first few sections of this chapter to get an idea of what you can do with ObjectPAL. Allow yourself to be intrigued.

Programming in ObjectPAL is in some ways similar to programming in other languages and in other ways different. ObjectPAL is similar to traditional languages because it uses variables, provides control structures like **if...then...else**, **for** loops, and **while** loops, performs calculations, and gives you a way to create functions (in ObjectPAL, functions are called methods). ObjectPAL differs from traditional languages because it is object-based.

When you use a traditional language, programming is an all-or-nothing proposition: either you take control of the application from beginning to end, or you don't program at all. With ObjectPAL, however, you need not face such a daunting task. Because ObjectPAL centers on objects, you can program as many or as few objects as you want.

The objects you write ObjectPAL code for are the objects you've been working with all along. Do you need to have Paradox for Windows check a value that was just entered in a field and beep if the value is wrong? Programming this function is simple; you change the snippet of built-in code that runs when the field's value changes. The operation takes only a little time to learn, and it is easy to use in other situations after you learn how the operation works.

Naturally, not everything you want to do with ObjectPAL is so simple, but how much or how little programming you do is entirely up to you.

This chapter and the other ObjectPAL chapters of this book assume that you know Paradox well. If you read and worked through the examples in the first two parts of this book, you have an excellent base from which to proceed. In particular, you should be very familiar with the mechanics of creating and modifying forms. Before you program a field, you need to know how to place that field on the form. This requirement holds true for all aspects of programming with ObjectPAL. Because ObjectPAL centers on objects, you should know all Paradox objects well before you try to program them.

The ObjectPAL chapters are intended primarily to help readers who have little or no programming experience get up and running in ObjectPAL with minimal trouble. If you are an experienced programmer, these chapters also serve as a fast-paced introduction to the ObjectPAL language. If you work through all four chapters, you learn to create Paradox for Windows applications complete with buttons, dialog boxes, mouse support, menus, and animation.

This chapter introduces ObjectPAL by giving you a conceptual overview of the benefits and structure of the language. A short example illustrates the general concepts you need to know to learn ObjectPAL quickly and use it effectively. This chapter also describes the ObjectPAL Editor and Debugger, known collectively as the ObjectPAL *integrated development environment* (IDE). A hands-on tutorial teaches you the basic functions of the Editor and Debugger, and also enriches your understanding of ObjectPAL programming techniques. If you are an experienced programmer, you may first want to read the last section in this chapter, "Quick Overview for Programmers," which gives an overview of the ObjectPAL language.

What Is ObjectPAL?

ObjectPAL is a high-level, event-driven, object-based, visual programming language. You can use ObjectPAL to create a completely customized application, one with entirely new buttons, menus, dialog boxes, prompts, warnings, and help. You can create a user interface for a database application, or you can use ObjectPAL to create an application that has nothing to do with a database.

Formal definitions and ambitious goals aside, a good way to get to know ObjectPAL is to think of it as a tool that extends the power of interactive Paradox. (In this chapter and in the following chapters, references to *interactive Paradox* mean the set of things that you can accomplish in Paradox without ObjectPAL.)

If you think of ObjectPAL as an extension of Paradox, you can think of ways to use ObjectPAL to perform tasks that would be awkward, difficult, time-consuming, or impossible to perform without it. Suppose that you want to create a unique but sequenced ID number every time a user in a network setting opens a new invoice record. If the last invoice created has the ID number 1203, for example, you would want the next invoice number to be 1204. Without ObjectPAL, you could create a single-record, single-field table in a shared data directory and store the most recently used invoice ID number in that field. Users could be instructed to open that table, start editing, lock the record, change the ID number to the next number in the sequence, unlock the record, leave Edit mode, close the table, return to the invoice table, and enter the new ID number. ObjectPAL, however, could perform those nine steps automatically whenever a user creates and posts a new invoice.

Performing detailed changes on fields can be difficult when you use queries interactively. For example, if a phone-number field is entered or imported to a table without parentheses around the area code (or a dash that separated the area code from the rest of the number), correcting the format with a query would be impossible. Your alternative would be to fix one record at a time. With ObjectPAL, however, you could write a routine that examines the Phone field of each record and changes any fields that weren't entered correctly.

Sometimes, you want to peer over users' shoulders, in a sense, and warn them when they are about to do something potentially damaging to the database (such as changing a key field). Although the structure of your database, how you link the tables, how you enforce referential, and the type of field validation you define can go far toward protecting the integrity and validity of data, sometimes a more specialized protection is required. This kind of monitoring is impossible do without ObjectPAL.

Keep in mind, however, that many of the things you need to do with a database you can do with Paradox interactively. If you are turning to ObjectPAL only as a means of solving a particularly thorny data-handling problem, you first should make sure that you cannot use interactive Paradox to solve that problem. Even many advanced users of interactive Paradox have only begun to tap the power of queries and calculations. Remember, too, that data validation, table lookups, choice lists, and many other powerful user-interface features are available in interactive Paradox.

ObjectPAL Is Object-Based

ObjectPAL works with objects. Objects are the things you create and work with when you design forms and reports, such as fields, lines, ellipses, boxes, and TableFrames. The first thing to remember about objects is something that you already know: *Objects have properties*.

When you create an object, you create it with properties. An object's properties define the appearance of the object. The properties of a box, for example, include size, position, color, and frame. All the properties that you can give an object when you use Paradox interactively, you can create or change when you work with an object in ObjectPAL. You can create a big blue box interactively, for example, and then use ObjectPAL to change it to a small red box.

The next thing you need to remember about objects is that *objects exist in a context*. The context of an object is the object that contains it, and the object that contains that object, and so on. Suppose that in a form, you create a box called *boxOne*. If you draw a circle called *circleOne* inside *boxOne*, the context of *circleOne* is first *boxOne* and then the form. The path back to the highest level of context is called the *containership hierarchy*. In ObjectPAL, the containership hierarchy is expressed as follows:

```
boxOne.circleOne
```

To read this hierarchy from the top down, you would say, "The box called *boxOne*, which contains *circleOne*." Typically, you would find reading the hierarchy the other way more useful, saying, "*CircleOne* contained by *boxOne*." It is crucial that you understand an object's context when you manipulate the object, because instructions in ObjectPAL statements also expect (or assume) a context. If you draw a second box in the form and, from the perspective of that form, you want to change the color of *circleOne* in *boxOne*, you would write the instruction as follows:

```
boxOne.circleOne.Color = LightBlue
```

This instruction says, "Set the Color property of the *circleOne* that is contained by *boxOne* to *LightBlue*." When the program is drawing *boxTwo* and you want to change a property of an object that is neither contained by *boxTwo*, nor contains *boxTwo* (in *boxTwo*'s containership hierarchy), you must state explicitly the containership hierarchy of the object to be changed.

Because the context of the instruction is different from the context of the object that the instruction affects, the instruction must be very specific about which object is to be changed. If you draw another circle inside *boxOne* and name that circle *circleTwo*, you could change the color of *circleOne* with the following instruction:

```
circleOne.color = "LightBlue"
```

Because *circleOne* and *circleTwo* have the same containership hierarchy (*boxOne*), you can create an instruction from *circleTwo* that directly refers to *circleOne*.

You can think of the hierarchy of objects on a form as a family tree. An object can see its ancestors (the objects that contain it), its siblings (objects that share the same parent, or container), and its offspring (the objects it contains). Objects can't see aunts, uncles, and cousins.

ObjectPAL Is Event-Driven

In Windows, no program has absolute, permanent control. No program can ever assume that it has first-hand knowledge of the specific hardware of a system or presume to know about other programs or what those programs are doing. Any application can be stopped at practically any time—whenever the user clicks on an another application.

This interface is possible for two reasons. First, every application is totally dependent on Windows to provide processing time, monitor space, and other resources. Ultimately, Windows is in control of every Windows program. Second, the nature of Windows encourages (and sometimes forces) Windows applications to be event-driven. An event-driven interface is one that responds only to specific system or user actions, such as mouse moves. The application takes control of the system (through Windows) long enough to respond to an event; the application then waits for the next event. To extend this concept farther, you can think of every object as being a small application.

Accordingly, a more elaborate description of objects takes into account their event-driven nature. That description might read as follows: Objects have a context that determines their relationship to other objects, a set of properties that determine their characteristics, and built-in methods that determine their behavior in response to events.

When you draw a rectangle in a form, you are not merely drawing, but also taking the first step in programming. The box is an object with properties that exists in the context of a form. But the box also has a behavior because Paradox built this box to respond to events.

By default, the box's response to most events is nothing. You use ObjectPAL to tell the box to do something other than, or more than, the default response when a certain event occurs. For example, you can change the color of the box when the user moves inside the borders of the box and change the color back again when the user leaves the box.

As an ObjectPAL programmer, you redefine the response of objects. To say the same thing in different terms, you don't tell the box *to* respond, because Paradox built the box to be responsive; you merely tell the box *how* to respond. Furthermore, you don't have to figure out how you want that box to respond to every possible event; you only tell the box how to respond if you need to change the default response for a particular event.

Every object has a set of default responses. To modify the default response of an object, you modify one or more of that object's built-in methods. Most of the time you will spend in ObjectPAL, you will spend modifying built-in methods.

ObjectPAL groups all the objects that you draw with the SpeedBar into a category called *UIObjects*. (Categories of objects are called *types* in ObjectPAL. Some other languages call them classes.) A page of a form is a UIObject. Forms are also UIObjects. (Forms have behavior that goes beyond their behavior as a UIObject; for the time being, however, think of them as UIObjects.)

UIObjects and forms come with their own sets of built-in methods. These built-in methods are triggered automatically in response to events or actions. When you click inside the boundaries of an object, for example, Paradox calls the **mouseClick** built-in method for that object.

The set of built-in methods built into an object varies according to the object. Most UIObjects have the same basic set, with a few notable exceptions; for example, fields have a **changeValue** built-in method, but boxes don't. The **changeValue** method is run whenever the value in a field changes. Having a **changeValue** method for a box doesn't make sense because a box object never contains data values (unless a field is placed inside the box).

Paradox makes finding and modifying an object's built-in methods easy. You right-click the object to bring up the properties menu, click Methods, click the built-in method you want to modify, and then click OK. An ObjectPAL Editor window opens, and Paradox positions the cursor at the point where you should start typing.

ObjectPAL Is Easy: An Example

The following exercise shows how you can change an object's properties at run time in response to an event, how objects contain one another, and how the containership hierarchy affects the way you write code. In this exercise, you write the program so that when the user clicks one of the objects, Paradox executes the built-in method that you modified. To write this program, follow these steps:

1. Choose File, New, Form. The Data Model dialog box appears.
2. In the Data Model dialog box, click OK (don't link any tables). The Page Layout dialog box appears.
3. Click OK in the Page Layout dialog box to create a default form.
4. In the form, draw a box several inches square, and then right-click the box to display the pop-up properties menu.
5. Click the default name at the top of the properties menu to open the Object Name dialog box.

> **NOTE** If you intend to directly refer to an object in ObjectPAL code, you should replace the default name with a unique name. (This rule also applies to form pages.) Usually, you shouldn't rename objects that are bound to a table because they conveniently take the name of the data they're bound to. For example, a TableFrame takes as its object name the name of the table to which it is bound.

6. Rename the object *boxOne*.
7. Draw a small circle inside *boxOne*.
8. Using the same technique you used in steps 4-6, rename the circle *yellowCircle* and then change its color to yellow.

III — PROGRAMMING PARADOX FOR WINDOWS

9. Draw a second circle inside *boxOne*.

10. Rename the second circle *greenCircle* and change its color to green.

11. Click *boxOne* until Paradox selects the box, and then choose For<u>m</u>, Object <u>T</u>ree, or click the Object Tree button in the SpeedBar to open an Object Tree.

12. Move the Object Tree away from *boxOne*. Your form should look like figure 13.1. The Object Tree graphically shows the relationship of *boxOne*, *yellowCircle*, and *greenCircle*.

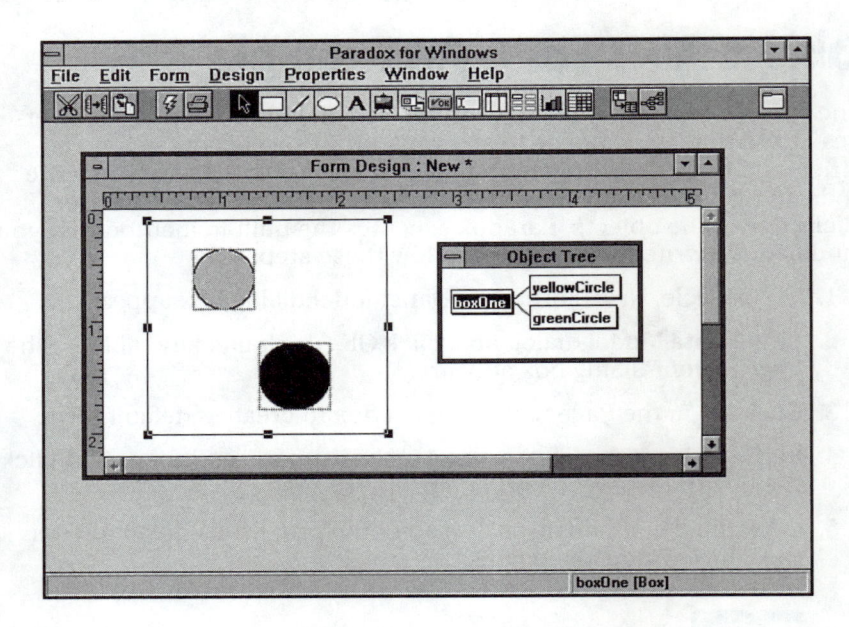

FIG. 13.1

The Object Tree shows the relationship of objects on a form.

Follow these steps to add another object to the form and open the ObjectPAL Editor:

1. Draw another box in the form and name it *boxTwo*.

2. Draw a circle inside *boxTwo* and name it *grayCircle*. Change the color to gray.

3. Right-click *grayCircle* and click Methods on the properties menu. Paradox opens the Methods dialog box, which lists all the built-in methods for *grayCircle*.

4. Because you want Paradox to respond when you click *grayCircle*, choose **mouseClick**. Paradox calls the **mouseClick** method for *grayCircle* whenever you click *grayCircle*.

13 — GETTING STARTED WITH OBJECTPAL

5. Click OK. Paradox opens an ObjectPAL Editor window. The window contains the default code that begins and ends the built-in method (see fig. 13.2).

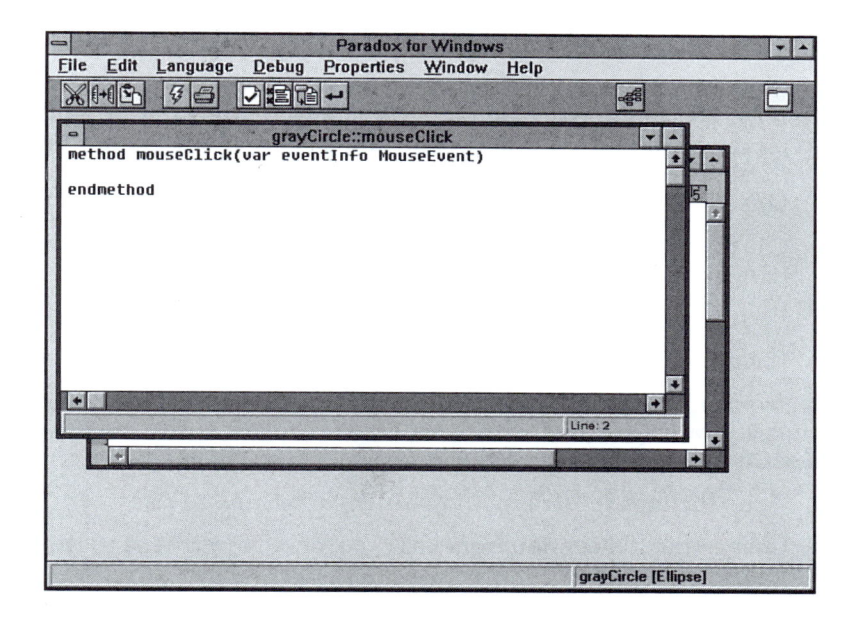

FIG. 13.2

The ObjectPAL Editor window with the **mouseClick** method.

6. Paradox positions the text cursor in the blank line. Leave the cursor where it is and type the following statement in the blank line:

   ```
   self.Color = LightBlue
   ```

   The preceding statement changes the color of *grayCircle* in *boxTwo*. The term *self* in an object's path name refers to the context of the instruction. Because the instruction is in a built-in method attached to *grayCircle*, *self* is *grayCircle* (of *boxTwo*).

   LightBlue is a constant value that represents a color to ObjectPAL. ObjectPAL provides these constants so that you don't have to remember the number that represents the color. All the basic colors have constants.

7. Check the method for syntax errors by clicking the Check Syntax button in the SpeedBar.

   Notice that both the menu and the SpeedBar change when you open an ObjectPAL Editor window. (The ObjectPAL menu and SpeedBar are explained in the "The ObjectPAL Editor" section later in this chapter.)

8. Correct any errors the compiler warns you about. The entire method should contain the following lines of code:

```
method mouseClick(var eventInfo MouseEvent)
   self.Color = LightBlue
endmethod
```

9. Run the form. You can run a form from the ObjectPAL Editor window by clicking the View Data button on the SpeedBar. If you prefer, close the Editor window and choose the View Data button from the SpeedBar, or choose Form, View Data (F8 also will toggle you to View Data mode).

10. Click *grayCircle*. As soon as you click the circle, the color changes to light blue.

11. Return to Design mode.

12. Change the light blue circle back to gray.

Now, from *grayCircle*'s built-in **mouseClick** method, you will try to change a property of another object. Follow these steps to modify **mouseClick**:

1. Open the **mouseClick** method for *grayCircle* in *boxTwo*.

2. Change the instruction from `self.color = LightBlue` to the following:

   ```
   greenCircle.color = LightBlue
   ```

3. Check the syntax. The method should look like the one shown in figure 13.3.

4. Run the form. Click the gray circle. Notice that the green circle in *boxOne* changes to light blue.

5. Return to Design mode when you finish.

You may be wondering if all object names on a form must be unique. The answer is no. All objects in the same immediate container must have unique names, but objects in different containers can have the same names. In the next example, you'll see how ObjectPAL sorts out distinct objects that have the same name.

1. Create another circle inside *boxTwo*, name it *greenCircle*, and set the circle's color to green.

2. Run the form.

3. Click *grayCircle*. This time when you click *grayCircle*, the *greenCircle* in *boxOne* stayed green, but the *greenCircle* in *boxTwo* changed to light blue. ObjectPAL chose the circle that was related most closely to the current object.

13 — GETTING STARTED WITH OBJECTPAL

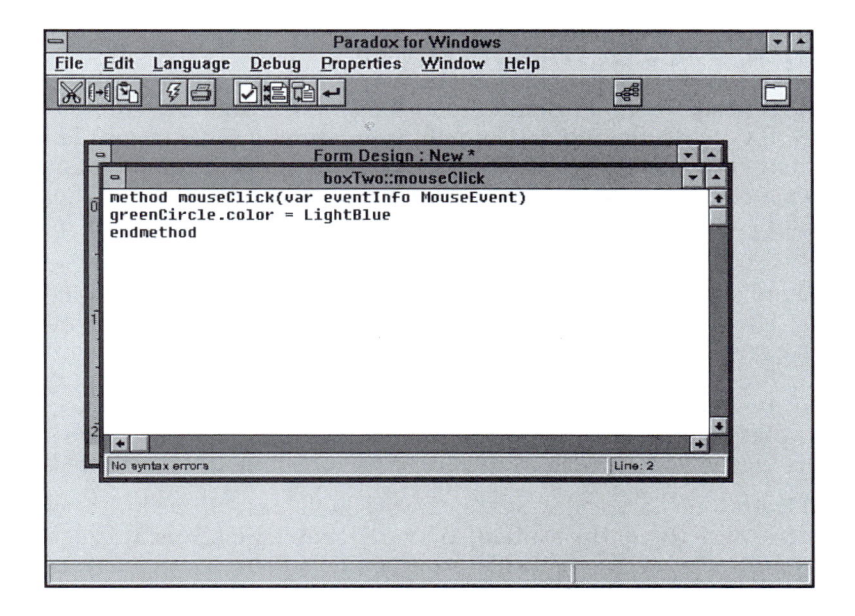

FIG. 13.3

The revised **mouseClick** method.

4. Return to Design mode and change the color of *boxTwo*'s *greenCircle* back to green.
5. Open the **mouseClick** method for *grayCircle*.
6. Replace the line

   ```
   greenCircle.Color = LightBlue
   ```

   with this line:

   ```
   boxOne.greenCircle.Color = LightBlue
   ```

   This tells ObjectPAL that you want to change the color of the *greenCircle* object in *boxOne*.
7. Check the syntax and run the form.
8. Click *grayCircle*. This time, the *greenCircle* in *boxOne* changes colors.
9. Return to Design mode and save the form as OP1. (You will use this form in later examples.)

ObjectPAL Is Modular

At the beginning of this chapter, you learned that you can use ObjectPAL to do as little or as much programming as you want. This flexibility is available because objects are inherently modular. In other words, *objects are self-contained*. You can change the behavior of one object in a form without changing the behavior of all the objects in the form.

The implications of this feature are wider reaching than you might think. The trivial side of this feature is that the nature of objects makes them easy to program. The nontrivial side is that you can use ObjectPAL to build complex systems. In a non-object-based language, a general rule is that the bigger or more complex a system becomes, the more likely it is to become unstable—and not merely because the system is bigger, has more lines of code, and consequently has more bugs.

With traditional languages, systems were built with all the intelligence at or near the top of the system; in overly simplistic terms, this scheme followed the rules of structured programming. Processes in a system were seen as linear, and programming was approached in linear fashion. But analysis of real-world complex systems (systems such as traffic patterns and the stock market) revealed that these systems embodied organic principles: nothing traveled in a straight line, and little change came from the top of the system. In a real-world system, control flows not from the top of the system, but from the bottom—from the interaction of all the little pieces, or *subsystems*.

Object-based programming enables you to develop systems with a more organic approach. In an object-based system, you build the intelligence into the little pieces (the objects). If you focus on correctly modeling the behavior of the subsystems, the complete system is likely to feel much more intuitive and much more like a real-world application.

Furthermore, an object-based system supports an iterative development process—a process in which you return to the program again and again to refine it. You can return to an object and make it smarter without jeopardizing the entire system. You can go back over the code for an object and modify that code because the object is relatively self-contained. To seasoned programmers, the implication of this capability is obvious: maintaining and improving an object-based system no longer requires the programmer to know everything about the system. In a well-designed system, one small change is exactly that—one small change.

You don't need to know object-oriented design principles to start programming in ObjectPAL. If you start with small chunks and then work your way up, your system will be better-designed than if you try to control everything from the top. The beauty of ObjectPAL is that the best way to use it is also the easiest. With ObjectPAL you can do the following:

- Place objects in a form
- Set properties for those objects
- If necessary, attach custom code to some of the built-in methods for those objects

You can attempt to write programs the old-fashioned way—starting at the top and working your way down to the bottom—but you will never appreciate the full power of ObjectPAL if you do. On the other hand, if you keep your application modular so that the code which affects an object is as close to that object as possible, your application will be well-designed and easy to maintain.

ObjectPAL Is Visual

Programming in ObjectPAL is visual programming. To create a dialog box, you place fields, choice lists, drop-down edit lists, buttons, and icons in a form, and then you tell Paradox that the form should be treated as a dialog (Properties, Form, Window Style). After you're happy with the look and feel of the dialog box, you use ObjectPAL to change the behavior of only those objects whose default behavior does not suit your needs.

This work is very different from the work you would have to do to create a dialog box in a non-visual environment. In many other languages—even those languages that include a function call to create a dialog box—you create the dialog box while you're working in some kind of text editor. To run the dialog box, you must compile the code, debug it, run it again, and so on until the dialog box works. Every time you blindly change the position of an element, you must access the code, a procedure that potentially creates more bugs.

As you learned in the previous sections, when you place objects in a form, you are giving those objects a context. The form enables you to see the user interface to your program as you program. You can see the relationships of the objects to one another not only in the form but also in the Object Tree. The Object Tree provides a conceptual view of the relationships among objects.

The Object Tree also is designed to let you access the code for an object. When the Object Tree for a form is open, you can see all the objects in the form and all the objects inside those objects. To inspect an object's properties, right-click the object's name in the Object Tree.

III — PROGRAMMING PARADOX FOR WINDOWS

The following exercise shows you how to use an Object Tree to access an object's methods. For this exercise, you use the form OP1.FSL that you created earlier in this chapter. Follow these steps:

1. Open form OP1.
2. Select the page by clicking anywhere on the page outside an object.
3. Right-click the page and rename it *pageOne*.
4. Open an Object Tree by clicking the Object Tree button in the SpeedBar (or choose For*m*, *O*bject Tree). The Object Tree should resemble figure 13.4.

   In the Object Tree, an underlined object name indicates that the object has defined methods.

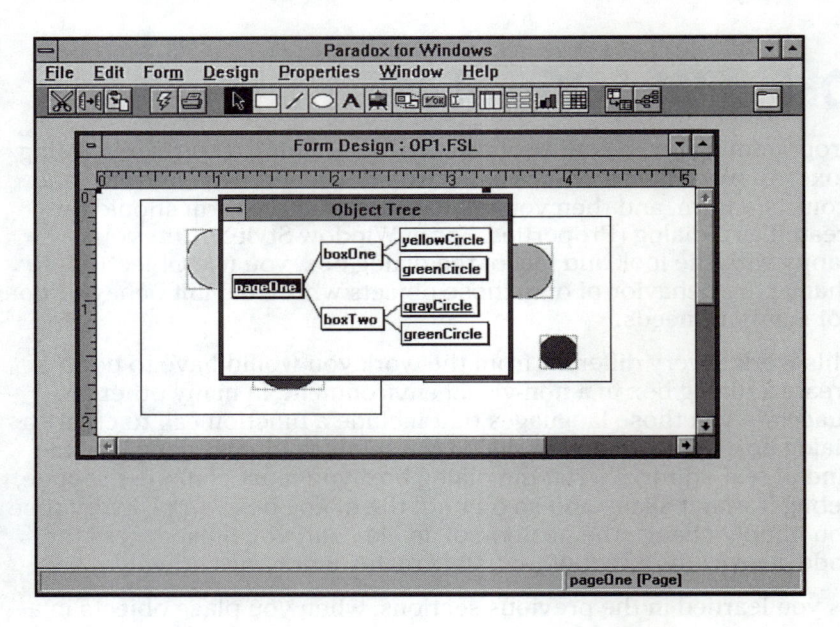

FIG. 13.4
The Object Tree for a page.

In the Object Tree for *pageOne* of the OP1 form, the *grayCircle* object is underlined because you attached code to the built-in **mouseClick** method of *grayCircle*. To access *grayCircle*'s methods from the Object Tree, follow these steps.

1. Right-click *grayCircle* in the Object Tree. Paradox opens the pop-up properties menu.

2. Click Methods in the properties menu to open the Methods dialog box. If a built-in method has been changed, an asterisk (*) appears next to the name of the method.

3. For now, click Cancel to close the Methods dialog box, then save and close the form.

The ObjectPAL Environment

Most of the ObjectPAL environment is the same as the one you've been working with all along; you use interactive Paradox to build a form that becomes the basis of your application. Two special tools, however, come in handy when you write ObjectPAL code: the ObjectPAL Editor and the ObjectPAL Debugger.

The *ObjectPAL Editor* enables you to write and check code (and actually does some of the writing for you). The *ObjectPAL Debugger* enables you to step through code one instruction at a time, watch for certain changes, correct errors, and fine-tune your application. The following sections describe these two tools.

The ObjectPAL Editor

The ObjectPAL Editor is where you write ObjectPAL code. When you choose to modify a method or other code container from the Methods dialog box, Paradox opens an Editor window. Your entry point to the ObjectPAL Editor is the Methods dialog box.

The Methods Dialog Box

The Methods dialog box opens when you choose Methods from the properties menu. This dialog box gives you access to code written for a specific object.

Most of the time, you use the Methods dialog box to modify built-in methods. You also can use this dialog box to write other kinds of code, including custom methods, custom procedures, constants, variables, user-defined variable types, and declarations of library methods and functions (see fig. 13.5).

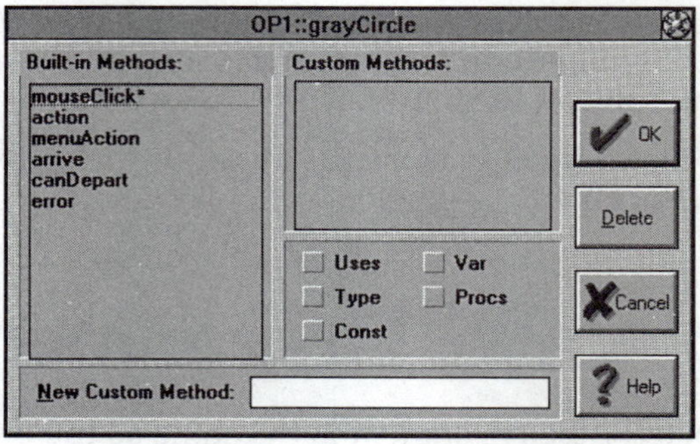

III — PROGRAMMING PARADOX FOR WINDOWS

FIG. 13.5

The Methods dialog box.

The Methods dialog box contains the following sections:

- The Built-in Methods section of the dialog box lists the built-in methods available for this object. To open a built-in method, double-click the method name, or select the method name and click OK.

  To select a number of methods, either Shift+click a contiguous group, or Ctrl+click each method. Paradox opens each method in a separate Editor window.

- An entry in the New Custom Method field creates a new method attached to the current object. Paradox does not automatically call custom methods in response to events.

- Any custom methods defined for an object appear in the Custom Methods section of the dialog box. (See Chapter 14 for details on how to use custom methods.)

- The Var box opens a variable window, called a Var window, in which you declare variables that are global to the object. You also can declare variables for a method in the **var** section of that method.

  Declaring variables from the Methods dialog box makes the variables global to the object. If a variable is global to an object, you can use the variable in any of the methods attached to the object and in any of the objects contained by this object. (Where you can use a method, variable, constant, procedure, or type depends on where that item is defined. The availability of data objects is broadly termed *scoping*. See Chapter 14 for more information about scoping.)

- The Const box opens a constant-declaration window, called a Const window.

Constants declared in a Const window are global to the object. You also can declare constants in a **const** section of a method, but they will not be global to the object. (Chapter 14 describes how to declare a constant.)

- The Type box opens a window in which you can declare user-defined data types. Data types declared in a Type window are available to all methods attached to this object and to all objects contained by this object. You also can declare user-defined types in a **type** section of a method (see Chapter 14 for information on defining new types).

- The Procs box opens a window that enables you to define procedures global to the object. Procedures are like methods except that procedures are not bound to an object type. Procedures defined in a Procs window are available to all methods attached to this object and to all objects contained by this object. You also can declare procedures in **Proc** sections of a method (see Chapter 14).

- The Uses box opens a window that enables you to declare methods and functions called from an ObjectPAL library or a dynamic link library. You also can declare library methods and functions in the **Uses** section of a method.

Neither ObjectPAL libraries nor dynamic link libraries are covered in these chapters.

The ObjectPAL Editor Window

An ObjectPAL Editor window opens from the Methods dialog box whenever you select a code container to modify. *Code containers* are built-in methods, procedures, custom methods, variable windows, type windows, const windows, and Uses windows.

When you open an Editor window, the main menu changes, as shown in figure 13.6.

The ObjectPAL Editor menu is available only when an ObjectPAL Editor window is open. The File, Window, and Help menus are standard menus.

In terms of text-handling, the ObjectPAL Editor works like most standard Windows editors. Common operations work in standard ways. To select text, for example, drag the mouse or hold down the Shift key while you press a cursor-movement key.

III — PROGRAMMING PARADOX FOR WINDOWS

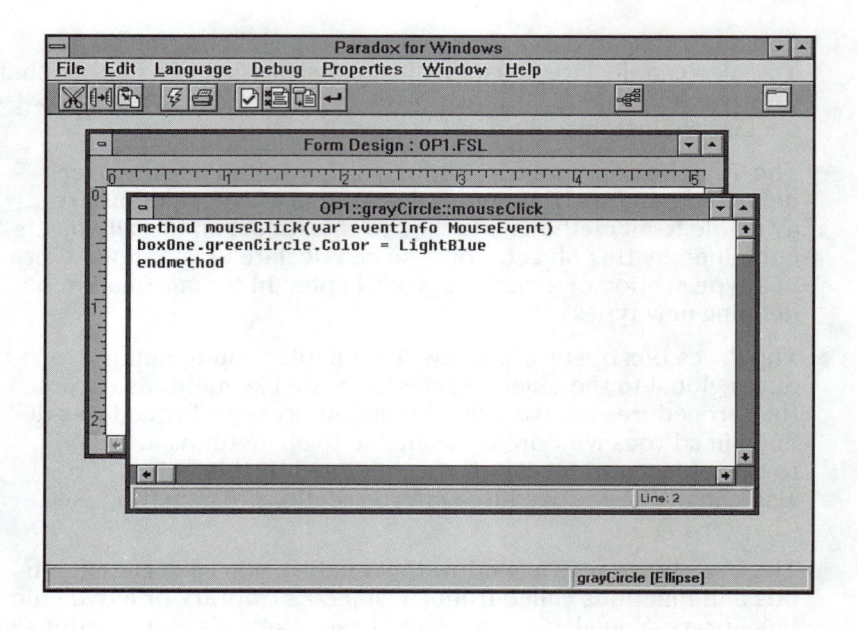

FIG. 13.6

The ObjectPAL Editor menu.

The ObjectPAL Editor window always opens in Insert mode. In Insert mode, anything you type is inserted at the current cursor position. To move around in the ObjectPAL Editor window, use the cursor-movement keys or the scroll bar.

Table 13.1 summarizes common ObjectPAL editing actions.

Table 13.1. ObjectPAL Editor Keys

Action	Key combination or menu command
Select Text	Shift+cursor movement key extends text selection Drag the mouse Edit, Select All to select the entire window
Copy Text	Ctrl+Ins copies text to the Clipboard Edit, Copy
Cut Text	Shift+Del cuts text to the Clipboard Edit, Cut
Paste Text	Shift+Ins pastes text from the Clipboard Edit, Paste

13 — GETTING STARTED WITH OBJECTPAL

Action	Key combination or menu command
Delete Text	Del erases selected text Edit, Delete
Search	Edit, Search and Edit, Search Next finds a string
Replace	Edit, Replace and Edit, Replace Next finds and replaces a string
Move to	Edit, Go To jumps to a specific line number

You also can use another editor, such as the Windows Notepad, to write ObjectPAL code (choose Properties, Alternate Editor from the ObjectPAL Editor menu). If you do use another editor, however, syntax checking and other special features of the ObjectPAL Editor menu will not be available.

The Language Menu

The Language menu helps you write and check ObjectPAL code. To check the code in a window for syntax errors, choose Language, Check Syntax. The compiler examines the code for the form. If the compiler finds an error, an error message appears in the status line of the open Editor window. Paradox positions the insertion point at the point of the error.

Some types of errors affect code in other methods for an object and also may affect code for other objects. When this problem occurs, the compiler opens each method that needs to be corrected.

The Language menu is available as a (floating) pop-up menu from any ObjectPAL Editor window. Right-click anywhere in the window to display the Language menu (see fig. 13.7).

In the Language menu, Check Syntax compiles the code on a form. Next Warning shows the next compiler warning. Methods opens the Methods dialog box for the current object. Object Tree displays the Object Tree for the selected object.

The second group of menu items in the Language menu are designed to provide help while you're writing ObjectPAL. Choose Keywords to see a list of keywords, such as **proc** and **if**. When you click a keyword, the application inserts the keyword into the current ObjectPAL Editor window at the insertion point.

FIG. 13.7

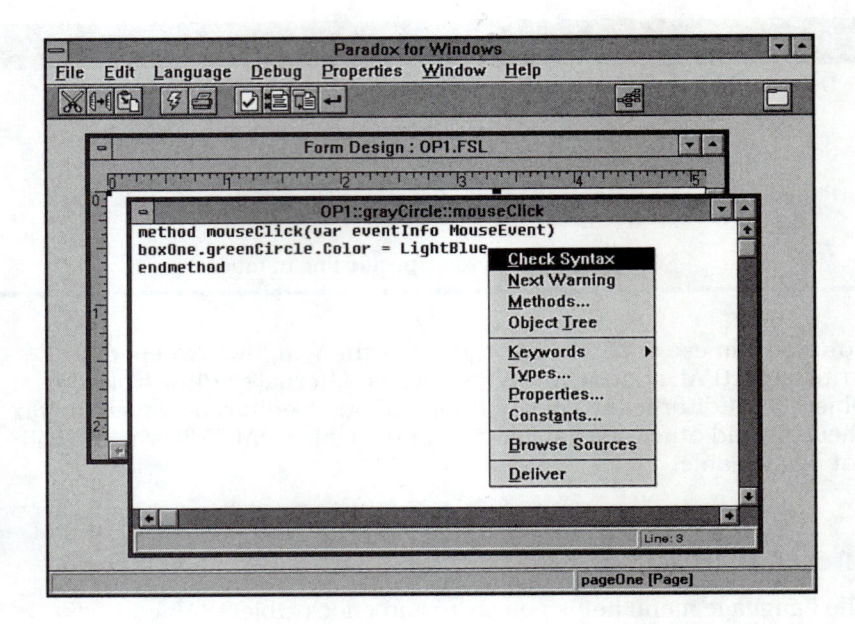

The Language pop-up menu.

The Types and Methods Dialog Box

Choose Types from the Language menu to display the Types and Methods dialog box (see fig. 13.8).

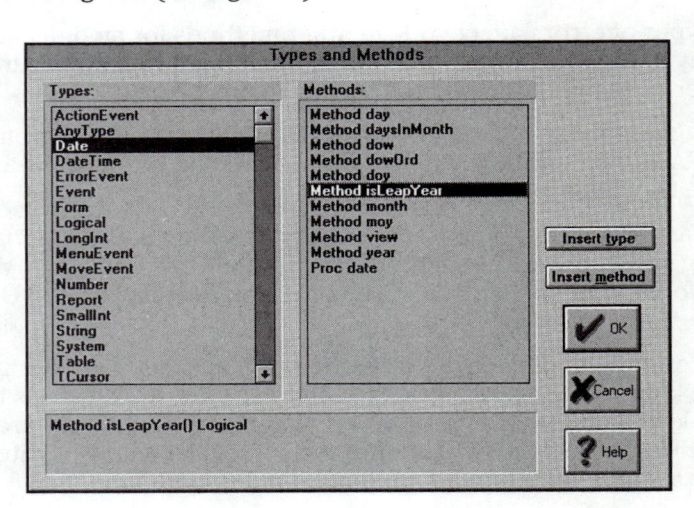

FIG. 13.8

The Types and Methods dialog box.

This dialog box is extremely useful while you're creating methods. The Types section of the dialog box lists all the ObjectPAL types. When you select a type, the Methods section of the dialog box lists the available methods for and procedures associated with that type. With the type of object or variable selected, you can click the Insert type button to insert the type name into the current ObjectPAL Editor window. (This feature actually isn't very useful, however, because you typically use an object's name in code. An object is an instance of a type, not the type itself.) The type name is inserted when you click the Insert type button, even if you click Cancel to close the dialog box.

When you select a method or procedure from a type, Paradox displays the syntax (or prototype) of that method in the syntax section of the dialog box (the unlabelled box at the bottom of the dialog box). With the method name selected, click the Insert Method button to insert the method in the current ObjectPAL Editor window. If you insert a method, you see the syntax of that method in the status line of the ObjectPAL Editor window when you return from the dialog box.

The syntax of a method tells you what arguments the method expects and what data type (if any) the method returns. This feature is particularly handy while you're learning the language. If you don't know the exact name of a method or whether a method is available for a certain object, browse through the Types and Methods dialog box.

> **TIP**
>
> Remember that the Paradox for Windows Help system contains entries for every ObjectPAL method and procedure.

The Display Objects and Properties Dialog Box

Choose Properties from the Language menu to open the Display Objects and Properties dialog box (see fig. 13.9).

In a fashion similar to the Types and Methods dialog box, the Display Objects and Properties dialog box lists all the UIObjects (display objects, such as bit maps and buttons).

When you select an object, all the property names for that object appear in the Properties section of the Display Objects and Properties dialog box. If you select a property, all the possible values for the selected property appear in the Values section of the dialog box.

FIG. 13.9

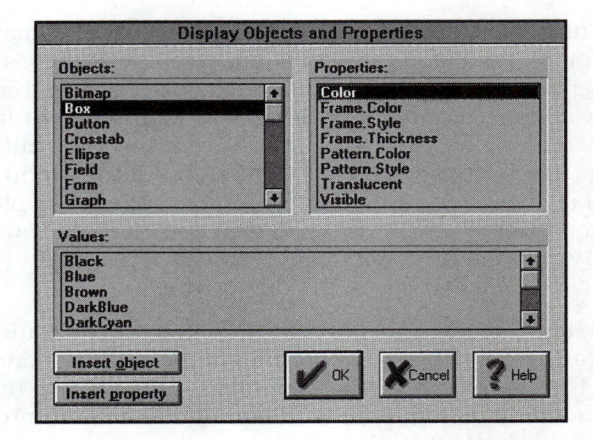

The Display Objects and Properties dialog box.

The Properties and Values sections are valuable resources while you're learning ObjectPAL, because objects have many properties. The Next property for a field object, for example, tells Paradox which field to move to when a user presses Tab (this is a read-only property); the Prev property indicates the preceding field.

The Constants Dialog Box

Choose Constants from the Language menu to open the Constants dialog box. The Constants dialog box enables you to view the various types of constants and to insert a constant directly into your code (see fig. 13.10).

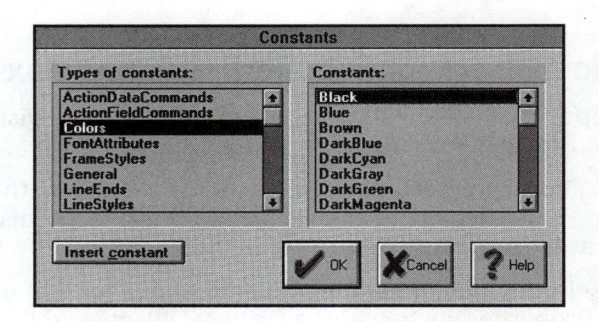

FIG. 13.10

The Constants dialog box.

A constant is a value of a certain data type that does not change throughout a program. Colors are constants, as are most property settings. Run-time errors also are constants. (Variables, on the other hand, are expected to change through a program. The difference between the two is explained in more detail in Chapter 14.)

13 — GETTING STARTED WITH OBJECTPAL

Source Code Reports

Typically, when you need to change part of an application, you open the form, click the object that you want to change, and then modify a snippet of code. Sometimes, especially if you have a large application, you may want to see all the code in one place. Language, Browse Sources from the ObjectPAL Editor menu creates a report that shows all the source code for all the objects in a form.

To see all the source codes for an entire form, follow these steps:

1. Select the form by pressing Esc.
2. Display the properties menu for the form.
3. Choose Methods.
4. Select a method to edit (any method will do).
5. Choose Language, Browse Sources. Paradox creates a report that shows all of the source code for the form (see fig. 13.11).

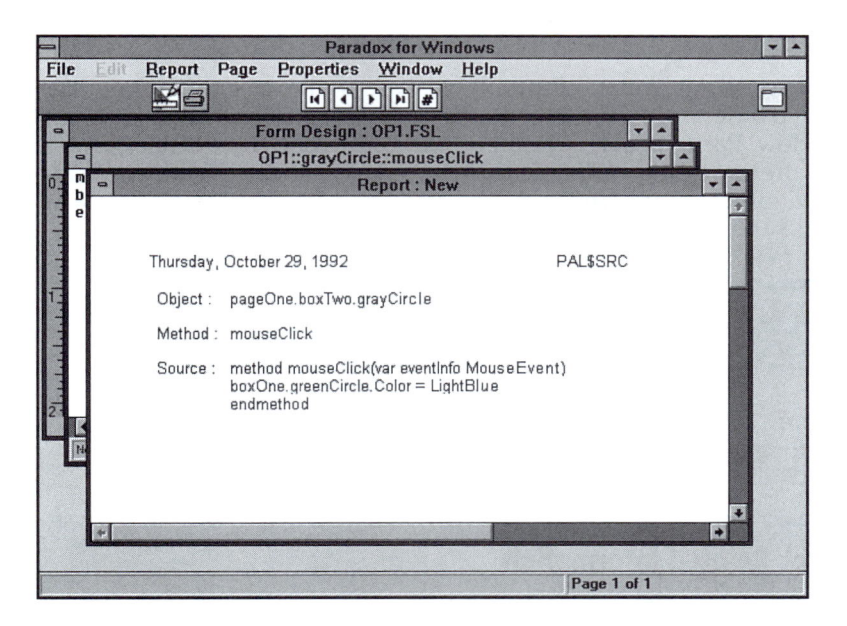

FIG. 13.11

A Browse Sources report.

The ObjectPAL equivalent of Language, Browse Sources is a method called **enumSource**. This procedure creates a table that contains one record for each defined method for each object in a form. The method definitions are stored in memo fields.

Language, Deliver creates another version of the current form and gives that version an FDL file-name extension. Users cannot enter Design mode in a delivered form and thus cannot change source code. Naturally, you should deliver only a complete and debugged form.

The Properties Menu

With the Properties menu, you set properties for the desktop, choose a default ObjectPAL Editor window size, set up an alternate editor, and toggle the display of compiler warnings.

Properties, Desktop opens the Desktop Properties dialog box, in which you can set or change characteristics of the desktop. For example, you can change the title of the desktop from *Paradox for Windows* to a custom title, such as *Inventory Control Application*.

Paradox opens an Editor or Debugger window to a default size. To change this size, first open an Editor window and set it to the size you want. Next, choose Properties, Window Sizing. In the Editor Window Size dialog box, choose Use Current Sizing From Now On.

Properties, Alternate Editor enables you to link to a different editor. With a different editor linked, whenever you attempt to open an Editor window, Paradox asks whether you want to use the default editor or the alternate editor. This feature is useful because even if you want to use another editor while you're creating code, you certainly will need to use the default editor to debug and fine-tune your code.

NOTE Because the ObjectPAL Editor provides a great deal of language help, you probably shouldn't use another editor until you're familiar with the ObjectPAL language.

Properties, Show Compiler Warning toggles the display of compiler warnings.

For Related Information

▶▶ "Declaring Constants," p. 564.

▶▶ "Creating Data Types and Records," p. 566.

▶▶ "Calling Procedures," p. 591.

▶▶ "Creating Custom Methods," p. 596.

ObjectPAL Debugger

The ObjectPAL Debugger is an integrated debugger. *Integrated* means that the debugger is available to you as you are writing and developing ObjectPAL code. Many programmers, particularly beginning programmers, bother to learn debuggers only when they absolutely must. Don't make this mistake. The Debugger can help you write and design better programs by showing you, line by line, exactly what is happening. (For an example of how to use the Debugger, see the "Adding a Program with ObjectPAL" section later in this chapter.)

Table 13.2 briefly describes the Debugger menu commands.

Table 13.2. Debugger Commands

Command	Action
Inspect	Opens a window to display the value of a variable
Stack Backtrace	Displays the methods and procedures most recently called and currently active (for example, if **methodOne** calls **methodTwo**, both methods are active and appear in the Stack window)
Set Breakpoint	At design time, marks a point in the code to stop at run time
List Breakpoints	Displays all current breakpoints and enables you to delete breakpoints
Trace Execution	Creates a window to show each line of code as the code is executed
Trace Built-ins	Enables you to choose built-in methods to trace
Enable DEBUG	At run time, halts execution when the program Statement reaches DEBUG statement; the combination of inserting a DEBUG statement and enabling the DEBUG statement works like a breakpoint
Enable Ctrl+Break To Debugger	At run time, halts program execution when user presses Ctrl+Break
View Source	Displays a list of defined methods; when you choose a method from the list, Paradox opens the method in an Editor window
Origin	Shows the method that contains the current breakpoint

continues

Table 13.2. Continued

Command	Action
Step Over	Executes one line of code but treats method and procedure calls as one line (useful if the method or procedure is fully debugged)
Step Into	Executes one line of code but steps into methods or procedures called (use this command to debug a procedure or method)
Quit This Method	Stops running method and closes all Debugger windows
Run	Available at design time or run time, this command starts or resumes execution, closing all Editor and Debugger windows

Adding a Program with ObjectPAL

As you learned earlier in this chapter, ObjectPAL's built-in features enable you to add small programs to an interactive application. This section shows you how to add a program that gives users help while they're working in a form. To create the form, follow these steps:

1. To begin, choose File, New, Form to create a new form.
2. Choose the Albums table from the Data Model dialog box. The Albums table was created in Chapter 2.
3. Click OK to select the default layout in the Design Layout dialog box.
4. Save the form as **AlbumsOP**, then run the form. Without any additional modifications, the running form should look like figure 13.12.

To add a Help button to the form, follow these steps:

1. Return to Design mode.
2. Click the Button tool in the SpeedBar.
3. In the upper right corner of the visible portion of the form, draw a button. Notice that Paradox labels the button LABEL. The default label text actually is a grow-to-fit, one-line, centered text field containing the word LABEL.

13 — GETTING STARTED WITH OBJECTPAL

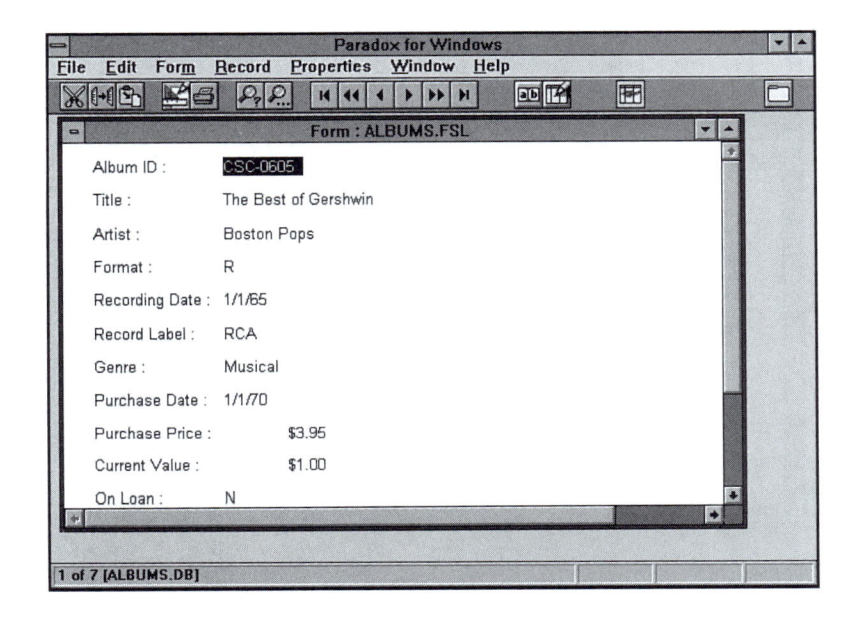

FIG. 13.12

The AlbumsOP form.

4. Select the label field for the button.
5. After the label is selected, click inside the text area to place the cursor inside the text field. Press End and then press Ctrl+Backspace to erase the default text.
6. When the field is clear, type **Help**. Adjust the field size, if necessary.

   The form should look like figure 13.13.

Naturally, to give users help with your form, you need to do more than just place and relabel a button. As it is, when you press the button, Paradox will push the button in, then release it, but Paradox won't do much else. To make the button do something, follow these steps:

1. Right-click the button to inspect its properties.
2. Rename the button *formHelp*.

TIP

Get into the habit of naming objects as you create them. Naming objects consistently helps you create a self-documenting application. In addition, the compiler insists that all objects not bound to a table be renamed before code refers to them.

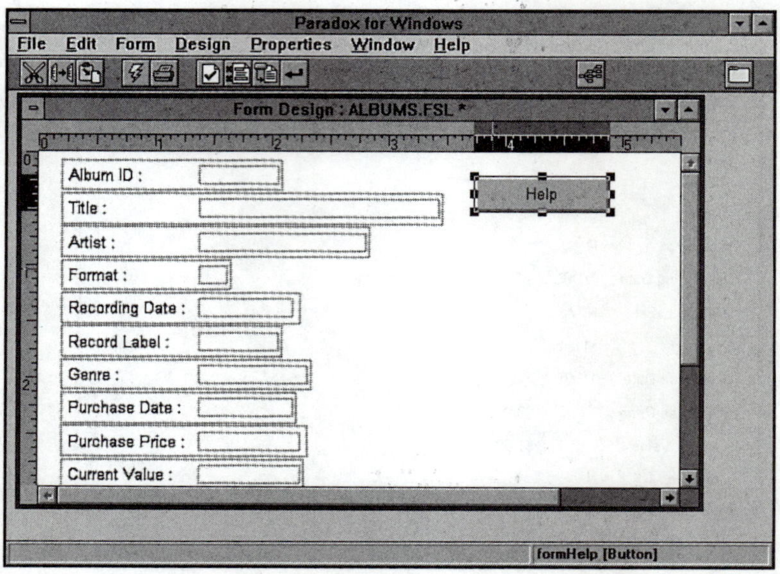

FIG. 13.13

The ALBUMS form with a Help button.

3. Choose Methods from the properties menu to open the Methods dialog box.

4. Choose **pushButton** from the list of methods (shown in the Built-In Methods section of the dialog box), then click OK. Your screen should look like figure 13.14.

5. Right-click in the window to display the Language menu.

6. Choose Types from the Language menu. Paradox displays the Types and Methods dialog box. The left section of the box lists the types (categories) of items for which you can write code.

7. Search through the Types list box for the System type. Press **S** to move to the type names beginning with S, and then press the down-arrow key to move through the type list until you find System.

   Alternatively, use the scroll bar to scroll through the list and then click System when it appears on-screen. Procedures and methods for the System type are listed in the Methods section of the Types and Methods dialog box.

13 — GETTING STARTED WITH OBJECTPAL

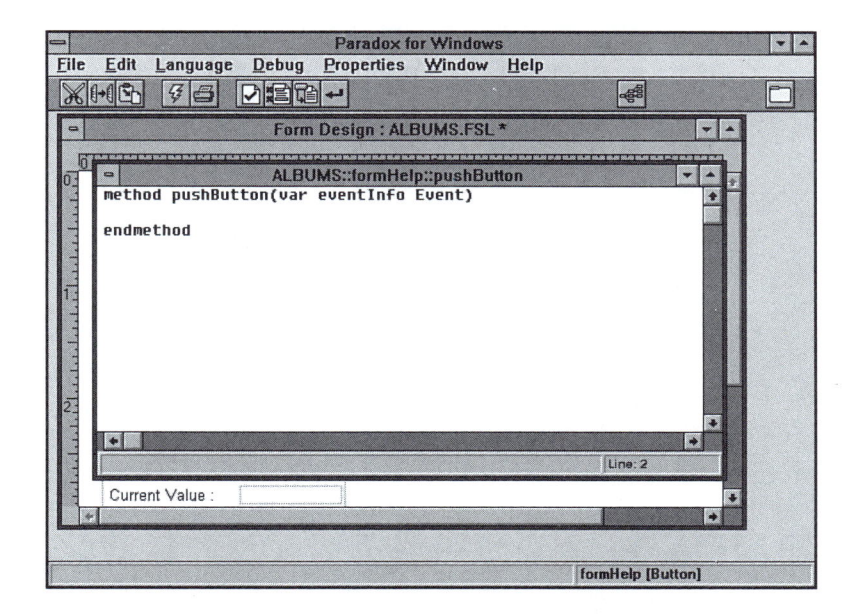

FIG. 13.14

The **pushButton** method for *formHelp*.

> **TIP**
>
> Paradox categorizes general-purpose procedures under the System type. Procedures do not actually belong to a specific type; their relationship with the System type is arbitrary. General procedures are not called in conjunction with an object name; thus, general procedures are not written to behave differently depending on the type of the object with which they are called. If you're looking for a general-purpose procedure, check the System type list.

8. Select the **msgInfo** procedure. When you select a procedure or method, the Syntax section of the dialog box lists the syntax of the method or procedure. The syntax of a method or procedure shows you what arguments the method or procedure expects and what type of value (if any) the method or procedure returns (see fig. 13.15).

9. Click the Insert Method button. Paradox inserts the word msgInfo at the cursor in the current ObjectPAL Editor window.

10. Click OK to close the dialog box. Your Editor window should look like figure 13.16.

FIG. 13.15

The Types and Methods dialog box with **Proc msgInfo** selected.

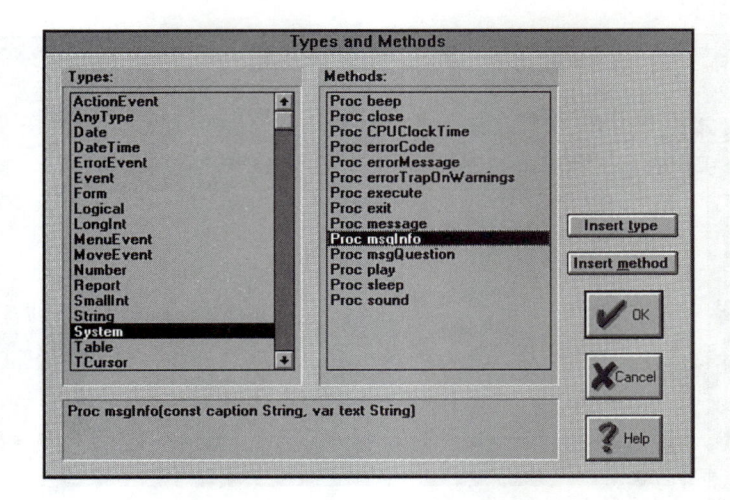

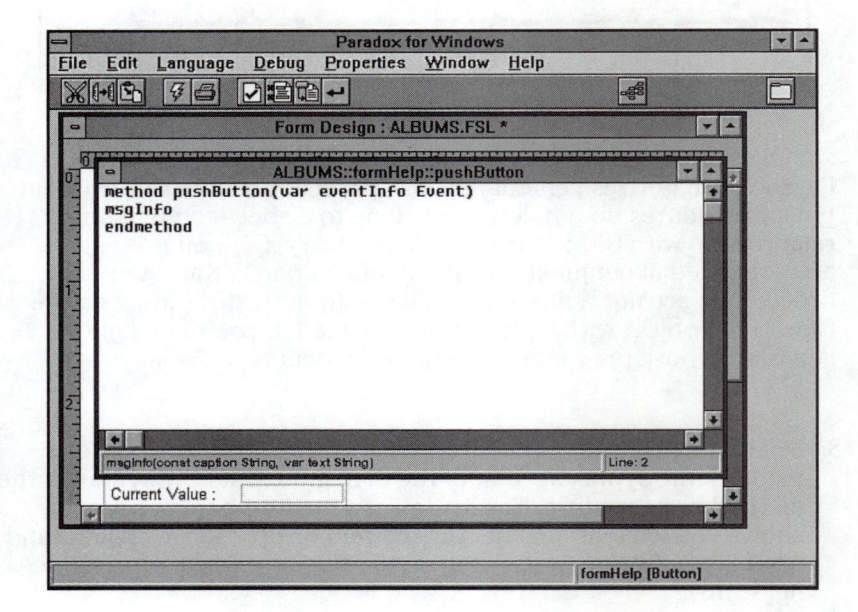

FIG. 13.16

Text inserted from the Types and Methods dialog box.

11. Notice that the syntax for **msgInfo** appears in the status line of the Editor window. The syntax tells you how to use the **msgInfo** procedure to display a message.

msgInfo takes two arguments. The first argument, described by the syntax as **const caption String**, specifies the string that the dialog box uses for the caption. The second argument, described by the syntax as **const text String**, specifies the string that the dialog box uses for the display text, or message.

12. Type the parentheses, comma, and arguments so that the entire method definition looks like this:

    ```
    method pushButton(var eventInfo Event)
    msgInfo("Form Help", "To add a new album, press Ins.")
    endMethod
    ```

13. Choose Check Syntax from the Language menu or click the Syntax Check button in the SpeedBar to check your code for errors. If typing errors appear, Paradox displays an error message in the status line and positions the text cursor at the point of the error. Correct the errors, if any, and check the syntax again.

14. Click the View Data button in the SpeedBar (or choose Run from the Debug menu). Paradox closes the Editor window, saves the changes to memory (but not to disk), and runs the form.

15. Click the Help button in the form. A message window appears, displaying the caption and text you specified (see fig. 13.17).

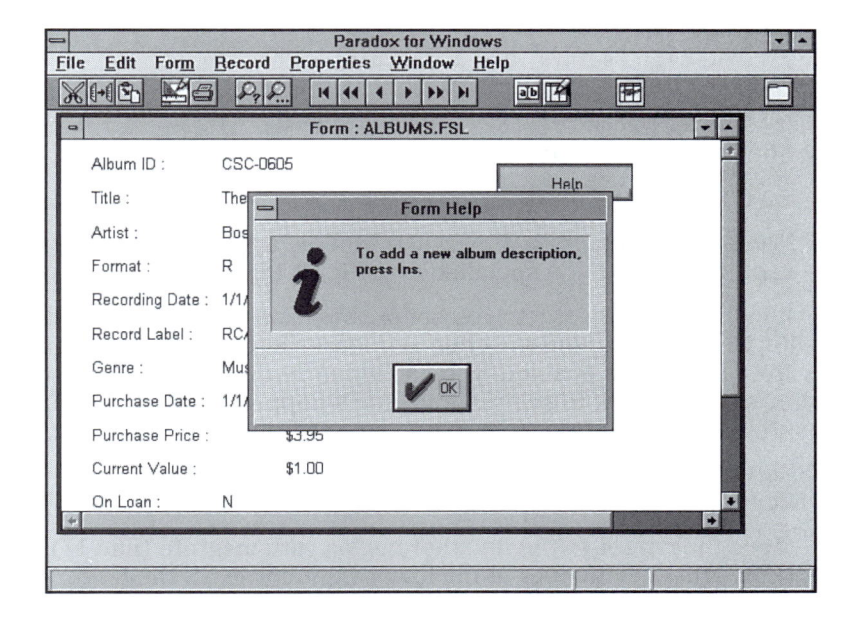

FIG. 13.17

A help message for the AlbumsOP form.

Previously, you entered a quoted string for the second argument. The **msgInfo** procedure also enables you to specify a string variable to display in the window. To assign the help text to a variable, follow these steps:

1. Return to Design mode and open the **pushButton** method for *formHelp*.

2. Modify **pushButton** so that it reads as follows (the text following the semicolons is comment text; you don't have to type it):

```
method pushButton(var eventInfo Event)
var                      ; opens the variable declaration section
    helpString    String  ; declares a variable of type String
endVar                    ; closes the variable declaration section

helpString =
"To add a new album, press
Ins. To search, move to a
field, then click the Speedbar
search button. For help on any
field, right-click the field."
; you can assign several lines of text to a single String variable
; the line breaks in the string above determine the line
; breaks in the displayed text

; this time, call msgInfo with helpString
msgInfo("Form Help", helpString)
endmethod
```

3. Check the syntax and correct any errors.

4. Save and run the form.

5. Press the Help button. A message window appears, displaying the caption and text you specified (see fig. 13.18).

The ObjectPAL Debugger lets you set *breakpoints*. A breakpoint tells Paradox to stop executing the code and start running the Debugger. After the Debugger is enabled, you can move through your program one line at a time, just to see exactly what's happening. Follow these steps to set a breakpoint:

1. Return to Design mode and open the **pushButton** method for *formHelp*.

2. Move the cursor to the line that begins with **msgInfo** (line 17). Notice the line number in the lower right corner of the Editor window.

3. Choose Debug, Set Breakpoint.

13 — GETTING STARTED WITH OBJECTPAL

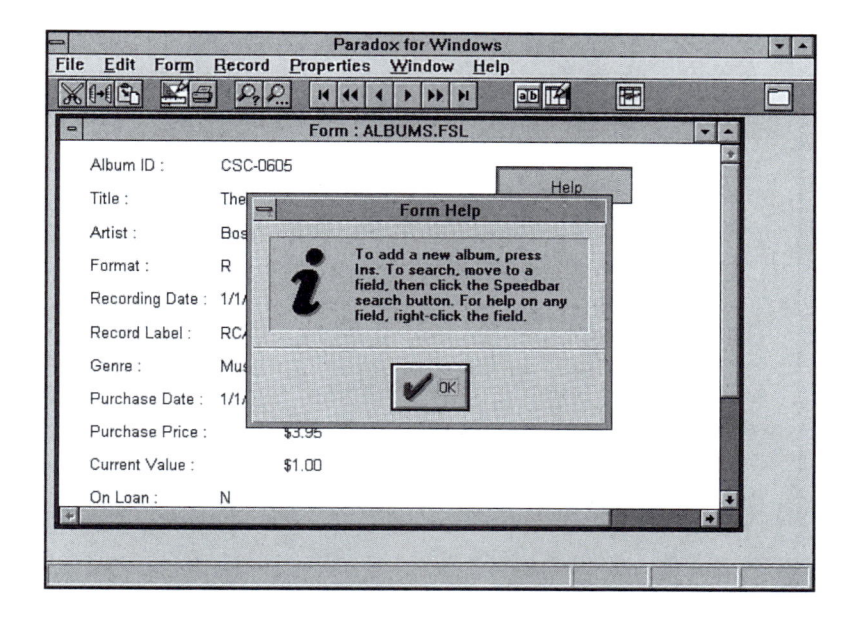

FIG. 13.18

A formatted help message for the AlbumsOP form.

4. Click OK to accept a breakpoint on the current line (line 17).

5. Save and run the form.

6. Click Help. Paradox executes the **pushButton** method for *helpForm* until it reaches line 17, the breakpoint line. Paradox does not execute the breakpoint line; it breaks after executing the previous line (line 16). When Paradox reaches the break, it opens the **pushButton** method in an ObjectPAL Editor window and positions the text cursor at line 17.

   Notice that the Editor window status line tells you why you stopped: Breakpoint at Line 17.

   The window should look like figure 13.19.

7. Choose Debug, Inspect. Paradox opens the Inspect dialog box. By default, the dialog box selects the words below or to the right of the cursor for inspection (see fig. 13.20).

8. Replace the existing text with the word **helpString**.

9. Press Enter or click OK. Paradox opens an Inspector window. The title of the Inspector window is the data type of the variable or constant displayed, as shown in figure 13.21.

III — PROGRAMMING PARADOX FOR WINDOWS

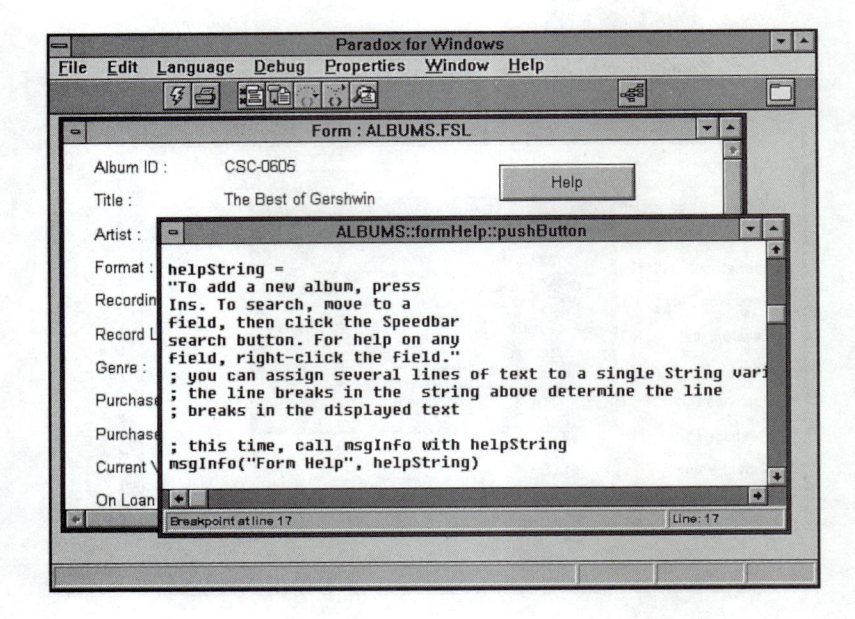

FIG. 13.19

An Editor window opened at a breakpoint.

FIG. 13.20

The Inspect dialog box.

FIG. 13.21

The Inspector window.

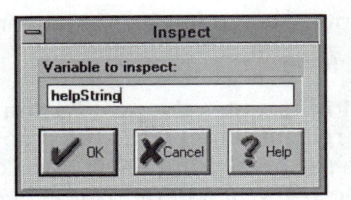

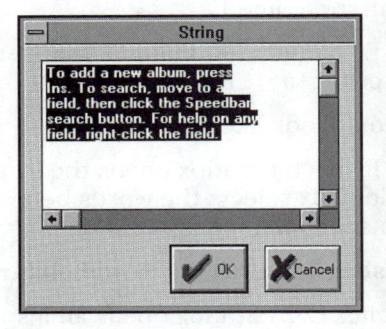

10. Click OK to close the Inspector window.
11. Choose Run from the Debug menu. The rest of the code for **pushButton** executes, showing you the Help dialog box you constructed with **infoMsg**.

12. Click Help again.
13. At the breakpoint, choose Debug, Inspect.
14. You can change a variable's value in the Inspector window by editing the displayed value. For example, click the first line of the string and change **album** to **CD**. From that point on, Paradox uses the changed string. Paradox does not change the value in your ObjectPAL program; the value changes only for the duration of the current program.
15. Click OK to close the Inspector window.
16. Choose Debug, Run or click the View Data button in the SpeedBar. When the Form Help dialog box appears, notice the text that you changed.

A Quick Overview for Programmers

Although ObjectPAL is designed so that it can be accessible to non-programmers, serious developers should note that ObjectPAL is a full-featured, high-level, extensible language. ObjectPAL is suitable for demanding programmers writing sophisticated applications. ObjectPAL is a real language, not merely a scripting language or a macro language.

Of the many types of users who will use ObjectPAL, some are already experienced programmers. The following sections describe ObjectPAL in terms that you are more likely to understand if you have programming experience. Some of these terms may be unfamiliar to you, but be assured that they are explained in more detail later in this chapter or in the following chapters.

Language Features

ObjectPAL supports the following functions:

- Built-in event handling
- Strong data typing
- User-defined data types
- Powerful data types such as resizable arrays, associative arrays (called *dynamic arrays*), and composite data types (called *Records*)

- Structured program control
- An extensive library of methods and procedures
- User-defined methods and procedures
- Calls to functions and procedures written in other languages, such as PASCAL, C, and C++
- Calls to an externally compiled help system (one compiled with the Windows Help Compiler)

Control Features

ObjectPAL enables you to trap for and change both keystrokes and mouse actions. Usually, however, you do not need to build this kind of low-level control. Instead, you can build code that responds to events. *Events* are something Paradox creates in response to a key press or a mouse click.

You can capture, respond to, change, create, and simulate all mouse events, including position, movement, right-clicks, left-clicks, double-clicks, and clicks in concert with a Shift, Alt, or Ctrl. You have similar control over all key presses.

You can open, position, size, minimize, maximize, and otherwise manipulate forms and all other display objects. You can use multiple forms as dialog boxes or as modules for an application.

Any property that you can set interactively for an object (for example, its color), you can set in ObjectPAL. At run time, ObjectPAL can control many properties that are not available from the properties menu, such as an object's position and focus status. For example, you can "follow" a user around a form by drawing a colored frame around the object that has focus.

You can create top-level menus with associated pull-down menus. You can hide the SpeedBar and even reset the main title of the main Paradox window.

Any table action that normally is available interactively can also be made available through ObjectPAL. A host of actions that are unavailable interactively also are available through ObjectPAL. For example, you can manipulate tables as Tables, TableViews, TableFrames, and TCursors. A *Table* is what you use for utility functions, such as Add and Subtract. A *TableView* is a table opened in a default window (what Paradox creates when you choose File, Open, Table). A *TableFrame* is a table object placed on a form. A *TCursor* is a handle to a table that you can use behind the scenes; TCursors come in handy for searching and sorting.

All the File system functions available interactively also are available under ObjectPAL control. You can call a built-in File Browser box to let a user choose a file. You can delete or rename files, if you need to, or make directories.

You can create queries (QBE files) interactively, then execute those queries under ObjectPAL control. You also can create query statements from scratch in ObjectPAL; these queries can include variables to be evaluated at run time.

Objects in ObjectPAL

The terminology of objects may be more confusing to experienced programmers than to novices, because the better you know a language or a paradigm, the more difficulty you have learning new terms for the language. Learning about object-based programming, however, is not difficult.

In everyday language, objects are just things—smart things. In programmers' terms, objects are data and code tightly bound together. You create objects either interactively or with ObjectPAL.

To make object-oriented programming work for you, just remember to start with the objects. In fact, start with the objects you already know best—the objects you place on a form. Don't start by trying to build complex multiform applications with low-level keyboard handlers, cascading menus, and flocks of dialog boxes. In fact, you will get to know ObjectPAL better if you try not to think too big, at least at first. Instead, for your first project, think about making specific objects on specific forms do what you want them to do. The possibilities for your next project will unfold as you go.

As you get to know ObjectPAL, you may wonder how it differs from an object-oriented language. Although ObjectPAL is object-based and much of its design is drawn from the principles of object-oriented programming (OOP), it is not a true object-oriented language.

What of the OOP terms *inheritance*, *encapsulation*, and *polymorphism*? If you have experience with OOP, you might think that ObjectPAL provides a class library, from which you can inherit classes and modify them as needed. But ObjectPAL is, rather, a hybrid library of classes (referred to in Paradox for Windows as *types*). You can create objects or instances of the classes (types) provided by ObjectPAL, but you cannot inherit those classes to create new classes. Furthermore, you cannot create your own classes from scratch.

The principle of encapsulation, in which data is stored with code, is incorporated into ObjectPAL by way of objects. When you write code in ObjectPAL, you write that code to and for specific objects. When you copy or move an object, all of the code stays with it.

Polymorphism means that methods (some languages call them functions) with the same name behave differently depending on the object they are called with. Polymorphism exists in ObjectPAL and is incorporated into the run-time library. Form objects and report objects, for example, each have an **open** method. The different **open** methods share the same name and do the same thing; ObjectPAL sorts out which is which when it compiles the program.

For Related Information
▶▶ "Declaring Variables," p. 555.

Chapter Summary

This chapter described how you can put ObjectPAL to work for you. After reading this chapter, you should understand how ObjectPAL differs from other programming languages and how you can use those differences to your advantage. The exercises in this section were an economy-class excursion into the land of ObjectPAL, designed to acquaint you with the ObjectPAL environment as quickly as possible. Read the next three chapters for the deluxe tour.

The next chapter, Chapter 14, explains the basic elements of the language, including how to use variables, how to construct loops to repeat sets of actions, how to use conditional statements, and how to define your own functions. Chapter 15 explains the major programming tasks you will want to use in ObjectPAL. Chapters 16, 17, and 18 provide short but complete ObjectPAL applications and explain how to tie together the different parts of a program.

CHAPTER 14

Understanding ObjectPAL Basics

This chapter explains ObjectPAL language building blocks. In this chapter, you learn how to create variables, how to construct control structures, and how to test for conditions. You also discover how to create procedures and custom methods.

This chapter is written to serve the needs of beginning and experienced programmers. To discuss basic programming concepts at great length, however, is beyond the scope of this book.

As you work through this chapter, you may want to keep a form open to try out examples. A few of the examples use tables built in previous chapters. The easiest way to try out examples is to create a button, rename it, and attach the example code to the button's **pushButton** event method.

> **NOTE** The examples in this chapter and the following chapters assume that you have the Advanced ObjectPAL option set to On. To set this option, choose Properties, Desktop, to open the Desktop Properties dialog, then choose the Advanced button in the ObjectPAL Level group.

Understanding Program Style Basics

Before you get started, you need to know how ObjectPAL code must look for the syntax checker to understand it and how ObjectPAL code should look for ordinary humans to be able to read it. You can write a variable declaration section, for example, like the following one:

```
var myStringVariable String myNumberVariable Number endvar
```

The ObjectPAL syntax checker does not object to this style, but it is not as easy to read as the following section:

```
var
    myStringVariable    String
    myNumberVariable    Number
endvar
```

Spaces

ObjectPAL usually allows any number of spaces wherever one space is allowed. In a comma-separated list of arguments, for example, you normally use one space after the comma for each item, as in

```
sound(174, 150)
; first number is frequency (pitch),
;   second number is duration
```

but you can write the same statement

```
sound(174  ,  150)
```

The following renditions are equally correct:

```
sound(174,150)       ; no space between comma and second argument
sound ( 174 , 150 )  ; extra spaces all over the place
sound(174,
        150)         ; arguments separated by carriage return
```

Maximum Characters

The maximum number of characters allowed on a line is 132. If you want to assign a long string to a variable, you can break up the string over several lines and *concatenate* (add together) the parts, as in the following example:

```
myStringVariable = "The first part of a very long string, plus " +
                   "the second part of a very long string, plus " +
                   "the third part of the string."
```

Alternatively, you can assign a string with embedded carriage returns by breaking the string exactly where you want the line breaks, as in the following example:

```
myStringVariable =
"The first part of a very long string, plus
the second part of a very long string, plus
the third part of a string, with line breaks."
```

The second and following lines of a broken string are read from the first character of the line. If you indent the second and following lines in the assignment, they also are indented when you display the message. Thus, the assignment

```
myStringVariable = "The first part of a very long string, plus
                   the second part of a very long string, plus
                   the third part of a string, with line breaks."
```

will display as

```
The first part of a very long string, plus
                   the second part of a very long string, plus
                   the third part of a string, with line breaks.
```

You cannot place comments in the middle of a string assignment constructed in this manner.

Using Uppercase and Lowercase

ObjectPAL is not case-sensitive: whether a letter in a command, method name, type name, procedure name, or variable is uppercase or lowercase is of no consequence. Both of the following lines declare the same variable with the same data type:

```
myStringVariable String
```

and

```
MYSTRINGVARIABLE STRING
```

You later can reference the variable *myStringVariable* as either uppercase, lowercase, or a combination of both. For maximum readability, use a combination of uppercase and lowercase, starting each new word fragment in a variable name with an uppercase letter.

Case matters only when you are dealing with text strings directly.

```
myStringVariable = "UPPERCASE"
```

is not the same as

```
myStringVariable = "uppercase"
```

Comments

ObjectPAL, like most programming languages, allows you to add comments to your programs. ObjectPAL provides two ways to indicate that text is a comment—or to *comment out* parts of your program. To tell ObjectPAL that the rest of the text on a line is a comment, precede the comment text with a semicolon, as in the following example:

```
myStringVariable = "uppercase"    ; this is comment text
```

To mark several lines of text as a comment, you may find braces easier to use. All the following code is commented out:

```
{     ; the open brace marks the beginning of comment lines
myStringVariable = "UPPERCASE"
myStringVariable = "uppercase"
}          ; the close brace marks the end of comment lines
```

ObjectPAL code uses the semicolon and the braces only to set off comments. Neither symbol is used for any other purpose.

Indentation

The indentation used for ObjectPAL is a matter of personal preference. Proper indentation improves code readability, however, perhaps more than any other single style convention.

Consider the following **if** statement:

```
if x = 1 then
   x = 2
else
   x = 1
endif
```

The line following the first **if** clause is indented to show that it will be executed only if the clause is true. The line following the **else** clause is indented to show that it will be executed only if the clause is false. The following statement is a less readable form:

```
if x = 1
then
x = 2
else
x = 1 endif
```

Indentation becomes critical to readability in more complex **if** statements. The indentation in the following example shows you where **if** statements are nested inside of other **if** statements.

```
if x > 1 then
   if x = 4 then
      if y = 3 then
         x = y + x
      else
         y = x + y
      endif
   else
      if z = 7 then
         x = z - 1
      else
         x = z
      endif
   endif
else
   x = 0
endif
```

If the same statements are written without indentation, sorting through which **if** belongs to which **else** and determining which **if** is nested is very difficult.

The number of spaces you indent to show the nesting of control is a matter of preference. If you are programming for or with a group of programmers, the group may set indentation standards.

Declaring Variables

Because they are used to hold data that changes or is expected to change when the program runs, *variables* exist in virtually all programming languages. If your program asks a user a question, for example, the question presumes that the answer cannot be known until run-time. Because you don't know what the answer will be, you store the answer in a variable. A program usually takes different sets of actions, depending on the value of a variable.

Variables also are used in a program as *handles*—or alias-names. When you want your application to open a form, for example, you must assign the form's name to a variable. You use the form's full file name only once; thereafter, you use the handle or variable.

Don't let the term *handle* intimidate you. You may have heard advanced programmers speak of handles as though they are some very abstract construct. A handle is very simple. Your name, for example, is the handle that other people use to address you; it's not who you are, it's just a name that refers to you. Some people have different handles for the same thing: to a nurse, you are the "patient with a hernia in 4B"; to the postman, you are the resident of "231 Elm Street"; to your children, you are "Mom" or "Dad." In ObjectPAL, you use handles in the same way—as a shorthand way of referring to a thing.

Variable Types

Variables are classified into types (also called *data types*). As a field type in a table structure tells Paradox what kind of information a field can hold, the type of a variable determines the kind of information the variable can hold.

A variable's type helps the compiler know how much storage to set aside for the variable. Variable types also enable the compiler to check your code for errors—called *type mismatches*. A type mismatch indicates that a variable is used in a way inconsistent with its type. This is similar to what happens in interactive Paradox if you try to type letters into a numeric field. If you have declared a variable to be a Number type and then try to assign letters to it, the compiler gives you an error message.

The process of checking for and requiring correct usage of data types is called *strong typing*. Strong typing is a feature of industrial-strength languages, such as C and Pascal. Although ObjectPAL implements strong typing, it also gives you a "back door": a data type called AnyType. Variables of type AnyType are acceptable in place of any other type. This does not mean that your data will be safe if you do something foolish like pass a string data type to a numeric data type via an AnyType variable. For this reason, use AnyType variables only when the programming situation demands them. ObjectPAL also does not require that you declare and type all variables before you use them. In the middle of your program, for example, you may have these statements:

```
i = 2 ; assign a number to i
msgInfo("What's i?", i) ; show i in a dialog
```

ObjectPAL figures out what data type to give the variable *i* based on what data you assign to *i*. Declaring variables before you use them is still safer and faster. Therefore, the example shown above should be:

```
var
  i SmallInt
endVar
```

```
i = 2                        ; ... some other code
                             ; assign a number to i
msgInfo("What's i?", i)      ; show i in a dialog
```

When you are first learning a language, strong typing feels more like a curse than a blessing—you have to listen to the compiler complain about your code. The blessing of strong typing is that the compiler is helping you design better code. If you write a procedure and intend it to take two arguments, a String and a Number, you have to tell the compiler the data type of both arguments. When the procedure is called by another part of the program, the compiler checks the data type of the arguments being passed. If the data types don't match—if you pass two Strings instead of a String and a Number, for example—the procedure is being used for something it was not intended. The compiler then gives you a syntax error.

Type methods and procedures provided for your use by ObjectPAL also expect a certain number and type of arguments when called. If the arguments you use to call the method or procedure don't match the definition of the method or procedure, the compiler notifies you.

Variable Declarations

Before you can use a variable in code, you must declare it. Variables are created usually in an area of a method called a *Var section*, but you also can create them in something called a *Var window*. (Where you need to declare variables is discussed in greater detail later in this chapter.)

When you declare a variable, you give it a name and a type. Variables of the same type can be declared on the same line. Declaring variables is a relatively straightforward process, as shown in the following example:

```
var
   colorOfForm            String
   searchDialogForm       Form
   numberOfSearches       Number
   CtrOne, CtrTwo         SmallInt
endVar
; lines or parts of lines preceded by a semi-colon are comments
; commenting your code is considered good programming style
```

The keywords **var** and **endVar** mark the beginning and end of the Var section. The line

```
colorOfForm    String
```

declares one variable, named *colorOfForm*, of the String data type. *colorOfForm* can hold text data. The line

```
CtrOne, CtrTwo        SmallInt
```

declares two variables, *CtrOne* and *CtrTwo*, both SmallInt data types. *CtrOne* and *CtrTwo* can hold whole numbers (integers) from –32768 to 32767.

Arrays are a special kind of a variable with a unique declaration syntax. The syntax for declaring an array is described in the section "Working with Arrays," later in this chapter.

Naming Variables

A variable's name is something you dream up as its creator. You can use terse names such as *x* or *y*, but creating more descriptive names is advisable.

Programmers traditionally used short, nondescriptive variable names—partly as a function of the way programs were created and maintained. When using punch cards, for example, punching in long variable names was a tedious task. Because a variable name also takes up storage, its length has an impact on the size of the compiled program.

The current thinking is that the advantages of longer names outweigh the disadvantages of slightly larger programs. Descriptive variable names make your code more readable. If someone else inherits your code—or if you return to your code after an extended absence—longer variable names can help you sort out what the program is trying to do.

Using Variables

After you have declared a variable, you assign a value to it. When you first assign a value to a variable, it is called *initializing a variable*. To initialize a variable, assign it any value that is consistent with its type. To initialize a SmallInt variable, named *CtrOne* (to be used as an index or counter), you might assign it the value 0 or 1, as in

```
CtrOne = 0
```

After the variable is initialized, it is said to be *assigned*. When a variable has a value, it can be used in expressions and tests. ObjectPAL provides the **isAssigned** method to test whether a variable has been assigned a value. To find out if *CtrOne* has been assigned a value, write the following:

```
ctrOne.isAssigned()
```

14 — UNDERSTANDING OBJECTPAL BASICS

isAssigned returns True if the variable has been assigned a value and False if not.

If you aren't certain that a variable is assigned, always test it with the **isAssigned** method before you use the variable in an expression or condition. The following code fragment tests whether the variable *buttonPushCounter* has been assigned a value yet. If it hasn't been assigned a value, the value of **buttonPushCounter** is set to 1.

```
if isassigned(buttonPushCounter) then
   buttonPushCounter = buttonPushCounter + 1 ; increments counter
else
   buttonPushCounter = 1
endif
```

If you attempt to use an unassigned variable in a test or expression, a run-time error results.

Using Variables as Handles

You usually manipulate objects on a form with the names you assign to them in the Properties menu. If you create an object and name it *objectOne*, for example, the following statement changes the color of *objectOne*:

```
objectOne.color = "Black"
```

Sometimes, however, you cannot take quite so direct an approach. To open a new form, for example, you first must declare an object of the type Form. Then you open the form, using the file name and the variable. The variable becomes a handle to the file. All actions subsequently are directed to the secondary form through the variable (handle).

```
method pushButton(var eventInfo Event)
var
  secondForm   Form
  ; secondForm is the variable name, the type is Form
  TitleFromOther String
  ; TitleFromOther is another variable of type String
endvar

; when SecondForm is first opened, the full file name is used
secondForm.open("albums.fsl")

; now, all actions on albums.fsl are through variable secondForm
secondForm.action(DataNextRecord)
TitleFromOther = secondForm.Title.value
secondForm.close()              ; close second form
msgInfo("Title", TitleFromOther)

endmethod
```

After the form ALBUMS.FSL is opened by using the variable name *secondForm*, *secondForm* is used as a handle to the form.

Types

Data types available in ObjectPAL are described in the following table. Any basic data type shown in Table 14.1 can be used on the right side of a variable declaration.

Table 14.1. Data Types

Type	Description
Basic Data Types	Types in this category correspond roughly to the field types available in Paradox interactively. Additional types available through ObjectPAL but not available interactively include Array, DynArray, Logical, Time, DateTime, SmallInt, LongInt, and Point.
AnyType	One of the basic data types. A variable of type AnyType can be used in place of many of the basic data types. Storage requirements vary.
Array	A fixed or resizable array holds a set of similar data types.
Currency	Numbers in the range of 10^{4930} to 10^{-4930} displayed in a currency format—for example, $16.33. Calculations on currency values are carried out to the sixth decimal place, then rounded back to two decimal places.
Date	Holds dates in the range 1/1/100 to 12/31/9999.
DynArray	Dynamic arrays hold a set of dissimilar data types. Each element has an associated tag.
Graphic	Holds graphic bit maps.
Logical	Evaluates to True or False. Used to store the success or failure of an operation or test.
LongInt	Holds numbers in the range from –2,147,483,648 to 2,147,483,648. Long and small integers have no decimal places.
Memo	Holds longer text fields. Strings hold shorter fields. Memos can be up to 512M.

14 — UNDERSTANDING OBJECTPAL BASICS

Type	Description
Number	Stores floating-point values up to 18 significant digits. Range is from 10^{-4930} to 10^{4930}. Requires storage of 8 bytes.
OLE	An OLE object is a document that was created by an OLE server. OLE stands for object linking and embedding.
Point	Stores an *x, y* coordinate pair, indicating screen position relative to window or object. *x*-values indicate horizontal position, *y*-values indicate vertical position. Coordinates start at 0,0 at upper left of window or object.
Record	Stores a group of related variables.
SmallInt	Holds numbers in the range of –32,768 to 32,767.
String	Holds up to 64K characters.
Time	Stores Date and Time, down to a millisecond.
Design Objects	Types in this category are used on a form to create the user interface design. A user interacts with these types of objects directly: they are not behind-the-scenes controls. A TableFrame, for example, is a UIObject placed on a form, with which a user interacts.
Menu	Holds menu items to display across the top menu. Replaces default menu.
PopUpMenu	Holds menu items to display in a local (pop-up) menu or in a cascaded (drop-down) menu.
UIObject	Any of the objects you create with the SpeedBar in Design mode—including boxes, ellipses, lines, editable fields, and buttons.
Data Models	Types in this category are used to access and manipulate data stored in tables.
DataBase	Holds the path to a directory of tables. Although it's not an alias, it can be used to specify a table in a particular directory.
Query	A file, statement, or String that contains a valid Paradox QBE or standard SQL query.

continues

Table 14.1. Continued

Type	Description
Table	A handle to the data stored in a table on disk. Table objects are used to add, copy, subtract, calculate column totals, and otherwise perform large operations on tables. Editing a table object is not allowed (instead, use a TCursor).
TCursor	Contains a pointer to the data in a table. TCursors work behind the scenes to let you edit and search through tables, among other operations.
Display Managers	Types in this category are used to manage the display of data.
Application	A handle to the main Paradox window. Required to set properties or title information for the parent window.
Form	A handle to a particular form. Required to open, close, and set properties of a form.
Report	A handle to a Report window. Required to open, close, size, and position a Report window.
TableView	A handle to a TableView window created in response to a File, Open, Table sequence of commands (not a TableFrame placed on a form). Required to open, close, size, and position a TableView window.
Data Objects	Objects used to access and manipulate data not stored in tables.
DDE	A handle to a dynamic data exchange (DDE) conversation.
FileSystem	A handle to the file system, with which you can get information about files, directories, and drives.
Session	A session represents a single user's rights, locks, and activities in Paradox. Typically, only one session is open at a time. To open and manipulate other sessions (other virtual users), you must declare and open a session. Each session takes one user count in a network setting.

14 — UNDERSTANDING OBJECTPAL BASICS

Type	Description
System	A handle used to inquire about system resources, such as font sets.
TextStream	A handle to an ANSI-only text file. TextStreams are used to read and write from files.
Events	Events hold information about user-generated or system-generated activities. Events are passed to event methods via the *eventInfo* parameter specified in the event method's definition.
ActionEvent	Contains information about an event generated by navigating or editing a table.
Event	Contains information about events not specific to the other event types.
KeyEvent	Contains information about events caused by a keystroke.
MenuEvent	Contains information about events caused by choosing a menu item.
MouseEvent	Contains information about events caused by moving or clicking the mouse.
StatusEvent	Contains information about message window events.
ValueEvent	Contains information about events that change the value of a field.
DLL Data Types	Data types in this category are required only while declaring the prototype of a function to be called from a DLL. Functions called from DLLs must be declared in the Uses window of an object.
CDOUBLE	A double-wide floating-point number (64 bits).
CLONG	A long integer value (32 bits).
CLONGDOUBLE	A long double-wide floating-point number (80 bits).
CPTR	A pointer value (16 bits).
CWORD	A word value (16 bits).

Declaring Constants

A constant is a named value that does not change during the execution of a method or procedure. Because programming is all about handling changing states, not constant states, you will not use constants as much as variables. A judicious use of constants, however, makes your code more readable and easier to modify.

Suppose that you have a form you open as a dialog box in several places in your application. When you open the form, you must provide the form's name, as shown in the following example.

```
method pushButton(var eventInfo Event)
var
    formDialog    Form
endvar

formDialog.openAsDialog("serchdlg.fsl")
msgInfo("Status", "Serchdlg.fsl should be open now. Closing it...")
formDialog.close()
endmethod
```

This example will suffice if you call the form SERCHDLG.FSL once or twice only. To change the name of the form, you need to hunt down only one or two occurrences of the string "SERCHDLG.FSL" and change each occurrence to the new file name. What if you end up using this form all over your application? Changing each occurrence can be a time-consuming and potentially error-prone process.

To prevent this from happening, you can use constants to hold the name of something you expect to use frequently in a method, procedure, or application. To rework the example shown above, you can declare a constant named *searchDialog* to contain the form's file name. Then, whenever you need to open the form, you use the constant name *searchDialog* instead of the full file name of the form. The following example shows how.

```
method pushButton(var eventInfo Event)
var
   formDialog     Form     ; a form handle
endvar

const
   searchDialog = "serchdlg.fsl"
   ; file name of form to use as dialog
endconst
```

```
; now, use the constant instead of the hard-coded file name
formDialog.openAsDialog(searchDialog)

msgInfo("Status",
        "The search dialog should be open now. Closing it...")

formDialog.close()
endmethod
```

In this arrangement, to change the file name of the form the application opens as a search dialog, you need to change the constant's value only once, at the top of the method or procedure.

You probably will realize the design value of using constants instead of variables only in larger applications, methods, or procedures. In a large application, for example, you may want to design a standard color scheme. You can declare global constants equal to color names, then routinely set the colors of objects to the constant as you open the object. See the next section for an explanation of the difference between local and global constants.

You may have noticed that you aren't required to give a constant a data type when you declare it. Paradox infers the data type of the constant from the type of data that you assign to it. If you assign a string, Paradox infers that the data type of the constant is a string. This usually works well, but not in all situations. Date types, for example, are actually stored as strings. In the declaration

```
dateConst = 1/1/92
```

Paradox computes 1 divided by 1, divided by 92, and stores the result in dateConst. This is almost certainly not what you intended. But in the declaration

```
dateConst = "1/1/92"
```

Paradox assigns the string "1/1/92" to *dateConst*; this is a little better, but still not perfect. To tell Paradox explicitly the data type of a constant, you must use a *cast* in the declaration. A cast tells the compiler how to handle a value. To cast a value to a particular data type, use the name of the data type with the assigned value as though it was a method, as in the following example.

```
dateConst = date("1/1/92")
```

Now dateConst will store a date as a date data type. This technique works for other data types as well.

Creating Data Types and Records

In addition to the data types provided by ObjectPAL, you can create new data types to use. The new data types aren't exactly entirely new variable types; rather, they are aliases for existing types.

To declare a new data type, set the new data type name equal to a standard data type. Type declarations take the following form:

```
type
   newTypeName = NormalTypeName
   newTypeNameTwo = NormalTypeName
endtype
```

The following Type section, for example, declares a new data type called ShortID:

```
type
  ShortID = String    ;declare a new data type called ShortID
endtype
```

Variable declarations with user-defined types are the same as those with regular data types. You can declare a variable of type ShortID with the following:

```
var
  tempID   ShortID
endvar
```

Declaring a user-defined type like this one is not very useful, although it enables you to change the type of an entire set of variables just by altering the declaration in the Type section. To change the type of ShortID from a String to SmallInt, for example, you need to change the type of ShortID in the Type section. You then need to check every reference to variables of type ShortID to make sure that they are used in a manner consistent with their new type. If a variable of type ShortID is assigned a number, the statement would be

```
tempID = "2879"
; string assignment, the string is enclosed in quotes
```

if type ShortID was a String, but

```
tempID = 2879      ; numeric assignment, no quotes required
```

if type ShortID was a SmallInt.

You realize the actual value of user-defined types when you declare compound data types with the RECORD keyword. The following type section creates a new data type called AlbumRec:

```
TYPE
   AlbumRec = RECORD
                       AlbumName   String
                       Performer   String
                       Label       String
                       Price       Currency
                       ENDRECORD
ENDTYPE
```

After you have created the AlbumRec data type, you can declare an AlbumRec variable like the following example:

```
var
  tempAlbum    AlbumRec
endvar
```

To work with the components of the tempAlbum variable, use dot notation. To assign a value to the AlbumName element, for example, write

```
tempAlbum.AlbumName = "Synchronicity"
```

The RECORD compound data type, combined with the TYPE statement, enables you to create very flexible data structures to group-related variables.

Understanding Scope

The *scope* of a variable or constant is the area of a program where the variable or constant has meaning. ObjectPAL determines the scope of a variable according to where you declare the variable. Scoping rules for variables also apply to constants.

Scope and the Containership Hierarchy

The scope of a variable is controlled largely by the *containership hierarchy*. For any given form, you can declare a variable or constant a number of places, including on the form itself, a page of the form, an object on a page, an object within another object, and so on.

To open the Methods dialog for these objects, you simply select the object, right-click the object to display the Properties menu, and choose <u>M</u>ethods. One very important object cannot be accessed in such a straightforward manner: the form itself. The form is the highest-order object in any containership hierarchy. To open the Properties menu for the form, right-click the title bar of the form, or follow these steps:

1. Press Esc to deselect all other objects.
2. Open the Object Tree. The object farthest to the left on the Object Tree is the form.
3. Right-click the form's default name on the Object Tree to display the Properties menu.
4. Change the default name of the form to something more meaningful.
5. Choose <u>M</u>ethods from the Properties menu. Paradox opens the Methods dialog box for the form.
6. From the Methods dialog for the form, you can define various types of global code and data objects.

You can declare variables for any object (including a form) in two ways: in the **Var** section of a method or procedure or in the Var window for an object. Variables declared in a **Var** section have a different scope than variables declared in a Var window. Similarly, constants declared in a **Const** section have a different scope than constants declared in a Const window.

Var Section Declarations

Variables declared in a **Var** section of a method or procedure are said to be *local* to the method or procedure in which they are called. This means that a variable declared in a **Var** section of a particular method is available to the method in which it is defined as well as to any methods or procedures called by that method. When the method stops executing, the variable loses its meaning—or becomes invisible. When a variable becomes invisible, it is said to be "out of scope."

The following definition for a **pushButton** event method declares a counter called *beepCounter*. *beepCounter* controls the number of beeps that sound when the button is pushed.

```
method pushButton(var eventInfo Event)
var
   BeepCounter     SmallInt
endvar

for BeepCounter from 1 to 3
  ; for loop sets BeepCounter to 1 at start
  ; then adds 1 to BeepCounter every time
  ; loop is executed
  beep()
```

```
    msgInfo("BeepCounter Is:", BeepCounter)
    ;  BeepCounter will be 1, then 2, then 3
 endfor            ; stops when BeepCounter is 3
 endmethod
```

The *beepCounter* variable is declared as a SmallInt because it never needs to hold values larger than 32,767. *beepCounter* has meaning only while **pushButton** runs. When **pushButton** stops running, *beepCounter* becomes undefined. The next time you execute **pushButton**, *beepCounter* is declared and then initialized as though it is a brand new variable.

To create a variable with a slightly different scope, place a **Var** section before the method definition. To declare a variable that counts the number of times a method was called, for example, you can write the following code:

```
; Notice the variable declaration outside of the method, but
; within the same Editor window.
var
   buttonPushCounter      SmallInt
endvar

method pushButton(var eventInfo Event)
; First time method is called, buttonPushCounter will have no value.
;  So, "if" statement checks to see if buttonPushCounter has been
;  assigned a value. Then sorts out what to do.
if isassigned(buttonPushCounter) then
   buttonPushCounter = buttonPushCounter + 1  ; increments counter
else
   buttonPushCounter = 1
endif
msgInfo("I have been pushed:", strval(buttonPushCounter) + " times")

endmethod
```

Variables declared in this fashion retain their values from one call of a method to the next. The first time the **pushButton** method shown above is called, *buttonPushCounter* is unassigned until it is set to 1 inside the **if** statement. The next time **pushButton** is called, *buttonPushCounter* is set to 2, then 3, and so on.

If you declare the method shown in the following example, *buttonPushCounter* always equals 1.

```
method pushButton(var eventInfo Event)
var
   buttonPushCounter      SmallInt
endvar

if isassigned(buttonPushCounter) then
```

```
    buttonPushCounter = buttonPushCounter + 1    ; increments counter
else
  ; first time method is called buttonPushCounter will have no value
  buttonPushCounter = 1
endif
msgInfo("I have been pushed:", strval(buttonPushCounter) + " times")

endmethod
```

In this version of the method, *buttonPushCounter* is always 1. This is true because it is declared inside the method definition: *buttonPushCounter* is declared, then assigned the value 1, then displayed in the **msgInfo** statement. When the method ends, *buttonPushCounter* becomes undefined, and all storage required by *buttonPushCounter* is released. The next time **pushButton** runs, *buttonPushCounter* is declared anew, assigned 1, and so on.

A constant declared inside a method definition behaves virtually the same as one declared outside the definition. In either case, the constant has the same value through successive calls because the constant's value is not allowed to change. Constants declared in a method window have the same scope as variables declared in a method window.

Var Window Declarations

Variables declared in a Var window and constants declared in a Const window are available to all methods in the object for which they are defined. This means that a variable *x* declared in a Var window for a button object called *buttonOne* is available to the **pushButton** method, the **mouseEnter** method, and all the other event methods, custom methods, and procedures for *buttonOne*. In addition, *x* is available for all of the methods for all of the objects contained by *buttonOne*.

To see how to create a variable in a Var window, create a button called *buttonOne*. (Open a new form, if necessary.) Then follow these steps:

1. Open the Methods dialog box for *buttonOne*. Several check boxes appear in the lower right quadrant of the dialog box.

2. Click the Var check box (see fig. 14.1) and choose OK. Paradox opens a Var window.

3. Type this line between the Var and endVar keywords:

   ```
   actionCounter     SmallInt
   ```

4. The Var window now should look like figure 14.2.

14 — UNDERSTANDING OBJECTPAL BASICS

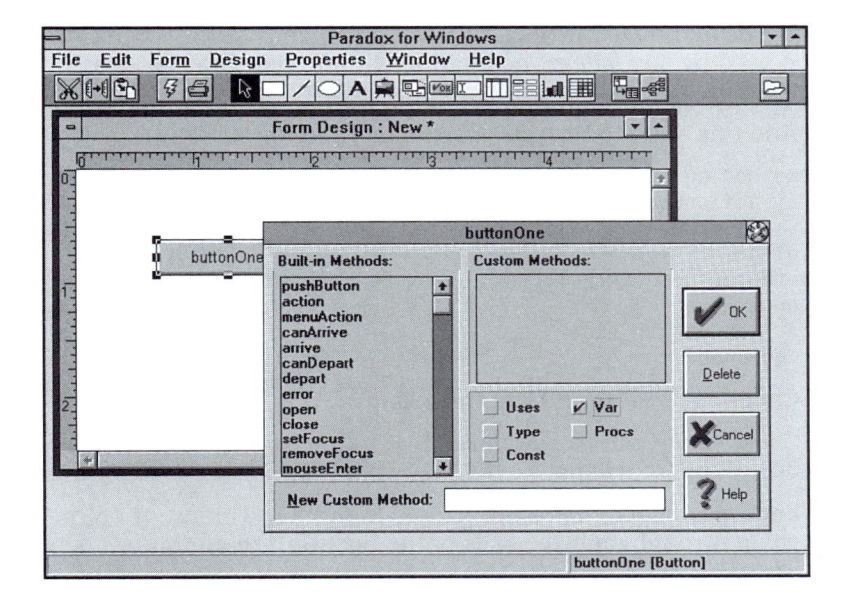

FIG. 14.1

The Method dialog box with Var checked.

After you declare the variable *actionCounter* in the Var window for the *buttonOne* object, *actionCounter* is available to every event method and procedure defined for *buttonOne*.

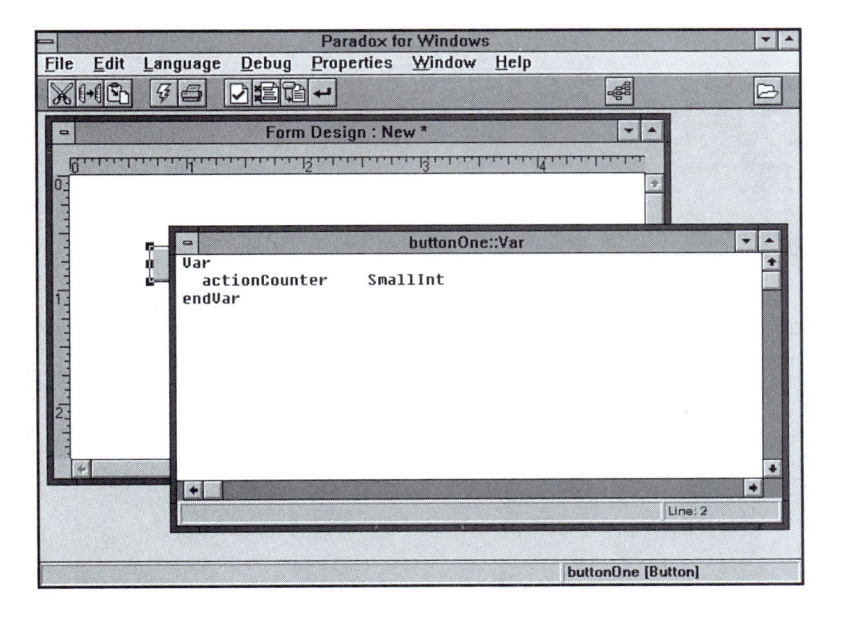

FIG. 14.2

The Var window with a variable declaration.

Because *actionCounter* is declared in the Var window for *buttonOne*, it can be used by any *buttonOne* method without being declared again in a **Var** section for the method.

1. Add this code to the **pushButton** method for *buttonOne*:

   ```
   method pushButton(var eventInfo Event)
   if actionCounter.isAssigned() then
      actionCounter = actionCounter + 1
   else
      actionCounter = 1
   endif
   actionCounter.view()
   endmethod
   ```

2. Check the syntax and run the form.

3. Click *buttonOne* several times. Every time you click it, a View window pops up telling you the value of *actionCounter* (see fig. 14.3).

   Because *actionCounter* is declared in the Var window, it holds its value through multiple calls of the **pushButton** method.

> **TIP** Remember the **view** method when you're trying to test code; it comes in handy when you need to watch variables. Every data type has a **view** method in its type.

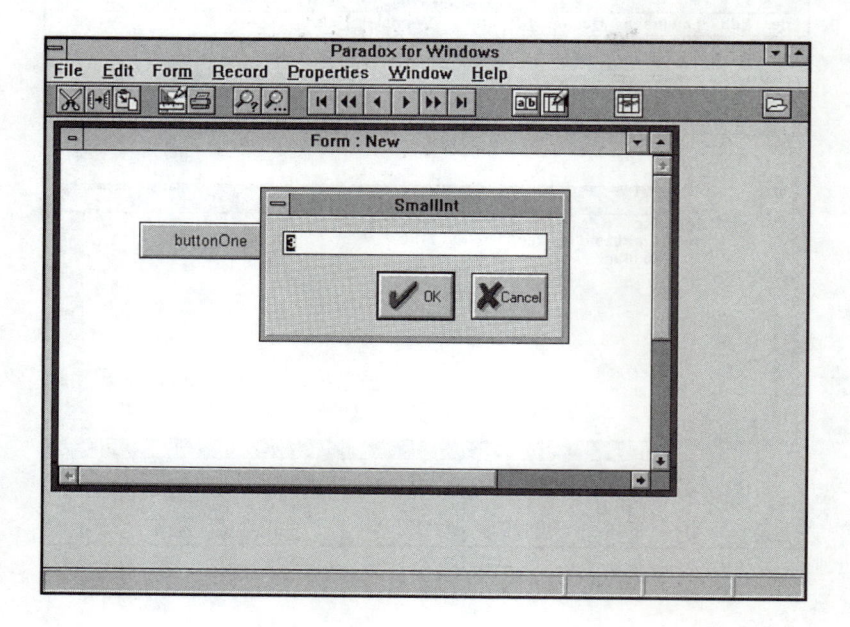

FIG. 14.3

A View window with the value of actionCounter displayed.

14 — UNDERSTANDING OBJECTPAL BASICS

4. Return to Design mode.

5. Change the definition for **mouseEnter** so that it looks like the definition for **pushButton**. (You can either cut and paste between the two definitions or just type in the new definition.) The definition for **mouseEnter** should look like this:

   ```
   method mouseEnter(var eventInfo MouseEvent)
   if actionCounter.isAssigned() then
     actionCounter = actionCounter + 1
   else
     actionCounter = 1
   endif
   actionCounter.view()
   endmethod
   ```

6. Check the syntax, then save and run the form.

7. Move the mouse pointer into *buttonOne*. As soon as you move within the boundary of *buttonOne*, a View window pops up to display the value of *actionCounter*. The first time you move the mouse pointer into *buttonOne*, the *actionCounter* variable is set to 1.

8. Click *buttonOne*.

   Notice that the value of *actionCounter* is now 2. *actionCounter* is available to and can be changed by both methods. Neither method declared *actionCounter*, but it is available to both of them. The value of *actionCounter* persists across multiple methods and multiple method calls for the same object.

The preceding example illustrates an important point about variables. The length of time a variable remains assigned is called *persistence*. Persistence saves the state of an object across time and space. Because persistent objects consume storage, good design practice dictates that variables and all data objects be persistent for the shortest amount of time necessary to accomplish the desired task.

A counter that controls the number of times a loop is executed, for example, should go away when the loop ends. A counter like this normally is declared in a **Var** section of a method. The **for** statement at the top of the loop assigns the variable its first value. The variable then is released automatically at the end of the method.

If you rigidly apply the rule of shortest persistence, you explicitly release the counter variable from memory at the very end of the loop. Waiting for Paradox to release it automatically at the end of the method is good enough, however. Although this means that the variable persists slightly longer than it needs to, this is acceptable. If you declare the same loop counter in a Var window for the object, the variable has a much longer persistence than necessary. The longest persistence for a variable is obtained by declaring the variable in the Var window for the form itself.

Variables created by Paradox during an ObjectPAL program cease to exist when the program ends. As a programmer, you can write those variables to an object that has a longer persistence, such as a table or a text file.

Tables are the data objects with the longest persistence in a Paradox application. Many tables exist from one invocation of the application to the next. They usually persist from one session on the system to the next session—existing even when the system on which they are stored is turned off. Some Paradox tables may outlive the current version of Paradox—possibly outliving Paradox itself. (See the next section to learn how variables are scoped and how scope relates to persistence.)

Scoping Variables and Constants

To make a variable available to the entire form, declare the variable in the Var window of the form itself. A variable that is available for the entire program is called a *global variable*. Relying on global variables for program control is considered a dangerous programming practice. The more parts of a program that have access to a variable, the greater risk that some part will change the value of that variable in a way that will make the rest of the program unreliable.

A variable available only within the method where it is declared is called a *private variable*. Using private variables as much as possible is considered good programming practice. A side benefit of using private variables relates to the efficiency of a program. A private variable takes up storage only while the method where it is declared is active. As soon as the method ends, all storage required to hold the method's variables is released (except for those variables declared in a method window before the method definition).

Declaring global constants, when needed, is considered good design. Constants, whether global or local, cannot be changed after they have been set. No procedure or method, therefore, has the ability to change the value of a constant in such a way that puts other procedures or methods at risk. This can make a program more robust. A side benefit to constants is that Paradox stores constants more efficiently than variables.

Scope is not exactly the same as persistence, although the two concepts are related. Scope pertains to whether an object is visible; persistence refers to whether an object exists. An object can exist (persist) but still be invisible to (outside the scope of) the currently executing code.

Using Operators

An *operator* is something that performs a calculation or other operation on one or more variables or other kinds of data. To assign a value to a variable, you use the assignment operator (the equal sign, =). To add a variable and a value, assign the result to another variable and then use the plus operator (+) and the assignment operator (=). To illustrate, consider the following section of code:

```
method pushButton(var eventInfo Event)
var
   buttonPushCounter      SmallInt     ; declare a variable
endvar

buttonPushCounter = 1    ; assign the value 1 to buttonPushCounter
msgInfo(" buttonPushCounter is:", buttonPushCounter)    ; displays 1

endmethod
```

The statement **buttonPushCounter = 1** is an example of an assignment operation. In ObjectPAL, as in most programming languages, assignment is always from right to left. The value to the right of the equal sign is assigned to the variable or constant on the left of the equal sign. Operators can be combined in a single statement, as follows:

```
method pushButton(var eventInfo Event)
var
    buttonPushCounter     SmallInt      ; declare a variable
    SomeValue             SmallInt      ; declare another variable
endvar

SomeValue = 3                           ; example of assignment
buttonPushCounter = 1 + SomeValue  ; assignment and addition
msgInfo(" buttonPushCounter is:", buttonPushCounter)   ; displays 4

endmethod
```

The statement **SomeValue = 3** sets the variable *SomeValue* equal to 3. The next statement **buttonPushCounter = 1 + SomeValue** adds 1 to the current value of *SomeValue* and stores the result (4) in *buttonPushCounter*.

Table 14.2 describes ObjectPAL operators and provides examples of how to use them.

Table 14.2. ObjectPAL Operators

Symbol	Meaning	Example	Value of x
=	Assignment	x = 3	3
	String Assignment	x = "Robert Hall"	Robert Hall
	Date Assignment	x = Date("1/1/93")	1/1/93
	Equal to (comparison)	x = (3 = 3)	True
+	Addition,	x = 3 + 5	8
	Date Addition	x = Date("1/1/92") + 1	1/2/92
	String Concatenation	x = "Bor" + "land"	Borland
–	Subtraction	x = 5 – 3	2
	Date Subtraction	x = Date("1/1/92") – 1	12/31/91
*	Multiplication	x = 5 * 3	15
/	Division	x = 8 / 4	2
( )	Precedence	x = (5 + 3) * 2	16
<>	Not equal to	x = 3 <> 4	True
		x = 3 <> 3	False
<	Less than	x = 3 < 4	True
		x = 4 < 3	False
<=	Less than or equal to	x = 4 <= 4	True
		x = 3 <= 4	True
		x = 5 <= 4	False
>	Greater than	x = 5 > 4	True
		x = 5 > 5	False
>=	Greater than or equal to	x = 5 >= 4	True
		x = 5 >= 5	True
		x = 5 >= 6	False
NOT	Logical negation	x = NOT 5 >= 4	False
		x = NOT 5 >= 6	True
AND	Logical AND	x = 5 = 5 AND 3 = 3	True
		x = 5 = 3 AND 3 = 3	False
OR	Logical OR	x = 5 = 5 OR 3 = 3	True
		x = 5 = 3 OR 3 = 3	True
		x = 5 = 3 OR 4 = 3	False

14 — UNDERSTANDING OBJECTPAL BASICS

To create more complicated expressions, you can use a variety of operators. The following code gives one example.

```
method pushButton(var eventInfo Event)
var
    TotalValue        Currency
    DaysOfOrdering    SmallInt
    BonusPercent      Number
    Bonus             Currency
endvar

TotalValue = 32565.32   ; notice there are no commas in number
DaysOfOrdering = 21
BonusPercent = 0.15
; leading zero not required, but improves readability
; In the following calculation,
; TotalValue / DaysOfOrdering * BonusPercent is
; calculated first, then added to 100.00, then assigned to Bonus
Bonus = 100.00 + TotalValue / DaysOfOrdering * BonusPercent

msgInfo("Bonus is:", Bonus)                ; displays 332.61

; In the following calculation, 100.00 is added to
; TotalValue, the result is divided by DaysOfOrdering
; and multiplied by BonusPercent, then
; assigned to Bonus. The parentheses around
; 100.00 + TotalValue change the order of evaluation
Bonus = (100.00 + TotalValue) / DaysOfOrdering * BonusPercent

msgInfo("Bonus is:", Bonus)                ; displays 233.32
endmethod
```

Notice in the above example that the first calculation produced a different result than the second calculation, although all the variables except *Bonus* stayed the same. The placement of parentheses around elements of an expression changed the evaluation of the expression. To understand why this happened, you need to know about something called *operator precedence*.

Operator precedence tells the compiler which element of an expression to evaluate first, second, and so on. It also tells the compiler which *operands* (the things to work on) belong to which *operators* (the things doing the work). Elements with the same precedence are evaluated left to right. Table 14.3 lists operators from the highest precedence (evaluated first) to the lowest precedence.

Table 14.3. ObjectPAL Operator Precedence

Symbols	Example	Value of x
()	x = (3 + 5) * 8	64
/ *	x = 3 + 5 * 8	43
+ –	x = 3 – 5 * 8 + 45	8 (Evaluates the same as 3 – (5 * 8) + 45)
= <> < > <= >=	x = 3 = 4 x = 3 <> 4 x = 3 < 4 x = 3 > 4 x = 3 <= 4 x = 3 >= 4	False True True False True False
NOT	x = NOT 3 = 4	True
AND	x = 3 < 4 AND 3 <= 4	True
OR	x = 3 < 4 OR 3 >= 4	True
= (Assignment)	x = 1	1

If you find operator precedence difficult to determine in complicated expressions, simply use parentheses to indicate the order of evaluation.

Creating Control Structures

Control structures determine the flow of execution within a method or procedure. Sometimes you want a particular instruction to execute only if a condition is true. At other times you want to perform a set of instructions a fixed number of times. To obtain this kind of control, you need control structures. The following sections describe the various control structures available to you in ObjectPAL.

If Statements

An **if** statement is the simplest control structure available to you. An **if** statement starts by evaluating an expression. If the expression evaluates to True, one set of instructions executes. If the expression evaluates to False, a different set of instructions executes (or none at all). In general, an **if** statement takes the following form:

```
if ConditionIsTrue then
   ; execute these instructions
else        ;  Condition is False
   ; execute these instructions instead
endif
```

The following simple **if** statement tests the color of the current object:

```
if self.color = DarkBlue then
   self.color = LightBlue
endif
```

If the color of the current object is dark blue, the **if** statement is True. When an **if** statement is True, the line or lines of code following the **if...then** clause are executed.

The first line of the **if** statement evaluates the following expression:

```
self.color = DarkBlue
```

The equal sign in the above expression is used as a comparison operator, not as an assignment operator. When the equal sign is used as a comparison operator, the expression can evaluate to either True or False. This illustrates a key point about constructing **if** statements: the expression used in the condition must evaluate to a logical value, either True or False.

If statements must include a **then** clause, but the **else** clause is optional. The following example uses an **if...then...else** statement to toggle the color of an object between light blue and dark blue.

```
; expression compares self.color and LightBlue

if self.color = LightBlue then
  ; the next line executes if self.color = LightBlue
  ; evaluates to True
  self.color = DarkBlue
else
  ; the next line executes if self.color = LightBlue
  ; evaluates to False
  self.color = LightBlue
endif
```

If statements can be nested within one another. The nesting can go to as many levels as the system can handle—eventually, you run out of memory.

The following code places another **if** statement after the **else** clause of the original **if** statement. The effect is to cycle the color of the object from dark blue to red to light blue.

```
if self.color = LightBlue then
   self.color = DarkBlue
else
   ; the nested if statement only executes if
   ; self.color = LightBlue is False
   if self.color = DarkBlue then
      self.color = Red
   else
      self.color = LightBlue
   endif
endif
```

You can read this statement as "If the current color is light blue, change it to dark blue. If the current color is dark blue, change it to red. If the current color is any other color, change it to light blue." Try attaching this code to the **mouseClick** event method of an ellipse or a box. Every time you click the object, its color changes.

Immediate If Statements

An immediate **if** (**iif**) statement is like an **if** statement, but it takes the form of a function or method call. An **iif** statement evaluates a condition, then returns one value if the condition is True and a different value if the condition is False. In general, an **iif** takes the following form:

```
iif(conditionToTest, ReturnValueIfTrue, ReturnValueIfFalse)
```

This **if** statement toggles the color of **self** back and forth from LightBlue to DarkBlue:

```
if self.color = LightBlue then
   self.color = DarkBlue
else
   self.color = LightBlue
endif
```

Rewritten as an **iif**, the statement looks like this:

```
self.color = iif(self.color = LightBlue,  DarkBlue, LightBlue)
```

The entire **iif** statement evaluates to a single value. In this case, if *self.color* is equal to LightBlue, then the condition is True, and the **iif** returns DarkBlue. If *self.color* is not equal to LightBlue, then the condition is False, and the **iif** returns LightBlue. The **iif** does not return the logical True or False of the condition itself. Nothing prevents you from writing an **iif** to do so, such as in the following example:

```
isColorBlue = iif(self.color = LightBlue, True, False)
```

Still, if that's what you want to do, you can simply write

```
isColorBlue = (self.color = LightBlue)
```

isColorBlue is assigned a logical True or False. Note that the parentheses around **self.Color = LightBlue** aren't required for correct evaluation. This statement works equally well to assign the result of the comparison **self.Color = LightBlue** to *isColorBlue:*

```
isColorBlue = self.color = LightBlue
```

Switch Statements

Switch statements behave like a series of **if** statements. If many different conditions need to be tested, a **switch** statement is easier to use and more readable than a series of **if** statements.

The following example rewrites the nested **if** example shown in the previous section.

```
switch
   case self.color = LightBlue : self.color = DarkBlue
                                 beep()
   case self.color = DarkBlue  : self.color = Red
   case self.color = Red       : self.color = LightBlue
   otherwise                   : self.color = LightBlue
endswitch
```

The **switch** and **endswitch** statements open and close the control structure. Each line beginning with a **case** tests a condition and executes the instructions following the colon if the condition given in the **case** statement is True. Paradox starts by testing the first **case** in the switch. If the condition is True for the first **case**, Paradox executes the instructions following the colon. The next line to be executed after a True **case** is the first statement following the **endswitch** command. If the condition is not True for the first **case**, Paradox tests the second **case**, and so on, through the list of **cases**.

Notice that you can place several instructions after the colon. If a **case** is true, Paradox executes all of the instructions up to the next **case**, **otherwise**, or **endswitch**. The optional **otherwise** clause is executed only if no other **case** is true.

Try Statements

Paradox enables you to control whether the editing changes caused by a block of instructions are accepted. A block of instructions that changes a record is called a *transaction*. If Paradox encounters a **fail** method in the middle of a **try** transaction, any unposted records are deleted, records with unposted changes are returned to their original states, and any open tables are closed.

The structure of a **try** statement is as follows:

```
try
   ; transaction to try
   ; fail is called to move execution to commands following onfail
onfail
   ; block of instructions to handle recovery
   ; [fail()]
endtry
```

The key thing to understand about a **try...onfail...endtry** construct is that control moves to the **onfail** block when Paradox encounters a critical error (not just a warning). The **fail** method takes this one step further by reversing the effect of the most recent edits. The **onfail** block does not explicitly need to reverse the previous edits or close tables. These activities occur automatically when **fail** is executed.

fail is not called automatically when an error occurs. The code in the **try** block should attempt a critical operation. If the operation itself fails, then control moves to the **onfail** block. In the **onfail** block, you might want to call **fail** to reverse previous editing.

try...onfail is an advanced feature, to be used when you are constructing a full transaction processing system. An exhaustive discussion of **try** statements is beyond the scope of this book.

For Loops

A **for** loop repeats a set of instructions a specific number of times. Use a **for** loop when you know exactly how many times you want to repeat a set of actions. To construct a more flexible type of loop that continues while a condition is true, use a **while** loop (explained in the next section).

The general structure of a **for** loop is as follows:

```
for counterVar
   ; from startNumber to endNumber
   ; step byNumber (optional)
   ;    body of for loop contains instructions to be repeated
endfor
```

The simplest **for** loop uses constants to determine the starting number and the ending number. The loop in the following example tells Paradox to beep five times.

```
var
   loopCounter     SmallInt
endvar
```

```
for loopCounter from 1 to 5
   beep()
endfor
```

This code tells Paradox to execute the instructions between the **for** statement and the **endfor** statement five times.

for loopCounter opens the **for** loop and sets the counter to a variable called *loopCounter*. Every time the loop runs, *loopCounter* increases in value by 1. If no different step value is specified, adding 1 to the loop counter is the default action. To accomplish the same thing, the **for** statement can be rewritten to start at 5 and count back to 1 in steps of –1:

```
for loopCounter from 5 to 1 step -1
```

The loop can be rewritten to step from 1 to 50 in steps of 10, as in

```
for loopCounter from 10 to 50 step 10
```

In either case, the loop executes five times.

from 1 to 5 determines the limits of the loop. The first time the loop executes, the variable *loopCounter* has the value of 1; the next time the loop executes, the variable *loopCounter* has the value of 2; and so on, until *loopCounter* reaches 5.

beep() is the only instruction in the body of the loop. The body of the loop executes once for each loop. The loop runs five times, so Paradox beeps five times. **endfor** marks the end of the loop.

A **quitloop** command in the middle of a **for** loop causes the loop to terminate. A **loop** command in the middle of a **for** loop causes Paradox to skip the remainder of the instructions in the loop and return to the top of the loop.

Scan Loops

A **scan** loop is very much like a **for** loop, with one important difference: **scan** loops are built to work with tables. Instructions in a **scan** loop execute once for every record in the table. A **scan** loop takes this general form:

```
scan TableName:
; body of scan loop contains instructions that execute
; once for each record in the table
endscan
```

In this type of **scan** loop, instructions in the body of the **scan** loop execute once for each record in the table. A more involved **scan** loop lets you test for records that meet a condition, as in the following:

```
scan TableName for Condition:
 ; body of scan loop
endscan
```

Scan loops make it easy to process a table. Suppose that you just imported a name and address table from a straight ASCII file. The phone numbers were given with all 10 digits packed together, as in

>   4155551212

You probably want to see the phone numbers with parentheses around the area code, a space between the area code and the exchange, and a dash between the exchange and the last four digits, as in:

>   (415) 555-1212

You cannot construct a query to do this type of processing, but a **scan** loop works great. Assuming that you have a table called NAMEADDR.DB, with a field named Phone, you can attach this code to a button's **pushButton** method to massage the table:

```
method pushButton(var eventInfo Event)
var
   nameAddrTC     TCursor
   phoneStr       String
endvar
; assume that nameAddr.db file is in working directory
if nameAddrTC.open("nameaddr.db") then
   nameAddrTC.edit()
   scan nameAddrTC:
     phoneStr = nameAddrTC.Phone
     ; assignment to temporary variable is not required
     phoneStr.view()   ; to see what it looks like before changes
     nameAddrTC.Phone = "(" + phoneStr.substr(1, 3) + ") " +
                       phoneStr.substr(4, 3) + "-" +
                       phoneStr.substr(7, 4)
     nameAddrTC.Phone.view()
     ; to see what it looks like after changes
   endscan
else
   msgStop("Status", "Couldn't open table.")
endif

endmethod
```

ObjectPAL has several types of table objects, including Tables, TCursors, TableFrames, and TableViews. In the **scan** loop, you can specify either a Table type or a TCursor type. If you want to edit the table in the body of the **scan** loop, you must specify a table opened as a TCursor. If you don't want to edit the table, you can use a Table object.

> **NOTE** A **scan** loop always starts at the beginning of the table and works its way to the end. **Scan** loops do not start at the current record.

You can abort a **scan** loop with the **quitloop** command. Paradox executes instructions in a loop until it reaches a **quitloop** command. Execution resumes with the first statement after the **endscan** command. The **loop** command also is valid in a **scan** loop. When Paradox encounters a **loop** command in the body of a **scan** loop, it returns to the top of the loop, moves to the next record, and executes the **scan** statement from top to bottom.

While Loops

A **while** loop repeats a set of instructions while a particular condition remains true. A **while** loop has the following general form:

```
while ConditionToTest
;    body of while loop contains instructions to be repeated
endwhile
```

Remember, when using a **while** loop, you must do something in the body of the loop to change the condition at the top of the loop. If you don't do anything to change the condition, the condition remains True, and the loop executes infinitely. In the following example, the loop runs while a variable is not equal to 1. For every iteration of the loop, the value of the tested variable is decreased. Eventually, *loopvar* becomes 1, and the loop ends.

```
var
    loopVar    SmallInt
endvar

loopVar = 30
while loopVar <> 1
    loopVar = loopVar - 1
endwhile
```

As it does in **for** loops, the **quitloop** command exists to give you an escape hatch to a **while** loop. Paradox executes instructions in a loop until the loop condition becomes False, or until Paradox reaches a **quitloop** command. Execution resumes with the first statement after the **endwhile** command. This enables you to construct a loop condition that is always True, and then break out of the loop in response to a condition test in the middle of the loop. The following example shows how you might use the **quitloop** command.

```
var
   loopVar      SmallInt
endvar

loopVar = 30
while True           ; this looks odd, but it works
   loopVar = loopVar - 1    ; decrement loopVar
   if loopVar = 1 then      ; test loopVar
      quitloop              ; break out of the loop
   endif
endwhile
; next instruction to execute
```

As with **for** loops, when Paradox encounters a **loop** command in the body of a **while** loop, it skips the rest of the instructions in the loop and returns to the top of the loop.

In the previous two examples, the **while** loops weren't very realistic. Because you knew the number of times the loop would execute (based on *loopVar*), you could have used a **for** loop more effectively. The next example gives you a more realistic situation that calls for a **while** loop.

Assume that you want to step through all the records in a table. To do this with a **for** loop, you need to find out the number of records in the table and set the starting loop number and the ending loop number accordingly. But this works only if the number of records in the table doesn't change during processing. What happens if the loop itself adds or deletes records? If you're in a network environment, users potentially can alter the number of records in the table while the loop is running.

To solve this predicament, the following **while** works it way through a table, testing for the end of the table. When Paradox reaches the end of the table, the condition becomes false, and the loop ends.

```
method pushButton(var eventInfo Event)
var
  albumTC    TCursor           ; Pointer to table
  albumTitles array[] String   ; array to hold titles
                               ; empty brackets mean this
                               ; array is resizable
endvar

albumTC.open("albums.db")   ; open the table to the TCursor
; a TCursor acts like an alias to a table name

while not albumTC.atLast() ; atLast returns true at end of table
   albumTC.nextRecord()        ; nextRecord moves to the next record
```

```
   albumTitles.addLast(albumTC.Title) ; add an element to the array
   ; nextRecord is the command that eventually makes
   ; the loop condition false
endwhile

; open a window to view the contents of the array
albumTitles.view("Contents of albumTitles")
; if included, a string argument sets title of View window
endmethod
```

The statement **albumTC.atLast()** returns True only when Paradox reaches the end of a table—specifically, when a move past the end of a table is attempted. The **while** loop condition must be True for the loop to execute and False for the loop to quit. To make the condition true, **not** is used to switch the False returned by **albumTC.atLast()** to True. When the end of the table arrives, **albumTC.atLast()** returns True, which is switched to False, and the loop terminates.

Calling Methods and Procedures

Methods and procedures, like functions in most languages, are self-contained pieces of code; they exist to perform a single action or a small set of related actions. The **beep** procedure, for example, merely tells Paradox to sound a beep.

The **open** method for the Form type is one example of a more complicated action. The effect of the **open** method is to display a form and open any tables placed on the form. What Paradox does to be able to open the form and its tables is hidden from you as an ObjectPAL programmer. You don't need to know what's going on internally to be able to use the method reliably.

This is the nature of an application language: you can write your own Paradox applications without knowing how Paradox itself was written.

In ObjectPAL, you can call three different types of methods:

- *Methods* are written specifically for certain types of objects.
- *Built-in methods* are attached to objects and called automatically by Paradox in response to events.
- *Custom methods* can be defined for objects.

You also can call *library procedures*, which are general-purpose functions not written specifically for use with a particular type. You also can write your own procedures.

Understanding Parameters and Arguments

Although methods and procedures are relatively self-contained, they often need some information to do their job. When methods or procedures are designed to require some outside information, they are defined with one or more formal *parameters*. A parameter holds information. The information passed is called an *argument*. If a parameter is like a mailbox, the argument is the mail.

The prototype of a method or procedure tells you what arguments the method or procedure expects. The following prototype for the **sound** procedure shows you what arguments **sound** expects:

```
sound(const freqHertz LongInt, const durationMillisecs LongInt)
```

sound expects two arguments—*freqHertz* and *durationMillisecs*. Both arguments must be of type LongInt, which means that you cannot pass them a number like 1.2. Because *freqHertz* and *durationMillisecs* are declared as constants (**const**), the sound procedure doesn't change the values of the arguments passed to it. The **const** keyword doesn't mean that you must pass the procedure constants.

The declaration of a parameter has three parts: a keyword indicating how the argument is passed, the name of the parameter, and the type of the parameter. In the parameter declaration

```
const freqHertz LongInt
```

const, in this context, is a keyword that determines how the argument is passed. The keyword that comes before the variable name can be one of the following:

- **const** indicates that the argument is passed as a constant. A procedure or method is not allowed to change the value of arguments passed as constants. Note that an argument does not have to be a constant to be passed as a constant. You can pass a literal (such as "LiteralString") as a constant, you can pass a variable as a constant, and you can pass a constant as a constant.

- **var** indicates that the argument is passed as a variable. A procedure or method is allowed to change the value of the argument. This type of parameter passing is also called *pass by reference*. The argument passed is actually a pointer to the real data. Any changes to the argument during the executing of the method or procedure result in changes to the data.

- The absence of a passing control indicates that the argument is passed as a copy of the original data. Any changes to the argument do not affect the original data. This also is called *pass by value*.

freqHertz is the name of the parameter. The method or procedure handles the argument passed to this parameter by its parameter name throughout the body of the method or procedure.

LongInt is the type of the variable or constant passed as an argument. The compiler checks procedure or method calls against the prototype of the procedure or method to make sure that they are passed the correct data type.

Understanding Return Values

Many methods and procedures return a value. If they do, you can call the method or procedure in an expression. The procedure or method is said to *evaluate to* its return value. In the following statement, the **getProperty** method evaluates to the current color of the field object *Album_ID*:

```
Title.Color = Album_ID.getProperty("Color")
```

Taken as a whole, this statement sets the color property of the *Title* field object to the same color as the *Album_ID* field object. The prototype for **getProperty** is

```
getProperty(const propertyName String) AnyType
```

AnyType at the end of the prototype indicates that **getProperty** returns a value of type AnyType. In this case, it returns a numeric value: the color of the *Album_ID* object. **getProperty** can return any valid data type.

Calling Methods

Methods are pieces of code written to perform a specific action on or for a certain type of object. Methods always are called with an object of the same type. In general, the syntax for calling a method is

```
objectName.methodName(ArgumentsIfAny)
```

Often a method returns a value. This means that if you assign the method call to a variable (as shown below), the variable holds the return value of the method.

```
returnValueIfAny = objectName.methodName(ArgumentsIfAny)
```

Many methods return a logical value of True or False to indicate success or failure. For example, **open**, one of the Form type methods, returns a logical True if Paradox is able to open the requested form. The following method illustrates the use of **open**:

```
var
   formToOpen      Form
   formOpened      Logical
   statusString    String
endvar

; attempt to open form ALBUMS.FSL
; if operation succeeds, formOpened will be set to True
formOpened = formToOpen.open("albums.fsl")

; check the value of formOpened
; "if formOpened" is the same as "if formOpened = True"
if formOpened then       ; set the statusString accordingly
   statusString = "I opened the second form."
else
   statusString = "I could not open the second form."
endif

;display the statusString in a message info dialog
msgInfo("Status", statusString)

formToOpen.close()        ; close the form
```

In the statement

```
formOpened = formToOpen.open("albums.fsl")
```

formOpened is the variable receiving the return value of the method call. *formToOpen* is the Form object (a variable of type Form) that you must call the method with. **open** is the name of the Form type method. The **open** method takes one argument, the name of the form to open, and returns one logical value. "albums.fsl" is the value of the argument required by the **open** method.

Because methods are written for a specific type of object, several methods can have the same name, but belong to different types. The Form and TCursor types contain an **open** method, for example. The compiler knows which one you mean by looking at the type of the object with which you're calling the method. In the preceding example, the compiler knows to call the **open** method from the Form type because you called **open** with a Form object.

To find the set of methods available for an object, you first must know the object's type name. The most common types you will work with are Forms, UIObjects, Menus, PopUpMenu, TCursors, and the basic data types, such as String and Number. The Types and Methods dialog box shows you all the methods available for each type. (The Types and Methods dialog box is described in detail in Chapter 13.)

Calling Procedures

Library procedures, like methods, are discrete pieces of code that perform a specific operation. Unlike methods, procedures are not written for types. Because procedures are not written for types, you don't need to call them with a particular object.

To call a procedure, use the procedure name and provide any arguments the procedure expects. A procedure sometimes takes no arguments and returns no value, such as:

```
beep()
```

On the other hand, some procedures, like **rgb**, take several arguments.

```
rgb(const red SmallInt, const green SmallInt, const blue SmallInt) LongInt
```

rgb takes three SmallInts that should have a value between 0 and 255. Combined, the three numbers specify a color. Don't be fooled by the fact that **rgb** returns a LongInt. The number returned is a numeric constant that translates to a color. You can set the color of an object with this statement:

```
method pushButton(var eventInfo Event)

; set the color of Title to yellow
Title.color = rgb(255, 255, 0)

; show the return value of rgb()
msgInfo("RGB returns", rgb(255, 255, 0))

; show the return value of Title.color
msgInfo("Field color is", Title.color)

endmethod
```

Calling DLL Functions

ObjectPAL enables you to call functions from a *dynamic link library (DLL)*. A dynamic link library contains a related group of functions that Windows applications call at run-time.

DLLs differ from libraries written for other environments because the linking of calling code to called code (the DLL function) happens dynamically at run-time.

III — PROGRAMMING PARADOX FOR WINDOWS

In other programming situations, called code is linked to calling code at compile-time. If the main program calls a function 10 times, the compiler and linker copy and link the function to the main program in 10 different places. (This makes for bigger, slower code.)

To use a function from a DLL, you must declare the DLL and the function in a Uses window. To open a Uses window for an object, right-click the object to open the Properties menu, choose Methods, check the Uses box, and click OK (see fig. 14.4).

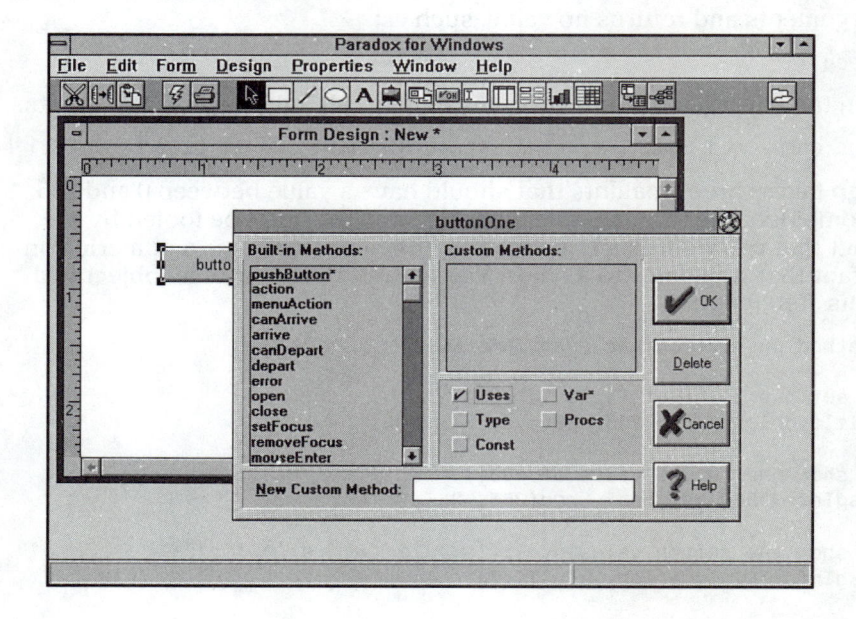

FIG. 14.4

Opening a Uses window from the Methods dialog box.

When you click OK after checking the Uses box on the Methods dialog box, Paradox opens the Uses window (see fig. 14.5).

To make DLL functions available to the current object, declare them in the Uses window of that object. If you want the DLL functions to be available to all the objects on the form, declare them in the Uses window of the form.

The DLL and function declaration take the following form:

Uses *DLLName*
    functionFromDLL(parameterName CType, parameterName CType, etc.)
    anotherFunctionfFromDLL(parameterName CType)
endUses

14 — UNDERSTANDING OBJECTPAL BASICS

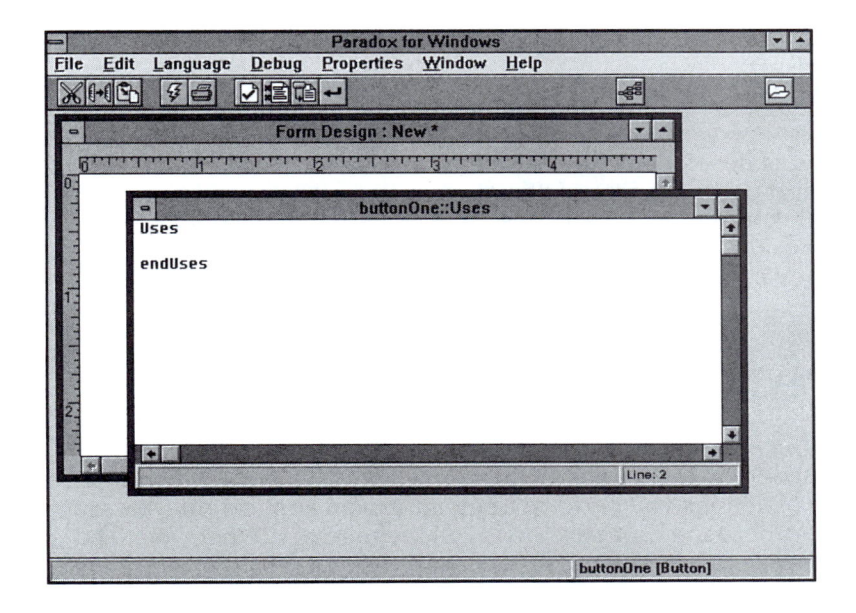

FIG. 14.5

The Uses window.

The USES block requires the file name of the DLL or the module name of the DLL, if it has already been opened by Windows. For each function you want to use, you must provide the function prototype. The function prototype is a description of the function, including the function name, the names of the function's parameters, the data type of the parameters, and the data type of the value returned.

The following USES block declares a function **DivFloat** from a DLL named MATHLIB.DLL, which divides one floating point number by another:

```
Uses "MATHLIB.DLL"
   DivFloat(numerator CDOUBLE, denominator CDOUBLE) CDOUBLE
endUses
```

The function name to be called is **DivFloat**. **DivFloat** takes two floating-point number arguments and returns a numeric value. To call the function **DivFloat** from a method, write the following:

```
method pushButton(var EventInfo Event)
var
   firstNum     Number
   secondNum    Number
   divResult    Number
endvar
firstNum = 1.359
secondNum = 5.87542
```

```
divResult = divFloat(firstNum, secondNum)
divResult.view()
endmethod
```

DLL is a very powerful feature because it enables you to use function libraries developed and tested by someone else. An outside developer or third-party supplier of libraries can provide you with a DLL, and you can link it right in. All you need to know are the prototypes of the functions you want to call. (These prototypes usually are supplied with the libraries.)

Creating Custom Procedures

Custom procedures work just like library procedures, with one big difference—you must write them yourself. If you have a task composed of a set of actions you perform frequently in an application, you can write a procedure that bundles those actions together. When you need to do the task, you just call the procedure.

To define a custom procedure for an object, open the Methods dialog for that object. Click the **proc** check box and click OK. Paradox opens an Editor window that has the following default text already written:

```
proc

endproc
```

A procedure definition takes the following general form:

```
proc ProcName(PassingControl ParameterName Type) OptionalReturnType
var
;   this section optional
endvar
const
; this section also optional
endconst

; body of procedure
return OptionalReturnValue
endproc
```

The parameter list in the parentheses following the procedure name is optional. If you declare more than one formal parameter, separate the parameters by a comma.

The scoping rules for procedures are roughly the same as they are for variables:

14 — UNDERSTANDING OBJECTPAL BASICS

- If the procedure is defined within a method, it is available only within the scope of that method.

- If a procedure is defined in a **proc** window (via the Methods dialog) for an object, it is available to all methods in the object as well as to all methods in all other objects contained by the original object (determined by the containership hierarchy).

- If a procedure is defined in the **proc** window of the form designer, it is global to the form.

Suppose that you want to create a tune to play in response to data-entry errors. You can write that procedure once, then cut and paste it to wherever else you want to use it. Or, you can write it as a procedure global to the form and call it from any method contained by that form.

This example assumes that the procedure **errorSound** was defined in the Proc window for a form object.

```
proc errorSound(const Severity SmallInt)
; constants will hold the frequency for different notes
const

  noteA1  = 110
  noteA#1 = 116
  noteB1  = 123
  noteC1  = 130
  noteC#1 = 138
  noteD1  = 146
  noteD#1 = 155
  noteE1  = 164
  noteF1  = 174
  noteF#1 = 184
  noteG1  = 195
  noteG#1 = 207
  noteA2  = 220
; the following constants will hold duration times
  sixteenth = 75      ; sixteenth note
  quarter   = 150     ; quarter note
  dottedq   = 225     ; dotted quarter
  half      = 300     ; half note
endconst

; play Dragnet
sound(noteA1, (int(dottedq * Severity)))
sound(noteB1, (int(sixteenth * Severity)))
sound(noteC1, (int(quarter * Severity)))
sound(noteA1, (int(quarter * Severity)))
sleep(quarter * Severity)   ; rest
sound(noteA1, (int(dottedq * Severity)))
sound(noteB1, (int(sixteenth * Severity)))
```

```
sound(noteC1, (int(quarter * Severity)))
sound(noteA1, (int(quarter * Severity)))
sound(noteD#1, (int(half * Severity)))

endproc
```

Note that **errorSound** takes one argument, *Severity*. *Severity* is used in the body of the method to control the length of each note. A higher *Severity* value makes the tune play slower. Now place a button on the form and label it "Dragnet". In the **pushButton** event method for the *Dragnet* button, call **errorSound** as shown:

```
method pushButton(var eventInfo Event)
errorSound(1)    ; "1" indicates the severity of the error to sound
sleep(1000)      ; sleep creates a pause
errorSound(2)    ; "2" will make ErrorSound play more slowly
endmethod
```

As in library procedures, custom procedures can return values to the method or procedure that called them. The **return** command, if followed by a value or expression, returns the value to the calling procedure or method.

The **return** command also causes a method or procedure to halt execution. When Paradox encounters a **return** command, it stops executing the method or procedure and returns program control to the method or procedure that called it.

Creating Custom Methods

Custom methods have a single but important advantage over custom procedures: they are scoped differently. A custom method can be written for any object on a form, including the form itself. When defined with an object, the method is called by referencing the object name (subject to the same containership hierarchy rules as the objects themselves).

To define a custom method for an object, open the Methods dialog for that object. Type the name you want to give the new method in the New Custom Method text box. Click OK. Paradox opens an ObjectPAL Editor window that has the following default text already written:

```
method NewCustomMethod()

endmethod
```

(The default text shows the new custom method name you typed in the New Custom Method text box.) If you want to declare formal parameters for the custom method, add parentheses after the method name and include the parameter list.

Suppose that you create the following custom method for the *pageOne* object of a form:

```
method giveStatus()
   msgInfo("Status", "I am a custom method for pageOne")
endmethod
```

If, on *pageOne*, you also have a button called *AlertSounds*, you can call **giveStatus** from the **pushButton** method of *AlertSounds* with

```
method pushButton(var eventInfo Event)
   giveStatus()
endmethod
```

If you attempt to call **giveStatus** the same way from a button on *pageTwo* of the same form, you run into trouble because *pageOne* is not in the same containership hierarchy as *pageTwo*. If you call a custom method defined in an object that is lower on the same containership hierarchy or in a different containership hierarchy, you must specify the object name to which the custom method is attached. From *pageTwo* of the same form, for example, the call to **giveStatus** looks like the following:

```
pageOne.giveStatus()
```

The custom method definition often is more complex than the example shown here. It usually includes formal parameters, for example. If so, you must pass arguments to those formal parameters that match the parameter specification of the custom method.

Assume that you have modified **giveStatus** on *pageOne* to look like this:

```
method giveStatus(const RepeatTimes SmallInt)
var
   x          SmallInt              ; to control counter of for loop
   StatusStr  String                 ; to build the string to display
endvar

for x from 1 to RepeatTimes    ; RepeatTimes is the formal parameter
                               ; passed into giveStatus
   StatusStr = "Calling the custom method for pageOne"
             + strval(x) + " of " + strval(RepeatTimes)
   msgInfo("Status", StatusStr)
endfor
endmethod
```

Because **giveStatus** now has formal parameters, you have to pass it arguments when you call it. From pageTwo (or anywhere else outside the containership hierarchy of pageOne), the call needs to look more like this:

```
method pushButton(var eventInfo Event)
pageOne.giveStatus(2) ; one argument of the correct type supplied
endmethod
```

or this:

```
method pushButton(var eventInfo mouseEvent)
var
   statusRepeats    SmallInt
endvar

statusRepeats = 2
pageOne.giveStatus(statusRepeats)
endmethod
```

Like other methods, custom methods can return values to the method or procedure that called them. The **return** command, if followed by a value or expression, returns the value to the calling procedure or method. The method declaration must include the data type of the value to be returned. The following revision of **giveStatus**, for example, returns a Logical value.

```
method giveStatus(const RepeatTimes SmallInt)  Logical
var
  x         SmallInt      ; to control counter of for loop
  StatusStr String        ; to build the string to display
endvar

for x from 1 to RepeatTimes
  ; RepeatTimes is the formal parameter
  StatusStr = "Calling the custom method for pageOne"
            + strval(x) + " of " + strval(RepeatTimes)
   msgInfo("Status", statusStr)
endfor
return True
endmethod
```

The **return** command also causes a method or procedure to halt execution. When Paradox encounters a **return** command, it stops executing the method or procedure and returns program control to the method or procedure that called it.

Working with Arrays

Arrays are variables that contain bundles of data. Unlike single variables, which contain one piece of data, arrays can contain many pieces of data. If a single variable is an egg, an array is a carton of eggs. Each piece of data in an array is called an *element* (not an egg!).

When you declare an array, you generally provide the name of the array, the number of elements, and the type of all the elements. To access a particular element, you give the array name and the index of the element you want. For an array called *allValues* to access the fourth element, for example, you write **allValues[4]**. To read this aloud, you say, "allValues sub four."

Arrays come in three types: fixed, resizable, and dynamic. A *fixed array* has a specified number of elements of the same type. A *resizable array* has an indeterminate number of elements of the same type. A *dynamic array* has an indeterminate number of elements of different data types.

Declaring Fixed Arrays

A fixed array has a specified, unchangeable number of elements. To declare a fixed array, provide the array name, the number of elements, and the data type. To declare an array of 12 Easter eggs (each element holds a string with a different color or pattern), write the following:

```
var
   EasterEggs  Array[12]    String
endvar
```

The preceding example declares EasterEggs as an array of 12 strings. To assign a value to an element, you include the index of the array, as in this statement:

```
EasterEggs[1] = "Blue and Red"
EasterEggs[2] = "Green"
```

Table 14.4 describes the methods in the Array type. Note that both arrays and resizable arrays are part of the same type. Many of the methods in the Array type, such as **grow** and **insertFirst**, however, work with resizable arrays only. This is true because some Array methods have the effect of growing the array. Table 14.4 includes a column that indicates if a method is appropriate for a resizable array only.

Declaring Resizable Arrays

A resizable array works like a fixed array with one exception: you can change the number of elements. To declare a resizable array, leave the size blank, as in the following example:

```
var
   PartsInStock   Array[]   String
endvar
```

Before the array can hold any data, you must give the array an initial size, using the **setSize** method. Table 14.4 describes the methods in the Array type.

Table 14.4. Array Methods

Method	Resizable?	Description
addLast	Yes	Adds an element to the last position of an array. Increases the array size by one.
append	Yes	Adds the entire contents of one array to the end of another array.
contains		Searches through each element of an array for a string or pattern of characters. Returns True or False.
countOf		Searches through each element of an array for a string or pattern of characters. Returns the number of times the search string was found.
empty		Empties an array.
exchange		Switches the contents of two cells in an array. Useful for sorting.
fill		Assigns a value to every element in an array [with a value].
grow	Yes	Makes an array larger by a number of elements.
indexOf		Searches an array for a particular value (must be the entire value, not a matching pattern or partial string). Returns the position of the first element that matches.
insert	Yes	Inserts one or more new elements into an array. Grows a resizable array by the number of items inserted.

14 — UNDERSTANDING OBJECTPAL BASICS

Method	Resizable?	Description
insertAfter	Yes	Searches an array for a particular value. If found, a new element with a specified value is inserted after matched element. If successful, grows a resizable array by 1.
insertBefore	Yes	Searches an array for a particular value. If found, a new element with a specified value is inserted before matched element. If successful, grows a resizable array by 1.
insertFirst	Yes	Inserts a new element into the first position of a resizable array.
isResizable		Returns True if specified array is a resizable array; otherwise, returns False.
remove	Yes	Removes several elements from an array, starting with a specified element. Adjusts index of array accordingly. Shortens a resizable array by the number of elements.
removeAllItems	Yes	Searches for and deletes all elements with the specified value. If successful, shortens a resizable array by the number of elements found.
removeItem	Yes	Searches for and deletes the first element that matches the specified value. If successful, shortens a resizable array by 1.
replaceItem		Searches for a value in an array and, if found, replaces it with a specified value. Does not change the size of an array.
setSize	Yes	Sets or resets the size of an array. If current array size is smaller than specified, **setSize** grows the array; if current array size is larger than specified, **setSize** truncates the array.
size		Returns the size of a fixed or resizable array.
view		Opens a dialog box and displays the contents of the array.

Declaring Dynamic Arrays

Dynamic arrays, like fixed and resizable arrays, are bundles of data. Like resizable arrays, dynamic arrays can shrink and grow after they have been declared. But dynamic arrays take the concept of an array one step further. Instead of indexing the array with numbers, you index a dynamic array with tags. A *tag* is really just a name. Any expression that evaluates to a String suffices as a tag.

In addition, you can store different data types in the same dynamic array. Valid data types for dynamic arrays include the following:

- SmallInt
- LongInt
- String
- Date
- Number

In the following example, a DynArray holds the notes of a scale. References to a particular element are by that element's tag name.

```
var
  durationF  SmallInt    ; multiplier for duration
  mScale DynArray[] Number
endvar

mScale["A1"]  = 110
mScale["A#1"] = 116
mScale["B1"]  = 123
mScale["C1"]  = 130
mScale["C#1"] = 138
mScale["D1"]  = 146
mScale["D#1"] = 155
mScale["E1"]  = 164
mScale["A2"]  = 220

sound(mScale["A1"], 200)
sound(mScale["A2"], 200)
...
```

Table 14.5 describes the methods in DynArray.

Table 14.5. DynArray Methods

Method	Description
contains	Searches all elements of a dynamic array for a search string or pattern. Returns True if a match is found.
getKeys	Creates a resizable array of strings containing the tag names of each element in the array.
removeItem	Searches a dynamic array for an element with a given value (not a partial value). Deletes the element if found.
size	Returns the number of elements in the dynamic array.
view	Opens a dialog box and displays the contents of the dynamic array.

Chapter Summary

In this chapter, you learned all the basic language elements of ObjectPAL. You now should be familiar with the various data types. In addition, you now know how to call ObjectPAL methods and procedures and how to construct custom methods and procedures. In the next chapter, you learn how to use the ObjectPAL language to create modules of an application.

CHAPTER 15

Sample Application: Using ObjectPAL

This chapter, along with the next three chapters, takes you through the steps of building a Paradox for Windows application with ObjectPAL. In these chapters, you learn how to interact with the user by using fields, messages, and dialog boxes. In addition, you learn how to manipulate forms, tables, reports, and queries under ObjectPAL control.

You will gain the most from this chapter and the following three if you follow the steps to create the sample application. You can read through the steps, of course, but you will have a better understanding of the concepts if you take a hands-on approach.

This chapter discusses the goals of using a graphical user interface and provides tips for designing forms, buttons, dialog boxes, and icons. As you work through this chapter, you will discover how to display the results of calculations, how to provide user help by displaying messages, and how to use the built-in dialog boxes to prompt or query the user.

This chapter assumes that you have read the previous two chapters and that you have a basic understanding of how to use the interactive features of Paradox for Windows. Before you begin this chapter, you definitely should know how to use the ObjectPAL Editor to create methods and procedures, and you should be familiar with basic editing techniques, such as cutting and pasting.

Designing a Graphical Interface

The user interface of an application consists of all the elements that allow users to control the flow of the application. Buttons, fields, dialog boxes, and menus are all part of the user interface. Buttons enable users to request an action or set of actions. Fields enable users to enter values to search for or store. You also can use fields to display output. Dialog boxes ask users to provide more detailed instructions. Menus provide users with a set of options that require just a few clicks of the mouse.

A *graphical user interface* uses graphics instead of words to interact with the user. Studies show that people can recognize symbols much more quickly than they can recognize words. To prove this phenomenon to yourself, place 40 names of animals on one wall and place 40 pictures of animals on another wall. Then, ask two people to stand, one facing each wall. If you ask them to find a particular animal, the person facing the pictures almost always locates the animal much faster. Thus, the goal of designing a user interface is to use, whenever possible, graphical information rather than verbal information to present choices to users.

Suppose that your application requires the user to confirm a data-entry form before proceeding to the next step. You can provide a menu option called Check Data Entry that checks the data in each field for consistency and accuracy. The Check Data Entry menu option represents a *verbal user interface*. To approach the same procedure using a graphical user interface, you can place a button with a check mark on it. When the user clicks the button, the application checks the data and proceeds to the next step.

Some graphic images depict the action they represent, and some do not. The system icon in the upper-left corner of every Windows window, for example, represents the system menu, but it is not a picture of a menu. In no way does the image resemble the system menu or depict any of its actions. Unless someone tells you that double-clicking the system icon for any window closes the window, you probably cannot guess its function.

The Microsoft Windows Terminal application, on the other hand, is an example of an image that depicts the action it represents. A picture of a telephone in front of a PC represents this application in the Accessories group. One glimpse at the icon gives you a good idea of what the application does.

Like the Microsoft Windows Terminal application, a picture can easily represent some actions, but not all. Depicting an action is desirable, when possible, because users can more easily recognize the action from the picture. And easy recognition makes your application easier to use.

If you cannot create or find an icon or a bit map that accurately depicts an action, however, you can use a symbol (such as ? or !) or a word (such as "Query" or "Do-It!"). As with the Windows System symbol, if you use the symbol or word consistently throughout your application, users are able to locate it quickly and to use it confidently. Although the system icon does not depict the action it represents, it remains effective across all Windows applications because it is used consistently.

To take full advantage of the graphical properties of objects, consider using the attributes of objects to provide visual clues to a user about the nature or contents of the object. The following list gives some tips and examples of visual clues:

- Use data-dependent colors to indicate different data ranges or values. To illustrate, use red to indicate negative numbers and black to indicate positive numbers. On an order and shipping form, use different colors to indicate different shippers—for example, purple for Federal Express, brown for UPS, and red for Express Mail.

- Group action buttons at the bottom of all dialog boxes, and try to make buttons the same size. Label the button, even if you also place an icon on the button.

- Place a title at the top of different form pages, at the top of dialog boxes, and at the top of list boxes. Label drop-down boxes.

- Label fields that you can edit and fields used to display results or status.

- Color display-only fields differently than fields you can edit. The user will become accustomed to the color difference and will not attempt to edit fields colored as display-only.

- Use formatting elements such as special frames, boxes, lines, and ellipses creatively but sparingly. Avoid clutter. Group, box, and separate objects only to improve immediate comprehension of the form, page, or dialog.

- When designing any information display, remember that seven is a magic number because humans can easily remember seven bits of information. If your form contains more than seven elements, think about how you can group them together or consider moving a set of options to a dialog box.

The consistent use of an object's color, shape, size, and position relative to other objects makes an object easy to recognize and locate. The easier and friendlier your application, the more grateful your users are (and the more likely you are to get that raise!).

Interacting with the User

In one sense, the entire purpose of any application is to interact with the user; without users, no programs would be needed. In a more limited sense, interacting with the user takes the form of messages and fields to obtain information from the user and to respond to the user.

To discover some of the ways you can interact with a user, you will learn how to build a mortgage calculator. The mortgage calculator serves as a sample application to illustrate many of the things you can do with ObjectPAL. You will learn to revise and enhance the mortgage calculator in the following chapters.

You expect a user to perform the following steps while using the mortgage calculator:

1. Type in a loan amount.
2. Choose an interest rate.
3. Select the term of the loan.
4. Calculate the monthly loan payment.
5. Change one or more of the fields and then recalculate the payment.

The mortgage calculator is fairly straightforward as long as the user does exactly what you expect. But what if the user types in a loan amount and then tries to calculate the payment without specifying the term of the loan or the interest rate? A good application tells the user to fill in the interest rate field and the term field. The following sections show you how to make your application prompt the user for this information.

First you must build the form. Then, you create the framework for the mortgage calculator by placing and naming objects on a form. The objects roughly correspond to the steps shown earlier. In the next section, you create the following objects:

- A field in which you expect the user to type in a loan amount
- A field with a drop-down list of common interest rates
- A field that allows the user to choose from a list of common mortgage terms
- A button to calculate the monthly payment
- A field to display the results of the calculation

When you're done placing and naming the fields, you can start adding ObjectPAL code. This coding provides users with help along the way and calculates payments after the user enters field values.

Creating and Naming Objects for the Mortgage Calculator

To create the mortgage calculator form, follow these steps:

1. Choose File from the main menu; then choose New, Form to open a new form.
2. Click OK in the Data Model dialog box (don't bind a table to the form).
3. Click OK in the Page Layout dialog box to accept the default page layout.
4. Choose File, Save to name the form. Type **MORTCALC** as the new file name; then choose OK.
5. Right-click the current page of the form to inspect properties. Currently, this is the only page of the form. Rename the page *pageOne*.
6. Inspect properties for *pageOne* and set the color to light gray.
7. Create a text object centered at the top of the page.
8. In the text object, type **Mortgage Calculator** (see fig. 15.1).
9. From the Properties menu, set the text font size to 12 or 14 points. Set the font color to a light color, such as white or yellow.
10. Name the text object *mcLabel*.
11. Draw a box around *mcLabel*. The box creates a margin of color around the label.

III — PROGRAMMING PARADOX FOR WINDOWS

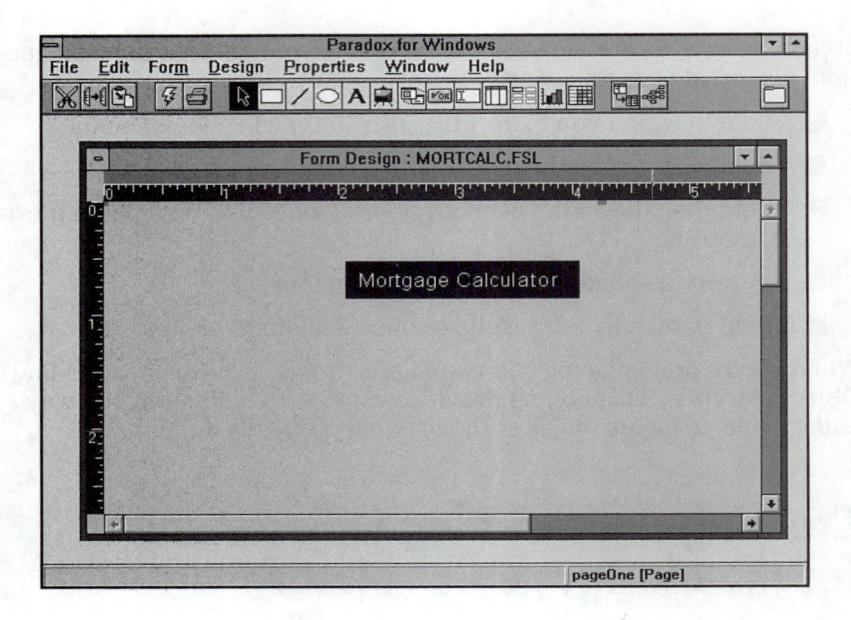

FIG. 15.1

The Mortgage Calculator.

12. Name the box *mcLabelBox*.
13. Set the color of *mcLabelBox* to dark blue.

To create a field for the user to enter a loan amount and another field to display the result of the calculation, follow these steps:

1. Place a field under *mcLabelBox*.
2. From the properties menu for the new field, set the name to *loanField*.
3. Choose Display Type, Labeled from the properties menu. Paradox creates two objects inside the field: one display region for the label and one edit region to change and display the contents of the field.
4. Rename the label to *loanFieldLabel*. Replace the default text in *loanFieldLabel* with **Loan Amount:**.
5. Set the color of *loanField* to dark gray.
6. Set the color of *loanEdit* to white.
7. Place another field. Name the field *paymentField*. Set the field type to Labeled. Set the color of *paymentField* to dark gray.
8. Erase the default text in the label and replace it with **Monthly Payment:** (see fig. 15.2).

15 — SAMPLE APPLICATION: USING OBJECTPAL

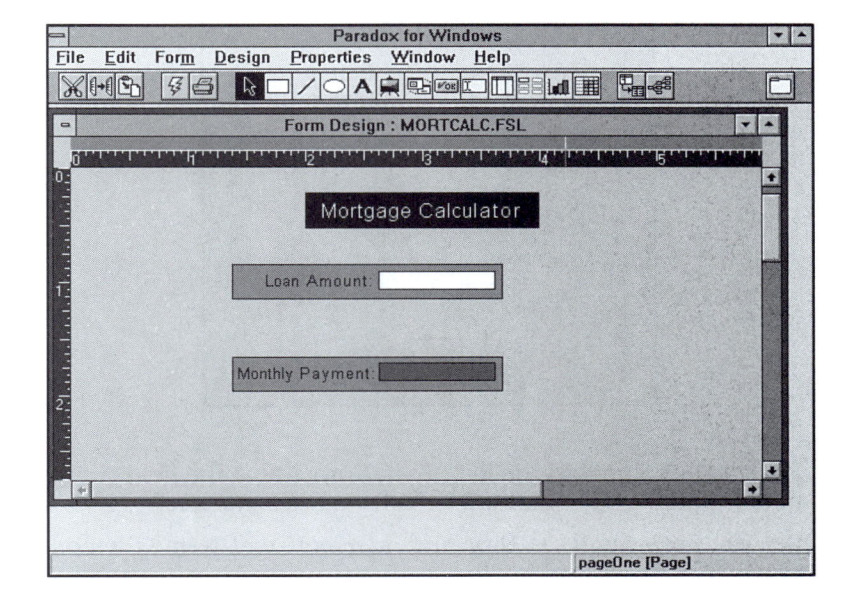

FIG. 15.2

Placement of *paymentField* and *loanField*.

9. From the properties menu, set the color of the edit region of the field to dark cyan to indicate that it is a display-only field.

10. Uncheck the Tab Stop option. Tab Stop is checked by default, which means that the user can tab to this object. When Tab Stop is not checked for a field, Paradox prevents the user from moving to the field with the keyboard or mouse.

11. Create a new field between *paymentField* and *loanField*. Name the field *rateDrop*.

12. Set the display type of *rateDrop* to Drop-Down Edit. Paradox opens a dialog box to define the items in the drop-down list. A drop-down edit field enables the user to type in a specific value or click the down arrow next to the field to choose a value from a prepared list. A drop-down edit field gives you the flexibility of presenting common choices, so the user doesn't need to type the value unless an uncommon value is required.

13. Create a list of common interest rate percentages, starting with 6.5 percent and proceeding in half-percent increments to 15 percent (see fig. 15.3). When the list is complete, choose OK to close the dialog box.

III — PROGRAMMING PARADOX FOR WINDOWS

FIG. 15.3

The Drop-Down Edit list for *rateDrop*.

14. Place a text object to the left of *rateDrop*. Name the field *rateFieldLabel*. Type **Annual % Rate:** in *rateFieldLabel*.

15. Draw a box around *rateDrop* and *rateFieldLabel*. Name the box *rateField*.

16. Adjust the size of *rateField*, *loanField*, and *paymentField* so that they are the same size. Adjust the labels within the fields and box so that the colons line up. Adjust the edit fields and drop-down list so that they are the same size and have the same alignment (see fig. 15.4.).

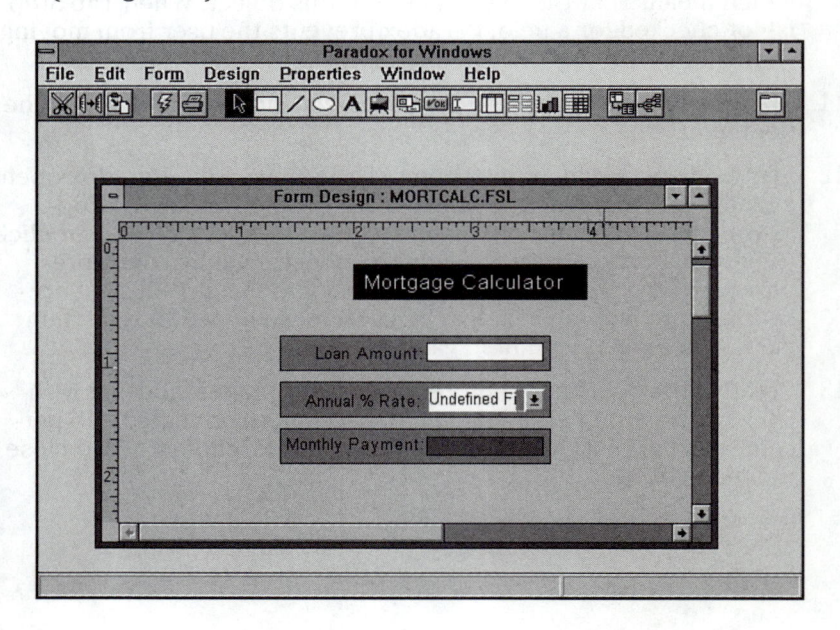

FIG. 15.4

The Mortgage Calculator with a rate field.

Next, add a drop-down edit box that lets the user choose the term of the loan by following these steps:

1. To the right of *loanField*, *rateField*, and *paymentField*, draw a field approximately three-fourths of an inch wide and 1 1/2 inches high. Rename the field *termField*.

2. Set the display type of *termField* to Drop-Down Edit. Paradox opens a dialog box that allows you to define the list. Enter a list of common mortgage terms (in years) including 3, 4, 5, 10, 15, and 30. Paradox creates a new list object contained by *termField*. Display the Object Tree for *termField* (it's hard to get the handles otherwise), and rename the contained list *termList*.

3. Place a text object above *termField*. Type **Term:** in the text object, resizing it if necessary.

4. Draw a box around *termBoxLabel* and *termField*. Name the box *termBox*. Set the color of *termBox* to dark gray.

5. Place a button under *termBox* and *paymentField*. Rename the button *calcButton*. Replace the default label on *calcButton* with **Calculate**.

6. Draw a box around all of the objects placed so far. Rename the box *mcBox*. Color the box yellow or another light color.

Your mortgage calculator now should look similar to the one in figure 15.5. The form you created by following the preceding steps doesn't have to look exactly the same, although all the objects should be placed in about the same position. What matters is the relationship of the objects to each other, because this relationship affects how you refer to the objects with ObjectPAL.

Figure 15.6 shows the Object Tree for this version of the mortgage calculator. Before you change the built-in methods for some of these objects, please check the Object Tree for your form to make sure it matches the Object Tree shown in figure 15.6. (Renaming the labels of fields, buttons, and edit regions is optional.)

Using Messages To Describe Objects

Most designers and application developers believe that what they've designed is intuitive and obvious to the user. They are not always right. The user can glean only so much information from the labels and placement of the fields in an application. You can accomplish a great deal with a good design, but it may not be enough. Consequently, programs need to communicate more freely with the user by way of prompts, dialog boxes, and help messages.

III — PROGRAMMING PARADOX FOR WINDOWS

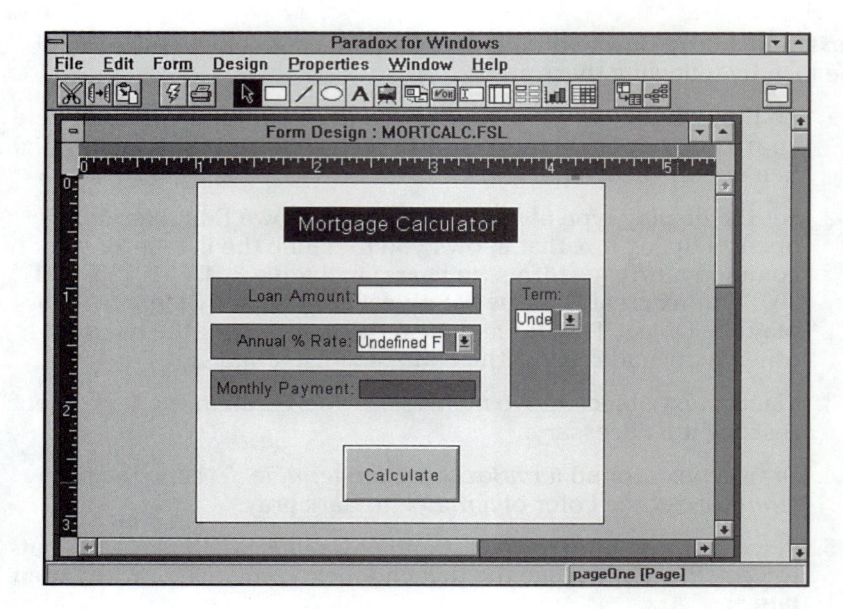

FIG. 15.5

The mortgage calculator form after creating the fields.

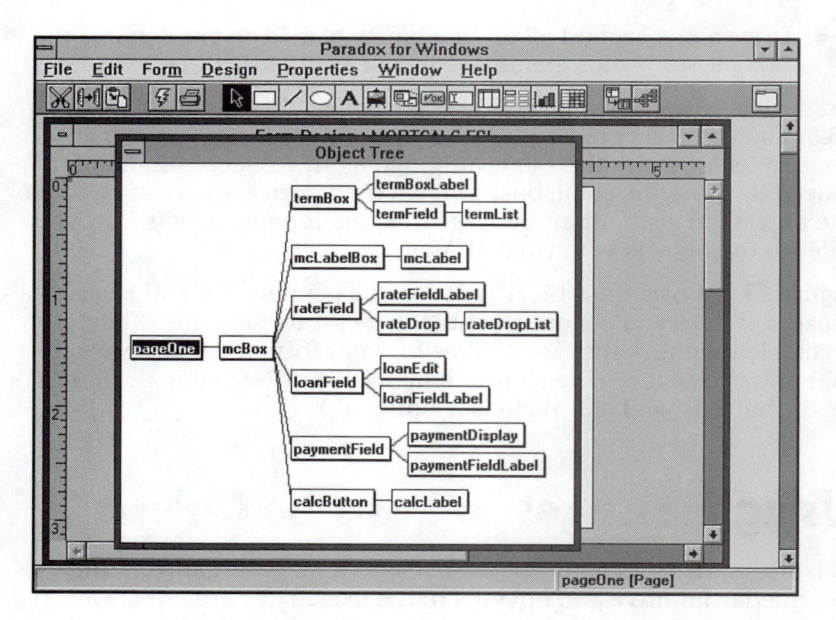

FIG. 15.6

The Object Tree for the mortgage calculator.

Think of the objects in an application as part of a big, friendly party; everyone knows everyone else and introductions are not necessary. Then along comes a new addition to the crowd—the user. All but the boldest of socialites wander through the crowd hoping someone says, "Hi! My name is..." Similarly, the internal life of an application is clear to itself and to its designers, but it is not always clear to the user.

Many people approach new software in the same way they approach a party where they don't know anyone; they hope someone makes an introduction. By using messages, you can instruct the objects on a form to give hints to the user about their purpose and function—to introduce themselves. When the mouse pointer crosses into the boundary of a Paradox SpeedBar button, for example, a short description of the object appears in the status bar. Paradox's user-friendly style is not standard across all windows applications, but you can make it a standard in yours.

To display a message in the status bar in response to an event, you must modify two built-in methods for every object you want to change. To make the message appear when the mouse pointer enters an object's territory, you must change the **mouseEnter** built-in method. To clear the message when the mouse pointer exits an object's territory, you must change the **mouseExit** built-in method. In the **mouseEnter** and the **mouseExit** built-in method, you will use the message procedure to write a string to the status bar.

Follow these steps to instruct *mcBox* to introduce itself:

1. Open the mortgage calculator form in Design mode.
2. Right-click *mcBox* to inspect properties.
3. Choose <u>M</u>ethods from the properties menu. Paradox opens the Methods dialog box.
4. Click the **mouseEnter** method from the list of built-in methods. Click the **mouseExit** method as well.
5. Click OK to open an ObjectPAL Editor window for both methods.
6. Move to the ObjectPAL Editor window for **mouseEnter**.
7. Between the **method** and **endmethod** lines, insert the following line:

    message("Enter amount, rate, and term, then calculate.")

8. Check the syntax, and correct any typing errors.
9. Make the **mouseExit** ObjectPAL Editor window active.
10. Between the **method** and **endmethod** lines, insert the following line:

    message("")

11. Check the syntax.

III — PROGRAMMING PARADOX FOR WINDOWS

12. Save and run the form.
13. Move the mouse pointer into *mcBox*. Notice that the status bar displays a message shown in figure 15.7.
14. Move the mouse pointer out of *mcBox*. The status bar clears. Notice that the message doesn't clear as you move into the objects contained by *mcBox*. Although you cross the border into another object, you don't actually exit from *mcBox*; consequently, Paradox doesn't call the **mouseExit** built-in method.

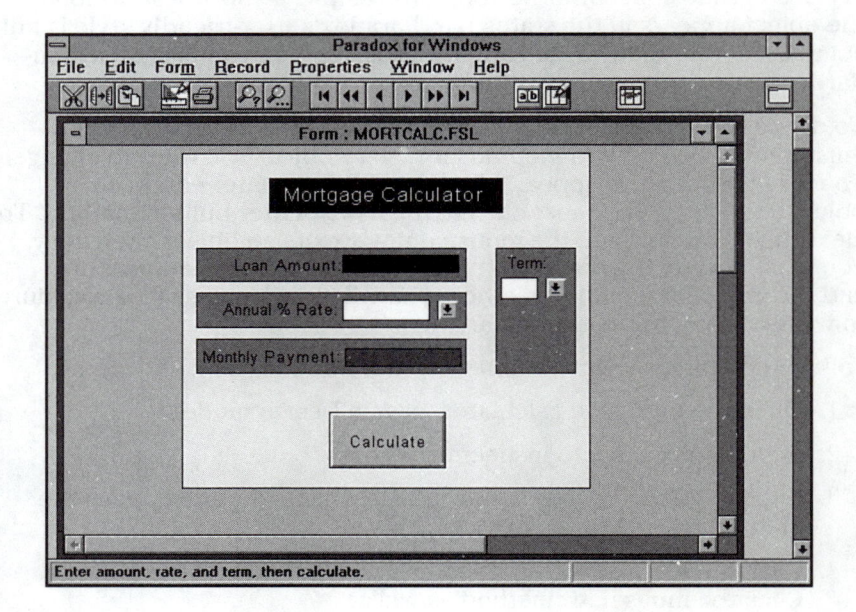

FIG. 15.7

Displaying a message in the status bar.

Although this message helps the user get a general idea of what to do, adding more specific messages to each field helps the user even more. To add specific messages, follow these steps:

1. Return to Design mode.
2. Open the Methods dialog box for *loanField* (select the field, choose Properties, and then choose Methods).
3. Select **mouseEnter** and **mouseExit** from the list of methods.
4. Click the ObjectPAL Editor window for **mouseEnter** to make it active.
5. Insert the following line:

   ```
   message("Type or edit loan amount.")
   ```

15 — SAMPLE APPLICATION: USING OBJECTPAL

6. Click the ObjectPAL Editor window for **mouseExit** to make it active.
7. To clear the status bar when the mouse exits *loanField*, insert the following line:

   `message("")`
8. Check the syntax for both windows.
9. Save and run the form.
10. Move the mouse into *mcBox*. Notice that the correct message for **mouseEnter** displays in the status bar.
11. Move the mouse into *loanField*. Again, Paradox displays the correct message *loanField* because moving into *loanField* triggered the **mouseEnter** built-in method for *loanField*.
12. Move the mouse out of *loanField* but still within the border of *mcBox*. Notice that the status bar clears the message for *loanField* but doesn't display the message for *mcBox*.
13. Return to Design mode.

When the mouse leaves *loanField*, Paradox triggers the **mouseExit** method for *loanField*. A departure from *loanField*, however, is not an entry to *mcBox*. Because *loanField* is embedded in *mcBox*, the mouse has been in *mcBox* all along, so Paradox doesn't trigger the **mouseEnter** method for *mcBox*.

To change this behavior, you can make the **mouseExit** method for *loanField* display the message for *mcBox*. (You also can call the **mouseEnter** method for *mcBox* directly from *loanField's* **mouseExit**, which is not wise. If the **mouseExit** method for *mcBox* is later modified to do something more than simply display the help message, the effect of calling *mcBox's* **mouseExit** cannot be predicted.)

To have the **mouseExit** method for *loanField* display the help message for *mcBox*, you can take one of two approaches:

- You can type the full message string in the **mouseExit** method for *loanField*. This approach has the advantage of being straightforward and easy to read. The disadvantage of this approach is that you end up typing in the same string a number of times.

- You can create a string constant for the help message and declare the constant so that it is global to all objects contained by *mcBox*. To display the message, use the constant in place of the quoted string and add an argument to the message procedure. The same message can be used in *mcBox's* **mouseEnter** and from the **mouseExit** method for other objects.

III — PROGRAMMING PARADOX FOR WINDOWS

The disadvantage of this approach is that it makes the code somewhat more difficult to read. Every time you see a reference to the constant, you may have to think about what's in that constant. But the advantage to this approach is that you don't need to retype the message string a number of times. If you need to change the string, you can change the constant just once, and the change is reflected wherever the constant is used.

Follow these steps to declare and use a constant for *mcBox's* help message:

1. Open the Methods dialog box for *mcBox*.
2. Check the Const box and click OK.
3. In the ObjectPAL Editor window, define a constant named *mcBoxMsg* to contain the message for *mcBox*. Type the following statement between the **Const** and **endConst** keywords (see fig. 15.8).

   mcBoxMsg = "Enter amount, rate, and term, then calculate."

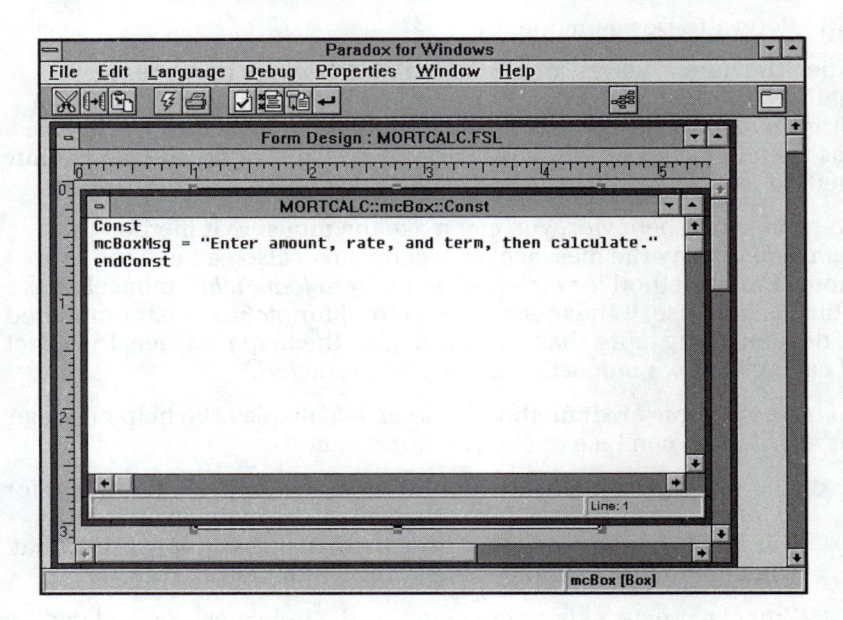

FIG. 15.8

The Const window for *mcBox*.

4. Check the syntax.
5. Open the **mouseEnter** method for *mcBox*.

6. Replace the string argument in **message** with the constant. The entire method should look like this:

   ```
   method mouseEnter(var eventInfo MouseEvent)
   message(mcBoxMsg)
   endmethod
   ```

7. Check the syntax.
8. Open the **mouseExit** method for *loanField*.
9. Replace the string argument in **message** with the constant, like this:

   ```
   message(mcBoxMsg)
   ```

10. Check the syntax.
11. Save and run the form.
12. Move the mouse into *mcBox*. Paradox displays the message contained in the constant *mcBoxMsg*.
13. Move the mouse into *loanField*. Paradox displays the correct message for *loanField*.
14. Move out of *loanField*. The message for *mcBox* is redisplayed.
15. Return to Design mode.

Repeat this process for all the other fields on the mortgage calculator. For the fields listed below, modify the **mouseEnter** method to include a statement that displays a message. Also, change the **mouseExit** method to include a statement that displays the message for *mcBox* (use the constant *mcBoxMsg*). Table 15.1 lists suggested messages for each field.

Table 15.1. Suggested Field Messages

Field	Message
rateField	"Type a rate or choose one from the list."
paymentField	"Calculated payment amount displays here."
termField	"Choose a loan term from the list."
calcButton	"Push to recalculate monthly payment."

Defining the Calculate Button

In addition to being easy to use, the mortgage calculator actually has to do something—calculate a monthly payment. After you fill in all three fields, you should be able to click the Calculate button to calculate the monthly payment.

The next point may seem obvious in this example, but it is critical: When you're trying to decide what to program or where to put your code, think about what you expect the user to do to initiate an action. Then, look for the built-in method that corresponds to what you expect the user to do.

In the mortgage calculator, you expect the user to enter the loan amount, the rate, and the term and then click the Calculate button. When the user clicks a button, Paradox executes that button's **pushButton** built-in method. Consequently, for the mortgage calculator, start by thinking about how you want to change the default behavior of the **pushButton** method for the Calculate button.

You want the Calculate button to do at least the following two things:

- Calculate the payment
- Display the result

To calculate the payment, you can use the **pmt** method (**pmt** is a method from the Number type). The **pmt** method takes three arguments: the loan amount, the percentage rate for the period, and the number of periods.

To use the **pmt** method, you first must get the arguments. The information you need is contained in the three fields *loanField*, *termField*, and *rateField*. One of the properties of any field is its value. To acquire the value of a field, use this general syntax:

```
varName = fieldName.Value
```

or more simply, use this:

```
varName = fieldName
```

In the second variation, Paradox assumes that you want the Value property. (The specific reference to the Value property is often used in these examples, but only because it makes the examples easier to read. To reference a field object's Value, you only need to use the field name.)

Because **fieldName.Value** evaluates to a value, you can use that value in more complicated expressions or as an argument in a method. For example, the statement

```
returnVar = fieldName.Value * 100
```

takes the value found in field *fieldName*, multiplies it by 100, and places the result in the variable *returnVar* (this assumes that *fieldName* is holding some kind of number, and that *returnVar* is a variable of a numeric type).

So, to calculate the payment using values from the fields, the code for **pushButton** might look like this:

```
method pushButton(var eventInfo Event)
var
  realRate   Number
  ; store value from rate field for easier calculation
  realTerm   Number   ; to store value from term field
  loanAmt Number
  mPayment   Number   ; monthly payment
endvar

realRate = rateField.rateDrop.Value    ; get the rate

realRate = realRate/100                ; convert to percentage
realRate = realRate/12                 ; convert to monthly rate

realTerm = termBox.termField.value * 12  ; convert term from years
                                         ; to months
; calculate monthly payment and assign result to payment field
loanAmt = loanField.Value
mPayment = loanAmt.pmt(realRate, realTerm)

msgInfo("mPayment is", mPayment)

endmethod
```

After you calculate the payment, you must display it to the user. You have several options for displaying the payment. You can display it in the status bar or in a **msgInfo** dialog (a dialog box created by the msgInfo procedure that you can use to display a short text string). As you have seen, Paradox uses the status bar to display help messages; the status bar changes whenever the user moves the mouse across an object. If the user doesn't read the result before moving the mouse, the message disappears. Consequently, displaying the result in the status bar isn't such a great idea.

Displaying the payment in a **msgInfo** dialog is a slightly better option than displaying the payment in the status bar because the dialog won't close until the user closes it.

The most sensible way to display the result, however, is in a field. The result stays in the field until the user recalculates the payment or closes the form. The purpose of the *paymentField* object that you placed earlier is to display the result of the mortgage calculation.

III — PROGRAMMING PARADOX FOR WINDOWS

You saw earlier how you can use a field's Value property to access the value held in the field. By the same token, you can assign a value to a field via the field's Value property. (Another way of saying this is that Value is a read/write property.) The following statement assigns 100 to *fieldName*:

```
fieldName.Value = 100
```

Use the same technique in the **pushButton** method for *calcButton* to assign the result of the monthly payment calculation to *paymentField*. To make the Calculate button calculate the payment when the user selects it, change the **pushButton** method for *calcButton* so that it contains the following code:

```
method pushButton(var eventInfo Event)
var
  realRate Number    ; store value from rate field
  realTerm Number    ; to store value from term field
  loanAmt Number
  mPayment Number ; monthly payment
endvar

realRate = rateField.rateDrop.Value      ; get the rate
realRate = realRate/100                  ; convert to percentage
realRate = realRate/12                   ; convert to monthly rate

realTerm = termBox.termField.value * 12  ; convert term from years
                                         ; to months

; calculate monthly payment and assign result to payment field
loanAmt = loanField.Value
paymentField.Value = loanAmt.pmt(realRate, realTerm)
endmethod
```

When you're done, check the syntax and give the mortgage calculator a trial run by following these steps:

1. Run the form.

2. Type **100000** in the Loan Amount field.

3. Choose 12.5 from the Annual % Rate drop-down list.

4. Choose 30 from the Term drop-down list.

5. Click the Calculate button. The **pushButton** method for *calcButton* sets the Monthly Payment field to the result of the calculation (see fig. 15.9).

6. Change the term to 15 years.

7. Click Calculate. Notice that Monthly Payment changes.

8. Erase the value in the Loan Amount field.

15 — SAMPLE APPLICATION: USING OBJECTPAL

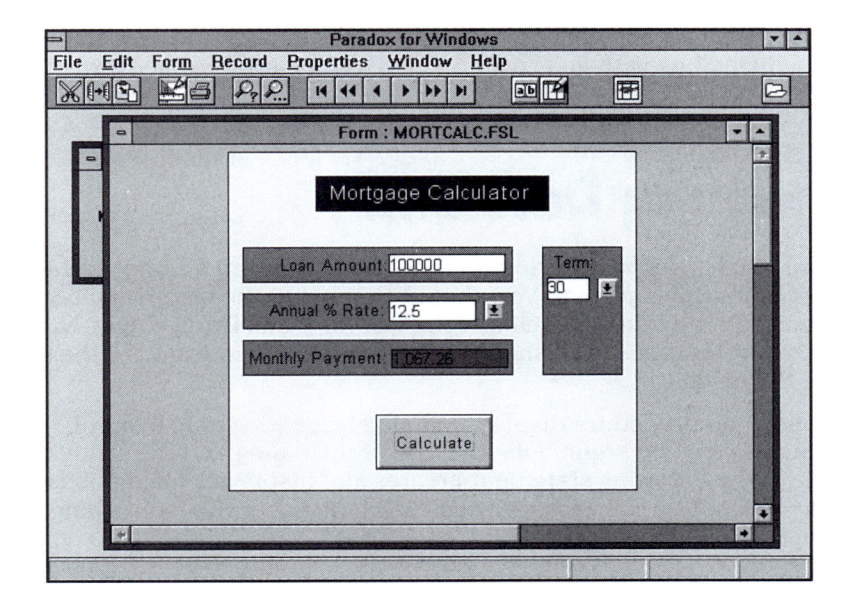

FIG. 15.9

Displaying the results of the calculation.

9. Click Calculate. Paradox displays a 0 (zero) in the Monthly Payment field.

10. Return to Design mode.

In the preceding example, you may have noticed that the method uses the *realRate* and *realTerm* variables to store intermediate results of calculations. This technique is not required by ObjectPAL, but it is used here to improve readability. A more compact way to write the loan calculation follows:

```
method pushButton(var eventInfo Event)
; pmt is called as a procedure instead of as a method
paymentField = pmt(loanField,
                  Number(rateField.rateDrop)/1200,
                  termBox.termField * 12)
endmethod
```

Notice that the rate argument is cast to the Number type. This is necessary because, like all undefined fields, the *rateDrop* field does not have a specific type associated to it. ObjectPAL decides to treat the value as a certain type according to the value. If a field contains an integer, ObjectPAL will treat it as an integer and treat the result of the calculation as an integer. If you remove the Number cast from this calculation and run it again, you will see that the final result is not what you expect. (Try it!)

The next section explains how to test for blank fields and how to display a dialog box with an error message when Paradox discovers a blank field.

Checking Data Entry

Before you let the **pushButton** method for **calcButton** attempt to calculate the monthly payment, you should check that the user has placed values in all the required fields. If the test for blank fields comes back positive, your application should abort the calculation and tell the user to fill the fields.

The **msgStop** procedure displays a dialog box with a stop symbol. **msgStop** takes two arguments: the title of the dialog and the string to display. The following statement creates and displays a dialog box with a title of Oops! and a message which alerts the user that something's wrong:

```
msgStop("Oops!", "Please fill in Loan Amount, " +
        "Annual % Rate, and Term, before you press Calculate.")
```

msgStop doesn't actually halt method execution; it's just a way for you to give a message to the user and tell them why what they're trying to do doesn't work. To stop a method, you can use the **return** command.

The new definition of **pushButton** for *calcButton* follows:

```
method pushButton(var eventInfo Event)
if loanField = "" OR
   rateField.rateDrop = "" OR
   termBox.termField = " " then
  msgStop("Oops!", "Before you click Calculate, " +
          "please fill in Loan Amount, " +
          "Annual % Rate, and Term.")
else
  ; pmt is called as a procedure instead of as a method
  paymentField = pmt(loanField,
                     Number(rateField.rateDrop)/1200,
                     termBox.termField * 12)
endif
endmethod
```

To test the mortgage calculator, follow these steps:

1. Check the syntax of the revised **pushButton** method.
2. Save and run the form.
3. Enter a loan amount, rate, and term.

4. Click Calculate.

5. Erase the entry for Loan Amount.

6. Click Calculate. The **pushButton** method for *calcButton* displays the **msgStop** dialog box with the title and message specified (see fig. 15.10).

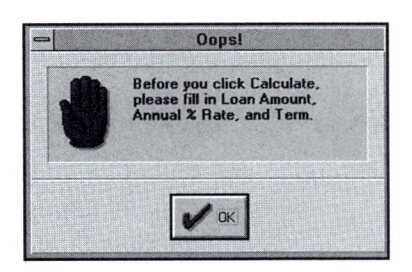

FIG. 15.10
Displaying a Stop message.

7. Click OK to accept the dialog box. Notice that the **pushButton** method for *calcButton* doesn't take any other actions. In the code example shown above, the next line after

    endif

is

    endmethod

If the condition at the beginning of the **if** statement is true, the lines following **then** are executed; afterward, execution skips down to the end of the **if** statement (**endif**). If the condition at the beginning of the **if** statement is False, the lines following **then** are skipped, and the lines following **else** are executed.

You can use a number of other built-in dialog boxes to interact with the user. You will learn how to create your own dialog boxes, of course, but these require more work than using the built-in dialog boxes.

Table 15.2 describes all the built-in dialog boxes. Each dialog is called by a procedure that takes two arguments: a dialog box title (string or string expression) and the dialog box text (string or string expression). Some of the dialog boxes return a value that tells you which button the user pressed to close the dialog (for example, Yes, No, or Cancel).

III — PROGRAMMING PARADOX FOR WINDOWS

Table 15.2. Built-In Dialog Boxes

Procedure	Buttons and return values
msgAbortRetryIgnore	See figure 15.11. Abort button returns "Abort"; Retry button returns "Retry"; and Ignore button returns "Ignore." Closing the dialog with the System icon, from the Control menu, or by pressing the Esc key returns "Cancel."
msgInfo	See figure 15.12. Dialog has an OK button but does not return any values.
msgQuestion	See figure 15.13. Yes button returns "Yes." No button returns "No." Closing the dialog with the System icon, with Close from the Control menu, or by pressing Esc returns "Cancel."
msgRetryCancel	See figure 15.14. Retry button returns "Retry." Cancel button returns "Cancel." Closing from System icon, with Close from the Control menu, or by pressing Esc returns "Cancel."
msgStop	See figure 15.15. Dialog has an OK button but does not return any values.
msgYesNoCancel	See figure 15.16. Yes button returns "Yes." No button returns "No." Cancel button returns "Cancel." Closing from the System icon, with Close from the Control menu, or by pressing Esc returns "Cancel."

FIG. 15.11
The msgAbortRetryIgnore dialog.

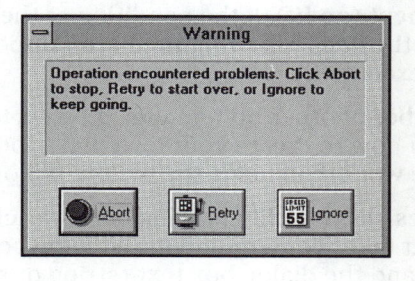

FIG. 15.12
The msgInfo dialog.

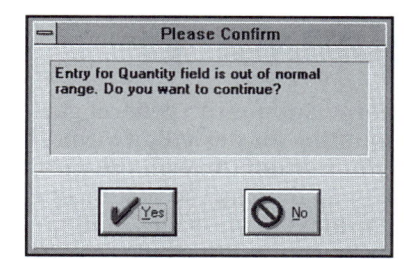

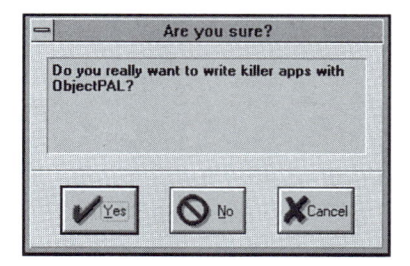

FIG. 15.13

The msgQuestion dialog.

FIG. 15.14

The msgRetryCancel dialog.

FIG. 15.15

The msgStop dialog.

FIG. 15.16

The msgYesNoCancel dialog.

Chapter Summary

In this chapter, you learned about the general goals of a graphical user interface and read about tips for designing forms, buttons, dialog boxes, and icons. As you worked through creating the mortgage calculator, you found out how to display the results of calculations, how to give the user help by displaying messages, and how to use the built-in dialog boxes to prompt or query the user.

In the next chapter, you will create another form to calculate the estimated payment that a household can afford. You also will find out how to open one form from another form and how to control the second form.

CHAPTER 16

Sample Application: Working with Multiple Forms

This chapter describes how to work with multiple forms under ObjectPAL control. In interactive Paradox, you can open several forms at the same time, but no link exists between them. Therefore, Paradox cannot update a field in one form from a field in another. (Paradox can look up values from a table while filling a form, but that's not the same as updating fields between forms.)

By using ObjectPAL, however, you can establish interaction between forms. Generally speaking, no higher program construct exists than the form; that is, you cannot write a program that manipulates several forms independently (at least not easily). One form can control another form, but no object is logically higher than both forms. The object highest in the hierarchy to which you can attach code is the form. (If you are particularly ambitious, you can attempt to write a script that controls forms, but this should be considered an advanced technique. In particular, PAL programmers should resist the temptation to design ObjectPAL programs that are controlled by scripts. If you are a PAL programmer, you will get along better with ObjectPAL if you don't try to force your programs into a PAL design.)

Think of multiple forms as "peers." From Paradox's point of view, the choice of which form opens and controls the other is purely arbitrary; a hierarchy does not represent the relationship of the forms to each other. This lack of hierarchy makes working with multiple forms a little tricky at first.

> **NOTE** This is the second of four chapters that build an ObjectPAL sample application. If you have already built the mortgage calculator form in the preceding chapter, you are ready to proceed with this chapter. If you have not, go back and build the mortgage calculator form now.

Creating the Payment Calculator Form

To discover how to work with multiple forms, you will create a new form in this chapter as a companion to the mortgage calculator form you created in the preceding chapter. The new form enables you to estimate the monthly mortgage payment that an individual or household can afford. After the payment is estimated, the mortgage calculator can work from the payment, interest rate, and term to determine the maximum loan amount for which an individual or household can qualify.

To create and name the new form, follow these steps:

1. Choose File, New, Form, and click OK in the succeeding two dialog boxes to accept the default settings.

2. Choose File, Save As and rename the form MPAYCALC.

3. Create the form shown in figure 16.1. Figures 16.2 and 16.3 show the object tree for the form, and table 16.1 describes the objects.

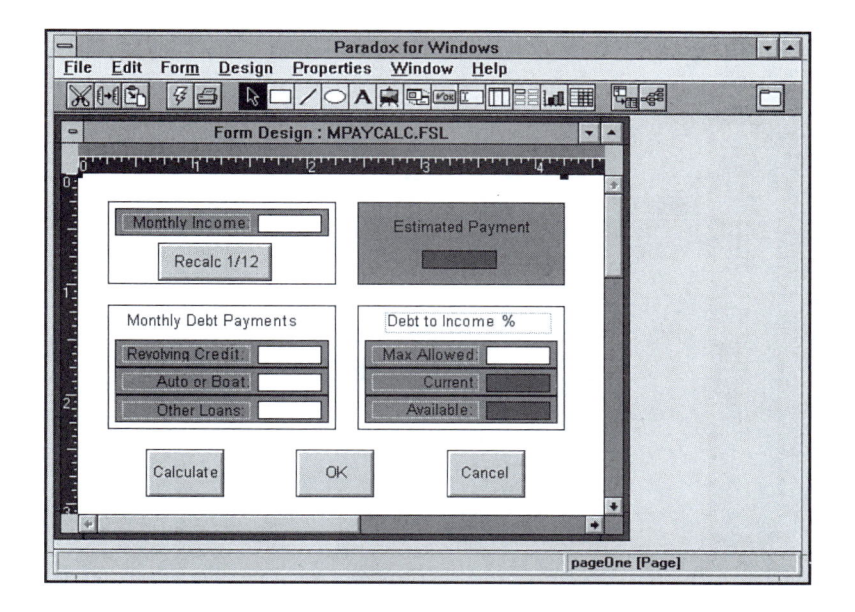

16 — SAMPLE APPLICATION: WORKING WITH MULTIPLE FORMS

FIG. 16.1

The payment calculator form.

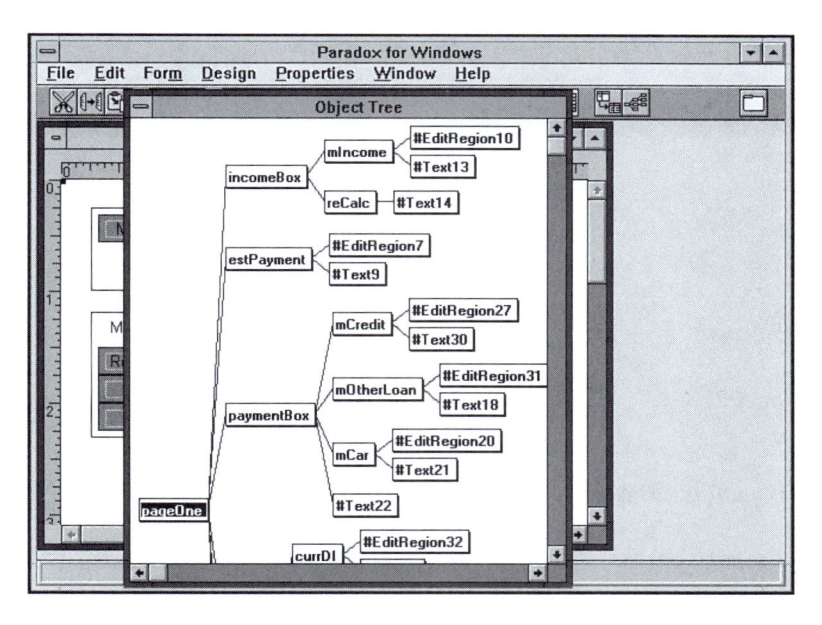

FIG. 16.2

The payment calculator form object tree (top portion).

III — PROGRAMMING PARADOX FOR WINDOWS

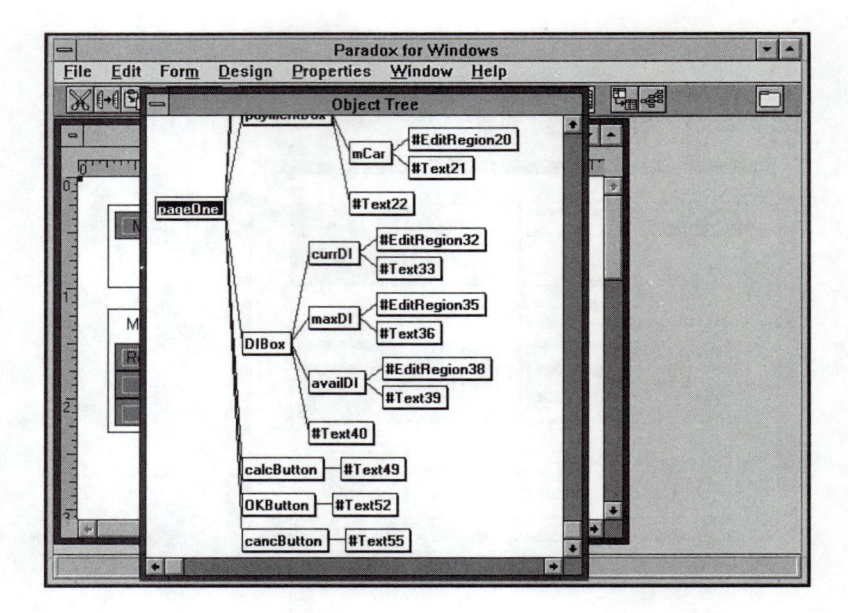

FIG. 16.3

The payment calculator form object tree (bottom portion).

Table 16.1. Objects in the Payment Calculator

Object name	Description
incomeBox	Box holding *mIncome* field and *reCalc* button
incomeBox.mIncome	Undefined field labeled "Monthly Income:"
incomeBox.reCalc	Button labeled "Recalc 1/12"
estPayment	Undefined field labeled "Estimated Payment:"
paymentBox	Box holding *mCredit*, *mCar*, *mOtherLoan*, and a text box with text of "Monthly Debt Payments"
paymentBox.mCredit	Undefined field labeled "Revolving Credit:"
paymentBox.mCar	Undefined field labeled "Auto or Boat:"
paymentBox.mOtherLoan	Undefined field labeled "Other Loans:"
DIBox	Box holding *maxDI*, *currDI*, and *availDI*; also includes text box "Debt to Income %"

16 — SAMPLE APPLICATION: WORKING WITH MULTIPLE FORMS

Object name	Description
DIBox.maxDI	Undefined field labeled "Max Allowed"
DIBox.currDI	Undefined field labeled "Current:"
DIBox.availDI	Undefined field labeled "Available:"
calcButton	Button labeled "Calculate"
OKButton	Button labeled "OK"
cancButton	Button labeled "Cancel"

Defining the Calculations

The payment calculator calculates the monthly payment from a different perspective than the mortgage calculator. Instead of telling you what the monthly loan payment is, the payment calculator calculates the monthly payment a household can afford.

Before you begin programming the payment calculator, you should understand a few assumptions about how lenders qualify buyers for a loan:

- Lending institutions qualify a potential buyer based on ability to pay, although credit history, job history, and other factors are considered.

- Lending institutions measure a household's ability to pay by the amount of monthly income available for debt payments.

- With few exceptions, the total percentage of a household's income considered available for loan repayment is usually limited to about one-third of the household's total monthly income.

- The qualifying process doesn't count how much of the household's income is spent on other kinds of expenses, such as utilities and medical care.

Therefore, if you know the gross monthly income of a household and you know the percentage of that income spent on other debts, you can calculate how much is left for a mortgage payment.

When users work with the payment calculator, you expect them to follow these steps:

1. Enter a monthly income, or enter an annual income and click the Recalc 1/12 button. This button calculates the monthly income from the annual income.

2. Enter various amounts in the monthly debt payment fields.

3. Enter the maximum debt-to-income ratio the lending institution allows (usually between 30 and 35 percent).

4. Click the Calculate button to calculate the estimated monthly payment. Additionally, clicking Calculate will update the remaining two debt-to-income percentages.

5. Return to the mortgage calculator by clicking OK or Cancel.

   When you click OK, Paradox carries the calculated payment to the estimated payment field on the mortgage calculator. When you click Cancel, Paradox does not carry the calculated payment to the mortgage calculator.

In the following sections, you will redefine the **pushButton** methods for *recalc*, *calcButton*, *OKButton*, and *cancButton*. You also can set starting values for some of the editable fields so that the user does not have to make an entry if the default value is acceptable.

recalcButton Methods

The **pushButton** method for *recalcButton* checks that the Monthly Income field has a value and then divides that value by 12. The purpose of this button is to let the user enter a yearly salary, then click the button to divide the yearly salary by 12. The result of the calculation is displayed in the Monthly Income field.

The definition of **pushButton** for *recalcButton* follows:

```
; reCalcButton::pushButton
method pushButton(var eventInfo Event)
var
   stopString     String       ; stores message
endvar

; first, check to see if mIncome is blank
if mIncome.isBlank() then
   ; if it is blank, display a message, but don't calculate
   stopString = "Enter a yearly income in the monthly " +
                "income field before pressing this button."
   msgStop("Stop", stopString)
else
   ; if it's not blank, calculate the monthly income and
   mIncome = number(mIncome)/12 ; write the result back to
                                ; the mIncome field
endif
endmethod
```

16 — SAMPLE APPLICATION: WORKING WITH MULTIPLE FORMS

The Var section of this method declares one variable: *stopString*. *stopString* is a string variable you can use to display the string in the **msgStop** dialog box. Assigning the string to a variable and then using the variable to display the message is not necessary but makes the code more readable. An alternative is to provide the string in the **msgStop** method call like this:

```
msgStop("Stop", "Enter a yearly income in the monthly income field
 before pressing this button")
; The example line above is broken. In an Editor Window,
; it would display all on one line.
```

The problem with this method is that you end up with a long line of code (depending on the length of the string). Unless you maximize the Editor Window displaying the method, you cannot read the string without scrolling to the right. Another option is to assign the string to the *stopString* variable by breaking the lines as they would break in the dialog when it displays, as in the following example:

```
stopString = "Enter a yearly income in the
monthly income field before
pressing this button."
```

The problem here is that the text on the second and third lines must be at the left margin. If the assignment occurs in an indented block, it cannot be indented with the rest of the block. In the **pushButton** method for *recalcButton*, the string is assigned to the variable *stopString* by concatenating (adding) several shorter strings. (The string concatenation operator + is the same as the numeric addition operator +.)

To test the *recalcButton*, follow these steps:

1. Check the syntax for *recalcButton*'s **pushButton** method. If necessary, fix any errors.
2. Save and run the form.
3. Enter a yearly combined income in the Monthly Income field. (Try $60,000.)
4. Press the Recalc 1/12 button. Verify that the calculation worked properly. (If you entered $60,000 in the previous step, the monthly income should be $5,000.)
5. Clear the amount in the Monthly Income field.
6. Press the Recalc 1/12 button again. The Stop message appears asking you to fill in a monthly income before you calculate (see fig. 16.4).

After you finish checking the payment calculator, return to Design mode.

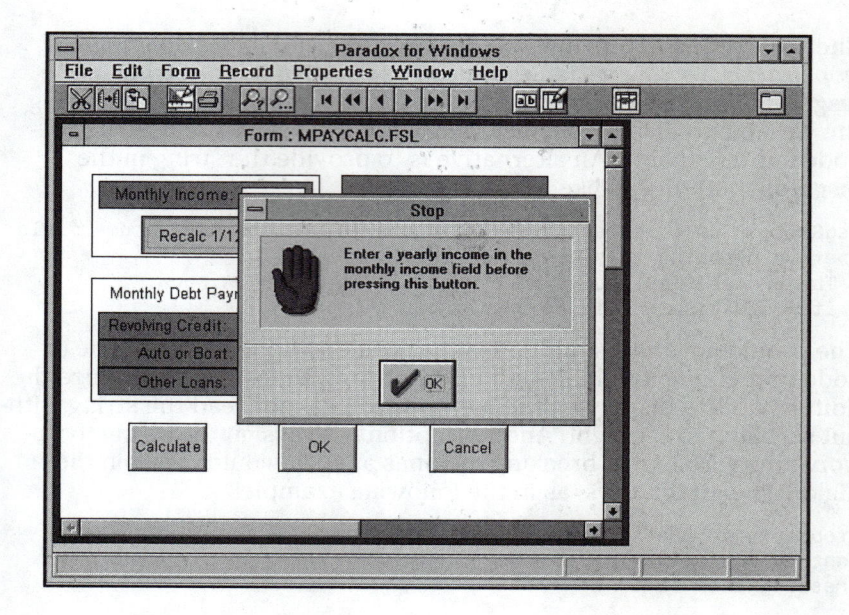

FIG. 16.4

The payment calculator with a Stop message.

calcButton Methods

The *calcButton* button calculates the monthly payment for which a household can qualify. The **pushButton** method for *calcButton* checks that the Monthly Income field has a value. If the field has no value, the method stops the calculation and tells the user why. Otherwise, the method calculates the current debt-to-income ratio and the available debt-to-income ratio. The method then multiplies the available debt-to-income percentage by the monthly income to come up with a qualifying monthly payment.

The following is the full definition of the **pushButton** method for *calcButton*:

```
; calcButton::pushButton
method pushButton(var eventInfo Event)
var
  tempIncome Number   ; temporary variable
  allDebt    Number   ; to hold all three monthly debt payments
  qAnswer    String   ; stores answer to question
endVar

; check for a blank value in mIncome
if incomeBox.mIncome.isBlank() then
  msgStop("Stop", "Please enter an income first.")
else       ; if mIncome is not blank, continue with calculations
```

16 — SAMPLE APPLICATION: WORKING WITH MULTIPLE FORMS

```
    tempIncome = number(incomeBox.mIncome)
        ; Value property is assumed
    allDebt = 0
    if NOT paymentBox.mCredit.isBlank() then
      allDebt = allDebt + paymentBox.mCredit
    endif
    if NOT paymentBox.mCar.isBlank() then
      allDebt = allDebt + paymentBox.mCar
    endif
    if NOT paymentBox.mOtherLoan.isBlank() then
      allDebt = allDebt + paymentBox.mOtherLoan
    endif

    ; set the value of current debt to income ratio
    if allDebt = 0 then
      DIBox.currDI = 0
    else
      DIBox.currDI = allDebt/tempIncome
    endif
    ; check for current debt-to-income so large that payment
    ;   calculated would end up as a negative number
    if DIBox.currDI > number(DIBox.maxDI) then
      qAnswer = msgQuestion("Status",
        "Current Debt-to-Income % exceeds maximum. Continue?")
      if qAnswer = "No" then
        return
      endif                        ; otherwise continue
    endif
    DIBox.AvailDI = number(DIBox.maxDI) - number(DIBox.currDI)
    estPayment = number(DIBox.AvailDI) * tempIncome
  endif
endmethod
```

The Var section of the preceding **pushButton** method declares a number of temporary variables. The *allDebt* variable stores the sum of all debt payments entered in the *mCredit*, *mCar*, and *mOtherLoan* fields. The *qAnswer* variable stores the user's answer to the dialog box displayed with **msgQuestion**.

The line

```
DIBox.CurrDI = allDebt / tempIncome
```

calculates the current debt-to-income ratio as that portion of monthly income currently used to pay off debt.

The line

```
if DIBox.currDI > number(DIBox.maxDI) then
```

checks to see if the current debt-to-income is greater than the maximum allowed. If the current debt-to-income percentage is greater than the maximum, the resulting affordable payment turns out to be a negative number (which is about as affordable as you can get). Because a negative number is probably not what the user wants or may be the result of an error, this method asks the user whether to continue with the calculations.

```
qAnswer = msgQuestion("Status", "Current Debt-to-Income % " +
         "exceeds maximum. Continue ?")
if qAnswer = "No" then
  return      ; quit the method
endif
```

The return value of **msgQuestion** is a string that tells you which button the user pressed to close the dialog box. The method assigns the string returned to the *qAnswer* variable. If the user presses the No button (don't continue), then the method should stop executing and return control to the caller. If the user presses the Yes button (please continue with calculation), then the method should continue processing. The statement

```
if qAnswer = "No" then
```

checks *qAnswer* to determine if the user pressed No. If so, the

```
return
```

statement halts execution of the method and returns to the dialog box. If *qAnswer* is something other than "No", execution continues through the end of the method. The line

```
DIBox.AvailDI = number(DIBox.maxDI) - number(DIBox.currDI)
```

calculates the available debt-to-income percentage and assigns it to the *availDI* field. If the monthly income is $3,000, for example, and the current monthly payments to debt total $300, the current debt-to-income ratio is $300/$3,000, or 10 percent. If the maximum allowed debt-to-income is 33 percent, that leaves 23 percent ($690) for other debts, such as a mortgage payment.

The line

```
estPayment = tempPayment * DIBox.availDI
```

takes the available debt-to-income percentage and multiplies it by monthly income to determine the amount of the estimated payment. The method then displays the estimated payment in the *estPayment* field.

To test the *calcButton*, follow these steps:

1. Check the syntax of the changed **pushButton** method. If necessary, fix any errors.

16 — SAMPLE APPLICATION: WORKING WITH MULTIPLE FORMS

2. Save and run the form.
3. Enter **$2,000** in the Monthly Income field.
4. Enter a maximum D/I percentage in the debt-to-income Maximum Allowed field of 35 percent.
5. Click Calculate. The payment calculated should be $700.00 (see fig. 16.5).

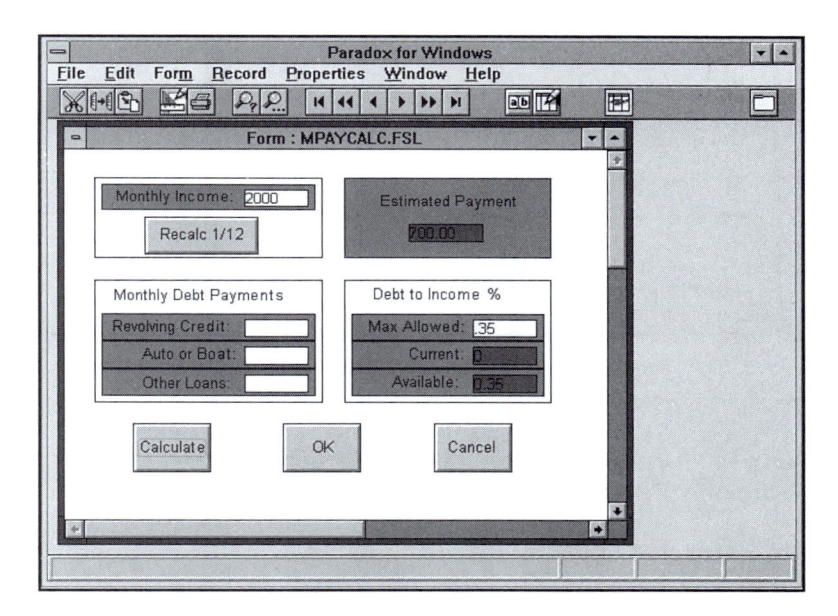

FIG. 16.5

The payment calculator with a payment displayed.

6. Enter **$400** in the Revolving Credit field.
7. Enter **$300** in the Auto or Boat field.
8. Enter **$100** in the Other Loans field. (Monthly Income still is $2,000 and Maximum Allowed debt-to-income ratio is still 35 percent.)
9. Click Calculate. The **msgQuestion** Status dialog box appears (see fig. 16.6) because the current total payments to debt exceed the maximum debt-to-income allowed.
10. Click Yes to continue. Notice that both the payment and the available DI numbers are negative (see fig. 16.7).
11. When you finish testing, return to Design mode.

III — PROGRAMMING PARADOX FOR WINDOWS

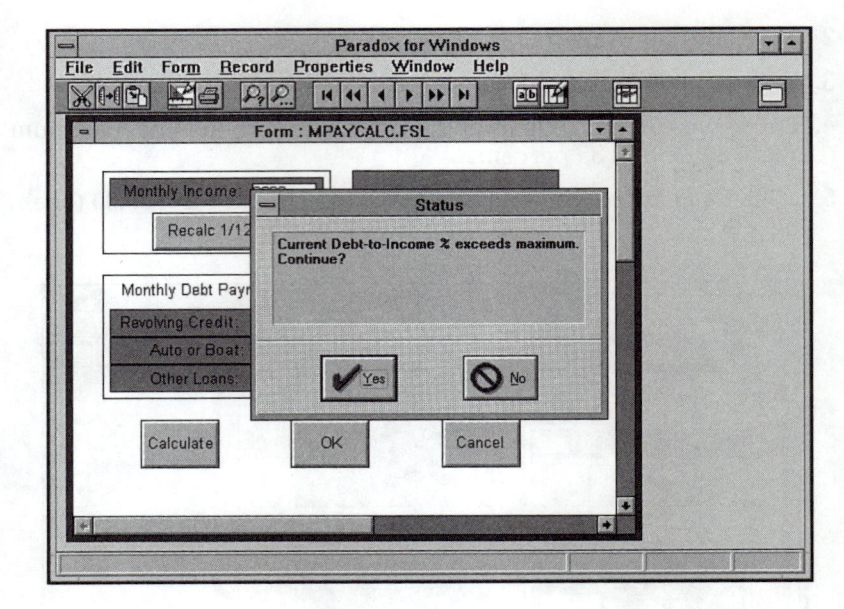

FIG. 16.6

The payment calculator with a question dialog box.

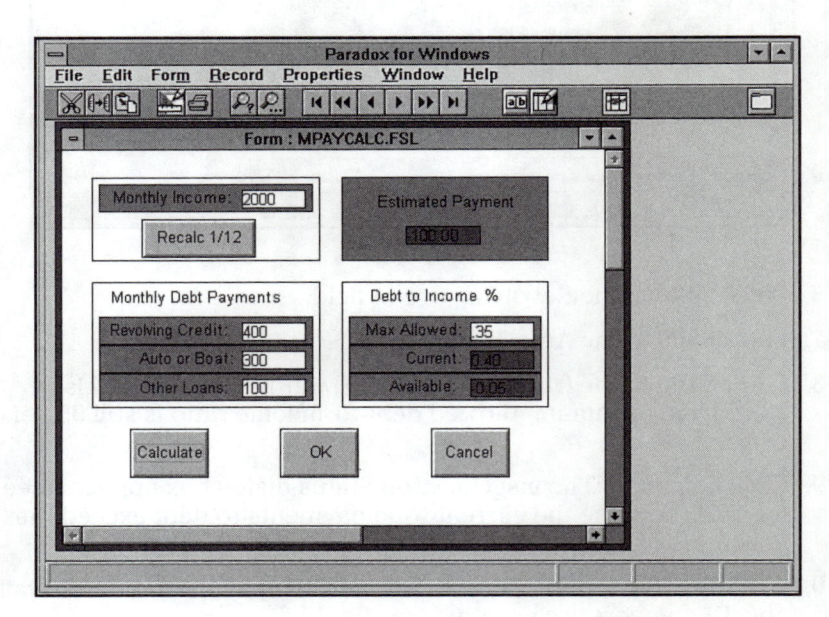

FIG. 16.7

The payment calculator with a negative payment.

OKButton Method

The **pushButton** method for *OKButton* checks that Paradox has calculated a monthly payment and then returns to the mortgage calculator. The **pushButton** method also indicates to the mortgage calculator that the user clicked OK to exit the payment calculator.

The definition of *OKButton*'s **pushButton** method follows:

```
method pushButton(var eventInfo Event)
if estPayment.isBlank() then
   msgInfo("Yo!", "You really should calculate " +
                  "a payment before you click OK. " +
                  "If you want to leave without " +
                  "calculating a payment, " +
                  "click Cancel.")
else
   formReturn("OK")    ; leave the form and return "OK"
endif
endmethod
```

Checking for a blank value in the *estPayment* field is roughly the same as in the previous two examples. If the user clicks OK when the *estPayment* field is empty, the message shown in figure 16.8 appears.

The line

```
formReturn("OK")
```

causes control to return to the calling form's method. Additionally, it returns the value "OK" to the calling method. In the next section, you learn what changes are necessary for the mortgage calculator to call the payment calculator and to handle the return value.

cancButton Method

The **pushButton** method for *cancButton* returns to the mortgage calculator. The **pushButton** method also indicates to the mortgage calculator that the user clicked the Cancel button to exit. This method is the shortest in this example:

```
method pushButton(var eventInfo Event)
formReturn("CancButton")   ; return control to the calling
                           ; form and pass a value back
endmethod
```

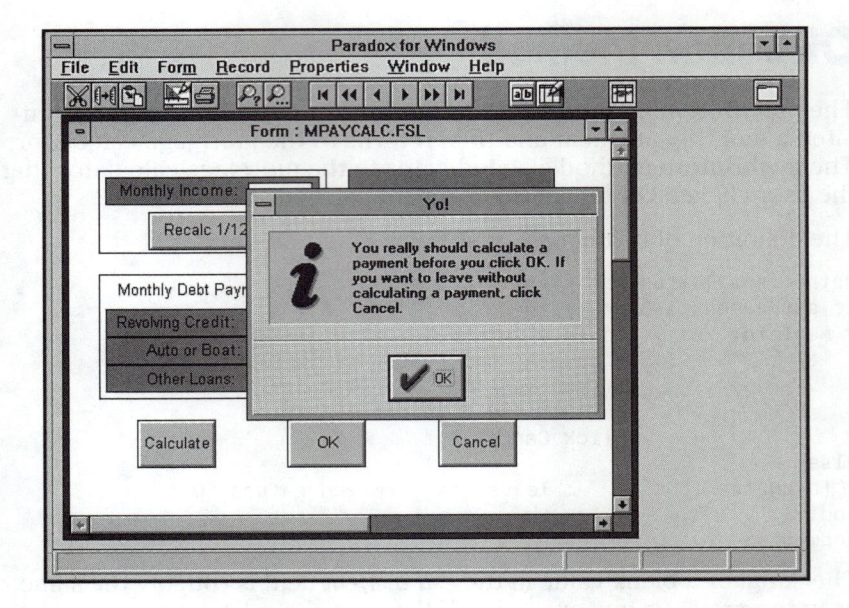

FIG. 16.8

The warning message for a blank payment field.

A Starting Value for maxDI

To make this form easier for users, you can set a default value in the *maxDI* field. That way, unless the maximum debt-to-income is something other than 33%, the user doesn't have to enter a value. The following **arrive** method for pageOne of the form sets the starting value for *maxDI* to 0.33 (33 percent):

```
; pageOne::arrive
method arrive(var eventInfo MoveEvent)
maxDI.Value = .33   ; set a starting value for maxDI
endmethod
```

If you have added all the method definitions shown in the preceding sections to the payment calculator, the payment calculator is now complete. Run the payment calculator and test it with different sets of numbers.

When you click the OK and Cancel buttons, they don't actually return control to the mortgage calculator because the payment calculator form was not called from the mortgage calculator. The next section explains the changes you must make to the mortgage calculator to make it open the payment calculator upon request. When you're done testing the payment calculator, save and close it.

Calling the Payment Calculator from the Mortgage Calculator

Now that the payment calculator does what you want, you can return to the mortgage calculator and revise it so that it opens the payment calculator. To do so, you must place several new buttons on the mortgage calculator.

Follow these steps to revise the mortgage calculator:

1. Start by opening the mortgage calculator form (MORTCALC.FSL).
2. Move *calcButton* over to the lower right corner of the mortgage calculator box.
3. Rename *calcButton* to *calcPayButton*.
4. Relabel *calcPayButton* to "Calculate Payment from Loan". This button calculates a payment amount based on the loan amount, the rate, and the term.
5. Place a new button to the left of *calcPayButton*. Name the button *calcLoanButton*.
6. Relabel *calcLoanButton* "Calculate Loan from Payment". This button calculates a loan amount based on the payment amount, rate, and term.
7. Place a new button to the left of *calcLoanButton*. Name the button *getPayment*.
8. Relabel *getPayment* "Estimate Qualified Payment". The *getPayment* button opens the payment calculator so that the user can determine the amount of the payment for which the household can qualify. After returning from the payment calculator with the correct payment, the user can press *calcLoanButton* to calculate the amount of the loan.

The mortgage calculator now looks like figure 16.9, and the object tree for the mortgage calculator looks like figure 16.10. (Renaming the labels of buttons and fields is optional because you don't need to refer to these names in code.)

getPayment Methods

The *getPayment* button's **pushButton** method should be defined so that it opens the payment calculator and waits for a return value. If the called form returns "OK", the **pushButton** method should get the estimated payment, close the payment calculator, and display the payment in the *paymentField*. If the payment calculator returns "cancButton", the **pushButton** method simply closes the payment calculator.

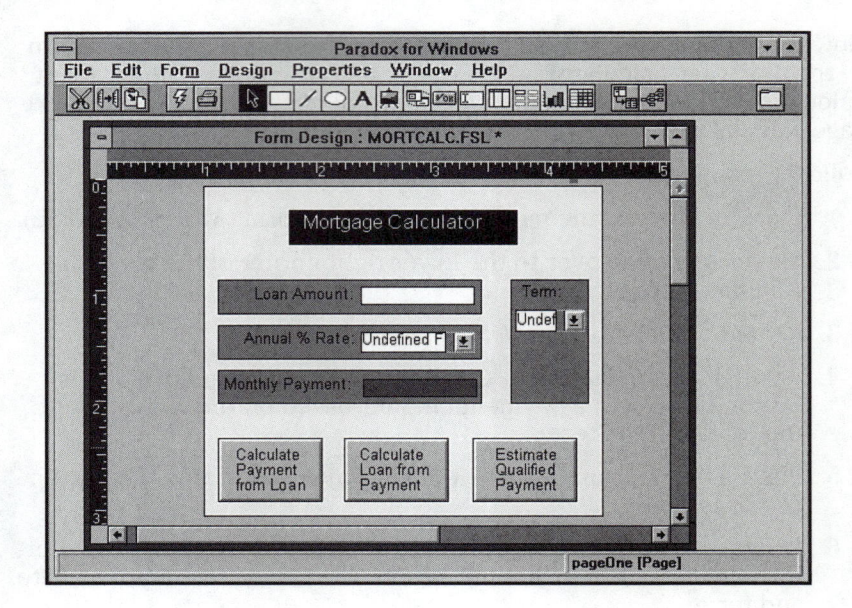

FIG. 16.9

The revised mortgage calculator.

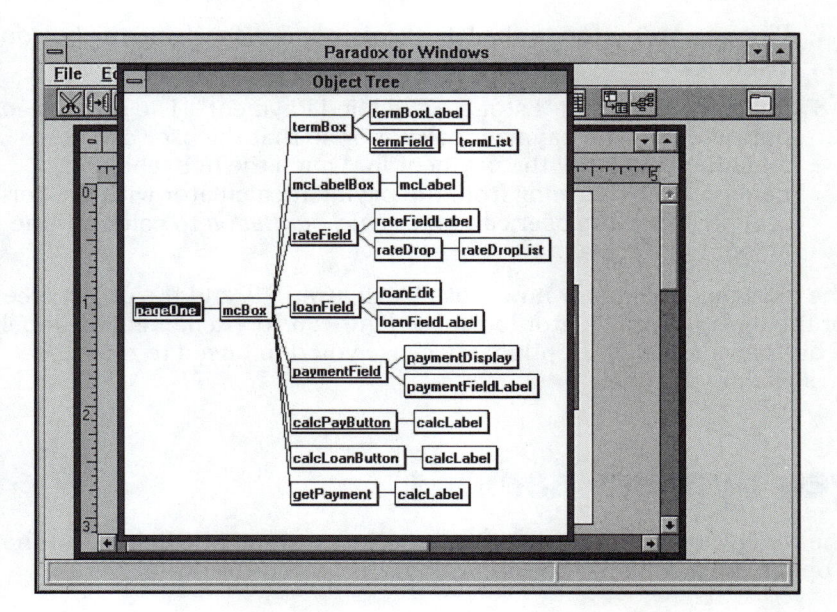

FIG. 16.10

The object tree for the revised mortgage calculator.

16 — SAMPLE APPLICATION: WORKING WITH MULTIPLE FORMS

The definition for *getPayment*'s **pushButton** method follows:

```
method pushButton(var eventInfo Event)
var
  paymentCalc    Form    ; a handle to the payment calculator form
  buttonPressed  String  ; to store the return value from mpaycalc
endvar

; first, open the payment calculator form
; assumes mpaycalc is in the same directory
if paymentCalc.open("mpaycalc.fsl") then
  ; wait for the form to return a value
  ; processing in the payment calculator stops until
  ; paymentCalc returns
  buttonPressed = paymentCalc.wait()
  if buttonPressed = "OK" then
    paymentField.Value = paymentCalc.pageOne.estPayment
  endif
  paymentCalc.close()
endif
endmethod
```

The statement

```
if paymentCalc.open("mpaycalc.fsl") then
```

opens the form MPAYCALC.FSL and attaches it to the object handle *paymentCalc*. It is the same as

```
; assign result (True/False) to a variable
x = paymentCalc.open("mpaycalc.fsl")
if x = True then
```

The **open** method returns a logical value True if it is successful and False if not. The **if** statement condition

```
if paymentCalc.open("mpaycalc.fsl") then
```

examines the return value of **open**. If the open attempt was successful, Paradox executes the line following the **if** statement. The next line (after the comments),

```
buttonPressed = paymentCalc.wait()
```

makes the mortgage calculator wait until the user closes the payment calculator. The target window for all key presses and mouse movements is the open payment calculator window. *buttonPressed* is assigned the value that the payment calculator returns. The **wait** in the preceding line links execution between the two forms along with the

```
formReturn("OK")
```

statement in the **pushButton** method for *OKButton* in the payment calculator, and the

```
formReturn("CancButton")
```

statement in the **pushButton** method for *cancButton* in the payment calculator.

The method then examines *buttonPressed* (the value the payment calculator returns).

```
if buttonPressed = "OK" then
  paymentField.Value = paymentCalc.pageOne.estPayment
endif
```

If the user closes the payment calculator by pressing *OKButton*, *calcButton* uses the estimated payment calculated by the payment calculator. The *calcButton* method then assigns the value in the *estPayment* field on the payment calculator to *paymentField* on the mortgage calculator. This concept is an important one to remember: even though the second form is not the active form anymore, you still can examine it. Although you can return only a single value through the **formReturn** method, you still have access to much more information from the second form itself. After the second form is closed with the line

```
paymentCalc.close()
```

you cannot obtain any more information from it.

Note that the user can close the payment calculator with the system menu in the upper left corner of the window. Then, the value the form returns is not "OK" or "CancButton" but another value entirely. In the next section, you see what to do to handle the various return values.

In the **mouseEnter** method for *getPayment*, add this line to display a help message for the *getPayment* button:

```
message("Find payment from income and expenses.")
```

In the **mouseExit** method for *getPayment*, add this line to display the message for *mcBox*:

```
message(mcBoxMsg)
```

calcLoanButton Methods

The Calculate Loan from Payment button must have a **pushButton** method that works backward from the payment to calculate the amount of loan for which a household can qualify. The following code defines the **pushButton** method for *calcLoan*.

16 — SAMPLE APPLICATION: WORKING WITH MULTIPLE FORMS

```
; calcLoanButton::pushButton
method pushButton(var eventInfo Event)
var
  pmtc      Number   ; payment in calculations
  lc        Number   ; Loan in calculations
  intc      Number   ; interest rate in calculations
  termc     Number   ; term in calculations
  powtermc  Number   ; negative term used in calcs
endvar

;  get the values and assign them to variables
if NOT (paymentField.isBlank() OR
        rateField.rateDrop.isBlank() OR
        termBox.termField.isBlank()) then
  pmtc  = paymentField
  intc  = rateField.rateDrop
  termc = termBox.termField
  if NOT ((pmtc <= 0) OR (intc <= 0) OR (termc <= 0)) then
    ; convert to months and monthly percentage
    intc = intc/100/12     ; convert to monthly percentage
    termc = termc * 12     ; convert to months

    ; calculate loan amount
    termc = 0 - termc   ; convert to negative for calculation
    lc = (1 - pow((1 + intc), termc)) * pmtc / intc
    ; display result in loanField
    loanField.Value = lc
  else
    msgStop("Sorry", "Monthly Payment ," +
          "and Term cannot be 0 or negative.")
  endif
else
  msgStop("Stopped", "Monthly Payment, Annual % Rate, " +
        "and Term must be filled in before you can calculate.")
endif
endmethod
```

First, the method tests the fields on which the calculation depends for blank values. The lines

```
if NOT (paymentField.isBlank() OR
        rateField.rateDrop.isBlank() OR
        termBox.termField.isBlank()) then
```

test for unassigned fields and proceed only if all the fields are not (NOT) blank. The effect of the combined OR tests is to return True even if only one of the fields is blank. That result is passed through the NOT to reverse the logic (turning a True result to False or a False result to True). Therefore, if one of the fields is blank, the OR statement becomes True and the entire statement becomes False. If the statement is False, execution resumes at the **else** clause near the end of the method.

Next, the fields are assigned to variables and tested for zero or negative values. The lines

```
if NOT ((pmtc <= 0) OR (intc < 0) OR (termc <= 0)) then
```

check all of the variables for 0 or negative numbers. If one or more of them is 0 or negative, the combined OR statement returns True, which is turned to False by the NOT. If the entire statement is True, execution proceeds with the following lines.

```
intc = intc/100/12      ; convert to monthly percentage
termc = termc * 12      ; convert to months
```

The lines above convert *intc* and *termc* to the values that the formula expects. The formula to calculate a monthly payment from a loan is as follows:

$$\text{Payment} = \frac{p * i}{1 - (1 + i)^{-t}}$$

where *p* is principal (loan amount), *i* is interest rate per period, and *t* is the term, or the number of periods (months). Given that formula, the formula to solve for the loan amount is:

$$p = \frac{(1 - (1 + i)^{-t}) * \text{Payment}}{i}$$

where *p* is principal, *i* is interest rate per period, and *t* is the number of periods. If you substitute the method's variable names, you get the following:

$$lc = \frac{(1 - (1 + intc)^{-termc}) * pmtc}{intc}$$

To solve the *(1 + intc)$^{-termc}$* part of the expression, you must use the **pow** method, which raises a number to the power given. To raise *(1 + intc)* to the power of *-termc*, the expression is:

pow((1 + *intc*), (0 - *termc*))

Therefore, the entire expression becomes:

```
; calculate loan amount
lc = (1 - pow((1 + intc), (0 - termc))) * pmtc / intc
```

which doesn't look much like the original formula, but it gets the job done. Paradox assigns the result of the calculation to *lc* and displays it in *loanField*.

In the **mouseEnter** method for *calcLoan*, add this line to display a help message:

```
message("Find loan amount based on payment.")
```

In the **mouseExit** method, add this line to display the message for *mcBox*:

```
message(mcBoxMsg)
```

Chapter Summary

In this chapter, you learned how to work with two forms at the same time. In addition, you now understand how to handle calculations with ObjectPAL and how to display results.

In the next chapter, you learn how to open the payment calculator form as a dialog. You also create a table to hold mortgage information for several clients and then bind that table to the form.

17 CHAPTER

Sample Application: Working with Dialog Boxes and Tables

This chapter illustrates how to open a form as a dialog box, how tables and forms interact under ObjectPAL control, and how to control data entry to a form. Be sure that you have created the sample application described in Chapters 15 and 16 before beginning this chapter.

Opening the Payment Calculator as a Dialog Box

The following characteristics identify a form as a dialog box:

- *Modality*. Determines if any other form can accept keystrokes or mouse clicks.
- *Layer*. Determines whether the form opens as the top-layer form and remains on top until you close it.
- *Window characteristics*. Determines the size and position of the form and whether the form displays scroll bars, a title, and minimize and maximize buttons.

These three attributes are discussed in the following sections.

Modal versus Non-Modal Forms

A *modal* form, dialog, or menu is one that does not disappear until you tell it to; it remains active until you specifically or implicitly close it. A modal form keeps the focus; you cannot move to another form or application while a modal form is displayed. Dialogs close, for example, when a method calls **formReturn** or when the user double-clicks the system icon. Menus close when you choose a *terminal* menu item—a menu item with no more submenus.

You can make a dialog or form behave modally by using the **wait** method after you open the dialog. The mortgage calculator application, for example, opens the payment calculator, which causes Paradox to open the form and bring it to the top. The following line from the **pushButton** method for the *getPayment* button on the mortgage calculator form makes the payment calculator modal:

```
buttonPressed = paymentCalc.wait()
```

Consequently, the payment calculator form remains in focus until it is closed. Because the payment calculator is modal, the payment calculator is the exclusive recipient of any keystrokes and mouse clicks. You cannot click someplace else on the desktop to make another form or window object active.

Layer

Unless you specify otherwise, when you open a form, Paradox opens it in a default-sized window as the top layer. A newly opened form appears on top of all other windows and becomes the active window. The **open** method always runs a form; the form is not opened in a Form Design window (the **load** method opens a form in a design window).

The confusing aspect of working with multiple forms is that you are tempted to think the original form—the form from which you open the second form—no longer has any control. While Paradox sends all events to the newly opened form, the original form retains control under ObjectPAL. Unless you tell the first form to wait until the other form is closed, the active method in the original form continues execution.

If you have several forms open at the same time, you can tell Paradox to display a specific form as the topmost form with the **bringToTop** method (defined for the Form type).

Form Window Characteristics

Paradox displays a newly opened form in its full size or in the default size of the window—whichever is smaller. Therefore, the easiest way to control a form's display size is to change the page layout of the form itself. If the payment calculator form is four inches wide and three inches high, for example, the form appears full size, but in a medium-sized window.

Another way to change an open form's size is to specify the size of the window as arguments to the **open** method. The **open** method for the Form type enables you to specify how you want to open a form. Specifically, you can open the form with a particular kind of window style, and you can open it to show at a certain location and a certain size.

You can call the **open** method in the following three ways. Each way corresponds to a syntax of open.

- To open a form with the default window style at the default location and as the default size, use this form of open:

    ```
    open(formFileName)
    ```

    where *formFileName* is the full file name and path (optional) of the form.

- To specify a window style for the open form, use this form of open:

  open(*formFileName*, *WindowStyle*)

  where *formFileName* is the file name of the form to open, and *WindowStyle* is a constant specifying the window style to use.

  You can specify a combination of window styles, if you like. Because the WindowStyle constant resolves to a number, you can combine two or more window styles by adding them together. For example

  open(*formFileName*, WinStyleHScroll + WinStyleVScroll)

  opens the form named in *formFileName* with a horizontal scroll bar and a vertical scroll bar.

- To specify a window style, location, and size for the form, use this form of open:

  open(*formFileName*, *WindowStyle*, *x*, *y*, *w*, *h*)

  where

  formFileName is the name of the form

  WindowStyle specifies one or more window-style constants that change the way the form appears when you open it (such as maximized or minimized)

  x is the horizontal coordinate of the upper-left corner

  y is the vertical coordinate of the upper-left corner

  w is the width of the window

  h is the height of the window. The coordinate and size arguments are specified in twips (1/1,440 of an inch).

  To display a window 3 inches wide and 2 inches high located near the top left of the main window, for example, use this statement:

  formVar.open("myform.fsl", WinStyleDefault, 700, 700, 4200, 2800)

In general, two ways exist to open a given form as a dialog:

- Set the property of the form to Form as Dialog by choosing Properties, Form, and selecting Dialog Box from the Window Style options. Use the **open** method to open the form. The form opens as a dialog because of its property setting.

17 — SAMPLE APPLICATION: WORKING WITH DIALOG BOXES AND TABLES   655

- Open a form not otherwise set as a dialog with the **openAsDialog** method.

Either combination of actions produces the identical effect: the form specified opens as a dialog. By far, the easiest way to open a form as a dialog box is to set the form's properties to those of a dialog box in the Form Window Properties dialog box.

Calling the Dialog Box

Now that you're familiar with how to open forms as dialog boxes, you're ready to change the properties of the payment calculator so that it behaves like a dialog box.

Follow these steps to set the properties for the payment calculator:

1. Open the payment calculator form in a design window.
2. Choose Properties, Form, Window Style to open the Form Window Properties dialog box (see fig. 17.1).

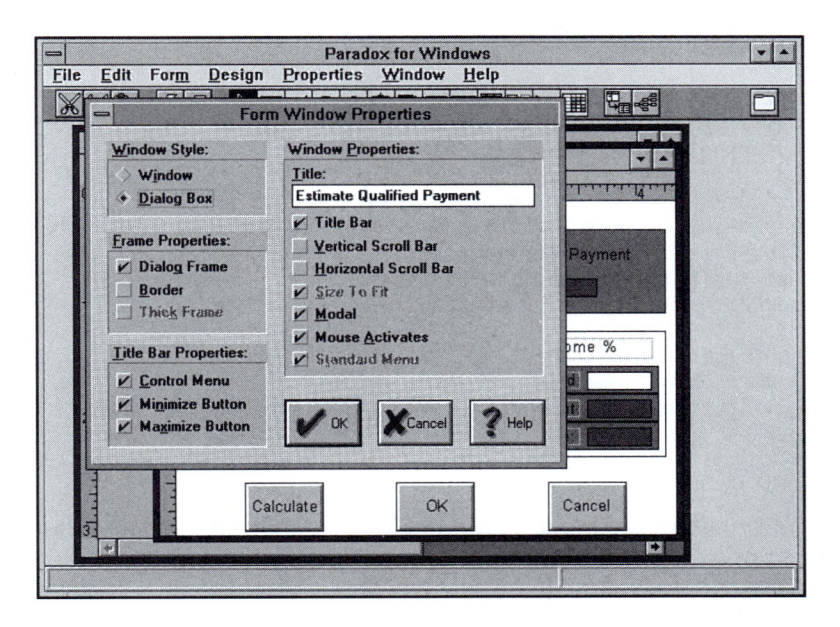

FIG. 17.1

The Form Window Properties dialog box.

3. Choose Dialog Box from the Window Style options.
4. Type the title **Estimate Qualified Payment** in the Title text box.

5. Choose Modal from the Window Properties option group.
6. Choose Title Bar from the Window Properties option group.
7. In the Title Bar Properties group, choose Control Menu, Minimize Button, and Maximize Button.
8. Click OK to close the dialog box and accept the settings.
9. Choose Form, Page, Layout to open the Page Layout dialog box.
10. Set a custom page size to 4.5" by 3.25". When the form opens, it will open to these dimensions.

The following code is the new code for *getPayment*'s **pushButton** method. The changed lines are shown in boldface:

```
method pushButton(var eventInfo Event)
var
  paymentCalc     Form     ; handle to the payment calculator form
  buttonPressed AnyType
  ; to store the return value from mpaycalc
  ; value returned will be a String if the
  ; payment calculator was closed with one of the
  ; buttons, but will be Logical if closed from
  ; the system menu
endvar
; first, open the payment calculator form
; assumes mpaycalc is in the same directory
if paymentCalc.open("mpaycalc.fsl") then
  ; wait for the form to return a value
  ; processing in the mortgage calculator stops until
  ; paymentCalc returns
  buttonPressed = paymentCalc.wait()
  if string(buttonPressed) = "OK" then
    paymentField.Value = paymentCalc.pageOne.estPayment
  endif
  if NOT (string(buttonPressed) = "False") then
    paymentCalc.close()
    ; if buttonPressed is False, the form is closed already
  endif
endif
endmethod
```

The argument to the **open** method merely specifies the name of the form to open (MPAYCALC.FSL). Paradox opens the form to a default position on the desktop and sizes the window to the form's page size.

The line

```
if string(buttonPressed) = "OK" then
```

17 — SAMPLE APPLICATION: WORKING WITH DIALOG BOXES AND TABLES

compares the string value of *buttonPressed* to the string "OK". You use the string procedure to cast *buttonPressed* to a String data type. This procedure is necessary to compare *buttonPressed* to the string "OK".

You declare the *buttonPressed* variable as an AnyType so that it can accept whatever type of value the dialog box returns. If the user closes the dialog box from the dialog box's system menu, Paradox returns a Logical value. If the user closes the dialog box with the OK or Cancel button, the payment calculator form passes back the string "OK" or "CancButton" to the mortgage calculator. Consequently, the *buttonPressed* variable must be able to accept a Logical data type as well as a String data type.

To discover whether the user pressed the OK button to leave the payment calculator dialog, however, you must compare the value of *buttonPressed* to the string "OK". You cannot compare a value of type AnyType to a string without first converting the AnyType to a string. The **string** procedure takes one argument and returns it as a String type without changing the value of the original argument. In other words, *buttonPressed* doesn't become a String data type from then on. The technique of temporarily converting a value from one data type to another is called *casting*.

Check the syntax of the new **pushButton** method for *getPayment*, and test the mortgage calculator. When the payment calculator dialog box opens, it looks like the dialog box in figure 17.2.

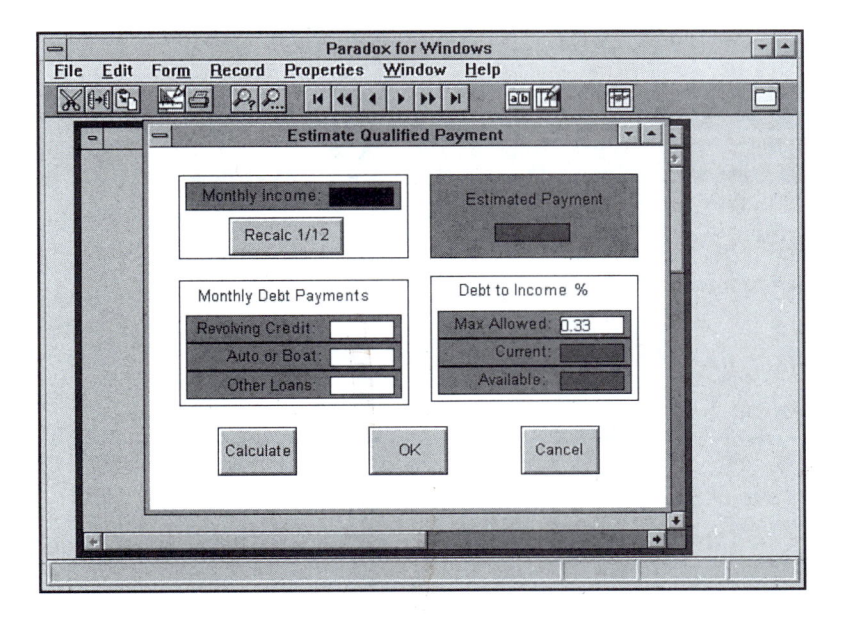

FIG. 17.2

The Estimate Qualified Payment dialog box.

Using Tables with the Mortgage Calculator

As you last left the mortgage calculator, it consisted of a group of undefined fields and several buttons. In the current design of the mortgage calculator, you assume the user approaches it in much the same way people use a desktop calculator. With a desktop calculator, you enter the numbers and find the result. You don't expect to return later and be able to retrieve the last numbers you entered. This setup is fine for a casual home user. After all, how often does one family need to calculate a mortgage?

If the users of the mortgage calculator are loan officers or mortgage brokers, however, they may want to enter information for a client and return to that information at a future date. To accomplish this objective, the calculator must store and retrieve information from a table.

The first step to make your calculator store and retrieve information from a table is to bind the fields on the form to fields in a table. With this approach, information in the table changes whenever you change information on the form.

To create a table for the mortgage calculator, perform the following steps:

1. Start by creating a table with the fields shown in table 17.1.

Table 17.1. The Mortgage Table

Field name	Type	Size	Key
First Name	A	12	*
Last Name	A	15	*
Loan Amount	$		
Rate	N		
Term	N		
Payment	$		

2. Save the table with the name Mortgage.

3. Open the Mortgage table and create four new records. Fill each record as shown in table 17.2.

Table 17.2. The Mortgage Table Records

Field name	Record 1	Record 2	Record 3	Record 4
First Name	Jim	Lyn	Peggy	Robert
Last Name	Weir	Hunter	Rich	Haley
Loan Amount	323,833.57	130,000.00	205,874.92	225,000.00
Rate	9	10.5	8.5	9.5
Term	30	30	30	30
Payment	2,490.00	654.00	1,583.00	1,891.00

Next, change the mortgage calculator forms by following these steps:

1. Open the mortgage calculator form.

2. Enlarge the box *mcBox*. Move the previously created fields down and the Mortgage Calculator title up to create space between the title and the old fields.

3. Place two new fields next to each other under the title. Change the Display Type property for both fields to Unlabeled.

4. Click the Data Model button and attach the MORTGAGE.DB table.

5. Inspect properties for the new field on the left and choose Define Field.

6. Bind the new field on the left to the First Name field from the Mortgage table. Paradox automatically names the new field *First_Name*. Do not change the default name.

7. From the Properties menu, set the alignment of *First_Name* to Right.

8. Bind the new field on the right to the Last Name field from the Mortgage table. Paradox automatically names the new field *Last_Name*.

9. Bind *loanField* to the Loan Amount field from the Mortgage table.

10. Bind *rateField.rateDrop* to MORTGAGE.Rate. Click OK when the List dialog box opens to accept the list defined earlier.

11. Bind *termBox.termField* to MORTGAGE.Term. Click OK when the List dialog box opens to accept the list defined earlier.

12. Bind *paymentField* to MORTGAGE.Payment.

III — PROGRAMMING PARADOX FOR WINDOWS

The mortgage calculator should now look something like figure 17.3. Figure 17.4 shows the Object Tree for the revised mortgage calculator.

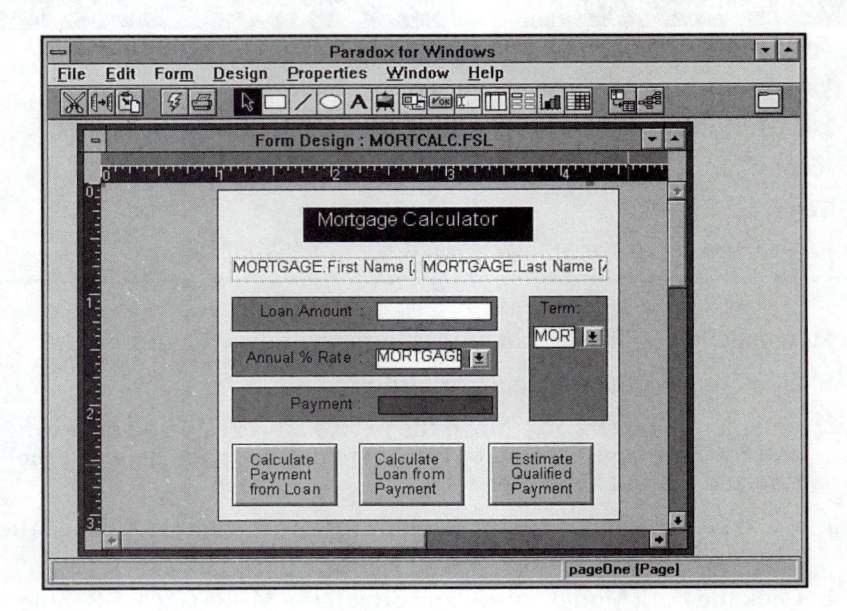

FIG. 17.3

The mortgage calculator bound to the Mortgage table.

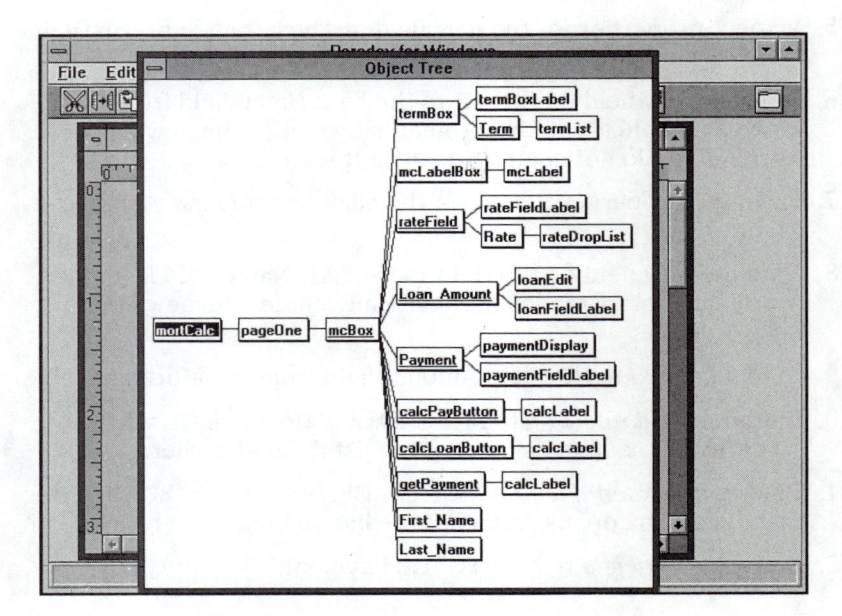

FIG. 17.4

The revised mortgage calculator Object Tree.

17 — SAMPLE APPLICATION: WORKING WITH DIALOG BOXES AND TABLES

To change the **pushButton** methods for *calcPayButton*, *calcLoanButton*, and *getPayment* to reference the new field names, do the following:

1. Change the **pushButton** method for *calcPayButton* so that it references the correct field names. In the following method, the changed lines are shown in boldface:

    ```
    ;mortCalc::calcPayButton::pushButton
    method pushButton(var eventInfo Event)
    if Loan_Amount.isBlank() OR
       rateField.Rate.isBlank() OR
       termBox.Term.isBlank() then
      msgStop("Oops!", "Before you click Calculate, " +
                      "please fill in Loan Amount, " +
                      "Annual % Rate, and Term.")
    else
      ; calculate the monthly payment and
      ; assign the result to Payment field
      Payment = pmt(Loan_Amount, Number(rateField.Rate)/1200,
                    termBox.Term * 12)
    endif
    endmethod
    ```

2. Change the **pushButton** method for *calcLoanButton* so that it references the correct field names. The revised method follows with the changed lines shown in boldface:

    ```
    ; calcLoanButton::pushButton
    method pushButton(var eventInfo Event)
    var
      pmtc     Number   ; payment in calculations
      lc       Number   ; Loan in calculations
      intc     Number   ; interest rate in calculations
      termc    Number   ; term in calculations
      powtermc Number   ; negative term used in calcs
    endvar

    ; get the values and assign them to variables

    if NOT (Payment.isBlank() OR
            rateField.Rate.isBlank() OR
            termBox.Term.isBlank()) then
      pmtc  = Payment
      intc  = rateField.Rate
      termc = termBox.Term
      if NOT ((pmtc <= 0) OR (intc <= 0) OR (termc <= 0)) then
        ; convert to months and monthly percentage
        intc = intc/100/12    ; convert to monthly percentage
        termc = termc * 12    ; convert to months
    ```

III — PROGRAMMING PARADOX FOR WINDOWS

```
      ; calculate loan amount
      termc = 0 - termc     ; convert to negative for calculation
      lc = (1 - pow((1 + intc), termc)) * pmtc / intc

      ; display result in loanField
      Loan_Amount = lc
    else
      msgStop("Sorry", "Monthly Payment ," +
                       "and Term can't be 0 or negative.")
    endif
  else
    msgStop("Sorry", "Monthly Payment, Annual % Rate, " +
                     "and Term must be filled in before you +
                      can calculate.")
  endif
endmethod
```

3. Change the **pushButton** method for *getPayment* so that it references the correct field names. The revised method follows with changed lines shown in boldface:

```
; getPayment::pushButton
method pushButton(var eventInfo Event)
var
  paymentCalc    Form    ; handle to the payment calculator form
  buttonPressed AnyType
  ; to store the return value from mpaycalc
  ; value returned will be a String if the
  ; payment calculator was closed with one of the
  ; buttons, but will be Logical if closed from
  ; the system menu
endvar

  ; first, open the payment calculator form
  ; assumes mpaycalc is in the same directory
  if paymentCalc.open("mpaycalc.fsl") then
    ; wait for the form to return a value
    ; processing in the mortgage calculator stops until
    ; paymentCalc returns
    buttonPressed = paymentCalc.wait()
    if string(buttonPressed) = "OK" then
      Payment = paymentCalc.pageOne.estPayment
    endif
    if NOT (string(buttonPressed) = "False") then
      paymentCalc.close()
      ; if buttonPressed is False, the form is closed already
    endif
  endif

endmethod
```

17 — SAMPLE APPLICATION: WORKING WITH DIALOG BOXES AND TABLES

4. Save the changed form.

Before you go through the following steps, save any open files that you have in Paradox as well as open files in other applications. The current mortgage calculator and payment calculator code contain several design flaws that cause Paradox to report errors. A remote chance exists that these errors may cause your system to hang. (Welcome to the world of software development!) Although your system freezing is unlikely, you should save any open files now to be safe.

To try out the revised mortgage calculator, perform the following steps:

1. If the mortgage calculator is open, run it. If it isn't open, open it in View mode.

   Notice that data from the Mortgage table displays in the bound fields. When Paradox opens the form, it opens any tables bound to the form. Paradox automatically displays the form with the first record showing.

2. Try to change the number in the Loan Amount field. Paradox displays a message that you must be in Edit mode to make any changes. This requirement is different from when you were in the previous version of the calculator. In the previous version, you used unbound fields, and Paradox allowed you to make changes without starting Edit mode.

3. Click the Edit button in the SpeedBar. Try to change the Loan Amount field again. As soon as you change a value, Paradox displays the message Locking record for data entry. Commit the change you made by clicking the Edit button again.

4. Click the Calculate Payment from Loan button. The Calculate Payment from Loan button calculates the payment based on the information in the other fields and attempts to write the result to the Payment field. Even under ObjectPAL control, however, you cannot change the value of a field unless the table is in Edit mode. When you click the Calculate Payment from Loan button, Paradox doesn't change the value of the Payment field.

5. Click the Edit button in the SpeedBar again. Click the Calculate Payment from Loan button. The Payment field now shows the new payment amount. You need to change the **pushButton** method for *calcPayButton* to check if the form is in Edit mode before attempting the calculation.

6. Change the payment shown in the Payment field.

7. Click the Calculate Loan from Payment button. The Loan Amount changes according to the new information. Again, if you aren't in Edit mode when you click the Calculate Loan from Payment button, Paradox will not make the change.

8. Click the Next Record button in the SpeedBar. Paradox moves to the second record in the Mortgage table.

9. Click the Estimate Qualified Payment button to open the payment calculator.

10. Enter a yearly salary.

11. Click the Recalc 1/12 button to calculate monthly salary from yearly salary.

12. Click Calculate to display a new monthly payment.

13. Click OK to return to the mortgage calculator. Notice that the new monthly payment appears in the Payment field. (If the mortgage calculator isn't in Edit mode, nothing happens.)

14. Click the Calculate Loan from Payment button to recalculate the loan amount based on the new payment.

15. Return to Design mode.

Controlling Data Entry in the Mortgage Calculator

As you worked through the mortgage and payment calculators, you saw that the mortgage calculator should be opened in Edit mode. You can change the mortgage calculator so that it opens in Edit mode by following these steps:

1. With the mortgage calculator open in Design mode, right-click the form's title bar to inspect properties for the form.

2. Rename the form object to *mortgageCalc*.

3. Inspect properties again for the *mortgageCalc* object (the form). Choose Methods from the properties menu. Open an Editor window for the built-in **arrive** method for pageOne of the mortgage calculator.

4. Change the **arrive** method so that it looks like this:

   ```
   ; pageOne::arrive
   method arrive(var eventInfo Event)
   self.action(DataBeginEdit)
   endmethod
   ```

   The line

   ```
   self.action(DataBeginEdit)
   ```

   uses one of the action constants, DataBeginEdit, to start Edit mode. Although the object referenced in this case is the page object (designated with the built-in *self* variable), technically, you can specify any field on the page, the page itself (*pageOne*), or the form (*mortgageCalc*).

   > **NOTE** The **action** method is one of the most powerful methods in ObjectPAL. The **action** method takes as its argument one of approximately 150 action constants. You can use action constants to start and end Edit mode, insert records in a table, navigate through fields and records, make text selections, and much more. See the Constants dialog for a list of action constants.

5. Although Paradox opens the form in Edit mode, the user still can press the Edit button to toggle out of Edit mode. Consequently, before you attempt any operation that fails if the form isn't in Edit mode, check the status of the form. If the form isn't in Edit mode, start Edit mode.

6. Add the following lines to the **pushButton** event for *calcLoanButton* directly after the Var section:

   ```
   ;... preceded by Var section
   if mortgageCalc.Editing = False then
      mortgageCalc.action(DataBeginEdit)
   endif
   ;... followed by calculations
   ```

   The **if** statement checks the Editing property of the form object *mortgageCalc*. If the form is in Edit mode, the Editing property is True; otherwise, it is False.

   Add the same fragment of code to the **pushButton** event for *calcPayButton*.

7. Save the mortgage calculator changes.

8. Save and run the mortgage calculator. Verify that Paradox opens the mortgage calculator in Edit mode.

Chapter Summary

In this chapter, you learned how to link a table to an existing form. This chapter also showed you more about working with tables bound to forms. It also introduced the flexible and powerful **action** method, with which you can emulate user actions such as moving a record forward, starting and ending an edit session, and canceling changes.

In the next chapter, you learn how to define menus for the mortgage calculator application and how to trap and handle menu events.

CHAPTER 18

Sample Application: Adding Menus

You can add many features to the mortgage calculator to make it a better application. For the purposes of this discussion, however, you have one major task left to accomplish.

To complete the sample application, you replace the default menu with custom menus. The menus should provide the user with a way to search for records, undo changes, print reports, get help, and display system information.

Understanding Menus

If you're asking yourself, "Where do I attach the code that defines a menu?," it's a good question. Menus should be available to the user regardless of their location within a form or page of a form. You therefore usually attach a menu code to a page of a form or to the form itself. Because the mortgage calculator has only one page, you can attach the menus to the page.

III — PROGRAMMING PARADOX FOR WINDOWS

The mortgage calculator will use primarily top menus. A *top menu* replaces the regular Paradox menu bar. All top menus in Windows work alike. A top menu usually is composed of several menu items arranged horizontally across the top of the window. Each horizontal menu item can open up a vertical menu—sometimes called a *pull-down menu* or *cascaded menu*. ObjectPAL also enables you to create *pop-up menus*. A good example of a pop-up menu is the properties menu. When you open it with a right-click, the properties pop-up displays as a vertical list of menu items somewhere on the workspace.

The top menu for the mortgage calculator should include the following menu choices:

- *File* displays a pull-down menu with the following item:

    Exit saves any data, leaves Edit mode, closes the form, and returns to Paradox.

- *Undo* cancels the changes to the current record.
- *Search* opens the Search dialog. In the Search dialog, the user can search for a client by first or last name.
- *Reports* displays a pull-down menu with the following items:

    Current Client prints a one-page report with just the data for the current client.

    All Clients prints a report that includes information for all the clients.

- *Help* displays a pull-down menu with the following items:

    Help gives the user field-specific help if it is available or application-wide help if no specific help is available for the current field.

    About opens a dialog that provides information about the application and about system resources.

Creating Menus

To create the top menu and the pull-down menus that cascade from it, attach the following code to the **arrive** method for *pageOne* of the mortgage calculator:

```
;pageOne:: arrive
method arrive(var eventInfo MoveEvent)
var
   mainMenu      Menu        ; to display the main menu
   reportPop     PopupMenu   ; for the Reports menu
```

```
    helpPop        PopupMenu     ; for the Help menu
    filePop        PopupMenu     ; for the File menu
endvar

; define the item for the File pull-down menu
filePop.addText("E&xit")

; define the items for the Reports pull-down menu
reportPop.addText("&Current Client")
reportPop.addText("&All Clients")

; define the items for the Help pull-down menu
helpPop.addText("&Help")
helpPop.addText("&About")

; add pull-down menus and single menu items in the order
; you want them to appear
mainMenu.addPopup("&File", filePop)
mainMenu.addText("&Undo")
mainMenu.addText("&Search")
mainMenu.addPopup("&Reports", reportPop)
mainMenu.addPopup("&Help", helpPop)

; the next line displays the menu but doesn't
; actually handle menu choices
mainMenu.show()

; make sure the form is in Edit mode
self.action(DataBeginEdit)

endmethod
```

The first thing to note about the preceding example is that pull-down menus are called pop-up menus by ObjectPAL. (From now on in this chapter, they are referred to as pop-ups.)

From ObjectPAL's point of view, a pop-up menu that can be displayed anywhere on-screen is no different from a pull-down menu. By default, a pop-up appears next to and slightly below the object from which it was invoked. If not enough room is left on the workspace to cascade the pop-up down, it is cascaded up. Each top menu item provides a point from which the pop-up can be displayed.

The Var section of the method code shown above declares *mainMenu* as a Menu and also declares three separate PopupMenus. *filePop* holds the single menu item for the File menu, *reportPop* holds the list of Reports menu choices, and *helpPop* contains the list of menu choices for the Help menu. The PopupMenu variable names and the Menu variable names do not have to have the same first name; in other words, ObjectPAL doesn't bind the PopupMenu to the Menu via the name. The PopupMenus were named in this manner for readability only.

You must construct the pop-up menu associated with each top menu item before you construct the top menu itself. The **addText** method adds one menu item to a PopupMenu. **addText** takes only one argument: the name of the menu. This structure means that, among other things, you cannot specify the position of the item you want to add. (If you want to change the ordering of menu items under script control, you can create an array of menu items, sort them as you please, then add the array to the PopupMenu with **addArray**.) The following lines add three menu items to the *reportPop* PopupMenu:

```
reportPop.addText("&Current Client")
reportPop.addText("&All Clients")
```

ObjectPAL enables you to create a menu hot key for each item you define. To make a letter in the menu item the hot key, precede the letter with an ampersand (&) character. This line, for example, makes *x* the hot key for the Exit item:

```
filePop.addText("E&xit")
```

After the menu is displayed, the user can move the cursor to Exit and press Enter, click Exit, or press **x**.

Add a menu item to the top menu with the **addText** method. This line adds the Search menu item to the top menu:

```
mainMenu.addText("&Search")
```

PopupMenus are added to the top menu with the **addPopUp** method. **addPopUp** takes two arguments: the name of the PopupMenu to add (previously constructed) and the name of the top menu item to which the PopupMenu should be bound.

The following line, for example, adds the *filePop* PopupMenu to the main menu and creates a top menu item called File:

```
mainMenu.addPopup("&File", filePop)
```

To display the top menu, *mainMenu*, as well as all its associated pop-ups, use the **show** method. You must construct the menu before you can use **show** to display it. Because *mainMenu* is constructed and shown from the **arrive** method of *pageOne*, Paradox displays *mainMenu* as soon as the form opens and arrives. This menu will be displayed until it is explicitly removed, or until the focus moves to another form (but only if that form does not have the Standard Menus option set; see the Form Window Properties dialog box). Moving to another page will not remove the menu.

After you define the **arrive** method, you need to check the syntax, save the form, and run the form. The top menus appear as shown in figure 18.1.

18 — SAMPLE APPLICATION: ADDING MENUS

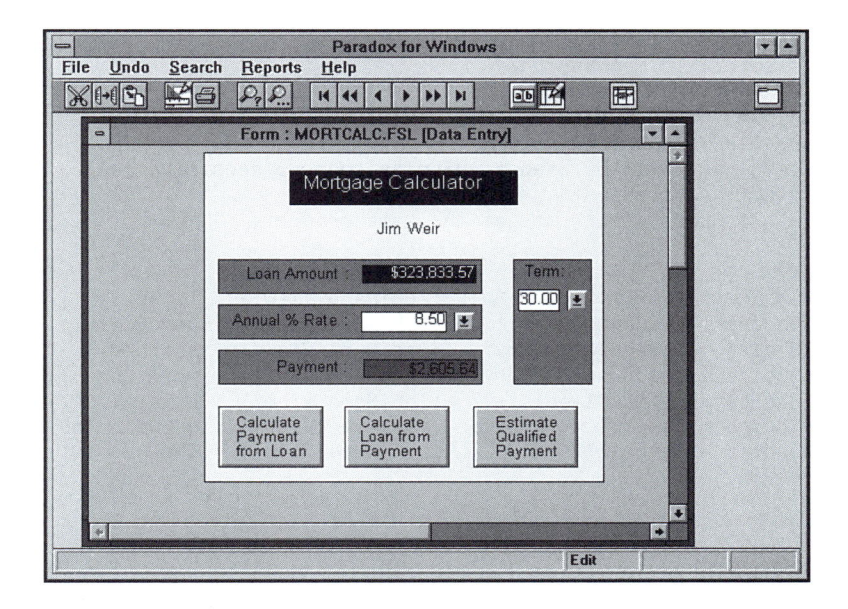

FIG. 18.1
The mortgage calculator menus.

Handling Menu Actions

Notably absent from the method definition shown in the preceding section is any code that controls what happens when the user chooses a menu item. The **arrive** method defines only the display of the menu, not the menu handling. To figure out where to put the menu handling, you have to know what event is caused by a menu choice. Any menu action creates a menu event. The **menuAction** built-in method for an object responds to menu events.

Here is where handling events gets a little tricky. Previously, you have seen that events are generated for specific objects. You wrote code to handle the event for the object that received the event. But events also can occur for an entire group of objects because of the Event model.

The complete definition of **menuAction** for *pageOne* follows:

```
; pageOne::menuAction
method menuAction(var eventInfo MenuEvent)
var
  mChoice,
  objName    String
  obj        UIObject
endvar
```

III — PROGRAMMING PARADOX FOR WINDOWS

```
; get the menu choice from the event packet
mChoice = eventInfo.menuChoice()

; get the name of the object that was active
; when the menu was chosen
; the active name will be used to display context-sensitive help
eventInfo.getTarget(obj)
objName = obj.Name            ; get the Name property

switch
  case mChoice = "E&xit"            : objName.View() ; fileExitM()
  case mChoice = "&Undo"            : objName.View() ; undoEditM()
  case mChoice = "&Search"          : objName.View() ; searchM()
  case mChoice = "&Current Client"  : objName.View() ; printCurrM()
  case mChoice = "&All Clients"     : objName.View() ; printAllCM()
  case mChoice = "&Help"            : objName.View() ; getHelpM(objName)
  case mChoice = "&About"           : objName.View() ; showAboutM()
endswitch

endmethod
```

When a menu event occurs, Paradox fills the variable *eventInfo* with information about the menu event. Paradox then calls **menuAction** and passes *eventInfo* as an argument. Among other things, *eventInfo* contains the name of the menu that the user chose. The following line gets the menu name and stores it to a variable called *mChoice*:

```
mChoice = eventInfo.menuChoice()
```

The next line, **eventInfo.getTarget(obj)**, creates a handle to the target. The *obj* variable contains information about the target object. The target object is the object that received the event. This object can be the target whether or not it has the focus (it can have focus only if it can receive a keyboard event; even if an object cannot receive a keyboard event, it still can be the target object).

In this case, **obj.Name** returns the object name of the target object. The target variable (*obj*) also can be used to refer to all the other properties of the object. The Name property of the active object is required so that when the user chooses Help from the menu, help can be retrieved for the current object.

The next set of statements comprises a *switch statement*. A **switch** statement is like a series of **if** statements, where each **case** statement acts like a single **if** statement. The following line, for example, tests the value of *mChoice*; if it is "E&xit", the statement following the colon is executed:

```
case mChoice = "E&xit"   : objName.View()    ;fileExitM()
```

Each of the **case** statements, if the condition evaluates to True, will execute a custom method; until the custom method is defined to handle the menu choice, the statement merely views the current object name. As you work through the following sections, you define each custom method. After the custom method that handles a menu choice is defined, you can delete the instruction to view the object name and call the custom method instead.

Closing the Form with fileExitM

The **fileExitM** custom method is called by the **menuAction** method when the user chooses Exit from the File menu. Before you let the user leave the application, you need to save the most recent changes. In some cases, the user will not want to save changes, so you need to find out whether the current record has been modified and give the user a chance to keep or discard the changes to that record. After you get a response from the user and take the corresponding action, you can close the form.

The **fileExitM** custom method should be defined as a custom method to the *pageOne* object. To define **fileExitM**, follow these steps:

1. Open the Methods dialog for *pageOne*.

2. In the New Custom Method box, type **fileExitM** and press Enter. Paradox opens an Editor window for the **fileExitM** method.

3. Enter the following method definition for **fileExitM**, working around the default text:

   ```
   ;pageOne:: fileExitM   (Custom Method)
   method fileExitM()
   var
     qAnswer String    ; answer to question
   endvar

   if mortgageCalc.Touched = True then
     qAnswer = msgQuestion("Please confirm",
       "Do you want to keep changes to this record?")
     if qAnswer = "No" then
       mortgageCalc.action(DataCancelRecord)
     endif
   endif

   mortgageCalc.action(DataEndEdit)
   mortgageCalc.close()

   endmethod
   ```

III — PROGRAMMING PARADOX FOR WINDOWS

4. When you finish entering the method, check the syntax and close the Editor window. When you open the Methods dialog for *pageOne* again, you will see the new custom method listed in the Custom Methods list (see fig. 18.2).

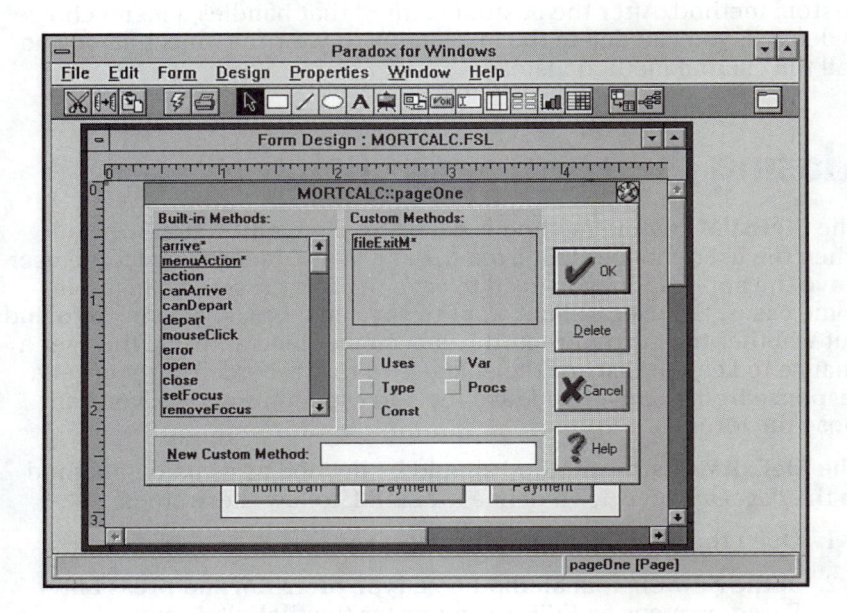

FIG. 18.2

Viewing methods in the Custom Methods list.

5. Choose the built-in **menuAction** method for pageOne.
6. Replace the line

    ```
    case mChoice = "E&xit" : objName.View()
    ; fileExitM()
    ```

    with

    ```
    case mChoice = "E&xit" : fileExitM()
    ```

7. Check the syntax, then save and run the form.
8. Edit a field to make changes.
9. Choose File, Exit. Notice that the **fileExitM** method asks whether to close without saving (see fig. 18.3).

The **fileExitM** method finds out whether a record has been changed by examining the state of the Touched property for the form. (Note that fields, records, multi-record objects, and tables also have a Touched property, which you can check to find out whether the item has been changed.) If **fileExitM** discovers that the record has been changed, the user is asked whether changes to the current record need to be saved. If the user clicks No, the form is sent an action of DataCancelRecord. Changes to the record currently bound to the form are not posted.

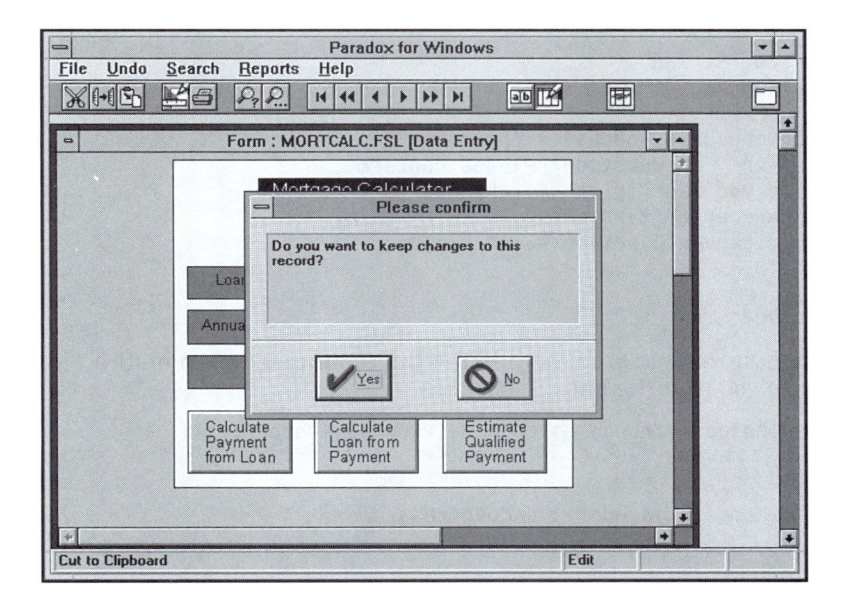

FIG. 18.3
Prompting the user to save or discard changes.

The **action** method takes as its argument one of the action constants. See the Constants dialog box for a list of action constants. An action usually does something to the table bound to the current object. In this case, the actions affect the underlying Mortgage table.

Restoring a Record with undoEditM

You can expect that the user will want to ask "what if" questions of the mortgage calculator—questions such as "What will my payment be if the interest rate goes up 2 percent?" Or, "How big of a loan could I qualify for if I had no other credit payments?"

Allowing the user to make changes is no problem: that's what the application does already. To restore a record to its original state, use the DataCancelRecord action constant with the **action** method. The following custom method definition asks the user to confirm whether or not to undo all changes to the record. If the user answers Yes, changes to the record are canceled.

The following is the complete custom method for **undoEditM**. Inspect properties for *pageOne*, then use the Methods dialog box to create a new custom method named **undoEditM**; then define **undoEditM**.

```
; pageOne::undoEditM         ; custom method
method undoEditM()
var
  qAnswer String
endvar

if mortgageCalc.Touched = True then
  qAnswer = msgQuestion("Please confirm",
    "Do you want to cancel changes to this record?")
  if qAnswer = "Yes" then
    mortgageCalc.action(DataCancelRecord)
  endif
endif
endmethod
```

Change the switch statement in the built-in **menuAction** method for *pageOne* so that the line

```
case mChoice = "&Undo" : objName.View() ; undoEditM()
```

reads

```
case mChoice = "&Undo" : undoEditM()
```

Searching for a Record with searchM

Although only 4 records are in the Mortgage table at the moment, a loan officer or mortgage broker having more than 4 clients is conceivable. Finding the record you want in a table of 4 records is no problem; navigating through 40 records is a little tedious. The mortgage calculator application therefore should give the user a way to search for the record of a particular client.

To accomplish the search, you need to create and display a dialog box. The Search dialog box enables the user to enter a first name or last name, check a radio button to indicate whether the search is for first or last name, and then click OK.

To create the form for the Search dialog, do the following:

1. Choose File, New, Form to open a new form.

2. Click OK to accept the Data Model dialog box without choosing a table.

3. In the Page Layout dialog box, set the page size to 3.5 inches wide by 1.3 inches high. When the form opens, choose File, Save As and enter the file name **"Msearch"**.

18 — SAMPLE APPLICATION: ADDING MENUS

4. Deselect all objects on the form by pressing Esc.
5. Right-click the form's title bar to display form properties, then rename the form designer object to *searchDialog*.
6. Rename the page to *pageOne*. Set the page color to dark blue.
7. On the left side of the form, place an undefined field. Set the Display type to Radio Buttons.
8. In the Define List of Items dialog box, add the two items **"First Name"** and **"Last Name"** and then choose OK. Rename the object *firstOrLast*.
9. Set the color of *firstOrLast* to gray.
10. Define the **open** method for *firstOrLast* as follows:

    ```
    method open(var eventInfo Event)
    self = "First Name"
    endmethod
    ```

11. Place a text object above the radio buttons. The text field should contain the words Search By:.
12. Place an undefined field near the top right of the form. Name the field *searchNameField*. Replace the default label with "Name".
13. Create two buttons under *searchNameField*. Rename the left button *OKButton*, and label it "OK". Rename the right button *cancelButton* and label it "Cancel".
14. Define the **pushButton** method for *OKButton* as follows:

    ```
    method pushButton(var eventInfo Event)
    var
      nameTemp String
    endvar
    if NOT pageOne.searchNameField.isBlank() then
      nameTemp = pageOne.searchNameField
      formReturn(nameTemp)
    else
      msgStop("Status",
              "Please enter a name to search for, " +
              "or press Cancel to leave the dialog box.")
    endif
    endmethod
    ```

15. Define the **pushButton** method for *cancelButton* as follows:

    ```
    method pushButton(var eventInfo Event)
    formReturn("Cancelled")
    endmethod
    ```

III — PROGRAMMING PARADOX FOR WINDOWS

16. Open the Form Window Properties dialog box. Choose Dialog Box from the Windows Style options, choose Dialog Frame under Frame Properties, choose all three Title Bar properties, and set Title Bar and Modal from the Window Properties group.

17. Resize the fields, buttons, and text boxes as appropriate. When you're done, the Search dialog should look similar to figure 18.4, with an object tree that looks like figure 18.5. After you adjust the appearance of the Search dialog, save and close it.

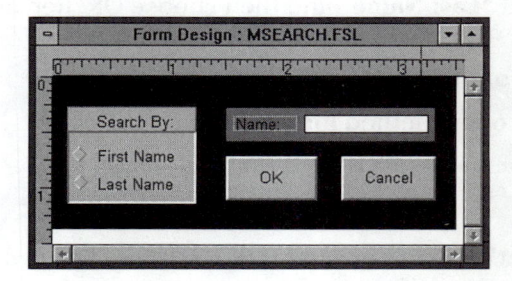

FIG. 18.4

The Search dialog form.

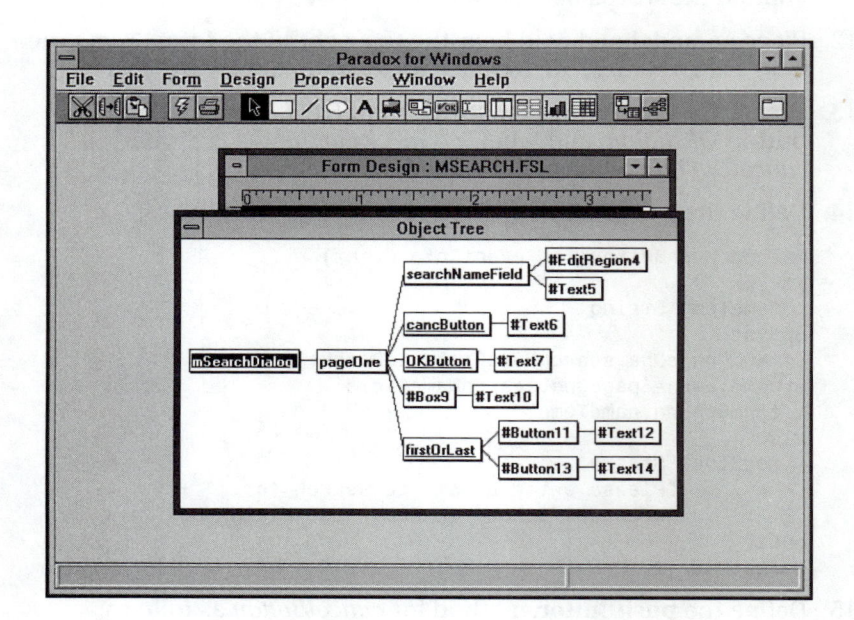

FIG. 18.5

The Search dialog form's Object Tree.

Now that you have created the Search dialog, you're ready to define the custom method **searchM**. Back in the mortgage calculator form (MORTCALC.FSL), open the Methods dialog for *pageOne* and enter the name **searchM** in the New Custom Method box; then choose OK.

18 — SAMPLE APPLICATION: ADDING MENUS

The following lines comprise the method definition for the custom method **searchM**:

```
; pageOne::searchM (Custom Method)
method searchM()
var
  searchForm        Form      ; search dialog
  searchName        String    ; name to search for
  searchFirstLast   String    ; search by first or last name
endvar

; if record has changed, ask user whether to save changes
if mortgageCalc.Touched = True then
  qAnswer = msgQuestion("Please Confirm",
    "Do you want to keep changes to this record?")
  if qAnswer = "No" then
    mortgageCalc.action(DataCancelRecord)
  endif
endif

if searchForm.open("msearch.fsl") then
  searchForm.setTitle("Search") ; set the title for dialog
  ; cast AnyType searchName to String as dialog returns
  searchName = string(searchForm.wait())
  if searchName = "False" then
    ; user closed form with system icon
    return
  endif
  ; find out if search should be on first name or last name
  searchFirstLast = searchForm.pageOne.firstOrLast
  searchForm.close()
  if searchName <> "Cancelled" then
    if searchFirstLast = "First Name" then
      if NOT pageOne.locate("First Name", searchName) then
        msgInfo("Status",
          "Sorry! Couldn't find a client with that first name.")
      endif
    else
      if NOT pageOne.locate("Last Name", searchName) then
        msgInfo("Status",
          "Sorry! Couldn't find a client with that last name.")
      endif
    endif
  endif
endif
endmethod
```

The **searchM** method first determines whether the current record should be saved (because the user will move to another record if the search is successful). If the user chooses No, changes to the record are discarded.

Next, the method attempts to open the form MSEARCH.FSL as a dialog. When you test this method, note that the dialog opens at its full size and in a convenient location. Although you can specify a size and location when you open the form, making the form's page an appropriate size eliminates the need to specify a size.

The **setTitle** method used in the next line places a caption in the title bar of the newly opened form. In this case, the title is set to "Search" (note that you can also set a title for a form in the Form Window Properties dialog box). As a rule, you should avoid long or overly descriptive titles for dialog boxes. If you browse around in the Windows applications on your desktop, you find that most professional software designers use short names for dialog boxes. This approach gives the dialog box an uncluttered look and makes referring to the dialog box by title easier.

You might remember from the **getPayment::pushButton** method that you used a variable of type AnyType to store the return value of a dialog. You did so because, depending on how the user closes the dialog box, the returned value can be either a String or a Logical value. If the user closes the dialog box by pressing one of the buttons, the **pushButton** methods for those buttons return a String; however, if the user closes the dialog box by double-clicking the system menu icon, the dialog box returns a Logical value. Thus, by setting the variable to AnyType, you assure that it can hold either of the two types of values.

Another way to accomplish the same thing is to declare the variable as a String and cast the return value to a String type. The *searchName* variable in the **searchM** method is the data type String. The entire **searchForm.wait( )** statement returns a value (either Logical or a String). This value is then cast to a String data type and assigned to the *searchName* variable with the following line of code:

```
searchName = string(searchForm.wait())
```

After *searchName* has the return value, you must check it to find out whether the user closed the dialog from the system menu. If the user closes the dialog from the system menu, the **searchForm.wait( )** statement returns the Logical value False, which is then cast to the String value "False". By convention, when a user closes a dialog from the system menu, the behavior should be the same as canceling the dialog. Consequently, the following lines quit the method without searching for any values:

```
if searchName = "False" then
  ; user closed form with system icon
  return
endif
```

Also, when the user closes a form or dialog with the system menu, the form itself is closed. In this case, if *searchName* is "False", you don't need to close the dialog box before proceeding. This is different from what you need to do if the user chooses Cancel to close the dialog. If the user clicks the Cancel button, you need to close the dialog box explicitly.

The next line gets the only other value you need from the Search dialog before you close it:

```
searchFirstLast = searchForm.pageOne.firstOrLast
```

As soon as the value of the *firstOrLast* radio buttons is obtained, the method closes the Search dialog.

If the value returned by the dialog to the *searchName* variable is not "Cancelled", the method then looks for the client name in either the First Name or Last Name field of the Mortgage table.

After you have entered and checked the **searchM** method, you need to change the case statement for the Search menu item in the **menuAction** method for *pageOne*. The entire switch/case statement should look like this:

```
switch
  case mChoice = "E&xit"          : fileExitM()
  case mChoice = "&Undo"          : undoEditM()
  case mChoice = "&Search"        : searchM()
  case mChoice = "&Current Client": objName.View() ;printCurrM()
  case mChoice = "&All Clients"   : objName.View() ;printAllCM()
  case mChoice = "&Help"          : objName.View() ;getHelpM(objName)
  case mChoice = "&About"         : objName.View() ;showAboutM()
endswitch
```

After you change and check the **menuAction** method, test the form. When you choose the Search menu item, the Search dialog opens (see fig. 18.6).

Printing the Current Form with printCurrM

To be able to print a report for just the current client, you need to accomplish several related tasks:

- Create a report that contains the correct fields in some aesthetic arrangement.
- Acquire the current record.
- Bind the acquired current record to the report.

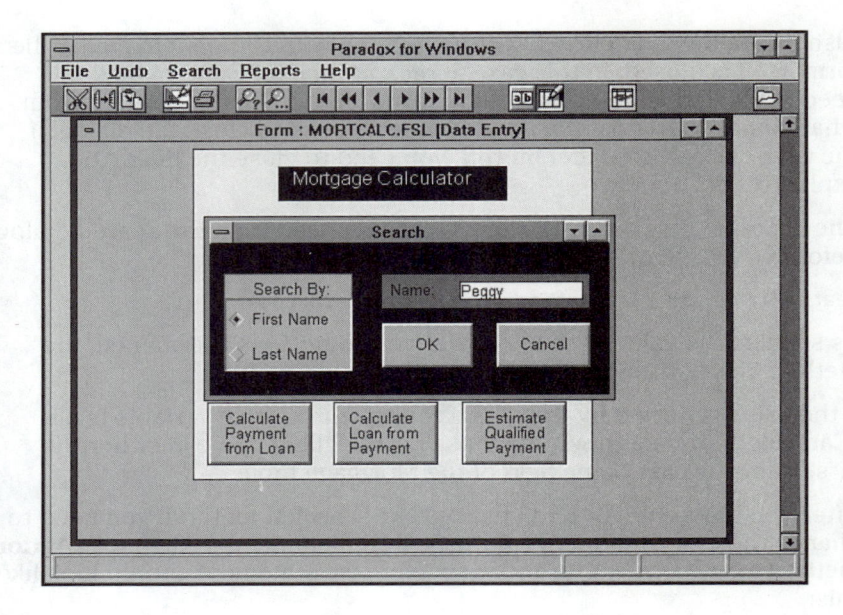

FIG. 18.6

The Search dialog opened at run time.

To understand why the following technique was chosen, you need to know a few things about reports and queries under ObjectPAL control.

Three types of queries exist:

- *Query files*, which you create interactively and save to a QBE file
- *Query strings*, which you create in ObjectPAL by assigning a symbolic query to a string
- *Query statements*, which you create in ObjectPAL by assigning a symbolic query to a query variable

Of these three types of queries, only one can be created so that it uses query variables: the query statement. Because you need to grab only the current record from the Mortgage table, you need to use two variables in the query statement: one to specify the first name, and the other to specify the last name. Because you need to use query variables, you cannot simply create a query file interactively and then bind the query to a report.

Knowing that you cannot bind a table to a report at run time is also important. Thus when you design the report that will be used for eventual output, the table name to which the report should be bound must already exist. Things get a bit awkward at this point. Although you need to fill the table with the current record—and only the current record—while the mortgage calculator is running, the table itself must exist when you go to create the report. The solution to this problem is to

18 — SAMPLE APPLICATION: ADDING MENUS

create the table ahead of time and then design the report and bind it to the table. At run time, write the results of the query to the table created previously. When you write a query answer to a table that already exists, the data in the table is replaced with the new data.

In summary, the **printCurrM** custom method creates and executes a query statement. The results of the query statement are written to a specified table. Because the table specified already exists, the new data replaces the old data in the table. The table does not need to exist before you run a query and write the results to the table. In this sample application, however, the table's existence was necessary so that the report could be bound to the table and created interactively.

Before you define the **printCurrM** method, follow these steps to create the required table and the report:

1. Choose File, Utilities, Copy.
2. Choose the Mortgage table as the table to copy.
3. Enter **MORTQONE** as the name of the copied table.
4. Choose File, New, Report to create a new report.
5. In the Data Model dialog box, choose MORTQONE.DB.
6. Arrange the records in the file any way you like.
7. Save the report as MORTQONE.RSL.
8. Close any open tables or reports and return to the mortgage calculator in Design mode.

Next, create a new custom method for *pageOne* called **printCurrM**. Define the method as shown in the following lines:

```
; pageOne::printCurrM
method printCurrM()
var
   qAnswer     String   ; store answer to question about saving data
   queryOne    Query    ; query statement
   cFirst      String   ; to store current first name
   cLast       String   ; to store current last name
   oneReport   Report   ; handle to the report
endvar

; if current record has changed, ask user whether to save changes
if mortgageCalc.Touched = True then
   qAnswer = msgQuestion("Please Confirm",
      "Do you want to keep changes to this record?")
   if qAnswer = "No" then
      mortgageCalc.action(DataCancelRecord)
   endif
endif
```

III — PROGRAMMING PARADOX FOR WINDOWS

```
    cFirst = First_Name   ; get current first name
    cLast = Last_Name     ; get current last name

    ; create the query statement--note that all fields
    ; from mortgage.db are included
    queryOne = Query

    mortgage.db | First Name    | Last Name     | Loan Amount | Rate  |
                | Check ~cFirst | Check ~cLast  | Check       | Check |

    mortgage.db | Term   | Payment |
                | Check  | Check   |

    endQuery

    ; execute the query statement and write the results to mortqone.db,
    ; mortqone was previously created, but only to provide a basis for
    ; the one mortqone.rsl report
    executeQBE(queryOne, ":WORK: mortqone.db")

    ; the user can print the form after it's open
    oneReport.open("mortqone.rsl")

    ; when the user closes report window, the method ends and returns
    ; to the mortgage calculator

    endmethod
```

After you check the syntax of **printCurrM** and close the Editor window, you need to change the case statement in the **menuAction** method for *pageOne* so that the statement calls **printCurrM**. The entire switch/case switch should now look like this:

```
  case mChoice = "E&xit"            : fileExitM()
  case mChoice = "&Undo"            : undoEditM()
  case mChoice = "&Search"          : searchM()
  case mChoice = "&Current Client"  : printCurrM()
  case mChoice = "&All Clients"     : objName.View() ;printAllCM()
  case mChoice = "&Help"            : objName.View() ;getHelpM(objName)
  case mChoice = "&About"           : objName.View() ;showAboutM()
endswitch
```

The **printCurrM** method has several noteworthy aspects. To create a query statement, you must first declare a variable with the data type Query. This line in the Var section creates a query variable called *queryOne*:

```
queryOne    Query       ; query statement
```

Next, you need to assign the query statement to the variable. The following lines do precisely that:

```
queryOne = Query

mortgage.db | First Name    | Last Name     | Loan Amount | Rate  |
            | Check ~cFirst | Check ~cLast  | Check       | Check |

mortgage.db | Term  | Payment |
            | Check | Check   |

endQuery
```

As you can see, a query statement is rather an odd creature. It is a representation of a query that you could otherwise create interactively. (In fact, you can create a query interactively, save it to a query file, then choose Edit, Paste From File to paste it into an ObjectPAL method.) The table name to query appears to the left of each group of query statement lines. In this case, the table name to query is MORTGAGE.DB. If the table to be queried exists in a directory other than the current directory, you must specify either a directory alias or the full path to the table.

Each field to be included in the answer table also must be shown. If you want to create only a list of client names and loan amounts, for example, the query statement looks like this:

```
queryOne = Query

mortgage.db | First Name | Last Name | Loan Amount |
            | Check      | Check     | Check       |

endQuery
```

Each field name and condition is separated by a vertical bar. The vertical bars in a group of lines in a query statement are shown aligned, but this is only for readability. (PAL programmers should take note that the old alignment requirement has been lifted.)

The entire statement is delimited by the keywords **Query** and **endQuery**. You need to place these keywords as shown in this example.

To run the query, use the **executeQBE** method. This method can take one or two arguments. The first argument is the Query variable name, in this case *queryOne*. The second argument optionally specifies a file name to write the results of the query to; if you don't specify a path name or alias for the file, the current work directory is assumed. If you don't include this argument, the query is written to the ANSWER.DB table in the current private directory (:PRIV:).

III — PROGRAMMING PARADOX FOR WINDOWS

To open and display a report, use the **open** method for the Report class. In the preceding example, the **open** method was called in its simplest form:

```
oneReport.open("mortqone.rsl")
```

The **open** method is called with the variable *oneReport* (declared as an object of class Report); MORTQONE.RSL is the name of the report to run. As with the **open** method for forms, other syntax forms exist for the **open** method for reports. You can open a report with a certain window style, and you can specify the size and position of the report window to open.

Printing a Client Report with printAllCM

A client report should print all the information in the table, grouped by client, and should provide a detailed list of current clients and status for the user. The code for selecting and printing a report is a simple one. You can use the technique shown here to add other reports to the Reports menu if you like.

To create a report for the Mortgage table, follow these steps:

1. Choose File, New, Report to open a new report.

2. In the Data Model dialog box, select MORTGAGE.DB.

3. Design the report to show all of the information for each client, grouped by client.

4. When you're done, save the report as MORTGAGE.RSL.

5. Return to the mortgage calculator in Design mode.

6. Define a new custom method for *pageOne*. Name the method **printAllCM**. The **printAllCM** method should be defined as follows:

   ```
   ; pageOne::printAllCM (custom method)
   method printAllCM()
   var
      reportAll   Report
   endvar
   
   ; open the report
   if NOT reportAll.open("mortgage.rsl") then
      msgStop("Error", "Could not find requested report.")
   endif
   
   endmethod
   ```

7. Check the syntax and close the Editor window.

8. Change the **menuAction** method for *pageOne* so that the statement calls the custom method **printAllCM**. The entire switch/case statement for the **menuAction** method should look like this:

```
switch
  case mChoice = "E&xit"            : fileExitM()
  case mChoice = "&Undo"            : undoEditM()
  case mChoice = "&Search"          : searchM()
  case mChoice = "&Current Client"  : printCurrM()
  case mChoice = "&All Clients"     : printAllCM()
  case mChoice = "&Help"            : objName.View() ;getHelpM(objName)
  case mChoice = "&About"           : objName.View() ;showAboutM()
endswitch
```

After you finish adding and changing the methods, you can save, run, and test the form.

Getting Help with getHelpM

When choosing Help from the Help menu, the user should get either the specific help message available for the current object or a more general help message for the entire application.

The **menuAction** method calls the **getHelpM** custom method if the user chooses Help from the Help menu. The **getHelpM** method takes one argument, *objName*, which the **menuAction** method previously set to contain the name of the object for which help is requested.

The help text to be displayed is contained in a table called MORTHELP.DB. The MORTHELP.DB table has the following structure:

    ObjectName   A20
    HelpMemo   A255

A record exists for every object that requires specific help. An additional record, with an ObjectName field of "defaultHelp", contains general help for the form. When the user requests help for an object, the **getHelpM** method searches the MORTHELP.DB table for help specific to that object. If no specific help is found, **getHelpM** gets the default help string.

Add the records shown in table 18.1 to the MORTHELP.DB table. This table includes only a few records for testing purposes. At your leisure, you can complete the table with more specific help messages for each object.

Table 18.1. The MORTHELP.DB Table

ObjectName	HelpMemo
defaultHelp	Enter loan amount, term, and a yearly interest rate; then click Calculate Payment from Loan. Press F1 from a field or button for more help.
getPayment	Click Estimate Qualified Payment to open the Estimate Qualified Payment dialog box. Then enter monthly income, monthly credit payments, and calculate the maximum payment for which you can qualify.
mcBox	Enter loan amount, term, and a yearly interest rate; then click Calculate Payment from Loan. Press F1 from a field for more help.

The easiest way to display help for the form is to use in a **msgInfo** dialog box the message shown above. If the message is longer than a few lines, however, the text area in the **msgInfo** dialog box isn't large enough to display the message. Instead, you can create another object in the mortgage calculator to display the message.

To create a new object called *appHelpBox*, follow these steps:

1. With the mortgage calculator open in Design mode, move to the lower part of page one.

2. Draw a box approximately three inches wide by two inches high. Rename the box *appHelpBox* (see fig. 18.7).

3. Inside *appHelpBox*, place a large text field. Rename the new text field *appHelpText*. Add a vertical scroll bar to the text field.

4. Under *appHelpText* inside *appHelpBox*, create a new button. Rename the button *closeBox*. Label the button "Close".

5. Define a **pushButton** method for closeBox, as follows:

```
method pushButton(var eventInfo Event)
; make the box disappear
appHelpBox.Visible = No
; move it back to its original position at the bottom
; of the page
appHelpBox.setPosition(1000,10000,4700,2300)
endmethod
```

18 — SAMPLE APPLICATION: ADDING MENUS

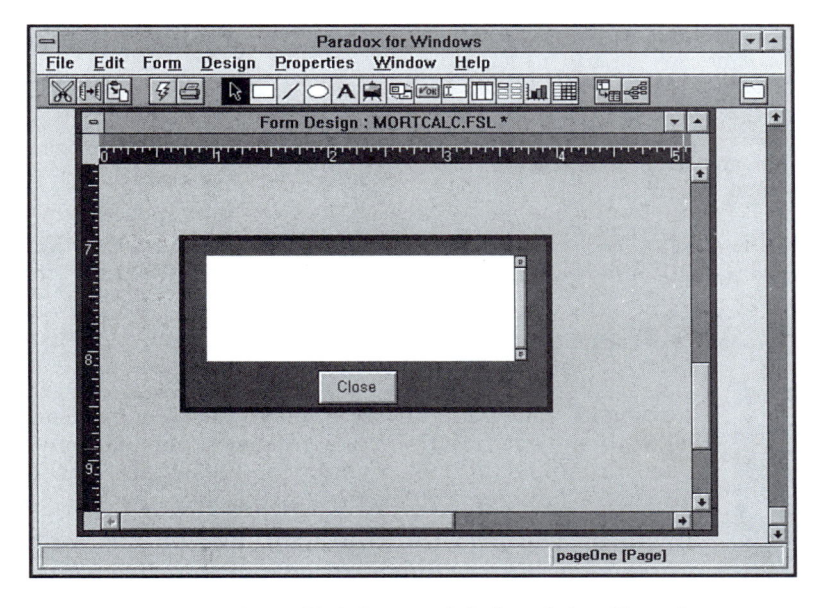

FIG. 18.7

The appHelpBox object.

After you have created *appHelpBox* and defined the Close button, you can define the **getHelpM** custom method. (Create **getHelpM** as a new custom method for the page.) This is the complete definition of **getHelpM**:

```
; pageOne::getHelpM::(Custom method)
method getHelpM(var objName String)
var
  helpTC    TCursor
endvar

helpTC.open("morthelp.db")            ; open help table
if NOT helpTC.locate("ObjectName", objName) then
  ; if you cannot find specific help for object, get default help
  helpTC.locate("ObjectName", "defaultHelp")
endif

pageOne.appHelpBox.appHelpText = helpTC.HelpMemo
helpTC.close()

; now, move the box into position (twips)
appHelpBox.setPosition(1000,2000,4700,2300)
; appHelpBox.closeButton takes care of moving box
;   back and setting it to invisible.
; Technically, the box doesn't have to be moved, it
;   can be placed where you want it to display
;   and be toggled from visible to invisible.
```

```
;   This method, however, is a bit awkward in Design mode.
; Also, the box should never be moved so that it is
;   entirely within the borders of mcBox. If it can be
;   physically contained by mcBox, it will be bound to
;   mcBox and become embedded to mcBox.
pageOne.appHelpBox.Visible = Yes
endmethod
```

First, this method declares a TCursor named *helpTC* and opens the MORTHELP.DB table. This command opens the table and binds it to the TCursor:

```
helpTC.open("morthelp.db")         ; open help table
```

> **NOTE** Knowing in some general way when you can accomplish a task with one of the action constants, and when you must use a TCursor, is difficult. If you are confused about when you need a TCursor, you're not alone: it is confusing.
>
> Sometimes, you can work with a table only by declaring a TCursor, binding it to the table, and manipulating the table through the TCursor. In other situations, the action constants enable you to work on a table through the form. If you have a table or group of tables bound to a form, for example, **action(DataNextRecord)** enables you to move to the next record in the table. If, in the course of editing the user creates a key violation, you'll need a TCursor to get to the key violation record (with the **attachToKeyViol** method).

The statement in the next line searches the ObjectName field of *helpTC* for the value *objName*:

```
helpTC.locate("ObjectName", objName)
```

If the locate operation succeeds, it returns True; otherwise, it returns False. If the locate fails, applying a NOT to it makes the entire condition True; commands in the **if** statement then are executed. In this case, the entire statement becomes True when the MORTHELP.DB table does *not* contain a record with *objName* in the ObjectName field. This situation indicates that no specific help is available for the object that was active when the user asked for help. In this case, the next command searches for the default help for the form:

```
helpTC.locate("ObjectName", "defaultHelp")
```

The *appHelpBox* object contains one field, *appHelpText*, and one button, *closeButton*. The field is used to display the current help string. The user can click the Close button to close and remove the box. After

18 — SAMPLE APPLICATION: ADDING MENUS

finding the correct help text, **getHelpM** sets the value of *appHelpText* to the help text found. Then the box is moved to the visible area of the form with this line:

```
appHelpBox.setPosition(1000,2000,4700,2300)
```

The box is set to visible with this line:

```
appHelpBox.Visible = Yes
```

After the user clicks Close, the box is moved back to its previous position (at the bottom of *pageOne* of the form) and set to be invisible again.

Change the **menuAction** method for *pageOne* so that it calls the **getHelpM** custom method:

```
; pageOne::menuAction
method menuAction(var eventInfo MenuEvent)
var
  mChoice,
  objName String
  obj UIObject
endvar

; get the menu choice from the event packet
mChoice = eventInfo.menuChoice()

; get the name of the object that was active
; when the menu was chosen
; the active name will be used to display context-sensitive help
eventInfo.getTarget(obj)
objName = obj.Name        ; get the Name property
switch
  case mChoice = "E&xit"           : fileExitM()
  case mChoice = "&Undo"           : undoEditM()
  case mChoice = "&Search"         : searchM()
  case mChoice = "&Current Client" : printCurrM()
  case mChoice = "&All Clients"    : printAllCM()
  case mChoice = "&Help"           : getHelpM(objName)
  case mChoice = "&About"  : objName.View() ; showAboutM()
endswitch

endmethod
```

To test the **getHelpM** method, follow these steps:

1. Save and run the mortgage calculator.

2. Use the Tab key to move to the Estimate Qualified Payment button.

3. Choose Help, Help from the menu. The method moves the appHelpBox into position, and shows the help available for the Estimate Qualified Payment button (see fig. 18.8).

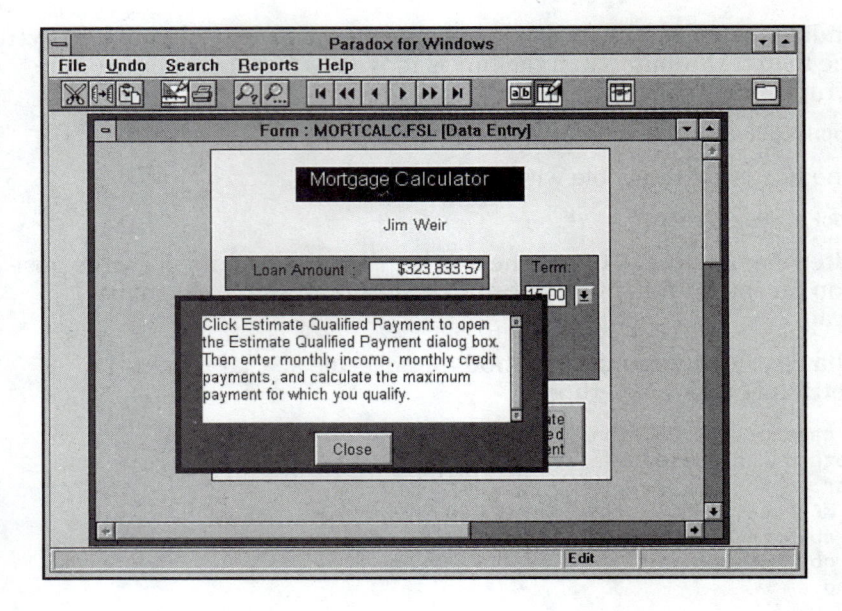

FIG. 18.8
The appHelpBox object.

Showing an Animated About Box with showAboutM

An About box, by convention, tells you something about the application. No set rule defines precisely what an About box must contain—many About boxes tell you little about an application that you didn't already know. (About boxes occasionally have hidden features, such as a credits list that pops up when you press a hidden or disguised button or type a code name.)

You can think of an About box as something similar to the copyright page of a book. The full name of the application, the date and version number of the application, a confidentiality statement (if necessary), the publisher or owner of the application, and the author or developer's name are all appropriate components of an About box. Additionally, you can include system statistics such as available resources, the amount of time the user has been in the application, the current time, the current user name (in a network setting), and so on.

In the About box for the mortgage calculator, you draw a two-paned window and a shade. When the About box opens, the shade is drawn. Over the next several seconds, the shade rises, revealing the contents of the window. Also, the About box shows the available memory on your system.

18 — SAMPLE APPLICATION: ADDING MENUS

Before you define the **showAboutM** custom method, you need to create a new form by following these steps:

1. Open a new form. Do not bind a table to the form.

2. Set the page size to 4 inches wide by 3 inches high.

3. Open the Object Tree for the form and rename the form *mortAboutBox*.

4. Rename the page to *pageOne*. Set the page color to dark blue, the pattern to the vertical lines (pinstripes), and the color of the pattern to dark brown. (This combination gives the impression of wallpaper.)

5. Draw a box on the left side of the page. The box should be approximately 2 inches wide by 2.5 inches high. Rename the box *windowFrame*. Set the color of the box to light gray.

6. Draw another box 1.75 inches wide by 2.25 inches high inside *windowFrame*. Rename the box *windowPanes*. Set the color of the box to dark gray.

7. Draw two boxes inside *windowPanes* to look like the upper and lower panes of a window. Leave a small margin between the two boxes. The boxes should be approximately 1.12 inches (1 1/8 inches) wide by .87 inch high (7/8 inch). Set the color of the panes to black.

8. In the lower pane, place a text box. The text box should be black with the text appearing in white or some other light color. You can include in the text box whatever copyright or version information you want.

9. If you prefer, you can draw some decorative elements in the upper pane. The upper pane shown later in figure 18.9 shows a moon and several stars. The moon was created by drawing an ellipse in a light color and overlaying that ellipse with a smaller ellipse set to black. (Drawing these elements is optional.)

10. In the center of the margin between the upper and lower panes, draw a small ellipse to look like a knob.

11. Within the *windowFrame* box and slightly above the upper pane, draw a long, thin box to look like a curtain rod, 1 7/8 inches wide by 1/16 inch high. Adding a vertical line near each end of the curtain rod improves the illusion.

12. Just below the curtain rod, draw another long thin box, slightly narrower than the curtain rod. Rename the box *shadeBox*.

13. In the Properties menu for *shadeBox*, set the Contain Objects property to off (unchecked).

14. To the right of *windowFrame*, draw a box 1 inch wide by 3/4 inch high. Rename the object *systemStats*. Set the color to a light color. Set the frame style as shown in figure 18.9.

15. Place an undefined field inside *systemStats*. Rename the field *sysMem*. Set the Display Type of *sysMem* to unlabeled. Set the Tab Stop property to off (unchecked).

16. Redefine the **arrive** method for *sysMem* as follows:

    ```
    ; MORTABOU::sysMem:: arrive
    method arrive(var eventInfo Event)
    var
       sysInfoBag  Dynarray[]  AnyType  ; a dynamic array
                                        ; to hold system information
    endvar
    ; the sysInfo method writes system information to a dynamic array
    sysInfo(sysInfoBag)
    ; get the value of the element with the tag "Memory"
    self.value = sysInfoBag["Memory"]

    endmethod
    ```

17. Adjust the size and shape of the various objects to look approximately like figure 18.9.

18. Create a button under *systemStats*. Rename the button *closeButton*. In the **pushButton** method for *closeButton*, include the following code:

    ```
    ; closeButton::pushButton
    method pushButton(var eventInfo Event)
    formReturn("OKButton")
    endmethod
    ```

19. The **arrive** method for *shadeBox* sets a timer that generates a timer event at a specified interval. Setting a timer doesn't do much in itself. After you know that **timer** methods respond automatically to timer events, however, you can start to create animation effects. To set a timer for *shadeBox* when the form is opened, redefine the **open** method for *shadeBox* as follows:

    ```
    method open(var eventInfo Event)
    self.setTimer(25)
    endmethod
    ```

    The **setTimer** method sets a timer in milliseconds. This particular timer goes off 40 times per second.

20. The **timer** method for *shadeBox* is called automatically whenever the timer goes off. If the timer is set to 500, for example, the **timer**

method executes every half second until the timer is turned off. In the **timer** method for *shadeBox*, you place the code that moves the shade. Redefine the **timer** method for *shadeBox* as shown in the following lines:

```
var
  incH   SmallInt   ; to increment height
  ; if this variable were set inside the method definition,
  ; it would be unassigned at the beginning of the method
  ; this way, it retains its value from one call of timer()
  ; to the next
  startX LongInt
  startY LongInt
  startW LongInt
  finalH LongInt
  startPosition Point
  startSize     Point
endvar

method timer(var eventInfo TimerEvent)
const
  changeH = 100
  startH = 3190
endconst

if NOT incH.isassigned() then
  ; all lines up to the else will only execute the first time
  ; this method is called
  startPosition = self.Position   ; get the starting position
  startX = startPosition.x()      ; take the x value
  startY = startPosition.y()      ; take the y value
  startSize = self.Size           ; get the starting size
  startW = startSize.x()          ; get the x value (width)
  finalH = startSize.y()          ; get the y value (height)
  incH = startH
else
  ; the next line changes the value of the height of the shade
  incH = incH - changeH
endif

; the setPosition method sets the position and size of the object
self.setPosition(startX, startY, startW, incH)

; when the changed height is the same as the original height,
; turn the timer off
if incH <= finalH then
  self.killtimer()
endif

endmethod
```

The variable *incH* (which sets the amount to increment or decrement the height) is declared above the method definition so that the variable retains its value between subsequent calls of the method. This approach is necessary because you need some way to track the current height of the shade as it is pulled up.

The variables *startX*, *startY*, and *startW* are declared outside the method for performance reasons. They are declared only once, the first time the method is called. In addition, assignment to the variables occurs only once, inside the **if** statement. A still faster way to set up the starting positions is to define constants. If you're certain of the starting position and width, as well as the final height, you can declare *startX*, *startY*, *startW*, and *finalH* as constants. As the shade is pulled up, only the height changes (*incH*), until it reaches the *finalH* value. The variable *finalH* is set to the height that *shadeBox* should be when it is fully raised. This height is the starting position height in Design mode.

The *x* and *y* coordinates are measured from the upper left corner of the object that contains *shadeBox*, not from the upper left corner of the window or page. Starting with the upper left corner of *windowFrame*, then, the upper left corner of *shadeBox* is 180 twips (1/1440 of an inch) to the right and 255 twips down. Instead of hard-coding these values as constants, the method is written so that if you place *shadeBox* in a slightly different position with respect to *windowFrame*, the method still works correctly.

The *changeH* constant specifies the amount that *shadeBox* should shrink every time it moves. For a smoother motion, you could set *changeH* to a smaller number, but because the shade would move less for every timer event, you also might need to increase the speed of the timer.

The *startH* constant specifies the height of *shadeBox* when the shade is all the way down, covering both window panes. You may need to adjust this number if you drew the panes slightly differently.

The condition in the following if statement tests *incH* to see whether it has been assigned a value:

```
if NOT incH.isassigned() then
```

The first time the method runs, *incH* does not have a value. Because *incH* is declared outside the method, however, it retains its value between **timer** method calls. If *incH* is unassigned, it should be set with the starting height of *shadeBox*, contained by the constant *startH*. In subsequent **timer** method calls, *incH* should be reduced by the amount in constant *changeH*.

18 — SAMPLE APPLICATION: ADDING MENUS

The heart of the method, the line that changes the size of *shadeBox*, is executed every time the method calls:

```
self.setPosition(startX, startY, startW, incH)
```

As you can see, the **setPosition** method takes four arguments: the *x* and *y* coordinates of the upper left corner of the object, the width of the object, and the height of the object. The position of the object doesn't change, but the size does. The size is set with the last two arguments, *startW* and *incH*. Because you don't want the width of *shadeBox* to change, *startW* maintains the object at its original width. The height of *shadeBox* is set with the *incH* variable, which was either set (the first time through) or changed (all subsequent times) within the **if** statement.

21. After you finish defining the methods, save the form as MORTABOU.FSL. As soon as you switch from Design mode to View mode, the shade should drop and then slowly rise.

> **TIP**
> If you find that objects appear on top of the shade, return to Design mode and make sure that the *shadeBox* property of Contain Objects is not set (is unchecked). Also, use the Bring to Front menu choice from the Design menu to make sure that no objects are set to display in front of *shadeBox*.

Now that you have created the About box, you can define the **showAboutM** method that calls the About box. Open the mortgage calculator in Design mode and create a new custom method called **showAboutM**. Define **showAboutM** as shown in the following lines:

```
; pageOne::showAboutM()
method showAboutM()
var
  aboutBoxDlg  Form
  buttonPressed String
endvar

; assumes dialog properties have been set for the form
if aboutBoxDlg.open("mortabou.fsl") then
  aboutBoxDlg.setTitle("About Mortgage Calculator")
  buttonPressed = string(aboutBoxDlg.wait())
  if buttonPressed = "OKButton" then
    aboutBoxDlg.close()
  endif
else
  msgStop("Error", "Could not locate the About box.")
endif

endmethod
```

Now, go back to the **menuAction** method for *pageOne* and change the switch/case statement so that it calls **showAboutM**. The entire **menuAction** method definition should look like this:

```
; mortcalc::pageOne::menuAction
method menuAction(var eventInfo MenuEvent)
var
   mChoice    String
   objName    String
endvar

; get the menu choice from the event packet
mChoice = eventInfo.menuChoice()

; get the name of the object that was active
; when the menu was chosen
; the active name is used to display context-sensitive help
;objName = active.getProperty("Name")
objName = active.Name

switch
   case mChoice = "E&xit"              : fileExitM()
   case mChoice = "&Undo"              : undoEditM()
   case mChoice = "&Search"            : searchM()
   case mChoice = "&Current Client"    : printCurrM()
   case mChoice = "&All Clients"       : printAllCM()
   case mChoice = "&Help"              : getHelpM(objName)
   case mChoice = "&About"             : showAboutM()
endswitch

endmethod
```

Save the mortgage calculator and test it. When you choose Help, About, the About box displays and the shade rises to reveal the windows underneath. Figure 18.9 shows the About box with the shade down. Figure 18.10 shows the About box with the shade up.

Improving the Mortgage Calculator Application

Although the sample application presented in the last four chapters presents many techniques and features of ObjectPAL and Paradox, you can do many things to improve the mortgage calculator. The following list provides a few ideas:

18 — SAMPLE APPLICATION: ADDING MENUS

- Turn off the display of the SpeedBar so that the user cannot choose Edit, Table View, or any other unexpected actions. The **hideSpeedBar** and **showSpeedBar** methods are included in the Form class to enable you to manipulate the SpeedBar. If you do turn off the SpeedBar, you need to add buttons or menu items that enable the user to cursor through the table. Most of what you need to do can be accomplished with one of the various action commands, such as DataNextRecord.

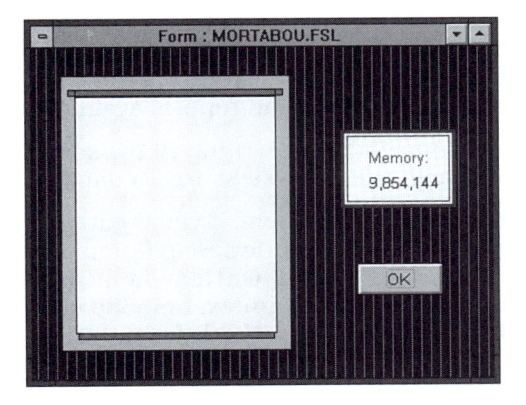

FIG. 18.9
The About box with the window shade down.

FIG. 18.10
The About box with the window shade up.

- Provide buttons or menu items that enable the user to insert new records or delete records. You can use the action constants DataInsertRecord and DataDeleteRecord.
- Set a title for the mortgage calculator that replaces the default "Paradox for Windows" title.

- Create data-dependent properties for the fields in the Mortgage table. You might, for example, want to set a range of valid numbers for the Loan Amount field.

- Make a small calculator available when the user right-clicks a field. The user then can easily enter several separate numbers to go into an aggregate field. If the loan qualification is based on two incomes, for example, you may want to enable the user to type two numbers and then place the sum of those numbers into the monthly income field.

- Package the application. Choose Form, Deliver from the Form Design window and Report, Deliver from the Report Design window to safeguard the forms and reports against changes.

- Document the application by writing all the source code to a report with the Language, Browse Sources command.

- Develop a compiled help system. If you create a help system compiled with the Microsoft Windows Help Compiler, you can access that help system with the **helpOnHelp**, **helpQuit**, **helpSetIndex**, **helpShowContext**, **helpShowIndex**, **helpShowTopic**, and **helpShowTopicInKeyword** methods from the System class.

Chapter Summary

In this chapter, you learned how to create menus and respond to menu choices by the user. In addition, you learned how to create and use custom methods and how to achieve animation effects.

APPENDIX A

Installing Paradox for Windows

This appendix describes how to install Paradox for Windows. As with most Windows software, installing Paradox is easy. You can expect to be up and running in about half an hour.

To run Paradox for Windows, you first must install Windows. See the Windows documentation or Que's *Using Windows 3.1*, Special Edition.

Installation Requirements

Make sure that your computer meets the requirements of Paradox for Windows, as shown in table A.1. If you are already running Windows 3.x and are happy with your machine's performance, you probably have met these requirements. If you plan to run Paradox on a network, be sure that your network appears in the list following table A.1. If you are not sure what kind of network you are using, consult the network administrator.

Table A.1. Paradox for Windows Installation Requirements

Element	Requirement/Comments
Processor	The 80286 is a minimum to run the program, but will result in quite slow performance. For better results, use a 386 or higher microprocessor.
Memory (RAM)	4M is the minimum. Additional memory noticeably improves performance, so start with 8M.
Storage	Hard disk required. Around 15M of free disk space needed for the Paradox program files and additional space for the database and related temporary files that Paradox uses in daily operation.
Display	EGA or higher; color VGA or Super VGA recommended.
Operating System	DOS 3.3 or higher. DOS 5.0 or higher is recommended.
Microsoft Windows	Version 3.1 or higher. Standard and 386 Enhanced modes are supported, but not Real mode. If you are using Windows 3.0, you should upgrade to 3.1 to take advantage of improvements in performance and reliability.
Mouse	A mouse or other pointing device is required for design but optional for data entry. Most users need a mouse to get the most out of Windows, so consider this required equipment.
Network	Paradox runs stand-alone or on Windows-compatible networks (see following list).

The following networks are supported by Paradox for Windows:

- Novell Advanced Netware
- Banyan Vines
- 3COM 3Plus/3Plus Open
- Microsoft LAN Manager
- Other 100-percent Windows-compatible networks

Now that you have met the requirements for Paradox, you are ready to load the software.

Making a Backup Copy of the Program Disks

Before you begin the installation, make a copy of each of the program disks and place the original disks aside for safekeeping. Follow these steps to make a backup copy:

1. Write-protect the original program disks. For 3.5-inch disks, slide the write-protect tab on the right side of the disk upward. For a 5.25-inch disk, place a write-protect sticker (included in the box of disks) over the write-protect tab. The disk is now protected from accidental erasure.

2. Gather enough blank, formatted floppy disks to copy all the program disks.

3. Run the DISKCOPY command from the DOS prompt, followed by the source drive and destination drive for the disk copy. Enter **DISKCOPY A: B:** at the DOS prompt, for example, to copy disks from drive A to drive B. This command will work even if you have only one floppy disk drive. See your DOS or Windows documentation for more information.

4. Insert and remove the floppy disks as prompted by DOS. Remember that the source disk is the original program disk and the destination disk is the new disk.

With a backup copy of the program disks in hand, you are ready to run the INSTALL program.

Running the Install Program

To run the Paradox for Windows INSTALL program, follow these steps:

1. Place the copy of Paradox system disk 1 in a floppy disk drive.

2. From the Windows Program Manager, choose File, Run. The Run dialog box appears (see fig. A.1).

3. Enter the name of the program to run, in this case A:INSTALL, in the Command Line field of the Run dialog box. If you are installing from the B drive, substitute B: for A: throughout these instructions.

USING PARADOX FOR WINDOWS, SPECIAL EDITION

4. Click OK to run the install program. The Paradox for Windows Installation dialog box appears, as shown in figure A.2.

5. Fill in your name, company, and serial number in the spaces provided in the Paradox for Windows Installation dialog box. The following section describes the installation options for Paradox for Windows.

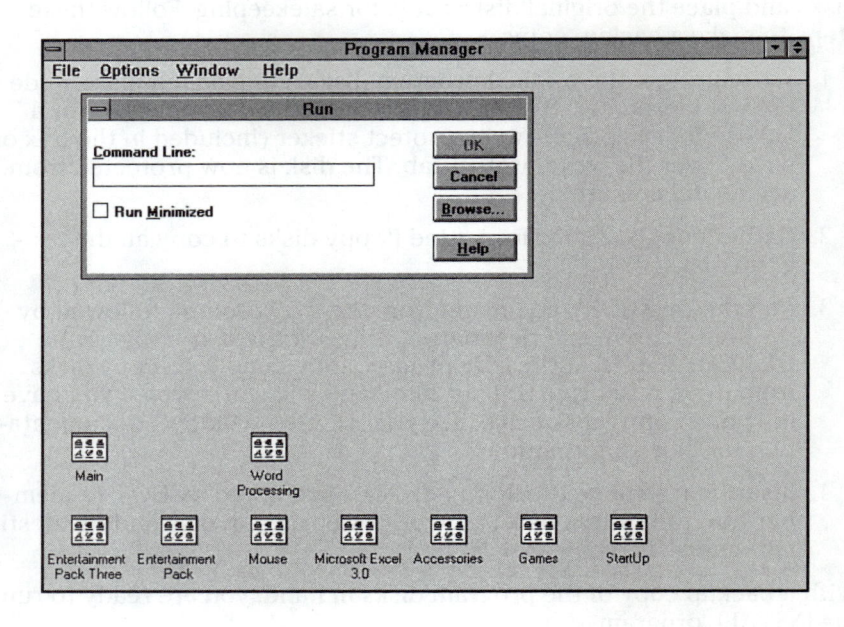

FIG. A.1

The Run dialog box.

Installing Sample Files

By default, Paradox installs sample tables, ObjectPAL examples, and a sample application. These are useful to illustrate the capabilities of Paradox for Windows and may be used to follow along with Paradox documentation. If you do not want to install sample files, click the box beside your choice to remove the check mark.

To change the subdirectory where Paradox installs the sample files, click the Subdirectories button. The Subdirectory Options dialog box appears (see fig. A.3). Change the names of the subdirectories where the samples will be installed and click OK.

A — INSTALLING PARADOX FOR WINDOWS

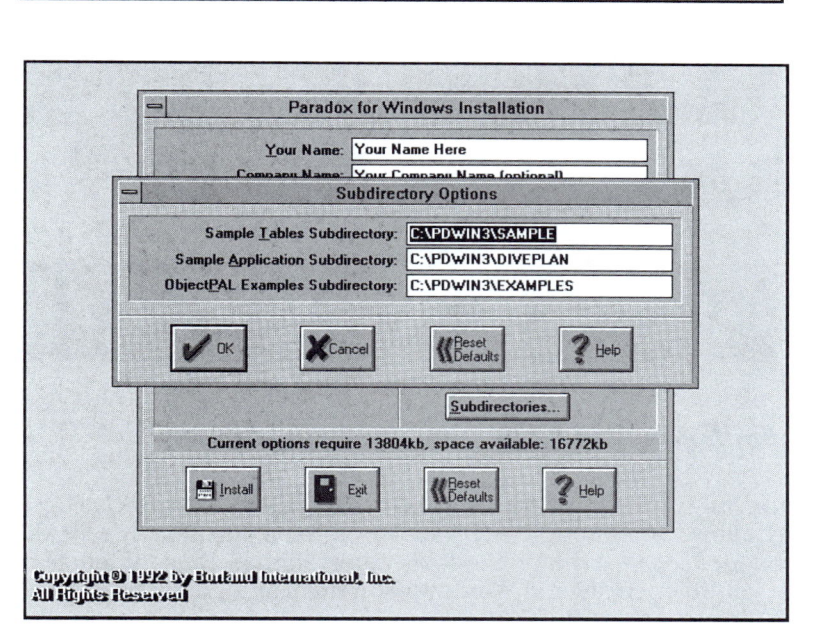

FIG. A.2

The Paradox for Windows Installation dialog box.

FIG. A.3

The Subdirectory Options dialog box.

USING PARADOX FOR WINDOWS, SPECIAL EDITION

When you have completed the Paradox for Windows Installation dialog box, click Install to begin the installation process. To clear the entries in this dialog box and start afresh, click Reset Defaults.

As installation proceeds, the Installing dialog box shows you progress in installation, counting the bytes transferred and showing the percentage of installation completed (see fig. A.4). Road signs periodically appear alerting you to new features advertising Borland products and services, and recommending that you register your software. When Paradox finishes copying the files from a disk, a New Disk dialog box appears asking you to insert the next disk (see fig. A.5). Insert the next disk and press Enter or click OK to continue.

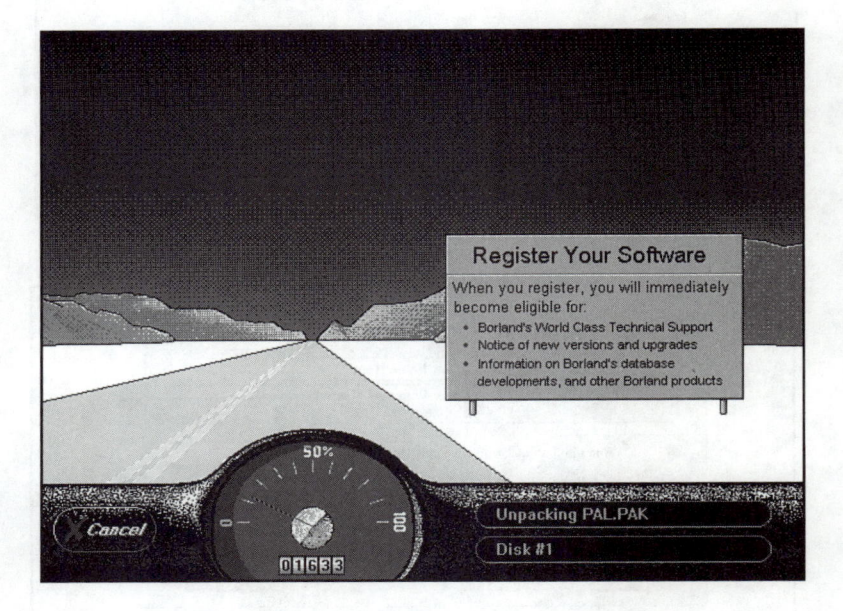

FIG. A.4

The Installing dialog box.

Installing SHARE

Before you run Paradox, you should install SHARE. The DOS SHARE utility allows you multiple accesses to the same file. Loading SHARE is a good idea for nearly any Windows application because Windows enables you to open several Windows at a time, and potentially open the same file more than once.

Either type the following line at the DOS prompt or add it to your AUTOEXEC.BAT file:

　　\DOS\SHARE

A — INSTALLING PARADOX FOR WINDOWS

707

This example assumes that you have loaded the DOS program files (including SHARE.EXE) in the DOS subdirectory. If SHARE.EXE is located elsewhere on your computer, modify this line accordingly.

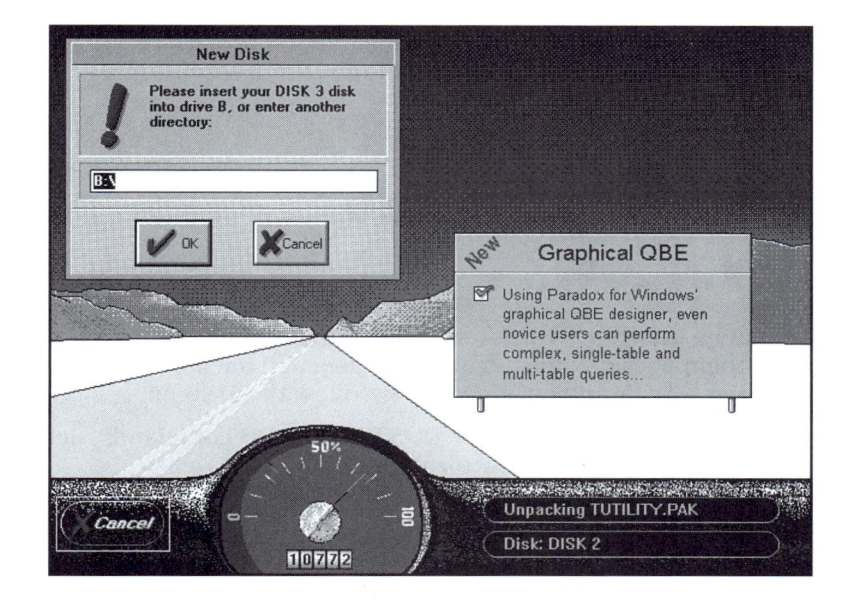

FIG. A.5
The New Disk dialog box.

Modifying CONFIG.SYS and AUTOEXEC.BAT Files

The CONFIG.SYS and AUTOEXEC.BAT files are used by DOS to set up the configuration of your computer. The CONFIG.SYS file contains parameters to set up the DOS environment and load some system software such as memory-management programs. Your CONFIG.SYS file should have a statement reading "FILES=60" (or greater). The FILES statement sets file handles—the number of files that may be opened simultaneously by DOS. Databases require more file handles than most applications.

To modify CONFIG.SYS or AUTOEXEC.BAT files, use the DOS EDLIN or EDIT text editors, or the Windows Notepad.

Viewing the README File

Borland sends last-minute information on your release of Paradox for Windows in a file called README.TXT. The README.TXT file is displayed automatically at the end of the installation process. Read through the file on-screen or print it and read it for recent release notes.

Deinstalling Paradox for Windows

Unfortunately, installing Windows applications is much easier than removing them. Paradox has no utility to deinstall itself from your computer. To remove Paradox from your PC, follow these steps:

1. Using the File Manager or the DOS DEL and RD commands, delete all the files in the following directories:

   \PDOXWIN
   \PDOXWIN\DIVEPLAN
   \PDOXWIN\MINIAPPS
   \PDOXWIN\SAMPLE
   \ODAPI

2. If you did not choose the default directories for Paradox installation, delete the appropriate directories.

3. Delete the Paradox for Windows program group by choosing File, Delete in the Program Manager.

APPENDIX B

Using the Graphical User Interface

Paradox for Windows is a fully graphical database program that runs under the graphical user interface of Microsoft Windows. A graphical user interface, or GUI (pronounced "gooey"), is much easier to use than a character-based interface for many operations and provides better printed and on-screen graphics. The Windows graphical user interface brings many advantages to Paradox and helps you easily accomplish the following tasks:

- Link to and use data from other Windows applications by using dynamic data exchange (DDE) and object linking and embedding (OLE)
- Use the SpeedBars (the Borland term for toolbars) and dialog boxes to automate common operations
- Run Paradox for Windows and other Windows applications at the same time
- Incorporate graphics images from other Windows applications in databases

This appendix presents the components of the Windows graphical user interface and shows you how to use these components effectively. You learn how to do the following tasks:

- Use the mouse
- Change the size, position, and arrangement of windows
- Use pull-down and cascade menus
- Use Object Inspectors
- Use dialog boxes
- Use SpeedBars

Customizing Database Objects

Paradox for Windows has many new options for customizing your databases. Several Paradox for Windows commands enable you to use colors and fonts to enhance your tables, forms, and reports in a WYSIWYG (what-you-see-is-what-you-get) display.

Paradox for Windows makes all customization features easily accessible through the Object Inspectors—context-sensitive dialog boxes specific to the selected item. Using some of the options, you can choose display format and set field label alignment, fonts, and font options for text (such as bold, italic, and underline). Figure B.1 shows examples of some of these options.

Using color in a database makes data easier to see and understand. Paradox for Windows enables you to specify the color of fields within a table and to specify whether values outside a specified range of values are displayed in a different color. You can display positive values in one color, for example, and negative values in another color.

You can choose from standard Paradox for Windows colors or make your own colors by selecting from a palette of 16.7 million colors. Most of the choices are patchwork colors, created from the colors the system can display. If you use a color printer, you may need to experiment with color selections to determine the combinations that produce the best results. If you use a black-and-white printer, colors are converted to shades of gray.

B — USING THE GRAPHICAL USER INTERFACE

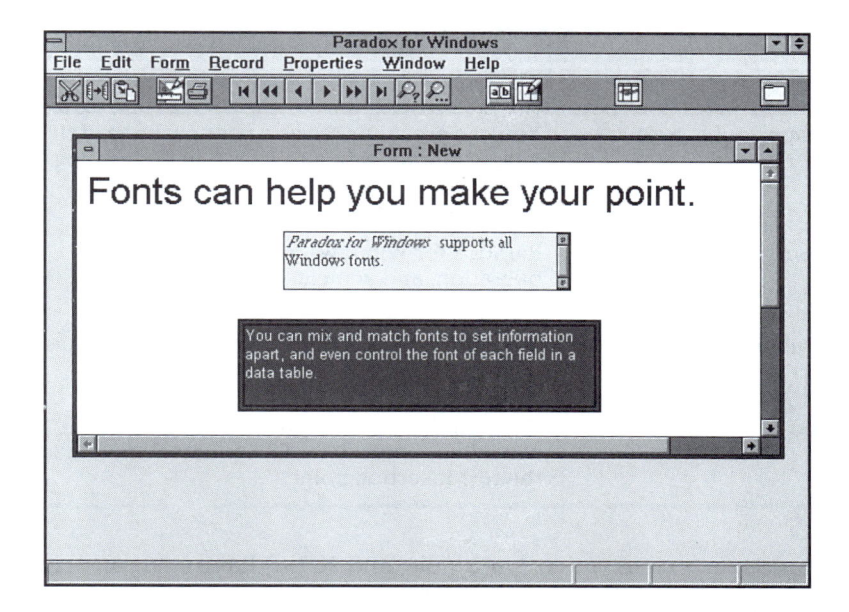

FIG. B.1 Different font and style options can improve the appearance of forms and reports.

Using the Mouse

Among the most exciting Paradox for Windows features is mouse capability. As with the keyboard, the mouse enables you to select commands and manipulate objects on-screen. You can perform many tasks—such as moving through windows, setting column widths, and moving in dialog boxes—more quickly with the mouse. Several Paradox for Windows features, such as SpeedBars, can be activated only with a mouse.

You move the mouse pointer around the screen by moving the mouse on a flat surface. The mouse pointer moves in the same direction as your hand. Usually, the mouse pointer is an arrow shape; as you perform different tasks in Paradox for Windows, the mouse pointer changes shape. Table B.1 explains the various shapes of the mouse pointer.

Table B.1. Mouse Pointer Shapes

Shape	Meaning
Arrow	You can perform normal operations, such as selecting blocks and menu commands.
White double arrow	You can resize the window.

continues

Table B.1. Continued

Shape	Meaning
Black double arrow	You can create or resize a window pane. If the mouse pointer is in a row or column heading and close to a grid line, you can widen a column or heighten a row.
Hourglass	Paradox for Windows is in the middle of an operation, and you can do nothing with the mouse.
Grabbing hand	The pointer is over a moveable graphic image.
Hand pointing up	The pointer is over a highlighted Help topic.
I-beam	The pointer is over data in the edit line; you can edit or enter data. This is sometimes called the text insertion point.

Most mouse devices (mice, trackballs, and so on) have a left and right button. You use the left mouse button to select cells and blocks, use menus, and enter information in dialog boxes. You use the right mouse button to activate the Object Inspector feature.

Table B.2 describes mouse terminology you need to know as you read this book and as you use Paradox for Windows.

Table B.2. Mouse Terms

Term	Meaning
Click	Quickly press and release the left mouse button.
Right-click	When inspecting object properties, click the right mouse button.
Double-click	Quickly press and release the left mouse button two times. Be sure not to move the mouse as you click.
Drag	Press and hold down the left mouse button and then move the mouse. This moves the mouse pointer, usually to highlight a block or after grabbing an object.
Grab	Move the mouse pointer to the object to move; press and hold down the left mouse button as you drag the object.
Point	Position the mouse pointer over the object you want to select or move.

B — USING THE GRAPHICAL USER INTERFACE

Term	Meaning
Select	Highlight cells or blocks or select graph objects.
Drag and drop	Point to a selected block, hold down the left mouse button, and move the selected block to a new location. To copy the selected block, hold down Ctrl while you press the left mouse button, move the mouse pointer to the target cell, and release the mouse button.

Using the Control Menus

You use the Paradox Desktop window to display and work with Paradox database objects. The Paradox Desktop is the main menu of Paradox for Windows, as shown in figure B.2. The small rectangle in the upper left corner of the screen is the Paradox for Windows Control menu box, which leads to the Paradox for Windows Control menu. This menu, which is similar to the Control menu in all Windows applications, enables you to manipulate the size and position of the Paradox window, close Paradox for Windows, and switch to other Windows applications (see fig. B.3).

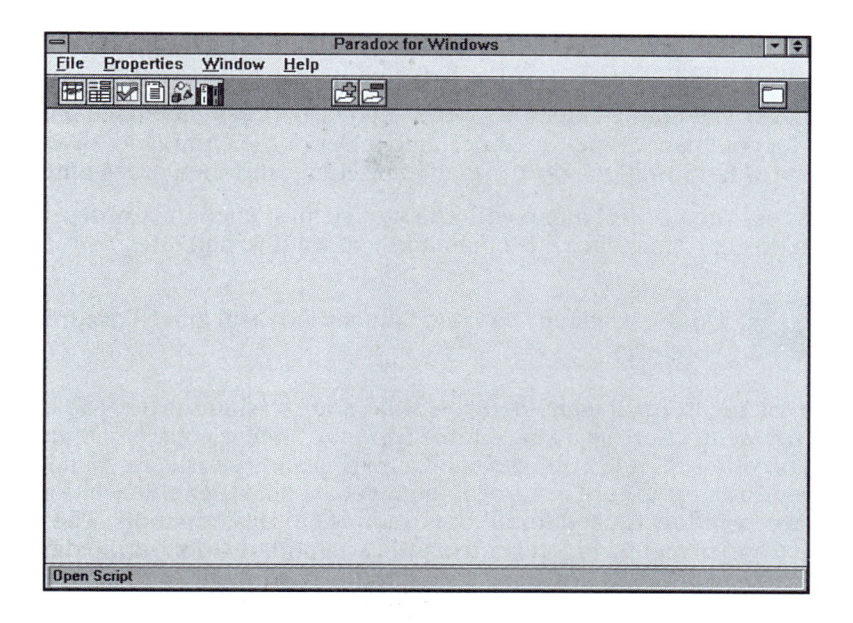

FIG. B.2

The Paradox for Windows Desktop.

USING PARADOX FOR WINDOWS, SPECIAL EDITION

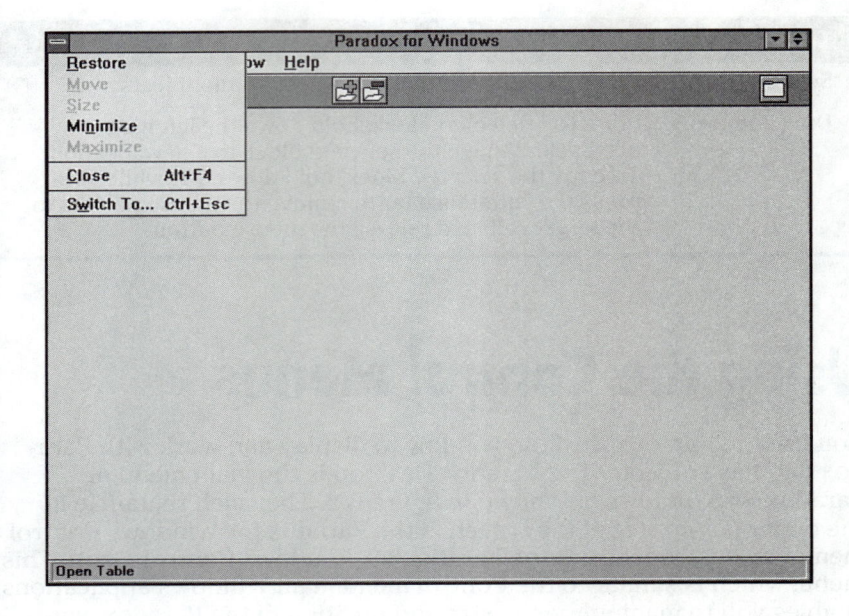

FIG. B.3

The Paradox for Windows Control menu.

Although the menu shown in figure B.3 has seven options, three are dimmed, which indicates a function currently unavailable. If you run Paradox for Windows in a partial-screen window or if you reduce the screen to an icon, different choices may be dimmed, which indicates that these choices are currently unavailable.

To access the Control menu with the keyboard, press Alt+space bar. To select a command, type the underlined letter of the command, or use the arrow keys to highlight the command name and then press Enter.

To access the Control menu with the mouse, first click the Control menu box and then click the command you want to activate.

NOTE Double-clicking the Control menu box will close Paradox for Windows.

Whereas the Control menu controls the Paradox window, the Table Control menu controls a single table window. Similar control menus exist on other Paradox objects such as forms and reports. Because all the windows for other Paradox objects behave like the table window, the table window is used for all the examples in this appendix. The Table Control menu, which controls the size and position of the database table window, is accessed through the Table Control menu box—the small rectangle in the upper left corner of the table window. Although similar to the Paradox for Windows Control menu, the Table

Control menu applies only to the table window. In addition, the Switch To option, which switches between Windows applications, also is replaced by the Next option, which switches between Paradox windows. Figure B.4 shows the Table Control menu.

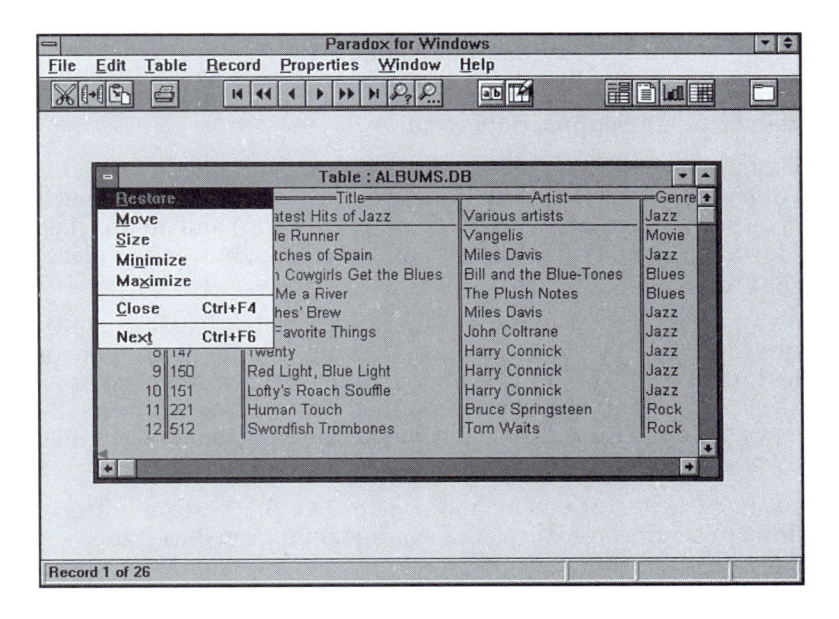

FIG. B.4

The Table Control menu.

To access the Table Control menu with the keyboard, press Alt+- (hyphen). To select a command, type the underlined letter of the command, or use the arrow keys to highlight the command and then press Enter. You also can use the shortcut keys—Ctrl+F4 to close the table window and Ctrl+F6 to activate the next table window—without first accessing the Table Control menu.

To activate the Table Control menu with the mouse, click the Table Control menu box, and then click the command you want to activate.

Changing the Size and Position of a Window

You can change the size and position of the Paradox Desktop window or a database object window by using the mouse or the keyboard. You can enlarge a window to fill the entire screen, reduce a window to a smaller but still active size, or shrink the window to an icon.

Maximizing and Restoring a Window

When maximized, the Paradox window fills the screen. When you maximize a table window, it fills the work area of the Paradox window. The Control menu of each window—both the Paradox window and each table window—has a Maximize command.

To maximize a window by using the keyboard, select the Maximize command from the appropriate menu.

To maximize a window by using a mouse, you don't need to use the Control menus. At the top right corner of the screen and of each window, you see a down triangle (the Minimize button) and an up triangle (the Maximize button). Click a window's Maximize button to enlarge the window.

When you maximize a window, the up triangle in the Maximize button changes to an up triangle and a down triangle, and the button becomes the Restore button. This button appears only if the workspace or a window is maximized. When you first load Paradox for Windows, the Paradox window is maximized, and the Restore button appears instead of the Maximize button.

If you select the Restore command or you click the Restore button, Paradox for Windows restores the window to its previous size.

Minimizing a Window

To shrink the Paradox window to an icon in the Program Manager, select the Minimize command from the Paradox for Windows Control menu, or click the Minimize button. If you are using other Program Manager applications and you want to run Paradox for Windows in the background, you can either minimize the Paradox window or use Ctrl+Esc or Alt+Tab to switch to the other application.

You can shrink a database table window in the Paradox window to an icon by selecting the Minimize command from the database's Control menu or by clicking the window's Minimize button. Minimizing table windows may be useful if you are working with several tables, forms, or reports. Each kind of window is identified by a special icon; the table icon, for example, has a grid with rows and columns, and a report icon shows a piece of paper. Figure B.5 shows examples of these two icons.

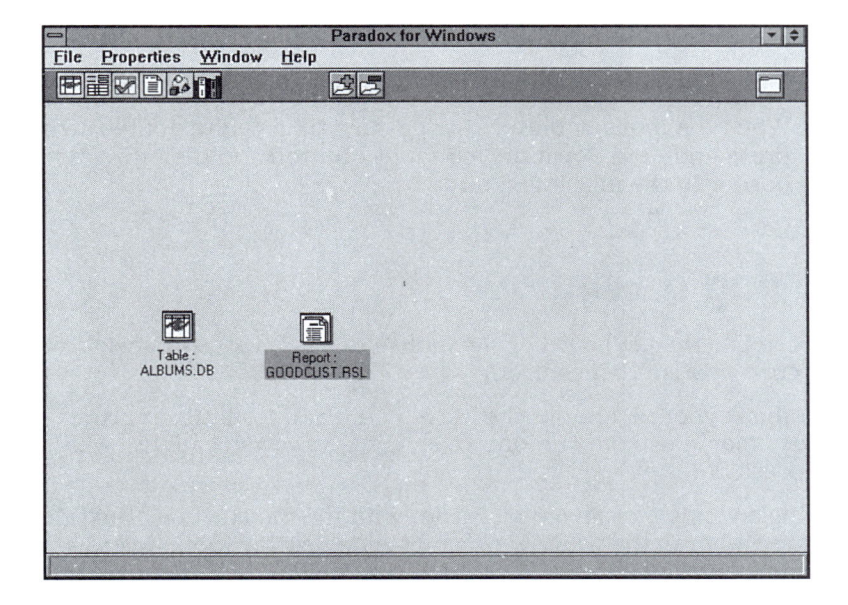

FIG. B.5
Windows reduced to icons in the Paradox Desktop window.

Sizing a Window

To change the size of a window, use the Size command from the appropriate Control menu and the cursor-movement keys, or use the mouse. Either method enables you to control the exact size of a window. You also can control the display of table windows by using the Window Tile and Window Cascade commands. The Window Tile command places all active table windows on-screen in non-overlapping positions. The Window Cascade command displays active table windows overlapping with the current window in front, and the title bar of every other active table window displayed above and behind the current window. For more information on the Window Tile and Window Cascade commands, see "Manipulating Windows" later in this appendix.

To change the size of a window using the keyboard, follow these steps:

1. Press Alt+- (hyphen) to activate the window Control menu.
2. Select Size.
3. Press the arrow key that points to the window border you want to adjust.
4. Move to the edge of the window by using the arrow keys.
5. Press Enter.

To size a window with the mouse, follow these steps:

1. Move the mouse pointer to the border you want to move.
2. When the mouse pointer changes to a thick white double arrow, press and hold down the left mouse button and then drag the border to the new location.

Moving a Window

You can use the keyboard or the mouse to move icons or a window that currently isn't maximized.

With the keyboard, choose the Move command from the appropriate Control menu, use the cursor-movement keys to relocate the window, and press Enter.

Moving a window or an icon is easier with the mouse. Click the title bar or icon and drag the window or icon to the new location. Release the left mouse button to leave the window or icon in the new position.

Closing a Window

Each Control menu has a Close command that enables you to close Paradox for Windows or a table window. To quickly close Paradox for Windows (or any Windows application window), press Alt+F4. To close a table window (or any Windows document window), press Ctrl+F4.

To close the Paradox window with the mouse, double-click the Paradox for Windows Control menu box or select the Close command from the Paradox for Windows Control menu. To close a table window, double-click the Table Control menu box or select the Close command from the Table Control menu.

If any files were created or changed, a dialog box prompts you to save changed files when you select the Close command for the Paradox window or a table window. Figure B.6 shows a dialog box similar to the one you see on-screen.

Accessing the Task List

With the Switch To command on the Paradox for Windows Control menu, you can switch to the Task List, which is a Program Manager utility that manages multiple applications. For example, you can use the Task List to switch to the Print Manager to pause or resume printing, assign a priority level to the printer, and remove print jobs from the print queue. To switch to the Task List without using the Paradox for Windows Control menu, press Ctrl+Esc.

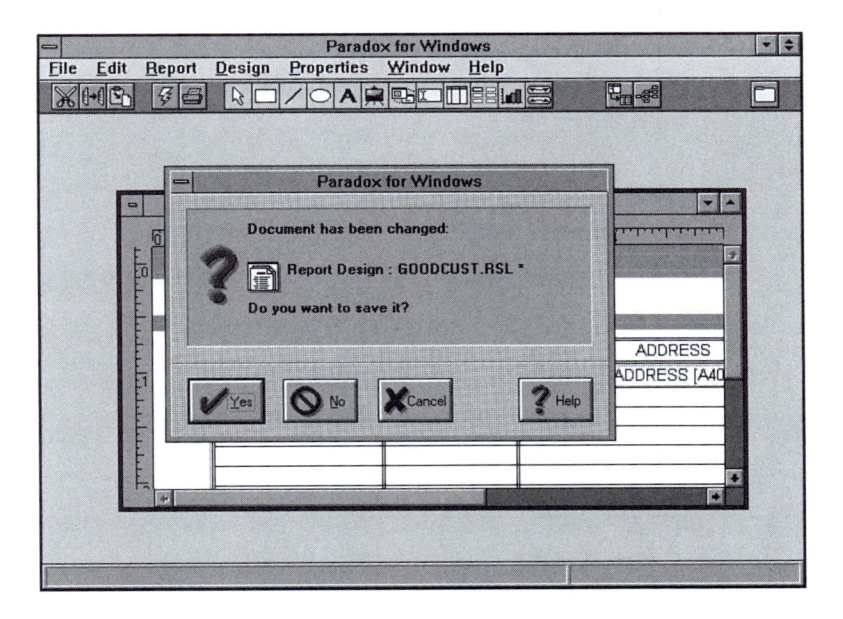

FIG. B.6
The File Exit dialog box.

Figure B.7 shows the Task List window. For more information about the Task List, refer to the Windows Program Manager documentation.

You also can switch between Windows applications by pressing Alt+Tab. If the first application that appears at the top of the screen is not the correct application, hold down the Alt key and continue to release and press Tab until the desired application title appears. To switch to the new application, release Alt.

Paradox for Windows doesn't allow you to access the Task List while a report is being sent to the printer or to the Print Manager. To switch to another application while Paradox for Windows is printing, refer to the "Sizing a Window" section earlier in this chapter.

Manipulating Windows

The Window command on the Paradox for Windows menu leads to other commands that enable you to size and arrange open windows in the table window and to make another table window active (see fig. B.8). These commands are discussed in the following sections.

USING PARADOX FOR WINDOWS, SPECIAL EDITION

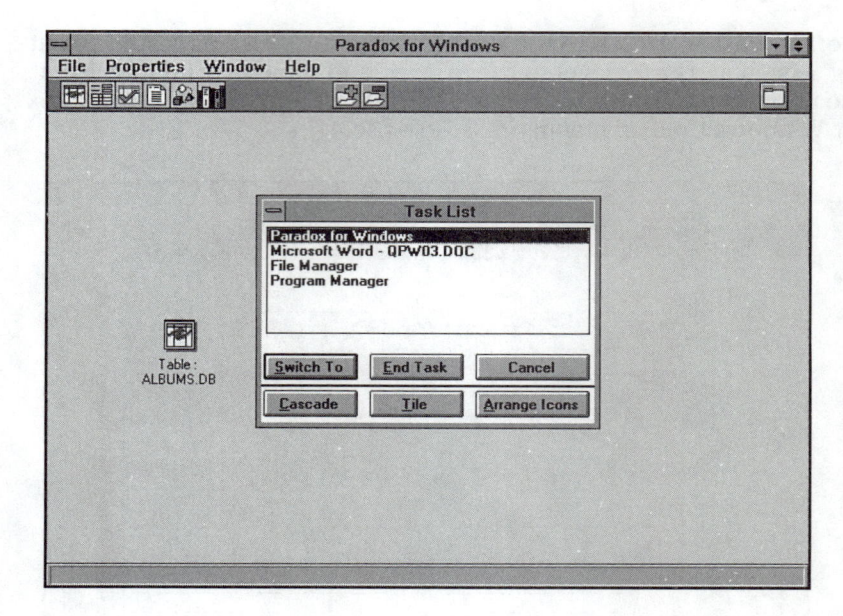

FIG. B.7
The Windows Task List.

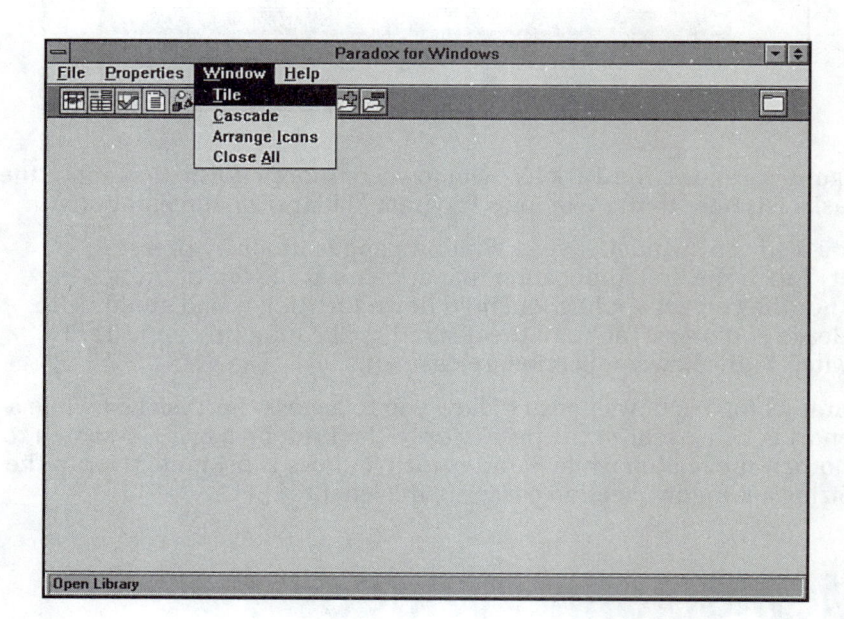

FIG. B.8
The Window menu.

Cascading Windows

The Window Cascade command arranges open windows to appear on top of one another, with only the title bars showing (see fig. B.9). The active window always appears on top.

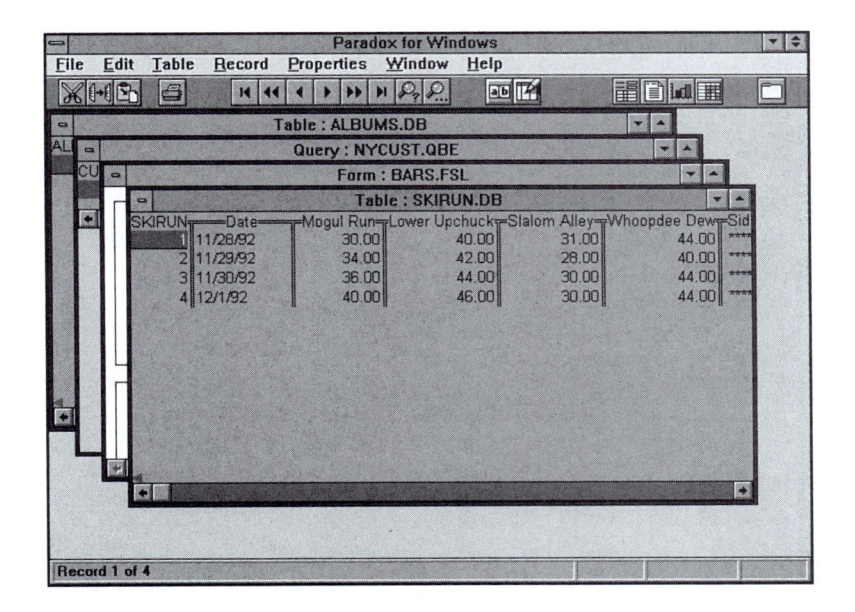

FIG. B.9

Cascaded windows.

Tiling Windows

When you choose Window Tile, Paradox for Windows sizes and arranges all open windows side by side, like floor tiles (see fig. B.10). The active window's title bar has a dark background (in standard Windows color settings).

Choosing a Window Display Mode

Besides the cascade and tile display mode options, you can drag the windows to any size or position you desire. You can display two tables side by side or up and down, use different forms with views of the same table, or maximize a window to fill the entire workspace. With all these choices, you may find choosing the best display mode difficult. The following guidelines can help you select the best display mode.

- Maximizing the window provides the largest visible work area.
- Tiling the windows enables you to view portions of several tables at the same time.
- Cascading the windows provides a large visible workspace (although not as large as maximizing a window) and makes switching between windows easy.

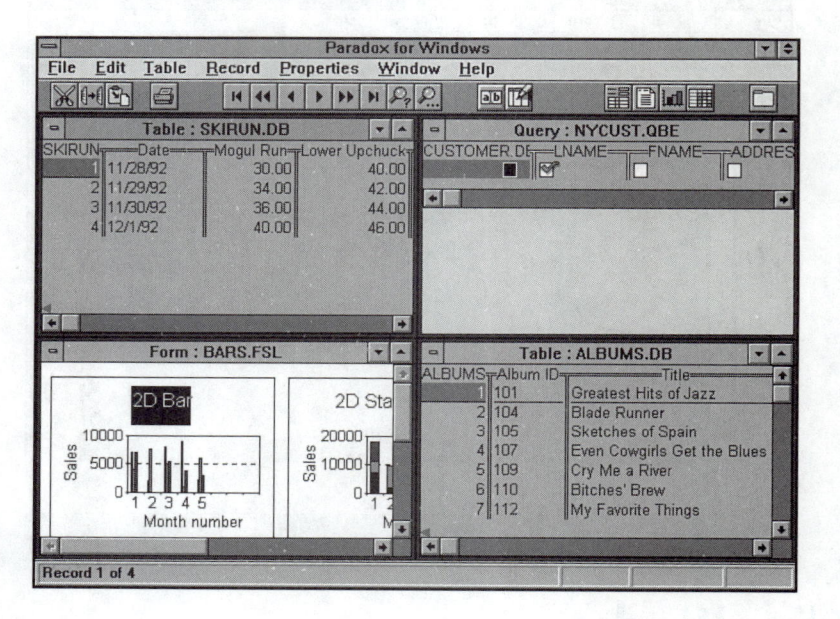

FIG. B.10

Tiled windows.

Making Another Window Active

When you choose the Window command from the Paradox main menu, the Window menu appears (refer to fig. B.8). Paradox for Windows lists open windows at the bottom of that menu, with a check mark next to the active window's name. To make another window active, press the number to the left of the window name or click the name with the mouse.

You can make another window active without using the Window menu. To cycle through the open windows, activating each window in turn, press Ctrl+F6. You also can activate a window by clicking with the mouse anywhere inside the window.

Using the Paradox for Windows Main Menu

The Paradox for Windows main menu always appears on the horizontal menu bar.

To access a command on the menu bar with the keyboard, you must first activate the menu by pressing the Alt key. An inverse video highlight, the menu pointer, appears in the menu bar. To move the menu pointer in the main menu, use the left- and right-arrow keys.

When you activate the main menu and press the right-arrow key, the menu pointer moves across the menu bar and highlights commands.

You can select a command in one of two ways: use the arrow keys to highlight the menu item and press Enter, or type the underlined letter of the menu item, usually the first letter. You cannot access the Control menus by typing an underlined letter. After the Control menus appear on-screen, however, you can type the underlined letters of the commands on the menus.

If you use the mouse to select commands, you don't need to activate the main menu first. Just click the command you want to use.

Using Pull-Down Menus and Cascade Menus

The commands on the menu bar lead to pull-down or cascade menus. Paradox for Windows uses pull-down menus to organize its first level of commands. If a command has a second level of commands, a cascade menu appears at the side of the pull-down menu (see fig. B.11). Cascade menus look and function just like pull-down menus.

> **TIP**
>
> Menu items appear with a triangle, an ellipsis (...), or nothing beside them. If the menu item has a triangle, a cascade menu appears when the item is selected. If the menu item has an ellipsis, Paradox for Windows needs more information to complete the command, and a dialog box appears when the item is selected. If the menu item has no marker, the item is the last selection in the command sequence. If you press Enter, Paradox for Windows executes the command. Figure B.11 shows all three kinds of menu items.

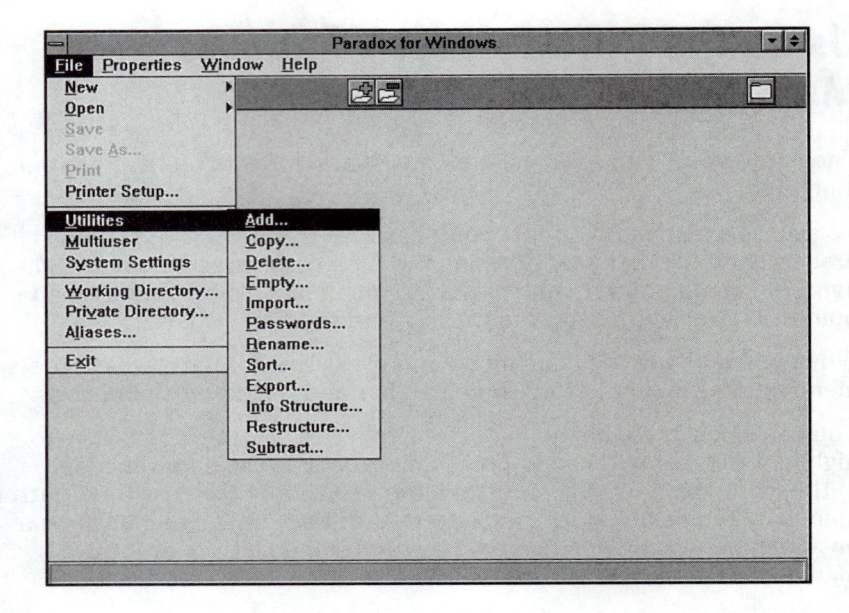

FIG. B.11

A pull-down menu with a cascade menu.

To move the menu pointer through the pull-down and cascade menus, click the command, use the up- and down-arrow keys, or type the underlined letter of the command you want to select.

By pressing Esc, you can cancel a command at any time. Depending on the selected command, the Esc key sometimes cancels the command completely, and sometimes steps back through your previous keystrokes, one menu level at a time. To cancel the command by using the mouse, click anywhere outside a menu. If a dialog box is displayed on-screen, click the Cancel button to cancel the command.

Occasionally, a menu item appears dimmed. A dimmed command is currently unavailable. When you have not opened or created an object, for example, the Save and Save As commands are unavailable and dimmed. If you select one of these commands with the keyboard or the mouse, nothing happens.

Using Object Inspectors

The Object Inspectors are an exciting new feature of Paradox for Windows. Object Inspectors are menus that appear when you point at an object with the mouse and click the right mouse button or select the appropriate Object Inspector from the pop-up properties menu. These menus include all of the major options that apply to the selected object. If you point to a text field and right-click, for example, the properties menu shown in figure B.12 appears. This menu contains settings for alignment, background color, font, text color, and data-dependent properties.

Paradox for Windows provides Object Inspectors for many types of objects.

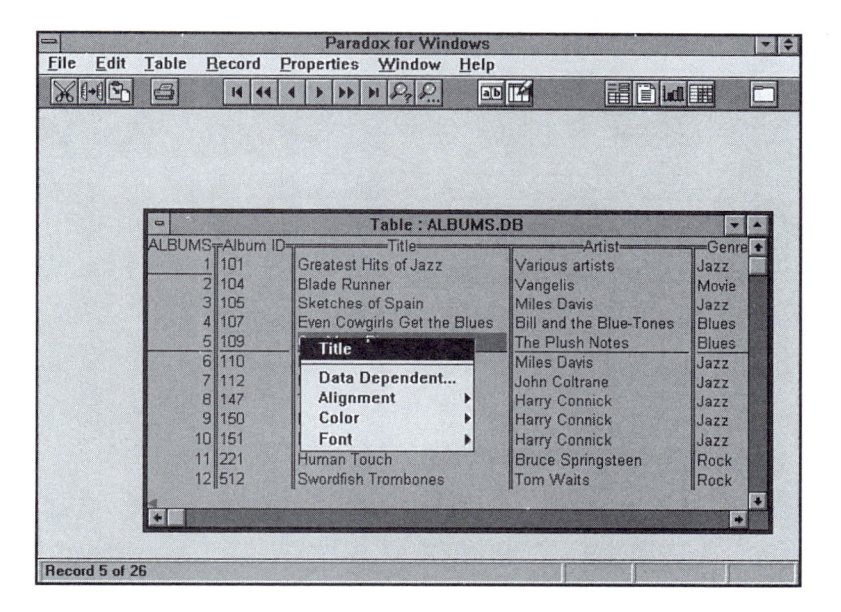

FIG. B.12

The Text field properties menu.

Using Dialog Boxes

When Paradox for Windows needs more information about a command, a dialog box is displayed. To execute the command, you must complete the dialog box and either confirm the information by choosing OK or cancel it by choosing Cancel. The following sections explain how to use dialog boxes.

Navigating within a Dialog Box

A dialog box is composed of fields, which organize choices. Before you can specify a choice, you first must select the field. Using the keyboard, you can select a field in two ways: type the underlined letter of the field or use the Tab and Shift+Tab keys to move the highlight to the field. The highlight functions much like a menu pointer: when you highlight a choice in a dialog box, you can select the choice. Not all fields have an underlined letter or can be surrounded by the highlight. This kind of field acts as a label for the choices below it. You don't need to worry about selecting these fields; you can bypass them and select the choices directly. When you select an option, the markers and the highlight move to show you the next choices. Figure B.13 shows a dialog box that contains several different kinds of fields.

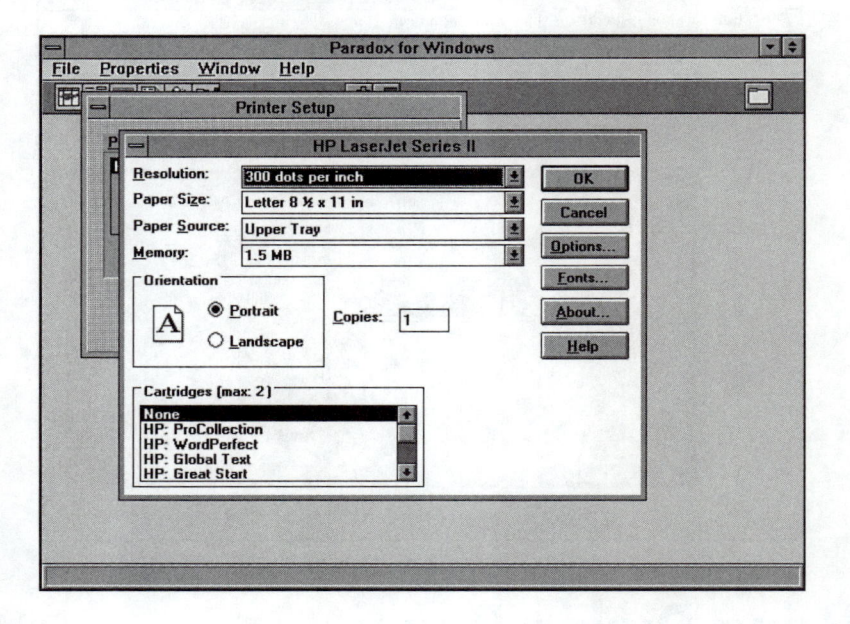

FIG. B.13

A dialog box.

If a button, such as the Options button in the Printer Setup dialog box, has three periods (an ellipsis) following the button name, an additional dialog box appears if you press the button. The Resolution field is a pull-down menu, as indicated by the arrow at the right side of the field. Click the arrow to view all the choices for the field.

Using a dialog box is usually a straightforward process, especially when it is a simple dialog box that contains a limited number of selections. Table B.3 describes the keys you use to navigate within a dialog box.

Table B.3. Cursor-Movement Key Actions in a Dialog Box

Key(s)	Action(s)
←	Moves to the preceding choice in a field
→	Moves to the following choice in a field
↑	Moves to the preceding choice in a field; in a list box, highlights the item one level up
↓	Moves to the following choice in a field; in a list box, highlights the item one level down
End	Moves to the last choice in a list box
Enter	Completes the command and closes the dialog box; toggles a selection in a check box
Esc	Closes the dialog box without completing the command; equivalent to selecting Cancel
Home	Moves to the first choice in a list box
PgDn	Scrolls down a list box
PgUp	Scrolls up a list box
Shift+Tab	Moves to the preceding field
Tab	Moves to the next field
Alt+letter	Moves to an option with the underlined letter that you press

You use Tab and Shift+Tab to move from field to field, and you use the cursor-movement keys to move from choice to choice. You press Enter to select the field or choice.

If you use a mouse, you do not need to select the field first; click the choice you want to select. Moving in a dialog box also is easier with the mouse. You can complete all sections of the dialog box before you confirm the choices by clicking OK.

Entering Information in a Dialog Box

A dialog box often contains many sections, but you rarely need to fill in every field of a dialog box. Usually, you only have to change a few fields from their default settings. Every dialog box has a title bar and command buttons. The title bar displays the command name or a description of the dialog box. When you choose a command button, you execute or cancel the command. Command buttons usually are labeled OK or Cancel.

To confirm the selections in a dialog box and execute the command, select OK. To cancel a command and close the dialog box, click Cancel or press Esc (or Ctrl+Break).

Option buttons indicate choices within a field. You can select only one option button at a time in a field; the Orientation field in the Printer Setup dialog box, for example, lists two possible settings. You can select only one choice in this field—Portrait or Landscape (refer to fig. B.13).

> **T I P**
>
> Option buttons are also known as radio buttons, because they function in a manner similar to the buttons on an automobile radio. When you select an option button, any other option button in the same field is deselected; you can select only one option button in a field at a time.

To select an option button with the keyboard, select an option by pressing Alt+ the underlined letter, or select the field by using the Tab key. Use the cursor-movement keys to move through the options and to select an option. If you select a different option button, Paradox for Windows deselects any existing selected option button.

Check boxes are square boxes that turn choices on or off. If a choice is turned on, a check mark appears in the box. To select or deselect a check box with the keyboard, first select the field using the Tab key, and then use the cursor-movement keys to move through the choices. Press Enter to select the choice and put a check mark in the check box. If the check box already contains a check mark and you press Enter, the check mark disappears, and the choice is turned off. If you use the mouse, click a check box to turn on or off the desired selection.

List boxes display lists of choices. You can select only one choice in a list box. With the keyboard, use the cursor-movement keys to highlight the choice you want, then press Enter. With the mouse, click the choice. A list box often has a text box on top that displays the currently selected choice.

If a list box has more choices than can appear on-screen, you can see all the choices by using the cursor-movement keys, including the PgUp, PgDn, Home, and End keys (see table B.3) to scroll through the list box. If you use the mouse, you can click the scroll boxes (the up and down arrows) or drag the elevator box in the scroll bar to scroll the list box.

Drop-down boxes are similar to list boxes. Drop-down boxes are used when a dialog box lacks enough room to display list boxes without covering other information. You can drop the box and see other choices in a drop-down box by clicking the mouse pointer on the down arrow. Using the keyboard, press the down-arrow key to drop the box.

Text boxes may appear with or without list boxes. When text boxes appear alone, you must enter information. Usually, you must type this information, but sometimes you can use the mouse to enter the information. Paradox for Windows, for example, often uses text boxes to ask for a table name. You can specify a table by pointing with the mouse on a list or by using the keyboard to type the name of the table.

To correct errors in text boxes by using the mouse, move the mouse pointer to the mistake, click to display the cursor, use Del and Backspace to erase the incorrect characters, and type the correct information. Characters you highlight before you begin typing are replaced by the new characters you type.

Moving a Dialog Box

Occasionally, a dialog box covers data that you need to see before you can complete the command.

You cannot use the keyboard to move a dialog box. To move the dialog box using the mouse, move the mouse pointer to the dialog box title bar, grab the title bar by pressing and holding the left mouse button, and drag the dialog box to another location.

Using SpeedBars

SpeedBars are groups of buttons that appear on the third line of the screen and serve as mouse shortcuts to many Paradox for Windows features (you cannot use SpeedBars from the keyboard). Different SpeedBars appear, depending on the current window. When you work with a database table, for example, the SpeedBar shown in figure B.14 appears.

To use the Paradox for Windows SpeedBars, point to the appropriate button with the mouse pointer and click the left mouse button. To print a table, for example, click the Print button on the SpeedBar.

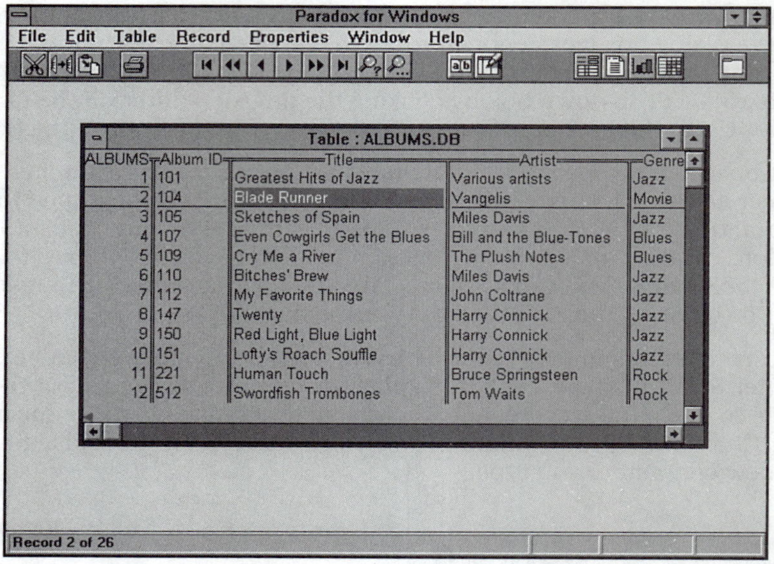

FIG. B.14

The Table SpeedBar.

Through Paradox for Windows, you have learned about the Windows graphical user interface. Because Paradox for Windows was designed as a Windows application, you can easily apply many of these skills to other Windows programs.

INDEX

Symbols

! (all values) special operator, 200
(number digit) picture character, 80, 401
& [any character (convert to uppercase)] picture character, 401
( ) (parentheses), 80
    group operators arithmetic operator, 199
    query arithmetic operator, 380
" " (quotation marks), 80
, (comma)
    alternative values picture character, 402
.. (multiple unknown) wild-card character, 188, 200
... (ellipsis), 54, 723
; (following character is literal, not picture, string character) picture character, 401
* (asterisk)
    multiplication query arithmetic operator, 199, 380
    repeat following character numerous time picture character, 402
+ (addition) query arithmetic operator, 380
- (subtraction) query arithmetic operator, 199, 380
-> (hyphen followed by greater-than symbol), 80
/ (division) query arithmetic operator, 199, 380
< (less than) comparison operator, 190, 200
<= (less than or equal to) comparison operator, 190, 200
= (equal to) comparison operator, 190, 200
> (greater than) comparison operator, 190, 200
>= (greater than or equal to) comparison operator, 190, 200
? [any letter (upper- or lowercase) picture character, 401
@ (single character) wild-card operators, 188, 200
    any character (convert to lowercase) picture character, 401
[ ] (square brackets), 80
    (optional items enclosed) picture character, 402
_ (underscore character), 80
{ } (curly braces), 80
    grouping operators picture character, 402
← keyboard shortcuts
    left one character, 134

move to preceding choice in field, 727
↑ keyboard shortcuts
highlight item one level up, 727
move to preceding choice in field, 727
previous field, 127
up one line, 134
↓ keyboard shortcuts
down one line, 134
highlight item one level down, 727
move to following choice in field, 727
next field, 127
→ keyboard shortcuts
move to following choice in field, 727
right one character, 134
1-D Summary graph type, 443
2-D Summary graph type, 443
25-character field names, 79
3-D bar graphs, 440
3COM 3Plus/3Plus Open, 5, 702

A

About box, 692-698
About menu, 668
accessing
DDE (Dynamic Data Exchange) values, 457-460
Help, 63-64, 687-691
Paradox main menu commands, 723
password levels, 416
tables with indexes, 95-98
Task List (Program Manager) utility, 718-719
utilities, 477
accumulators, 432
action method, 665, 675
activating windows, 722
Add (File menu) command, 418, 478

Add Band Report Design window SpeedBar button, 274
Add Table (Query menu)
button, 177-178
command, 174-175
Add Table dialog box, 474
adding
buttons, 237
columns, 289-290
crosstabs, 243
fields, 210, 237-243, 269, 280-283
graphics, 229-237, 278-279
graphs, 243
to forms, 364
to reports, 283
ObjectPAL
comments, 554
programs, 538-547
objects, 237
table objects, 282-283
tables to queries, 174
text, 222-229, 278
addLast array method, 600
addPopUp method, 670
addText method, 670
Adjust Size (Design menu) command, 250
aggregators
crosstabs, 432
cumulative, 432-433
defining, 432-433
normal, 432-433
unique, 432-433
Alias Manager dialog box, 498-500
aliases, 93, 208, 498-501
Working directory, 500
Aliases (File menu) command, 498
Align (Design menu) commands
Bottom, 250
Center, 250
Left, 250
Middle, 250

INDEX

Right, 250
Top, 250
aligning
  objects, 249-251
  text, 225
ALL grouping operator, 384
allDebt variable, 637
alphanumeric
  fields, 382
  types, 83-84
Alt (highlight first menu item) keyboard shortcut, 47
Alt+Backspace (Edit/Undo) keyboard shortcut, 47, 135
Alt+Esc (move to next Windows application on Desktop) keyboard shortcut, 47
Alt+F4 (close application window) keyboard shortcut, 47
Alt+H (open Help window) keyboard shortcut, 47
Alt+hyphen (open Control menu of current window) keyboard shortcut, 47
Alt+*letter* (move to option with underlined letter) keyboard shortcut, 727
Alt+Q (Query menu) command, 175-176
Alt+space bar (open Paradox Control menu) keyboard, 47
Alt+Tab (restore minimized application) keyboard shortcut, 47
Alt+underlined *letter* (select menu item) keyboard shortcut, 47
American Standard Code for Information Interchange, *see* ASCII
AND conditions, 374
Answer table, 200
  editing, 201-203
  printing, 203
  sorting, 201
Answer Table Properties dialog box, 201-202

menu command, 184, 201
Query SpeedBar button, 177-178
append array method, 600
applications
  linking, 456
  Microsoft Windows Terminal, 607
  mortgage calculator, 676-681, 698-700
approximate matches
 operators, 186-189
  LIKE, 187
  wild-card, 188-189
area, 438
area graphs, 441
arguments, 588-589
arithmetic operators
  – (subtraction), 199
  ( ) (group operators), 199, 380
  * (multiplication), 199, 380
  + (addition) query, 380
  - (subtraction) query, 380
  / (division), 199, 380
arrays, 558, 599-603
  dynamic, 602-603
  fixed, declaring, 599
  methods
    addLast, 600
    append, 600
    contains, 600
    countOf, 600
    empty, 600
    exchange, 600
    fill, 600
    grow, 600
    indexOf, 600
    insert, 600
    insertAfter, 601
    insertBefore, 601
    insertFirst, 601
    isResizable, 601
    remove, 601
    removeAllItems, 601
    removeItem, 601
    replaceItem, 601

setSize, 601
size, 601
view, 601
resizable, 600-601
arrive method, 642, 664, 670, 694
AS operator, 195, 200
ASCII (American Standard Code for Information Interchange), 84, 488
assigning variables, 558
persistance, 573
attaching ObjectPAL code, 233
Auto Refresh (File menu) command, 507
AUTOEXEC.BAT file, 707
automatic links, 470
Auxiliary Passwords dialog box, 415
AVERAGE summary operator, 383, 387
Avg summary function, 239, 280
axes, 437

B

Backspace (Delete previous character) keyboard shortcut, 135
backups for program disks, 703
Band Labels (Properties menu) command, 285
bands
    deleting, 285
    Group, 284
    Page, 284
    Record, 284
    Report, 284-287
    resizing, 285
Banyan Vines, 5, 702
bar graphs, 437-438, 450-451
    3-D, 440
    clustered, 439
    stacked, 439
basic ObjectPAL data type, 560-561

beepCounter variable, 569
binary fields, 79, 83, 87
bits, 85
Blank as Zero (File menu) command, 508
BLANK operator, 196-197, 200
Blank style option, 211, 271
blank values, 196-197
Borrow Table Structure dialog box, 106
borrowing table structures, 104-110
Box SpeedBar tools
    Forms, 215
    Report Design window, 273
boxes, 54
    drawing, 219-222, 276-278
    properties, 220, 276-277
braces, curly ({ }), 80
brackets, square ([ ]), 80
breakpoints, 544
BringToFront option, 249
BringToTop method, 653
Browse Sources (Language menu) command, 700
Browser dialog box, 230
Browser, *see* File Browser
built-in
    dialog boxes, 625
    methods, 518, 587
        editing, 527
        menuAction, 671
        mouseEnter, 615
        mouseExit, 615
Button Forms SpeedBar design tool, 216
buttonPressed variable, 657
buttons, 44, 55, 61-62
    adding, 237
    Form view SpeedBar
        Copy to Clipboard, 131
        Cut to Clipboard, 131
        Design, 131
        Edit data, 126, 131
        Field view, 131
        First record, 131

Last record, 131
Locate field value, 131
Locate next, 131
Next record, 131
Next set of records, 131
Open folder, 131
Open Table, 12
Paste from Clipboard, 131
Previous record, 131
Previous set of records, 131
Print, 131
Table view, 131
option, 728
Query SpeedBar
  Add Table, 177
  Answer Table Properties, 177
  Copy to Clipboard, 177
  Cut to Clipboard, 177
  Field View, 177
  Join Tables, 177
  Open Folder, 177
  Paste from Clipboard, 177
  Remove Table, 177
  Run Query, 177
Report Design window SpeedBar
  Add Band, 274
  Data Model, 274
  Object Tree, 274
  Print Report, 273
  View Data, 273
Table view SpeedBar
  Copy to Clipboard, 130
  Cut to Clipboard, 130
  Edit Data, 131
  Field View, 130
  Last Record, 130
  Locate Field Value, 130
  Locate Next, 130
  Next Record, 130
  Next Set of Records, 130
  Open Folder, 131
  Paste to Clipboard, 130
  Previous Record, 130

Previous Set of Records, 130
Print, 130
Quick Crosstab, 131
Quick Form, 131
Quick Graph, 131
Quick Report, 131
see also tools

C

CALC operator, 199
calcButton method, 636-639, 646
calcLoanButton methods, 647-649
calculated fields, 238-239, 280-281
calculations
  defining, 633-634
  loans, 646-649
  monthly payments, 636-639
  numeric, 381
  queries, 379-385
  payments, 620-624
  records, 380-382
calling
  dialog boxes, 655-666
  DLL (Dynamic Link Libraries) functions, 591-594
  methods, 589-590
  ObjectPAL, 591-594
  open method, 653-654
  payment calculator from mortgage calculator, 643-649
  procedures, 591
cancButton method, 641
canceling commands, 728
candidate keys, 90
Cascade commands
  Table menu, 413
  Window menu, 721
cascaded menu, 668
cascading
  menus, 723
  windows, 721
case statement, 673

casting values, 657
center tabs, 256
changeH constant, 696
CHANGETO operator, 199, 393
character field type, 87-88
check boxes, selecting, 728
Check operators
    descending, 199
    group, 199
    mark, 199
    plus, 199
check marks, 178-179
Check Syntax (Language menu)
    command, 543
check-box field, 358-360
checking data types, 556
child tables, 411
clicking, 712
clients, 455
    reports, printing, 686-687
Clipboard, 138-141
Close (Control menu) command, 718
closing
    dialog boxes, 680, 728
    Paradox for Windows, 37, 718
    windows, 718
clustered bar graphs, 439
CMY (Cyan, Magenta, Yellow)
    method, 246
code
    containers, 529
    ObjectPAL, 552-553
        attaching, 233
        comments, 554
        indentation, 554
        maximum characters, 552-553
        spaces, 552
    objects, 524
    type mismatches, 556
cold links, 469
color, 244-246
    custom, 245
    font, 160
    graphs, 449-450

screens, 160, 263
text, 227
columns, 50
    adding, 289-290
    crosstabs, 422
    deleting, 289-290
    editing, 195
    graphs, 441
    moving, 157, 289-290
    resizing, 26-27, 157-159, 289
    see also fields, 69
combining
    alphanumeric fields, 382
    table duplications, 76
    window styles, 654
commands
    accessing
        Paradox main menu, 723
    Alt+Q (Query menu), 175-176
    canceling, 728
    Control menu
        Close, 718
        Minimize, 716
        Size, 717
        Switch To, 464, 718
    Debug menu
        Inspect, 545
        Set Breakpoint, 544
    Design menu
        Adjust Size, 250
        Adjust Size, Maximum Height, 251
        Adjust Size, Maximum Width, 251
        Adjust Size, Minimum Height, 251
        Adjust Size, Minimum Width, 251
        Align, Align Bottom, 250
        Align, Align Center, 250
        Align, Align Left, 250
        Align, Align Middle, 250
        Align, Align Right, 250
        Align, Align Top, 250
        Group, 248
        Ungroup, 249

INDEX

Ditto keystroke, 142
DOS
   DEL, 708
   DISKCOPY, 703
   RD, 708
Edit menu
   Paste Link, 467
   Undo, 144
Edit mode menu
   Record, 152
File menu
   Aliases, 498
   Delete, 708
   Exit, 37
   Multiuser, Display Locks, 502
   Multiuser, Set Locks, 503
   Multiuser, Set Retry, 506
   Multiuser, User Name, 504
   Multiuser, Who, 505
   New, 77
   New, Form, 208, 343, 519, 630
   New, Query, 172
   New, Report, 267
   ODAPI, 509
   Open, Form, 474
   Open, Table, 35, 96
   Print, 422
   Printer Setup, 293
   Private Directory, 501
   Run, 703
   Save, 203, 259
   Save As, 203, 630
   System Settings, Auto Refresh, 507
   System Settings, Blank as Zero, 508
   System Settings, Drivers, 508
   Utilities, 110, 477
   Utilities, Add, 418, 478
   Utilities, Copy, 496
   Utilities, Delete, 497
   Utilities, Empty, 497
   Utilities, Export, 493
   Utilities, Import, 486
   Utilities, Rename, 495
   Utilities, Sort, 482
   Utilities, Subtract, 480
   Working Directory, 500
Grid properties menu
   Row Lines, 166
Language menu
   Browse Sources, 700
   Check Syntax, 543
   Properties, 533
   Types, 540
Locate menu
   Replace, 146
   Value, 146
New menu
   Table, 77
ObjectPAL Debugger
   Enable Ctrl+Break To Debugger, 537
   Enable DEBUG, 537
   Inspect, 537
   List Breakpoints, 537
   Origin, 537
   Quit This Method, 538
   Run, 538
   Set Breakpoint, 537
   Stack Backtrace, 537
   Step Into, 538
   Step Over, 537
   Trace Built-ins, 537
   Trace Execution, 537
ObjectPAL Editor
   Constants, 534
   Edit, Copy, 530
   Edit, Cut, 530
   Edit, Delete, 531
   Edit, Go To, 531
   Edit, Paste, 530
   Edit, Replace, 531
   Edit, Replace Next, 531
   Edit, Search, 531
   Edit, Search Next, 531
   Edit, Select All, 530
   Properties (Language menu), 533

commands (continued)
   Options menu
     Properties, 230
   Paradox main menu
     Window, 722
   Properties menu
     Answer Table, 184, 201
     Answer Table, Sort, 184
     Band Labels, 285
     Current Object, 218
     Data Dependent, 162
     Expanded Ruler, 255
     Form, 654
     Form, Deliver, 700
     Form, Window Style, 655
     Grid Settings, 254
     Methods, 520, 567-568, 664
     Preferred, Report, 267
     Restore, 166
     Save, 166
     Show Grid, 257
     Snap to Grid, 257
     Sort, 201
     View Properties, 166
     Zoom, 258
   Query menu
     Add Table, 174-175
     Field View, 175
     Remove Table, 175
     Run, 175
     Run Query, 371
     Wait for DDE, 175
   Record menu
     First, 262
     Last, 262
     Next, 262
     Next set, 262
     Previous, 262
     Previous set, 262
   Report menu
     Deliver, 700
   Save As, 109
   Table menu
     Info Structure, 109
     Restructure, 100, 203, 405
     Sort, 181

   Update Rule, Cascade, 413
   Update Rule, Prohibit, 413
   Window, 719
   Window Cascade, 721
   Window Tile, 721
comments
   ObjectPAL
     adding, 554
     code, 554
comparing records, 385-388
comparison operators
   < (less than), 190, 200
   <= (less than or equal to),
     190, 200
   = (equal to), 190, 200
   > (greater than), 190, 200
   >= (greater than or equal to),
     190, 200
composite keys, 70, 92-93
concatenation strings, 552, 635
conditions of multi-table
   queries, 374-375
CONFIG.SYS file, 707
Const window, constants,
   declaring, 570-575
constants, 534
   changeH, 696
   declaring, 564-565, 570
     Const window, 570-575
     ObjectPAL, 564-565
   defining, 696
   global, 574
   scopes, 567-575
     containership hierarchy,
       567-568
   startH, 696
   WindowStyle, 654
Constants (Language menu)
   command, 534
containership hierarchy scopes,
   516-517
   constants, 567-568
   variables, 567-568
contains array method, 600
contains DynArray method, 603

INDEX

Control menus, 41-42
  commands
    Close, 718
    Minimize, 716
    Size, 717
    Switch To, 464, 718
  menus, 713-715
control structures
  loops
    for, 582-583
    scan, 583-585
    while, 585-587
  statements
    if, 578-580
    immediate if (iif), 580-581
    endswitch, 581
    switch, 581
    try, 581-582
controlling
  ObjectPAL
    keyboard shortcuts, 548-549
    mouse, 548-549
  printers, 293
conversion types
  dBASE, 116
  fields, 115-116
converting values, 657
Copy commands
  File menu, 496
  ObjectPAL Editor, 530
Copy to Clipboard SpeedBar buttons
  Form SpeedBar, 131
  Query, 177-178
  Table, 130
copying
  tables, 496-497
  values, 143
Count summary function, 238, 280
COUNT summary operator, 383
countOf array method, 600
Create dialog boxes
  Paradox for Windows Table, 82

Create Table or Restructure Table, 81. 347, 400
creating
  crosstabs, 422-436
  data
    models, 343-346
    types, 566-567
  drop-down edit fields, 351-354
  expressions, 577
  forms, 207-215, 693-694
  multi-table, 336-349
  payment calculator, 630-642
  graphs, 436-451
  joins, 376-379
  menus, 668-670
  methods, custom, 596-598
  mortgage calculator
    fields, 610
    forms, 609-613
    tables, 658-664
  ObjectPAL dialog boxes, 525
  objects, 57-59, 688
  OLE (Object Linking and Embedding) objects, 462-466
  passwords, 414
  procedures, 594-596
  queries, 172-174
    INSERT, 390
    multi-table, 366-373
  records, 566-567
  reports, 267-272, 686
  Search dialog box forms, 676-681
  tables, 17-21, 76-94, 311-313
    graphs, 332
  variables, 557
cross tabulation, *see* crosstabs
Crosstab Forms SpeedBar
  design tool, 216
crosstabs, 55
  adding, 243
  aggregators, 432
    cumulative, 433
    normal, 432
    unique, 433

columns, 422
creating, 330-332, 422-436, 425
data model, 435-436
fields, 434
multi-table, 435-436
one-dimensional, 422-428
printing, 422
properties, 433-434
rows, 422
two-dimensional, 428-430
viewing, 427
Ctrl+← keyboard shortcuts
left one word, 135
previous word first letter, 129
Ctrl+→ keyboard shortcuts
next word first letter, 128
right one word, 135
Ctrl+A (Search Next) keyboard shortcut, 47
Ctrl+Backspace keyboard shortcuts
delete previous word, 135
delete word left of cursor, 129
Ctrl+C (Copy selected object) keyboard shortcut, 48
Ctrl+D keyboard shortcuts
ditto, 142
repeat last entry, 47-48
Ctrl+End (end of field) keyboard shortcut, 127-128
Ctrl+Enter (Super tab) keyboard shortcut, 48
Ctrl+Esc (switch to other application) keyboard shortcut, 47
Ctrl+F (Field view) keyboard shortcut, 47
Ctrl+F2 (Persistent Field view) keyboard shortcut, 48
Ctrl+F5 (Post/Keep locked) keyboard shortcut, 49
Ctrl+F6 (activate windows) keyboard shortcut, 722
Ctrl+F7 (Quick graph) keyboard shortcut, 49
Ctrl+F11 (First record) keyboard shortcut, 49

Ctrl+F12 (Last record) keyboard shortcut, 49
Ctrl+G keyboard shortcuts
Grid menu, 47
grid properties, 160
Ctrl+H (current column header) keyboard shortcut, 47, 160
Ctrl+Home keyboard shortcuts
beginning of field, 128
beginning of memo field, 134
first record in first field, 127
Ctrl+Ins (Edit/Copy) keyboard shortcut, 47, 135
Ctrl+L (Lock record) keyboard shortcut, 47-48
Ctrl+M keyboard shortcuts
current data column, 160
field properties for current column/object, 48
Ctrl+PgDn (right one screen) keyboard shortcut, 134
Ctrl+PgUp (left one screen) keyboard shortcut, 134
Ctrl+R (rotate) keyboard shortcut, 48, 157
Ctrl+T (Memo view) keyboard shortcut, 48
Ctrl+Z (Locate value) keyboard shortcut, 48, 146
cumulative aggregators, 432-433
curly braces ({ }), 80
currency
field type, 83-85
record marker, 165
Current dialog boxes
Drivers, 508
Users, 505
current forms, printing, 681-686
Current Object (Properties menu) command, 218
cursor, 261
custom, 596-598
methods, 587
fileExitM, 673-675
getHelpM, 687, 691
printCurrM, 683-686

INDEX 741

showAboutM, 693
undoEditM, 676
procedures, 594-596
customizing database objects, 710
Cut ObjectPAL Editor command, 530
Cut to Clipboard SpeedBar buttons
    Form, 131
    Query, 177-178
    Table, 130
cutting values, 143

D

data
    editing, 143-145
    entering, 22-27
        dialog boxes, 727-729
        graphic fields, 137-143
        in Form view, 27-29
        mortgage calculator, 664-665
    exchanging, 455-471
    importing from spreadsheets, 486-488
    integrity, 4
    model crosstabs, 340-346, 435-436, 561-562
    ObjectPAL types, 560-563
        basic, 560-561
        data models, 561
        data objects, 562
        design objects, 561
        display managers, 562
        DLL (Dynamic Link Libraries), 563
        events, 563
    objects, scoping, 528
    OLE (Object Linking and Embedding) fields, 142
    organizing normalization, 74
    properties, 166
    types, 556, 566-567
    validating, 99-104
    viewing, 124-125
Data Dependent (Properties menu) command, 162
Data Dependent Properties dialog box, 162
Data Model
    Forms SpeedBar design tool, 243
    Report Design window SpeedBar button, 274
Data Model dialog box, 208-209, 343
data-dependent properties, 162-164
data-entry
    date formats, 132
    locks, 155
    modes
        Edit, 125-127
        Field view, 128-130
        Form view, 124-125
        Non-field view, 128-130
        Table view, 124-125
        View, 125-127
database management systems (DBMSs), 170-171
databases
    flat-file, 68
    objects, customzing, 710
    relational, 68
        primary keys, 70
        referential integrity, 68, 72
        tables, 50-51
    reports, 303
    tables, 69-70
date
    field types, 83-88, 132-133
    format, data-entry, 132
DB (Paradox database table) file type, 476
dBASE, field types
    character, 87-88
    date, 87-88
    float number, 87-88
    logic, 87-88

memo, 87-88
number, 87-88
table types
logical fields, 78
view deleted records, 78
types, conversions, 116
dBASE IV, indexes, 97-98
DBF (dBASE-compatible database table) file type, 476
DBMSs (database management systems), 68, 170-171
DDE (Dynamic Data Exchange), 456-461
automatic links, 470
capacity, 470
memory requirements, 470
servers, 470
speed, 470
storage requirements, 470
values, accessing, 457-460
debt-to-income ratio, 637
Debug menu commands
Inspect, 545
Set Breakpoint, 544
Debugger, *see* ObjectPAL, Debugger
decimal tabs, 256
declarations of variables
ObjectPAL, 557-560
Var section, 568-570
Var window, 570-574
declaring
arrays
fixed, 599
resizable, 600-601
Const window constants, 570-575
constants, 570
dynamic arrays, 602-603
ObjectPAL
constants, 564-565
variables, 555-563
default derivation formulas in tables, 3
default value validity checks, 101-102

Define dialog boxes
Crosstab dialog box, 423-425
Field Object dialog box, 238
functions, 238-23
Graph, 442
Group, 299
Link, 344
List, 356
List of Items, 677
Secondary Index, 96, 347
Table Object, 290
defining
aggregators, 432-433
calculations, 633-634
constants, 696
fields, summary, 239
forms, 360-361
primary keys, 90-93
variables, 696
deinstalling Paradox for Windows, 708
Del (Delete) keyboard shortcut, 47, 129, 135
DEL DOS command, 708
Delete commands
File menu, 497, 708
ObjectPAL Editor, 531
DELETE operator, 199, 392
deleting
bands, 285
columns, 289-290
fields, 210-241, 270, 288
repeating, 74-75
records, 145
from multiple tables, 480-481
referential integrity, 413
tables
fields, 74-75, 118
from queries, 175
records, 392-393
Delimited ASCII Import dialog box, 490
Deliver commands
Form menu, 700
Report menu, 700

INDEX

deselecting objects, 217, 275
Design (Form SpeedBar) button, 131
design
  documents, 205, 462
  layout fields, 210-211
  object types, 49
    boxes, 54
    buttons, 55
    crosstabs, 55
    ellipses (...), 54
    fields, 55
    graphics, 55
    graphs, 55
    lines, 54
    multi-record objects, 55
    OLE objects, 56
    tables, 55
Design Layout dialog box, 209, 345
Design menu
  commands
    Adjust Size, 250
    Adjust Size, Maximum Height, 251
    Adjust Size, Maximum Width, 251
    Adjust Size, Minimum Height, 251
    Adjust Size, Minimum Width, 251
    Align, Align Bottom, 250
    Align, Align Center, 250
    Align, Align Left, 250
    Align, Align Middle, 250
    Align, Align Right, 250
    Align, Align Top, 250
    Group, 248
    Ungroup, 249
  options
    Bring to Front, 249
    Send to Back, 249
design objects, text, 54
design objects ObjectPAL data type, 561

design tools
  Forms SpeedBar
    Box, 215
    Button, 216
    Crosstab, 216
    Data Model, 243
    Ellipse, 215
    Field, 216
    Graph, 216
    Graphic, 215
    Line, 215
    Multi-record, 216
    Object Tree, 243
    OLE (Object Linking and Embedding), 215
    Selection Arrow, 215
    Table, 216
    Text, 215
Designer Properties dialog box, 61, 252
designing reports, 302-305
Desktop, 40-46
  Control menu, 41-42
  icons
    Maximize, 42
    Minimize, 42
  menu bar, 42-44
  menus
    File, 43
    Help, 43
    Properties, 43
    Window, 43
  message area, 46
  SpeedBar, 44
  title bar, 41
detail tables, 337
dialog boxes, 60, 626, 655-666, 725-729
  built-in, 625
  closing, 680, 728
  creating
    ObjectPAL, 525
  data, entering, 727-729
  fields, 725-727
  moving, 729

directories
   private, 501
   switching, 208
   tables, viewing, 478
   Working in aliases, 500
DISKCOPY DOS command, 703
disk, program backups, 703
Display Locks (File menu) command, 502
Display Locks option, 154
display manager ObjectPAL data type, 562
Display Objects and Properties dialog box, 533
displaying
   forms, 653-655
   messages, help, 649
   ObjectPAL messages, 615-619
   table structures, 109
   windows options, 721-722
Ditto keystroke command, 142
DLL (Dynamic Link Library)
   functions, calling, 591-594
   ObjectPAL, 591-594
DLL ObjectPAL data type, 563
documents, design, 205, 462
DOS
   commands
      DEL, 708
      DISKCOPY, 703
      RD, 708
   utilities
      SHARE, 706-707
double-clicking, 712
drag and drop, 713
dragging, 712
drawing
   boxes, 219-222, 276-278
   ellipses, 219-222, 276-278
   lines, 219-222, 276-278
Drivers (File menu) command, 508
drop-down
   boxes, 729
   edit box, 613
   edit fields, creating, 351-354

duplicate records
   replacing, 479
duplications
   fields, 179-181
   records, preventing, 70, 479
   tables, combining, 76
dynamic arrays, 602-603
Dynamic Data Exchange, *see* DDE
DynArray methods
   contains, 603
   getKeys, 603
   removeItem, 603
   size, 603
   view, 603

E

Edit data SpeedBar buttons
   Data, 126
   Form, 131
   Table, 131
Edit data-entry mode, 125-127
   data
      editing, 143-145
   records
      inserting, 152-153
Edit data-entry mode menu
   commands
      Record, 152
edit fields
   drop-down, 351-354
Edit menu
   commands
      Paste Link, 467
      Undo, 144
Edit mode
   starting, 665
EDIT text editor, 707
editing
   AUTOEXEC.BAT file, 707
   columns, 195
   CONFIG.SYS file, 707
   data, 143-145
   fonts, 156
   graphic properties, 141-142

INDEX

methods
    built-in, 527
mortgage calculator, 643, 658-664
objects, responses, 518
records, 393-394
referential integrity, 414
tables, 156-167
    fields, 115-118
    with queries, 388-394
editing Answer table, 201-203
Editors, ObjectPAL, 527-536
EDLIN text editor, 707
Ellipse
    Forms SpeedBar design tools, 215
    Report Design window SpeedBar tool, 273
ellipses, 54, 723
    drawing, 219-222, 276-278
    properties, 220, 276-277
embedded objects, 247-248, 461
Empty (File menu) command, 497
empty array method, 600
Enable Ctrl+Break To Debugger ObjectPAL Debugger c, 537
Enable DEBUG ObjectPAL Debugger command, 537
encapsulation, 549, 550
End (current record last field) keyboard shortcut, 127-128, 134, 727
endswitch statement, 581
Enter (Insert carriage return/line fine) keyboard shortcut, 135, 415, 727
entering
    data, 22-27
        dialog boxes, 727-729
        graphic fields, 137-143
        in Form view, 27-29
        into memo fields, 133-136
        mortgage calculator, 664-665
    field values, 399

entities, 17, 69
    weak, 342
enumSource method, 535
equal to (=) comparison operator, 190
error queries, 176
Esc (close menu) keyboard shortcut, 47, 135, 727
event-driven interfaces, ObjectPAL, 517-519
eventInfo variable, 672
events, 548
    receiving, 672
    target objects, 672
events ObjectPAL data type, 563
EVERY summary operator, 387
exact matches, searching, 185-186
EXACTLY summary operator, 387
exchange array method, 600
exchanging data, 455-471
exclusive table criteria, 373
executeQBE method, 685
executing
    mortgage calculator, 663
    programs
        INSTALL, 703-708
    queries, 685
Exit (File menu) command, 37
Expanded Ruler (Properties menu) command, 255
expanded rulers, 255-256
exploding pie graphs, 451
Export (File menu) command, 493
exporting tables to spreadsheets, 492-493
expressions, 577
extendability, 4
extensions of files, 476-477

F

F (Form) file type, 476
F1 (access context-sensitive help) keyboard shortcut, 47-48

F2 (Field view) keyboard shortcut, 48
F3 (Super back tab) keyboard shortcut, 48
F4 (Super tab) keyboard shortcut, 48
F5 (Lock record) keyboard shortcut, 49
F6 (Inspect properties) keyboard shortcut, 49
F7 (Quick form) keyboard shortcut, 49
F8 (View data) keyboard shortcut, 49
F9 (Enter/exit edit mode) keyboard shortcut, 49
F10 (Menu) keyboard shortcut, 49
F11 (Previous record) keyboard shortcut, 49
F12 (Next record) keyboard shortcut, 49
fail method, 581
FDL (Form) file type, 476
Field
    Forms SpeedBar design tool, 216
    Report Design window, SpeedBar tool, 273
field types
    dBASE
        character, 87-88
        date, 87-88
        float number, 87-88
        logic, 87-88
        memo, 87-88
        number, 87-88
    unsupported, 88-89
Field view (Form SpeedBar) button, 131
Field View (Query menu) command, 175
Field View (SpeedBar, Query) button, 177-178
Field View (Table SpeedBar) button, 130

Field view data-entry mode, 128-130
fields, 17, 50, 55, 323
    adding, 210, 237-243
        to reports, 280-283
    alphanumeric, 382
    binary, 79
    calculated, 238-239, 280-281
    check marks, 178-179
    check-box, 358-360
    creating, 610
    crosstabs, 434
    data, OLE (Object Linking and Embedding), 142
    date, 132-133
    deleting, 210, 241, 270, 288
        tables, 74-75, 118
    design layouts, 210-211
    dialog boxes, 725-727
    drop-down edit, 351-354
    editing tables, 115-118
    fonts, editing, 156
    graphic, 79, 198
    inserting tables, 118
    key, 482
    labels, 210, 262-263
    list, 354-355
    locating, 146-147
    logical, 79
    maxDI, 642
    memo, 133-136, 198
        formatted, 79, 136-137
    messages, 619
        ObjectPAL, 619
    names
        25-character, 79
        referencing, 661
        specifying, 79-82
    OLE (Object Linking and Embedding), 79, 467
    Read Only, 238
    reformatting, 242
        reports, 282
    regular, 237-238, 280, 287
    repeating
        deleting, 74-75

INDEX

reports, 269
required, 100
rights, 415-417
selecting, 178-184
sizing tables, 89
sorting, 181
special, 240-241, 281-282
   defining, 351-361
summary, defining, 239
switching tables, 126
system, 240
types, 82-89
   alphanumeric, 83-84
   binary, 83, 87-119
   conversions, 115-116
   currency, 83-85
   date, 83-87
   formatted memo, 83, 86
   graphic, 83, 86
   memo, 83, 86
   number, 83-85
   OLE (Object Linking and Embedding), 83, 86-87
   short number, 83-85
values
   duplicates, 179-181
   entering, 399
File Browser feature, 474-477
File Browser window, 59
File dialog boxes
   Export, 474
   Import, 474, 486
File menu commands, 43, 668
   Aliases, 498
   Delete, 708
   Exit, 37
   Multiuser, 502-506
   Multiuser, Display Locks, 502
   Multiuser, Set Locks, 503
   Multiuser, Set Retry, 506
   Multiuser, User Name, 504
   Multiuser, Who, 505
   New, 77, 172
   New, Form, 208, 343, 519, 630
   New, Query, 172
   New, Report, 267

   New, Table, 77
   ODAPI, 509
   Open, Form, 474
   Open, Table, 35, 96
   Print, 422
   Printer Setup, 293
   Private Directory, 501
   Run, 703
   Save, 203, 259
   Save As, 203, 630
   System Settings, Auto Refresh, 507
   System Settings, Blank as Zero, 508
   Table, Info Structure, 109
   Table, Restructure, 100
   Utilities, 110, 418, 477
   Utilities, Add, 418, 478
   Utilities, Copy, 496
   Utilities, Delete, 497
   Utilities, Empty, 497
   Utilities, Export, 493
   Utilities, Import, 486
   Utilities, Rename, 495
   Utilities, Sort, 482
   Utilities, Subtract, 480
   Working Directory, 500
file servers, 153
fileExitM custom method, 673-675
files
   AUTOEXEC.BAT, editing, 707
   CONFIG.SYS, editing, 707
   extensions, 476-477
   graphics, selecting, 138
   locks, 502
   queries, 682
   README.TXT
      viewing, 708
   samples, installing, 704-706
   text, importing, 488-492
   types
      DB (Paradox database table), 476
      DBF (dBASE-compatible database table), 476

F (Form), 476
FDL (Form), 476
FSL (Form), 476
FTL (Compiled Form), 476
MB (Memo/BLOB data associated with table), 476
PX (Primary Index), 476
QBE (Query By Example), 476
RDL (Report), 476
RSL (Report), 476
SDL (Script), 476
SQL (SQL query), 476
SSL (Script), 476
TV (Table View Settings), 477
VAL (Validation checks associated with table), 477
X01 (Table index), 477
Y01 (Table index), 477
fill array method, 600
filters, 362-364
financial reports, 303
FIND operator, 199
finding, *see* locating
First (Record menu) command, 131, 262
fixed arrays, 599
fixed decimal point number, 84
fixed-length text, 488
flat-file databases, 68
flickering screens, 253
float number field type, 87, 88
floating decimal point number, 84
fonts, 160
  color, 160
  editing, 156
  selecting, 226
  size, 160
  style, 160
  typeface, 160
footers in reports, 286
for loops, 582-583
foreign keys, 70, 314

Form commands
  File menu, 343, 474, 519, 630
  Properties menu, 654
Form Design window, 215-237
  graphics, 229-237
  menus, Properties, 218
  objects
    deselecting, 217
    moving, 217
    selecting, 217-218
  text, 222-229
Form menu command, Deliver, 700
Form SpeedBar buttons
  Copy to Clipboard, 131
  Cut to Clipboard, 131
  Design, 131
  Edit data, 131
  Field view, 131
  First Record, 131
  Last record, 131
  Locate field value, 131
  Locate next, 131
  Next record, 131
  Next set of records, 131
  Open folder, 131
  Paste from Clipboard, 131
  Previous record, 131
  Previous set of records, 131
  Print, 131
  Table view, 131
Form view, 27-29
Form view data-entry
  keyboard shortcuts, 127
  mode, 124-125
Form Window Properties dialog box, 655, 678-680
format codes, 405
formats, date, 132
formatted memo fields, 83, 86, 136-137
formReturn method, 646
forms, 51, 206-207
  creating, 207-215, 693-694
    mortgage calculator, 609-613
    Search dialog box, 676-681

current, printing, 681-686
defining, 360-361
displaying, 653-655
filters, 362-364
graphs, adding, 364
layering, 653
modal, 652
multi-table, 324-326, 336-349
non-modal, 652
objects
   forms, 361-364
   tables, 361-364
opening, 653-655
payment calculator, 630-642
renaming, 496, 564
saving, 259
testing, 260-262
window styles, 654
Forms SpeedBar design tool
   Data Model, 243
   Object Tree, 243
formulas, default derivation in tables, 3
frames, 438
FSL (Form) file type, 476
FTL (Compiled Form) file type, 476
functions
   calling
      DLL (Dynamic Link Library), 591-594
   summary
      Avg, 239, 280
      Count, 238, 280
      Max, 238, 280
      Min, 238, 280
      Std, 238, 280
      Sum, 238, 280
      Var, 239, 280

G

general procedures, 541
getHelpM custom method, 687, 691
getHelpM method, 691
getKeys DynArray method, 603
getPayment method, 643-646
getPayment::pushButton method, 680
global
   constants, 574
   variables, 574
Go To ObjectPAL Editor command, 531
grabbing, 712
Graph tools
   Forms SpeedBar design, 216
   Report Design window, 274
Graph area, 438
Graphic SpeedBar tools
   Forms, 215
   Report Design window, 273
Graphic data type, 4
graphic field type, 83, 86
graphic fields, 79, 198
   data, entering, 137-143
graphic properties, editing, 141-142
graphical user interface (GUI), 39, 606-608, 709-730
graphics, 55
   adding, 229-237
      to reports, 278-279
   legends, 438
   moving, 138-142
   scaling, 232
   selecting files, 138
graphics programs
   Harvard Graphics, 437
   Lotus Freelance, 437
   Microsoft Powerpoint, 437
graphs, 55
   adding, 243
      to forms, 364
      to reports, 283
   area, 437, 441
   axes, 437
   bar, 438, 450-451
      3-D, 440
   bars, 437
      clustered, 439
      stacked, 439

color, 449-450
columns, 441
creating, 332, 436-451
frames, 437
grid lines, 437
labels, 437
legends, 437
line, 440
marker, 441
objects, 442-443
pattern, 449-450
pie, 440, 450-451
pies, exploding, 451
printing, 451-452
properties, 444-445
scales, 437
scatter, 441
series, 437, 450
slices, 441
tick marks, 437
titles, 437
types
   1-D Summary, 443
   2-D Summary, 443
   Tabular, 443
x-y, 441
greater than (>) comparison operator, 190
greater than or equal to (>=) comparison operator, 190
grid
   lines, 438
   properties, 165-166
Grid properties menu command, Row Lines, 166
Grid Settings
   dialog box, 254
   Properties menu command, 254
grids, 257
Group (Design menu) command, 248
Group band, 284
grouping
   objects, 248-249
   operators
      ALL, 384

      UNIQUE, 384
   records, 382-385
      in reports, 299-301
grow array method, 600
GUI (graphical user interface), 4, 39, 709-730

H

handles, 56, 217, 555, 559-560
   TCursor, 549
Harvard Graphics graphics program, 437
headers in reports, 286
heading properties, 165
height, rows, 159
Help
   accessing, 63-64, 687-691
   menu, 43, 668
   messages, 649
helpOnHelp method, 700
helpQuit method, 700
helpSetIndex method, 700
helpShowContext method, 700
helpShowIndex method, 700
helpShowTopic method, 700
helpShowTopicInKeyword method, 700
hideSpeedBar method, 699
hierarchy, containership, 516, 517
Home (Beginning of field) keyboard shortcut, 127-128, 134, 727
hot key, 43
HSV (Hue, Saturation, Value) method, 246
hyphen followed by greater-than symbol (->), 80

I

icons
   Maximize, 42
   Minimize, 42
IDE (integrated development environment), 514

if statements, 578-580, 665, 690
immediate if (iif) statements, 580-581
Import (File menu) command, 486
importing
   data from spreadsheets, 486-488
   text files, 488-492
incH variable, 696
inclusive table criteria, 373
indentation, ObjectPAL code, 554-556
indexes
   dBASE IV, 97-98
   pointers, 95
   secondary, 95, 314-315, 346-348
   tables, accessing, 95-98
   unique, 97
indexOf array method, 600
indicators, keys, 91
Info Structure (Table menu) command, 109
inheritance, 549
initializing, variables, 558-559
inner joins, 377
insert array method, 600
INSERT operator, 199, 390-391
insertAfter array method, 601
insertBefore array method, 601
insertFirst array method, 601
inserting
   records, 152-153, 389-391
   tables fields, 118
Inspect (Debug menu) command, 545
Inspect dialog box, 545
Inspect ObjectPAL Debugger command, 537
inspecting object properties, 57
Installation dialog box, 704
installing
   file samples, 704-706
   requirements, 702
Installing dialog box, 706
integers, 84

integrated debugger, 537
integrated development environment (IDE), 514
integrity, referential, 68, 316-318, 397
   databases, 72
   tables, 410-414
interacting ObjectPAL users, 608-624
interfaces, event-driven, ObjectPAL, 517-519
intersection of search criteria, 191-193
Inventory Control Application, 536
isResizable array method, 601

J-K

Join Tables (SpeedBar, Query) button, 177-178
joins
   creating, 376-379
   inner, 377
   outer, 377-378
justification, 160

key fields, 482
keyboard, 46-49
keyboard shortcuts
   ← (Left one character/move to preceding choice in field), 134, 727
   ↑
      highlight item one level up, 727
      move to preceding choice in field, 727
      previous field, 127
      up one line, 134
   → (move to following choice in field/right one character), 134, 727
   ↓
      down one line, 134
      highlight item one level down, 727

move to following choice in field, 727
next field, 127
Alt (highlight first menu item), 47
Alt+*letter* (move to option with underlined letter), 727
Alt+Backspace (Edit/Undo), 47, 135
Alt+Esc (move to next Windows application on Desk, 47
Alt+F4 (close application window), 47, 718
Alt+H (open Help window), 47
Alt+hyphen (open Control menu of current window), 47
Alt+space bar (open Paradox Control menu), 47
Alt+Tab (restore minimized application), 47
Alt+*underlined letter* (select menu item), 47
Backspace (Delete previous character), 135
controlling ObjectPAL, 548-549
Ctrl+← (left one word/ previous word first letter), 129, 135
Ctrl+→ (right one word/next word first letter), 128, 135
Ctrl+A (Search Next), 47
Ctrl+Backspace (Delete previous word), 135
Ctrl+Backspace (Delete word left of cursor), 129
Ctrl+C (Copy selected object), 48
Ctrl+D (repeat last entry (ditto), 47-48, 142
Ctrl+End (end of field), 127-128
Ctrl+Enter (Super tab), 48
Ctrl+Esc (switch to other application), 47

Ctrl+F (Field view), 47
Ctrl+F2 (Persistent Field view), 48
Ctrl+F5 (Post/Keep locked), 49
Ctrl+F6 (activate windows), 722
Ctrl+F7 (Quick graph), 49
Ctrl+F11 (First record), 49
Ctrl+F12 (Last record), 49
Ctrl+G
  Grid menu, 47
  grid properties, 160
Ctrl+H (current column header), 47, 160
Ctrl+Home
  beginning of field), 128, 134
  first record first field, 127
Ctrl+Ins (Edit/Copy), 47, 135
Ctrl+L (Lock record), 47-48
Ctrl+M (Field properties for current column/object), 48, 160
Ctrl+PgDn (right one screen), 134
Ctrl+PgUp (left one screen), 134
Ctrl+R (rotate), 48, 157
Ctrl+T (Memo view), 48
Ctrl+Z (Locate value), 146
Del (Delete), 129, 135
Del (Edit/Clear or Edit/ Delete), 47
End (current record last field), 127-134
End (End of field), 128, 727
Enter (Insert carriage return/ line fine), 135
Enter (toggle selection in check box), 135, 727
Esc (close dialog box/menu), 47, 135, 727
F1 (access context-sensitive help), 47
F1 (Help), 48
F2 (Field view), 48
F3 (Super back tab), 48

INDEX

F4 (Super tab), 48
F5 (Lock record), 49
F6 (Inspect properties), 49
F7 (Quick form), 49
F8 (View data), 49
F9 (Enter/exit edit mode), 49
F10 (Menu), 49
F11 (Previous record), 49
F12 (Next record), 49
Form view data-entry, 127
Home (Beginning of field/line), 127-128, 134, 727
Memo view data-entry code, 134-135
PgDn (scroll down list box), 134, 727
PgUp (up one screen), 134
Shift+↓ (Select down one line), 135
Shift+Ctrl+Enter (Super backtab), 48
Shift+Ctrl+H (Heading properties for all columns), 47
Shift+Ctrl+L (Commit record), 47-48
Shift+Ctrl+M (Field properties for all columns), 48
Shift+Ctrl+Z (Locate and replace), 48, 146
Shift+Del (Edit/Cut), 47
Shift+End (Select to end of line), 134
Shift+F2 (Memo view), 48
Shift+F3 (Page back), 48
Shift+F4 (Page forward), 48
Shift+F5 (Commit record), 49
Shift+F6 (Multi-object inspect), 49
Shift+F7 (Quick report), 49
Shift+F8 (Object properties), 49
Shift+F11 (Previous set), 49
Shift+F12 (Next set), 49
Shift+Home (select to beginning of line), 134
Shift+Ins (Edit/Paste), 47, 135
Shift+Tab (move to preceding field), 727
Shift+Tab+← (previous field), 127
Tab, 135, 727
Table view data-entry, 127
keys
　candidate, 90
　composite, 70, 92-93
　foreign, 70, 314
　indicators, 91
　Keyviol, 417
　primary, 50, 70, 79
　　defining, 90-93
　tables, sorting, 79
　violations, 417-418
Keyviol key, 417

L

labels, 438
　fields, 210, 262-263
　mailing, 295-298
　text, 262-263
LAN, *see* local area network
landscape (horizontal) printer orientation, 294
Language menu, 531-536
　commands
　　Browse Sources, 700
　　Check Syntax, 543
　　Properties, 533
　　Types, 540
　dialog boxes
　　Display Objects and Properties, 533
Last (Record menu) command, 262
Last Record SpeedBar buttons
　Form, 131
　Table, 130
layering forms, 653
layout
　page reports, 267-271
　screens, 263-264

layout styles
  reports, 271-274
left tabs, 256
legends, 438
less than (<) comparison
  operator, 190
less than or equal to (<=)
  comparison operator, 190
levels, accessing passwords, 416
library procedures, 587
LIKE operator, 187, 200
Line SpeedBar tools
  Forms, 215
  Report Design window, 273
lines, 54
  drawing, 219-222, 276-278
  graphs, 440
  properties, 221, 277
linking
  applications, 456
  tables, 313-324
    in queries, 369-371
    updating, 413
links
  automatic, 470
  cold, 469
  see also relationships
list boxes, selecting, 728
List Breakpoints ObjectPAL
  Debugger command, 537
List dialog box, 659
list fields, 354-355
load method, 653
loans, calculating, 646-649
local area network (LAN), 153
local variables, 568
Locate And Replace dialog box, 151
Locate Field dialog box, 146
Locate Field Value SpeedBar
  buttons
    Form
    Table, 130
Locate menu commands
  Replace, 146
  Value, 146

Locate Next SpeedBar buttons
  Form, 131
  Table, 130
Locate Record Number dialog
  box, 149
locating
  fields, 146-147
  objects, 59
  records, 145-152
    numbers, 149-150
  values, 147-149
locking, 154
  options, 154-155
  read-only, 154
  records, 155
locks, 502
  tables, 503-504
logic field type, 87-88
logical fields, 79
lookup tables, 318-320, 404-410, 409
loops
  for, 582-583
  scan, 583-585
  while, 585-587
Lotus Freelance graphics
  program, 437
lowercase in ObjectPAL, 553-555

M

mailing labels, 295-298
major object types, 49
  forms, 51
  queries, 52-53
  reports, 51-52
  script, 53-54
  tables, 50-51
manipulating ObjectPAL tables, 548-549
many-to-many relationship, 339, 368
many-to-one relationships, see one-to-many
marker graphs, 441
master tables, 337

INDEX

matches
  approximate, 186-189
    LIKE operator, 187
      wild-card operator, 188-189
  exact, searching, 185-186
Max summary
  function, 238, 280
  operator, 383
maxDI field, 642
Maximize icon, 42
maximizing windows, 716
maximum characters
  ObjectPAL code, 552-553
Maximum Height (Design menu) command, 251
maximum values, 400
  validity checks, 100-101
Maximum Width (Design menu) command, 251
MB (Memo/BLOB data associated with table) file type, 476
memo fields, 133-136, 198
  data, entering, 133-136
  formatted, 79, 136-137
  types, 83-88
Memo view data-entry code keyboard shortcuts, 134-135
menuAction built-in method, 671, 687, 691, 698
menus
  About, 668
  actions, 671-698
  bar, 42-44
  cascaded, 668
  cascading, 723
  Control, 713-715, 718
    Table, 714
  creating, 668-670
  File, 668
  Help, 43, 668
  Language, 531-536
  Object Inspectors, 724-725
  options, selecting, 44
  Paradox for Windows main menu, 719
  Path, 208
  pop-up, 668
  Properties, 43, 536
  pull-down, 723
  Query, 175-176
  Reports, 668
  Search, 668
  shared, 247
  top, 668
  Type pull-down, 477
  Undo, 668
  Window, 43
messages
  areas, 46
  displaying, 615-619
  help, displaying, 649
  ObjectPAL fields, 619
methods, 587-591
  action, 665, 675
  addPopUp, 670
  addText, 670
  arrays
    addLast, 600
    append, 600
    contains, 600
    countOf, 600
    empty, 600
    exchange, 600
    fill, 600
    grow, 600
    indexOf, 600
    insert, 600
    insertAfter, 601
    insertBefore, 601
    insertFirst, 601
    isResizable, 601
    remove, 601
    removeAllItems, 601
    removeItem, 601
    replaceItem, 601
    setSize, 601
    size, 601
    view, 601
  arrive, 642, 664, 670, 694
  bringToTop, 653
  built-in, 518, 587

editing, 527
menuAction, 671
mouseEnter, 615
mouseExit, 615
calcButton, 636-639, 646
calcLoanButton, 647-649
calling, 589-590
cancButton, 641
custom, 587
creating, 596-598
fileExitM, 673-675
getHelpM, 687, 691
printCurrM, 683-686
showAboutM, 693
undoEditM, 676
DynArray
contains, 603
getKeys, 603
removeItem, 603
size, 603
view, 603
enumSource, 535
executeQBE, 685
fail, 581
formReturn, 646
getHelpM, 691
getPayment, 643-646
getPayment::pushButton, 680
helpOnHelp, 700
helpQuit, 700
helpSetIndex, 700
helpShowContext, 700
helpShowIndex, 700
helpShowTopic, 700
helpShowTopicInKeyword, 700
hideSpeedBar, 699
load, 653
menuAction, 687, 691, 698
mouseEnter, 646, 649
mouseExit, 646, 649
msgStop, 635
ObjectPAL pushButton, 540
OKButton, 641
open, 587, 686
calling, 653-654

openAsDialog, 655
pmt, 620
pow, 648
printAllCM, 686-687
pushButton, 643-646, 652, 661, 677, 694
recalcButton, 634-635
searchM, 679-681
selecting, 528
setPosition, 697
setTimer, 694
setTitle, 680
show, 670
showAboutM, 697
showSpeedBar, 699
stopping, 624
timer, 694
wait, 652
Methods
dialog box, 520, 527-529, 615
ObjectPAL property, 229
Properties menu command, 520, 567-568, 664
Microsoft
LAN Manager, 5, 702
Powerpoint graphics program, 437
Windows Terminal application, 607
Min summary
function, 238, 280
operator, 383
Minimize
Control menu command, 716
icon, 42
minimizing windows, 37, 716
Minimum Height (Design menu) command, 251
minimum values, 400
validity checks, 100-101
Minimum Width (Design menu) command, 251
modal forms, 652
modes, data-entry
Edit, 125-127
Field view, 128-130

INDEX 757

Form view, 124-125
Non-field view, 128-130
Table view, 124-125
View, 125-127
monthly payments, 620-624
   calculating, 636-639
mortgage calculator application, 698-700
   data entry, 664-665
   editing, 643, 658-664
   executing, 663
   fields, 610
   forms, 609-613
   monthly payments, 620-624
   payment calculator, calling, 643-649
   records, searching, 676-681
   tables, 658-664
   testing, 624-625
MORTHELP.DB table, 687-688
mouse, 46-49, 711-713
   controlling ObjectPAL, 548-549
   pointer shapes, 711-712
mouseEnter built-in method, 615, 646, 649
mouseExit built-in method, 615, 646, 649
moving
   columns, 289-290
      in tables, 157
   cursor, 261
   dialog boxes, 729
   graphics, 138-142
   objects, 217
      in reports, 274
   windows, 718
msgAbortRetryIgnore procedure, 626
msgInfo procedure, 541, 626
msgQuestion procedure, 626
msgQuestion Status dialog box, 639
msgRetryCancel procedure, 626
msgStop method, 635
msgStop procedure, 626

msgYesNoCancel procedure, 626
multi-record forms, data model, 343-346
Multi-record SpeedBar tools
   Forms, 216
   Report Design window, 273
Multi-Record
   objects, 55
   regions, 242, 283
   style option, 211, 269, 271
multi-table
   crosstabs, 435-436
   forms, 324-326, 336-349
      nested, 348-349
      secondary indexes, 346-348
   query conditions, 326-329
      AND, 374
      OR, 374-375
      creating, 366-373
      joins, 376-379
   reports, 302
multiple
   objects, 247-253
   tables, 73-74
   windows, 62-63
Multiuser (File menu) command, 502-506

N

names, fields, 79-82
naming
   tables, 93
   variables, 558
navigation, 4
nested multi-table forms, 348-349
Network dialog boxes
   Refresh Rate, 507
   Retry Period, 506
   User Name, 504
networks
   3COM 3Plus/3Plus Open, 5
   Banyan Vines, 5
   local area (LAN), 153

Microsoft LAN Manager, 5
Novell Advanced NetWare, 5
New (File menu) command, 77, 172, 208, 267, 343
New Disk dialog box, 706
new features of Paradox for Windows
    data integration, 4
    extendability, 4
    Graphic data type, 4
    GUI features, 4
    navigation, 4
    OLE (Object Linking and Embedding) data type, 4
New menu, commands, Table, 77
Next (Record menu) command, 262
Next Record SpeedBar buttons
    Form, 131
    Table, 130
Next set (Record menu) command, 262
Next Set of Records SpeedBar buttons
    Form, 131
    Table, 130
NO summary operator, 387
Non-field view data-entry mode, 128-130
non-modal forms, 652
normal aggragators, 432-433
normalization data, 74
NOT operator, 196, 200
Novell Advanced NetWare, 5, 702
number field type, 83-88
numbers
    fixed decimal point, 84
    floating decimal point, 84
    integers, 84
    powers, 648
    records, locating, 149-150
numeric calculations, 381

O

Object Database Application Programming Interface, 509
Object Inspectors, 724-725
Object Linking and Embedding, see OLE
Object Tree, 525
    Forms SpeedBar design tool, 243
    Report Design window SpeedBar button, 274
object types
    design
        boxes, 54
        buttons, 55
        crosstabs, 55
        ellipses (...), 54
        fields, 55
        graphics, 55
        graphs, 55
        lines, 54
        multi-record objects, 55
        OLE objects, 56
    major
        forms, 51
        queries, 52-53
        reports, 51-52
        scripts, 53-54
        tables, 50-51
object-based programming, 524
ObjectPAL, 1, 515-527, 605-700
    arrays
        dynamic, 547
        resizable, 547
    built-in event handling, 547
    code, 552-553
        attaching, 233
        comments, 554
        indentation, 554-556
        maximum characters, 552-553
        spaces, 552
        type mismatches, 556
    comments, 554
    constants, declaring, 564-565

INDEX

data types
  basic, 560-561
  creating, 566-567
  data models, 561
  data objects, 562
  design objects, 561
  display managers, 562
  DLL (Dynamic Link
    Libraries), 563
  evemts, 563
dialog boxes, 525
DLL (Dynamic Link Libraries)
  functions, 591-594
drop-down edit box, 613
Editor window, 529
event-driven, 517-519
field messages, 619
File menu commands
  New, Form, 538
function calls, 547
graphical user interface,
  606-608
    messages, 615-619
handles, TCursor, 549
help sytem, 547
hierarchy, containership,
  516-517
IDE (integrated development
  environment), 514
keyboard shortcuts,
  controlling, 548-549
Language menu commands
  Check Syntax, 543
lowercase, 553-555
messages, 615-619
methods, 547
  built-in, 518
  pushButton, 540
  selecting, 528
mortgage calculators
  creating, 609-613
  fields, 610
  testing, 624-626
mouse, 548-549
msgInfo procedure, 541
objects, 549-550

  code, 524
  properties, 516-523
  responses, 518
  subsystems, 524
operators, 576
procedures, 547
  calls, 547
  general, 541
programs, 538-547
properties, Methods, 229
records, 566-567
scripts, writing, 283
strong data typing, 547
structured program control,
  547
tables, manipulating, 548-549
types, data, 560-563
uppercase, 553-555
user-defined data types, 547
users, interacting, 608-624
variables
  arrays, 558
  assigning, 558
  creating, 557
  declarations, 557-560
  declaring, 555-563
  handles, 559-560
  initializing, 558-559
  naming, 558
  types, 556-557
ObjectPAL Debugger, 537-538
  breakpoints, 544
  commands
    Enable Ctrl+Break To
      Debugger, 537
    Enable DEBUG, 537
    Inspect, 537
    List Breakpoints, 537
    Origin, 537
    Quit This Method, 538
    Run, 538
    Set Breakpoint, 537
    Stack Backtrace, 537
    Step Into, 538
    Step Over, 537
    Trace Built-ins, 537
    Trace Execution, 537

ObjectPAL Editor, 527-536
  code containers, 529
  commands
    Constants, 534
    Edit, Copy, 530
    Edit, Cut, 530
    Edit, Delete, 531
    Edit, Go To, 531
    Edit, Paste, 530
    Edit, Replace, 531
    Edit, Replace Next, 531
    Edit, Search, 531
    Edit, Search Next, 531
    Edit, Select All, 530
    Properties (Language menu), 533
  Language menu, 531-536
  Methods dialog box, 527-529
  Properties menu, 536
  source code reports, 535-536
objects, 49-56, 462-466
  adding, 237
  aligning, 249-251
  code, 524
  creating, 57-59, 688
    OLE (Object Linking and Embedding), 462-466
  customzing in databases, 710
  data, scoping, 528
  deselecting, 217, 275
  embedding, 247-248, 461
  graphs, 442-443
  grouping, 248-249
  locating, 59
  moving, 217, 274
  multiple, 247-253
  multi-record, 55
  ObjectPAL, 549-550
  OLE (Object Linking and Embedding), 56, 279
  payment calculator
    calcButton, 633
    cancButton, 633
    DIBox, 632
    DIBox.availDI, 633
    DIBox.currDI, 633
    DIBox.maxDI, 633
    estPayment, 632
    incomeBox, 632
    incomeBox.mIncome, 632
    incomeBox.reCalc, 632
    OKButton, 633
    paymentBox, 632
    paymentBox.mCar, 632
    paymentBox.mCredit, 632
    paymentBox.mOtherLoan, 632
  properties, 56, 218, 275, 469-471
    inspecting, 57
    ObjectPAL, 516-523
  prototype, 252-253
  renaming, 481-485
  responses, editing, 518
  selecting, 56, 217-218
    in reports, 274-275
  sizing, 56, 249-251
  spacing, 249-251
  subsystems, ObjectPAL, 524
  tables, 242, 361-364
    adding, 282-283
    resizing, 289
    TableFrame, 548
  target, 672
  text properties, 223-229
  types
    design, 49
    major, 49
objects types
  design tables, 55
ODAPI (File menu) command, 509
OKButton method, 641
OLE (Object Linking and Embedding), 4, 461-471
  capacity, 470
  clients, 470
  field type, 83, 86-87
  fields, 79, 467
    data, 142
  Forms SpeedBar design tools, 215
  links, automatic, 470

INDEX 761

memory requirements, 470
objects, 56, 462-466
    adding, 237
    creating, 462-466
    embedded, 461
    properties, 469-471
Report Design window,
    SpeedBar tools, 273
report objects, 279
servers, 470
speed, 470
storage requirements, 470
one-dimensional crosstabs, 422-428
one-to-many (many-to-one) relationships tables, 71, 339, 368
one-to-one relationship, 71, 339, 368
Open (File menu) command, 96, 474
Open a Table dialog box, 109, 122
Open Document dialog box, 474-475
Open Folder SpeedBar buttons
    Form, 131
    Query, 177-178
    Table, 131
Open menu commands, Table, 96
open method, 587, 686
    calling, 653-654
Open Table (SpeedBar) button, 122
Open Table dialog box, 475
openAsDialog method, 655
opening
    forms, 653-655
    payment calculator, 643
    tables, 122-123
operands, 577
operator precedence, 577
operators, 575-578
    arithmetic
        – (subtraction), 199
        ( ) (group operators), 199, 380
        * (multiplication), 199, 380
        + (addition) query, 380
        - (subtraction), 380
        / (division), 199, 380
    AS, 195
    BLANK, 196-197
    CHANGETO, 393
    comparison
        < (less than), 190, 200
        <= (less than or equal to), 190, 200
        = (equal to), 190, 200
        > (greater than), 190, 200
        >= (greater than or equal to), 190, 200
    DELETE, 392
    grouping
        ALL, 384
        UNIQUE, 384
    INSERT, 391
    LIKE, 187
    NOT, 196
    ObjectPAL, 576
    precedence, 578
    reserved symbols
        Check descending, 199
        Check group, 199
        Check mark, 199
        Check plus, 199
    reserved words
        CALC, 199
        CHANGETO, 199
        DELETE, 199
        FIND, 199
        INSERT, 199
        SET, 199
    special
        ! (all values), 200
        , (AND), 200
        AS, 200
        BLANK, 200
        LIKE, 200
        NOT, 200
        OR, 200
        TODAY, 200

summary, 382-385
    AVERAGE, 383, 387
    COUNT, 383
    EVERY, 387
    EXACTLY, 387
    MAX, 383
    MIN, 383
    NO, 387
    queries, 383-384
    SUM, 384
TODAY, 198-200
wild-card, 188-189
    ..(multiple characters), 200
    @ (single character), 200
options
  buttons, 728
  Design menu
    Bring to Front, 249
    Send to Back, 249
  Display Locks, 154
  locking, 154-155
  Picture, 102
  Set Locks, 154
  Set Retry, 154
  styles
    Blank, 211, 271
    Multi-Record, 211, 269-271
    Single-Record, 211, 271
    Tabular, 211, 271
  User Name, 154
  Who, 154
  windows, 721-722
Options menu command, Properties, 230
OR conditions, 374-379
OR special operator, 200
ordering, see sorting, 181-184
orientation of printers
  landscape (horizontal), 294
  portrait (vertical), 294
Origin ObjectPAL Debugger command, 537
orphan records, 72
outer joins, 377-378

P

page bands, 284
  footers, 286-287
  headers, 286-287
page layout reports, 270-271
Page Layout dialog box, 270, 519
Paradox for Windows
  background, 2
  closing, 37, 718
  commands
    accessing, 723
    Window, 722
  deinstalling, 708
  installing requirements, 702
  new features
    data integrity, 4
    extendability, 4
    Graphic data type, 4
    GUI features, 4
    navigation, 4
    OLE (Object Linking and Embedding) data type, 4
  starting, 14-17
  table types
    25-character field names, 78
    binary fields, 78
    formatted memo fields, 78
    graphic fields, 78
    OLE (Object Linking and Embedding) fields, 78
    primary keys, 78
    referential integrity, 78
    table lookup, 78
    table sort by key, 78
    validity checks, 78
parameters, 588-589
  passing by reference, 588
parentheses ( ), 80
passing by reference, parameters, 588
Password Protection dialog box, 414
passwords
  access levels, 416

INDEX

creating, 414
Paste ObjectPAL Editor
  command, 530
Paste from Clipboard SpeedBar
  buttons
    Form, 131
    Query, 177-178
    Table, 130
Paste From Graphic File dialog
  box, 230
Paste Link (Edit menu)
  command, 467
pasting values, 143
Path menu, 208
pattern graphs, 449-450
payment calculator
  calling from mortgage
    calculator, 643-649
  creating forms, 630-642
  loans, 646-649
  objects
    calcButton, 633
    cancButton, 633
    DIBox, 632
    DIBox.availDI, 633
    DIBox.currDI, 633
    DIBox.maxDI, 633
    estPayment, 632
    incomeBox, 632
    IncomeBox.mIncome, 632
    IncomeBox.reCalc, 632
    OKButton, 633
    paymentBox, 632
    paymentBox.mCar, 632
    paymentBox.mCredit, 632
    paymentBox.mOtherLoan,
      632
  opening, 643
  properties, 655-656
payments, calculating, 620-624
PCs (personal computers)
  Paradox for Windows,
    deinstalling, 708
persistance variables, assigning,
  573

PgDn keyboard shortcuts
  down one screen, 134
  scroll down list box, 727
PgUp keyboard shortcuts
  scroll up list box, 727
  up one screen, 134
Picture Assistance dialog box,
  104
picture characters, 103-104,
  401-402
  # (number digit), 401
  & [any character (convert to
    uppercase)], 401
  , (alternative values), 402
  ; (following character is
    literal, not picture string
    character), 401
  * (repeat following character
    numerous times), 402
  ? [any letter (upper- or
    lowercase), 401
  @ [any character (convert to
    lowercase)], 401
  [ ] (optional items enclosed),
    402
  { } (grouping operators), 402
Picture option, 102
pictures, 401-403
pie graphs, 440, 450-451
  exploding, 451
pmt method, 620
pointers
  in indexes, 95
  shapes, 711-712
pointing, 712
polymorphism, 549-550
pop-up menu, 668
PopupMenu variable, 669
portrait (vertical) printer
  orientation, 294
pound sign (#), 80
pow method, 648
power numbers, 648
precedence operators, 577-578
Preferred (Properties menu)
  command, 267

preventing duplicate records, 70
previewing reports, 291-292
Previous (Record menu)
 command, 262
Previous Record SpeedBar
 commands
  Form, 131
  Table, 130
Previous set (Record menu)
 command, 262
Previous Set of Records
 SpeedBar buttons
  Form, 131
  Table 130
primary keys, 50, 70, 79
 defining, 90-93
Print (File menu) command, 422
Print SpeedBar buttons
 Form, 131
 Table, 130
Print File dialog box, 35, 292
Print Report (Report Design
 window) SpeedBar button, 273
printAllCM method, 686-687
printCurrM custom method,
 683-686
Printer Setup
 dialog box, 726
 File menu command, 293
printers
 controlling, 293
 orientation
  landscape (horizontal), 294
  portrait (vertical), 294
printing
 Answer table, 203
 client reports, 686-687
 crosstabs, 422
 forms
  current, 681-686
 graphs, 451-452
 Quick Reports, 35-36, 266
 reports, 266-267, 292-294
private
 directories, 501
 variables, 574

Private Directory
 dialog box, 501
 File menu command, 501
procedures, 587-591
 calling, 591
 custom, 594-596
 general, 541
 library, 587
 msgAbortRetryIgnore, 626
 msgInfo, 626
 msgQuestion, 626
 msgRetryCancel, 626
 msgStop, 626
 msgYesNoCancel, 626
 ObjectPAL
  msgInfo, 541
 string, 657
Program Manager utility
 Task List, 718-719
programs
 adding ObjectPAL, 538-547
 comment out, 554
 disk backups, 703
 INSTALL, executing, 703-708
 object-based, 524
Prohibit (Table menu)
 command, 413
properties, 50, 56, 216
 boxes, 220, 276-277
 data, 166
 data-dependent, 162-164
 ellipses, 220, 276-277
 graphics, 141-142
 graphs, 444-445
 grid, 165-166
 heading, 165
 inspecting in objects, 57
 lines, 221, 277
 ObjectPAL
  Methods, 229
  objects, 516-523
 objects, 218, 275, 469-471
 payment calculator, 655-656
 report tables, 290-291
 tables, 156
 text object, 223-229
 tools, 275

INDEX 765

properties, crosstabs, 433-434
Properties menu commands, 43, 536
   Answer Table, 184, 201
   Answer Table, Sort, 184, 201
   Band Labels, 285
   Data Dependent, 162
   Expanded Ruler, 255
   Form, 654
   Form, Window Style, 655
   Grid Settings, 254
   Language menu, 533
   Methods, 520, 567-568, 664
   Options menu, 230
   Preferred, Report, 267
   Restore, 166
   Save, 166
   Show Grid, 257
   Snap to Grid, 257
   Sort, 201
   View Properties, Save, 166
   Zoom, 258
prototype objects, 252-253
pull-down menus, 723
pushButton method, 540, 643-646, 652, 661, 677, 694
PX (Primary Index) file type, 476

Q

Q&A (Symantec), 170
qAnswer variable, 638
QBE (query by example), 2-3, 30-34, 169-204
   advantages, 170-171
   Answer table, 200-203
      editing, 201-203
      printing, 203
      sorting, 201
   file types, 476
   queries
      creating, 172-174
      saving, 203
      tables, 174, 175
      writing, 171-172

Quick Start
   crosstabs, creating, 330-332
   Form view data entry, 27-29
   multi-table
      forms, 324-326
      queries, 326-329
   Paradox for Windows
      closing, 37
      starting, 14-17
   QBE (query by example), 30-34
   Quick Reports, printing, 35-36
   tables
      columns, 26-27
      creating, 17-21, 311-313
      linking, 313-324
queries, 52-53, 152
   arithmetic operators
      ( ) (grouping, 380
      * (multiplication), 380
      + (addition), 380
      - (subtraction), 380
      / (division), 380
   calculations, 379-385
   creating, 172-174
   errors, 176
   executing, 685
   files, 682
   INSERT, creating, 390
   multi-table, 326-329
      conditions, 374-375
      creating, 366-373
   operators, summary, 383-384
   renaming, 496
   saving, 203
   set, 386-388
   statements, 682-684
   tables
      adding, 174
      deleting, 175
      editing, 388-394
      linking, 369-371
   writing, 30, 171-172
Query (File menu) command, 172

query by example, *see* QBE
Query Editor dialog box, 172-174
Query menu, 175-176
   commands
      Add Table, 174-175
      Field View, 175
      Remove Table, 175
      Run, 175
      Run Query, 371
      Wait for DDE, 175
   options
      Add Table, 175
Query SpeedBar, 177-178
   Add Table, 177-178
   Answer Table Properties, 177-178
   Copy to Clipboard, 177-178
   Cut to Clipboard, 177-178
   Field View, 177-178
   Join Tables, 177-178
   Open Folder, 177-178
   Paste from Clipboard, 177-178
   Query, 177-178
   Remove Table, 177-178
   Run Query, 177-178
Quick Table SpeedBar buttons
   Crosstab, 131
   Form, 131
   Graph, 131
   Report, 131
   printing, 35-36, 266
Quit This Method ObjectPAL Debugger command, 538
quotation marks (" "), 80

R

range limits in tables, 3
ranges values, 189-191
RD DOS command, 708
RDL (Report) file type, 476
Read Only fields, 238
read-only locking, 154
README.TXT file
   viewing, 708

recalcButton methods, 634-635
   testing, 635
receiving events, 672
Record (Edit mode menu) command, 152
Record band, 284
Record menu commands
   First, 262
   Last, 262
   Next, 262
   Next set, 262
   Previous, 262
   Previous set, 262
records, 17, 50
   calculations, 380-382
   comparing, 385-388
   creating, 566-567
   deleting, 145
      from multiple tables, 480-481
      preventing, 70
      replacing, 479
      tables, 392-393
   editing, 393-394
   grouping, 382-385
      in reports, 299-301
   inserting, 152-153, 389-391
   locating, 145-152
   locking, 155
   numbers, 149-150
   orphans, 72
   restoring, 675-676
   searching, 676-681
   set operations, 385
   transferring tables, 478-480
   unlocking, 155
   viewing, 79
   see also rows
referencing field names, 661
referential integrity, 3, 68, 316-318, 397
   deleting, 413
   editing, 414
   in databases, 72
   tables, 410-414

INDEX

Referential Integrity dialog box, 411
reformatting
 fields, 242
 report fields, 282
refreshing, 154
regions, multi-record, 242, 283
regular fields, 237-238, 280, 287
relational databases, 68
 primary keys, 70
 record duplications, 70
 referential integrity, 68
 tables, 50-51
relationships, 339-346
 data models, 340-343
 many-to-many, 339, 368
 one-to-many (many-to-one), 71, 339, 368
 one-to-one, 71, 339, 368
 see also links
remove array method, 601
Remove Table
 Query menu command, 175
 Query SpeedBar button, 177-178
removeAllItems array method, 601
removeItem array method, 601
removeItem DynArray method, 603
Rename (File menu) command, 495
renaming
 forms, 496, 564
 objects, 481-485
 queries, 496
 reports, 496
 scripts, 496
 tables, 110, 495-496
repeating fields, deleting, 74-75
Replace commands
 Locate menu, 146
 Next ObjectPAL Editor, 531
 ObjectPAL Editor, 531
replaceItem array method, 601
replacing duplicate records, 479

Report commands
 File menu, 267
 Properties menu, 267
Report band, 284
Report Design window, 272-279
 SpeedBar buttons
  Add Band, 274
  Data Model, 274
  Object Tree, 274
  Print Report, 273
  View Data, 273
 SpeedBar tools
  Box, 273
  Ellipse, 273
  Field, 273
  Graph, 274
  Graphic, 273
  Line, 273
  Multi-record, 273
  OLE (Object Linking and Embedding), 273
  Selection Arrow, 273
  Table, 273
  Text, 273
Report Layout dialog box, 287
Report menu commands, Deliver, 668, 700
reports, 51-52
 bands, 284-287
  deleting, 285
  resizing, 285
 boxes, drawing, 276-278
 creating, 267-272, 686
 databases, 303
 designing, 302-305
 ellipses, 276-278
 fields
  adding, 269, 280-283
  calculated, 280-281
  deleting, 270, 288
  reformatting, 282
  regular, 280, 287
  special, 281-282
 financial, 303
 footers, 286
 graphics, 278-279

graphs, 283
headers, 286
layout, 267-269
    pages, 270-271
    styles, 271-274
lines, 276-278
mailing labels, 295-298
multi-record regions, 283
multi-table, 302
objects
    deselecting, 275
    moving, 274
    OLE (Object Linking and Embedding), 279
    selecting, 274-275
previewing, 291-292
printing, 266-267, 292-294
    clients, 686-687
Quick, printing, 35-36
records, grouping, 299-301
renaming, 496
saving, 291-292
source code, 535-536
styles, 305-306
table properties, 290-291
text, 278
types, 266
required fields, 100
reserved symbols operator
    Check descending, 199
    Check group, 199
    Check mark, 199
    Check plus, 199
reserved words, 190
    in tables, 94
    operators
        CALC, 199
        CHANGETO, 199
        DELETE, 199
        FIND, 199
        INSERT, 199
        SET, 199
resizing
    arrays, 600-601
    bands, 285
    columns, 26-27, 157-159, 289

    object tables, 289
    rows, 159, 290
    table columns, 26-27
responses, editing objects, 518
Restore (Properties menu) command, 166
restoring
    records, 675-676
    windows, 716
restricting search criteria, 185-200
Restructure (Table menu) command, 100, 203, 405
Restructure dialog boxes
    dBASE IV Table, 97
    Paradox for Windows Table, 96
    Table, 315, 347
    Warning, 406
restructuring tables, 111-118, 481-485
return values, 589
RGB (red, green, blue) method, 246
right tabs, 256
right-clicking, 712
rights, 414
    fields, 415-417
    table, 415
    tables, 415-416
Row Lines (Grid properties menu) command, 166
rows, 50
    crosstabs, 422
    resizing, 159, 290
    see also records
RSL (Report) file type, 476
rulers, 254-256
Run commands
    File menu, 703
    ObjectPAL Debugger, 538
    Query menu, 175, 371
Run dialog box, 703
Run Query SpeedBar button, 177-178

S

sample files, installing, 704-706
Save commands
   File menu, 203, 259
   Properties menu, 166
Save As (File menu) command, 109, 203, 630
Save Referential Integrity As dialog box, 318
Save This Object? dialog box, 34
saving
   forms, 259
   queries, 203
   reports, 291-292
   tables, 93-94, 109-110
scales, 438
scaling graphics, 232
scan loops, 583-585
scatter graphs, 441
scoping
   constants, 567-575
   data objects, 528
   variables, 571-575
      Var section, 568-570
screens
   color, 160, 263
   flickering, 253
   layouts, 263-264
scripts, 53-54
   renaming, 496
   writing, 53
      ObjectPAL, 283
SDL (Script) file type, 476
Search & Replace dialog box, 223
search criteria
   intersection, 191-193
   restricting, 185-200
Search dialog box, 676
   forms, creating, 676-681
Search menu, 668
Search ObjectPAL Editor commands, 531
search-and-replace, 150-152

searching
   exact matches, 185-186
   records, 676-681
   value ranges, 189-191
searching, *see* locating
searchM method, 679, 681
searchName variable, 680
secondary indexes, 95, 346-348
Select All ObjectPAL Editor command, 530
Select Fields dialog box, 210, 269
Select File dialog box, 59, 138,
selecting, 713
   check boxes, 728
   fields, 178-184
   fonts, 226
   graphic files, 138
   layout style reports, 271-274
   list boxes, 728
   menu options, 44
   methods, 528
   object, 217-218
   objects, 56
      in reports, 274-275
   styles, 211-215
   table types, 77-79
Selection Arrow SpeedBar tools
   Forms design, 215
   Report Design window, 273
Send To Back option, 249
series, 438
   graphs, 450
servers, 455
   file, 153
Set commands
Breakpoint
      Debug menu, 544
      ObjectPAL Debugger, 537
   Locks (File menu), 503
   Retry (File menu), 506
Set Locks option, 154
set operations, 385
SET operator, 199
set queries, 386-388
Set Retry option, 154

Set Working Directory dialog box, 500
setPosition method, 697
setSize array method, 601
setTimer method, 694
setTitle method, 680
SHARE (DOS) utility, 706-707
shared menus, 247
Shift+↓ (Select down one line) keyboard shortcut, 135
Shift+Ctrl+Enter (Super backtab) keyboard shortcut, 48
Shift+Ctrl+H (Heading properties for all columns) keyboard shortcut, 47
Shift+Ctrl+L (Commit record) keyboard shortcut, 47-48
Shift+Ctrl+M (Field properties for all columns) keyboard shortcut, 48
Shift+Ctrl+Z (Locate and replace) keyboard shortcut, 48, 146
Shift+Del (Edit/Cut) keyboard shortcut, 47
Shift+End (Select to end of line) keyboard shortcut, 134
Shift+F2 (Memo view) keyboard shortcut, 48
Shift+F3 (Page back) keyboard shortcut, 48
Shift+F4 (Page forward) keyboard shortcut, 48
Shift+F5 (Commit record) keyboard shortcut, 49
Shift+F6 (Multi-object inspect) keyboard shortcut, 49
Shift+F7 (Quick report) keyboard shortcut, 49
Shift+F8 (Object properties) keyboard shortcut, 49
Shift+F11 (Previous set) keyboard shortcut, 49
Shift+F12 (Next set) keyboard shortcut, 49

Shift+Home (select to beginning of line) keyboard shortcut, 134
Shift+Ins (Edit/Paste) keyboard shortcut, 47, 135
Shift+Tab (move to preceding field) keyboard shortcut, 727
Shift+Tab+← (previous field) keyboard shortcut, 127
short number field type, 83-85
Show Grid (Properties menu) command, 257
show method, 670
showAboutM custom method, 693, 697
showSpeedBar method, 699
Single-Record style option, 211, 271
Size (Control menu) command, 717
size array method, 601
size DynArray method, 603
sizing
    fonts, 160
    objects, 56, 249-251
    table fields, 89
    windows, 717-718
slices of graphs, 441
Snap to Grid (Properties menu) command, 257
Sort commands
    File menu, 482
    Properties menu, 184, 201
    Table menu, 181
Sort dialog boxes
    Answer, 184
    Sort Table, 201, 482-483
sorting
    Answer table, 201
    fields, 181-184
    tables, 481-485
source code reports, 535-536
spacing
    ObjectPA code, 552
    objects, 249-251
special fields, 240-241, 281-282
    defining, 351-361

INDEX

special operators
  ! (all values), 200
  , (AND), 200
  AS, 200
  BLANK, 200
  LIKE, 200
  NOT, 200
  OR, 200
  TODAY, 200
specifying field names, 79-82
SpeedBar buttons, 44
  Forms
    design tools
    Box, 215
    Button, 216
    Copy to Clipboard, 131
    Crosstab, 216
    Cut to Clipboard, 131
    Data Model, 243
    Design, 131
    Edit data, 126, 131
    Ellipse, 215
    Field, 216
    Field view, 131
    First Record, 131
    Graph, 216
    Graphic, 215
    Last record, 131
    Line, 215
    Locate field value, 131
    Locate next, 131
    Multi-record, 216
    Next record, 131
    Next set of records, 131
    OLE (Object Linking and Embedding), 215
    Open folder, 131
    Paste from Clipboard, 131
    Previous record, 131
    Previous set of records, 131
    Print, 131
    Selection Arrow, 215
    Table, 216
    Table view, 131
    Text, 215
  Query, 177-178
    Add Table, 177-178
    Answer Table Properties, 177-178
    Copy to Clipboard, 177-178
    Cut to Clipboard, 177-178
    Field View, 177-178
    Join Tables, 177-178
    Open Folder, 177-178
    Paste from Clipboard, 177-178
    Remove Table, 177-178
    Run Query, 177-178
  Report Design window
    Add Band, 274
    Data Model, 274
    Object Tree, 274
    Print Report, 273
    View Data, 273
  Table
    Copy to Clipboard, 130
    Cut to Clipboard, 130
    Edit Data, 131
    Field View, 130
    Last Record, 130
    Locate Field Value, 130
    Locate Next, 130
    Next Record, 130
    Next Set of Records, 130
    Open Folder, 131
    Paste to Clipboard, 130
    Previous Record, 130
    Previous Set of Records, 130
    Print, 130
    Quick Crosstab, 131
    Quick Form, 131
    Quick Graph, 131
    Quick Report, 131
SpeedBar design tools
  Report Design window
    Box, 273
    Ellipse, 273
    Field, 273
    Graph, 274
    Graphic, 273

Line, 273
Multi-record, 273
OLE (Object Linking and Embedding), 273
Selection Arrow, 273
Table, 273
Text, 273
spreadsheets
   data, importing, 486-488
   tables, exporting, 492-493
SQL (Structured Query Language) file type, 70, 476
square brackets ([ ]), 80
SSL (Script) file type, 476
Stack Backtrace ObjectPAL Debugger command, 537
stacked-bar graph, 439
startH constant, 696
starting
   Edit mode, 665
   Paradox for Windows, 14-17
statements
   area, 185
   case, 673
   endswitch, 581
   if, 578-580, 665, 690
   immediate if (iif), 580-581
   queries, 682, 684
   switch, 581, 672
   try, 581-582
Std summary function, 238, 280
Step ObjectPAL Debugger commands
   Into, 538
   Over, 537
stopping methods, 624
stopString variable, 635
strings
   concatenation, 552-553, 635
   procedures, 657
   queries, 682
strong typing, 556
Structure Information Paradox for Windows Table dialog box, 109

Structured Query Language, see SQL
structures
   tables
      borrowing, 104-110
      displaying, 109
styles
   fonts, 160
   options
      Blank, 211, 271
      Multi-Record, 211, 269, 271
      Single-Record, 211, 271
      Tabular, 211, 271
   reports, 305-306
   selecting, 211-215
   windows, combining, 654
Subdirectory Options dialog box, 704
subsystems, 524
Subtract (File menu) command, 480
Sum summary function, 238, 280
SUM summary operator, 384
summary
   fields, 239
   functions
      Avg, 239, 280
      Count, 238, 280
      Max, 238, 280
      Min, 238, 280
      Std, 238, 280
      Sum, 238, 280
      Var, 239, 280
   operators, 382-385
      AVERAGE, 383, 387
      COUNT, 383
      EVERY, 387
      EXACTLY, 387
      MAX, 383
      MIN, 383
      NO, 387
   queries, 383-384
   SUM, 384
Super Tab (F4), 46
switch statements, 581, 672

INDEX   773

Switch To (Control menu) command, 464, 718
switching
    directories, 208
    tables fields, 126
systems
    fields, 240
    requirements, 4-5
System Settings (File menu) command, 507

T

Tab (move to next field) keyboard shortcut, 135, 727
Table
    commands
        File menu, 35, 96
        Info Structure, 109
        New menu, 77
        Open menu, 96
        Restructure, 100, 203, 405
        Sort, 181
        Update Rule, Cascade, 413
        Update Rule, Prohibit, 413
    Control menu, 714
    dialog boxes
        Add, 418, 475
        Copy, 496
        Delete, 475, 497
        Empty, 475, 497
        Export, 493
        Rename, 110, 495
        Type, 77
    Forms SpeedBar design tool, 216
    Report Design window SpeedBar tool, 273
    SpeedBar buttons
        Copy to Clipboard, 130
        Cut to Clipboard, 130
        Edit Data, 131
        Field View, 130
        First Record, 130
        Last Record, 130
        Locate Field Value, 130
        Locate Next, 130
        Next Record, 130
        Next Set of Records, 130
        Open Folder, 131
        Paste to Clipboard, 130
        Previous Record, 130
        Previous Set of Records, 130
        Print, 130
        Quick Crosstab, 131
        Quick Form, 131
        Quick Graph, 131
        Quick Report, 131
Table view
    data-entry
        keyboard shortcuts, 127
        mode, 124-125
    Form SpeedBar button, 131
TableFrame table object, 548
tables, 50-51, 55
    accessing with indexes, 95-98
    adding to queries, 174
    child, 411
    columns, 69
        editing, 195
        moving, 157
        resizing, 26-27, 157-159
    copying, 496-497
    creating, 17-21, 76-94, 311-313
        for mortgage calculator, 658-664
    criteria
        exclusive, 373
        inclusive, 373
    data, 22-27
    deleting from queries, 175
    detail, 337
    duplications, combining, 76
    editing, 156-167
        with queries, 388-394
    exporting to spreadsheets, 492-493
    fields, 50, 323
        adding, 210, 237-243
        calculated, 238-239
        deleting, 74-75, 118, 210, 241

774 USING PARADOX FOR WINDOWS, SPECIAL EDITION

editing, 114-118
fonts, 156
inserting, 118
key, 482
labels, 262-263
Read Only, 238
reformatting, 242
regular, 237-238
sizing, 89
summary, 239
switching, 126
system, 240-241
types, 82-87
formulas, default derivation, 3
graphs, 332
in databases, 69-70
keys
    composite, 70
    foreign, 70
linking, 313-324, 413
    in queries, 369-371
locks, 503-504
lookups, 79, 318-320, 404-410
manipulating ObjectPAL, 548-549
master, 337
MORTHELP.DB, 687, 688
multi-joins, 376-379
multiple, 73-74
naming, 93
objects, 242, 361-364
    adding, 282-283
    resizing, 289
    TableFrame, 548
opening, 122-123
primary keys, 70
    defining, 90-93
properties, 156
    reports, 290-291
range limits, 3
records, 50
    deleting, 392-393, 480-481
    editing, 393-394
    inserting, 152-153, 389-391
    locking, 155

    orphans, 72
    transferring, 478-480
referential integrity, 316-318, 410-414
    checks, 3
    deleting, 413
    editing, 414
relationships, 72
    one-to-many (many-to-one), 71
    one-to-one, 71
renaming, 110, 495-496
reserved words, 94
restructuring, 111-118, 481-485
rights, 415-416
rows, 69
    resizing, 159
saving, 93-94, 109-110
secondary indexes, 314-315
sorting, 481-485
    by key, 79
structures
    borrowing, 104-110
    displaying, 109
TableView, 548
types
    25-character field names, 78
    binary fields, 78
    formatted memo fields, 78
    graphics fields, 78
    logical fields, 78
    OLE fields, 78
    primary keys, 78
    referential integrity, 78
    selecting, 77-79
    table lookup, 78
    table sort by key, 78
    validity checks, 78
    view deleted records, 78
validity checks, 79, 322-324
values, 323, 371-373
viewing in other directories, 478
TableView table, 548
tabs, 256

INDEX

Tabular
   graph type, 443
   style option, 211, 271
tags, 602
target objects, 672
Task List (Program Manager)
  utility, accessing, 718-719
TCursor, 549, 690
testing
   calcButton method, 638
   data, 624
   forms, 260-262
   mortgage calculator, 624-625
   recalcButton methods, 635
Text
   Forms SpeedBar design tools, 215
   Report Design window SpeedBar tools, 273
text, 54
   adding, 222-229
      to reports, 278
   aligning, 225
   boxes, 729
   color, 227
   editors, 707
   files, importing, 488-492
   fixed-length, 488
   labels, 262-263
   object properties, 223-229
   wrapping, 225
Text Options dialog box, 490
tick marks, 438
Tile (Window menu) command, 721
tiling windows, 721
timer method, 694
title bar, 41
titles, 438
TODAY operator, 198-200
tools, 44 (*see also* buttons)
   properties, 275
   Report Design window SpeedBar
     Box, 273
     Ellipse, 273
     Field, 273

     Graph, 274
     Graphic, 273
     Line, 273
     Multi-record, 273
     OLE (Object Linking and Embedding), 273
     Selection Arrow, 273
     Table, 273
     Text, 273
top menus, 668
Trace ObjectPAL Debugger commands
   Built-ins, 537
   Execution, 537
transactions, 581
transferring table records, 478-480
try statements, 581-582
TV (Table View Settings) file type, 477
two-dimensional crosstabs, 428-430
type mismatches, ObjectPAL code, 556
Type pull-down menu, 477
typeface fonts, 160
types, 549
   conversions
     dBASE, 116
     fields, 115
   data, 556
     checking, 556
     ObjectPAL, 560-563
   fields
     alphanumeric, 83-84
     binary, 83, 87, 119
     currency, 83-85
     date, 83-86
     formatted memo, 83, 86
     graphic, 83, 86
     memo, 83, 86
     number, 83-85
     OLE (Object Linking and Embedding), 83, 86-87
     short number, 83-85
     unsupported, 88-89

files
- DB (Paradox database table), 476
- DBF (dBASE-compatible database table), 476
- F (Form), 476
- FDL (Form), 476
- FSL (Form), 476
- FTL (Compiled Form), 476
- MB (Memo/BLOB data associated with table), 476
- PX (Primary Index), 476
- QBE (Query By Example), 476
- RSL (Report), 476
- SDL (Script), 476
- SQL (SQL query), 476
- SSL (Script), 476
- TV (Table View Settings), 477
- VAL (Validation checks associated with table), 477
- X01 (Table index), 477
- Y01 (Table index), 477

graphs
- 1-D Summary, 443
- 2-D Summary, 443
- Tabular, 443

object, major, 50-54
ObjectPAL variables, 556-557
objects
- design, 49
- major, 49

reports, 266
tables, selecting, 77-79
Types (Language menu) command, 540
Types and Methods dialog box, 533, 540

U

UIObjects, 518
underscore character (_), 80
Undo (Edit menu) command, 144
Undo menu, 668
undoEditM custom method, 676
Ungroup (Design menu) command, 249
unique aggregators, 432-433
UNIQUE grouping operator, 384
unique index, 97
unlocking records, 155
unsupported field types, 88-89
updating linked tables, 413
uppercase, ObjectPAL, 553-555
user interface
- graphical, 606-608
- verbal, 606

User Name
- File menu command, 504
- options, 154

users
- interacting, ObjectPAL, 608-624
- names, viewing, 505

utilities
- accessing, 477
- Program Manager Task List, 718-719
- SHARE (DOS), 706-707

Utilities (File menu) command, 110, 418, 477-480

V

VAL (Validation checks associated with table) file type, 477
validity checks, 79, 99-104, 322-324, 398-401
- default values, 101-102
- required fields, 100
- values
  - maximum, 100-101
  - minimum, 100-101

Value (Locate menu) command, 146
values
- accessing DDE (Dynamic Data Exchange), 457-460
- blank, 196-197

INDEX

casting, 657
converting, 657
copying, 143
cutting, 143
duplicate fields, 179-181
entering in fields, 399
locating, 147-149
pasting, 143
ranges, 189-191
return, 589
search-and-replace, 150-152
tables, 371-373
validity checks
  default, 101-102
  maximum, 100-101, 400
  minimum, 100-101, 400
Var section declaration variables, 568-570
Var summary function, 239, 280
Var window declaration variables, 570-574
variables
  allDebt, 637
  arrays, 558
  as handles, 559-560
  assigning, 558
    persistance, 573
  beepCounter, 569
  buttonPressed, 657
  creating, 557
  defining, 696
  eventInfo, 672
  global, 574
  incH, 696
  initializing, 558-559
  local, 568
  naming, 558
  ObjectPAL
    declarations, 557-560
    declaring, 555-563
    types, 556-557
  PopupMenu, 669
  private, 574
  qAnswer, 638
  scopes, 567-575
    containership hierarchy, 567-568

searchName, 680
stopString, 635
Var section, 568-570
Var window, 570-574
verbal user interface, 606
view array method, 601
View Data Report Design window SpeedBar button, 273
View data-entry mode, 125-127
view DynArray method, 603
View Properties (Properties menu) command, 166
viewing
  crosstabs, 427
  data, 124-125
  README.TXT file, 708
  records, deleted, 78-79
  tables in other directories, 478
  user names, 505
violation keys, 417-418

W

Wait for DDE (Query menu) command, 175
wait method, 652
weak entities, 342
what-you-see-is-what-you-get (WYSIWYG), 710
while loops, 585-587
Who (File menu) command, 505
Who option, 154
widths of columns, 157-159
wild-card characters, 189
  .. (multiple unknown), 188, 200
  @ (single character), 188, 200
Window menu, 43
windows
  activating, 722
  cascading, 721
  closing, 718
  displaying options, 721-722
  File Browser, 59
  Form Design, 215-237
  Form Window Properties, 680
  maximizing, 716

minimizing, 37, 716
moving, 718
multiple, 62-63
ObjectPAL Editor, 529
Report Design, 272-279
restoring, 716
sizing, 717-718
styles, 654
tiling, 721
Windows
    Clipboard, 138-141
    commands, 719
        Cascade, 721
        Paradox main menu, 722
        Style (Properties menu), 655
        Tile, 721
WindowStyle constant, 654
words, reserved, 190
    in tables, 94
Working Directory
    File menu command, 500
    in aliases, 500
wrapping text, 225
writing
    ObjectPAL scripts, 283
    queries, 30, 171-172
    scripts, 53
WYSIWYG (what-you-see-is-what-you-get), 710

X-Z

x-axis, 437
x-y graph, 441
X01 (Table index) file type, 477

y-axis, 437
Y01 (Table index) file type, 477

Zoom (Properties menu) command, 258